"So much has been written about the JFK assa
conspiracy theories about it. What remains undiagn
Oswald (or any other purported assassins) but of t]
selves. What's in it for them? The short answer is power. ~~~ ~~
this book, the most important contribution to the literature to come along in a
generation. Michel Gagné is reflective and thoughtful in both his thinking and his
writing".

Michael Shermer, Ph.D. *Publisher of* Skeptic *magazine,*
columnist for Scientific American, *Presidential Fellow of*
Chapman University, USA, and author of Heavens on Earth,
The Moral Arc, The Believing Brain, *and*
Why People Believe Weird Things

"Michel Gagné is skeptical of JFK conspiracy theories, and he is also a teacher of
logic. Thus he recognizes in conspiracy arguments fallacies that are not peculiar to
the JFK case, but crop up in all sorts of debates. His volume is a cogent and incisive
treatment of the whole assassination landscape, with particular attention to recent
conspiracy arguments not dealt with in earlier volumes from people like Posner
and Bugliosi".

John McAdams, Ph.D.[†] *Formerly Professor of Political Science,*
Marquette University, USA, and author of JFK Assassination Logic:
How to Think about Claims of Conspiracy

"Michel Gagné tackles the problem of conspiracism head on. He considers the
many reasons why people believe in conspiracies. He systematically, critically, and
successfully analyzes the most prominent interpretations of the assassination of JFK,
the actors involved, and their respective motivations. *Thinking Critically About the
Kennedy Assassination* offers a contemporary application of critical thinking to a
controversial and hotly debated subject".

Jeffrey Ian Ross, Ph.D. *Professor, School of Criminal Justice,*
University of Baltimore, USA

THINKING CRITICALLY ABOUT
THE KENNEDY ASSASSINATION

Thinking Critically About the Kennedy Assassination uses the tools of critical thinking, historical research, and philosophical inquiry to debunk the many myths and conspiracy theories surrounding JFK's shocking and untimely death.

As we approach the 60th anniversary of the violent public assassination of President John F. Kennedy, over half of all Americans surveyed continue to believe that he was killed by a conspiracy involving multiple assassins. Through its reasoned and detailed analysis of the content and evolution of JFK conspiracy narratives, this book also serves as a comprehensive case study of paranoid reasoning and modern mythmaking. The book's opening chapters lay out the "official" academic consensus concerning the Kennedy assassination (better known as the "Lone Gunman Theory") and discuss the origins of popular interpretations of Kennedy's life and death, such as the nostalgic myth of "Camelot," the unsympathetic "Irish Mafia" narrative, and the many conspiracy theories critical of both. Subsequent sections scrutinize the alleged motives of leading conspiracy suspects, the ballistic, forensic, and medical evidence related to JFK's murder, and the most popular "proofs" of an enduring government cover-up. The book concludes that no clear evidence exists to suggest that JFK was the victim of a conspiracy and ends with a discussion of the causes and consequences of paranoid thinking in contemporary public discourse.

This volume will appeal to students of history, politics, psychology, and cultural and media studies, and to a broader audience interested in American history, critical thinking, and conspiracy thinking.

Michel Jacques Gagné teaches courses in critical thinking, political philosophy, philosophy of religion, and ethics in the Humanities Department of Champlain College Saint-Lambert, a junior college (CÉGEP) located near Montreal, Canada. He has an M.A. in History (Concordia University, Canada, 2005), with a thesis on civil rights protests in Northern Ireland during the 1960s, and undergraduate degrees in Education (McGill University, Canada, 1999) and History and Political Science (with joint-honors, McGill University, Canada, 1995). He has published articles in *Skeptic*, the *National Post*, the *Encyclopedia of Religion and Violence*, and *History Studies: The History Society Journal at the University of Limerick*. He is also the creator and host of the *Paranoid Planet* podcast, which discusses conspiracy theories and related phenomena. He resides with his wife and two children in Montreal, Canada.

CONSPIRACY THEORIES

Series Editors: **Peter Knight,** *University of Manchester,* and **Michael Butter,** *University of Tübingen.*

Conspiracy theories have a long history and exist in all modern societies. However, their visibility and significance are increasing today. Conspiracy theories can no longer be simply dismissed as the product of a pathological mindset located on the political margins.

This series provides a nuanced and scholarly approach to this most contentious of subjects. It draws on a range of disciplinary perspectives, including political science, sociology, history, media and cultural studies, area studies, and behavioral sciences. Issues covered include the psychology of conspiracy theories, changes in conspiratorial thinking over time, the role of the Internet, regional and political variations, and the social and political impact of conspiracy theories.

The series will include edited collections, single-authored monographs, and short-form books.

Russia Today and Conspiracy Theories
People, Power and Politics on RT
Ilya Yablokov and Precious N Chatterje-Doody

Conspiracy Theories and Latin American History
Lurking in the Shadows
Luis Roniger and Leonardo Senkman

Plots: Literary Form and Conspiracy Culture
Edited by Ben Carver, Dana Craciun and Todor Hristov

Thinking Critically About the Kennedy Assassination
Debunking the Myths and Conspiracy Theories
Michel Jacques Gagné

THINKING CRITICALLY ABOUT THE KENNEDY ASSASSINATION

Debunking the Myths and Conspiracy Theories

Michel Jacques Gagné

Routledge
Taylor & Francis Group

LONDON AND NEW YORK

Cover image: © Getty Images

First published 2022
by Routledge
4 Park Square, Milton Park, Abingdon, Oxon OX14 4RN

and by Routledge
605 Third Avenue, New York, NY 10158

Routledge is an imprint of the Taylor & Francis Group, an informa business

© 2022 Michel Jacques Gagné

British Library Cataloguing-in-Publication Data
A catalogue record for this book is available from the British Library

Library of Congress Cataloging-in-Publication Data
Names: Gagné, Michel Jacques, author.
Title: Thinking critically about the Kennedy assassination: debunking the myths
and conspiracy theories / Michel Jacques Gagné.
Description: Abingdon, Oxon; New York, NY: Routledge, 2022. |
Series: Conspiracy theories |
Includes bibliographical references and index.
Identifiers: LCCN 2021043811 (print) | LCCN 2021043812 (ebook) |
ISBN 9781032119786 (hardback) | ISBN 9781032114477 (paperback) |
ISBN 9781003222460 (ebook)
Subjects: LCSH: Kennedy, John F. (John Fitzgerald), 1917–1963–Assassination. |
Conspiracies–United States–History–20th century.
Classification: LCC E842.9.G27 2022 (print) |
LCC E842.9 (ebook) | DDC 364.152/4–dc23
LC record available at https://lccn.loc.gov/2021043811
LC ebook record available at https://lccn.loc.gov/2021043812

ISBN: 978-1-032-11978-6 (hbk)
ISBN: 978-1-032-11447-7 (pbk)
ISBN: 978-1-003-22246-0 (ebk)

DOI: 10.4324/9781003222460

Typeset in Bembo
by Newgen Publishing UK

To future former conspiracists

CONTENTS

FIGURES

AUTHOR'S PREFACE

Man is obviously made to think. It is his whole dignity and his whole merit; and his whole duty is to think as he ought.

Blaise Pascal
Pensées *(1958) Section 2, p. 45*[1]

In December 2011, I had one of those *Eureka!* moments, and just like the Greek philosopher Archimedes mine also occurred in the bath, though it had nothing to do with the density of objects in water. Rather, it was about something that happened in Dallas in 1963—or, rather, something that happened to *me* because of what happened in Dallas a decade before I was born—triggered by my recent decision, after years of dogged resistance, to finally open a book I'd spent two decades vilifying, and which I had never actually bothered to read.

That book was the 1964 *Report of the President's Commission on the Assassination of President Kennedy*, better known as the *Warren Report*, an 888-page summation of the American government's official investigation into the violent death of President John Fitzgerald Kennedy. Having recently started teaching a course on critical thinking and its application to conspiracy theories, I found myself no longer able to hate this book from a distance. And that is why, for no better reason than to fully verse myself in the "lies" of my perceived enemies, I took the book home for my Christmas vacation.

I confess that when it came to the subject of Kennedy's assassination, I had so far almost exclusively consumed only such books, films, and alternative internet radio programs (we now call them podcasts) that held a conspiracist view of reality—a worldview that largely reflected my own. These sources, produced by leading "JFK buffs" such as Mark Lane, Jim Garrison, Fletcher Prouty, Oliver Stone, James Fetzer, and Len Osanic—names you will find cited throughout this book—told me that

John Kennedy, an internationally admired and peace-loving statesman determined to end the Cold War, eradicate racism, and bring forth an age of peace and goodwill, was gunned down by warmongering fascists inside his own government, and that the fallout from this mad coup d'état had now metastasized into a global political cancer.

As a bilingual French Canadian who grew up under the dark cloud of the Cold War, of Mutually Assured Destruction, "acid rain", wide-scale government deregulation, North American Free Trade, and the increasing Americanization of my country's economy, media, and culture—all of which were easily blamed on our powerful southern neighbor—it was enticing to believe that a man like John Kennedy, widely described as a champion of international cooperation, might somehow have made the present more idyllic, both in his country and mine, had he only survived long enough to win a second term.

By the time, I finally resolved to spar with the Warren Report on my own, without a mediating conspiracist digesting it for me, I had for several years been speaking about JFK's death with my students, colleagues, and friends with right-eous indignation, holding it up as a proof that on at least one occasion a conspiracy theory turned out to be true. Alas, I was soon to discover that my rock-hard evidence of a government plot was as solid as a shack built over a fault line.

I now place a large part of the blame for my lack of judgment on various personal anxieties fueled by having grown up under the highly mediatized threat of nuclear war, unresolved childhood feelings of helplessness, limited career prospects (or so it seemed at the time), and a growing pessimism about the political process. These feelings were all to a certain extent justified. The problem was that they collectively instilled in me a sense of estrangement from the dominant culture, feelings of alienation that made me seek "alternative" explanations for catastrophic events, narratives that I found appealing because they vindicated my insecurities and my impression of being a victim of history.

I pin much of the rest of the blame on filmmaker Oliver Stone's *JFK* (1991), an imaginative and highly seductive conspiracy thriller about Kennedy's assassination—a murder perpetrated, this film alleges, by a cabal of greedy American militarists trying to take over the world. A unique and wonderfully crafted artwork, Stone's film bamboozled my vulnerable undergraduate mind—a mind educated enough to grasp the sensational factoids of world history but also naive enough not to grasp the chaotic chains of cause and effect that underlie most catastrophic events. In contrast to the complicated and morally ambivalent social science textbooks I was required to read in college, Stone's film offered me a simple, attractive, and compelling explanation for the problem of evil, one that implanted in me a paranoid view of all things.

I was certainly not the first wide-eyed idealist to tumble down that rabbit hole. I am also certain that hundreds of thousands will follow. But unlike most of the people this book is about, I'm glad to say I found my way out. This did not happen at once nor by chance. My falling out with conspiracism occurred gradually, over a decade into my teaching career. It came as a result of teaching basic logic to students in a junior college, a task that, if I was to preach by example, required me to surrender my own rigid assumptions about how the world worked to the same dispassionate and careful analysis that I was asking my students to perform on theirs. Simply put, I came to accept my own right to be wrong.

As a person trained in the study of history and not formal logic, I had until then focused my search for truth on the verification of facts—namely by assessing whether or not some reported event happened the way various authorities claimed that they did—and not on how such facts, including those that are unshakably true, can be strung together arbitrarily, carelessly, or malevolently to produce a compelling story that rings true but isn't. Teaching and studying logic helped me develop a "filter" for testing historical claims, one that helped me see that not all verified facts are necessarily connected, and that even the wisest historians with a commitment to Truth (with a capital T) sometimes fall prey to emotional reasoning. In other words, studying the past through a philosopher's eye taught me to better detect pseudohistory (or what we can rightly call bullshit), much of which, I'm sad to say, permeates the conspiracy genre.

And that is why, to make a short story long, I wound up in a bathtub with a copy of the Warren Report and a life-changing paradigm shift. This little Copernican revolution hit me from two sides with two mutually reinforcing propositions. The first held that historic events—especially world-shaking ones like JFK's murder—are, much like quantum mechanics, more complex, and chaotic when studied up close than any novice researcher might at first assume. The second held that once we accept the reality of the first proposition—that history is sloppy, full of random coincidences, and shaped by the poorly informed choices of human free agents—complex events like the Kennedy assassination are actually quite simple to grasp, provided we do not insist on making every detail fit a tidy narrative as if it were a novel or movie.

We are often told that history is stranger than fiction. Indeed, it rarely follows the rules of traditional storytelling, with its carefully crafted menagerie of heroes and villains, its linear narratives, its economy of time and characters, and its underlying moral lessons. To study history as if it came from a novel will invariably lead careless researchers to connect, simplify, stereotype, demonize, exaggerate, speculate, overgeneralize, and cleverly reimagine the people and facts that don't neatly fit into the story they *wish* to be true. To put it another way, it was the logical principle of Ockham's razor—which states that the explanation with the fewest unproven assumptions has the greatest chances of being right—that convinced me time and again that I had been putting my trust in a haphazardly engineered myth that did not reflect the messy and emotionally unsatisfying jumble of causes that history is actually made of. I thereby began to realize that my acceptance of certain conspiracy theories had less to do with the strength of the evidence and more to do with my emotional and existential needs for an inspiring story that gave my life meaning. That JFK could be murdered for no greater reason than that a disgruntled young Marxist decided one morning to take his rifle to work and turn himself into someone important simply did not compute. Like millions of other "JFK buffs," I longed for a more meaningful story, one that, at the very least, would make a more satisfying film script.

After considering these two propositions, I began to carefully weigh conspiracy-based arguments against those favoring a single gunman until there remained little doubt in my mind which argument offered a simpler, sufficient, noncontradictory, and more harmonious account that corresponded with all of the *provable*, *necessary*, and *pertinent* facts of the case. After this, every JFK conspiracy theory I came across seemed to require a good deal more faith—a logic-bending, fact-ignoring, fiction-generating, neurotic type of faith—than it took to believe that Lee Harvey Oswald shot President Kennedy without assistance from a sixth-floor window using a bolt-action rifle. This was not the story I *wanted* to hear. It was, however, the only one I could *prove*.

My 2013 op-ed piece in the *National Post*, "How Oliver Stone Turned Me into a Conspiracy Theorist," was my official *mea culpa* and an attempt to get other recovering conspiracists talking about the JFK assassination. It was also the seed that sprouted the germ that turned into this book. My 2017 *Skeptic* magazine article, "From Camelot to Conspiracy: Memory, Myth, and the Death of JFK," further elaborated my take on the psychology of "JFK buffs" and the sorts of myths they produce. This book aims to equip historians of all stripes, be they accomplished academics, college students, or amateur researchers, with a practical method and a ton of examples to help them wade through the quagmire of conspiracy claims and other forms of disinformation that congest twenty-first-century media. If it can keep just a few budding minds from tumbling into the rabbit hole of paranoia, or even better, help them climb out, this book will have served its purpose.

To conclude, I have learned in the process of writing this book—the sort of book my professors should have got me to read while in college—that there are three secrets to not losing your marbles when trying to answer a question like "Who shot Kennedy?" These are (a) to be ready to follow sound logic and clear evidence *wherever* these lead, even at the cost of being proved wrong, (b) to engage in meaningful and respectful exchanges with those who hold a different viewpoint, especially qualified experts, and to give the benefit of the doubt to official investigations—yes, even the Warren Commission—that they did not deliberately set out to "brainwash" the public, and (c) to avoid speculating too much about what could have possibly happened beyond what the evidence and laws of logic tell us. In other words, we must learn to tolerate uncertainty regarding what is not known (and may never be), not because that's what the "official" storytellers want you to believe, but because that is how one avoids crossing the mirror and getting trapped in a shadowy realm of one's own invention.

Michel Jacques Gagné
July 31, 2021

Note

1 Pascal, B. (1958: English edition; original published 1670), *Pensées*, E.P. Dutton & Co., Inc., New York, Section 2, p. 45, par. 146, available at www.gutenberg.org/files/18269/18269-h/18269-h.htm#SECTION_II

ACKNOWLEDGMENTS

This book took nearly two decades to gestate and over five years to write. I am grateful to Jonathan Kay who, as managing editor of *The National Post*, came to visit my classes in 2012 to discuss his own book on 9/11 conspiracists, which gave me the desire to produce a comparable work on the subject of JFK. I am also thankful to *National Post* editor Matt Gurney for assisting in the publication of my essay on JFK conspiracism on the 50th anniversary of the Kennedy assassination (November 22, 2013), which got the ball rolling for this project, and to Michael Shermer, editor of *Skeptic* magazine, for publishing my essay "From Camelot to Conspiracy" in the Winter 2017 issue, which summarizes some of the conclusions of this book. I would also like to thank the following academics for their assistance with past publications: Professor Jeffrey Ian Ross, School of Criminal Justice at the University of Baltimore, and editor of *Religion and Violence: An Encyclopedia of Faith and Conflict from Antiquity to the Present* (2011); Adrian Cormican and Dr. Connor Reidy, coeditors of *History Studies: The History Society Journal of the University of Limerick* (Volume 8, 2007); Professor Ronald Rudin and Professor Mary Vipond, department of History, Concordia University, Montreal, Qc.; and Professor Sean Farrell, Department of History, Northern Illinois University. Some recognition is also due to those who helped me revise this text, including Professors Jeff Ross and the late John McAdams, who wrote this book an endorsement before he passed away in early 2021; and to Joan Lillo, who produced some of the diagrams in this book. A large thank you is also due to Craig Fowlie, Hannah Rich, Sarahjayne Smith, and the rest of the Routledge staff who helped prepare this manuscript for publication.

I would also like to thank conspiracy researchers David Lifton and Rex Bradford for helping me locate and vet some photographic evidence, and some of my colleagues and personal friends for helping me edit this manuscript, find sources, produce diagrams, or simply allowing me to rant about my obsessions. These include

Paul Catanu, Stephen Hawkins, Nicole Haché, Cornelia Penner, Jonathan Powers, James Jervis, David Millar, Michael Nasra, David Thurmann, Brian Dunning, Fred Litwin, David Howell, Anthony Granato, Paul Huston, Scott Halse, Patti Kingsmill, and Stephen Wishart.

I especially thank my wife Shirley and two children, Éliane and Jean-Daniel, for their patient support through the writing and editing process. I love you all.

PHOTOGRAPHIC CREDITS

- All images of Warren Commission and HSCA exhibits, courtesy of US National Archives and Records Administration (NARA), JFK Assassination Records (Public Domain).
- Photographs of John and Jacqueline Kennedy (Figures 3.3, 3.4, 11.7, and 11.8) and Limousine at Parkland Hospital (Figure 14.1) courtesy of JFK Library (Public Domain) (White House photographers Cecil Stoughton, Abbie Rowe, and Robert Knudsen).
- Dallas news photos (Figures 11.3, 11.6, and 14.2) courtesy of *Fort Worth Star-Telegram* Collection, Special Collections, University of Texas at Arlington Library, Arlington, Texas.
- Dallas Police Department photos of TSBD, November 22, 1963 (Figures 12.1, 12.2, and 13.5) and Oswald "backyard photos" (Figures 16.1, 16.2, and 16.3) courtesy of University of North Texas Libraries, *The Portal to Texas History*, Dallas Municipal Archives.
- Zapruder Film Frames (Figures 13.2 and 17.1) courtesy of The Sixth Floor Museum at Dealey Plaza (Zapruder Film ©1967 (Renewed 1995) The Sixth Floor Museum at Dealey Plaza).
- James Altgens photograph (Figure 13.3) courtesy of AP-The Canadian Press.
- Diagrams of single- and magic-bullet theories (Figures 13.6 and 13.7), and Zapruder film, frame, and lens (Figure 17.2) by Joan Daniel Lillo, 2018.
- All other images are in the public domain.

A NOTE ON NOMENCLATURE

In producing a book of this genre, an author is forced to refer to persons, groups, or ideas with popular descriptors that may be interpreted by some as derogatory. Though sometimes used pejoratively by other authors, this book's use of the words "conspiracist," "conspiracy theorist," and "JFK buff" is based on objective definitions with no derogatory intent. While this tome does criticize conspiracy theories and people who traffic in them, I have made every effort to avoid resorting to personal attacks. I therefore hope that the text will speak for itself and that all my readers, including those who reject my conclusions, will make good use of the principle of charity, as I have attempted to do myself.

ABBREVIATIONS

AGVA   American Guild of Variety Artists
ARRB   Assassination Records Review Board
ARVN   Army of the Republic of (South) Viet Nam
CIA   Central Intelligence Agency
DA   District Attorney
DCI   Director of Central Intelligence
DPD   Dallas Police Department
EOP   external occipital protuberance
FBI   Federal Bureau of Investigation
FOIA   Freedom of Information Act
HSCA   House Select Committee on Assassinations
IRS   Internal Revenue Service
JBS   John Birch Society
JFK   John Fitzgerald Kennedy
KGB   *Komitet gosudarstvennoy bezopasnosti* (Soviet Committee for State Security)
LBJ   Lyndon Baines Johnson
NARA   National Archives and Records Administration
NODA   New Orleans District Attorney
NPC   Naval Photographic Center
NPIC   National Photographic Interpretation Center
NSAM   National Security Action Memorandum
OSS   Office of Strategic Services
RFK   Robert Francis Kennedy
SAIC   Special Agent In Charge (Secret Service)
SDS   Students for a Democratic Society
SOP   standard operating procedures

TSBD	Texas School Book Depository
UNTL	University of North Texas Libraries
USAF	US Air Force
USSR	Union of Socialist Soviet Republics (aka: the Soviet Union)
UTAL	University of Texas at Arlington Libraries
WC	Warren Commission

1

INTRODUCTION

Knowledge and conspiracy theories

1.1   A tale of two movies

In December 1991, filmmaker Oliver Stone shocked the world with a controversial historical drama on the assassination of President JFK. This was not the first time an ambitious theory had been proposed to explain the reasons for Kennedy's death. It was, however, the most influential attempt in several decades to promote the idea that the 35th president of the United States was not killed by an unhinged lone gunman but as a result of a massive homegrown conspiracy.

The film's title, *JFK*, was simple, though its plot was ambitious and convoluted. It purported to offer a truer account of the facts of Kennedy's murder than the comprehensive findings of two government investigations: the 1963–64 Warren Commission and the 1977–79 House Select Committee on Assassinations (HSCA), both of which pinned the blame, in part or in whole, on a young Marxist and former Marine named Lee Harvey Oswald. Stone's *JFK* rejected these conclusions and claimed instead that Oswald was framed to cover up a right-wing conspiracy operating from within several branches of the federal government in tandem with private weapons contractors and mainstream media.

An immediate box office success, *JFK* garnered several Academy Award nominations, including Best Picture. It was also immediately panned by journalists and academics who accused Stone of perverting a highly significant, if not sacred event in American history to promote a paranoid political agenda. Especially worrisome to Stone's many critics was the fact that *JFK* was a visually stunning and soul-stirring movie, a finely crafted piece of art with a large cast of Hollywood superstars, an inspiring score, and a storyline that unfolded more like a music video than a typical period drama. It was thus highly influential in shaping the public's understanding of what happened on that sunny 1963 Dallas afternoon. And as this book will show, it was also almost entirely wrong.

DOI: 10.4324/9781003222460-1

To summarize, *JFK* tells the story of Jim Garrison, a stubbornly virtuous district attorney (DA) who, a few years after Kennedy's death, discovers a chain of suspicious clues concerning the President's murder—most of which are conveniently located within his own jurisdiction of New Orleans parish in Louisiana, where Lee Harvey Oswald spent parts of his youth and brief adult life. Something about Oswald's behavior in New Orleans a mere few months before Kennedy died convinces the high-minded DA that the President's alleged assassin was not the angry lone nut described by the Warren Commission but an American intelligence asset secretly posing as a disgruntled communist. Garrison then rounds up several suspects, witnesses, and pieces of evidence that point to a local group of anti-Cuban radicals with ties to the CIA, the FBI, the Pentagon, and the Washington political establishment. All of this forces him to conclude that President Kennedy, "like Caesar," was publicly executed by traitors inside his own government, men who should have been implementing his dream of a peaceful and tolerant post-Cold War America, namely through a massive withdrawal of US troops from Vietnam. However, Garrison soon discovers that their involvement in the assassination (and in scuttling JFK's plans for Vietnam) has been covered up by near-invincible forces with the complicity of a ruthless new president, Lyndon Baines Johnson. Undeterred, Garrison chases every lead until he bags a suspect: a gay New Orleans businessman named Clay Shaw whom he is convinced was Oswald's CIA "handler". But Garrison's investigation is frustrated repeatedly by invisible conspirators who bug his offices, intimidate and murder his witnesses, tamper with the evidence, and threaten his reputation, life, legal staff, and family. The film ends on a pessimistic note with Shaw beating the charge of conspiracy—proof that the judicial system is rigged by the Washington warmongers. Yet it also offers its viewers a glimmer of hope in a scrolling postscript that informs them that: (a) Shaw's victory was a sham due to the covered-up fact that he "worked" for the CIA during the 1950s; (b) thousands of Kennedy-related files are "locked away" in sealed government archives; and (c) the war in Vietnam was one of the most lucrative conflicts ever for weapons developers. The film ends with the ambiguous phrase "What is past is prologue," an oblique call to arms for the upcoming struggle to release these files and open a new, and this time fair, investigation of Kennedy's murder.

The historical accuracy of this film and its place in the corpus of JFK myths is one of several themes discussed in this book, largely due to its enduring impact in shaping the way regular people "remember" President Kennedy's death. The film also continues to serve as a recruitment tool for new converts—through social networks like *YouTube*, for instance—and as a point of reference for the myriad online conversations of "Kennedy buffs" (amateur JFK conspiracy researchers). According to historian Michael Kurtz, who believes there was a conspiracy, "with the exception of *Uncle Tom's Cabin*, *JFK* probably had a greater direct impact on public opinion than any other work of art in American History".[1] According to novelist Norman Mailer, who authored a biography of Lee Oswald and concluded he did act alone, *JFK* was "one of the worst great movies ever made" because it was "wrong on so many historical points yet draws in the viewer in a way that only a great film can".[2]

Three decades after its initial release, *JFK* remains a nail-biting thriller that can keep viewers spellbound for over three hours, thanks largely to its narrative structure and cinematography. The film is marked, for instance, by a suspenseful stream of dramatic scenes depicting Garrison's 1967–69 inquest, interspersed with genuine newsreel of Kennedy's time in the White House and black and white scenes that look much like historical footage but are in fact carefully crafted—if not necessarily accurate—reenactments of real events. All of this happens at a dizzying rate that offers little time for reflection. It is largely due to this fast-paced stream of images and information that the film managed to galvanize popular outrage, albeit in different ways. For those with a strong dislike of powerful institutions and only a shallow knowledge of the film's historical contents, it is easy to come away from *JFK* believing that all rival accounts of Kennedy's death are little more than government propaganda and corporate whitewashing. For the small minority of academics and journalists who followed the details of Kennedy's life closely—many of whom were also incensed by the film's overt anti-Americanism—*JFK* is easily dismissed as an elaborate deception, a voyage into the fantasy world of left-wing historical revisionism and anti-statist paranoia.

Nearly a decade after the release of Stone's *JFK*, a remarkable psychological thriller titled *Memento* hit a few hundred theater screens. It was the first major production of filmmaker Christopher Nolan, now a celebrated Hollywood icon. *Memento* tells the story of a former insurance claims investigator named Leonard (Lenny) Shelby, who suffers from anterograde amnesia (the inability to create new lasting memories) caused by a head injury he suffered during a home invasion that left his wife raped and, presumably, dead. Remembering nothing since that fateful day, Leonard awakens every morning determined to murder his wife's attacker. He therefore develops an intricate system of memory aids (mementos) to help him "remember" the recent past, including Polaroid pictures and self-administered body tattoos. Throughout his quest, Leonard is resolved never to become like Sammy Jankis, a man who shared the same mental condition but ended up unintentionally killing his wife and being committed to an asylum.

The film opens at the end of the story, with Leonard murdering Teddy, a corrupt policeman claiming to be his best friend. It then works its way backward through time to reveal—spoiler alert!—that Leonard has long ago murdered his wife's assailant and that he is now, because of his condition, aimlessly chasing false leads fed to him by self-interested grifters. In one of the film's most revealing scenes, Teddy offers Lenny the following insight, confident that his malleable "friend" will soon forget it all:

TEDDY: You tell everyone about Sammy Jankis. Everyone who'll listen. […] Great story. Gets better every time you tell it. So you lie to yourself to be happy. Nothing wrong with that, we all do. Who cares if there's a few little things you'd rather not remember?

LENNY: What the fuck are you talking about?

TEDDY: I dunno… your wife surviving the assault… her not believing about your condition… […] I guess I can only make you believe the things you want to be true, huh? […]

LENNY: Why do you keep lying to me?

TEDDY: I'm not. I was the cop assigned to your wife's death. I believed you, I thought you deserved the chance for revenge. I helped you find the other guy who was in your bathroom that night. […] We found him and you killed him. […] You didn't remember, so I helped you start looking again, looking for the guy you already killed. […] Does it even matter who? I stopped asking myself why a long time ago. No reason, no conspiracy; just bad fucking luck. […] When you killed him, I've never seen you so happy—I was convinced you'd remember. But it didn't stick, like nothing ever sticks. Like this won't stick.[3]

Then, in a moment of lucid cognizance, Lenny destroys evidence of this painful truth—that he is Sammy Jankis—and decides to turn Teddy into his wife's aggressor. Amnesia sets in again and the film ends with Leonard chasing another false clue, which the audience knows will invariably lead him to murder his only friend.

Now widely considered a cult classic, *Memento* never received upon its release attention or earnings comparable to *JFK*. Indeed, Nolan struggled to find a US distributor. Though it was nominated for two Academy Awards, *Memento* did not capture a major prize. It was nevertheless a masterful murder mystery as riveting and original as *JFK*. The two films also shared several esthetic similarities, like a purposeful combination of grayscale and colorized sequences, the use of multiple timelines and flashbacks that induced confusion, the use of still photography as a prop, hidden clues, characters with dual identities, a narrative that forced the audience to engage mentally to solve the puzzle onscreen (a task that can necessitate multiple viewings), and an obsessive attention to detail. To all this, Nolan's film added the destabilizing trick of presenting half of the film's scenes in reverse chronological order so that the end of the film was the middle scene in the story, its most revealing one. The climactic scene of *Memento* finds Leonard discovering his own helplessness due to the unreliability of his intricate system for "remembering" the past, rendering him a powerless time-traveler perpetually stuck in a meaningless moment. But instead of accepting his humbling condition, Leonard dreams up a more empowering past, one that transforms his vulnerabilities into a self-affirming righteous anger that gives him strength to go on.[4] Under such conditions, what would the rest of us do?

At first sight, these two stories seem diametrically opposed. Unlike *JFK*, the conspiracy unveiled in *Memento* turns out to be no more than a tragic example of human wretchedness. Nolan's Lenny, unlike Stone's restyled Jim Garrison, is no inspiring hero. His disorder notwithstanding, he is a man compromised by his flawed character: a lack of empathy for others, an unwillingness to accept his own weakness and ignorance, and a propensity to betray anyone, including himself, to exact his revenge. In the end, *Memento*'s Lenny, unlike *JFK*'s Garrison, is not the victim of a massive conspiracy conducted by the authorities but of a massive self-delusion.

Yet, seen from another angle, *Memento* and *JFK* essentially tell the same story—that of a man tilting at windmills, chasing the self-empowering myth that the whole world is out to deceive him. The essential difference between the two stories is that they come to us from opposing viewpoints. *JFK* has us remain in the mind of the protagonist until the end, convincing us that the hero is sane while the rest of the world has gone mad. *JFK* keeps us looking outward at the shadowy enemies that threaten our country, community, and way of life. It perversely revels in the "discovery" that the world is a sinister place full of malefactors while the hero on screen—a thinly veiled projection of ourselves—is incorruptibly good. It gives us a real group of villains to blame (the "military industrial complex") for the state of our world and our feelings of alienation, exonerating us from all culpability. *Memento*, on the other hand, dramatically wrenches us out of the mind of the protagonist. It has us perceive his flaws from a distance so that we might better perceive the true enemy—not a conspiracy of powered elites but the fallout of our flawed humanity: self-deception, wrath, greed, and pride. It offers its viewers a shocking reminder that our memories, feelings, and beliefs often betray us that we sometimes just see what we want to see, especially when we would sooner replace a past filled with pain with a more empowering story.

By conducting a thorough analysis of the theories that hold that President Kennedy was killed by a government plot, this book takes a deep look into the world of paranoid storytelling and aims to help you, the reader, better avoid manipulation, poor logic, and self-deception in your pursuit of the truth.

1.2 Do you want to know a secret?

To conspire literally means to "breathe together".[5] A conspiracy is generally defined as a secret shared by small groups of like-minded individuals, usually to cover up some illegal or dishonest behavior.[6] Although a conspiracy could be well intentioned (surprise birthday parties are, in a sense, a kind of conspiracy), the word is generally used to refer to some immoral and secretive act. Secrets are also, by definition, not factually proven. Once they become known to the wider public, they are no longer secrets and become merely "scandals". This gives us our first insight into the logical problem posed by conspiracy theories (CTs). In other words, to claim that one *knows* they are a victim of a *secret* plot is a logical contradiction that opens that person up to accusations of paranoia: "a tendency on the part of an individual or group toward excessive or irrational suspiciousness and distrustfulness of others".[7] Hence, the person making knowledge claims about the existence of a secret plot (assuming they don't have some kind of insider knowledge) is either making unjustified assumptions and does not in fact *know* what they claim to be true, or the conspiracy has been exposed and is simply no longer secret.[8]

Conspiracists—those who produce and believe in conspiracy claims—tend to get out of this bind by claiming that proof of a conspiracy *does* exist, people just need to pay closer attention to it. Anyone who disagrees with their conclusions must therefore be willfully blind or lack the necessary acumen to see the evidence for what it is. For these reasons, the conspiracist often thrusts committed unbelievers (we will call them skeptics) into one of two bags: they are either gullible dupes, in which case they need to be educated, or else they are conniving shills, in which case they must be shamed and exposed. On the other hand, many skeptics believe that conspiracists are delusional cranks and nut jobs living in a fantasy universe. Unsurprisingly, debates between conspiracists and skeptics tend not to produce amicable relations.

But what if the greatest educational benefit of studying CTs is not just to determine what the evidence objectively tells us about secret cabals and occult forces but also to understand why certain people come to believe that the world is the chessboard of powerful clandestine agents, while others find such theories ridiculous? What if limiting our focus to establishing the true facts of some controversial event like the Kennedy assassination is itself part of the problem, because such efforts tend to ignore the root cause of conspiracy theorizing, which is the way subjective minds select, simplify, reinterpret, distort, and fabricate historical "facts" that help us produce meaningful narratives about the past, stories that are grounded partly in truth but also shaped by the hopes, fears, and frustrations we have about our place in the world and human history? This is why any investigation of questions like "who killed President Kennedy?" must remain attentive to psychological research about the formation of memories and belief systems and to the personal, political, and existential concerns that each "conspiracy researcher" brings to the table.

It may be impossible to establish with absolute certainty that a conspiracy ever actually happened, but it is certainly possible to establish whether or not a conspiracy is *known* to have happened, or whether or not it could have occurred without being exposed by the proper authorities. Hence, the debate over conspiracism is also an epistemological one. That is, it concerns the theoretical study of knowledge: how do we know that our beliefs are true, and if so, how can we prove this to others beyond a reasonable doubt? Knowledge is habitually defined as *justified* true belief.[9] Our study of JFK CTs as knowledge claims will thus necessarily require us to consider the reliability of the tools we use to make sense of our world and the past: physical artifacts, our human senses, personal memory, eye and earwitness reports, written records, and observation technology such as photography, film, sound recordings, and X-rays. More importantly, it will require us to consider the strengths and limits of human reasoning—one of humanity's most powerful faculties, but also one that can be misled. The human mind is an effective tool to gather multiple observations and synthesize them into a coherent whole—or what we might call a story, theory, or narrative. JFK CTs, like all historical narratives, are stories that aim to give our lives context, meaning, and purpose. But if they are built on false data, faulty assumptions, fallacious logic, or emotional manipulation, such stories can lead us away from the Truth and toward self-serving delusions.

The major sin committed by CTs, this book will argue, is not that they lie (though some of them do) but that in their yearning to be right, they connect facts together with faulty logic, like a shattered vase that's arbitrarily rebuilt with little concern for its original form, convincing even themselves that the object they hold in their hands is genuine and not an aberration. This book thus serves as a critique of the way conspiracists justify and promote false narratives using faulty logic and various forms of deception—including *self*-deception.[10]

Our study of CTs as knowledge claims will also lead us to consider the structure of arguments, the primary tool of philosophy that allows rational creatures like us to solve practical problems using language, logic, and structured debate. For this reason, this book is primarily interested in the structure of conspiracy narratives—the inferences and assumptions that shape them—and secondarily in the reliability of the evidence used to support conspiracy claims. If no clear evidence or compelling logic exists to support such beliefs, we should desist claiming that something is *known* and conclude instead that what is being offered to us is not Truth but merely a belief system, not unlike a political ideology or a religious faith. As we will see, conspiracists rarely submit their convictions to the scrutiny of formal logical analysis in the way that responsible mathematicians or philosophers are compelled to do. This may be because careful critical thinking threatens to undermine the fragility of their untested theories, which can, in turn, trigger a personal crisis of faith—a crisis which the theory itself was originally designed to ward off.

1.3   Why do they believe?

Many authors have attempted to explain the principal causes of conspiracism. One of the first academics to do so was historian Richard Hofstadter in his influential 1964 essay, "The Paranoid Style in American Politics".[11] Witnessing the rising popularity and influence of right-wing reactionaries during the 1950s and early 1960s,[12] Hofstadter observed that conspiracist thinking in the United States has been a staple of American culture since colonial days. What changed over the years was not the level of actual danger threatening American citizens but the object of their anxieties. Overestimated Cold War fears of a furtive communist plot to infiltrate American institutions were in fact largely a rehash of earlier moral panics[13] directed at the British, at slave owners and abolitionists, Jesuits, Irish and Italian migrants, Mormons, Freemasons, and other secret societies, rich industrialists, international bankers, munitions makers, and other presumed threats to the established social, economic, and moral orders:

> The paranoid spokesman sees the fate of conspiracy in apocalyptic terms—he traffics in the birth and deaths of whole worlds, whole political orders, whole systems of human values. He is always manning the barricades of civilization. He constantly lives at the turning point. Like religious millenialists he expresses the anxiety of those who are living through the last days and he is sometimes disposed to set a date for the apocalypse.[14]

In Hofstadter's view, conspiracism is essentially the fruit of economic and political angst, a fear of being dispossessed by suspicious minority groups set to the tune of Christian millennialism—the belief that the end of the world is approaching and will culminate in an epic battle between the forces of good and evil. It is a popular and convincing narrative across the wider American citizenry, especially those with European and Protestant roots raised to believe in America as a divinely ordained "New Jerusalem," and also to those in precarious economic situations who might easily be swayed by fearmongering populists. The American conspiracism depicted by Hofstadter is inspired by traditional religious ideas of a powerful devil or Antichrist figure (an "amoral superman") charging the gates of Christian civilization, but who invariably turns out to be an inverted "projection of the self".[15] For these reasons, Hofstadter concluded, conspiracism is an essentially conservative ideology. While this perspective has had much-staying power and helps explain some of the currents in American conservatism today, many other forms of conspiracism have emerged since his essay was written which are neither directed at outsiders nor appeal to the right wing. As this book will show, JFK conspiracists are largely left-leaning liberals in their political views, and their fears are almost exclusively directed at an incumbent enemy who already controls the state, not a horde of foreigners kicking in the doors of civilization. Hofstadter's conclusions therefore fail to explain why conspiracism can also take hold among this demographic.

Four decades later, political scientist Michael Barkun offered a similar analysis.[16] Concerned with right-wing conspiracism of the extreme libertarian and racist varieties, Barkun highlights the similarities between radical fundamentalist Christian millennialists and those who promote more secular theories about secret societies, the "New World Order" (an apocalyptic global dictatorship), the September 11, 2001, terrorist attacks, and alleged alien abductions. These types of conspiracists, Barkun explains, have since the 1960s produced a hybrid ideology—which he calls "improvisational millennialism"—that does not abide by any particular Christian doctrine but merely asserts its rejection of "liberal" authorities such as the United Nations, the federal bureaucracy, and much of the mainstream media.[17] This form of conspiracism appeals to nontraditional subcultures, namely those that espouse occultism and the New Age, insofar as it draws its inspiration from an "ill-defined potpourri" of alternative scientific, historical, and metaphysical truth claims—what he calls "stigmatized knowledge"[18]—to challenge the legitimacy of the "official" historical narratives promoted by powerful institutions like state and federal governments, universities, academic journals, and mainstream publications. In addition to government secrets and skullduggery, recurring themes in this literature include "suppressed" ancient wisdom and mysteries, alternative health care, the paranormal, and various types of pseudoscience, from young-earth creationism to crystology. "The improvisational style" of this literature, he explains, "is characterized by relentless and seemingly indiscriminate borrowing".[19]

If Barkun is correct, conspiracism should be understood neither as a religious nor a political ideology, but as an attempt by alienated communities to position themselves as the legitimate guardians of freedom and truth in their society. In other words, CTs serve as a tool of legitimization, an escape hatch from the dictates of the dominant culture for those who feel estranged, not as a definite statement on the nature of reality. This allows a CT to remain flexible and evolve, to be reshaped or abandoned when it no longer inspires the group. These evolving counternarratives also offer believers a sense of resilience, empowerment, moral superiority, and group solidarity against the (allegedly) corrupt elites who perpetuate their power through "official stories" and the obsequious masses who swallow them whole.

> Conspiracy theories therefore function both as a part of suppressed knowledge and as a basis for stigmatization. [...] Those who believe in conspiracy theories are convinced that only they know the true manner in which power is held and decisions are made. [...] Stigmatization itself is taken to be evidence of truth—for why else would a belief be stigmatized if not to suppress the truth?[20]

Barkun's analysis gives us some understanding of how elements of Christian millennialism came to be recycled by secular and esoteric communities in the latter half of the twentieth century, and how the xenophobic conspiracism described by Hofstadter during the 1960s has grown more concerned that an evil consortium is now trying to take over the world from *inside* the halls of American government. However, it fails to account for how some conspiracy beliefs that are less esoteric and religious than those described by Barkun—namely those discussed in this book—have been accepted as true by as many as 60–80% of Americans over the past half century.[21] The concept of stigmatized knowledge might be appropriate to describe marginalized groups such as religious cults, political extremists, and groups who reject vaccinations, deny the Holocaust, or claim that shapeshifting reptilian aliens live among us, but not a community as wide and as varied as those who promote JFK CTs.

More recently, political scientists Joseph Uscinski and Joseph Parent have offered a broader and more empirically cogent description of conspiracism as an expression of political angst.[22] In a statistical survey of print and electronic conspiracy chatter during the past century, these authors have demonstrated that the focus of conspiracism in the United States fluctuates over time in a fairly predictable fashion, much as Hofstadter claimed. However, its overall intensity has remained rather stable during this time and, possibly, for as long as the country exists. Moreover, they note that conspiracism is neither primarily right wing nor left wing, nor does it affect one generation much more than another. Instead, such theories "flourish across space just as much as they do across time"[23] on both sides of the political spectrum and in equivalent measures, albeit at opposite times and over different concerns. To wit, while conservatives fear the growing size and power of government, progressives express an equivalent disdain for the concentration of wealth. And while those on the right will more likely blame Democrats for their misfortunes or see communists lurking in bushes, those on the left are just as quick to blame Republicans for ruining their lives or imagine fascists running the world from corporate boardrooms. "Conspiracy theories permeate all parts of American society and cut across gender, age, race, income, political affiliation, educational level, and occupational status".[24] Indeed, Americans of all stripes have an aversion to despotism and many share the same hyperactive sense that their freedoms are constantly under attack, they just don't agree on whom they should blame for this state of affairs. This suggests that belief in CTs is deeply influenced by the filter of values through which we observe our society.

According to Uscinski and Parent, three major forces determine what kind of conspiracy one is likely to believe in. These are (a) the level of one's feelings of vulnerability, (b) the political ideology one espouses, and (c) one's social identity (race, gender, class, etc.).[25] However, the most important factor determining the popularity of a specific conspiracy claim is the political affiliation of the person who lives in the White House. In other words, Americans are most likely to believe in CTs when they feel themselves locked out of power for a sustained period of time, and since the president of the United States happens to be the most visible symbol of power in America, he (or she) is the one Americans look upon to determine which way the political wind is blowing. The further away their own political values lie from the center of power, the more likely they are to believe that this power has been usurped by some secret cabal.

> The targets and timing of resonant conspiracy theories follow a strategic logic, based on foreign threat and domestic power. In this way, conspiracy theories are used by vulnerable groups to manage perceived dangers: they are early warning systems that keep watch over the most sensitive areas and prepare solutions to potential attacks. At bottom, conspiracy theories are a form of threat perception, and fears are fundamentally driven by shifts in relative power. Because defeat and exclusion are their biggest inducement, conspiracy theories are for losers (speaking descriptively, not pejoratively).[26]

This analysis holds that belief in CTs, far from being a fringe phenomenon, is widespread and relatively benign so long as the revolving doors of political power offer equivalent opportunities to groups on different sides of the political spectrum. For Uscinski and Parent, conspiracy theorizing is thus a normal bi-product of American political culture. But their study also helps us perceive that a sustained period of estrangement from the centers of power (for instance, when a party remains in office for two or more terms) can generate a greater sense of vulnerability among the losers of elections and to a spike in certain forms of conspiracy theorizing.[27] Like Barkun, these authors recognize that in extreme cases CTs offer a powerful incentive for marginalized "losers" to resort to violence against the state, the wealthy, or mistrusted minorities.[28] What Uscinski and Parent fail to explain, however, is why many individuals remain ardent conspiracists even when they manage to be in power.

Another set of authors see conspiracism as a manifestation of deeper psychological conditions that affects a certain percentage of predisposed individuals.

Robert Robins and Jerrold Post have been intrigued by the paranoid mindset that makes many conspiracy believers adamantly refuse to change their minds in the face of clear and conclusive evidence that they are wrong.[29] They offer seven indicators of this irrational mindset: (a) extreme suspiciousness of others, (b) centrality (an exaggerated sense of self-importance), (c) grandiosity (contempt directed at those who hold rival beliefs), (d) hostility toward their perceived opponents, (e) fear of the loss of autonomy (a compulsive and unrealistic desire for independence and safety), (f) projection of one's weaknesses and obsessions on others—especially concerning the enemy's motives, and (g) delusional thinking, the tendency to believe in disproven or improbable claims "in the presence of strong contradictory evidence".[30]

Conspiracist neuroses affect not only the disenfranchised, they explain, but also the powerful—President Richard Nixon and Soviet dictator Joseph Stalin are two well-known examples. Hence, it is their self-perception of weakness, not their actual standing in society, that makes such individuals vulnerable to the paranoid mindset. But conspiracism is not in itself irrational, they explain, it is an "adaptive response" to irrational feelings which aims to produce rational explanations where these are lacking.[31] Conspiracists are in fact hyperrational, ascribing a hidden cause to all accidents, a sinister purpose to all tragedies, and to all enemies a set of evil intentions and powerful tools to help them achieve their goals. In doing so, the conspiracist is trying to validate feelings of helplessness, not by reassessing their own state of mind—the usual stuff of psychotherapy—but by reengineering the world around them:

> Although distorted, the paranoid system is coherent, an integrated syndrome, each aspect supporting the others. The syndrome as a whole can be personally reparative ('I must be important because others conspire against me') and may even be politically useful. The syndrome is also self-validating. Political failure confirms the paranoid's suspicions. [...] The reason the paranoid cannot afford to question his fixed conclusion of danger is that it is psychologically essential to his emotional well-being. He cannot face the underlying shame of his insignificance; 'proving' that he is the center of a conspiratorial plot reassures him.[32]

British psychologist Patrick Leman similarly argued that conspiracism rises out of a condition called anomie: feelings of general disaffection, rejection, or disempowerment from society. While anomie may be caused by one's actual political standing or economic condition, it is just as likely to affect the successful and wealthy who see themselves as outcasts. Furthermore, people who indulge in conspiracy theorizing tend to have acquired an emotional predisposition to victimhood, for example, by having experienced a particular trauma that makes them susceptible to believe in conspiracies in general, not only those that explain their social conditions or personal anguish. This helps explain why "people who believe in one theory are more likely to believe in others".[33]

One variety of conspiracist triggers, Leman explains, are "flashbulb memories": sudden, violent, disturbing, and newsworthy events that have a long-lasting effect on one's emotional state, for instance, by not allowing the grieving person to find a satisfactory meaning, purpose, or emotional closure in that event. The deaths of John Kennedy, Martin Luther King, Jr., and Princess Diana, for example, produced this type of traumatic experience not just in small groups on the political fringe but also across large communities, even whole generations. "Some of these iconic, shared events can provide fertile ground in which conspiracy theories are sown".[34] And so, the grief that follows the seemingly meaningless death of an iconic figure can trigger a bout of conspiracist ideation that functions as a *meaning*-seeking, rather than a *truth*-seeking, psychological mechanism.

Canadian journalist Jonathan Kay presents a similar exposition in his study of 9/11 Truthers.[35] Conspiracism, he argues, is first and foremost a coping mechanism for people who grieve or feel powerless and who are looking for rational answers to the problem of evil—the question of why bad things happen to good people. The larger the tragedy, the less clear its causes, the more popular conspiracism becomes:

> Conspiracy theories [...] are more likely to blossom when great tragedies or national traumas—the French Revolution, World War I, the assassination of JFK, 9/11, the 2008 financial crisis—rupture a society's intellectual foundations, and shatter citizens' faith in traditional authority figures. [...] Conspiracism is not so much a psychological ailment in and of itself as it is a symptom of a mind in flight from reality.[36]

Conspiracism, then, offers its despondent adherents a cheap emotional remedy that exchanges meaningless facts for a more meaningful story in which they are the innocent victim, the uncompromising hero, and the prophet of ultimate victory.

Kay also identifies seven personality types (excluding the mentally ill) that are easily seduced by conspiracist thinking.[37] These are as follows: (a) those muddling through a midlife crisis—mostly men—whose lives or careers are not satisfying; (b) "failed historians": fringe ideologues whose outlandish theories have failed to attract a mass audience; (c) "damaged survivors," such as the mothers of children with autism or sufferers of rare and incurable conditions, yearning to put a face on the cause of their ills; (d) "cosmic voyagers"—mystics who dabble in esoteric studies, New Age religions, and pseudoscience; (e) "cranks": retired intellectuals and other aging puzzle-solvers whose minds lack the stimulation once found in thought-intensive occupations; (f) "evangelical doomsayers": religious millennialists who, like the more secular crank, devours texts, albeit religious ones, looking for hidden secrets and codes; and (g) radical firebrands, mostly undergraduate students, charging the barricades of political, social, and economic injustice with angry rhetoric and subversive ideas derived from secondary sources. In other words, argues Kay, CTs are not the fruit of a lack of education, but of a reasonably educated mind in an emotional crisis, intuitively connecting disparate facts to construct a meaningful explanation for their predicament. The die-hard conspiracist is not as passive observer; he or she places themselves inside the story as a victim, crusader, or both. This allows them to maintain the belief that their suffering is purposeful, that history has not left them by the wayside, and that they have the knowledge and power to change it.

The political and psychological explanations discussed earlier represent some of the leading and, I believe, most compelling attempts to make sense of conspiracism as a social, political, and psychological phenomenon. While mental illness accounts for some conspiracist ideations, cognitively impaired individuals rarely produce the sort of complex arguments that attract a wide and sustained following.[38] For this reason, mental illnesses like schizophrenia could only account for a very small percentage of conspiracy theorizing.

Other authors, such as psychologist Rob Brotherton,[39] have offered biological explanations for the popularity of CTs. Such authors tend to focus on the human brain's rational pattern-seeking nature—what Brotherton calls our "hyperactive intention detector"—using analogies drawn from evolutionary psychology:

> The pattern detection software built into our brain is exquisitely sensitive, but there's no built-in quality control program to keep it in check. […] Our brain evolved to interpret patterns quickly and decisively, which means treating every connection as meaningful by default. […] Imagine one of our early ancestors strolling through the forest one day when she hears a rustle in the bushes and every bird in the area stops chirping. To discount it as a mere chance, or to spend too long mulling over potential explanations, could be a costly mistake. There might be a dangerous predator in the area. The better an early hominid was at spotting patterns and quickly inferring plausible causes, the more likely she was to survive and pass on her pattern-prone genes. Our ancestor's legacy to us is a brain programmed to see coincidences and infer causes.[40]

For this reason, he argues, humans evolved a natural propensity to look for intelligible patterns in the irrational "noise" of our daily lives. Most of us override this inborn self-defense mechanism through social interaction, prior experience, common sense, and education (namely of the scientific method), allowing us to live in civilized society without being frightened at every turn that something or someone is trying to attack us.

Recent advances in the biological sciences have made such explanations popular. However, our understanding of the internal processes of the human brain is still in its infancy and blaming our brains for producing in us certain conscious beliefs and not others seems overly deterministic. It also lacks a sufficient body of supporting evidence. For instance, why should one person's brain and not someone else's be attracted to complex conspiracist explanations unless some other environmental or psychological condition first triggers it? Would this mean that people with stronger conspiracist views have stronger pattern-prone genes, giving them superior survival skills? Or might this mean that they are less evolved than cooler-headed skeptics?

And why should the patterns identified in the noise be those of one type or another unless some nonbiological factors also propel us to look for particular patterns, such as a government cover-up instead of, say, a satanic deception? In the final analysis, biological explanations might offer us a partial explanation for the overactive imaginations of certain people but they leave too many questions unanswered about the process through which different types of CTs emerge, why certain people are more susceptible than others to believe in them, and why some theories are more popular than others, without resorting to faulty analogies, circular reasoning, and unfalsifiable pseudoscience.

Finally, a recent movement within the field of analytical philosophy, led by Charles Pigden, argues that conspiracy theorizing has been unnecessarily pathologized given the wide number of possible (and sometimes exposed) secretive plots and may in fact be a healthy and natural form of skepticism.[41] This movement arose in reaction to Austrian philosopher Karl Popper's contention that CTs are flawed by design as they constitute fatalistic doctrines of the extreme left and extreme right, whose revolutionary totalitarian ideologies are grounded on fears of a grandiose secret plot by an invisible godlike enemy.[42] While it is true that many conspiracy claims do end up being true (e.g., the Watergate Affair), critics point out that Pigden and his followers overgeneralize their categories of theories and believers, ignoring the many psychological, sociological, and political forces that habitually shape popular conspiracy narratives.[43] In response, English philosopher Quassim Cassam suggests that the term Conspiracy Theories ("with a capital C and a capital T") should not be applied to reasoned academic, forensic, and journalistic inquiries (e.g., into the actions of a Guy Fawkes or an Al Qaeda), lest the term lose all practical meaning. It should instead be restricted to those types of popular stories that are the product of intellectual vices that revel in self-serving propaganda. "Conspiracy Theories," he notes, "are political gambits whose real function is to promote a political agenda".[44] Echoing Popper, Cassam argues that CTs are "implausible by design" and marked by five recurring and distinctive characteristics: (a) they are speculative, relying on conjecture instead of sound logic; (b) they are contrarian, born to discredit an "official" or dominant viewpoint; (c) they are esoteric, favoring hidden and outlandish causes over simpler and obvious ones; (d) they are amateurish, preferring the crowd-sourced explanations of laypersons, or the musings of sages speaking outside their field of research, to the careful analysis of qualified experts; and (e) they are premodern in the sense that they favor deterministic explanations and hypercompetent beings over the chaotic forces of history and human error that modern scholarship, time after time, has revealed to underlie catastrophic events.[45]

In sum, if there is an overall consensus to be found in these arguments, it is that CTs are primarily fueled by minds grappling with the need to make sense of a complex, unpredictable, and unjust world and cope with unbearable feelings of powerlessness and vulnerability.

The purpose of the abovementioned discussion was not to produce an exhaustive analysis of conspiracism nor to insist that it must be seen as a political ideology, a psychological condition, or a vestigial biological faculty, but rather to ground our discussion of JFK theories within the broader context of the inter-disciplinary study of conspiracism. Without negating the value of the arguments cited previously, this book will argue that conspiracist reasoning is largely the product of an existential quest for meaning, one that relies on elaborate myths grounded partly in historical truth and partly in the imagination, and whose ultimate purpose is to offer direction and purpose to the lives of those who feel rejected or abandoned by the society in which they live. As we will see, JFK conspiracy claims are only one of several classes of myths that have been spun from the life and death of the tragic and enigmatic figure that was John Kennedy, though they do represent one of the best examples of mythmaking in contemporary American culture.

Although CTs need not be political, they quite often are. This is because they invariably bring up questions about power—such as who gets to decide what is truth and what's not, whose contributions should be acknowledged and whose should be ignored, or who should be elected, appointed, promoted, demoted, lambasted, or fired. This sort of power is found in nonpolitical spaces like private industry, professional orders, religious institutions, old boys' clubs, universities, and labor unions. But ultimately questions about power must at some point migrate into political themes, namely about who controls the state apparatus, because the modern state remains the legitimate provider of justice, punishment, and welfare in almost all parts of the world. It is also, in most open societies, the guarantor of commerce, free movement, and open communications. Even in a democracy that champions freedom and rights, the state's presence is felt everywhere in our lives. CTs are not the only people who question the limits and nature of government power. But more exceptionally, they wonder what those who have power might do under the veil of secrecy to manipulate those who have less of it. In short, CTs fix the blame for umpteen undesired conditions—from sudden deaths to health epidemics, urban poverty, drug trafficking, and even the weather—on those who wield political power (or appear to) and tend to emanate from those who *are* powerless, *feel* powerless, or are *fearful of losing* power. CTs are an example of what happens when people base their convictions on fears, unjustified suppositions, and wishful thinking instead of sound reason and investigation. The ongoing popularity of CTs—and JFK theories are still among the most popular—demonstrates that critical thinking is still urgently needed.

Unfortunately, critical thinking is a skill few people formally develop, which helps explain not just the successes of conspiracism, but also those of false advertising, of duplicitous politicians, of "fake news," of get-rich-quick schemes, of miracle diets, urban legends, pseudoscience, and a myriad internet scams. This book is intended to help you recognize misleading claims and to help you decide what you ought to believe when you're faced with the promise of simple solutions. Beware of those who would sell you "The Truth" about anything. The real truth is always more complicated—but also harder to repudiate—than an ambitious theory about some faceless villains keeping a secret from you.

Beyond our discussion of Kennedy's death, this book is designed to help you better evaluate the information that you receive. As a member of a democratic society, a citizen of a free country, and a human being entitled to the dignity of not being manipulated, your mind is your most important organ, and you should train it appropriately.

1.4   The nature and structure of this book

What I have attempted to deliver in this book is a comprehensive and systematic autopsy of one of the most enduring myths of our age. For practical reasons, I have narrowed my focus to a cross section of books, websites, and documentaries that represent a general consensus among JFK buffs, many of which shaped the narrative of Oliver Stone's famous film, along with some more recent works by popular conspiracy researchers like James Fetzer, James Douglass, Vincent Palamara, and David Mantik, and information gleaned from popular websites like *Black Op Radio, JFK Lancer, JFKfacts.com, 22 November 1963*, and *Spartacus Educational*.

An astounding number of books have been written about President John Kennedy. One source estimates this number at about 40,000 publications.[46] Readers may therefore rightfully wonder why the world needs another JFK book and whether it might shed more light on our understanding of the man's life, death, and historical significance.

The truth is that most of these sources are either historical biographies that largely ignore the details of Kennedy's death, or speculative conspiracist accounts focused almost entirely on his assassination. Indeed, there exist very few books in circulation that offer a comprehensive examination of, and a rebuttal to, the plethora of existing conspiracist tomes. While not all of these skeptical works endorse the Lone Gunman Theory (as this book does), they do tend to be more cautious in their hypotheses of what happened in Dallas. Such early works include the original *Warren Report* (1964), William Manchester's *Death of a President* (1967), and the 1979 *Report of the HSCA*, which argued in favor of a small-scale conspiracy involving Lee Oswald and one or a few never-identified sidekicks. More recent skeptical works include Gerald Posner's *Case Closed* (1993), Patricia Lambert's *False Witness* (2000), Vincent Bugliosi's *Reclaiming History* (2007), and John McAdams' *JFK Assassination Logic* (2014)—which draws heavily on Professor McAdams' comprehensive debunking website.[47] Readers will find many references to these works throughout this book. Nevertheless, this book is not a rehash of their opinions. Rather, I drew many of my conclusions directly from government documents, including depositions and exhibits collected by the Warren Commission, HSCA, and Assassination Records Review Board, as well as FBI and Justice Department reports and official autopsy records. Other sources used include academic journals, professional newspapers, magazine and radio interviews, web-based articles that demonstrate strong professionalism, and several specialized works on ballistics and other pertinent fields. Readers will hopefully find that my skepticism is well-supported, nondogmatic, and open to review, and presented in a respectful tone (though this was sometimes challenging) with a willingness to consider multiple viewpoints, provided these were logically consistent and factually supported, not mere conjecture.

Unlike biographical authors who use a simple narrative style to prevent their research from clouding the quality of their prose, or conspiracists who strafe the reader with thousands of disjointed questions and factoids, skeptical authors must offer rigorous explanations and a clear trail of evidence to ensure that their readers follow their reasoning to the end. I therefore made my argument as comprehensive and as easy to follow as possible by minimizing the usage of technical jargon or defining terms clearly when jargon seemed necessary. I also relegated many details to the footnotes so as not to overwhelm readers. In fact, this book contains over a thousand footnotes. I make no apologies for it. Most conspiracists are notorious for insufficiently referencing their sources or misrepresenting the musings of other buffs as if these were hard facts. As much as possible, I have selected expert academic or journalistic sources whose authors are subject to a rigid editorial process. Many conspiracists perceive newspaper editors and peer-reviewed journals as the malevolent gatekeepers of the reigning establishment, guarding their shameful secrets from the public. Having published articles for both kinds of publication and learned a few practical lessons about the benefits of good "gatekeeping," I consider professional editors a much-needed balm on public discourse, especially in an age when anybody can broadcast their unfiltered rants globally without ever having to reason them through.

All responsible skeptics would probably agree that their claims must be logically consistent and not go beyond the available facts, and that if they agree on these points, that their conclusions will be close to the same. Hence, my purpose for writing this book was not to correct what previous skeptics have claimed (except where they can be proven wrong), but to supplement and update their work by clarifying certain points and presenting some evidence that their books had ignored. On the other hand, my focus is different from theirs insofar as this book is not intended to simply rebut the conspiracists' theories but to serve as a tool to promote critical thinking by highlighting glaring examples of faulty reasoning. In that sense, my intentions are more pedagogical than forensic. This book can therefore be regarded as a crash course in critical thinking as well as a book about Kennedy.

Finally, another reason that makes this book pertinent is that I am well placed to offer a rebuttal to the claims and assumptions of the conspiracists. Indeed, I promoted their theories for nearly two decades, that is until I was compelled to concede that, rather than seeing reality for what it was, I had been, much like *Memento*'s Leonard, closing my eyes to everything that did not resonate with my favored interpretation of how the world worked.

A particular (and commendable) trait of JFK CTs is the fact that they rarely include the more esoteric themes that creep into other types of conspiracy literature: claims about secret societies, ancient archeological mysteries, extraterrestrial visitors, supernatural beings, or mind control. For this reason, JFK CTs remain more accessible to a mainstream audience and more scientifically plausible in the eyes of the general public. This inevitably makes them more seductive than most conspiracy myths, and more difficult to dismiss by those who lack expertise in fields such as military history, police investigations, ballistics, health sciences, photography and film, and the like. I concede that I am not an expert in any of these disciplines, but I do have a particular insight into the history of the period and of the factual and logical errors regularly committed by conspiracy buffs by virtue of my background as a teacher of history, politics, religion, and philosophy, as well as by being a "recovering conspiracist".

While this book is addressed to a wide readership and not just academics or veteran conspiracists, my intended target audience is composed of young adults entering college. These are the people I habitually teach, a demographic that is highly susceptible to take conspiracy claims at face value and to attract others into their captivating vortex.[48] I therefore wrote it with the assumption that my audience was literate but not necessarily familiar with the history of the 1960s, forensic science, formal logic, ballistics, and other issues discussed. This choice compelled me to lay out my arguments systemically, to identify full names and titles clearly, to lay out all pertinent historical details, and to carefully explain concepts and terms at the risk of making my more advanced readers impatient. I have also included discussions relating to epistemology (the study of knowledge) and worldviews (the study of the interplay between perceptions, beliefs, and human behaviors), two fields of inquiry that are often neglected in skeptical works on conspiracism, as well as some discussions on argument structure, types of logic, types of fallacious reasoning, research methods, and historical theory. These explanations are spread throughout the text so as not to slow down the pace of the narrative. The appendices at the end of the book offer the novice philosopher additional tools to analyze arguments and identify misleading logic.

This book is divided into four sections. Part I, titled "Myth and counter-myth," examines various interpretations of Kennedy's life and death starting with the *Warren Report* (Chapter 2), and the myths that shaped popular conceptions of JFK's life and legacy: the "Irish Mafia" and "Camelot" myths (Chapter 3) and the evolving conspiracist narrative (Chapter 4).

Part II, "Motive," assesses the various suspects blamed by conspiracists for organizing, perpetrating, or covering up a conspiracy to murder President Kennedy. These suspects include Southern racists, Former Vice President Richard Nixon, and members of the FBI (Chapter 5), organized crime syndicated and Jack Ruby (Chapter 6), the CIA and anti-Castro Cubans (Chapter 7), the Joint Chiefs of Staff, White House "hawks," and the "military industrial complex" (Chapter 8), and Vice President Lyndon Johnson (Chapter 9). Part II ends with an assessment of Lee Oswald's life and possible motive (Chapter 10).

Part III of this book, "Means," is primarily concerned with the evidence recovered in Dallas and in Kennedy's body and car to establish whether or not a single shooter from the sixth floor of the Texas School Book Depository (i.e., Lee Harvey Oswald) could have perpetrated this crime on his own. It begins with a study of "suspicious" persons and happenings in Dealey Plaza on the day of the assassination (Chapter 11), followed by an assessment of the evidence gathered by Dallas Police, the FBI, and other law enforcement agencies to build a case against Oswald (Chapter 12). It ends with an in-depth assessment of the two most popular claims made by conspiracists: that a single (or "magic") bullet could not inflict seven wounds in the bodies of Kennedy and Texas Governor John Connally (who was riding in the same car) and that a second shooter on the "grassy knoll" participated in the assassination (Chapter 13).

Part IV of this book, "Opportunity," examines claims that a cover-up after the fact was conducted by the Secret Service (Chapter 14) and/or the autopsy doctors (Chapter 15). It also assesses the claims that photographs of Lee Harvey Oswald in his backyard holding the murder weapon were faked to incriminate him (Chapter 16) and that the Zapruder home movie that captured the assassination in gory detail was a forgery (Chapter 17). The book ends with a discussion on why conspiracists rewrite the past, and why modern CTs mimic the trappings of religious cults (Chapter 18).

"Pride goeth before destruction" states the Biblical book of Proverbs.[49] Perhaps that is because pride has the power to blind us from the truth, particularly regarding our fears of failure, of losing control, of being manipulated or rejected. Coming to grips with the causes of some of these feelings and finally writing this book was for me a therapy of the mind, a dose of humility, and a passage into a more pragmatic view of the world. I hope it serves you just as well.

Notes

1 Michael Kurtz: "Oliver Stone, *JFK* and History," in Robert B. Toplin, ed.: *Oliver Stone's USA* (2000), cited in Jonathan Nashel: *Edward Lansdale's Cold War* (2005), 201. For publisher info, refer to the Bibliography.

2 Norman Mailer: "Footfalls in the Crypt," *Vanity Fair*, February 1992, cited in Nashel (2005), 201.

3 Christopher Nolan, dir.: *Memento* (Newmarket Films, 2000).

4 See Andy Klein: "Everything You Wanted to Know about 'Memento'," *Salon*, June 8, 2001.

5 *Online Etymology Dictionary* (2021).

6 The *Merriam-Webster Dictionary* (2021) defines CT as "a theory that explains an event or set of circumstances as the result of a secret plot by usually powerful conspirators". This definition, which I will be using throughout this book, has the advantage of not presupposing that CTs are false or delusional.

7 Ibid.

8 This is why, for instance, historians do not label the Watergate *Scandal* or the Iran-Contra *Affair* as "conspiracies". See also Quassim Cassam: *Conspiracy Theories* (2019).

9 Jonathan Jenkins Ichikawa and Matthias Steup: "The Analysis of Knowledge," *Stanford Encyclopedia of Philosophy*, March 7, 2017.

10 On fallacious logic, see Appendix 1. On argumentation and types of logic, see Appendix 2.

11 Richard Hofstadter: "The Paranoid Style in American Politics," *Harper's Magazine*, November 1964.

12 Examples he gives include the communist witch-hunts of Senator Joseph McCarthy, the anti-Marxist John Birch Society and its founder Robert W. Welch, Jr., and the presidential campaign speeches of Senator Barry Goldwater.
13 Criminologist Scott Bonn defines a moral panic as "a situation in which public fears and state interventions greatly exceed the objective threat posed to society by a particular individual or group who is/are claimed to be responsible for creating the threat in the first place". Scott A. Bonn: "Moral Panic: Who Benefits from Public Fear?," *Psychology Today*, July 20, 2015.
14 Hofstadter, 82.
15 Ibid., 85.
16 Michael Barkun: *A Culture of Conspiracy* (2006). I will be citing the Second Edition (2013).
17 Ibid., 16–29.
18 Ibid., 26. "By *Stigmatized Knowledge*," Barkun writes, "I mean claims to truth that the claimants regard as verified despite the marginalization of those claims by the institutions that conventionally distinguish between knowledge and error—universities, communities of scientific researchers, and the like". Emphasis in the original.
19 Ibid., 18.
20 Ibid., 27–8.
21 Art Swift: "Majority in U.S. Still Believe JFK Killed in a Conspiracy: Mafia, Federal Government Top List of Potential Conspirators," *Gallup Politics*, November 15, 2013.
22 Joseph P. Uscinski and Joseph M. Parent: *American Conspiracy Theories* (2014).
23 Ibid., 3.
24 Ibid., 5.
25 Ibid., 11–6.
26 Ibid., 131.
27 This is reflected, for instance, in the spike in popularity of 9/11 "Truther" CTs among progressives during the George W. Bush administration (2001–08) and to their sudden decline during the Obama years (2008–16), during which xenophobic "Birther" theories about the legitimacy of Obama's birth certificate grew in popularity among conservatives.
28 Uscinski and Parent, 6–7. See also Barkun, 193. Examples of violent conspiracists include Oklahoma City bomber Timothy McVeigh, the "Unabomber" Ted Kaczynski, Norwegian mass murderer Anders Behring Breivik, the Boston Marathon bombers Tamerlan and Dzhokhar Tsarnaev, and JFK's alleged assassin Lee Harvey Oswald.
29 Robert S. Robins and Jerrold M. Post: *Political Paranoia: The Psychopolitics of Hatred* (1997).
30 Ibid., 7–13.
31 Ibid., 18–9.
32 Ibid., 14.
33 Patrick Leman: "The Born Conspiracy," *New Scientist*, July 14, 2007, Vol.195, No.2612.
34 Ibid.
35 Jonathan Kay: *Among the Truthers: A Journey Through America's Growing Conspiracist Underground* (2011).
36 Ibid., 149–50.
37 Ibid., 151–203.
38 Ibid., 183.
39 Rob Brotherton: *Suspicious Minds: Why We Believe Conspiracy Theories* (2015).
40 Ibid., 171.

41 Charles Pigden: "Popper Revisited, or What Is Wrong with Conspiracy Theories?," *Philosophy of the Social Sciences*, Vol.25, No.1, 1995, 3–34. See also Mark Pauly: "Conspiracy Theories," *Internet Encyclopedia of Philosophy* (2021), and works by Brian Keeley, Lee Basham, David Coady, and Matthew Dentith.

42 Karl Popper: *Conjectures and Refutations: The Growth of Scientific Knowledge* (1963).

43 See Michael Butter and Peter Knight: "The History of Conspiracy Theory Research," in Joseph Uscinski, ed.: *Conspiracy Theories and the People Who Believe Them* (2019). See also Gagné: "Who Watches the Watchers' Watchers? A Review of *Conspiracy Theories & the People Who Believe Them*, edited by Joseph E. Uscinski.," *Skeptic*, Vol.25, No.2, Spring, 2020, and Cassam: *Conspiracy Theories* (2019).

44 Cassam (2019), 7. See also Cassam: "Epistemic Vices and Conspiracy Theories," *Issues in Philosophy: Blog of the American Philosophical Association*, February 28, 2018.

45 Ibid., 16–29.

46 Cory Matteson: "JFK Assassination Produced about As Many Books as Questions," *Lincoln Journal Star*, November 16, 2013.

47 John McAdams, ed.: *The Kennedy Assassination*, 1995–2021, https://mcadams.posc. mu.edu/home.htm.

48 Kay, 316–20.

49 Proverbs 16:18, Authorized (King James) version.

PART I
Myth and counter-myth

Will the real JFK please stand up?

2

THREE DEAD IN DALLAS

The "official story"

2.1   Murder in Dealey Plaza

Dallas, Texas. November 22, 1963. 12:30 p.m. It was a bright, sunny, and windy late-autumn day. The sidewalks lining the motorcade route were crowded. Half the city, it seemed, had come out to welcome the charismatic young head of state and his fashionable wife Jacqueline. President JFK had come to Texas fresh from a quick tour of Florida with the unabashed intention to charm local voters and moneyed elites to help him secure the upcoming election. The previous contest, which saw Kennedy beat Richard Nixon—the more experienced but prickly outgoing Vice President—would be remembered as one of the tightest elections in American history. No one was more aware than JFK himself that he was still far from having secured a second mandate, and Texas was one of those states that could decide the outcome. The next election was nearly a year away but it sure couldn't hurt to get an early head start.

The young Catholic president, with his Bostonian accent, wealthy family connections, and Harvard education, was not the typical politician Texans voted to office. Indeed, he barely managed to win that state in the previous contest and had done so by selecting the veteran Texas congressman Lyndon Baines Johnson (LBJ) as his running mate, his rival in the preceding Democratic Party nomination. Relations between the two men had never been smooth. Some would later even suggest that Johnson's days in the Kennedy White House were numbered.[1] Whether or not this was the case, it was clear to both men that it would take much charm to keep the people of Texas and their 25 Electoral College votes from choosing a Republican in 1964. Indeed, the growing civil rights movement had polarized attitudes throughout the South, and both Kennedy and Johnson had come out in favor of increased legal rights for black Americans. Both men thus stood to lose many votes in this state if they didn't play their cards right.

DOI: 10.4324/9781003222460-3

But Kennedy was an ace at public relations. He spoke well, was attractive, and was educated and witty. He loved to ride in open-top motorcades, shake hands and greet crowds, and was unusually young—the first American president born in the twentieth century, the first in many years to raise little children in the White House. Most importantly, he was backed by a dedicated and well-oiled campaign machine—some called it his "Irish Mafia"—a brain trust of east coast intellectuals, corporate professionals, and Irish Catholics that included his younger brother Robert Francis Kennedy (aka: Bobby or RFK). The First Lady, with her ersatz European allure and enigmatic modesty, was a media darling who gave the White House the airs of a fairy-tale castle, hosting classical concerts and theatrical performances, exhibiting artworks, entertaining foreign dignitaries, running a daycare, and overseeing several important restoration projects, some of which had been the subject of TV specials. Parading through Texas with "Jackie" beside him could only make Kennedy's star shine brighter, and it was the principal reason for having her there. Showing his allegiance to popular local statesmen like Vice President Johnson, Texas Governor John Connally, and Senator Ralph Yarborough couldn't hurt either—all of whom had agreed to take part in the President's motorcades despite the deep animosities that festered between them.[2]

Theirs was a four-day lightning tour of Texas' major cities: San Antonio, Houston, Fort Worth, and now Dallas. Austin would be next, assuming all went smoothly, followed by a weekend at the Johnson family ranch. Kennedy had given multiple speeches, taken part in dinners and luncheons, mingled with public figures, and driven past crowds of adulating fans. Mrs. Nellie Connally was seated in front of the Kennedys as they rode down Main Street, alongside her husband the Governor, when she turned and exclaimed, "You can't say that Dallas doesn't love you today, Mr. President!"[3] Indeed, everything seemed to indicate that Kennedy was headed for re-election. But history had other plans.

Gunshots rang out as the President's limousine rolled slowly through Dealey Plaza, a grassy square surrounded by fountains and concrete pergolas, located at the western edge of downtown Dallas—the very point where the motorcade was scheduled to come to an end and then make its way to a luncheon at the nearby Dallas Trade Mart.

Between two and six shots (some say even more) were fired at Kennedy's limousine during a period of 5–12 seconds, depending on which witnesses you choose to believe and what evidence and interpretation you find most convincing. "My God! They're going to kill us all!,"[4] exclaimed Governor Connally, who was hit by a bullet (some say several) that struck him in the back, punctured his lung, fractured a rib, shattered his right wrist, and broke the skin on his left thigh. President Kennedy, seated almost directly behind him, was hit by two separate slugs (again, some say more), the first of which punctured his upper back, between his neck and right shoulder, and his throat beneath his Adam's apple. The second plowed through his skull, shattering his cranium and mangling his brain. Did all these shots come from behind? Were any fired from the front? These questions lie at the heart of every theory that purports to explain what happened that day.

Kennedy crumpled sideways onto his wife. Connally did the same. The two women, uninjured, cradled their bleeding husbands all the way to the hospital. Secret Service driver agent William Greer, turning briefly to witness the President lurch from the shots, drove off at great speed.[5] He was not yet aware of how serious the President's wounds were, nor that Secret Service agent Clint Hill, assigned to protect Mrs. Kennedy, had jumped onto the back of the car during the murderous sequence to protect the first couple, albeit in vain. The two wounded statesmen were rushed to nearby Parkland Memorial Hospital. Governor Connally would spend several hours in surgery and recover. But little could be done to save President Kennedy. He was declared dead a half hour later, at 1 p.m. Central Standard Time, after every attempt to revive him had failed.

Back in Dealey Plaza there was immediate confusion as local, federal, and state law enforcement, along with several curious civilians, began scouring the area for evidence of the shooter(s). Many headed toward the Texas School Book Depository (TSBD), a red brick commercial building that stood on the corner of Houston and Elm. Its seven stories loomed high over the section of Elm Street where the President's car had rolled past when the gunshots rang out. Many thought they had heard firecrackers, adding to the confusion. Others rushed up a grassy embankment located further down Elm Street, which would soon be immortalized by the media as "the grassy knoll". It was a small but steep slope that took up most of the north side of Elm Street west of the TSBD, where the street sloped underneath a concrete railway overpass (see Figure 2.1).[6] Behind the knoll, obscured by a wooden fence and some trees, stood a gravel parking lot and railyard. Did the shots come from there? Several witnesses thought so. Or maybe the crowd had just followed the first wave of curious onlookers who had run up the hill to catch a last glimpse of the President's car speeding northwards on the Stemmons Freeway.

A little over an hour later, the Dallas Police arrested a local man named Lee Harvey Oswald, a confessed Marxist and pro-Cuban activist who had defected to, and recently returned from, the communist Soviet Union. He had a police record. He had an FBI file. He was a former US Marine trained to shoot rifles at long-range targets. Oswald had just been spotted a few miles south of Dealey Plaza in the Oak Cliff district of Dallas by Johnny Calvin Brewer, a shoe store manager. Brewer had noticed a suspicious-looking man loitering outside his store, trying to elude a police cruiser. "He looked like he had been running," Brewer later testified, "he just stood there and stared".[7] Brewer then followed the man, who snuck into the nearby Texas Theater without purchasing a ticket. Having heard the police sirens and news of the shooting over the radio, Brewer phoned the authorities.

A crowd of policemen arrived in minutes. But Oswald had become a suspect even before Brewer's involvement because he was an employee of the TSBD where the police was now searching for evidence. According to TSBD employees, Oswald had spent all morning in the building's warehouse, located on its upper floors, filling book purchase orders. Numerous witnesses in the plaza told investigators that they heard shots coming from that part of the building. (Since it was the lunch

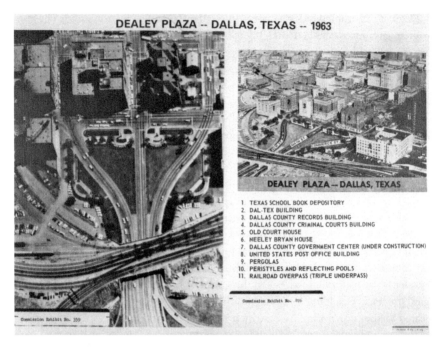

FIGURE 2.1 Aerial views of Dealey Plaza

Source: Warren Commission Exhibits 359 and 876 (HSCA JFK Exhibits F-10a,10b), National Archives and Records Administration.

hour, the warehouse was mostly empty during the motorcade's passage.) Some witnesses described a man similar to Oswald standing in the sixth-floor window, sporting a rifle or a piece of pipe shortly before the shots were fired.[8] Some TSBD employees, watching the motorcade from the windows on the fifth floor, said they heard gunshots and shells hit the floor above them.[9] Less than two minutes after the shooting, Oswald was spotted in the Book Depository's second-floor lunchroom by Dallas patrolman Marrion Baker and his impromptu guide, TSBD manager Roy Truly. Baker assumed that the shooter would not be a regular employee, so he and Truly left Oswald and rushed upstairs to inspect the roof. When the police subsequently sealed off the building, Truly took a head count and noticed that Oswald, whom he had seen only minutes before, was now missing. According to Truly, Oswald had probably been coming downstairs when he heard him and Baker come up, which made him duck into the second-floor lunchroom.[10]

To make the police even more suspicious, Oswald fit the description of a suspect who was seen firing a handgun at Dallas policeman J.D. Tippit, who was found dead about 40 minutes after the assassination.[11] Several witnesses would later confirm they saw Oswald shoot Tippit, reloaded his revolver, and/or flew the scene.[12] Tippit's murder occurred just a few blocks from the boarding house where Oswald resided.[13]

On the sixth floor of the Book Depository, beside a window overlooking the motorcade route, police detectives found three rifle bullet casings. They also identified Oswald's handprints on boxes that made up the walls of a makeshift "sniper's nest". The boxes had been arranged in such a way that someone loitering in the sixth-floor warehouse would not have seen the shooter take aim. A 6.5-millimeter Mannlicher-Carcano rifle was also found stashed between stacks of boxes that cluttered the sixth-floor warehouse. Having obtained from Mr. Truly the address of the missing employee (which was Oswald's wife's address: the two were now living separately), Dallas Police rushed over to discover a good deal more evidence.

Oswald's wife Marina and their two young children lived with Ruth Paine, a family friend who could speak Russian. Marina, who had migrated with Lee from the Soviet Union the previous year, spoke and understood little English. Paine lived in the suburb of Irving. Inside her garage, the police found a rolled-up blanket whose fibers matched those found on the rifle and inside a handmade paper bag recovered on the sixth floor of the TSBD which appeared to have been used to carry a disassembled rifle.[14] The Carcano, an Italian military rifle rarely used in Texas, was traced through its serial number to someone called Alek James Hidell. It had been purchased by mail the previous spring from a Chicago sports store and delivered to a Dallas post office box belonging to Oswald. Dallas Police soon discovered that A.J. Hidell was an alias used by Oswald.[15] The evidence in Ruth Paine's garage also included a set of "backyard photographs" of Lee dressed in black, holding a rifle like the one found in the TSBD. The pictures also showed him holding two Marxist newspapers and holstering a revolver like the one he had brandished during his arrest at the Texas Theater: a .38 Smith & Wesson Special. The same weapon was linked to the ammunition used to kill Tippit.[16]

The Dallas Police was quick to charge Oswald for Tippit's murder. He would be charged with the President's murder a few hours later. Dallas District Attorney (DA) Henry Wade made these charges public at a late-night press conference. The pieces fit. The evidence against Oswald was strong. Nothing seemed to suggest he was part of a larger team. As far as the Dallas DA, the local Police, and the FBI were concerned, it was an open-and-shut case.[17]

Case closed? Far from it.

2.2 "Curiouser and curiouser": the assassin's assassination

That afternoon, as the Dallas Police closed in on their only suspect, the Secret Service decided to evacuate acting president Lyndon Johnson back to Washington.[18] Johnson then insisted that Mrs. Kennedy not be left behind. The newly widowed First Lady, in turn, demanded that her husband's body not be left in Dallas. Hasty arrangements were therefore made to return everyone, including JFK's body, onboard Air Force One (the presidential jet) against the protests of Dr. Earl Rose, the Dallas County medical examiner. Homicide was a state crime, Rose told the Secret Servicemen, and President Kennedy's body had to, by law, undergo an autopsy in the county where he was killed.[19] A violent scuffle nearly broke out between Rose and Special Agent Roy Kellerman.[20] The Washington crowd pushed past the stubborn coroner and the president's whole entourage quickly returned to the airport. Was this a criminal getaway or were these the reasonable acts of security agents doing their jobs in the face of a possible larger attack? Such questions receive wildly divergent responses.

What followed these events has left many inquiring minds even more perplexed. Less than an hour after Johnson and the Kennedys' hasty departure, Parkland emergency doctors Kemp Clark and Malcolm Perry responded to journalists' questions during a press conference held at the hospital. Clark and Perry were, at this time, among the best-positioned professionals to describe the late president's wounds and cause of death.[21] However, some of the details they shared—a massive wound at the *back* of Kennedy's head and an *entrance* wound in his throat—gave many the impressions that JFK had been shot from the front, an account that was to be contradicted by the subsequent autopsy.

It was decided by Mrs. Kennedy during the flight back to Washington on the advice of her late husband's doctor, Vice Admiral George Burkley, that the autopsy should take place at a military facility, not a private hospital.[22] JFK's body was therefore transported directly, upon its arrival at Andrews Air Force Base, to Bethesda Naval Hospital where it underwent an autopsy and embalming procedures before being returned to the White House during the night. This process would raise the suspicions of numerous Kennedy buffs during the following years, suspicions that still fuel many debates over 50 years later. The first problem was that Bethesda Naval Hospital was a teaching hospital that catered primarily to servicemen; it was not equipped or staffed to perform *forensic* autopsies—the sort required for criminal trials.[23] JFK had, however, served in the Navy during World War II, so on that count Bethesda was not an unseemly choice.

Second, the staff performing the autopsy—Doctors Humes, Boswell, Finck, and Ebersole, with their assistants—were only given a few hours to perform their duties, after which all autopsy materials, including all tissue samples, X-rays, photographs, and their negatives, were returned to the Kennedy family (i.e., to Jackie and Attorney General Robert Kennedy).[24] The autopsy staff was thus unable to perform a full autopsy. For instance, the president's head was never shaved, no report was made on the state of his adrenal glands, and his brain, which was removed to be studied the following day, would be dissected without the rest of the evidence (namely the skull) present for comparative study. The inaccessibility of this evidence forced Dr. Humes to complete his report with the sole aid of his blood-stained handwritten notes, making it impossible to identify and correct possible inaccuracies in the original measurements. Still, a phone conversation that took place the next day between Humes and the doctors at Parkland did solve a few quandaries. The entrance wound in the president's back, for instance, could finally be linked to the wound in his throat (as an exit wound) which was not possible during the autopsy since the throat wound was destroyed by the doctors at Parkland who, trying to keep the president alive, had performed a tracheotomy. It would take five more years before Attorney General Ramsay Clark discovered that other inconsistencies had crept into the autopsy report, and that the jar that contained Kennedy's brain could no longer be found.[25] Yet more fodder for speculation.

By Sunday morning, November 24, the Dallas police had not yet managed to elicit a confession out of Lee Harvey Oswald, whose official stance was to claim on live television that he was a "patsy" (i.e., a scapegoat) for having previously lived in the Soviet Union. In other words, Oswald was claiming to be not a hunter but a victim of anti-communists. The Dallas DA nevertheless reached the conclusion that Oswald did murder Kennedy, that he probably did so alone, and that the courts would prove this beyond a reasonable doubt. The physical evidence they had compiled was now bolstered by a trove of FBI evidence providing a motive. The suspect, it turned out, had expressed hatred for the United States on several occasions, both publicly and in private correspondences. He had defected to the Soviet Union and lived there from 1959 to early 1962, during which he attempted to relinquish his US citizenship (but never finalized the procedure). He had also been arrested in New Orleans a few months earlier after taking part in a public scuffle with Carlos Bringuier, an anti-Castro Cuban exile whose operations Oswald had attempted to infiltrate under false pretense, and who confronted Oswald when Bringuier later spotted him distributing pro-Castro leaflets on a busy street corner. Oswald's support for the Cuban revolution and his admiration for Castro were well known by many who knew him. He had even been offered airtime to defend his Marxist beliefs on a New Orleans radio station. On the other hand, he did not appear to have any strong connections to any communist government or organizations save the New Orleans chapter of a pro-Castro group—the Fair Play for Cuba Committee—which he seemed to have founded himself and whose members included only Oswald and "Alek Hidell," his alter ego. No others were discovered, neither by the Dallas Police and FBI nor subsequently by the Warren Commission, which would paint him as a disgruntled and unstable loner.[26] All of this, along with more evidence yet to emerge, might have convinced the public for good that all this mess was the work of one man. But all bets were off when Oswald himself was shot during a routine prisoner transfer.

A boisterous and flighty nightclub owner named Jack Ruby (born Jacob Rubenstein) took an immediate and obsessive interest in the president's alleged murderer.[27] He closed his clubs down for a few days out of respect for the Kennedys, condemning other bar owners for not doing the same; he loitered around the Dallas police department all weekend, volunteering his services to out-of-town journalists; and he devoured newspapers, learning all he could about Oswald and the investigation. He stood near the young man more than once, corrected DA Wade for getting some facts wrong during a press conference, and fussed to others about Oswald's arrogant tone and smug smile. Not only was Ruby well known to the Dallas Police as a purveyor of adult entertainment and an acquaintance of local crooks, he was also a peculiar groupie who visited cops and journalists frequently in their workplaces, who offered them free food and drinks for their patronage, and who loved to mingle with local celebrities. Wherever there was a spotlight or news story unfolding, Ruby was usually nearby. But this time he had more than just handshakes and pleasantries on his mind.

On Sunday morning, November 24 at 11:20 a.m., Jack Ruby snuck down a ramp that led into the underground parking garage of Dallas City Hall building (where the local police headquarters were located), unnoticed by a police sentry guarding the way.[28] Oswald appeared from a hallway almost immediately, escorted by several policemen, to be transported to nearby Dallas County Jail. The parking garage was abuzz with journalists, photographers, and cameramen who had been compelled to wait there for hours; Oswald's departure time had been pushed back several times. But Ruby got there with only seconds to spare. It was either a feat of clockwork precision, worthy of Jules Verne's Phileas Fogg, or else one of the greatest coincidences in modern history. Oswald rounded the corner handcuffed to detective Jim Leavelle: a sitting duck to anyone with a gun and the will to use it. Ruby, who habitually carried a revolver because he frequently carried large sums of cash, managed to fire only a single shot before several policemen wrestled him down. Oswald was rushed to Parkland hospital where he died less than two hours later. Ruby was subsequently charged and, to no one's surprise, found guilty of murdering Lee Harvey Oswald. But that single gunshot fired in haste, a bullet that tore through multiple organs and caused its victim to hemorrhage to death,[29] guaranteed that Kennedy's alleged assassin would never stand trial and that his motive— if we assume he was guilty—would remain murky forever.

Ruby's murderous act compounded the public's confusion. The entire situation moved from tragic to surreal in less than three days. Anyone who was not suspicious of how quickly the Dallas Police closed in on Oswald and how quickly he became their only suspect now had good reason to be. Before Ruby's crime, one could reasonably accept the idea that a single, angry lone nut had just gotten lucky. It was infuriating but it fit the facts that were reported. They could also hold to the belief, as many officials in Texas and Washington did, that Oswald was a communist agent sent by the Soviets or Castro to retaliate against Kennedy's recent attempt to liberate Cuba—one more episode in the zero-sum game between Soviet communism and Western democracy. Only a small group might have concluded by then that Oswald had been a pawn in some massive right-wing conspiracy.[30] But Ruby's crime changed all that. Indeed, the nightclub owner had nothing to make him appear like a Soviet agent. Many saw him instead as the tip of a sinister criminal plot, a henchman for organized crime with ties to corrupt cops. What if Ruby had in fact been sent by the mafia to silence Oswald? Could this mean that the mob had also rubbed out the president and blackmailed local cops to cover their crime? And if so, what did that say about the vulnerability of American institutions against these criminal rackets? Or maybe the rabbit hole went deeper. What if racists inside the Dallas Police, FBI, Ku Klux Klan, or all of these working together, had plotted to murder Kennedy so that he might be replaced by a corruptible and manipulable Texan? Or something even deeper, like some powerful cabal entrenched in the American political power structure, in the intelligence community, the oil industry, the military, the federal bureaucracy, some network of secret societies, or even Lyndon Johnson himself?

On Monday November 25, President Kennedy was given a solemn state funeral in Washington that included a massive procession from the Capitol building to St. Matthew's Cathedral. His body was then laid to rest at Arlington National Cemetery with all of the decorum reserved for a national hero. This event, along with the period of public viewing that preceded it, was attended by hundreds of thousands of Americans and hundreds of foreign dignitaries, heads of state, diplomats, and royalty who marched through the streets of Washington behind the grieving Kennedy family—a "bodyguard's nightmare"[31] in light of the last days' events. Millions more watched the procession on live television, including inside the Soviet Union. Coincidently, 700 uniformed officers and 1,500 civilians made their way to Beckley Hills Baptist Church in Dallas to pay their respects to Officer Tippit. His widow would receive over $650,000 in donations from the public, members of the media and policemen, the Kennedy family, and Abraham Zapruder who donated a large portion of the profits he made selling his home video of the assassination to *Life* magazine.

That same afternoon, Lee Oswald was buried in a nondescript grave in a quiet suburban cemetery in Fort Worth, Texas. His funeral was attended by little more than a handful of policemen, a gaggle of journalists, and a few despondent family members: his estranged mother Marguerite, his older brother Robert, his wife Marina, and his two infant children.[32]

2.3 "Too many cooks messing with the broth"

One of Lyndon Johnson's first decisions as head of state was to appoint a presidential commission to investigate and explain what happened to President Kennedy and Lee Harvey Oswald that weekend in Dallas. Johnson's reasons for doing this have elicited much controversy. Many have argued that this decision was forced by powerful people responsible for these murders. Some claim he did so to hide evidence of his own corruption and involvement in the affair.[33] Others have argued that Johnson had little choice since letting multiple branches of government conduct separate investigations under the constant scrutiny of the news media would likely expose several embarrassing secrets concerning Kennedy's and his administration, secrets that could sully the country's international reputation, humiliate the Kennedy family, and tarnish JFK's legacy.[34] We will examine these allegations in subsequent chapters.

According to historian William Manchester, the Kennedy family's chosen biographer of these events, Johnson was persuaded by Deputy Attorney General Nicholas Katzenbach—then filling in for the grieving Robert Kennedy—that only a federal commission could responsibly deal with the issue. "The public must be satisfied that Oswald was the assassin," he wrote to Johnson's personal assistant, "that he did not have confederates who are still at large; and that the evidence was such that he would have been convicted at trial".[35] This was desirable for two basic reasons, wrote Katzenbach. First, the new president had to maintain the public's trust in the country's political and legal institutions. There was a need, he insisted, to dispel growing rumors popularized in the "Iron Curtain press" (i.e., foreign Marxist newspapers) that the assassinations of John Kennedy and Lee Oswald had been the fruit of a right-wing conspiracy.

Second, he argued, the Dallas authorities and the FBI had so far demonstrated a lack of objectivity and consistency in their investigations, leading many journalists to claim that these law enforcement bodies were manipulating evidence to reach a foregone conclusion that Oswald was a Soviet agent. Hence, neither the Dallas Police nor the FBI should be trusted to do this alone. They were too invested—as was the Secret Service—in their need to defend their reputations and cover up any errors they made, errors that might have cost Kennedy his life.[36] Whether Katzenbach's memo is evidence of his brilliant insight into the workings of para-noid minds, of the man's distrust of Southern conservatives, or of a massive govern-ment plot to conceal a *coup d'état*, is another contentious issue in JFK assassination literature.

Whatever Katzenbach's motives might have been, President Johnson agreed with him and began assembling a team of elder statesmen to oversee this endeavor, against the initial resistance of long-standing FBI director J. Edgar Hoover, a personal friend of LBJ.[37] The President's Commission on the Assassination of President Kennedy, better known as the Warren Commission, would be staffed by 15 high-profile lawyers and 12 junior counsels who performed the main work of deposing witnesses, gathering sworn affidavits, and vetting the evidence collected by several agencies. It would be chaired by Earl Warren, the popular Chief Justice of the US Supreme Court, a Kennedy ally and ardent defender of civil rights. Warren would be assisted in his oversight by a bipartisan panel of six men who currently or formerly held important positions in various branches of government. These were Democratic Senator Richard Russell, Jr., Republican Senator John Sherman Cooper; Democratic House Majority Whip Hale Boggs, Chair of the House Republican Conference Gerald Ford (the third highest-ranking Republican in Congress), former Director of Central Intelligence (DCI) Allen Dulles, and John J. McCloy, the former President of the World Bank and former US High Commissioner for Germany, who also recently served as one of Kennedy's inter-national negotiators for limiting nuclear weapons testing.

The Commission's team of investigators was led by chief counsel J. Lee Rankin. It took them nearly nine months to produce their Report, pushing the summer deadline set by President Johnson into the early fall, after questioning nearly 400 witnesses and compiling 26 volumes of depositions and affidavits, police photographs, FBI memoranda, forensics reports, and thousands of exhibits relating to Kennedy, Oswald, and Ruby. It was an ambitious task performed with an eye on the clock, which forced them to cut several corners. For instance, the 26 volumes were published without an index. This is largely because President Johnson had insisted that these proceedings end before the upcoming election campaign grew heated, to dispel rumors of communist agents and shady conspiracies that were feeding his rivals' campaigns.

The report was well received by all major media, which have continued to defend it, in part or in whole, until the present. It also raised the public's confidence that Oswald had acted alone to a temporary all-time high of 36%, against 50% who believed in some sort of conspiracy.[38] This increased sense of closure would contribute to Johnson easily defeating his Republican rival, the firebrand Arizona conservative Barry Goldwater, who had promoted several anti-communist conspiracy claims during the campaign trail.[39] But the years that followed would not be so kind to Johnson, nor would public opinion ever be as favorably disposed toward him and the Warren Commission as it had been in the autumn of 1964.

2.4   The Warren Report, Part 1: Oswald and Ruby

Nearly half of *The Warren Report* (Chapters 4–7) is devoted to explaining the life, personality, and actions of Lee Harvey Oswald. It is perhaps its strongest component, based on depositions from Oswald's immediate family, friends and acquaintances, and various professionals who dealt with him over the years. It also includes a thorough analysis of his personal items, such as his diaries and photographs, that suggested he was a troubled and frustrated loner who suffered illusions of grandeur and had a tough childhood, few friends, an unhappy marriage, and difficulties keeping a job. Yet, despite his laziness and antisocial personality, he was a bright autodidact with an interest in political philosophy.

Whether or not Oswald was mentally ill cannot be proven, though the Warren Commission suggested (as have Oswald biographers Priscilla Johnson, Norman Mailer, and Gerald Posner) that some form of sociopathy influenced his thoughts and behavior from a young age.[40] His Marxist convictions were also traced back to his teenage years and seemed genuine. So were his beliefs that American capitalism was decadent and predatory, and his later beliefs, after returning from Russia, that Soviet-style communism was corrupt and repressive. In all, *The Warren Report*'s profile of Oswald suggested that Kennedy's killer had no significant ties to any network of spies, whether American or communist.[41] His connections to other political organizations were also few and superficial. These included some American socialist newspapers like *The Militant* and *The Worker* for which he had subscriptions and to which he sometimes wrote letters,[42] and a visit to the Soviet and Cuban embassies in Mexico City a few weeks before the assassination.[43]

Confirming the conclusions of the FBI and Dallas Police, the Warren Commission established that Oswald did own a 6.5-millimeter Mannlicher-Carcano rifle, purchased by mail and delivered to a Dallas post-office box registered to Oswald, using the alias Alek Hidell.[44] In addition, the rifle's ammunition—an uncommon type of round-tipped, full-metal jacketed military bullet—closely resembled pieces of lead recovered from Connally's body and bullet fragments found inside the limousine.[45] Another bullet, labeled CE399, which seemed to have fallen out of Governor Connally's clothes when he was rushed into surgery, was recovered from a stretcher in Parkland hospital. Surprisingly, it seemed to have suffered almost no damage.[46] The three spent bullet casings found inside the "sniper's nest" also bore the firing pin markings produced by the same Mannlicher-Carcano rifle, and at least one witness could confirm that a man fitting Oswald's description had been sitting or standing at the sixth-floor window before and during the shooting, holding a similar rifle. The Commission also confirmed the authenticity of Oswald's palm and fingerprints recovered from the rifle, the paper bag, and the boxes that made up the "sniper's nest," as well as the fibers of the blanket in which the weapon was stored in Ruth Paine's garage, since the Oswalds returned to Dallas from New Orleans.

The Commission also discovered that the ammunition fired at Kennedy (an unspent cartridge was found in the rifle) shared a resemblance with a slug found at the site of an unsolved cold case dating back to the previous spring: a failed attempt to assassinate retired Major General Edwin Walker, a staunchly right-wing political activist who lived in Dallas and whose outspoken contempt for civil rights and communist Cuba had caused Oswald to state on several occasions that the man was a dangerous fascist, an American Hitler-in-waiting.[47] On the evening of April 10, 1963, Walker had been shot at and lightly wounded by a single bullet that broke through a window at the back of his house while he was inside doing his taxes. The window frame deflected the bullet which merely grazed Walker. The shooter remained unidentified until photographs of Walker's house were found among Oswald's possessions inside Ruth Paine's garage. Lee's erratic behavior during the days surrounding this incident was divulged by Marina during her Warren Commission testimony.[48] These findings helped explain why Oswald had produced those incriminating backyard photographs of himself posing with his rifle, revolver, and Marxist newspapers. They were to become, had the hit on Walker succeeded, a living testimony of his exploits as a "hunter of fascists".[49]

Moreover, the Commission confirmed Oswald's ownership of the .38 Smith & Wesson Special revolver whose bullets matched casings found near Officer J.D. Tippit's body. They tracked Oswald's movements from the TSBD until his arrest at the Texas Theater.[50] They took note of his presence in the Depository's lunch-room minutes after the shooting (when he was spotted by patrolman Baker), of his boarding a bus a few blocks from the TSBD, of his exiting the bus because it was caught in traffic and entering a taxi a few blocks away, of his hasty return to his boarding house in Oak Cliff where he put on a light-colored jacket[51] and picked up a revolver, of his hasty departure while ignoring his housekeeper's greeting, of the nine witnesses who confirmed seeing Oswald shooting Tippit or fleeing on foot, and of the wary shoe store manager who tracked him down to the Texas Theater. The timeline was feasible. The witnesses were credible. The evidence fit their scenario. The Commission found no reason to doubt that Lee Oswald had shot Kennedy and then a policeman during a failed getaway. The evidence was so overwhelmingly stacked against Oswald, stated attorney and anti-conspiracy author Vincent Bugliosi,[52] that it would have qualified on any other occasion as an open-and-shut case, had it not been for the historical importance of the victim and the public's desire for a more meaningful story.[53] G. Robert Blakey, another celebrated attorney, who 15 years later would oversee the second government investigation into these events (but who, unlike Bugliosi, has remained a staunch believer in a conspiracy), came to the same conclusion: Oswald was guilty beyond a reasonable doubt.[54]

As for Jack Ruby, the Warren Commission examined his early life, his psychological profile, his personal and professional relations, and his behavior during the days that led to his televised killing of Oswald.[55] What they discovered was the story of a peculiar man: a former Chicago street urchin who skipped school to hang out in boxing clubs; a bumbling self-made businessman who worked his way up the food chain; a mildly observant Jew without a wife, children, or steady girlfriend; an exuberant chatterbox who used big words out of context; a thug with a disconcerting obsession for his pet dachshunds (one of which he called his "wife"); and an impulsive boss who could be extremely generous one minute and explode into violent anger the next. Though he was arrested eight times by the Dallas Police between 1949 and 1963, all of these had been for minor charges such as carrying a concealed weapon, disturbing the peace, violating a peace bond, permitting dancers to perform after hours, violating state liquor laws, ignoring traffic summonses, and one case of assault. Most of these charges ended up being dropped. All of them could be attributed to the man's flighty temper and occupation as a peddler of erotic entertainment, which often compelled him (not unwillingly) to rough up unruly clients. Moreover, Ruby had only informal friendships with Dallas policemen and low-level members of organized crime, and no connections whatever with the FBI, the CIA, communist and right-wing organizations, or any other group that could be suspected of murdering Kennedy. In the end, the Commission concluded that despite the suspicious nature of Ruby's shooting of Oswald, it had been the act of a passionate and unstable man, one who was feeling the pinch of excessive debt and had a long-standing hatred of Marxists and anti-Semites. Oswald and Ruby, they concluded, were two men who resembled each other in almost no other way except in their irrational will to channel their anger through violence.[56]

But these conclusions, as the following chapters will show, were not to be shared by a growing number of amateur researchers who grew increasingly convinced that the Warren Commission had never intended to seek out the truth, but only to frame a patsy to whitewash a much larger crime.

2.5   The Warren Report, Part 2: bullet wounds and ballistics

While the evidence of Oswald's involvement seemed strong, the Warren Commission had more trouble proving that only three shots, all fired from the TSBD's sixth-floor window, had inflicted nine separate wounds to President Kennedy and Governor Connally.[57] There were three major reasons for this. First, the members of the Commission did not gain full access to the autopsy materials. They therefore derived many of their conclusions solely from the pathologists' reports and testimonies. Second, the Commission misinterpreted the timing and sequence of the shots. This led to a rather unlikely timeframe that made the involvement of a second shooter more likely. Finally, because it depended too heavily on the recollections of Governor Connally, who remained convinced that he and the president were struck by two different shots, the Commission found itself trying to defend a scenario that did not accord with the ballistic and video evidence.

2.5.1 The autopsy pictures

For reasons that were not fully disclosed to the members of the Warren Commission (we will discuss these in later chapters), access to the President's autopsy pictures and X-rays proved surprisingly hard to obtain. This was partly due to Chief Justice Warren's reticence to compel the Kennedy family to release these sensitive materials in fear that they might be leaked to the press.[58] This problem was compounded by the fact that the autopsy was rushed, that it was performed by a team of pathologists with insufficient experience with forensic investigations, and that its report contained missing and inconsistent data. In the end, the Kennedy family's decision to favor discretion over professional rigor might have helped them deflect some unwanted media attention, but it also caused decades of controversy.[59]

Eventually, the Commission did gain limited access to these restricted materials, but to put Bobby and Jackie Kennedy at ease, Chief Justice Warren—who observed the pictures in the company of lead counsel Rankin, both of whom found them disturbing—arranged for the other Commission members to see only schematic drawings based on the notes and memories of the pathologists. Due to some inaccuracies caused by the artist not having seen the autopsy pictures firsthand, these drawings were mistaken in their location of the two entry wounds on Kennedy, which elicited further suspicions by conspiracists[60] (see Figures 2.2 and 2.3).

2.5.2 The sequence of the shots

To set up a "clock" of the assassination, the Commission relied on the now-world-famous home movie taken by Abraham Zapruder, a Dallas businessman who stood on an elevated wall overlooking Elm Street at the time Kennedy and Connally were hit. Based on the speed of Zapruder's camera and the fact that the bolt-action Carcano required a minimum of two seconds to reload each cartridge, the Commission estimated that the total sequence of the shooting lasted between 4.8 and 5.6 seconds. This meant that Oswald could have fired no more than three bullets in all.[61] These calculations dramatically cut down the number of possible ways a single assassin could inflict nine wounds.

However, this also led the Warren Commission to make faulty assumptions. First, the Commission's staff reached the conclusion that the first shot would likely be the most accurate given that the shooter could have already loaded the rifle and waited for an optimal angle to shoot. Hence, it was assumed that the *first* shot struck Kennedy to the right of his first thoracic vertebra[62] at Zapruder frame 210, exiting his throat near his Adam's apple, accounting for two wounds. Second, since

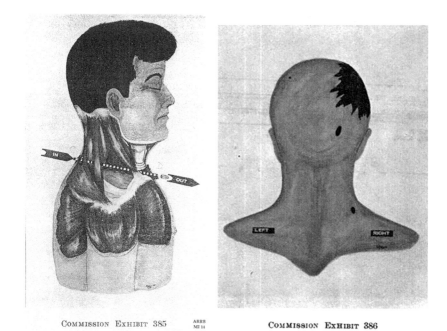

COMMISSION EXHIBIT 385   ARRB
                           MI 14   COMMISSION EXHIBIT 386

COMMISSION EXHIBIT 388

FIGURE 2.2 Drawings of JFK wounds (throat wound; back of neck and head; head wound)

Source: Warren Commission Exhibits 385, 386, and 388, National Archives and Records Administration.

FIGURE 2.3 Arlen Specter describes the path of bullet CE399

Source: Warren Commission Exhibit 903, Sixth Floor Museum at Dealey Plaza, National Archives and Records Administration.

Governor Connally claimed to have heard the first shot, turned sideways to look, and *then* felt the pain of the bullet that struck him in the back without hearing a second shot, he remained convinced—and the Commission with him—that he was hit by a different bullet than the first one that struck Kennedy. This alleged *second* bullet traversed Connally's torso, collapsed his lung, fractured a rib, and shattered his wrist before lodging itself in his thigh, accounting for five more wounds. Connally's opinion was reinforced by his wife's claim that she turned to see Kennedy clutching his throat before her husband began slumping toward her. The third shot, they all concluded, hit Kennedy in the head and burst out his right temple, accounting for two more wounds (for a total of nine).[63]

2.5.3 The Single Bullet Theory

Until July 1964, it appeared that three shots from behind were enough to account for all wounds suffered by Kennedy and Connally. Since the Warren Commission's ultimate purpose had been to demonstrate that Kennedy was not killed by a group of assassins, it was ready to close the books on its investigation, until an important new piece of evidence surfaced late during the hearings that forced the Commission to rethink its findings. A Dallas car dealer named James Tague, they discovered, who stood under the triple underpass during the shooting, was slightly injured by what might have been a bullet fragment or piece of flying curbstone.[64] A police report had been made of Tague's injury on November 22, 1963, but it was ignored in the mayhem until it resurfaced a half-year later when Tague contacted the authorities to inquire about it. Tague testified before the Warren Commission a month after its official deadline had passed. This late revelation reinforced the beliefs of several Commission staffers that one of the three shots fired by Oswald must have gone off course.[65] Having reviewed the Zapruder film, ballistic evidence, and autopsy reports, the Commission found it easier now to disagree with the testimonies of John and Nellie Connally and to conclude that Oswald's *second* shot missed its target, though it did not speculate as to why.

This realization meant that the first shot would have had to hit Kennedy *and* Connally, causing all injuries sustained by both men, except for Kennedy's head wounds. This came to be known as the Single-Bullet Theory, originally proposed by Arlen Specter, one of the Commission's junior counsels (and a future Assistant DA and US Senator), to help iron out contradictions between eyewitness reports and the ballistic evidence. Indeed, the wounds seemed to align rather well from Connally's back through Kennedy's throat, back up to the sixth-floor window (see Figure 2.3). Unfortunately, 1964 technology did not allow the Warren Commission to verify with sufficient exactitude whether the theory was ironclad. Unsurprisingly then, it was divisive from its inception, even among Commission members. But it was empirically defensible, based on a reliable principle of forensic science, which is to give precedence to the physical evidence over eyewitness recollections—a principle that many conspiracists, as we will see, tend to apply in reverse.[66] Any further inconsistencies could be blamed on the frequent unreliability of eye and earwitnesses, or the delayed reactions of the victims.

The *Warren Report*'s major failure in this matter—and in retrospect it was a significant blunder—was not to disclose the fact that the Single Bullet Theory was not accepted unanimously by its staffers and that significant opposition to it was expressed by some commissioners, especially Senator Russell, who favored Governor Connally's version.[67] This deliberate suppression of internal dissent would eventually surface and, along with numerous other omissions and miscalculations, further erode the credibility of the *Warren Report* among the conspiracy-minded.

A final problem faced by the Commission was bureaucratic resistance. Far from being a mouthpiece for the FBI or CIA, the Commission's staff had tense relations with these two agencies and often struggled to gain their assistance. FBI director Hoover was from the beginning opposed to civilian investigations that might undermine the FBI's own conclusions or expose its blunders—including the Bureau's repeated failure to identify Oswald as a genuine threat following his return from the Soviet Union.[68] The CIA, intent on concealing its illegal part- nership with organized criminals to get rid of Fidel Castro (see Chapters 6 and 7), had its own reasons to eschew Commission requests.[69] No clear evidence has surfaced to suggest that Commissioner Allen Dulles—the former Director of

Central Intelligence fired by Kennedy after the failed 1961 invasion of Cuba, but appointed to the Commission on the advice of his brother Robert Kennedy—tried to derail the Commission's investigations. However, it is now well established that part of his mandate was to make sure that nothing embarrassing to the CIA would surface in the Commission's proceedings.[70] If the reluctance of both agencies to collaborate with the Commission is to be taken as proof of a conspiracy to kill JFK (which many conspiracists do), then it is hard to see how this could also incriminate Earl Warren and his Commission. At best, logic should make us conclude that the Warren Commission was well meaning, if powerless to dig up clear proofs of an "inside job".

The Warren Commission disbanded in September 1964 after submitting its report to President Johnson, leaving no process or person to respond to any new evidence or objections concerning its findings. This would make it easier for it to be picked apart in the years that followed.

2.6 Pop goes the weasel

The conclusions of the Warren Commission were soon dubbed "the official story" by a rising number of critics convinced that the *Warren Report* was little more than a government whitewash and that someone else than Oswald was guilty of JFK's murder. The word "official" literally means "authoritative".[71] The expression "official story" should therefore logically mean that this is the best explanation currently available. It could also mean that this story is endorsed by officials—epistemic authorities with specialized training (such as medical and ballistics experts, historians, and attorneys) or who have been endowed with a special investigative function (such as news reporters or a committee of elected officials). In other words, the phrase "official story" should, used correctly, mean something like "the most likely hypothesis" or "the consensus of experts". However, that is not how the phrase is typically used by many critics of the Warren Commission. In much of the conspiracist literature, the expression "official story" has come to mean something more like "the lies that the government wants you to believe". Hence, if there exists such an "official" story, it is inferred that there must also exist an "unofficial" (i.e., alternative) story, one that may contain proofs of a scandal. The widespread misuse of this phrase is more than just derisive; it is logically manipulative because it carries the implicit assumption that the explanations offered by the Warren Commission were necessarily self-serving and arbitrary.

Expressions like this one are often called weasel words: vague or empty clichés that contain a hidden assumption or value judgment that manipulates the audience's perception of the issue.[72] Words like "modern" and "ancient," "open–minded" and "closed–minded," "science," and "religion" (etc.) are often used this way to score easy points without a proper justification. It would be less misleading to refer to the *Warren Report* as the "standard historical model"[73] of JFK's assassination. As we shall see, the Warren Commission's findings have been scrutinized, verified, and largely accepted by a wide range of historians, forensics and ballistics experts, and respected journalists, most of whom had no reason to protect any branch of the government or any secret cabals, nor to defend a set of conclusions they knew to be false. As the critical thinking podcaster and filmmaker Brian Dunning remarked, no one ever alludes to the "official story" of the 1944 invasion of Normandy, nor to the "official properties" of the element Boron.[74] One should therefore be wary of anyone using terms like "the official story" as a self-evident proof of conspiracy. This does not mean that we shouldn't examine the declarations of authority figures with a healthy dose of skepticism. Politicians do lie, intelligence and law-enforcement officials sometimes abuse their powers, and criminal conspiracies occur quite frequently. But we should not be too hasty to bring the whole edifice down. It is not the duty of experts who have carefully looked at the data and forged a consensus to prove all their opponents wrong. In the fields of physical science and history, much as it does in the courts, the burden of proof lies with those who impeach the consensus with a novel interpretation. Caution should always precede revolution.

When a given interpretation—having considered all available evidence and ruled out any contradictions—is shown to be the simplest and most probable, it merely becomes a historical fact, not an "official story".[75] There will always remain the possibility that certain facts were incorrectly assessed and that the theory requires revisions, but the discovery of error does not mean that the theory itself is a sham. Far from it, because a theory based on empirical data, such as the lone gunman scenario, seeks to achieve inductive strength. In other words, it seeks the greatest level of *probable* truth, not logical necessity.[76] When assessing the physical evidence and eyewitness reports of any criminal cold case—including the JFK assassination— we need to remember that we are dealing with *incomplete* data and that the data we do have has been processed and interpreted by numerous physical instruments, emotionally strained witnesses, and various types of experts, all of which are by nature imperfect. Thus, a responsible critical thinker should tolerate uncertainty to avoid reaching hasty conclusions, especially when the evidence is open to interpret- ation.[77] Human and mechanical error should be our first assumption when facing incongruous data, not manipulation by a hidden deceiver, largely because errors and accidents are known to occur far more frequently than massive deceptions.[78]

But before we can begin looking more closely at the historical facts that may support or disprove the claims of the *Warren Report*, we must take a look at the evo- lution of explanations, conspiracist and otherwise, for what happened to President Kennedy.

Notes

1 These included local Dallas papers, Kennedy's secretary Evelyn Lincoln, and also Mrs. Kennedy. Many JFK aides would deny it, namely Arthur Schlesinger and Robert Kennedy. Thurston Clarke: "'It Will Not Be Lyndon': Why JFK Wanted to Drop LBJ for Reelection," *The Daily Beast*, November 18, 2013. See also Vincent Bugliosi: *Reclaiming History* (2007), 14–6, and Chapter 9 of this book.

2 Ibid., 13–6.

3 Testimony of Mrs. John Bowden Connally, Jr. (Nellie Connally), *Warren Commission Hearings* (Henceforth WC), 1964, Volume IV. See also James Swanson: *End of Days: The Assassination of John F. Kennedy* (2013), 112.

4 Testimony of Gov. John Bowden Connally, Jr.; Testimony of Mrs. John Bowden Connally, Jr., WC IV. There is much controversy over what was said and done during this brief period, including the recollections of Mrs. Connally whose version of these events is widely quoted.

5 Testimony of William Robert Greer, Special Agent, Secret Service, WC II.

6 This landmark is generally nicknamed the "triple underpass" as the three streets that cross Dealey plaza (Elm, Main, and Commerce) converge in an hourglass figure under the railway above.

7 Testimony of Johnny Calvin Brewer, WC VII.

8 Testimonies of Arnold Rowland, Amos Lee Euins, Bob Jackson, Malcolm Couch, James Worrell, and Howard Brenner, WC II, III, and VI. See also Swanson, chap. 6.

9 Testimonies of Bonnie Ray Williams, Harold Norman, and James Jarman, Jr., WC III.

10 Testimonies of Marrion L. Baker and Roy Sansom Truly, WC III. See also Alfred Robbins: "Who Killed President Kennedy?," *New York Journal-American*, May 24, 1964. Conspiracists often highlight the fact that another TSBD employee, a clerical supervisor named Mrs. Robert A. Reid, subsequently saw Oswald holding a full bottle of Coke walk past her inside the second-floor office—an unusual route for a stock boy. An assassin on the lam, they suspect, would not bother to stop and buy a Coke. But if Oswald was trying to avoid looking suspicious while trying to exit the building, and given the fact that his wife and Wesley Frazier reported that Lee ate no breakfast and carried no lunch to work that morning, the act of buying a Coke is not inherently suspicious (except perhaps that Lee usually drank Dr. Pepper, which was available from a different machine located on the first floor). The entire question of whether Oswald had reason to buy a Coke at that time doesn't really help either side of the debate. It is a piece of errant data that can be interpreted in various ways. See Testimony of Mrs. Robert A. Reid, WC III, and Bugliosi, 49–50.

11 One witness used Tippit's patrol car radio to call for help. Testimony of Domingo Benavides, WC VI. See also Dale Myers: *With Malice: Lee Harvey Oswald and the Murder of Officer J. D. Tippit* (1998).

12 Testimonies of Helen Markham, WC VI; William Scoggins, WC III; William Arthur Smith, WC VII; Barbara Davis, WC III; Virginia Davis, WC VII; Ted Callaway, WC III; Sam Guinyard, WC VII; Warren Allan Reynolds, WC XI; and Affidavits of Harold Russell, WC VII; Mary Brock, WC VII; and B.M. Patterson, WC XV. See also Bugliosi, 74–82, 960–1, and endnotes: 531–6.

13 The Warren Commission established the time of Tippit's murder as 1:15 p.m. See William Manchester: *The Death of a President* (1967) and Bugliosi (2007) for a pro-Warren Commission timeline. Many conspiracists argue that Oswald could not have traveled by foot and public transit from Dealey Plaza to his boarding house in Oak Cliff and from there to the Texas Theater on Jefferson boulevard within an hour, suggesting that Tippit was killed by someone other than Oswald, presumably to frame him. Police transmissions of the civilian who called for help on Tippit's car radio (assumed by the Warren Commission to be Benavides, but which the HSCA concluded was probably T.F. Bowley) show Tippit was shot prior to 1:16 p.m. W.M. Drenas: "Car #10 Where are you?" (1998) and John McAdams: "The JFK Assassination Dallas Police Tapes: History in Real Time Part Two," *The Kennedy Assassination* website.

14 Buell Wesley Frazier, one of Ruth Paine's neighbors who also worked at the TSBD, frequently gave Oswald lifts to and from the Paine household to visit his family on

weekends. Against habit, he now came on a work day (Thursday). The morning of the assassination (Friday), Oswald carried a long paper bag to work instead of his smaller lunch bag. He told Frazier it contained curtain rods for his apartment. Testimonies of Buell Wesley Frazier and Linnie Mae Randle (Frazier's sister), WC II.

15 Manchester, 94; Swanson, chap. 7. A fake US Marines Certificate of Service Card and a Selective Service ID bearing Hidell's name and signature but a photograph of Oswald were found in his wallet when he was arrested. Oswald never explained what they were doing there, but also never denied they were his. See "Alek Hidell I.D. Cards," *The Portal to Texas History* website.

16 Five unused bullets were found in Oswald's pockets when he was arrested, facilitating the identification of the cartridges and slugs found near Tippit's body. According to Bugliosi, these discarded spent cartridges matched Oswald's revolver "to the exclusion of all others". The slugs extracted from Tippit were a "probable match". Bugliosi, 964.

17 Bugliosi, 189–94.

18 It was believed that the assassination may be part of a larger coordinated attack on the country. Former Secret Service agent Clint Hill, Interview by Duncan McCue: *CBC: The Current*, November 22, 2013.

19 The assassination of a president was not explicitly made a federal crime until 1965. Bugliosi, 93 (footnote).

20 Bugliosi, 92–3.

21 Press Conference at Parkland Memorial Hospital, Dallas, Texas, November 22, 1963, 2:16 p.m. CST.

22 Manchester, 349–50. See also interview of historian Robert Dallek on "Ideas: The Enright Files – John F. Kennedy," *CBC Radio 1*, November 4, 2013.

23 Lieutenant Colonel Pierre Finck, one of the three pathologists who took part in the autopsy (conducted by Commander James Humes) was experienced in the study of wound ballistics. Finck was chief of the Wound Ballistics Pathology Branch of the Armed Forces Institute of Pathology (AFIP) at nearby Walter Reed Army Medical Center. Bugliosi, 152 and endnotes, 175; Philip Shenon: *A Cruel and Shocking Act* (2015), chap. 1.

24 Testimonies of Comdr. James J. Humes, Comdr. J. Thornton Boswell, and Lt-Col. Pierre A. Finck, WC II. See also the depositions to the Assassination Records Review Board (ARRB) of Dr. James Joseph Humes, February 13, 1996, and of Dr. J. Thornton Boswell, February 26, 1996.

25 "1968 Panel Review of Photographs, X-Ray Films, Documents and Other Evidence Pertaining To the Fatal Wounding of President John F. Kennedy on November 22, 1963 In Dallas, Texas," (Clark Panel Report), February 26, 1968. See also Bugliosi, 369 and endnotes, 131.

26 Oswald's possible connections to a Soviet or Cuban conspiracy continue to raise speculations among some JFK researchers. See for example, Gus Russo and Stephen Molton's *Brothers in Arms* (2008), and Shenon (2015).

27 Ruby's background, peculiar personality, his behavior that weekend, and his subsequent trial are described in the *Warren Report*, chaps. 5 and 6 and appendix 16. See also Gerald Posner: *Case Closed: Lee Harvey Oswald and the Assassination of JFK* (2003), chaps. 15 and 16, Bugliosi, 1071–144, 1465–84 and endnotes, 947–8, and Swanson, chap. 9.

28 Testimony of (Dallas policeman) Roy Eugene Vaughn, WC XII. See also Bugliosi, 270–6, and endnotes 105–10.

29 This time, Dr. Rose did perform the necessary autopsy. See "Lee Harvey Oswald Autopsy Report, November 24, 1963," available at *The Portal to Texas History* (accessed 2018).

30 Many in the local FBI staff initially suspected right-wing extremists from the Ku Klux Klan or John Birch Society. Many Dallas policemen, more conservative than the largely

out-of-state FBI office, suspected the involvement of other Marxists. Once Oswald's profile became clearer, both theories became difficult to sustain. Bugliosi, 77–8 (and footnote), 85–6 and 89–90.

31 Bugliosi, 308.
32 Ibid., 307–19.
33 Shenon, 42–4; Robin Ramsay: *Who Shot JFK?* (2013), 100–12.
34 Kathryn Olmsted: *Real Enemies* (2009), 112–27.
35 Nicholas Katzenbach: "Memorandum for Mr. Moyers," November 25, 1963, FBI 62-109060 JFK HQ File, Section 18, available at *Mary Ferrell Foundation* website.
36 Manchester, 629–31.
37 Johnson initially suggested that the federal government let Texas Attorney General Waggoner Carr lead the investigation. "If you get too many cooks messing with the broth it messes it up," he told Hoover in a recorded telephone conversation on November 25, 1963. The two men spoke again on November 29 after the *Washington Post* called for a federal investigation and both houses of Congress discussed opening their own inquiries. This time, they discussed the public relations "three ring circus" that could result from this "rash of investigations". *Telephone Call: The President to J. Edgar Hoover, November 25, 1963, 10:30 a.m.* and *Telephone conversation between the President and J. Edgar Hoover, November 29, 1963, 1:40 p.m.* (*LBJ Library*). "LBJ Phone Calls—November 1963".
38 Art Swift: "Majority in U.S. Still Believe JFK Killed in a Conspiracy," *Gallup Politics*, November 15, 2013.
39 See Rick Perlstein: *Before the Storm: Barry Goldwater and the Unmaking of the American Consensus* (2002), chaps. 8 and 11.
40 A 1953 psychiatrist's report (when Lee was 13 years old) made the following remarks:

> He is [a] tense, withdrawn and evasive boy who dislikes intensely talking about himself and his feelings. He likes the [sic] give the impression that he doesn't care about others and rather likes to keep to himself so that he is not bothered and does not have to make the effort of communicating. It was difficult to penetrate the emotional wall behind which this boy hides and he provided us with sufficient clues, permitting us to see intense anxiety, shyness, feelings of awkwardness and insecurity as the main reasons for his withdrawal tendencies and solitary habits. Lee told us: 'I don't want a friend and I don't like to talk to people'.
> Youth House Psychiatrist's Report, 5/7/53, Bronx, Case No. 26996, by Psychiatrist Renatus Hartogs, M.D., Ph.D.

41 Ex-KGB agent and Soviet defector Yuri Nosenko, as well as Soviet sources released after the fall of communism, described Oswald in a similar light. See Posner, chap. 3, and Christopher Andrew and Vasili Mitrokhin: *The Sword and the Shield: The Mitrokhin Archive and the Secret History of the KGB* (1999).
42 *Warren Report*, 404–15.
43 Oswald's visits to these embassies in late September 1963 are discussed in the *Warren Report*, 299–311, Bugliosi, 1044–8, and Posner, chap. 9. Many conspiracists suggest Oswald was being set up as a fake communist agent using an impersonator in Mexico City, whose photograph was taken by the CIA and sent to the FBI following the assassination. However, numerous documents and eyewitnesses—including Meryl and John McFarland, who spoke with Oswald on the bus trip to Mexico City, and a Cuban embassy employee named Silvia Durán—confirm that Oswald was definitely in Mexico City trying to obtain a Cuban visa. But the Cuban embassy, after consulting Soviet authorities, would only issue him a tourist visa, and only on the condition that he first

obtain a Soviet visa to travel back to the USSR with his wife and children. Being either unable or unwilling to do this, Oswald returned to Dallas where Ruth Paine helped him obtain a job at the Book Depository. Regarding the erroneous photograph of Oswald in Mexico, the CIA later explained that its Mexico City station had simply photographed the wrong man and mistakenly sent that picture to its headquarters in Langley—a proof of their disorganization, not of a conspiracy.

44 Ibid., 181–2. Handwriting experts confirmed that "Hidell" was Oswald. Alek (or "Alik") was a nickname given to him by Soviet friends who thought "Lee" was too feminine, while the name Hidell was that of a former acquaintance in the US Marines. It also rhymed with "Fidel" (i.e., Castro). Oswald had also used the alias "O.H. Lee" to register at his Dallas boarding house, possibly to elude the FBI. Being a committed Marxist and former defector who wrote to Marxist newspapers, publicly defended Castro, purchased weapons through the mail and visited communist embassies, Oswald had sufficient reason to fear the FBI without being involved in a conspiracy.

45 "Small Fragment of Metal from the Wrist of Governor John Connally" (item 305166), and "Fragment of the Base of a Bullet Found in the Front of the Presidential Limousine Following the Assassination of President John F. Kennedy" (item 305151), *Records of the President's Commission on the Assassination of President Kennedy, 1954–1965*, National Records and Archives Administration (NARA).

46 Though not crushed, CE399 carried several signs of having been fired: its sides carried rifling marks, it was slightly bent, its rear end was significantly compressed, and matching fragments from its lead core were extracted from Connally's wounds. *Warren Report*, chap. 3, 79–81. (See also Figure 13.9.)

47 *Warren Report*, 183–7, 280–99. Bugliosi, 680–97. Walker campaigned to become governor of Texas in 1962. He was defeated by John Connally in the Democratic primaries.

48 Testimony or Mrs. Lee Harvey Oswald, WC I.

49 This phrase (written in Russian, possibly by Marina) appeared at the back of one of the backyard photos that had been given to George de Mohrenschildt, a Russian expatriate and family friend. The House Select Committee on Assassinations would later try, unsuccessfully, to link the handwriting to Marina Oswald. Lee Oswald's signature also appeared on the picture. Bugliosi, 794–5 and endnotes, 403–4.

50 *Warren Report*, chap. 4, 166–71.

51 Marina told the police that Lee only owned two jackets: a blue one, which he had left at the TSBD, and a gray one, which he wore during the Tippit murder and tossed away a few minutes later. It was found under a nearby car. *Warren Report*, chap. 4, 175–6.

52 In addition to publishing *Reclaiming History* (2007), a 1,700-page investigation of JFK conspiracy theories, Bugliosi served as prosecuting attorney in a television mock trial of Lee Harvey Oswald during the mid-1980s: *On Trial: Lee Harvey Oswald*, London Weekend Television Productions, 1986.

53 "CBC Ideas: The Enright Files: John F. Kennedy," *CBC Radio 1*, November 4, 2013.

54 G. Robert Blakey interview for "Who Was Lee Harvey Oswald?" (1993) *PBS: Frontline*, November 19, 2013.

55 *Warren Report*, chaps. 5 and 6 and appendix 16.

56 Ibid., 274.

57 For a fuller discussion of these wounds, see Chapter 13.

58 Posner, 407.

59 ARRB *Final Report* (1998), chap. 6, Part II, Section B1, 121.

60 Posner, 408. Although any discrepancy between the drawings, the autopsy report, and the autopsy face sheet (shorthand notes) could be ironed out by the Commission's staff,

devout conspiracists often preferred to interpret this as proof of foul play. McAdams: *JFK Assassination Logic* (2011), 219–21.

61 *Warren Report*, 96–7.

62 The autopsy report, which located each wound using visible markers on body's surface, placed the wound of entry "5 ½ inches (14 centimeters) from the tip of the right shoulder joint and approximately the same distance below the tip of the right mastoid process, the bony point immediately behind the ear". *Warren Report*, 87–92.

63 *Warren Report*, 85–117. See also McAdams: *JFK Assassination Logic*, chap. 15, and Posner, chap. 17.

64 Tague told the Commission that something had stung him on the face after hearing what he thought was a loud firecracker or "cannon-type sound". Realizing they were gunshots, he took shelter beneath the underpass. Deputy Sheriff E.R. "Buddy" Walthers approached him some minutes later stating he had seen "something fly off back on the street," and remarked that Tague had "a couple of drops of blood" on his cheek. Tague believed he heard three shots and that he was hit by the second. Testimony of James Thomas Tague, WC VII.

65 Many other witnesses, including Virgie Rackley (aka: Virgie Mae Baker) and Royce G. Skelton, also claimed they saw something ricochet off the pavement, and some Dallas policemen found what looked like a bullet mark on the Elm Street curb. However, it remains possible that Tague's injury had another unexplained cause. No part of the missing bullet was ever recovered. Frank S. DeRonja and Max Holland: "Technical Investigation Pertaining to the First Shot Fired in the Kennedy Assassination, 22 November 1963," 20 November 2011, *Washington Decoded*. According to these authors, it was the first shot, not the second, that missed.

66 For example, conspiracy author James Fetzer writes:

> A photograph is viewed merely as a graphic portrayal of oral testimony […] The practice of the Warren Commission and apologists for its findings appears to be the exact opposite, whereby photographs and films—including X-rays—have been used to discount the testimony of eyewitnesses, *which is not only the better evidence* but is actually required to lay a foundation for the admissibility of evidence.
>
> *Fetzer:* Murder in Dealey Plaza *(2000), 11. Emphasis added.*

Contrast this with the 1998 *ARRB Final Report*, which argued that:

> a significant problem that is well known to trial lawyers, judges, and psychologists, is the unreliability of eyewitness testimony. Witnesses frequently, and inaccurately, believe that they have a vivid recollection of events. Psychologists and scholars have long-since demonstrated the serious unreliability of peoples' recollections of what they hear and see. […] The deposition transcripts and other medical evidence that were released by the Review Board should be evaluated cautiously by the public. Often the witnesses contradict not only each other, but sometimes themselves. For events that transpired almost 35 years ago, all persons are likely to have failures of memory. It would be more prudent to weigh all of the evidence, with due concern for human error, rather than take single statements as 'proof' for one theory or another.
>
> *ARRB* Final Report, *123–4.*

67 Russell even threatened not to sign the final report unless he could submit a disclaimer, which he did. But Earl Warren did not include it in the final draft, wishing to maintain a united front. Commissioners Boggs and Cooper also expressed strong reservations. It should be noted however that these three had the lowest attendance record at the

Commission hearings and were therefore the least familiar with the forensic evidence. Posner, 409.

68 Posner, 405–7.

69 CIA: "Family Jewels," 1973. (A file pertaining to the Agency's collaboration with organized crime syndicates to undermine Communist Cuba, declassified in 2007). www.cia.gov/readingroom/collection/family-jewels.

70 Olmsted, 122–7; Shenon, 105.

71 *Merriam-Webster Dictionary.*

72 The expression is drawn from the traditional belief that weasels can suck an egg empty without damaging its shell. The *Macmillan Dictionary* defines "weasel word" as: "A word that someone uses to avoid saying what they really mean". The *Merriam-Webster Dictionary* defines it as: "a word used in order to evade or retreat from a direct or forthright statement or position".

73 Brian Dunning: "The JFK Assassination: How should we regard the conspiracy theories about the assassination of John F. Kennedy?," *Skeptoid: Critical Analysis of Pop Phenomena*, podcast episode #389, November 19, 2013.

74 Ibid.

75 Ibid.

76 For a brief discussion on inductive and deductive logic, see Appendix 2.

77 Wade and Tavris: *Psychology* (1990), 31–6.

78 Uscinski and Parent, 50. See also Section 10.3 of Chapter 10 of this book.

3

THE KENNEDY MYSTIQUE

From Irish Mafia to Camelot

3.1 The power of myth

A myth is a story made up of "ostensibly historical events that serves to unfold part of the world view of a people".[1] It is a story that may appear outlandish to outside observers but is believed to be true by the community that produced or perpetuates it. "Although myths are speculative," writes art historian Henry Sayre, "they are not pure fantasy. […] They serve to rationalize the unknown and to explain to people the nature of the universe and their place within it".[2]

What makes a myth true in the eyes of the believer is not its factual accuracy—otherwise it would just be plain history or science—but its explanatory power. It is an *interpretation* of reality, told in a narrative and sometimes symbolic form, that tells us how and why the world functions as it does. Myths help us make sense of the chaotic flow of human history by fitting separate events into a larger and coherent story. They inform us that the world is a rational place, that events have understandable causes, that our lives have a purpose, and that there are identifiable sources of "good" and "evil". They tell us what truth claims we ought to accept or be skeptical of. Myths offer us an historical narrative that is predictable and orderly, and hence more emotionally satisfying, than "scientific" accounts of the past. The popular medievalist and mythologist Joseph Campbell suggested that a myth "helps you to put your mind in touch with this experience of being alive," it helps you "relate to the world or to understand that world beyond what is seen".[3] Ultimately, myths invite us to reflect on the rightness or wrongness of our actions and motivations and those of other people, especially those who hold power over our lives.

Some myths are origin stories. The epic war between the Greeks and the Trojans, fancifully retold in Homer's *Iliad*, is an enduring example of a myth that purports to explain the origins of a nation. So is the Biblical account of the Exodus, in which the descendants of Jacob miraculously escape the clutches of Egypt's Pharaoh to

DOI: 10.4324/9781003222460-4

become God's chosen people in a divine ceremony in the Sinai desert. There exist many creative foundation myths of ancient cities like Babylon, Rome, and Memphis (the one in Egypt, not Tennessee) which archaic audiences took to be more or less true.[4] The amount of factual truth contained in such stories is usually lost in time, and they are often taken as fictions by modern audiences. Yet myths are not simply a thing of the past.

Many types of myths are widely accepted today. They offer simplistic and romanticized chronicles of how a particular nation or community was formed, survived and flourished, overcame adversity, and produced great leaders and heroes (or, in some cases, villains[5]). But unlike ancient stories of gods feuding over the physical realm, modern myths tend to be less supernatural and focus on human protagonists and malefactors. Modern myths are especially observable in totalitarian regimes whose leaders use propaganda to embellish their image. Consider for instance the state-sponsored account of the birth of late North Korean dictator Kim Jong Il, which was allegedly marked by "a double rainbow and a glowing new star [that] appeared in the heavens" over his birthplace on top of Mount Paektu, one of many stories that bestow a quasi-divine status on the Kim dynasty.[6] But myths also take hold in Western democracies. The claim that British King George III intended to establish "an absolute Tyranny over these [United] States [...] with circumstances of Cruelty & perfidy scarcely paralleled in the most barbarous ages," to reduce his American subjects to slavery, and hand their lands over to French Catholics and "merciless Indian Savages," was a self-serving exaggeration (to say the least) intended to inflame anger and trigger a revolution. It is an account that modern historians know to be inaccurate, but which has been irremediably etched onto the American psyche via the Declaration of Independence.[7]

Myths can be used to extol the virtues of historical figures and polish away their vices (e.g., George Washington, Abraham Lincoln, or Martin Luther King, Jr.). This allows such individuals to better embody the values of those who view them as heroes and even serve as projections of their ideal selves. Myths can also be used to demonize perceived enemies (e.g., George III, John Wilkes Booth, or Julius and Ethel Rosenberg), turning them into two-dimensional villains who represent everything the nation or group should detest. "Fictional origins and historical events are retrospectively woven into master narratives to 'invent' a people and provide them with a distinctive and uplifting past," writes political scientist Richard Ned Lebow.[8] While such myths are seldom historically accurate, they nonetheless must be historically *plausible* to be accepted, lest we dismiss them as utter nonsense. The most enduring myths hide in that gray area between brute historical fact ("Lincoln defeated the Southern Confederates") and wild flights of fancy ("Lincoln defeated a legion of vampires"). Somewhere between these two poles lies a powerful metaphor for what America is and should be. If that metaphor is inspiring, plausible, and hard to disprove, it will have a wide and enduring appeal.

But myths must offer their audience more than an inspiring story that connects them to the past. "Stylized representations of the past have the potential to create a 'we feeling,' and hence a sense of community among those who internalize these narratives," adds Lebow. "The narratives that construct these identities help to shape how people think of their countries and how they should behave".[9] To be effective, myths must inform our sense of identity, telling us who we are, what we are not, and which side to take in a moral debate. They must give us a sense that our life is lived rightly and that we joined the right camp in the war between good and evil. As a result, myths have the power to unite or divide large groups of people.

Modern myths can be hard to recognize for what they are, especially when they are widely accepted and retold in schools, in mainstream and social media, political speeches, movies, and literature. Most Western democracies have origin stories that get told and retold in schoolbooks and popular culture—stories that contain numerous glosses, inaccuracies, or an outright biased perspective.[10] If the account we are told coheres with our personal beliefs and self-perception, we may remain blind to the errors in the story and go on ignoring the parts that are unpleasant but true.

Inversely, popular narratives about the past don't always ring true. This may occur when they exclude us from the story or depict us, our community, and our values as a threat to the wider society, or fail to answer our most pressing questions about who we are and what our life purpose should be. The result is cognitive dissonance: "a state of tension that occurs when a person simultaneously holds two cognitions (thoughts, beliefs) that are psychologically inconsistent [...]. This tension is uncomfortable, and someone in a state of dissonance will be motivated to reduce it".[11] Myths, especially those that contain a conspiracy theory, can help us reduce that tension by offering us a new story, one that is close enough to reality to make us feel grounded in truth, with different heroes and villains that echo our beliefs more closely. Myths are the chameleons of history: they evolve to suit the psychological needs of those who believe them by asserting the goodness of their religious doctrines, the rightness of their political ideas, the legitimacy of their ethnic, sexual, or gender identity, or any other moral conviction.

Accounts of the life, death, and legacy of John Kennedy are rife with mythical themes. In fact, JFK has become one of modern history's most idealized political figures, partly because of his charisma, untimely death, and youthful image (like Peter Pan, he will never grow old), but also because his career was so short, and his brand of liberalism so pragmatic, that he can be made to reflect whatever hopes or anxieties others project upon him. Compared to many other famous assassinated statesmen—Julius Caesar, Cicero, King Henri IV, Abraham Lincoln, Mohandas Gandhi, Martin Luther King, Jr., etc.—Kennedy had yet to establish a clear legacy by the time he was killed. Much of what he stood for had not yet materialized; it existed only in speeches. In speaking of the many contradictory ways, JFK is remembered, political scientist James Piereson wrote: "People search for ways of making their beliefs consistent, either by denying or ignoring key facts or by reinterpreting facts in such a way as to make them consistent with deeply held convictions".[12] This is why, he explains, by cherry-picking his speeches or the events in his life, many have come to perceive JFK as a man of the left *and* a man of the right, as a Cold Warrior *and* an apostle of peace, as a committed Catholic *and* an affront to the Church, as a stooge of corporate greed *and* an agent of communism. In other words, JFK's life and persona were enough of a blank slate that he can easily be viewed by some as a national savior and by others as a traitor. Much of the same ambiguity enshrouds Lee Oswald, who also was young and enigmatic, whose thoughts and motives were a mystery even to those who knew him, and whose behavior in the days following Kennedy's death did not fit the popular stereotypes of Marxist revolutionaries. Which one of these two men was a hero, and which one was a villain? Could both be villains, or victims of a sinister plot brewing offstage? Answers largely depend on one's expectations.

The "official" story of JFK's death that was reported during the hours, days, and months that followed, was a nightmare of madness to many, one that didn't fit any obvious pattern. A hapless lone communist known to the FBI (but largely left to his own), who just happened to work in a building on the President's motor-cade route, had managed to evade detection by his coworkers and single-handedly murder the world's most powerful man, one whose youth and optimism—so the story went—heralded an era of progress, renewal, and cooperation. Worse, the assassin had no manifest motive, even though he had acted, of all places, in a very conservative state where racial tensions were high, where right-wing groups openly advertised their hatred of Kennedy, but whom, the public was told, had nothing to do with his death nor had any connection to Oswald. To make matters more confusing, JFK's murder was followed by another assassination that many took for a mob hit. This entire scenario screamed out for a rational narrative with a clear moral arc and appropriate balance of good and evil. Sadly, the official report of the president's death offered the public little of that. And that is why many myths had begun to take shape.

3.2   "A hand on the chicken switch": the myth of the Irish Mafia

The mythologization of John Kennedy began long before he died, even before he was president. In fact, the entire Kennedy family enjoyed (or suffered) a sort of mystique that made them the object of mass adulation, gossip, rumors, and hatred—the sort that is usually reserved for Hollywood stars and British Royals. This fascination with all things Kennedy increased exponentially following JFK's assassination. It remained strong over the following decades, fed by popular nostalgia, conspiracy theorizing, and a string of family tragedies that included the 1968 shooting of John's brother Robert (another deep well of conspiracy angst), and the tragic 1999 death of his son John F. Kennedy, Jr., a magazine editor and pop-culture icon who died in an accidental plane crash (i.e., unless you believe he was murdered by Hilary Clinton![13]).

Much of this fascination with John Kennedy as a heroic figure and a symbol of American progress was largely the creation of JFK's father, Joseph P. Kennedy, Sr., a wealthy and influential investor and federal bureaucrat whose ambitions and reputation (both positive and negative) fostered the emergence of several Kennedy myths. John Kennedy was Joe Kennedy's second son, the second of nine children. Throughout his long and accomplished career, Joe Kennedy sought wealth and success through hard work and upward mobility. Ever-mindful of the poverty and discrimination his Irish Catholic ancestors faced in their home country and then as immigrants, Joe Kennedy became a leading member of the Boston Irish community and an important political power broker during the interwar period (1918–39). After obtaining a Harvard education and contracting a high-profile marriage to Rose Elizabeth Fitzgerald (the daughter of Boston mayor John Francis "Honey Fitz" Fitzgerald), the elder Kennedy established lucrative business connections in New York and Hollywood and filled important positions in President Franklin Delano Roosevelt's administration as Chairman of the Securities and Exchange Commission and then as Ambassador to the Court of St. James (i.e., the United Kingdom).

One of the many enduring rumors concerning the wealthy Kennedy clan holds that the family patriarch built a large part of his fortune trafficking alcohol during the period of prohibition. It is known that Joe Kennedy invested in alcohol-related import ventures before and after prohibition, but it remains contested whether he pursued it illegally during that time. If he did, it largely evaded the attention of the authorities, either because Joe Kennedy was more discrete and less criminally driven than the infamous Chicago mobster Al Capone, or because he had numerous political, business, and family connections that allowed him to evade prosecution. According to Kennedy biographer Laurence Leamer,

> it is probably testimony to the sheer acumen of Joe Kennedy that no one has come up with any hard physical evidence linking him to bootlegging, but the circumstantial evidence strongly suggests that Joe was a financier and supplier of illegal liquor.[14]

Whether or not the Kennedy fortune was ill-gained, the perception that a liberal and Catholic "Irish Mafia" was gaining political power unnerved many conservatives and reactionaries.

With his rapid social ascension, his significant wealth, and his large family, it is not surprising that Joe Kennedy saw himself as the founder of a new dynasty. He made connections in elite circles (partly through the Democratic Party) and had high expectations for his children, especially his eldest son Joseph ("Joe Jr.") whom he was grooming to become the first Catholic US president. However, Joe Jr., who volunteered for military service in 1941, died during an ill-fated bombing raid against the Nazis. The charge to take up the family banner fell on the shoulders of John, the less academic and more "fragile" and "sheltered" of Joe Kennedy's two oldest sons.[15]

Like his father, John Kennedy studied at Harvard and, like his older brother, then volunteered for military service. He was almost killed as well while serving as a Navy Lieutenant in the Pacific when his motor torpedo boat (PT-109) was rammed by a Japanese destroyer. His prowess in saving the lives of several crew members would bolster his reputation as an exceptional and patriotic young leader. It would even inspire the production of a *PT-109* book, movie, and song, which were marketed during his tenure as president (a JFK action figure would follow).

Lieutenant John Kennedy returned home a decorated war hero in 1944 and began a brief stint in journalism. But he quickly resolved to enter (or was thrust) into politics, running for a vacant Congressional seat in 1946, which he secured with his father's connections and money. He was then elected Junior Senator for Massachusetts in 1952. In 1955, he published *Profiles in Courage*, a work of non-fiction that earned him a Pulitzer Prize (perhaps undeservedly[16]). As a congressman and senator, JFK served on high-profile committees that gave him insight into the workings of organized crime and foreign policy. Despite chronic back problems that mined his attendance record, Kennedy rose to prominence in the late fifties as a possible candidate for the presidency.

Nevertheless, Senator Kennedy was perceived as the underdog when he secured the Democratic nomination in 1960. Lyndon Johnson, his main rival at the convention, had much more experience and political savvy but lacked the charisma and glamour of the young Kennedy who defeated him handily and went on to defeat a strong Republican contender, incumbent Vice President Richard Nixon. It was, arguably, the first national contest in which television tilted the scales of popular opinion.[17] Nixon was the more popular and experienced realist who had sniffed out communist spies while in Congress and faced-off against Soviet leader Nikita Khrushchev on national TV while he was vice president. Furthermore, rumors surrounding Joe Sr.'s business practices, his support for Roosevelt's New Deal, and his promotion of the appeasement of Hitler before the war,[18] made many conservatives view the young Senator as a disguised socialist, even though he was always rigidly anti-communist.[19] Southern racists, traditionally drawn to the Democratic Party since the Civil War, perceived Kennedy as a carpet-bagging Ivy League oligarch, a group they believed had too long undermined Southern laws and traditions. Kennedy's Catholicism was also unpopular with large parts of the electorate. To many conservative Protestants and Masonic freethinkers, JFK was no less than an agent of the Papacy. Unsurprisingly, a conservative backlash took shape during the years 1947–63 against the entire Kennedy clan. It was not strong enough to halt JFK's ascent to the presidency, but it was bitter enough to radicalize anti-Kennedy sentiment on the political right. This anti-Kennedy movement, shaped by staunch anti-communist, anti-liberal, and anti-Catholic beliefs, gave shape to a string of character assassinations built from cherry-picked facts, half-truths, and unsubstantiated rumors about Kennedy's background, beliefs, and rise to power, a set of claims that is best be described as the Myth of the Irish Mafia.

The Irish Mafia narrative was hatched mainly in newspaper and magazine editorials while JFK was in office. Influential conservative journalists like William F. Buckley, Russell Kirk, John Chamberlain, and James Burnham used their media pulpits to critique Kennedy's youth and ineptitude, his allegedly anti-American policies, his softness on communism, or his moral corruption.[20] Anti-Catholic evangelists, outspoken opponents of civil rights like General Edwin Walker and

Birmingham Public Safety Commissioner Eugene "Bull" Connor, and right-wing organizations like the Young Americans for Freedom, the John Birch Society, and the Ku Klux Klan also publicly railed against Kennedy, depicting him as a dangerous liberal, communist, or antichrist.[21] A set of anti-Kennedy ads and handbills—some of which appear in the *Warren Report*—were also distributed in Dallas in advance of his fatal tour of Texas[22] (see Figure 3.1).

However, the most visible and influential element of this literature was *JFK: The Man and the Myth* (1963) by syndicated columnist Victor Lasky, which sold 300,000 copies and briefly made the bestseller list.[23] It was a one-sided, hyper-conservative critique of Kennedy's character and record in Congress, behind whose charismatic façade lurked a "shallow, immature and untrustworthy" operator.[24] It also alleged that JFK engaged in sexual misconduct (some of which was later proven true) and questioned his heroic wartime record. Lasky went on to write several other "Man and the Myth" books targeting other liberal figures, including Bobby Kennedy and other members of JFK's entourage. While Lasky's attack might not have greatly affected Kennedy's chances at reelection, there is little doubt that it fostered the emergence of several Kennedy counter-myths during the years that followed (see section 3.3).[25]

The Irish Mafia Myth would not fare well following Kennedy's murder. Railing against a dead man who was now hailed as a national martyr became a morally questionable act during the years, even decades, that followed his death. Self-censorship on these matters even hampered the career of Senator Barry Goldwater, the 1964 Republican presidential candidate, who until the assassination had spent much of his pre-campaign energies attacking Kennedy's ethics, competence, and support for civil rights. The Irish Mafia narrative would nevertheless return as a popular theme in the historical literature, though it grew more tempered than the vitriol produced by Lasky or shifted its focus to other members of the Kennedy clan.[26]

The first of these postmortem critiques was Richard Whalen's *The Founding Father: the Story of Joseph P. Kennedy* (1964), an exposé on the ambitious and amoral pragmatism of the Kennedy patriarch, his thirst for wealth and status, and alleged obsession to prove he was not a stereotypical Irishman.[27] While the Kennedys were a united family, Whalen argued, they were no paragons of Catholic values, but more like a small authoritarian regime caught between the Church and the marketplace; a royal-family-in-waiting ruled by a cold, commanding, and power-driven progenitor.[28] Similar works appeared in later years, including Ronald Kessler's *The Sins of the Father: Joseph P. Kennedy and the Dynasty He Founded* (1996) and David Nasaw's *The Patriarch: The Remarkable Life and Turbulent Times of Joseph P. Kennedy* (2013), which painted the man as a bootlegger, a ruthless bully, an absent father, an anti-Semite, a commanding family autocrat, a rogue diplomat, a master manipulator, and an inveterate womanizer.[29]

The Irish Mafia narrative went out of style during the Seventies and Eighties as memories of the Kennedy family and JFK's time in office became filtered through the tragic deaths of both Jack and Bobby.[30] This was due largely to the powerful nostalgic myth of Camelot (see next section) which presented JFK as a martyr for

WANTED

FOR

TREASON

THIS MAN is wanted for treasonous activities against the United States:

1. Betraying the Constitution (which he swore to uphold):
   He is turning the sovereignty of the U. S. over to the communist controlled United Nations.
   He is betraying our friends (Cuba, Katanga, Portugal) and befriending our enemies (Russia, Yugoslavia, Poland).
2. He has been WRONG on innumerable issues affecting the security of the U.S. (United Nations- Berlin wall -Missle removal - Cuba- Wheat deals -Test Ban Treaty, etc.)

3. He has been lax in enforcing Communist Registration laws.
4. He has given support and encouragement to the Communist inspired racial riots.
5. He has illegally invaded a sovereign State with federal troops.
6. He has consistantly appointed Anti-Christians to Federal office:
   Upholds the Supreme Court in its Anti-Christian rulings.
   Aliens and known Communists abound in Federal offices.
7. He has been caught in fantastic LIES to the American people (including personal ones like his previous marraige and divorce).

FIGURE 3.1 Anti-Kennedy leaflet and newspaper ad., November 1963

Source: Warren Commission Exhibits 996 and 1031, National Archives and Records Administration.

14—Section 1 · The Dallas Morning News · Friday, November 22, 1963

WELCOME MR. KENNEDY

TO DALLAS...

...A CITY so disgraced by a recent Liberal smear attempt that its citizens have just elected two more Conservative Americans to public office.

...A CITY that is an economic "boom town," not because of Federal handouts, but through conservative economic and business practices.

...A CITY that will continue to grow and prosper despite efforts by you and your administration to penalize it for its non-conformity to "New Frontierism."

...A CITY that rejected your philosophy and policies in 1960 and will do so again in 1964—even more emphatically than before.

MR. KENNEDY, despite contentions on the part of your administration, the State Department, the Mayor of Dallas, the Dallas City Council, and members of your party, we free-thinking and America-thinking citizens of Dallas still have, through a Constitution largely ignored by you, the right to address our grievances, to question you, to disagree with you, and to criticize you.

In asserting this constitutional right, we wish to ask you publicly the following questions—indeed, questions of paramount importance and interest to all free peoples everywhere—which we trust you will answer...in public, without sophistry. These questions are:

WHY is Latin America turning either anti-American or Communistic, or both, despite increased U. S. foreign aid, State Department policy, and your own Ivy-Tower pronouncements?

WHY do you say we have built a "wall of freedom" around Cuba when there is no freedom in Cuba today? Because of your policy, thousands of Cubans have been imprisoned, are starving and being persecuted—with thousands already murdered and thousands more awaiting execution and, in addition, the entire population of almost 7,000,000 Cubans are living in slavery.

WHY have you approved the sale of wheat and corn to our enemies when you know the Communist soldiers "travel on their stomachs" just as ours do? Communist soldiers are daily wounding and/or killing American soldiers in South Viet Nam.

WHY did you host, salute and entertain Tito — Moscow's Trojan Horse — just a short time after our sworn enemy, Khrushchev, embraced the Yugoslav dictator as a great hero and leader of Communism?

WHY have you urged greater aid, comfort, recognition, and understanding for Yugoslavia, Poland, Hungary, and other Communist countries, while turning your back on the pleas of Hungarian, East German, Cuban and other anti-Communist freedom fighters?

WHY did Cambodia kick the U.S. out of its country after we poured nearly 400 Million Dollars of aid into its ultra-leftist government?

WHY has Gus Hall, head of the U.S. Communist Party praised almost every one of your policies and announced that the party will endorse and support your re-election in 1964?

WHY have you banned the showing at U.S. military bases of the film "Operation Abolition"—the movie by the House Committee on Un-American Activities exposing Communism in America?

WHY have you ordered or permitted your brother Bobby, the Attorney General, to go soft on Communists, fellow-travelers, and ultra-leftists in America, while permitting him to persecute loyal Americans who criticize you, your administration, and your leadership?

WHY are you in favor of the U.S. continuing to give economic aid to Argentina, in spite of that fact that Argentina has just seized almost 400 Million Dollars of American private property?

WHY has the Foreign Policy of the United States degenerated to the point that the C.I.A. is arranging coups and having staunch Anti-Communist Allies of the U.S. bloodily exterminated?

WHY have you scrapped the Monroe Doctrine in favor of the "Spirit of Moscow"?

MR. KENNEDY, as citizens of these United States of America, we DEMAND answers to these questions, and we want them NOW.

THE AMERICAN FACT-FINDING COMMITTEE

"An unaffiliated and non-partisan group of citizens who wish truth"

BERNARD WEISSMAN,
Chairman

P.O. Box 1792 — Dallas 21, Texas

(Political Advertisement paid for by Bernard Weissman)

FIGURE 3.1 Continued

democracy and established itself as the dominant narrative of JFK's life, even among conservatives.[31] Studies of the "dark side" of the Kennedy family grew popular again after the end of the Cold War. Interestingly, several of these were not penned by conservatives but by authors on the political left weary of Kennedy hagiographies who held a more critical view of the man's foreign policy decisions, electoral machinations, and tawdry personal life. These books include Nigel Hamilton's *JFK: Reckless Youth* (1992), Noam Chomsky's *Rethinking Camelot: JFK, the Vietnam War, and U.S. Political Culture* (1993), and Seymour Hersh's *The Dark Side of Camelot* (1997), all of which shared the view that Kennedy should be perceived as the *cause* of conspiracy, not its *victim*. Hamilton's book offers a none-too-flattering account of JFK as a confused, rebellious, and passive-aggressive youth "emotionally crippled in his relations with women," a psychoanalytic deconstruction of "Kennedyland" as a "theme park of family values," and a critique of the family that spawned this mysterious politician with a "strangely split psyche".[32] It scrutinizes JFK's early love affairs with disreputable women and his strained relations with his distant and dysfunctional parents. As a result, he argues, the lovelorn young Kennedy became an unscrupulous politician obsessed with beautiful young creatures and adulating crowds, two fetish loves that could have equally led to his undoing.

Chomsky's volume responds to claims made by filmmaker Oliver Stone[33] that Kennedy, had he survived, would have pulled American troops out of Vietnam and brought the Cold War to an end during his second mandate. The historical record consistently demonstrates, insists Chomsky, that JFK's foreign policy toward South-East Asia and Latin America was consistent with the then-popular "domino theory"—the belief that any international expansion of communism must be countered with militarily force lest the Soviets take over the world. Kennedy thus completely misunderstood (or else plainly ignored) the plight of the people of South Vietnam, their dismal economic situation, and the reasons for their growing support of communism. True to his anarcho-syndicalist worldview, Chomsky scolds his fellow leftists who depict Kennedy as an apostle of peace instead of a sponsor of "U.S. backed state terror". Chomsky herein presents JFK not as a martyr, but as a puppet of predatory Western capitalism.[34]

Hersh's book focuses on the scandalous goings-on in the Kennedy White House and JFK's personal and family connections to organized crime. Kennedy took part in lascivious parties thrown by singer Frank Sinatra and his Las Vegas "Rat Pack," a community of womanizing entertainers with mafia connections. He also engaged in illicit affairs with international spies, Hollywood stars, underage aides, and mobsters' girlfriends. But most importantly, Hersh claims, Kennedy benefitted—with the blessing and help of his father—from the mafia's assistance in "stealing" the 1960 election and later in trying to murder Cuban leader Fidel Castro, a set of crimes that were covered-up—again, at the urging of Joe Sr.—by naming his inexperienced brother Bobby the country's Attorney General, making it easier for him to sidestep any investigation into these crimes. Kennedy's illegal attempts to kill Castro, Hersh suggests, ultimately caused his own downfall when Lee Harvey Oswald, a desperate admirer of Castro who somehow got wind of these murder attempts, turned his rifle toward the president.[35] JFK thus precipitated his own death despite Bobby's guilt-fueled beliefs that Jack had been a victim of a grander plot.

Other highly critical Kennedy books include Gary Willis' *The Kennedy Imprisonment: A Meditation on Power* (1982) and Thomas C. Reeves' *A Question of Character* (1997). Such volumes, however, were swimming against the current. The antipathy many conservatives felt toward John Kennedy during the 1950s and 1960s has largely dissipated—displaced perhaps by equivalent antipathies for the Clintons, Barack Obama, or Joe Biden—making the Irish Mafia narrative less and less compelling with time. However, these critical exposés have allowed many twenty-first-century researchers to temper their dislike or admiration of the man with a more nuanced picture of Kennedy and his times. Several recent biographies of JFK do not hesitate to highlight the ugly parts of his personal and political lives without ignoring the good. These include Richard Reeves' *President Kennedy: Profile of Power* (1993), John Hellmann's *The Kennedy Obsession: The American Myth of JFK* (1999), Laurence Leamer's *The Kennedy Men* (2001), Robert Dallek's *An Unfinished Life* (2004), and James Pierson's *Camelot and the Cultural Revolution: How the Assassination of John F. Kennedy Shattered American Liberalism* (2007). Such works help us see Kennedy not as a hero or demon but as a shrewd politician and a flawed human being with a proclivity for sexual escapades, a man who prioritized style over substance, and a liberal Cold Warrior with a genuine, if moderate, desire for racial equality.

3.3 "For one brief shining moment": the myth of Camelot

If the conservative Irish Mafia myth was hamstringed by the events of November 22, 1963, its liberal counterpart enjoyed the opposite fate. Indeed, Kennedy's death was a mythmaking bomb that turned a polarizing pragmatist into a national saint.

Ever-conscious of his family's public image, Joseph Kennedy had instilled in his children the importance of having a good reputation, not as a virtue in its own right but as a means of achieving worldly success. The Kennedy children were free to pursue their own dreams and desires, but unless these led to "serious" careers like the law, business, or politics, the young Kennedys knew not to expect much support from their father.[36] But if they made success and the family name their primary endeavor, they could count on their father's connections and funds to carry them farther than they ever would on their own. This lesson was not lost on the academically middling and sickly young Jack Kennedy, who from early adulthood yearned to step out of the shadow of his anointed older brother to earn the full respect of his father. But if this were ever to happen, Jack would have to carefully manage his public persona—what might today be called his "brand"—to match Joe Jr.'s golden-boy image. This was not something Jack would leave others to shape. He was determined to carefully manage his image himself.[37]

Running for office and giving inspiring speeches was only one part of this project. Another was to present himself as an American patriot and champion of democracy by publishing articles for prestigious journals and newspapers during his time in Congress, and also two books: one on the theme of resisting tyranny and the other on the duty to follow one's conscience. Demonstrating his "intellectual engagement with national issues," writes Hellmann, allowed the young Senator to "dramatically transform the impression of youthful daring and energy" that had first helped him woo the public: a genteel playboy image that he was growing too old to sustain and which he needed to groom "into one of maturing seriousness".[38] JFK's first major publication was *Why England Slept*, an updated version of his undergraduate senior thesis (first published in 1940, and again during his presidency in 1961). It presented a critique of British Prime Minister Neville Chamberlain's prewar policy of appeasing the Nazis and praise for Winston Churchill, who remained resolutely opposed to totalitarianism during the interwar years. The book served to bolster Kennedy's image as a Cold Warrior devoted to countering Soviet Communism, an image he freely promoted during his presidential campaign.

Another book he produced during this period (with much assistance from Ted Sorensen[39]) was *Profiles in Courage*, composed during his 1954 convalescence from a spine operation—a procedure that nearly killed him—which he underwent during his tenure as Senator. The book is a series of studies of American senators—men like John Quincy Adams, Daniel Webster, and Sam Houston—who displayed fortitude and determination in the face of strong opposition. The book depicted these men as political luminaries, archetypal statesmen, and, indirectly, examples of what Kennedy himself could become. As Hellmann remarked, a positive correlation between the book's author and the men showcased in *Profiles* could not have been hard to infer by its original readers:

> These elements positioned the contemporary reader to ask on every page if the young politician who had written the book would carry into the present the knowledge afforded by the examples of past senators. Would the young hero answer the call to moral courage?[40]

Had *Profiles in Courage* been written a decade later by anyone else, it would have screamed for a chapter on JFK—that is, on the heroic and nostalgic version of the man as he was remembered after his death, not as he was known before. But the transformation of Kennedy's image from a reckless and privileged youth into a political sage, a national hero, and a paragon of civic virtue equal to Abraham Lincoln would still require more work. This was accomplished during the days that immediately followed his death by none other than his wife Jacqueline, who made it her ultimate mission to carefully manage (cynics might say engineer) the way her murdered husband would henceforth be remembered.

As Mrs. Kennedy emerged from a state of shock during the hours that followed the assassination, she grew convinced, like many around her, that Jack had been killed by Southern racists opposed to his civil rights platform.[41] It was a rational conclusion: Dallas was known to harbor strong anti-Kennedy feelings and widespread opposition to racial equality. It was also home to two outspoken right-wing opponents of Kennedy: retired Army General Edwin Walker and oilman H.L. Hunt.[42] It was also the place where Lyndon Johnson's wife Lady Bird was spat on during the 1960 presidential campaign, and where Adlai Stevenson, a former presidential candidate serving as Kennedy's Ambassador to the United Nations, was attacked by protestors on October 24, 1963, a few weeks before JFK's fatal trip to Texas.[43] Southern antipathy had also been the reason for Kennedy's trip to Texas, to charm its conservative electorate. President Kennedy had in fact joked while traveling from Fort Worth to Dallas that morning that they were "heading into nut country" and flippantly stated that if anybody really wanted to kill him, all they had to do was climb up a tall building "with a telescopic rifle".[44] Many of his biographers have observed that Kennedy seemed to believe he was fated to live a short life and often quipped darkly about it. On the morning of November 22, 1963, this was just one more example of Kennedy's wry sense of humor. A few hours later, it would be nothing less than prophetic. For any or all these reasons, Jacqueline Kennedy harbored instant and fierce resentment against Southern reactionaries whom she believed had murdered her husband. When JFK's personal physician, Admiral George Burkley, recommended aboard Air Force One that she change out of her blood-spattered dress, Mrs. Kennedy replied, "No! Let them see what they've done". When, after landing at Andrews Air Force Base, Kennedy's staff began making arrangements to usher her out of the plane without attracting the media's attention, Mrs. Kennedy again refused. "We'll go out the regular way," she told Press Secretary Malcolm Kilduff, "I want them to see what they have done".[45] As William Manchester remarked:

> This was an entirely new relationship. The day had gone forever when the pols dismissed the President's wife as Jackie the Socialite. And she herself was a new Jackie, transformed by her vow that the full impact of the loss should be indelibly etched upon the national conscience. [...] The new Jackie contrasted so sharply with the First Lady they had known that even the inner circle of Kennedy intimates were slow to grasp the extent of the *volte-face*.[46]

Mrs. Kennedy resolutely remained in that blood-caked pink dress for the rest of the day and all through the evening, wearing it dutifully before the public and cameras like the stigmata of saints. She made herself visible to fellow travelers inside the plane, standing beside Lyndon Johnson for photographs while he was getting sworn-in (see Figure 3.2). She did so again for the journalists, dignitaries, and three thousand onlookers who watched her deplane at Andrews Air Force Base in Washington, and again while she paid her regards to her husband's remains inside the "hushed and cavernous" East Room of the White House.[47] Through all this, the former First Lady remained determined to show the whole world what her husband and she had been made to suffer at the hands of virulent racists.

Of course, Mrs. Kennedy was one of the few people in the United States who had not yet tuned in to the news to follow the story of the presumed assassin. It was only late that evening, during the autopsy in Bethesda, that she was informed by Bobby Kennedy that the Dallas Police had arrested a suspect—a confessed communist who appeared to have acted alone. This information was hard for Jackie to

FIGURE 3.2 Jacqueline Kennedy and Lyndon Johnson aboard Air Force One, 22 November 1963

Source: Cecil Stoughton / JFK Library.[48]

process. It robbed her husband's death of a purpose and invalidated her anger. "He didn't even have the satisfaction of being killed for civil rights," she told her mother that night, "It had to be some silly little Communist".[49]

Jacqueline Kennedy was not alone in wanting to blame someone else than an unhinged lone Marxist. Back in Washington, President Johnson and his entourage quietly wondered whether the Russians or Cubans had something to do with all this. Many conservatives in Texas and Washington had little doubt (in spite of thin evidence) that Oswald was a foreign-sponsored assassin.[50] Liberal-minded journalists and politicians, for their part, began thumping "the drumbeat of collective guilt," blaming the climate of violence and racism that reigned in Texas and throughout the South.[51] Even Chief Justice Warren, a long-time supporter of civil rights and the ultimate arbiter of the seminal 1954 *Brown v. Board of Education of Topeka* ruling, declared in a public statement delivered hours before Lee Oswald's identity became public that "a good and great president has suffered martyrdom as a result of the hatred and bitterness that has been injected into the life of our nation by bigots".[52] Two days later, during a memorial service held at Capitol Hill, the Supreme Court judge would again intone that Kennedy had been "a believer in the dignity and equality of all human beings; a fighter for justice; an apostle of peace". Warren then added, though it was now clear Oswald had been no Bircher or Klansman:

FIGURE 3.3 Kennedy family and JFK casket arriving at Capitol, 24 November 1963
Source: Abbie Rowe/JFK Library[53]

What moved some misguided wretch to do this horrible deed may never be known to us, but we do know that such acts are commonly stimulated by forces of hatred and malevolence such as today are eating their way into the bloodstream of American life.[54] Many others, including Kennedy's special assistant and speechwriter Arthur Schlesinger Jr., were quick to blame a "violent streak in the national culture [...], a climate of bigotry and intolerance cultivated by the radical right".[55]

This improvised mash-up of facts, feelings, and fictions by high-profile figures caused widespread confusion about the crime and its alleged perpetrator.

Was Oswald a Marxist, as Texas authorities claimed, or a right-wing bigot, as the East Coast establishment seemed to suggest? Could he in fact be both? Many Americans—including Jack Ruby[56]—lacked the political knowledge to grasp the difference between left-wing and right-wing extremism, and therefore accepted both claims as true. Those who identified as Marxists or socialists could rightly feel indignant for being mistaken for their sworn enemies. The same applied to diehard conservatives who suddenly found themselves wrongfully blamed for the acts of a communist zealot. Indeed, Oswald could be called many things, but "racist" was not one of them. Unfortunately, the climate of grief and anger that followed Kennedy's death did not leave much room for careful reflection or public debates on these types of distinctions. Declarations like those discussed previously, and the support they received from leading journalists, only confused the public's understanding of why their president was murdered. As James Piereson explains, Kennedy's most likely cause of death—that he was a victim of the politics of the Cold War—was obfuscated early in the game by a liberal fixation on Southern bigotry.[57]

In the weekend that followed the murder, Mrs. Kennedy was deeply involved in shaping the details of JFK's funeral, setting a tone that, she believed, would correctly establish his legacy as a great democratic defender of human rights (see Figure 3.3). As a result, JFK would receive official respects second only to those of Abraham Lincoln, the Great Emancipator and Civil War victor. It was clear that Mrs. Kennedy wished for the two men to be conjoined in the popular imagination, much like Jack had fostered a kinship between himself and his political heroes in *Profiles in Courage*. From the beginning of the funeral procession to the lowering of JFK's casket into its burial plot, the ceremony was a carefully stage-managed set of symbols: the black veil, the horse-drawn cortege, the kissing of the coffin, the Kennedy children's military salute (on their mother's cue), the bagpipers of the Scottish Black Watch Regiment (whose performance was the last one JFK attended, and whose history served as a powerful symbol of "a lost cause, which, in the end, triumphed"[58]), JFK's burial in Arlington National Cemetery, and the eternal flame that still graces his last resting place, located just a short walk from the Tomb of the Unknown Soldier. Like Gettysburg, the Ford Theater, and the USS Arizona, Kennedy's grave has become one of America's prime mythical spaces, a partly historical and partly manufactured heritage site. To borrow a phrase from French historian Pierre Nora, it has become a powerful "*lieu de mémoire*". According to Nora, *lieux de mémoire* (i.e., "realms of memory" or "memory spaces") are public landmarks inhabited by communal symbols like monuments or memorials that produce a sense of collective identity through the commemoration of an ostensibly shared but highly mythologized past. They are

> at once natural and artificial, simple and ambiguous, concrete and abstract. […] The fundamental purpose of a *lieu de mémoire* is to stop time, to inhibit forgetting, to fix a state of things, to immortalize death, and to materialize the immaterial…[59]

This served to repackage the story of JFK's death in a way that better served the worldview of his widow, family, and supporters. As Piereson explains:

> Here in a nutshell is the central myth of the Kennedy assassination: a climate of hate inspired by the far right [...] created the conditions for President Kennedy's murder. [...] Oswald merely played a part in a larger cultural drama. On this view, President Kennedy was a martyr, somewhat like Abraham Lincoln, to the causes of civil rights, racial justice, and an elevated liberalism.[60]

It is a testimony to Mrs. Kennedy's strength of character and theatrical sense that she did not allow the apparent meaninglessness of her husband's murder to deter her from shaping the legacy she thought he deserved. In her view, Jack had dedicated his life to fighting the forces of bigotry and ought to be remembered that way. But the funeral was only the first of her efforts to firmly establish this narrative. In the following weeks, Mrs. Kennedy enlisted the services of two famous and trusted writers to help her shape President Kennedy's story. The first was the Pulitzer Prize-winning *Life* journalist Theodore White, author of *The Making of the President, 1960* (1961), a laudatory chronicle of JFK's first (and only) presidential campaign. White was a former classmate of John's brother Joe Jr.—another heroic dead Kennedy—and a sort of family friend. The second was historian William Manchester, author of *Portrait of a President* (1962), a flattering primer on JFK's personal life. Both authors would help firmly establish the nostalgic myth of Camelot.

Jackie met with White at the Kennedy compound in Hyannis, Massachusetts, less than a week after JFK's funeral. The interview was published in the December 6, 1963, issue of *Life*.[61] She offered White an exclusive story providing he let her proofread and edit the text. White agreed, though he would later regret relinquishing his journalistic autonomy.[62] "It was Jacqueline Kennedy's tour de force," wrote James Swanson, "her finest hour—actually more than five hours—of press manipulation".[63] While the funeral had established a persuasive symbolic connection between JFK and Abraham Lincoln, this interview proposed an even more compelling analogy between the slain president and the mythical King Arthur. The Broadway musical *Camelot* had recently enjoyed a popular run and its audio record, Mrs. Kennedy told White, had been a source of enjoyment at the White House. Referencing its lyrics, Jacqueline painted a storybook image of her late husband, not as the pragmatic liberal that journalists and advisors knew him to be, but as a visionary idealist. She highlighted his love of music and literature, his sickly childhood and fondness for chivalry, his faith, his inspiration to children, and his aspirations to place a man on the Moon. "For a while," she told White,

> I thought that history was something that bitter old men wrote, but then I realized history made Jack what he was. [...] Jack had this hero idea of history, the idealistic view. [...] There'll be great presidents again [...] but there'll never be another Camelot again.[64]

James Piereson further noted:

> One must admire Mrs. Kennedy for the skill with which she deployed these images in the difficult aftermath of her husband's death. Our retrospective view of President Kennedy is now filtered through the legends and symbols she put forward at that time. The hardheaded politician devoted to step-by-step progress was transformed in death into the consummate liberal idealist. The Cold War leader who would "bear any price to insure the survival of liberty" was subsequently viewed as an idealistic peacemaker.[65]

White's interview, which reached a readership of 30 million, inaugurated several decades of nostalgic Camelot metaphors about the Kennedy White House, making it one of the most powerful and enduring myths in contemporary American culture. But this would have unforeseen and adverse repercussions. In turning JFK into a larger-than-life apostle of peace and describing his death as the end of an era, Mrs. Kennedy "inadvertently contributed to the unwinding of the tradition of American liberalism that her husband represented in life, […] leaving his successors with little upon which to build".[66]

Manchester's role in creating this myth was a bit more subtle. Robert and Jacqueline Kennedy requested in early 1964—while the Warren Commission was still investigating the murder—that this historian draft a chronicle of JFK's death. In doing so, they gave him privileged access to the family's records, as well as those of the Warren Commission (which he declined[67]), provided the family's privacy and dignity were respected. While there is no indication that Manchester intended to break their trust, he did maintain greater autonomy than either White or Chief Justice Warren, even exposing some plebeian details of the Kennedys' private habits.[68] Nevertheless, Manchester's investigation into the causes and context of JFK's death, published as *The Death of a President* (1967), was professional and thorough, independently reaching the same conclusions as the Warren Commission regarding the who and the how of the crime. The book sold over a million copies and remains, over a half-century later, one of the most influential accounts of the events that occurred on the weekend of Kennedy's death.

Thus did Jacqueline Kennedy, with the assistance of Theodore White, William Manchester, and Chief Justice Warren, lay the groundwork for an enduring and powerful myth that painted Jack Kennedy as a hero who died for an inspiring purpose: to teach a nation that they could be nobler, more peaceful, more just, and more cosmopolitan, irrespective of the fact that he was gunned down by a "silly little communist" with no history of racism.

Far too many accounts in the Camelot tradition exist for us to survey even a moderate sample. These include countless articles, photographic essays, and picture books produced by *Life* magazine and similar publications, as well as several memoirs by Kennedy's former colleagues, such as Theodore Sorensen's *Kennedy* (1965) and *The Kennedy Legacy* (1969), Arthur Schlesinger Jr.'s *A Thousand Days* (1965), Pierre Salinger's *With Kennedy* (1966), and Kenneth O'Donnell and David Powers' *Johnny,*

We Hardly Knew Ye (1972). Some recent biographies adopt the Camelot tone but are less blind than earlier works to JFK's flaws. These include Chris Matthew's *Jack Kennedy: Elusive Hero* (2011), James Swanson's *End of Days* (2013), Larry Sabato's *The Kennedy Half Century* (2013), Dean Owen's *November 22, 1963: Reflections on the Life, Assassination, and Legacy of John F. Kennedy* (2013), and Andrew Cohen's *Two Days in June: John F. Kennedy and the 48 Hours that Made History* (2014). Such publications, many of which coincided with the 50th anniversary of the assassination, suggest that the mixture of heroism and nostalgia contained in the Camelot myth still holds a great deal of sway over the popular imagination and also over many historians.

The role Jackie Kennedy played in shaping her dead husband's legacy had an enormous impact on future researchers. For many decades, the glittering myth of Camelot would serve as a powerful filter through which most Kennedy researchers—conspiracist or otherwise—would examine his life. Jackie Kennedy's discrete but unwavering efforts to have her husband remembered as an icon of courage, champion of freedom and civil rights, and a victim of hatred—in short, as one of the greatest presidents in US history—was successful in stamping out the uglier story about a rich, shallow, nepotistic, and morally fraught sophomore, a man of great words but little substance, one whose love of adulating crowds and lack of concern for his safety might have gotten him killed.

Indeed, the Camelot myth was very successful in quelling the conservative "Irish Mafia" trope, but as we will see, it also had the perverse effect of stoking another ideological furnace. For if the slain president had indeed been a paragon of virtue, as the Camelot story proclaimed, one could rightly wonder why anyone, including Oswald, would have wanted to kill such a luminary. In the minds of many who were racked by grief and desperately longed for a story that gave their life meaning, such questions could only point to a monstrous and pervasive evil, not to some angry lone nut.

Notes

1 *Merriam-Webster Dictionary*.
2 Henry M. Sayre: *The Humanities: Culture, Continuity & Change, Volume I,* Fourth Edition (2019), 20.
3 Joseph Campbell with Bill Moyers: *The Power of Myth* (1991), 6, 10. Interestingly, two individuals closely related to the JFK assassination—Lyndon Baines Johnson's former personal assistant and Press Secretary Bill Moyers as well as Jacqueline Kennedy (Onassis), then working as a publishing editor at Anchor Books—were involved in the production of this influential volume, based on a six-part 1988 PBS television special.
4 See, for example, Mary Beard: *SPQR: A History of Ancient Rome* (2015), chap. 2.
5 The recent popular transformation of John A. Macdonald, the first Canadian Prime Minister, from visionary nation-builder to genocidal bigot is a noteworthy example. Alex Ballingall: "Sir John A. Macdonald: Architect of genocide or Canada's founding father?," *The Toronto Star*, August 24, 2017.
6 Kim Jung Il was actually born in a small fishing village in Russia. "Kim Jong Il: 10 weird facts, propaganda," *CBS News*, December 19, 2011.

7 "Declaration of Independence: A Transcription". *U.S. National Archives* website.

8 Richard Ned Lebow: *The Politics and Ethics of Identity* (2012), 50.

9 Ibid., 50, 49.

10 Beard, chaps. 10 and 11.

11 Wade and Tavris, 360.

12 James Piereson: *Camelot and the Cultural Revolution* (2007), 103.

13 Bethania Palma: "Was JFK Jr. a U.S. Senate Frontrunner Before His 'Suspicious' Plane Crash?," *Snopes.com*, n.d. (accessed 2021).

14 Laurence Leamer: *The Kennedy Men, 1901–1963* (2001), 41.

15 Ibid., chap. 6.

16 The book was likely shadow-written by Theodore (Ted) Sorensen, Kennedy's friend and speechwriter. Sorensen never formally admitted to writing the book, though he admitted he "collaborated" on it, "made a first draft of most chapters," and received payment from Kennedy for his unacknowledged part in writing the manuscript. See Richard J. Tofel: "In His Own Words," (A Review of Ted Sorensen's *Counselor*), *The Wall Street Journal*, May 9, 2008.

17 Leamer, 450–2.

18 Ibid., 119–23.

19 Ibid., 246–7.

20 Piereson, xiv.

21 Bugliosi, 97–100; Perlstein, 104–10; Diane McWhorter: *Carry Me Home, Birmingham, Alabama* (2001), passim.

22 The two most popular examples of these are an unsigned handbill titled "Wanted for Treason," and a full-page newspaper ad titled "Welcome Mr. Kennedy to Dallas," published in the *Dallas Morning News* on November 22, 1963 by an anti-Kennedy group calling itself The American Fact-Finding Committee. Warren Commission Exhibits No.996 and No.1031.

23 Lasky's book was an acerbic response to two recent pro-Kennedy books: Theodore White's *The Making of the President, 1960* (1961) and William Manchester's *Portrait of a President* (1962).

24 Piereson, 27.

25 Piereson, chap. 2; Burt A. Folkart: "Victor Lasky; Wrote Political Critiques," *Los Angeles Times*, February 23, 1990.

26 Senator Edward "Ted" Kennedy, the youngest Kennedy brother, would become a "safer" target of anti-Kennedy sentiment following his controversial 1969 car accident at Chappaquiddick, Massachusetts, which caused the death of one of his young assistants, Mary Jo Kopechne. See, for example, Jack Olsen: *The Bridge at Chappaquiddick* (1970).

27 Thomas F. Curley: "The Founding Father: The Story of Joseph P. Kennedy, by Richard J. Whalen," *Commentary Magazine*, May 1, 1965.

28 Ibid.

29 Michiko Kakutani: "Just Wait Till Your Father Gets Home: David Nasaw's 'Patriarch,' on Joseph P. Kennedy," *The New York Times*, November 29, 2012; Kakutani: "Kennedy as President (Stick to the Facts, Please)," *New York Times*, October 1, 1993.

30 A notable exception is Peter Collier's and David Horowitz' *The Kennedys: An American Drama* (1984) which presents the Kennedy family as a histrionic cast of characters who, by choice or circumstance, earned their tragic fate. See Christopher Lehmann-Haupt's review in the *New York Times*, June 13, 1984.

31 See, for example, Bill O'Reilly and Martin Dugard: *Killing Kennedy: The End of Camelot* (2012).

32 Martin F. Nolan: "No Quarter for the Kennedys: *JFK: Reckless Youth*, By Nigel Hamilton," *Los Angeles Times*, November 22, 1992.
33 See Introduction, Chapter 4, and Chapter 8 of this book.
34 Noam Chomsky: *Rethinking Camelot* (1993), 23–7.
35 Seymour Hersh: *The Dark Side of Camelot* (1997), chap. 10 and epilogue.
36 Leamer, 51–3, 92, 265, passim.
37 See John M. Hellmann: *The Kennedy Obsession: The American Myth of JFK* (1997), pro-logue and chap. 1.
38 Hellmann, 1–2.
39 See note 16, above.
40 Hellmann, 4–5.
41 Kennedy had announced a civil rights bill during a televised speech on June 11, 1963. It was his first substantial attempt to overturn segregation laws and practices in the South. Until then, Kennedy had met civil rights protests and demands cautiously and in a piece-meal fashion. The announcement was followed by a spree of racist violence. "Report to the American People on Civil Rights, 11 June 1963," *John F. Kennedy Presidential Library and Museum* website; McWhorter, chaps. 21–27.
42 Bugliosi, 1260–6.
43 Manchester, 38.
44 Manchester, 121; Testimony of Kenneth P. O'Donnell, WC VII; Shenon, 358–9.
45 Ibid., 348.
46 Ibid., 347.
47 Bugliosi, 197–9; Ibid., 385.
48 www.jfklibrary.org/asset-viewer/archives/JFKWHP
49 Manchester, 407.
50 Shenon, chaps. 3, 5, 11, and 12.
51 Swanson, 241.
52 "Declaration of Chief Justice Earl Warren, November 22, 1963," Warren Papers, U.S. Library of Congress, cited in Shenon, 31.
53 www.jfklibrary.org/asset-viewer/archives/JFKWHP
54 Earl Warren: *Memoirs*, 353–4, cited in Shenon, 33. Warren would later accept, once he had surveyed the forensic evidence, the FBI's conclusions that Oswald the Marxist—and not a Klansman—was the president's murderer. Shenon, 94–6, 122–3.
55 Piereson, 98.
56 Jack Ruby's poor understanding of the differences between left-wing (anti-capitalist) and right-wing (anti-Semitic) radicalism exacerbated his hatred of Oswald during the weekend of November 22–24, precipitating his murderous act. Bugliosi, 1071–144.
57 Piereson, 98.
58 Manchester, 488.
59 Pierre Nora: *The Realms of Memory: Rethinking the French Past,* Volume I (1996), 14–5.
60 Piereson: *Camelot and the Cultural Revolution*, foreword to the 2013 edition.
61 Theodore H. White: "For President Kennedy: An Epilogue," *Life*, December 6, 1963.
62 James Piereson: "How Jackie Kennedy Invented the Camelot Legend after JFK's Death," *The Daily Beast*, 11/12/2013.
63 Swanson, 269.
64 White (1963).
65 Piereson: "How Jackie Kennedy Invented the Camelot Legend…"
66 Ibid.
67 After Chief Justice Warren extended the offer, lead counsel Rankin, expressed fear that Manchester's access to this material (some of which was classified) might complicate

their work and threaten their credibility, which Manchester respected. His book henceforth became a "parallel investigation" of the assassination instead of a vulgarization of the *Warren Report*. Shenon, 181–2.

68 Manchester later explained in a review of Oliver Stone's *JFK*: "I was answerable to no one. I accepted no money from the Government or the Kennedys, and I stipulated that the author's royalties would be donated to the John F. Kennedy Library in Boston". Manchester: "No Evidence for a Conspiracy to Kill Kennedy," *The New York Times*, January 17, 1992. Jackie threatened to sue Manchester in 1967 before the book went to press over passages she felt were unflattering. Manchester agreed to remove some and the lawsuit was dropped. Shenon, 299–300, 510–1; Philip Nobile: "JFK, Jackie joined mile-high club day before his death," *New York Post*, November 17, 2013.

4

CASE NEVER CLOSED

The evolving conspiracy narrative

4.1   To the barricades!

After the "Irish Mafia" and "Camelot" narratives discussed in Chapter 3, the third major strand of Kennedy mythmaking comes in the form of conspiracy theories. Such works are legion, and their claims are diverse and often contradictory. This may be why few authors have attempted to write a comprehensive historiography of the JFK conspiracy literature.[1] Nevertheless, most of these sources share similarities in tone, intent, and research methods. Many are emotionally charged, promote political agendas, or are narrated in the first person, depicting hypothetical scenarios based on *possible* rather than proven facts, and make liberal use of circular reasoning. This chapter contains an overview of the "alternative" or conspiracist literature on JFK using a generational (i.e., historical) approach to chart the evolution of this community and its attempts to challenge the "official story" (see Chapter 2). Its purpose is to show how JFK conspiracy theories evolved to incorporate newer realities and concerns such as the Vietnam War and the Watergate Scandal and respond to public inquiries into Kennedy's murder, namely the Warren Commission (1964), the House Select Committee on Assassinations (HSCA) (1977–79), and the Assassination Records Review Board (ARRB) (1994–98).

It is worth pointing out that JFK conspiracy myths have been deeply influenced by the Camelot narrative in at least two ways. First, the vast majority of conspiracist works have undiscriminatingly accepted the "saintly" view of President Kennedy as a great humanist and champion of international cooperation cut down by the "forces of hatred". While such occult forces are sometimes described by right-wing conspiracists as agents of communism, and by the more radical fringe as agents of the United Nations, most conspiracists describe Kennedy's killers (always in the plural) as a cabal of warmongering elites and racists entrenched in the American

DOI: 10.4324/9781003222460-5

power structure. Hence, there is a strong left-liberal or libertarian bias running through much of this literature, which focuses its search for culprits among traditional enemies of the left: the military, the intelligence community, law enforcement, conservative politicians and bureaucrats, private industry, and progressive statesmen perceived to be corrupt hypocrites or sellouts, like Lyndon Johnson and Earl Warren.

It can be hard for a novice historian to keep track of the long list of suspects conspiracists claim had the motive, means, and opportunity to murder the president. To wit, some researchers blame hundreds, even thousands, of anonymous minions and passive observers whom they think were aware of the plot but were too afraid or too corrupt to speak out. More cautious theorists name only a few dozen suspects whom, they assume, were required to shoot Kennedy multiple times from several angles, set up Oswald as the scapegoat, and cover their collective tracks. And yet, despite this large gaggle of suspects, the scenarios contained in such books also require that these same assassins had at their disposal unnatural powers of foresight, manipulation, and secrecy, greater than those known to belong to the world's most powerful spy agencies and organized crime syndicates (assuming, i.e., that magic or demons were not involved). Unsurprisingly, "conspiracy researchers" as they often call themselves, rarely attempt to put faces and names on most malefactors in this high-stakes operation. They are usually satisfied rounding up a small number of *possible* high-profile suspects who *might* have been part of some secret cabal, which itself *could* have been steering dozens, hundreds, or thousands of obsequious underlings, described collectively using a vague umbrella term like the "Secret Team," the "Deep State," the "Establishment," the "Military Industrial Complex," or simply "The Men Who Killed Kennedy".

Second, conspiracist authors almost universally reject the apolitical tendency of the Camelot myth to blur distinctions between right-wing and left-wing extremism, a narrative device that helped Jackie Kennedy, Earl Warren, and likeminded others symbolically hang Lee Oswald alongside Southern racists (see Chapter 3). This deliberate fudging of political categories was probably more careless than malicious, though it proved deeply aversive to leftists who admired Kennedy but did not perceive Marxism as a threat to democracy, and instead feared unfettered capitalism, conservative ideologues, and a resurgence of "fascism" in America, the sort that gave rise to witch hunts during the 1950s by men like Joseph McCarthy, Richard Nixon, and J. Edgar Hoover.

Indeed, to many on the political left, Oswald looked nothing like a political murderer. He simply did not look evil enough. Worse, he looked too much like them: a frustrated, alienated, and powerless man shortchanged by a rigged political system controlled by the wealthy establishment. So either Lee Oswald was not a *genuine* leftist—a person who should have been marching in the streets, calling for social justice and civil rights, not doling out terror with a rifle—or else he was just what he said, a "patsy," framed by the right-wing establishment to look like a Marxist lone nut. Admittedly, Oswald was a pathetic figure who could easily be cast as a collateral victim of the struggle against racism, militarism, and big capital.

Had he not, after all, protested his innocence until he was "silenced" by Ruby? It is therefore not surprising that the earliest JFK conspiracists were embattled leftists who had experienced the anti-communist backlash of the 1950s firsthand and still carried emotional scars from this ordeal, people who believed that the deaths of JFK and of the unprosecuted "patsy" would lead to a new wave of persecutions.

In the following years, these authors were joined by a coterie of progressives, liberals, and libertarians who, for various reasons, saw themselves as fellow victims of the establishment. By the late 1960s, the growth of the anti-nuclear, anti-Vietnam War, and decolonization movements—better known as the New Left, the political wing of the wider counterculture movement—provided the youthful, militant, and anxious readership that fueled the production of conspiracist literature. "Rather than inspire revulsion in left-wing radicalism," argues James Piereson, "Oswald's actions had the opposite effect. Many of the activists who mourned Kennedy's untimely death would turn into a version of the man who assassinated him".[2] The failure of the Warren Commission and subsequent inquiries to expose acceptable culprits for Kennedy's murder would radicalize this community. A long sequence of Republican presidents and *laissez-faire* Democrats in the White House would further convince the JFK buffs that their country had truly been taken from them and that a conspiracist reading of JFK's murder was the only appropriate way to explain this unsavory situation.

4.2   Mother's lawyer knows best

The first outspoken proponent of a conspiracy theory was in fact Lee Oswald's mother, Marguerite Oswald, who came to believe, even before Kennedy was elected, that her youngest son was involved in a government plot. Mrs. Oswald became convinced as early as 1959, after learning of Lee's defection to the USSR, that he was not the communist turncoat described in newspapers but a US government agent sent to spy on the Russians.[3] On the day of the assassination, after hearing Lee's name in the news (they hardly spoke since his return from Russia the previous year), Mrs. Oswald notified the local media of her existence and took advantage of everything they offered in exchange for an exclusive story: car rides, hotel rooms, meals, money, and anything that made her the center of attention. Nearly everyone who dealt with Marguerite Oswald before, during, and after that November weekend agreed that she was self-absorbed, jealous, demanding, vindictive, highly narcissistic, self-pitying, and generally out of touch with reality.[4] She even told several people that weekend, and long afterward, that Lee was the hero of this story, the one who tried to *prevent* Kennedy's assassination and who should be buried alongside the President in Arlington National Cemetery.[5]

Few took Mrs. Oswald seriously except for Mark Lane, a young attorney and civil liberties activist who can be aptly described as "patient zero" of JFK conspiracism. On December 19, 1963, Lane published a virulent critique of the Dallas Police in *The National Guardian*, a left-leaning publication.[6] The piece highlighted apparent inconsistencies in the evidence against Lee Oswald—flagrant mistakes that, Lane claimed, would have exonerated him had he lived to face trial. The article included a 15-point indictment of statements by Dallas District Attorney (DA) Henry Wade who, truth be told, got as many facts wrong as he got right during an impromptu press conference the evening of Lee Oswald's death.[7] For Lane, this was proof that the Dallas Police had charged the wrong man with falsified evidence and unreliable witnesses (see Chapter 12). Lane also argued that Oswald did not have a motive for shooting the president, nor had he even tried to leave the country. "If Oswald were a leftist, pro-Soviet and pro-Cuban," Lane argued, "did he not know that during the last year, with the assistance of President Kennedy, a better relationship was in the process of developing between the U.S. and the Soviet Union?"[8] From that point on, Lane described himself as Oswald's public defender and never attempted to study the evidence objectively, but only to present the "facts" that proved that his "client" had been set up. According to Vincent Bugliosi, Lane "elevated to an art form the technique of quoting part of a witness's testimony to convey a meaning completely opposite to what the whole would convey".[9] This method would not just infect Lane's other writings, it became symptomatic of the conspiracy literature in general.

Through early 1964, Lane and Marguerite Oswald crossed the United States and traveled to Europe, raising funds and presenting the legal defense they thought Lee should receive. Much of it was based on a selectively reading (and misreading) of witness statements and Dallas Police documents that were leaked to *Dallas Morning News* reporter Hugh Aynesworth, which Lane had managed to "borrow" and never give back.[10] Lane would also attempt, unsuccessfully, to attend Warren Commission's proceedings as the late Lee Oswald's legal counsel, and then as Marguerite Oswald's attorney—which earned him an invitation to be deposed about his conspiracy claims. Lane presented his case to the Commission, including his claims that Oswald was photographed *outside* the Texas School Book Depository during the assassination (see Chapter 10), that Kennedy was killed by a "grassy knoll shooter" (see Chapter 13), and that Oswald's damning back-yard photographs were fakes (see Chapter 16).[11] The Commission's lawyers were unimpressed. Lane's evidence, they concluded, was founded on loaded questions and hearsay. Hence, the Commission's lawyers dismissed Lane as a pesky oppor-tunist and unscrupulous shyster, but failed to anticipate his resolve and the impact he would have on others.[12]

Lane went on to become one of the most enduring and influential JFK theorists. He would assist New Orleans DA Jim Garrison in his 1967–69 inquest into Kennedy's murder (see Section 4.4) and produce popular conspiracy works like *Rush to Judgment* (1966), *A Citizen's Dissent: Mark Lane Replies to the Defenders of the Warren Report* (1968), the movie *Executive Action* (1973), the documentary *Two Men in Dallas* (1976), and *Plausible Denial: Was the CIA Involved in the Assassination of JFK?* (1991). Lane also represented James Earl Ray, the convicted murderer of Martin Luther King, Jr., and also the Peoples Temple, a religious sect led by the evangelical-socialist mystic Jim Jones, who instigated a mass suicide in Guyana in 1978. In both cases, Lane used the same sort of "evidence" he used to exonerate Oswald, using speculative theories to prove that his clients were victims of state persecution.

Lane made many converts in the United States and abroad, mostly on the political left. The most famous was the aging British philosopher Bertrand Russell who, like Lane, published a widely cited brief against the Warren Report before it was even published.[13] Other hard-line socialists soon also critiqued the freshly printed report: formerly blacklisted American journalist Thomas Buchanan (*Who Killed Kennedy?*, 1964), the German antifascist Joachim Joesten (*Oswald: Assassin or Fall Guy?*, 1964), former Progressive Party investigator and poultry farmer Harold Weisberg (*Whitewash: The Report on the Warren Report*, 1965—a self-published rant that fathered many sequels), the French *Figaro* journalist Léo Sauvage (*The Oswald Affair*, 1966), and American philosopher Richard Popkin (*The Second Oswald*, 1966). In addition to echoing Lane, these works claimed Oswald had been an informant for the FBI and CIA, that he was impersonated by an impostor for months, even years,[14] that Oswald shot Officer Tippit because the policeman was in on the plot and intended to murder the patsy to keep him from talking, and that Kennedy's murder was ordered and financed by Texas oilmen. While these authors never received attention comparable to Lane's, their books fed the rising swell of criticism and moral outrage of a younger brood of conspiracists.

4.3   The Dealey Plaza Irregulars

A second salvo took shape soon after the early leftist response when Texas journalists Hugh Aynesworth of the *Dallas Morning News* (who remained skeptical of most conspiracy claims), Lonnie Hudkins of the *Houston Post* (who endorsed several of them), and the *Washington Post's* Drew Pearson (a "yellow journalist" who loved fanning the rumor mill) published several articles that criticized parts of the "official story". When it became known that the FBI had Oswald under surveillance weeks before the assassination, for instance, many suspected he'd been an informant, "sheep-dipped" into the mafia or communist underworld. The *New York Times*, *The Nation*, and *Life* magazine also began publicizing such theories.[15]

New believers jumped on the bandwagon with little urging. For some, exposing a government cover-up became a full-time obsession. This new wave of JFK buffs was principally composed of young professionals, lawyers, and journalists, college students, citizen activists, and amateur sleuths with idealistic liberal views. They were devout admirers of Kennedy—not the politician so much as the fleeting symbol of youthful optimism—grieving a loved one whose death made their future uncertain. Many had no formal experience in writing or research. Several were women and housewives who had harbored a crush on the young president. Historian Kathryn Olmsted calls them the "Dealey Plaza Irregulars": an alliance of liberal dreamers with "the virtues of dedication, diligence, and almost messianic belief in the righteousness of their cause, [who] believed that they could expose the conspiracy on their own".[16] They formed discussion groups, not unlike contemporary trauma victims and UFO "abductees," critiquing the Warren Report and comparing theories. They congregated in hotspots like Dealey Plaza and Washington's National Archives, and social gatherings in Philadelphia, New Orleans, and universities across the country. "They developed a nation-wide grassroots network to pool their knowledge and prove that ordinary citizens could penetrate the national security state's culture of secrecy".[17] The Freedom of Information Act (FOIA)—passed, ironically enough, by President Johnson in 1966—facilitated their efforts in trying to expose the government's treachery. The steady trickle of official documents that were released (or stolen) over the following decades, offered a possible link to a "smoking gun" and ensured that a lucrative cottage industry of JFK conspiracy books would continue to finance their quest.

Some members of this group, like David Lifton, Shirley Martin, Maggie Field, and Lillian Castellano, pored over the Warren Commission's hundreds of depositions in search of anomalies and contradictions. They chased down and interviewed neglected witnesses. They conducted their own experiments. They were the grunts of the movement performing the tedious legwork, filing tons of declassified documents and alternative data, volunteering their time to more accomplished researchers like Penn Jones, Vincent Salandria, and Gaeton Fonzi, journalists and lawyers whose theories appeared in the alternative publications *Minority of One*, *Ramparts*, *Conspiracy Newsletter*, *Third Decade*, and (later) *Probe*, media outlets that served as the echo-chambers of conspiracy chatter long before internet websites, blogs, and social networks existed. Angered that the Warren Commission had published its 26 volumes with no index, a research analyst for the World Health Organization named Sylvia Meagher drafted a comprehensive subject index of these tomes to facilitate the research of others. Meagher, who grew convinced that anti-Castro Cubans had murdered Kennedy, also penned the influential *Accessories After the Fact: The Warren Commission, the Authorities, and the Report* (1967). A legal secretary named Mary Ferrell became the leading archivist of the movement. Her vast collection of official and alternative documents would, decades later, be one of the most visited JFK assassination websites. Others, like California housewife Mae Brussell, began alternative radio programs and newspapers devoted to JFK research.

Another influential work from this group was graduate student Edward Jay Epstein's *Inquest: The Warren Commission and the Establishment of Truth* (1966), a critique of the Warren Report based on interviews of its ex-members. Though critical of the "official story," Epstein did not offer a counter-theory and would, over the following decades, grow increasingly skeptical of many conspiracy claims. This book was followed by existentialist-philosopher-turned-private-detective Josiah Thompson's *Six Seconds in Dallas: A Micro-Study of the Kennedy Assassination* (1967). More academic and cautious than previous volumes, Thompson nonetheless argued in favor of a multi-assassin scenario in which Lee Oswald (or someone using his rifle) partnered with at least two other shooters firing together from different locations (a theory that has become known as "Triangulation of Crossfire"). Thompson's claims seemed authoritative by virtue of his having been one of the few civilians (and only conspiracist) to have had studied frames of the original Zapruder film, then in the possession of *Life* magazine. Like Epstein, Thompson would also grow critical of more ambitious authors who later claimed that the film was a forgery (see Chapter 17). Jones, Lifton, Fonzi, and Salandria would produce their own books, some more successful than others. Retired military officer and journalist Penn Jones' four-volume *Forgive My Grief* (1966, 1967, 1974, and 1976) would blame Lyndon Johnson and US military intelligence for JFK's murder and list over a hundred other "suspicious deaths"[18] (another popular theme in the literature) which, he claimed, proved that the conspirators were murdering witnesses of their conspiracy. Jones also claimed that as many as nine snipers took shots at Kennedy, one of whom stood in an Elm Street storm drain.[19]

David Lifton, an early convert to Mark Lane's theories, would prove to be one of the most ambitious authors of this vintage, both in his dedication and outlandish claims. A college-dropout and life-long bachelor (admittedly due to his JFK obsession[20]), Lifton took 15 years to publish his magnum opus: *Best Evidence: Disguise and Deception in the Assassination of John F. Kennedy* (1980). In it he argued that JFK's wounds were secretly altered somewhere between Dallas and Washington to make them *appear* as if he was shot from the back and not from the front (see Chapter 14). In other words, none of the autopsy evidence can be accepted as valid because, he claimed, it was all fabricated.[21]

Gaeton Fonzi, an investigative journalist from Philadelphia, would later serve as an investigator for the HSCA (see Section 4.7), where he became convinced that the CIA murdered Kennedy together with anti-Castro Cubans. Fonzi would have a falling out with the congressional members of the HSCA because, he felt, they were not prying deeply enough into the CIA's drawers. He went on to publish *The Last Investigation* (1993), a critique of the HSCA and indictment of the CIA. Vincent Salandria, a Philadelphia lawyer and American Civil Liberties Union (ACLU) member, would not publish his own work until 1999 (a set of essays titled *False Mystery*).

4.4 Fear and loathing in New Orleans: the trial of Clay Shaw

In the spring of 1967, Jim Garrison, the charismatic and controversial DA of New Orleans, opened an investigation into Kennedy's murder. Conspiracists across the country rejoiced that a high-profile lawman with the power to arrest and convict the "real assassins" was as critical of the Warren Commission as they were. An imposing figure both in stature and personality, Garrison's associates described him as incredibly smart and quick-witted, but also obsessive, self-righteous, narcissistic, unapologetic, and neurotic.[22] He had an Ayn Rand-inspired contempt for big government, especially federal institutions like the FBI, with whom he had been briefly employed but quit, disillusioned.[23]

Influenced by Mark Lane, Harold Weisberg, and Edward Jay Epstein, and prodded by his conspiracy-minded friend Senator Russell Long,[24] Garrison became convinced that Kennedy's murderers were hiding in plain sight inside his own jurisdiction and that they had cavorted with Oswald throughout the summer of

1963.[25] JFK buffs flocked to New Orleans to offer Garrison their assistance. *Life* editor Richard Billings[26] and the editors of *Ramparts* and *Playboy* applauded the news and offered the DA front-page coverage. Other media remained deeply skeptical.[27] Garrison's most outspoken critics were high-profile journalists covering the details of his inquest and also some members of his own staff.[28] Over the next two years, Garrison's probe would be one of the most ambitious and expensive attempts to prove that JFK died as a result of a conspiracy. It would also profoundly divide the conspiracist movement and ruin many reputations—including Garrison's own.

Garrison's investigation initially focused on David Ferrie, a local man who was questioned by the Warren Commission in 1964 and then dismissed as unimportant. An eccentric character afflicted by full-body baldness (*alopecia universalis*) for which he sported a wig and false eyebrows, Ferrie not only looked strange, he had a sordid personal life. A former high school teacher and novice Catholic priest, Ferrie was defrocked for homosexuality. He then became an airline pilot and was fired again after being arrested for soliciting sex from a minor. He later morphed into a right-wing zealot, attempting (unsuccessfully) to join an anti-Castro militia.[29] Ferrie finally settled on earning his keep as a pilot-for-hire and part-time private investigator. Based on this personal history, and some crank calls made by Jack Martin, a former colleague,[30] Garrison concluded that Ferrie and Oswald were somehow connected. Although Ferrie now worked as an investigator for the defense team of New Orleans crime boss Carlos Marcello, it was not his ties to the mafia that interested Garrison but his homosexuality and anti-communism. Indeed, Garrison all but ignored organized crime in his investigation, which would have been the simplest (as well as the riskiest) conspiracy connection to draw in a place like New Orleans.

Initially, Garrison believed that Kennedy died as a result of a "homosexual thrill-killing" masterminded by Ferrie.[31] Garrison's evidence was thin, but as several Garrison biographers note, he was not the type of lawman to let the lack of evidence get in the way of a conviction.[32] He soon connected Lee Harvey Oswald to a scruffy man who frequented Ferrie's apartment during the summer of 1963, a man that several of Ferrie's acquaintances knew as "Leon".[33] Garrison took this to mean that Oswald was one of Ferrie's male lovers. Since Ferrie had gone ice skating in Houston with some gay friends on the weekend of the assassination, Garrison became convinced that the true purpose of this "vacation" had been for Ferrie to serve as a getaway pilot, even if Houston was not much closer to Dallas than New Orleans and all of Ferrie's movements that weekend were accounted for.[34]

Garrison soon added Ferrie's former employer, the private investigator and ex-FBI agent Guy Banister, to his list of suspects. Garrison connected Banister to Oswald obliquely by virtue of a fake address—544 Camp Street—that Oswald had stamped on his pro-Castro leaflets (see Chapter 5). He was the first of many conveniently dead suspects blamed by the New Orleans DA From there, Garrison's list grew to include several anti-Castro Cubans, the FBI, the Dallas Police, the CIA, President Johnson, and a homosexual Jack Ruby who moved secretly through New Orleans using the nickname "Pinky".[35] As with Ferrie, Garrison ignored Ruby's connections to organized crime—by far the easiest way to link him to a conspiracy, though perhaps not the one Garrison had in mind.

Garrison's investigation hit a snag when Ferrie suddenly died.[36] The New Orleans coroner judged it a natural death.[37] Garrison would nonetheless tell the media that Ferrie's death looked like a guilty man's suicide.[38] No matter, this left the DA with no one to prosecute, but Garrison found a new lead within the thousands of pages of Warren Commission hearings.

His next suspect was Dean Andrews, an obese, jive-talking, and ambulance-chasing local attorney who wore sunglasses indoors and specialized in defending homosexuals and cross-dressers against public indecency charges. Andrews, the Warren Commission revealed, made phone calls to Dallas the weekend of the assassination claiming he was Lee Oswald's lawyer. But since Oswald made no mention of a New Orleans lawyer while in custody (or ever), Andrews' attempt to contact him elicited inquiries by FBI, Secret Service, and Warren Commission investigators. Andrews, it turned out, had been in the hospital at the time of his calls, heavily medicated and fighting pneumonia. He was unable to produce any proof of ever having been hired by Oswald. But instead of admitting he lied to the FBI (a federal crime), Andrews told the Secret Service that he had been hired to represent Oswald by a man named Clay Bertrand. When prodded for Bertrand's details, Andrews gave contradictory descriptions that suggest he made up the whole story.[39] As with Jack Martin and David Ferrie, the authorities closed the books on Andrews concluding he had just wasted their time with a shameless attempt to ride the president's murder to stardom. Garrison, however, concluded that Andrews knew more than he claimed and that Oswald and "Bertrand" were connected.

A thorough investigation by Garrison's staff found no trace of Bertrand in New Orleans. The DA therefore concluded that "Bertrand" was an alias used by an important member of the local homosexual underground. Garrison soon locked his sights on Clay Shaw, a wealthy New Orleans businessman with international connections, whose name happened to be Clay and who happened to be gay. On little more evidence, Garrison had Shaw arrested and took nearly two years to build a case against him. A mild-mannered, well-manicured six-foot-four man with broad-shoulders and wavy white hair, Shaw looked nothing like the young, ruddy-complexioned, five-foot-eight and 175-pound "rascal" described by Andrews. But none of that discouraged Garrison, who labeled Shaw a "Phi Beta Kappa sadist" and a criminal mastermind with ties to the CIA.[40]

Garrison then rounded up several controversial witnesses to connect Shaw to Ferrie and Oswald. These included convicted felon and heroin addict Vernon Bundy, who told a 1967 grand jury that he saw Shaw by the shore of Lake Pontchartrain—New Orleans' beach front—during the summer of 1963 handing money to a young "beatnik" holding a stack of pro-Castro leaflets.[41] Another was Perry Raymond Russo, a young bisexual Baton Rouge insurance salesman who befriended Ferrie in the early autumn of 1963. Russo, who became Garrison's primary witness, told the grand jury that he had attended an "assassination party" at Ferrie's home—a gathering of homosexuals and Cuban exiles that included

Shaw, Ferrie, and Oswald, whom he described as a dirty bearded character named "Leon"—and that discussion at this party centered on murdering the president with triangulated gunfire. These testimonies convinced the grand jury that the DA had cause to prosecute Shaw.[42] The ruling made Garrison an instant celebrity though he had presented no formal evidence of a conspiracy, only eyewitnesses who claimed seeing Ferrie, Shaw/Bertrand, and Oswald/Leon together. This was the "high-water mark of excitement and hope" for the conspiracists.[43] Garrison's witnesses, however, would be his undoing.

A few days after these hearings, the *Saturday Evening Post*'s James Phelan published an exposé based on admissions and documents Garrison shared with him. These revealed that Russo was drugged, hypnotized, and taken to Shaw's house and Ferrie's former apartment to help him "remember" the past.[44] In other words, Russo's grand jury testimony—the principal reason Shaw had been indicted—was largely fabricated by Garrison. *NBC*'s Frank McGee launched his own investigation of Garrison's inquest and discovered that Russo had failed a polygraph test, which the DA concealed from the grand jury, and that other Garrison witnesses, including Vernon Bundy and Ferrie's young lover Alvin Beauboeuf, had been bribed, intimidated, or threatened to produce corroborating statements.[45] A large part of Garrison's problem was his use of propinquity (i.e., guilt-by-association) in his search for suspects. He would see bloodlines, friendships, even the proximity of residences, as evidence of collaboration. "Garrison didn't believe coincidences happen," wrote Patricia Lambert, "Wherever reality failed to suit his needs, Garrison simply changed it".[46]

The Phelan article and the *NBC* probe had a marked impact on the public's perception of Garrison, especially outside New Orleans. Many journalists now made it their mission to expose him as a fraud. Many of his staff and volunteers quit or were fired after Garrison accused them of being FBI and CIA spies. Many who remained privately questioned his state of mind.[47] Several of Garrison's investigators conflicted with Garrison over his methods.[48] Yet despite these setbacks, Garrison remained popular as many believed he must have more proofs up his sleeve. Indeed, bad press only made him more tenacious. He solicited airtime on TV talk shows, gave lengthy interviews to *Playboy* and *Ramparts*, and made speeches on university campuses.[49] He also convinced the Federal Communications Commission (FCC) to force *NBC* to give him a half-hour of air time to respond to their allegations, which he used to lambaste the Warren Report as a "fairy tale".[50] The narrative he now presented focused less on Shaw, Ferrie, and Oswald as homosexual thrill-seekers, and more on an ambitious right-wing government plot in which the three men were minor operatives.[51]

With this ambitious new story, Garrison could more easily dismiss his journalistic opponents as agents of disinformation. The CIA, he told *Playboy*, killed JFK because he tried to normalize US–Soviet relations by making peace with Castro.[52] They did this, he said, using several assassins, none of whom were Oswald but which included three anonymous tramps who were detained, escorted, and photographed in Dealey Plaza (see Figure 11.3) and then let go without a hearing.[53] Shaw now was Oswald's

CIA "babysitter" in New Orleans, while George de Mohrenschildt played a similar role in Dallas.[54] Ruby graduated from gay hit man to "CIA bagman," anti-Castro gun-runner, and "self-hating Jew" in the service of "master racists".[55] Garrison also blamed Texas oilmen like H.L. Hunt and claimed that the CIA had stolen files from his office and bugged his phones. No evidence was offered to prove it.

In response to Garrison's media campaign, *CBS* newsmen Walter Cronkite and Dan Rather produced an ambitious four-part investigation of Kennedy's death that vindicated the Warren Report.[56] In 1968, Attorney General Ramsay Clark prodded the Justice Department to review the autopsy evidence, partly to respond to Garrison's claims that it was manipulated. The Clark Panel echoed the conclusions of the Warren Report, of William Manchester's *Death of a President*, and of the *CBS News* probe. The two camps were irreconcilable.

The Shaw trial began in January 1969 amidst a media circus. Perry Russo and Vernon Bundy offered upgraded versions of their grand jury testimonies, now compromised by the news that they had been bribed or drugged and hypnotized. Russo backtracked on several of his previous claims, admitting to 26 factual errors in his original interview conducted by Assistant DA Andrew Sciambra,[57] and that he never heard anyone agree to kill Kennedy.

Garrison brought in more controversial witnesses. These included a group of civilians from Clinton, Louisiana, who claimed they saw Oswald, Shaw, and Ferrie together in 1963 driving through their small rural town. Some of these erroneously reported seeing Marina Oswald holding a newborn baby (as she had appeared in post-assassination news photos[58]). Their testimonies were inconsistent and vague under cross-examination. Indeed, the entire Clinton joyride seemed to have had no obvious purpose save to help Garrison connect his suspects.[59] Even more controversial was witness Charles Spiesel, a New York accountant who frequently visited Louisiana and who claimed he attended another assassination party with Oswald, Ferrie, and Shaw—but not Russo. Under cross-examination, Spiesel was exposed as a disturbed paranoid who thought he was the victim of a conspiracy carried out by his psychiatrist, the New York police, former clients (15 of whom had filed malpractice suits against him), and total strangers whom he believed had secretly hypnotized him dozens of times and disguised themselves as his relatives.[60]

The rest of Garrison's case against Shaw had little to do with the accused; it focused on trying to prove that Kennedy was killed by multiple shooters. The Zapruder film, subpoenaed from *Life* magazine, was played to the jury over a dozen times. Several Dealey Plaza witnesses were called in, only some of whom claimed they heard shots or saw smoke from the "grassy knoll". Weapons specialists and photographic experts were also discordant. Marina Oswald, Ruth Paine, JFK autopsy pathologist Dr. Pierre Finck, Dallas Deputy Sheriff Roger Craig, and many others were called in to testify. None offered substantiated proofs that the Warren Commission was fraudulent. In the end, the Shaw trial offered the public four weeks of exceptional theater, if little else. The jury remained unimpressed with Garrison's evidence and acquitted Shaw of all charges after deliberating less than an hour. It was a massive failure for Garrison and for the conspiracist movement.

It financially ruined Clay Shaw, put an end to Dean Andrews' legal career, made a laughingstock of the New Orleans DA's office and many of Garrison's witnesses, and may have precipitated David Ferrie's fatal stroke.[61] Its impact on the historical evidence is also tragic: it made it harder for future researchers to separate fact from fiction. The New Orleans portion of the conspiracy narrative injected hundreds of unproven speculations, red herrings, and lies into what was already a maze of distractions. If Mark Lane can be faulted for digging that first rabbit hole, Garrison takes credit for turning it into an underground city.

After this, Garrison abandoned his quest to prosecute Kennedy's killers despite his bold promise to "nail every one of the assassins" even if it takes 30 years.[62] He would instead write three books on the subject. The first, *A Heritage of Stone* (1970), describes a conspiracy orchestrated by the CIA and the "military industrial complex" to stop JFK from ending the Cold War. It says nothing about his fruitless campaign to connect Clay Shaw to the crime nor his earlier theory of a homosexual thrill-killing. The second, *The Star-Spangled Contract* (1976), is a fictional conspiracy novel containing all of the paranoid themes Garrison fans are now familiar with: secret CIA murders, White House intrigues, creeping fascism, pulpy sex scenes, and a self-righteous lone-crusader fighting an evil bureaucracy. His third and final work, *On the Trail of the Assassins* (1988), is an imaginative and self-congratulating account of the Shaw trial retold in the style of a hardboiled detective novel (see Section 4.8).

Conspiracists are divided over Garrison's legacy. On one hand, JFK buffs such as Harold Weisberg and David Lifton accuse him of obscuring the real cover-up. Others, such as Jim DiEugenio (*Destiny Betrayed*, 1992), Lisa Pease (*Probe* magazine), and Joan Mellen (*A Farewell to Justice*, 2005), have remained staunch defenders of Garrison's claims that Shaw and Ferrie took part in the crime. In doing so, they have kept alive some of Garrison's most questionable "proofs," such as the far-fetched claims of Rose Cherami, whom Garrison claimed had advance knowledge of JFK's murder, and the fictitious stories on Shaw concocted and planted by Soviet agents.

Garrison's failure to convict anyone frustrated his followers, but it also left them an entire new subplot to dig through, one with multiple intrigues and colorful characters. Indeed, the Shaw trial left an indelible stamp on the folklore of JFK's death. It further fueled theories that the CIA, anti-Castro Cubans, the Warren Commission, and President Johnson were somehow involved in Kennedy's murder and that a massive cover-up is still ongoing. Some even managed to turn Garrison's failure into a victory, a proof not that his theories were false but that the enemy is so powerful it can scuttle the legal process. The monster was fed, the legend would grow.

4.5 Down with the Man!

The Shaw trial occurred at a time of increased turbulence in America and throughout the world. The liberal optimism that captured the imaginations of a whole generation just a few years earlier morphed into widespread cynicism. The shocking assassinations of Martin Luther King, Jr. and Bobby Kennedy (in April and June of 1968) did little to change the minds of those who believed President Kennedy was the victim of a conspiracy, in spite of Garrison's failure to prove it and the fact that these two statesmen's killers were captured alive, pleaded guilty, acted alone, and were angry loners.[63] On the contrary, many became convinced that the killings of King and Bobby had been the work of the same shadowy network that murdered JFK, and that their alleged assassins were also patsies.[64]

The civil rights movement had by 1968 spilled out of the South into the industrial north and California, igniting protests and riots in the black ghettos of New York, Newark, Detroit, Chicago, Washington, Oakland, and Los Angeles. Once a proponent of Christian love and racial reconciliation, the movement was radicalized by militant groups like the Student Nonviolent Coordinating Committee (SNCC) and the Black Panther Party for Self-Defense (BPP), which eclipsed King's reformist rhetoric with calls for "Black Power" and violent resistance.[65] Despite landmark federal legislation that ended legal segregation in the South and introduced ambitious anti-poverty programs (what President Johnson called his "Great Society" program), funding for these was hamstringed by the enormous expenses required to sustain an anti-communist war in Southeast Asia. The successes of these economic reforms were also undercut by Lyndon Baines Johnson (LBJ)'s unpopular decision to institute forced conscription.[66]

But there were other reasons for disillusioned young Americans to "turn on, tune in and drop out" as counterculture guru Timothy Leary proclaimed, and not necessarily through rock and roll, recreational drugs, and free love. Revolution was in the air, and not just in America. In the cities of Prague, Paris, Montreal, Tokyo, Saigon, London, Belfast, Chicago, San Francisco, and many others, throngs of impatient students, factory workers, and minority rights activists took to the streets to protest the war in Vietnam, the Cold War, nuclear weapons, economic disparities, racism, sexism, all types of colonialism, and capitalism itself.[67] Radical democracy was their weapon. Changing the world was their goal. Their way to do it was to bring down "the Man"—a faceless power broker with a suit and briefcase. Revolutionary international Marxism, the sort Kennedy condemned openly, was their guiding philosophy. They formed groups like the Youth International Party (or "Yippies") and Students for a Democratic Society (SDS). They called themselves the New Left; their opponents called them "Groucho Marxists" or "Trotskyites". Two years of civil unrest rocked the whole Western world, often with violent reprisals.[68]

With LBJ refusing to run for a second term (citing health reasons) and Bobby Kennedy having just been murdered, the Democrats were divided and without strong leadership. President Richard Nixon, newly elected by a landslide in November 1968, vowed to reverse Johnson's social reforms and, claiming to speak for the "silent majority," increased the country's military commitment to South Vietnam. News correspondents like Seymour Hersh and *Pentagon Papers* whistleblower Daniel Ellsberg exposed covered-up atrocities perpetrated by American troops in Vietnam—revelations that turned many Americans against the

war and against the new president, making them wonder what other secrets the
White House was keeping and whether John Kennedy, had he survived, might have
altogether prevented this war from happening.[69]

It was in this charged atmosphere that disillusioned JFK buffs entered the 1970s.
This rapid change in social and political consciousness fostered not only anger and
cynicism, but also a crisis of confidence against traditional institutions—political,
financial, religious, and academic. Many developed a sense that the world was controlled by some sinister force. It would be rash to blame this revolutionary fervor
solely on paranoid thinking, yet there is no doubt that much of the zeal animating
late-1960s protests was fueled by belief in conspiracies, some founded, some not.
Once the protesters disbanded, the dust settled, and little seemed to have changed,
many in the New Left found the JFK conspiracy research community a welcoming
place to rail against the "fascist police state" and demand that the state look again
at the Kennedy case.

Like the New Left, the JFK research movement had lost much steam by the end
of Nixon's first term. The number of conspiracist publications waned and support
for their cause inside Congress grew tepid. And yet, nearly two-thirds of Americans
now believed that the Warren Report was a fraud.[70] Devout JFK buffs continued
publishing theories in alternative publications like *Ramparts*. The rest of the load
of conspiracy chatter was picked up by TV talk shows and Hollywood studios.
Movies like *Executive Action* (1973), a thriller penned by former black-listed script-
writer Dalton Trumbo based on Mark Lane's JFK theories, and the *Parallax View*
(1974), a drama about the murder of a fictional presidential candidate in which the
protagonist discovers a government plot to turn angry lone nuts into brainwashed
assassins, echoed the paranoid and cynical zeitgeist. These were followed in 1974
by the novel *Winter Kills* by Richard Condon, author of *The Manchurian Candidate*
(another conspiracy thriller about a brainwashed assassin). Condon's second such
novel, which became a film in 1979, was a thinly veiled, semi-satirical take on the
JFK assassination inspired by the "Irish Mafia" myth.[71] Then followed a flurry of
pulpy conspiracy flicks that showed the US federal government embroiled in sinister plots, from murdering its own citizens to control Middle Eastern oil fields
(*Three Days of the Condor*, 1975) to faking space exploration missions (*Capricorn
One*, 1977). However, the main catalyst for 1970s political paranoia came from the
White House.

In mid-1972, the *Washington Post* began to reveal that President Nixon and
his closest advisors had perpetrated and covered up crimes, including break-ins at
Daniel Ellsberg's psychiatrist's office and Democratic Party headquarters (located
in the Watergate Hotel in Washington), as well as illegal wiretaps, laundering illegal
campaign funds, tax evasion, hush money payments, and secret bombings of neutral countries. The public could not be entirely faulted for thinking that all men
in power were devious and that secret *coup d'états*—like those that happened in
Vietnam and Chile (with US approval)—were possibly on their menu. The 1973–
74 Watergate Affair showcased a widely televised Senate investigation, a Supreme
Court directive forcing the President to surrender recordings of his private White

House conversations, Congressional impeachment procedures, and Nixon's resignation. The controversy was compounded a month later when the disgraced president was offered a full pardon by his unelected incumbent President Gerald Ford who, suspiciously enough in the eyes of the conspiracy minded, had served on the Warren Commission and helped construct the "official story" of JFK's murder. Ford tried to explain that this pardon was necessary for the nation to turn a fresh page and for the new administration to focus its efforts on rebuilding the trust of Americans. By accepting the pardon, Ford argued, Nixon recognized his own guilt and political exile.[72]

But that is not how much of the public understood Ford's ill-timed compassion, and post-Watergate paranoia ensured that, at least in the eyes of the man on the street, Nixon's escape from justice smacked of something more sinister. Watergate had no clear connection to Kennedy's murder, yet this scandal, which turned much of America into an army of paranoids, gave renewed life to the JFK movement. Instead of reassuring the public that the system worked to uncover high-level conspiracies, the Watergate scandal had the inverse effect. If prominent government members had truly performed all of these crimes and then lied under oath, and if Nixon could get away without serving so much as a day in a country-club prison, could anyone in Washington be trusted to speak the truth about Kennedy? As a result, the "official story" of JFK's death would, by the mid-1970s, be rejected by nearly 80% of Americans.[73]

One of the many responses to Vietnam and Watergate was the creation of the Assassination Information Bureau, a conspiracist lobby group chaired by Carl Oglesby. A former president of the SDS and figurehead of the New Left, Oglesby was an author, actor, musician, and activist with Marxist *and* libertarian convictions. Like many other 1960s protestors who moved from left-wing campus politics to full-time conspiracy research, Oglesby discovered "clues" in the Kennedy assassination and the Watergate Affair that suggested the New Left movement had not bled dry by its own excesses but by the secret machinations of two dueling cabals: one made up of Texas "oil baron cowboys" (who killed Kennedy), the other made up of New England "old-money Yankees" (who, in revenge, scuttled the cowboy-appointed Nixon).[74] For several years, Oglesby's organization pressured Congress to reopen the Kennedy case. That wish was fulfilled in 1976 when the House of Representatives voted to officially do so (see Section 4.7).

4.6 Birth of the expert

Several JFK buffs gained popularity in the mid-1970s as self-appointed experts in fields related to Kennedy's death: the US military, intelligence agencies, the federal bureaucracy, the Secret Service, the medical evidence, and the photographic evidence. The three most prolific of these were Fletcher Prouty, Peter Dale Scott, and Robert Groden. Many others have since joined their ranks.[75]

It should first be noted that many conspiracists use the term "expert" rather loosely compared to mainstream professionals. In academia, for instance, the term is generally reserved for someone who has achieved the highest level of education in his or her discipline (e.g., a doctorate degree), who occupies a tenured professorship or research chair, and has contributed to their field through peer-reviewed publications. Academic expertise is also not a blank check. When such individuals speak outside their field, they are generally considered less authoritative than more qualified peers. Other marks of expertise may include managing archives and primary documents, producing seminal pedagogical textbooks, or receiving commendations and awards from professional orders and institutions. Conspiracists, on the other hand, often attach the term "expert" to individuals who have merely spent more time than their counterparts reading a particular subject and expounding their views in popular media, which today could amount to producing a blog or a series of *YouTube* videos. True to the populist nature of conspiracism, there is no recognized procedure through which one becomes a "conspiracy expert"—no peer review process or obligation to study opposing views. The movement's widespread siege mentality further discourages them from debating leading historians and skeptics in public. This tends to produce skewed and inaccurate arguments.

The first "expert" to emerge was Leroy Fletcher Prouty, a retired US Air Force Colonel. Prouty's primary interests lay in clandestine intelligence operations (aka: "black ops") and an alleged secret power struggle between Kennedy and the CIA over Vietnam (see Chapter 8). Prouty had an impressive resume, having served as a pilot during the World War II, an airport manager in the Korean War, and a "Focal Point officer for the Department of Defense in support of CIA covert activities"[76] during the Eisenhower and Kennedy administrations (1955–64). After a second career in the rail industry, Prouty became the movement's leading military "expert" until his death in 2001, producing two books, several articles, and many interviews on "suspicious" events, from oil embargos to crashed civil airliners, most of which he blamed on CIA malfeasance.[77] Prouty's ease of speech, affable grandfatherly tone, and Toastmasters-honed storytelling genius imbued him with an unmerited semblance of authority as an elder statesman. He also served as an advisor for Oliver Stone's 1991 film *JFK*, inspiring its character "Mr. X," the mouthpiece of several questionable theories about the Vietnam War.

Prouty was a supporter of various religious cults and fringe groups, including the Church of Scientology, the LaRouche movement, and Jim Jones' Peoples Temple—whose 1978 mass murder-suicide he also blamed on the CIA.[78] Prouty also maintained affiliations with racist right-wing groups like the Liberty Lobby and the holocaust-denying Institute for Historic Review (IHR) which published Prouty's first book and used it to promote anti-Semitic theories.[79] Although he never promoted anti-Semitism, Prouty's historical claims were often careless, self-serving, and inspired by a similar form of paranoia.[80] Like Garrison before him, Prouty had a tendency to inculpate suspects who were unable to respond to his allegations, either because they were already dead or constrained by security clearances. He also had a habit of weaving himself into his own narrative, casting himself (often falsely) as an important player in the events he described (see Chapters 8 <u>and</u> 11). He also frequently referred to obscure and unverifiable documents that were classified, out of print, or nonexistent. All this compelled many naïve researchers to accept his claims blindly, claims that often turned out to be false.[81] Many of Prouty's non-JFK theories were just as outlandish—such as his claim that the scarcity of fossil fuels is a hoax perpetrated by oil barons, that oil is not made of organic matter,[82] and that CIA pilot Gary Powers' U-2 spy plane, captured by the USSR in 1960, was deliberately sabotaged by the CIA to scuttle President Eisenhower's attempts to deescalate Cold War tensions.[83]

Prouty's first book, *The Secret Team: The CIA and Its Allies in Control of the United States and the World* (1973), purports that the Agency's true purpose is to foment wars, instigate revolutions, cull the resource-rich and energy-hungry populations of the developing world with Malthusian indifference, and assassinate the foreign and domestic opponents of this program of world domination. But, he writes, the CIA is really just the toolkit of a more powerful clique he interchangeably calls the "Secret Team," the "high cabal," and the "military industrial complex," a consortium of federal and private institutions coordinated by, but not limited to, the US Joint Chiefs of Staff, the upper echelons of the intelligence community, powerful Washington bureaucrats and think tanks, large international banks, financial institutions, the news media, large publishing houses, petroleum cartels, and private military contractors. "The Secret Team," he writes,

> has very close affiliations with elements of power in more than three-score foreign countries and is able when it chooses to topple governments, to create governments, and to influence governments almost anywhere in the world. [...] In many ways and by many criteria the Secret Team is the inner sanctum of a new religious order.[84]

By withdrawing American troops from Vietnam (which numbered over ten thousand in late 1963), President Kennedy was spoiling decades-long, billion-dollar deception whose purpose was to trigger an epic conflict in Southeast Asia—a stepping-stone to the creation of a fascist new world order. There are no unforeseeable events in Prouty's universe, no good or bad luck, no successful whistleblowers, no free or compassionate thought on the part of the enemy or its puppet regimes; only a team of cold and calculating psychopaths united by bloodlust and greed. Prouty's description of Kennedy's foreign policy as a worldwide peacemaking project cut short by CIA henchmen struck a deep chord with many opponents of the Vietnam War. It henceforth became a central theme in many JFK theories.

Another high-profile "expert" to emerge in this period is Peter Dale Scott, a Canadian-born poet and English professor who briefly worked in the Department of External Affairs (Canada's State Department). Echoing Colonel Prouty, Scott perceived Vietnam policy and the "military industrial complex" as leading causes of JFK's murder. But in some ways, Scott's theories are even more ambitious.

In *The War Conspiracy* (1972), Scott argues that secret pressures from Wall Street, oil companies, weapons makers, government bureaucrats, and organized crime syndicates forced President Eisenhower to get the United States involved in Vietnam to help them plunder Indonesian resources following the ousting of France by communists. In a 1973 article published during the Watergate hype, Scott further suggested that the Kennedy assassination, the war in Vietnam, and the Watergate Affair were all part of a global-historical-economic conspiracy to enrich and empower a group of right-wing warmongers at everyone else's expense:

> In my opinion, it is no coincidence that the key figures in Watergate [...] had been drawn from the conspiratorial world of government narcotics enforcement, a shady realm in which the operations of organized crime, counter-revolution, and government intelligence have traditionally overlapped. [...] I believe that a full exposure of the Watergate Conspiracy will help us to understand what happened in Dallas and also to understand the covert forces which later mired America in a criminal war in Southeast Asia.[85]

Until that time, most JFK buffs limited their research to factoids pertaining directly to Kennedy. Scott offered them a more imaginative method of foraging proofs that disregarded the space and time boundaries of normal historical research. Put simply, Scott offered his readers a methodology based on drawing "connections" between unique or seemingly accidental events that, studied through a wide lens, appeared to reveal the international reach and ongoing involvement of an invisible hand plotting a global takeover.

But Scott did not limit his focus to Vietnam and Watergate. In time, he also included the Lincoln assassination, President Reagan's war on drugs, the Iran-Contra affair, the Oklahoma City bombing, the 9/11 attacks, and ongoing income disparities as proof of this ambitious multigenerational plot.[86] This complex method of connecting the dots between mysterious events, violent conflicts, horrible catastrophes, and all-too-convenient arrangements is what Scott calls "deep politics," a slightly more sophisticated way of saying "mega-conspiracy theory" without actually having to say it. Scott's 14 books and dozens of articles essentially follow the same pattern: they deeply probe under the surface of seemingly unrelated phenomena—what he calls "public events" and "the public state"—to expose the "Deep State," a clandestine realm of secret handshakes, covert operations, and back-room deals performed by the rich and powerful at the expense of the rest of society.[87]

And yet, Scott's Deep State is more than just a group of nefarious people. It is the pattern of overlapping conspiracies that underlies the political power structure, or as he cryptically explains it, the "socio-dynamic process of violent power itself".[88] One has to wonder whether Scott is not stealing a page from Saint Augustine, the fourth-century Christian apologist, who simply described this nefarious force as "original sin".[89] And like Augustine's devil, nothing is left to chance by the feckless, humorless, and hypercompetent enemy that rules Scott's world. All hoaxes, he alleges, have been deliberately planted by the Deep State to throw off truth-seeking researchers. When proof of his theory appears to be lacking, it is blamed on an ongoing cover-up. If any evidence seems to disprove it, it is called disinformation.

Even the French philosopher René Descartes could not have imagined an evil genius with so dogged a will to deceive.[90] Like the mystical study of Biblical codes and cereal boxes, Scott's bureaucratic conspiracy is convoluted and self-deceptive, with proofs of a coordinated grand evil design hiding everywhere in plain sight in the chaotic "noise" of history.[91] The "deep politics" of the political poet from Berkeley has, in sum, weaponized Garrison and Prouty's guilt-by-association techniques and used them to launch credulous JFK buffs into an alternate universe.

A third "expert" to emerge during the Watergate backwash is Robert Groden, whose publications include *JFK: The Case for Conspiracy* (written with Peter Model, 1977), *High Treason: The Assassination of J.F.K. and the Case for Conspiracy* (written with Harrison Livingstone, 1993), *The Killing of a President* (1993), and *The Search for Lee Harvey Oswald* (1995). A photo-optics technician with no formal training,[92] Groden has marketed himself for over four decades as an expert on the Kennedy assassination' photographic and film evidence. He has frequently claimed that four to seven gunmen hidden in different parts of Dealey Plaza fired at Kennedy ten or more times.[93] Some of Groden's other "proofs" of conspiracy include the following: (a) a conspicuous "crop mark" on Oswald's chin in some of his "backyard photographs" (see Chapter 16) which, Groden argues, proves that Oswald's face was pasted on someone else's body[94]; (b) still frames from a New Orleans newsreel that show Oswald distributing pro-Castro leaflets in front of the local Trade Mart while someone who (vaguely) looks like Clay Shaw is standing nearby[95]; (c) visual proofs that the Zapruder film and autopsy pictures were faked to hide the fact that JFK's head was struck *twice*[96]; (d) signs that the tracheotomy scar on JFK's corpse was intentionally widened to make it *appear* like a wound of exit[97]; (e) proofs that the autopsy pictures were falsified to hide a large *exit* wound at the back of JFK's head[98]; and (f) evidence that Mrs. Kennedy's Warren Commission statements describing a *frontal* head shot were redacted and her family threatened to keep this assertion a secret. Needless to say, Groden's purported "proofs" of a conspiracy are questioned even by many conspiracists.

Groden also produced some highly influential diagrams, one of which depicts the inferred path of CE399, the so-called "magic bullet" that—according to the Warren Commission—struck JFK in the back, exited his throat, and caused all of Governor Connally's injuries. According to Groden, this bullet would have had to zigzag through the air to accomplish this task, a scientific impossibility. Groden thereby transformed the "magic bullet theory" into a compelling visual meme that is still widely used to ridicule the official story.[99]

Groden has been an influential activist for the movement.[100] As a young man, he became obsessed with the Kennedy assassination and has remained so. He often referenced a day in 1965 when, visiting JFK's grave, he promised the dead president that he would find out who killed him no matter how long it took.[101] This event would determine the path of the rest of his life. After dropping out of high school to serve in the military, he was hired by EFX Unlimited, a New York film company that performed editing work for *Life* magazine (the proprietor of the original Zapruder film) and for the film *Executive Action* written by Mark Lane. It was there that

Groden obtained a second-generation copy of the Zapruder film. Few Americans had until then seen it in its entirety. It was a precious find, the first of Groden's vast collection of JFK records. He copied and edited new versions to project at symposiums until it was viewed by comedian and political activist Dick Gregory in 1975, who spoke of it to the media. The two men were subsequently called to testify to the Rockefeller Commission (see Section 4.7), where they argued, using the film, that several shooters fired at Kennedy. They then appeared with fellow JFK buff Ralph Schoenman on Geraldo Rivera's *Goodnight America* talk show, where the film was first shown to a national audience. These events increased the pressure on Congress to open a new investigation into the Kennedy assassination. They also earned Groden a stint as an unpaid consultant for the HSCA. Although the Committee's intention was merely to have him present the conspiracy viewpoint and not serve as an expert witness, this experience gave Groden a heightened status as an "assassination expert".[102] Yet Groden's alleged evidence would be rejected in whole by the Committee's expert photography panel.[103] However, Groden's privileged access to JFK's autopsy materials gave him the opportunity to abscond with several photos that had never been shown to the public and which he later sold to a sensationalist tabloid newspaper.[104]

Groden's paranoia increased with time. He told his young sons that the family phone was tapped and that a suspected arson fire next door was caused by a bomb intended for him.[105] He then moved from Philadelphia to Dallas, leaving behind his two children and a wife struggling with cancer, to pursue his obsession full-time, which includes managing a JFK photo-archive and proclaiming the conspiracist gospel in Dealey Plaza. He also served as a photographic advisor for Oliver Stone's *JFK*. This allowed him to further popularize his "proofs" of conspiracy, from faked photographs to zigzagging bullets, sometimes to his own embarrassment.[106] Since then, notes Dallas journalist Jim Schutze, Groden has been living alone in a "deceptively bland suburban home" curating his extensive repository of JFK documents:

> a dark, chaotic, cavernous archive of assassination evidence, snow-drifted with files and books, with only enough room left open for him to eat fast-food alone standing by the sink. [...] His cause has taken him into a deep solitude, as if he were a tethered astronaut staring back at Earth from outer space.[107]

Groden was recently engulfed in a long legal dispute with the city of Dallas and the Sixth Floor Museum at Dealey Plaza (located inside the former Texas School Book Depository) over his use of public space. The numerous grievances filed by the city, and the 81 code violations he's been charged with, include selling literature and DVDs without a license, posting a giant yellow "grassy knoll" banner (with arrows pointing to his kiosk), and painting a large "X" in the middle of Elm Street marking the spot of Kennedy's death. The city of Dallas failed to evict him from the Plaza and was forced to settle a $100,000 lawsuit filed by Groden for harassment and infringement of rights. It is perhaps unsurprising that Groden has depicted their efforts as proof of an ongoing plot to extinguish the truth, and not, as the city and nearby Museum argued, an attempt to free this historic landmark of a peddler of falsehoods causing traffic problems.[108]

4.7   The HSCA and its discontents

The mid-1970s was a period of renewed optimism for the movement, thanks to the establishment of three separate public inquiries into reports of malfeasance at the CIA and other government agencies, which many believed were connected to JFK's death. But despite several shocking new revelations, these investigations would fail to incriminate anyone else than Oswald, handing the JFK buffs another setback, and provoking yet another schism.

Although President Ford's reputation was marred by his controversial pardon of Richard Nixon, his short tenure as president (from August 1974 to January 1977) ushered in a period of increased government transparency.[109] These efforts were accompanied by a withdrawal of the rest of American troops from Vietnam, a limited amnesty for draft dodgers, and attempts to atone for the questionable deeds of federal intelligence agencies.

In 1975, Ford set up the US President's Commission on CIA Activities within the United States (better known as the Rockefeller Commission, chaired by Vice President Nelson Rockefeller) which investigated allegations that CIA agents had illegally spied on thousands of American citizens.[110] The *Rockefeller Report*, published later that year, exposed several illegal acts performed by the Agency, including MKULTRA, an abandoned psychological warfare (i.e., "mind control") program directed by Dr. Sidney Gottlieb, through which the CIA drugged unwitting Americans with LSD, a psychedelic drug, some of whom died as a result.[111] This commission also confirmed that the CIA partnered with organized criminals during the early 1960s to try to assassinate Fidel Castro. Furthermore, it examined the claims of Robert Groden, Jack White, Michael Canfield, Allan Weberman, and others that the Agency had been involved in Kennedy's murder. To the disappointment of many, the Rockefeller Report concluded that such claims were unfounded and upheld the Warren Commission's conclusion that Oswald acted alone.[112]

The revelations of the Rockefeller Commission provoked the Senate to set up the Select Committee to Study Governmental Operations with Respect to Intelligence Activities, chaired by Senator Frank Church. The Church Committee, as it became known, looked deeper into secret activities at the CIA, FBI, National Security Agency (NSA), Internal Revenue Service (IRS), and several military intelligence agencies. The Committee revealed in 1975–76 that the CIA had not only conspired to murder Castro, it had also run a secret terrorism campaign against Cuba (aka: Operation Mongoose), had facilitated the assassinations of foreign leaders (including Congolese Prime Minister Patrice Lumumba and Dominican dictator Rafael Trujillo), and had supported the 1973 military coup in Chile that overturned the democratically elected socialist government of Salvador Allende. The Church Committee also revealed that the CIA and FBI illegally opened the mail of thousands of US citizens and that the FBI, through its Counterintelligence

Program (COINTELPRO) that ran from 1956 to 1971, spied on and intimidated civilian protesters in the civil rights movement, New Left, and Black Panther Party. The Church Committee further chastised the CIA for having withheld crucial information from the Warren Commission concerning its plots against Castro and Oswald's movements in Mexico City—both of which might have changed that Commission's conclusions. It also scolded the FBI for hiding the fact that it had Lee Harvey Oswald under surveillance several weeks before the assassination, had known of his pro-Castro activities in New Orleans, and yet had failed to inform the Dallas police and Secret Service of this. The Church Committee thus fueled a growing mistrust of the CIA and FBI by revealing that these agencies had in fact engaged in conspiracies. However, it found no evidence that any government agent or agency intentionally caused Kennedy's death.[113]

The third and most comprehensive of these inquiries, and by far the most eager to find a conspiracy, was the HSCA. Made up of 12 Congressional members and a large team of lawyers, investigators, and panels of experts, the HSCA sat from 1976 to 1979 to investigate the deaths of President Kennedy and Reverend Martin Luther King, Jr.[114] The HSCA initially struggled to resolve various conflicts between its members that forced it to cycle through three different chairmen—Congressmen Thomas Downing, Henry Gonzales, and Louis Stokes—all of whom clashed with each other or Richard A. Sprague, the Committee's first lead counsel. Sprague was replaced by G. Robert Blakey, a young Cornell law professor previously employed by the Justice Department to prosecute criminal rackets for Attorney General Robert Kennedy. Blakey had strong feelings that the mafia was responsible for JFK's murder and hoped that the HSCA would prove it.[115]

Given budgetary concerns and the fact that the memories of witnesses are often dulled or corrupted by time, the HSCA focused on examining the physical evidence with recently improved forensic technologies unavailable to the Warren Commission. Panels of experts inspected photos and films, studied weapons ballistics (the study of bullets and their impact), and used forensic pathology (the medical study of the causes of violent deaths), dactyloscopy (the study of fingerprints), graphology (the study of handwriting), and acoustics (the study of sound patterns and echoes) to reconstruct the assassination sequence. They examined the evidence dug up by Jim Garrison's inquest, much of which was considered unfounded. The viewpoints of conspiracists Robert Groden, Jack White, and Richard E. Sprague (a colleague of Fletcher Prouty unrelated to the former lead counsel) were assessed, and even accepted by some panelists and committee members.[116]

In the end, the HSCA concluded that Lee Oswald was guilty beyond a reasonable doubt of firing three shots with a Mannlicher-Carcano rifle from the sixth floor of the Texas School Book Depository, missing once and striking JFK twice. All evidence, it asserted, pointed to Oswald being the sole cause of all of President Kennedy's and Governor Connally's wounds. Indeed, the HSCA ended up corroborating almost all of the Warren Commission's conclusions, including the Single Bullet Theory, the reliability of the autopsy report—with some corrections to the location of the head entry wound—and the authenticity of Oswald's backyard photos.[117] The HSCA also reported that the Warren Commission, whose methods had sometimes been hurried or flawed, had nevertheless operated in good faith and reached reasonable conclusions. This was surprising to many, including several of the Committee's congressional members, legal counsels, and investigators who had initially set out to expose a massive conspiracy. The Committee did, however, harshly blame the Secret Service for its failure to adequately protect Kennedy during his motorcades. It also scolded the FBI and CIA for not pursuing some leads that could have exposed potential collaborators. Nevertheless, the HSCA exonerated these agencies, along with the White House, Pentagon, the Soviets, Communist Cuba, anti-Castro Cubans (working "as a group") and organized crime syndicates (again, "as a group").[118] All in all, the HSCA was ready to conclude, as it reached the end of its investigation, that they found no trace of a conspiracy to murder John Kennedy. In fact, a preliminary draft of its report claimed just that. But things took a different turn.

The HSCA was compelled to change its conclusions at the 11th hour when its panel of acoustics experts[119] wowed them with charts and statistical data suggesting a *fourth* shot was fired at Kennedy. The sound of this shot, which they said originated from a different location and rifle than Oswald's, was captured by a Dallas police Dictabelt (a vinyl strip used to record radio chatter) when a motorcycle patrolman escorting the motorcade, or so they concluded, inadvertently left his two-way radio stuck in the open position. Because these four shots appeared to align with events on the silent Zapruder film, and because the suspicious fourth shot was believed to have come from the infamous "grassy knoll," the Committee identified Dallas police officer H.B. McLain as the one who recorded these sounds—even though McLain would remain adamant that he was not in the stated location at the required time and that the recording did not correspond with his movements during this period.[120] But to the members of the HSCA's acoustics panel, who backed up their theory using complex mathematical computations, this was sufficient to claim that a fourth shot had occurred. And since Oswald could not have fired four shots, there had to have been a second shooter on the "grassy knoll" who fired one shot, struck nothing, left no trace of his act, and was never photographed, filmed, or otherwise identified. Despite its controversial nature, the HSCA's acoustic proof of a second gunman was welcomed by lead counsel Blakey and many others who remained convinced in spite of the rest of their findings that Oswald did not act alone, and that a conspiracy, however small, had in fact occurred.[121]

Thus did the HSCA manage to "prove" that Oswald did not act alone. It was a far cry from the theories propounded by Lane, Garrison, Groden, and others, but it was enough to convince many of them, if they ignored the rest of the Committee's findings, that they had been right all along. However, it is rarely acknowledged by most conspiracists that the HSCA's acoustic evidence—the only thing it could produce to prove the existence of a conspiracy—was impeached almost immediately by subsequent expert studies. In 1982, the National Research Council (NRC) concluded that the Dictabelt's "acoustic impulses were recorded [...] approximately one minute *after* the assassination".[122] In 1988, the Department of Justice produced a rejoinder to the HSCA Report based on new studies performed by the FBI and the National Academy of Sciences, both of which echoed the NRC's conclusions that the four "shots" on the Dictabelt did not occur in Dealey Plaza at 12:30 p.m. Several independent expert studies later concluded the same.[123]

The HSCA's theory of a two-man assassination team made up of Oswald and an unknown accomplice drew flak from both sides of the debate. To those in the media, academia, and government who continued to endorse the Lone Gunman Theory, the HSCA's claim that one of JFK's killers got away was no less offensive than if the Committee had blamed half of the country for it. The Committee's shaky evidence of a phantom second shooter would inevitably lead skeptics to reject the HSCA's most controversial conclusion.[124] Defenders of the Warren Commission would henceforth speak of the HSCA with mixed feelings, disagreeing staunchly with its *Final Report* while simultaneously embracing the work and conclusions of most of its panels of experts.

But the toothpaste was out of the tube. Now that a government body had endorsed the idea of a conspiracy—no matter how small and poorly corroborated—many conspiracists, such as Henry Hurt, Anthony Summers, and James Fetzer, hailed the HSCA as a victory, ignoring much of the rest of its findings.[125] Others dismissed the whole thing as a poisoned apple. These include former HSCA staffers Gaeton Fonzi and Robert Tanenbaum, whose pet theories had been rejected by the Committee.[126] There were two major reasons for the dissonant reactions of the conspiracists. First, accepting all of the HSCA's conclusions entailed that they might have been right about the *existence* of a grassy knoll shooter, but that most of the "proofs" they produced to support it were false. This smacked of admitting their own incompetence. Second, accepting that Oswald was a willful participant in the affair was even more problematic because it attacked the very core of their belief that JFK died at the hands of a massive right-wing coup d'état. To incriminate Oswald as the only successful sniper in the attack—a man conspiracists had been depicting for years as a victim of the establishment—required them to exonerate the "fascist" government that had (rightly, it turns out) declared Oswald guilty. In other words, it had indeed been a crime of hatred performed by a leftist, not an act of state terrorism. By offering conspiracists the conclusion, they sought at the cost of sacrificing the story they used to support it, the HSCA inadvertently robbed them of their high-minded purpose, which was not to prove *any* conspiracy but *a particular kind* of conspiracy—a right-wing coup d'état—the only kind that would vindicate their moral outrage and sense of victimhood. Predictably, the early 1980s witnessed few publications propounding the coup d'état narrative.[127]

4.8   Release the files!

The 1980s saw the rise of a less ambitious brand of JFK buff, one who sought to balance the findings of the Rockefeller, Church, and HSCA reports with the enduring possibility that organized crime, if not the US government, was involved in Kennedy's murder. This group includes Seth Kantor (*The Ruby Cover-Up*, 1980),

Anthony Summers (*Conspiracy*, 1980), G. Robert Blakey and Richard Billings (*The Plot to Kill the President*, 1981—republished as *Fatal Hour*, 1992), Henry Hurt (*Reasonable Doubt*, 1985), John H. Davis (*Mafia Kingfish*, 1988), and David E. Scheim (*Contract on America*, 1992).[128] Such authors generally agreed that a low-scale conspiracy involving members of organized crime, aided by rogue intelligence assets (e.g., private mercenaries and/or anti-Castro Cubans connected to the CIA's Castro plots), recruited Lee Oswald and then rubbed him out. Such books delved at great length into the possible motives of corrupt Cuban exiles, CIA assets, and mobsters like Santo Trafficante, Carlos Marcello, and Sam Giancana. They also exposed a plethora of suspicious "connections" between these mafia bosses and smaller mob fish like David Ferrie, Jimmy Hoffa, Johnny Roselli, Edward Becker, and Charles "Dutz" Murret, who could somehow be linked to Lee Oswald (see Chapter 6) in a conspiracist version of the "six degrees of Kevin Bacon" game. The explanatory power of these "mafia hit" theories left many skeptics underwhelmed, as well as many JFK buffs who favored the coup d'état narrative. Invariably, such books offered a tantalizing look into the dark underworld of organized crime, but not enough evidence to convince a well-informed reader that Oswald could be a mafia hit man.

Hardened JFK buffs suffered two more disappointments in the early 1980s. The first followed a costly attempt by British conspiracist Michael Eddowes (author of *The Oswald File*, 1977), to have Oswald's body exhumed by a team of expert pathologists. Eddowes had set out to prove his theory that a Soviet impostor had replaced the American defector and was now buried in Lee Oswald's place.[129] A comparative study of Oswald's dental records and unique physical features revealed, to Eddowes' disappointment, that the exhumed body was positively the same as the one that defected to Russia in 1959.[130]

The second setback occurred in 1986 as a result of a widely televised mock trial of Lee Harvey Oswald that featured two high-profile lawmen: former Los Angeles prosecutor Vincent Bugliosi (famous for his prosecution of murderous cult leader Charles Manson) and defense attorney Gerry Spence (famous for his defense of nuclear power plant whistleblower Karen Silkwood). The intensive three-day, 300-minute televised trial took place in a London studio refurbished as an American courtroom with an American judge and jury, many of the original witnesses and experts questioned by the Warren Commission and HSCA, and several alleged witnesses of a conspiracy. The mock trial ended with a guilty verdict—the first trial Spence lost in 17 years. While the event was considered by some journalists as "frivolous, even distasteful" entertainment,[131] it nevertheless suggested that the Warren Commission had a strong enough case against Oswald.

While the 1968 assassinations of Bobby Kennedy and Martin Luther King, Jr. led many to conclude that JFK was the victim of an ongoing plot, more recent attempts to assassinate Alabama Governor and presidential candidate George Wallace (in 1972), President Gerald Ford (twice, both in 1975), and President Ronald Reagan (in 1981) have been largely ignored by Kennedy researchers. A possible reason for this is the fact that all three victims survived, making these shootings less impactful as "flashbulb memories".[132] A stronger explanation is the fact that, as natural enemies of the mostly left-leaning JFK buffs (Wallace was an outspoken segregationist while the two Republican presidents had previously served, respectively, on the Warren and Rockefeller Commissions), these assassination attempts did not harmonize well with left-leaning conspiracy narratives.[133] The fact that all four of these men's attackers survived, faced trial, and appeared to be deranged, could not help conspiracists rehabilitate Oswald, nor could they be easily turned into usable patsies.[134] On the other hand, the 1980 assassination of former Beatle John Lennon, whose politics were in line with those of most JFK buffs, would better serve them as proof of an ongoing plot, even if Lennon's assassin (Mark David Chapman) was a clear-cut example of an "angry lone nut".[135]

Conspiracist fervor waxed brighter in the wake of the Iran-Contra Affair (1986–87), a scandal that rocked the Reagan White House during his second term. The scandal began with the exposure of a secret arms deal between the United States and Iran—America's sworn enemy since 1979, now under a trade embargo—in exchange for money and hostages. The profits were then illegally channeled by Colonel Oliver North, one of Reagan's National Security Council staffers, to pro-American "freedom fighters" (read: anti-communist terrorists) trying to overturn Daniel Ortega, the democratically elected socialist president of Nicaragua. Twelve weeks of televised public hearings culminated with the convictions of several members of Reagan's administration on charges of perjury, obstruction of justice, withholding and destroying evidence, and conspiracy—most of which were overturned on appeals.[136] The remaining culprits were later pardoned by President George H.W. Bush, Reagan's successor and former vice president. Though Reagan's direct involvement in the affair was never clearly established by a special review board (the Tower Commission), subsequent revelations show he was far more involved than could be proved at the time.[137] These events seemed to confirm the belief shared by JFK buffs since the Vietnam War that "the men who killed Kennedy" were still firmly in charge of their country.

The election of the elder President Bush in 1988 ushered in a third consecutive Republican administration, a fifth one in six elections. More importantly, the rapid collapse of the Soviet Bloc in 1989 and the subsequent fragmentation of the USSR left Bush in charge of the world's only remaining superpower. His overthrow of Panamanian dictator Manuel Noriega (a former CIA asset), his war to liberate Kuwait from Iraqi dictator Saddam Hussein (another former US ally), and Bush's "sinister" past as a Texas oil tycoon, as DCI, and as an alleged member of several real and imagined secret societies, sent chills up the spines of the most paranoid. Bush's years in power thus witnessed an increase in conspiracy theorizing about Freemasons, the Skull and Bones society, the Bilderberg Group, the Council on Foreign Relations, and other "New World Order" inspired bogeymen.[138]

Riding this wave of increased suspicion, the JFK buffs went back on the offensive. The first major attempt to revive the movement was *The Men Who Killed Kennedy*, a TV documentary produced by British filmmaker Nigel Turner. First broadcast in two episodes in 1988, the program evolved into a nine-part, five-hour miniseries that for many years received regular airtime on the *History Channel*.[139] The plot was ambitious, convoluted, and often self-contradicting, each episode a *Rashomon*-type account of what allegedly happened to Kennedy—from a mafia hit, to a CIA "black op," to a military-style ambush involving fake policemen, sheep-dipped assassins, right-wing racists, French heroin smugglers, snipers lurking in storm drains, fake wounds, switched caskets, exploding and frangible bullets, even weaponized cancer cells.[140] The only perspective missing from Turner's program, ironically, was the one representing the "official story," reinforcing the widely held conspiracist view that *anything but* the Warren Report is acceptable fare.

Several popular books followed, as well as one hugely influential film that set the standard for decades to come. These were Jim Garrison's *On the Trail of the Assassins* (1988), brilliantly edited if not shadow-written by Zachary Sklar, a left-wing activist and journalism professor; Jim Marrs' *Crossfire: The Plot that Killed Kennedy* (1989); Robert Groden and Harrison Livingstone's *High Treason* (1989), and, capitalizing on the claims made by these authors, Oliver Stone's Hollywood blockbuster *JFK*, which he cowrote with Sklar.

Garrison had decided a decade earlier to write a memoir about his prosecution of Clay Shaw. His desire to dredge up the botched trial so many years later was sparked by the revelation, made by former DCI Richard Helms in 1979, that Clay Shaw served as an unpaid informant for the CIA's Domestic Contact Service during the early 1950s.[141] Helms made this admission while serving as a witness in a lawsuit by E. Howard Hunt, the former CIA agent and convicted Watergate conspirator, against the anti-Semitic right-wing Liberty Lobby concerning its claims that Hunt had been one of the tramps photographed in Dealey Plaza on November 22, 1963.[142]

Garrison struggled to find a publisher. His manuscript was eventually picked up by Sheridan Square Press, a small independent outfit whose owners Ellen Ray and Bill Schaap were longtime left-wing conspiracy buffs and old fans of Garrison.[143] Rewritten by Sklar, the book received wider attention than Garrison's earlier publications. It has since gone through several reprints. As a piece of historical memoir, however, Garrison's *Trail* deviates dangerously into pseudohistory, distorting verified facts, dredging up "evidence" that has long been debunked, and changing his earlier claims whenever these clashed with new interpretations. Oliver Stone nevertheless bought the book's movie rights and pitched it to Warner Brothers Studios with the intention of crowning his Vietnam War trilogy—*Platoon* (1986), *Born on the Fourth of July* (1989), and the forthcoming *Heaven and Earth* (1993)—with a Vietnam-inspired conspiracy thriller based on Garrison's updated memories. It was a bold recipe for financial success. It would also transform the public's confused memory of Kennedy's death into a Frankenstein monster.

Stone spared no effort to construct one of the most compelling historical dramas in Hollywood history. The film hit theaters just before Christmas 1991 and became an immediate success. Its nomination for four Golden Globes (winning two) and eight Academy Awards (winning two) is indicative of Stone's filmmaking genius.[144] The film also featured a moving soundtrack by famed *Star Wars* composer John Williams, and an impressive slate of Hollywood stars playing real, fictional, and composite characters. These included Hollywood favorites Kevin Costner as Jim Garrison, Gary Oldman as Lee Harvey Oswald, and Kevin Bacon as "Willie O'Keefe," a homosexual Southern racist based on Perry Russo, the real Garrison's controversial star witness. Stone also awarded cameo roles to many conspiracist celebrities, including to Jim Garrison who played a surly Chief Justice Warren. But *JFK*'s most effective feature was its editing work. The over three-hour-long motion picture includes a convincing collage of genuine newsreel footage mixed with dramatized reenactments that flicker onscreen in rapid succession, a veritable orgy of flashbacks and paranoid innuendos. The story told in *JFK* was highly compelling precisely because it was a remarkable piece of cinematography that weaved the theories of dozens of leading conspiracists seamlessly into a single grand narrative. "What made the movie such a powerful experience," wrote Patricia Lambert, "was its apparent authenticity. [...] What is clear is that [Stone] knew how to make a film that *appeared* to deliver it".[145]

The combination of esthetic beauty and careless research that permeates *JFK* left almost no one indifferent. It was acclaimed by some reviewers as a masterpiece. Many others called it shameless propaganda namely due of its demonization of President Johnson and Chief Justice Warren and its wholesale vilification of whole government agencies. Most importantly, it was the film's depiction of Oswald as a hapless victim, and its hagiographic portrayal of Garrison scrubbed clean of his real-life narcissism and vindictive paranoia, that made historians and veteran journalists furious.[146] Part-Matlock and part-Columbo, Stone's protagonist was turned into a "Capraesque All American Nice Guy and Defender of Democracy," an over-polished version of the sanitized self-portrait Garrison offered in *Trail*.[147]

In response to the backlash against *JFK*, Stone became an ardent public defender of the conspiracy theories that inspired his film. His principal targets were the *New York Times'* Tom Wicker and the *Washington Post*'s George Lardner, Jr., vocal critics whom he considered mouthpieces of the establishment. Stone launched his counteroffensive before the film was even released, as the screenplay was leaked to the press by fellow conspiracy author Harold Weisberg, who once assisted Garrison's inquest but quit disenchanted. Stone filed libel and copyright infringement suits against several newspapers, thereby gaining the right to rebut his critics in their own media the way Garrison had two decades earlier.[148] Most noteworthy was Stone's nationally broadcast public lecture at the National Press Club in Washington.[149] The event saw Stone accusing the entire journalistic profession of betraying their country for nearly three decades with a contrived "official story" of Kennedy's murder.

Stone's film and the controversy it elicited sparked a new wave of interest in the Kennedy assassination. It triggered an avalanche of new titles by weathered and fledgling researchers, many of whom described themselves as neglected witnesses or insiders of a conspiracy.[150] It also gave rise to diverse works aiming to debunk Stone's claims. The most popular of these, and by far the most reviled by conspiracists, was Gerald Posner's *Case Closed* (1993).

Though it did not spark the social and political revolution its creators anticipated, *JFK* spurred many elected officials to call for the release of all remaining classified documents relating to Kennedy's death. This provoked President Bush to draft the 1992 JFK Records Act which called for the collection, cataloging, and release of all evidence lingering in government files. The Act also gave birth to the ARRB, which examined a trove of classified papers, performed new depositions, commissioned a technical study of the Zapruder film, and published a report discussing its successes and failures in trying to complete the evidence trail. The ARRB made no special attempt to retry the case; its mandate was to explain what evidence could and could not be found. That being said, it unearthed no clear proof that the Warren Commission or HSCA was duped or behaved in bad faith.[151] Nevertheless, at least one of its leading staffers (Douglas Horn, Chief Analyst for Military Records) was a committed conspiracist who would go on to claim that the ARRB did uproot but failed to flag several proofs of conspiracy.[152] The JFK Records Act gave government agencies until October 2017 to release their remaining classified documents. Though this deadline has now been partly postponed at least twice, much of this task has been achieved.[153] Such documents—assuming none were removed, hidden, or destroyed—so far appear not to contain any proof of a murderous conspiracy. Unsurprisingly, many JFK buffs remain convinced otherwise.

Stone's film deeply influenced the popular imagination of JFK's murder for the following decades. It has contributed, among other things, to an onslaught of new print, television, film, and online conspiracist media. It also enjoyed a new surge in popularity after the September 11, 2001 terrorist attacks, convincing members and sympathizers of the "9/11 Truth Movement" that these attacks were masterminded not by Middle-Eastern jihadists, but by the "Men Who Killed Kennedy" (see Section 4.9).[154] Inversely, Stone's film also inspired a wave of movies and TV dramas, cold case investigations, historical documentaries, investigative journalism, and new academic research that counter his JFK theories. This becomes evident each year, and especially every ten years (e.g., in 1993, 2003, and 2013), during the month of November, leading up to the anniversary of the assassination, when JFK historians and other Lone Gunman Theorists become highly coveted media figures.[155]

4.9   Fabula Perpetua

The ARRB did not put an end to conspiracy theorizing. However, its report and the repeated statements of its leading members that they found no cover-up many conspiracists to conclude that if a plot to murder JFK did happen, proof of it is likely not to be found in government files.[156] Some of these, now resigned to accept the conclusions of the Warren, HSCA, and ARRB Reports, came full circle to believe that Oswald, though he was likely the only shooter, surely was aided by Communist Cuba. Unanswered questions concerning his brief trip to Mexico City in September 1963, during which Oswald is known to have met with Cuban and Soviet officials (and possibly Cuban intelligence assets), were enough for a group of middling conspiracists to continue believing in some cover-up involving the Cubans and/or CIA. This is the conclusion reached by investigative journalists Gus Russo (*Live by the Sword: The Secret War against Castro and the Death of JFK*, 1998; *Brothers in Arms*, 2008), Jefferson Morley (*Our Man in Mexico: Winston Scott and the Hidden History of the CIA*, 2008; *The Ghost: The Secret Life of CIA Spymaster James Jesus Angleton*, 2017), and Philip Shenon (*A Cruel and Shocking Act: The Secret History of the Kennedy Assassination*, 2013). All three of these authors claim that, while Oswald was no doubt guilty, the CIA is also to blame for having known in advance that Oswald was working with communist Cuba (perhaps as a double agent) and did nothing to stop him (see Chapter 10). Major suspects fingered by these authors include Mexico City CIA station chief Win Scott and the Agency's chief of counterintelligence James Angleton, both of whom, they suggest, were amoral agents who willfully hid proofs of Castro's involvement in Kennedy's murder.[157] Some prominent American statesmen, including former Senator, presidential candidate, and Secretary of State John Kerry, have endorsed similar theories.[158]

Hardened believers, on the other hand, influenced by ARRB contrarian Douglas Horne and retired University of Minnesota philosophy professor James Fetzer, denounced the Review Board for its suppression of several "smoking guns" which prove, they allege, a massive government conspiracy.[159] This led to the formation of Assassination Science, a community of "scholars" made up of conspiracy-minded doctors, physicists, lawyers, academics, and uncredentialed researchers who came together to prove that most of the medical, photographic, video, and eyewitness evidence of JFK's death was either stolen, edited, or brazenly faked by squadrons of government stooges (see Chapters 14–17). Alongside Fetzer and Horne, they include ophthalmologist Gary Aguilar, radiation oncologist David Mantik, neurologist Robert Livingston, physicist (and climate change skeptic) John Costella, attorneys Douglas Weldon and Bradley Kizzia, English professor Peter Dale Scott, and amateur sleuths David Lifton, Jack White, Vincent Palamara, and David Healy.

Fetzer has by far been the most prolific member of this group. He has organized conspiracy symposia, administered websites and blogs, hosted discussion forums, appeared in numerous internet, radio, and TV interviews, and published a long list of conspiracy-themed articles and books, including four collections of essays: *Assassination Science: Experts Speak Out on the Death of JFK* (1998), *Murder in Dealey Plaza: What We Know Now that We Didn't Know Then about the Death of JFK* (2000), *The Great Zapruder Film Hoax: Deceit and Deception in the Death of JFK* (2003), and *The 9/11 Conspiracy: The Scamming of America* (2007).[160] Fetzer's crossover into 9/11 and Moon Landing Hoax theories has made him one of the most visible recent proponents of superconspiracies[161] alongside fellow JFK buff Peter Dale Scott, internet talk show host Alex Jones, and British ufology guru David Icke.

As the new millennium opened, conspiracist fabulations were indelibly marked by the September 11, 2001, terrorist attacks and by popular fears that vaccines, AIDS, Jihadi terrorism, economic globalization, UFOs, and even the Biblical record of Jesus Christ's life are all the products of ongoing cover-ups. Unlike Fetzer, Scott,

Jones, and Icke, few veteran JFK buffs openly endorse such beliefs. Yet there is no doubt that four decades of JFK conspiracy theorizing have helped produce an imaginative template that inspires other movements to mimic its style. It has also fostered enough mistrust of traditional authorities to feed these other forms of anti-government hysteria. "It is impossible to overstate how influential the legacy of JFK's murder has been in the formation of the flourishing and variegated conspiracist subcultures of later decades," writes Jonathan Kay. "In fact, the death of JFK acts as a sort of universal hinge point for conspiracy theorists everywhere".[162]

That said, the relationship between JFK buffs and the 9/11 Truth movement was not just imitative, it was deeply organic. Young firebrand "Truthers" like Jason Bermas and Peter Joseph injected new blood and energy into the older, more cynical fold of JFK buffs while the veterans of JFK research provided a wealth of experience and "stigmatized knowledge"[163] to these vocal opponents of President George W. Bush's War on Terror, allowing Truthers to depict the 9/11 attacks not as an isolated incident but as part of a decades-old program of world domination. Younger converts to JFK conspiracism (including this author) needed little encouragement to join the Truthers. Veteran Kennedy buffs like Fetzer and Scott were also warmly welcomed in Truther conventions and social media discussions alongside that movement's own body of "experts," men like Richard Gage, David Ray Griffin, Michael Ruppert, Michel Chossudovsky, and Paul Zarembka, many of whom adopted JFK theories as further proof of their anti-Bush convictions.[164] The two movements were ideal bedfellows largely because their anxieties flowed from similar wells of despair: fears of government surveillance, secrecy, wars of Western aggression, covert operations, environmental catastrophes, and the unbridled growth of corporate wealth. For the better part of a decade, leaders of these sister movements became almost indistinguishable. "The more one studies the Left's reaction to the JFK assassination," writes Kay,

> the more striking is the similitude with the 9/11 Truth movement. [...] So many of the Truthers I interviewed also turned out to be JFK conspiracy buffs—and sometimes even interlaced the two subjects in bizarre ways. [...] Scratch the surface of a middle-aged 9/11 Truther, and you are almost guaranteed to find a JFK conspiracist.[165]

9/11 Trutherism waned during Barack Obama's presidency (2008–16) largely because the conservative Bush administration, having given way to a more progressive one, was no longer easy to scapegoat. Inversely, the election of an African American liberal with a Muslim-sounding name provoked a rise in right-wing paranoia and questions about his legitimacy as both a president and an American citizen. Although right-wing "Birtherism" eclipsed left-wing "Trutherism" as the conspiracy *du jour* after 2008, JFK theories nevertheless continued to thrive.

As the 50th anniversary of Kennedy's death approached, a veritable avalanche of anti-conspiracy books, films, documentaries, and TV dramas went into production. Some of these, like James Swanson's *End of Days* (2013) and the films *Parkland*

(2013) and *Killing Kennedy* (2013)—based on works by Vincent Bugliosi (*Reclaiming History*, 2007) and Bill O'Reilly (*Killing Kennedy: The End of Camelot*, 2012)—were more sentimental than pedagogic. Documentaries like National Geographic's *JFK: The Lost Bullet* (2011) and PBS NOVA's *Cold Case: JFK* (2013) attempted more directly to impart critical thinking and a better understanding of forensic science to a new generation of JFK buffs. As resolute as these attempts were to reclaim history from the conspiracists, the flow of JFK theories continued.

In fact, it went into hyperdrive. Dozens of new conspiracist titles were published in the lead-up to the 50th anniversary, 25 of which were produced by Skyhorse press, a conspiracy-fetishizing publishing house.[166] Some recent titles, like David Talbot's *Brothers* (2007), James Douglass' *JFK and the Unspeakable* (2008), and Oliver Stone and Peter Kuznick's miniseries and book *The Untold History of the United States* (2012, 2014), are pumped full of nostalgia for JFK and his brother Bobby, both of whom are depicted as saintly martyrs for pacifism with little regard for historical accuracy. Other titles, like Robin Ramsay's *Who Shot JFK?* (2007), Jesse Ventura's *They Killed Our President: 63 Reasons to Believe There Was a Conspiracy to Assassinate JFK* (2013), and Roger Stone's *The Man Who Killed Kennedy: The Case Against LBJ* (2014), throw all remaining caution to the wind by rehashing umpteen debunked theories, unsubstantiated rumors, and fictional Hollywood movie plots to support their conviction that all investigations of JFK's murder that remotely support the Lone Gunman Theory are part of a clandestine program to obfuscate the truth.

A few recent conspiracy books take us deep into parallel universes. These include Judyth Vary Baker's *Me & Lee: How I Came to Know, Love and Lose Lee Harvey Oswald* (2010), which depicts a sexual tryst between the author and Kennedy's alleged killer during his stay in New Orleans during the summer of 1963. According to Baker, the two lovebirds were coopted to produce a murderous cancer agent for the CIA to use against Castro. Another is Bonar Menninger's *Mortal Error: The Shot That Killed JFK* (1992, 2013), which claims that a Secret Service agent—Special Agent George Hickey—who rode in the follow-up car during the Dallas motorcade accidentally shot Kennedy through the head (without hundreds of spectators noticing) at the same time that another shooter inside the Texas School Book Depository just happened also to shoot (but miss) Kennedy. And one cannot fully ignore the deliciously titled *Dr. Mary's Monkey: How the Unsolved Murder of a Doctor, a Secret Laboratory in New Orleans and Cancer-Causing Monkey Viruses Are Linked to Lee Harvey Oswald, the JFK Assassination and Emerging Global Epidemics* (2007, 2014) by Edward T. Haslam, a book whose title pretty much summarizes its contents and merits.[167] Needless to say, even many JFK buffs have found such works laughable. But that has sadly not made them unprofitable.

In sum, JFK conspiracism has not shown any signs of going away. If anything, it has displayed a growing tendency to double down on irrational, unprovable, and disproven beliefs. But in the age of Trumpocracy, when conspiracy theories are being considered seriously and even produced at the highest levels of decision-making, this should not be entirely surprising to us. Unraveling this tangled mess of theories is the job of the rest of this book. It might also, one likes to hope, inject more sober thought into the political process.

Notes

1 A notable exception is Peter Knight's *The Kennedy Assassination* (2007), chaps. 5–7.
2 Piereson (2007), x.
3 She said this in a letter to the FBI in 1959. Bugliosi, 155–6; 295–7; 302–3.
4 These individuals include her two oldest sons, Lee's wife Marina, Marguerite's Russian translator Peter Gregory, Ruth Paine, Chaplain Pepper at Parkland Hospital, and several police, FBI, Secret Service, media, and Warren Commission personnel. Many reports were even less flattering. Bugliosi, 1–319, *passim*; Shenon, chap. 18.
5 See, for example, the 1964 interview with Marguerite Oswald in "The Men Who Killed Kennedy," Episode 4 (1995).
6 Mark Lane: "Oswald Innocent?—A Lawyer's Brief: A Report to the Warren Commission," *National Guardian*, Vol.16, No.11, December 19, 1963.
7 Bugliosi, 304–6.
8 Lane: "Oswald Innocent?"
9 Bugliosi, 1004, see also 1000–11, endnotes 557–8, and Shenon, chap. 20.
10 Shenon, 135–6.
11 One of these "proofs" concerned the rifle scope, which appeared in the photographs published in *Life* magazine (large, in color) but was missing in the ones published by the *New York Times* (smaller, black and white). The Commission concluded that these photos were altered by copy editors trying to make the image look sharper, not because of any malevolence. Shenon, 196.
12 Shenon, chap. 20, *passim*.
13 Bertrand Russell: "16 Questions on the Assassination," *The Minority of One*, September 6, 1964. The essay offered a long list of rhetorical questions based on incorrect facts fed to Russell by Lane and his own conspiracist personal secretary Ralph Schoenman. It has been reprinted and cited by numerous conspiracists, including James Fetzer in *Murder in Dealey Plaza* (2000). On Schoenman, see Fred Litwin: *I Was a Teenage JFK Conspiracy Freak* (2018), 114–6.
14 On this "Two Oswalds Theory," see Chapter 10.
15 Shenon, chaps. 14 and 15.
16 Olmsted, 111–2. The moniker is a wink to the "Baker Street Irregulars," street urchins from Arthur Conan Doyle's Sherlock Holmes novels who perform intelligence gathering for the detective.
17 Ibid., 112.
18 Penn Jones, Jr.: "Disappearing Witnesses," *The Rebel*, January 1984.
19 Ron Rosenbaum: "Still on the Case," *Texas Monthly*, Vol.11, No.11, November 1983, 153.
20 Bugliosi, 1057.
21 Ibid., 1057–70.
22 Posner, 424; Milton Brener: *The Garrison Case: A Study in the Abuse of Power* (1969); Adriane Quinlan: "After JFK Assassination, DA Jim Garrison's Investigation Rips into the Life of Clay Shaw," *New Orleans Times-Picayune*, November 21, 2013.
23 Garrison was diagnosed by FBI doctors with chronic anxiety with hypochondriasis, functional bowel symptoms, and psychogenic allergic manifestations, as well as a "marked mother dependency". "Garrison Record Shows Disability," *Associated Press*, December 29, 1967; See also Warren Rogers: "The Persecution of Clay Shaw," *Look*,

August 26, 1969, 54; "Dick Billings's Personal Notes on Consultations and Interviews with Garrison: December 1966–January 25, 1967," *JFK Online*; David Reitzes: "Milton Brener on New Orleans District Attorney Jim Garrison," *JFK Online*; Posner, 421.

24 Eric Norden: "Playboy Interview: Jim Garrison—A Candid Conversation with the Embattled District Attorney of New Orleans," *Playboy*, October 1967, 71–2; Robert Travis Scott: "Controversy, Mystery Still Surround the Death of Huey P. Long," New Orleans *Times-Picayune*, September 8, 2010. Long was the son of populist Louisiana Governor Huey "Kingfish" Long who was assassinated in 1935, a popular theme of local conspiracy chatter.

25 This was a shining example of the streetlight fallacy: an attempt to solve a problem by looking for evidence not where it is most likely to be (i.e., in Dallas or Washington) but where it is easiest to search, which in Garrison's case had to be New Orleans since his prosecutorial powers did not extend any further. The streetlight fallacy is often illustrated by the anecdote of a drunkard looking for his keys under a lamppost, not because that is where he dropped them but because the light makes it easier to search. David H. Freedman: "Why Scientific Studies Are So Often Wrong: The Streetlight Effect," *Discover Magazine*, December 10, 2010.

26 Billings served for six months as a member of Garrison's staff. He would break with the DA over the questionable evidence Garrison used to indict Clay Shaw.

27 See Posner, chap. 18; Patricia Lambert: *False Witness: The Real Story of Jim Garrison's Investigation and Oliver Stone's Film JFK* (1998), chap. 2; Brener (1969); and Donald H. Carpenter: "Jim Garrison: Trump before Trump," *Washington Decoded*, 11 March 2017.

28 These include the *New Orleans States-Item*'s Rosemary James, *Newsweek*'s Hugh Aynesworth (the former *Dallas Morning News* reporter who'd been bamboozled by Mark Lane), the *Saturday Evening Post*'s James Phelan, *Look* magazine's Warren Rogers, the *Washington Post*'s George Lardner, Jr., and *NBC*'s Frank McGee. Assistant DA Milton Brener and Garrison's special investigator William Gurvich also spoke out against his methods.

29 Lambert, 62–3; Carpenter (2017).

30 Jack Martin, a notorious alcoholic, had called the local police and FBI in November 1963 to identify Ferrie as Oswald's accomplice. The calls were apparently made in revenge after Ferrie told their employer, private investigator Guy Banister, that Martin had made expensive personal long-distance phone calls during Banister's absence—which led Banister to beat Martin in rage. The FBI, the New Orleans Police Department, the Houston Police Department, the Texas Rangers, and the Warren Commission all investigated Martin's allegations in 1963–64. Nothing was found to connect Ferrie to Oswald. Lambert, chap. 3; Shenon, 468–9. An old photograph of a Louisiana Civil Air Patrol cookout featuring Ferrie and a teenaged Oswald surfaced in 1993, proving that the two men were once seen together, but necessarily more than acquaintances. John Ciravolo, the owner of the photograph, did not consider it proof that Oswald and Ferrie would even remember each other. Lambert, 59 (footnote).

31 James Phelan: "Rush to Judgment in New Orleans," *Saturday Evening Post*, May 6, 1967. Ironically, it was Ferrie who first leaked the news of Garrison's inquest, angered by the DA's harassment. Lambert, chap. 5.

32 See works by Lambert, Posner, Carpenter, Phelan, Lardner, Holland, Bethell, Brener, and Billings.

33 "Leon" turned out to be James Ronald Lewallen, a former pilot and quality inspector for Boeing and NASA who was sometimes called "Lee," "Lou," and "Leon," and who temporarily resided with Ferrie. Lewallen had long hair, was often described as a beatnik, and looked almost nothing like Oswald. Posner, 437.

34 The FBI investigated Ferrie's connections to Oswald and confirmed the ice-skating story and that Ferrie's plane was at that time in no condition to fly. Lambert, chap. 5.

35 Phelan (1967); Norden, 174–6. The "Pinky" alias and the claim that Ruby and Oswald were lovers came from Melba Christine Marcades (aka: Rose Cherami), a heroin addict and prostitute who said she'd worked as a stripper at Ruby's Dallas nightclub (no evidence exists to prove this). Many conspiracists also say she had advance knowledge of the assassination, but it is unclear whether her claims were recorded accurately and prior to the assassination by Louisiana State Trooper Lieutenant Francis Frugé—who found Cherami by the roadside on November 21, 1963, with "severe symptoms of withdrawal". Frugé then escorted her to the East Louisiana State Hospital (ELSH), where she displayed "episodically psychopathic behavior". For a conspiracist interpretation see Jim DiEugenio: "Rose Cheramie [sic]: How She Predicted the JFK Assassination," *Probe*, July–August 1999 issue, Vol.6, No.5. For a skeptical view, see Posner, 444 (footnote), and Reitzes: "Impeaching Clinton—Part Two: Jackson," (2000), *JFK Online*. The HSCA, citing narcotics bureaus in Oklahoma and Texas, found Cherami's stories to be "erroneous in all respects". HSCA Vol. X, 197–204. Cherami's credibility was further challenged in 2003 when ELSH Doctor Donn Bowers stated in an open letter to researcher Bob Dorff that he wasn't present at the hospital the day Cherami allegedly discussed a plan to kill Kennedy and that he never had any contact with her. Reitzes: "Impeaching Clinton—Part Two," footnote 44.

36 Garrison said he had been on the verge of arresting Ferrie. Garrison's lead prosecutor James Alcock admitted to Patricia Lambert in 1994 that they had no plans to arrest Ferrie at that time because they had no case against him. Ferrie's apartment had also been monitored by Garrison's investigators, who saw no suspicious persons entering or exiting his residence the night of his death, save for the *Washington Post*'s George Lardner, Jr., who interviewed Ferrie that night concerning his dealings with Garrison's office. Lambert, 302, note #18.

37 Lambert, 62–5 and 302, note #12. Dr. Ronald A. Welch, who performed the autopsy, listed the cause of death as a berry aneurism. He also confirmed that Ferrie had a history of cardiovascular problems, and recently suffered several milder bleeds likely caused by stress.

38 Norden, 126. Oliver Stone's *JFK* suggests Ferrie was murdered.

39 See Dean Andrews' FBI interview, November 25, 1963 (Commission Exhibit 3094, WC XXVI), Secret Service Report regarding interview with Andrews, December 5, 1963 (Commission Exhibit 2103, WC XXVI) and Testimony of Dean Adam Andrews, Jr., WC XI. Andrews was also unable to produce any proof of having been hired by Bertrand. Posner, 427–9. He would later admit under oath (to Garrison) that he made the whole story up using a joke name he heard at a "fag wedding". The DA later charged Andrews with eleven counts of perjury. He was convicted of three and sentenced to eighteen months in prison, after which he was disbarred. Lambert, 120–1.

40 Billings: *New Orleans Journal*, March 3, 1967, 18, cited in Reitzes: "Impeaching Clinton—Part Two". See Also Fred Litwin: *On the Trail of Delusion: Jim Garrison: The Great Accuser* (2020). Allegations that Clay Shaw was a CIA agent did not originate with Jim Garrison. The connection was made for him by *Paese Sera*, an Italian Marxist newspaper that published a story on Shaw four days after his (highly publicized) arrest by Garrison's office, identifying Shaw as a fascist and a CIA operative. The story was picked up by other European newspapers before it found its way to Garrison. This corroborating evidence fed Garrison's certainty that Shaw was guilty. The story was later found to have been invented and planted by the Soviet KGB as part of a campaign of *dezinformatsiya*

(disinformation) to turn Europeans and Americans against the US government. Max Holland: "The Power of Disinformation: The Lie That Linked CIA to the Kennedy Assassination," (2001), Center for the Study of Intelligence, *Central Intelligence Agency*, April 14, 2007. The *Paese Sera* story has remained one of the main conspiracist "proofs" that Shaw was a CIA agent. See, for example, Joan Mellen: *A Farewell to Justice: Jim Garrison, JFK's Assassination, and the Case that Should Have Changed History* (2005), 236–42.

41 This helped Garrison "prove" that Oswald, not James Lewallen, was Ferrie's roommate "Leon". Lambert, 101 (and footnote).

42 Under 1967 Louisiana law, the defense did not have a right to study the evidence or know the identity of the prosecution's witnesses until these were disclosed to the grand jury. Garrison was also friendly with several grand jurors (including foreman Albert V. Labiche) who were subjected to lengthy anti-Warren Commission lectures by conspiracist authors Mark Lane, Harold Weisberg, and William Turner. Lambert, 119.

43 Bugliosi, 995.

44 Oliver Stone's *JFK* suggests that Russo (a composite character named "Willie O'Keefe") was invited over for sex. Russo was in fact made to visit Shaw's home at Garrison's urging under the pretense of selling him insurance. Shaw did not recognize Russo. Phelan (1967).

45 "The JFK Conspiracy: The Case of Jim Garrison," Reported by Frank McGee, *NBC*, June 1967.

46 Lambert, 201.

47 These included Thomas Bethell and Harold Weisberg. Tom Bethell: "Was Sirhan Sirhan on the Grassy Knoll?" *The Washington Monthly*, March 1975; "Inside the Garrison Investigation: The Thomas Bethell Diary" (1967–68), *The Kennedy Assassination*; George Lardner, Jr.: "On the Set: Dallas in Wonderland: How Oliver Stone's Version of the Kennedy Assassination Exploits the Edge of Paranoia," *The Washington Post*, May 19, 1991.

48 William Gurvich quit in protest and informed Bobby Kennedy that the whole case was a sham. HSCA interview with Gurvich, November 7 and 26, 1978, *The Kennedy Assassination*. Bill Boxley, whose real name was William Clarence Wood, Jr., was a former CIA employee fired by the Agency for alcoholism in 1953. Boxley/Wood became a liability to Garrison when it was discovered that he was feeding Garrison whatever "facts" he was told to produce. Boxley/Wood was renamed "Bill Broussard" in Stone's *JFK* and portrayed as a government informant. However, a 1968 internal CIA memo drafted by Ernest A. Rische, titled "Bill Wood, Agent for Jim Garrison, Making Inquiries in Houston," reveals that the CIA had had no relations with Wood since his forced resignation. Deputy Director, DCS, to Houston Office Chief, April 26, 1968, *The Kennedy Assassination*. This contradicts Garrison's claims that Wood/Boxley/Broussard infiltrated his office using a fake name on behalf of the CIA. (In fact, the fake name had been Garrison's idea.) See Garrison: *On the Trail of the Assassins* (1988), 222.

49 See Norden (1967) and William W. Turner: "The Inquest," *Ramparts*, June 1967. In January 1968, Garrison appeared on the *Tonight Show*, whose host Johnny Carson debated him at length with unusual candor. In February, he was interviewed on Dutch television by Willem Oltmans, a controversial left-wing journalist and conspiracist. Oltmans would become one of Garrison's staunchest promoters in Europe. Holland: "The Power of Disinformation".

50 "NBC Presents: Jim Garrison's Response," *NBC*, July 15, 1967.

51 Shaw did have a past with the CIA—as an unpaid informant concerning his foreign business contacts from 1948 to 1956. Shaw denied this fact until his death, a fact Garrison

would discover in the late 1970s, which provoked him to start writing his "memoirs" (*On the Trail of the Assassins*, 1988). The CIA had always been uncertain whether Garrison already knew about this (he didn't). Holland: "The Power of Disinformation".

52 Norden, 74.

53 *Tonight Show with Johnny Carson*, January 31, 1968.

54 Norden, 70.

55 Ibid., 172–6.

56 "A CBS News Inquiry: The Warren Report," *CBS*, June 25–28, 1967, *CSPAN*.

57 Lambert, 137.

58 Marina was still pregnant with Rachel during these Clinton "sightings". June Oswald was already a toddler.

59 These "witnesses" included barber Edwin Lea McGehee, local state representative Reeves Morgan, Town Marshall John Manchester, and Clinton Registrar of Voters Henry Earl Palmer, several of whom were members of the local Ku Klux Klan chapter and were desirous to see Garrison run as Vice President alongside Alabama governor George Wallace. See Lambert, 187 and 196, and David Reitzes: "Impeaching Clinton—Part Two". No physical record of Oswald's presence in Clinton was produced by the prosecution, only witnesses who disagreed on key details. Nor had any Clinton "witnesses" informed the authorities or their friends that President Kennedy's murderer had come to town a few weeks prior to the assassination to get a haircut, speak to the local state representative, register to vote, and apply for a job at a nearby psychiatric hospital. The Clinton mystery would be elucidated a quarter century later when Patricia Lambert tracked down Anne Hundley Dischler, one of Garrison's volunteer investigators, who provided her with her 1968 handwritten interview notes—evidence that the Clinton witnesses never met Oswald or Shaw but had instead been coached by Assistant DA Andrew Sciambra, the same man who manufactured Perry Russo's "memories" of an assassination party at Ferrie's apartment. Lambert, chap. 13.

60 Posner, 447; James Kirkwood: *American Grotesque* (1992), 231–45, cited in Reitzes: "The Clay Shaw Trial Testimony of Charles Spiesel (Summary)," *JFK Online*.

61 Garrison went on to charge Shaw with several counts of perjury, which were appealed until Shaw won a permanent injunction against Garrison in 1971. This final hearing revealed that Garrison received nearly $100,000 from private funders, most of which he spent without keeping accounts. He was also chastised for his illegal methods and fabrication of evidence. Garrison appealed to the District Court and US Supreme Court. His case was rejected both times. Shaw then initiated a multi-million dollar abuse-of-process lawsuit against Garrison and his funders but died before it reached a court room. Lambert, 175. Had Shaw had a surviving relative to sponsor the case on his behalf, it is likely that he would have won, preventing Garrison from further alleging his guilt, thereby preventing further books and films—including Oliver Stone's—from doing the same. Posner, 449–50.

62 Norden, 178.

63 Shenon, 471. King was shot by James Earl Ray while supporting a sanitation workers' strike in Memphis. Ray was a small-time criminal and escaped convict with strong racist beliefs and an admiration for George Wallace, the segregationist Alabama Governor. Gerald Posner: *Killing the Dream: James Earl Ray and the Assassination of Martin Luther King, Jr.* (1998). Robert Francis Kennedy (RFK) was shot at close range by Sirhan B. Sirhan inside the Ambassador Hotel in Los Angeles the night of the California Democratic presidential primary. Sirhan was a young Palestinian immigrant who later claimed he killed RFK to protest his pro-Israel policies. Dan E. Moldea: *The Killing of Robert F Kennedy: An Investigation of Motive, Means, and Opportunity* (1997).

64 See, for example, William F. Pepper: *An Act of State: The Execution of Martin Luther King* (2003), and William Klaber and Philip H. Melanson: *Shadow Play: The Untold Story of the Robert F. Kennedy Assassination* (1998).

65 Clayborne Carson: *In Struggle: SNCC and the Black Awakening of the 1960s* (1981); James R. Ralph, Jr.: *Northern Protest: Martin Luther King, Jr., Chicago and the Civil Rights Movement* (1993); Charles E. Jones, ed.: *The Black Panther Party [Reconsidered]* (1998).

66 Allan Nevins et al.: *A Pocket History of the United States* (1992), 575–83.

67 Mark Kurlansky: *1968: The Year that Rocked the World* (2004); Michel J. Gagné: *The Harp, the Hammer and the Plough: The Northern Ireland Civil Rights Movement and the World Beyond, 1963–1968*, Masters Thesis in History, Concordia University, 2005, https://spect rum.library.concordia.ca/8752/.

68 The most famous of these were the August 1968 protests at the Democratic Party Convention in Chicago and the "Kent State University Massacre" of May 4, 1970. Todd Gitlin: *The Sixties: Years of Hope, Days of Rage* (1993).

69 Nevins et al., 583–90.

70 According to ongoing Gallup research, this figure has fluctuated between 60% and 80% since the mid-1970s. The highest spikes in JFK conspiracism occurred in the mid-1970s in the wake of the Watergate Affair and following the September 11, 2001 terrorist attacks, two other conspiracy-generating national crises. Swift (2013).

71 Knight, 107–8; John F. Keener: "Biography, Conspiracy, and the Oswald Enigma," *Biography (University of Hawaii Press)*, Vol.20, No.3, Summer 1997. On the Irish Mafia myth, see Chapter 3 of this book.

72 Scott Shane: "For Ford, Pardon Decision Was Always Clear-Cut," *The New York Times*, December 29, 2006.

73 Swift (2013).

74 David Greenberg: "Dallas through the Looking Glass: The Plot to Link JFK's Death and Watergate," *Slate*, November 20, 2003.

75 These include Vincent Palamara (the Secret Service—see Chapter 14), David Mantik (the medical evidence—see Chapter 15), Jack White (film and photography—see Chapter 17), and John Newman (military history).

76 Len Osanic: "Who Is Col. L. Fletcher Prouty?" (n.d.), *The Col. L Fletcher Prouty Reference Site.*

77 See Len Osanic: *The Col. L. Fletcher Prouty Reference Site* (www.prouty.org) and Osanic's internet radio talk show, *Black Op Radio* (www.blackopradio.com).

78 Thomas G. Whittle and Jan Thorpe: "Revisiting the Jonestown Tragedy: Newly Released Documents Shed Light on Unsolved Murders," *Freedom Magazine*, Vol.29, No.4, Church of Scientology International (1998).

79 Chip Berlet: "Right Woos Left: Populist Party, LaRouchian, and Other Neo-Fascist Overtures to Progressives, and Why They Must Be Rejected," *Political Research Associates*, February 27, 1999.

80 Prouty's writings share a peculiar similarity to *The Protocols of the Elders of Zion*, an early twentieth-century anti-Semitic hoax produced by the Russian secret police to turn Orthodox Christians against Jews and communists (whom the tract suggested were in league together). Prouty's works were also strongly influenced (by his own admission) by a similar hoax titled *The Report from Iron Mountain on the Possibility and Desirability of Peace* (1967), used by the Liberty Lobby and Institute for Historic Review to promote their theories of Zionist world domination. Neither groups nor Prouty or Oliver Stone—all of whom cited this source as proof of a massive CIA/right-wing conspiracy to depopulate and control the world—seemed to realize that its author, Leonard Lewin, wrote it as a satire of political think tanks. Binjamin W. Segel: *A Lie and a Libel: The History*

of the Protocols of the Elders of Zion, edited and translated by R.S. Levy (1996); Leonard Lewin: *The Report from Iron Mountain on the Possibility and Desirability of Peace* (1967); Leonard Lewin: "The Guest Word: Report from Iron Mountain," *New York Times Book Review*, March 19, 1972.

81 Edward J. Epstein: *The Assassination Chronicles* (1992), 578–80, cited in John McAdams: "L. Fletcher Prouty: Fearless Truth Teller, or Crackpot?" (n.d.), *The Kennedy Assassination*; Robert Sam Anson: "The Shooting of *JFK*," *Esquire*, November 1991, cited in Reitzes: "The JFK 100: The Mystery Man, 'X'," 2012, *JFK Online*.

82 "Fletcher Prouty: Oil Is Not from Fossils," (n.d.), *Internet Archive*.

83 Prouty: *The Secret Team* (1973), chap. 18; Prouty: "Col. Fletcher Prouty Discusses the Gary Powers U2 Flight," *The Col. L Fletcher Prouty Reference Site* (n.d.).

84 Ibid., chap. 1 (n.p.).

85 Peter Dale Scott: "From Dallas to Watergate: The Longest Cover-Up," *Ramparts Magazine*, November 1973, 12–20.

86 Scott: *The War Conspiracy: JFK, 9/11 and the Deep Politics of War* (2013)—an updated version of his 1972 book; Scott: "The Doomsday Project and Deep Events: JFK, Watergate, Iran-Contra, and 9/11," *The Asia Pacific Journal*, Vol.9, No.47, Number 2, November 26, 2011; Scott: "The Fates of American Presidents Who Challenged the Deep State (1963–1980)," *The Asia Pacific Journal*, Vol.12, No.43, Number 4, October 20, 2014.

87 See Scott: *Deep Politics and the Death of JFK* (1993); Max Holland: "Paranoia Unbound," *The Wilson Quarterly*, Winter 1994, 87–90; and Greenberg: "Dallas through the Looking Glass". The phrase was revived by President Trump and his Alt-right supporters. See Evan Osnos: "Trump vs. the 'Deep State'," *The New Yorker*, May 14, 2018.

88 Scott: "The Fates of American Presidents…"

89 Saint Augustine: *The City of God*, Part II, Books XIV and XIX, *The Works of Aurelius Augustine, Bishop of Hippo*, Rev. Marcus Dods, ed., 1871.

90 René Descartes: "Meditations I and II," *Meditations on First Philosophy*, tr. by Elizabeth S. Haldane, *The Philosophical Works of Descartes* (1911).

91 Journalist Max Holland aptly described Scott's theories as "an unreadable compendium of 'may haves' and 'might haves,' non-sequiturs, and McCarthy-style innuendo, with enough documentation to satisfy any paranoid […] a virtual political Disneyland". Holland: "Paranoia Unbound".

92 Groden admitted this much when cross-examined during the 1996 O.J. Simpson civil trial. "Robert Groden—12/18/96 Testimony at Simpson Civil Trial," posted at McAdams, ed.: *The Kennedy Assassination*.

93 "Comments on the Panel's Report by Robert Groden, Consultant to the Committee," HSCA VI, 306–8. See also Robert Groden interview on *Black Op Radio*, September 18, 2008, posted on *DVP's JFK Archive*.

94 "Comments on the Panel's Report by Robert Groden…," 295.

95 Groden: *The Killing of a President*, 141; Groden: *The Search for Lee Harvey Oswald*, 74–5, excerpted in John McAdams: "Oswald Tied to Clay Shaw at New Orleans Trade Mart?" *The Kennedy Assassination*.

96 That is, once from the grassy knoll and once from the south side of the Plaza, leaving a small wound in his left temple that no one but Groden noticed. "Comments on the Panel's Report by Robert Groden…," 301.

97 "JFK Autopsy Photos Were Faked & Here's How & Why Feds Did It," *The Globe* (with special collaboration from Robert Groden), Vol.58, No.53, December 31, 1991.

98 "Comments on the Panel's Report by Robert Groden….," 299. Groden later claimed this hole was large enough for an X-ray technician at Parkland [Bethesda?] Hospital to put both his fists inside the gaping hole. "JFK Autopsy Photos Were Faked…"

99 The diagrams can be viewed at: http://mcadams.posc.mu.edu/bogus3.gif and http://mcadams.posc.mu.edu/bogus4.gif. See also Figure 13.6. It is unclear where and when the expression "magic bullet" originated. A private email chain between David Lifton, David Lesar, John McAdams, and myself (May 25–26, 2018) suggests it was first used in print by Mark Lane or Ray Marcus as early as 1966, but that several conspiracists already referred to it as "magic bullet," "super bullet," and "bastard bullet".

100 See ARRB Deposition of Robert J. Groden (in two parts), July 2 and August 20, 1996; Jim Schutze: "Dutch Film Portrays Our Own Robert Groden as Obsessed, Not Crazy," *The Dallas Observer*, July 16, 2015. See also the documentary film *Plaza Man* (2014) by Dutch filmmaker Kasper Verkaik, which offers an intimate portrait of Groden's public and personal life.

101 Joyce Carol Oates: "Twenty-Six Seconds of the JFK Assassination—And a Lifetime of Family Anguish," *The Washington Post*, November 17, 2016.

102 Other, more prominent members of the HSCA held conspiracist views, including forensic pathologist Cyril Wecht and lead counsel G. Robert Blakey.

103 "Comments on the Panel's Report by Robert Groden….," 294. See Chapter 16 of this book.

104 "JFK Autopsy Photos Were Faked…" The autopsy materials remain the property of the Kennedy family, not of the federal government or National Archives (where they are presently stored).

105 Schutze (2015).

106 In 1997, Groden was hired as an expert witness by the legal defense team of former footballer O.J. Simpson, who had recently been found not guilty of his estranged wife's murder. Simpson was now fighting a civil trial over her wrongful death. Groden argued that over 30 pictures of Simpson wearing a pair of rare Bruno Magli shoes, whose prints were identified at the murder scene, were faked in order to frame him, against the testimony of the photographer who took them. Simpson lost the case and Groden lost many feathers. Associated Press: "Jurors See 30 Photos of Simpson as He Wore Magli Shoes in 1993," *New York Times*, January 7, 1997.

107 Schutze (2015).

108 Amy Martyn: "Dallas Wants JFK Conspiracy Theorist to Remove 'Grassy Knoll' Sign from Grassy Knoll," *The Dallas Observer*, May 7, 2015; Rodger Jones: "JFK 'X' Reappears on Elm Street in Dealey Plaza," *Dallas News*, November 2013.

109 Nevins et al., 594–600.

110 Seymour Hersh: "Huge C.I.A. Operation Reported in U.S. against Antiwar Forces, Other Dissidents in Nixon Years," *The New York Times*, December 22, 1974.

111 Nicholas M. Horrock: "Destruction of LSD Data Laid to C.I.A. Aide in '73'," *New York Times*, July 18, 1975; Kim Zetter: "April 13, 1953: CIA OKs MK-Ultra Mind-Control Tests," *Wired*, April 13, 2010; John D. Marks: *The Search for the Manchurian Candidate: The CIA and Mind Control—The Secret History of the Behavioral Sciences* (1979).

112 The *Rockefeller Report* also argued (a) that conspiracy suspects Frank Sturgis and Howard Hunt had solid alibis; (b) that the three anonymous "derelicts" who were briefly detained and let go by Dallas Police had been found in a boxcar *a half-mile south* of Dealey Plaza and hence were not in the Plaza at the time of the shooting; (c) that suspicious silhouettes in the Zapruder and Nix films were "imaginative illusions"; and (d) that no connections were found linking Oswald or Ruby to the CIA and Watergate burglars. The Commission also offered a new revelation to account for Kennedy's backward motion after the fatal headshot: he was wearing a back brace that impeded his forward motion. *Report to the President by the Commission on CIA Activities within the United States* (1975), 251–68.

113 *Final Report of the Select Committee to Study Governmental Operations with Respect to Intelligence Activities, United States Senate* (1976), chaps. VIII, IX, and X. See also Bugliosi, 369–70.

114 On the HSCA's conclusions concerning King's murder, see "Findings on MLK Assassination," *Report of the Select Committee on Assassinations of the U.S. House of Representatives* (1979), *National Archives: JFK Assassination Records.* (Henceforth *HSCA Report.*)

115 Sprague, who assembled a huge staff (170 lawyers and researchers), intended to subject all suspects and witnesses to polygraph tests and voice stress evaluators, and to equip his investigators with miniature devices to secretly record their phone conversations. All this threatened to run the Committee's budget into the tens of millions of dollars and challenged the ethical principle of informed consent. Sprague stepped down from his post to prevent the Committee from imploding. It henceforth operated on a tighter budget with more moderate objectives. This also triggered the resignations of several staff members loyal to Sprague, including deputy chief counsel Robert Tanenbaum and investigator Gaeton Fonzi, both of whom held conspiracist views and became vocal critics of the HSCA's "timid" conclusions. Bugliosi, 370–8.

116 These included Dr. Cyril Wecht and Congressmen Thomas Downing and Christopher Dodd. See "Separate Remarks, Views and Dissent of Members of the Committee," chap. IV, *HSCA Report.*

117 "Summary of Findings and Recommendations," *HSCA Report.* See Chapters 13, 15, and 16 of this book.

118 Ibid.

119 These were Dr. James Barger, Mark Weiss, and Ernest Aschkenasy. Bugliosi, 376–80.

120 It should also be noted that this new acoustic evidence was extrapolated from a static-filled mess of noises etched on a 15-year-old strip of vinyl, which was almost impossible to decipher without a high-quality audio mixer. For this reason, some Committee members chose to record a dissenting view. See "Separate Views of Hons. Samuel L. Devine and Robert W. Edgar," and "Dissent and Additional Remarks of Hon. Harold S. Sawyer to the Final Report of the Select Committee on Assassinations," in "Separate Remarks, Views and Dissent of Members of the Committee," chap. IV, *HSCA Report.* See the lengthy 63-page (!) endnote on this matter in Bugliosi, endnotes 153–218.

121 "Summary of Findings and Recommendations". In using the words, "scientific evidence *does not preclude the possibility* of two gunmen….," the HSCA was in fact supporting its conclusions with an argument from ignorance fallacy (i.e., claiming that something is true because it is not proven false). Critical thinkers will realize that many things are scientifically *possible* but not in fact true.

122

> Since the recorded acoustic impulses are similar to static, efforts to attribute them to gunshots have depended on echo analyses; but in these analyses desirable control tests were omitted, some of the analyses depended on subjective selection of data, serious errors were made in some of the statistical calculations, incorrect statistical conclusions were drawn and the analysis methods used were novel in some aspects and were untested at such high levels of background noise. Furthermore, some of the recorded background sounds, such as the delay in the sounds of police sirens, are not what one would expect if the open microphone had been in the motorcade. For these and other reasons discussed in the report, the Committee concluded that the previous acoustic analyses do not demonstrate that there was a grassy knoll shot.

National Academy of Sciences: "Executive Summary," *Report of the Committee on Ballistic Acoustics*, National Academy Press, Washington, DC, 1982, posted at *JFK Online*. This research was initiated following the discovery by Steve Barber, an Ohio rock musician, that the Dictabelt recording contained the voice of Dallas sheriff Bill Decker, speaking "cross talk" over another channel (recorded on a different machine than the channel 1 Dictabelt). This conversation was shown to have happened some time after the shooting was over. Kathryn Olmsted, interview by Barry Glassner, *Book TV*, CSPAN, April 25, 2009.

123 In the late 1990s, computer animator Dale Myers used the home movies taken by several bystanders to establish that patrolman McLain had not yet arrived at the required location (near the corner of Houston and Elm) to record the sounds on the Dictabelt. "Peter Jennings Reporting: The Kennedy Assassination – Beyond Conspiracy," *ABC News*, 2003. In 2005, the Forensic Science Society published a peer-reviewed study that upheld the NRC's findings. R. Linsker et al.: "Synchronization of the Acoustic Evidence in the Assassination of President Kennedy," *Science & Justice*, Vol. 45, No. 4, 2005, 207–26. In 2013, political scientist Larry Sabato, author of *The Kennedy Half Century* (2013), commissioned a re-investigation of the Dictabelt recording by the media engineering firm Sonalysts Inc. By examining the two police channels recorded by the Dictabelt—only one of which (channel #2) was used for the motorcade (not channel #1, which recorded the alleged gunshots)—and the pattern of the vehicle's acceleration and auditory Doppler effects, Sonalysts' sound engineers concluded that the open microphone had recorded traffic noises several miles from Dealey Plaza, most likely at the Dallas Trade Mart where several other motorcycle policemen awaited Kennedy's arrival. Charles Olsen and Scott Martin: "Analysis of the Dallas Police Department Dictabelt Recording Related to the Assassination of President John F. Kennedy," March 25, 2013, in Larry J. Sabato: "The Kennedy Half Century: Acoustical Analysis of November 22, 1963 Dallas Police Recordings," October 15, 2013.

124 Posner, 235–40; Bugliosi, endnotes 153–218; Myers: "Epipolar Geometric Analysis of Amateur Films Related to Acoustics Evidence in the John F. Kennedy Assassination," 2010, *JFK Files: Secrets of a Homicide*.

125 For example, Henry Hurt: *Reasonable Doubt* (1985), 33–4, 100–2; Anthony Summers: *Not in Your Lifetime* (1998), chaps. 4 and 5; James Fetzer, ed.: *Murder in Dealey Plaza* (2000).

126 Fonzi: "Who Killed JFK?" *The Washingtonian*, November 1980; Fonzi: *The Last Investigation* (1993); Groden and Livingstone: *High Treason* (1990); Tanenbaum: "JFK Assassination Conspiracy Theories: An Analysis of Government Misconduct: The House Select Committee on Assassinations," Presentation given at Duquesne University, Wecht Institute of Forensic Science and Law, October 18, 2013, *CSPAN*.

127 With the notable exception of David Lifton's *Best Evidence* (discussed above and in Chapter 14).

128 This list can also include Lamar Waldron and Thom Hartmann's *Ultimate Sacrifice* (2005) and *Legacy of Secrets* (2008), as well as David Kaiser's *The Road to Dallas* (2008), which gave a new life to mob-centered JFK theories in the twenty-first century.

129 "Oswald's Body Is Exhumed; an Autopsy Affirms Identity," *The New York Times*, October 5, 1981.

130 Bugliosi, 1039–44. See also Chapter 10 of this book.

131 John Corry: "TV REVIEW; Showtime Stages 'Trial' of Lee Harvey Oswald," *New York Times*, November 20, 1986.

132 Patrick Leman: "The Born Conspiracy," *New Scientist*, July 14, 2007, 35–7 (see Chapter 1 of this book).

133 These events did spark conspiracy chatter among conservatives. See, for example, Niles Mercado: *Bush Killing Reagan: The Bush-Hinckley Conspiracy Bill O'Reilly Won't Tell About* (2015), and Roger Stone and Saint John Hunt: *Jeb and the Bush Crime Family: The Inside Story of an American Dynasty* (2016).

134 These were, respectively: Arthur Bremer, who inspired the film Taxi Driver; Lynette "Squeaky" Fromme, a leading member of the Manson Family cult; the leftist revolutionary Sara Jane Moore; and the schizophrenic John Hinckley, Jr., who saw himself as Bremer's Hollywood doppelganger.

135 Danielle Sloane: "Inside the Mind of John Lennon's Killer," *CNN*, December 8, 2015. Many conspiracists have used Chapman's mental health problems as "proof" that the CIA's MKULTRA "mind control" program was successful and never abandoned. See Fenton Bresler: *Who Killed John Lennon?* (1990).

136 Nevins et al., 640–2.

137 Malcolm Byrne, Peter Kornbluh, and Thomas Blanton: "The Iran-Contra Affair 20 Years on: Documents Spotlight Role of Reagan, Top Aides," November 24, 2006, *The National Security Archive*.

138 Satanism and secret societies had by now replaced communism and civil rights organizations as the principal targets of conservative paranoia. See, for example, Pat Robertson: *The New World Order* (1991). On the rise of this movement, see Jeffrey Victor: *Satanic Panic: The Creation of a Contemporary Legend* (1993); Daniel Pipes: *Conspiracy: How the Paranoid Style Flourishes and Where It Comes from* (1999); and Barkun (2013).

139 Some episodes—including Episode 9: "The Guilty Men," which accused Lyndon Johnson of murdering Kennedy—were retracted following the lodging of libel complaints against the movie's producers, namely by the Johnson estate and former colleagues of LBJ.

140 "The Men Who Killed Kennedy," Nigel Tuner Productions, Episodes 1–9, *History Channel*, 1988, 1995, 2003.

141 Deposition of Richard McGarrah Helms, E. Howard Hunt, Plaintiff, v. Liberty Lobby, Inc., Defendant, No. 80-1121-Civ.-JWK, US District Court, Southern District of Florida, cited in Max Holland: "The Power of Disinformation".

142 See Chapter 11. The erroneous claim that Hunt was one of these tramps, which was debunked by the HSCA's forensic photography panel, originated in Alan J. Weberman and Michael Canfield's *Coup d'Etat in America: The CIA and the Assassination of John F. Kennedy* (1975).

143 Austin Wilson (Associated Press): "Media No Longer Laughing, Jim Garrison Says: Judge Revives View of JFK Assassination," *Los Angeles Times*, March 12, 1989; Interview with Zachary Sklar on *Black Op Radio*, Show #38, May 17, 2001. It was Ray and Schaap who introduced Garrison to Sklar, and these two to filmmaker Stone. Sheridan later declared bankruptcy after losing a libel suit over another conspiracy book, Ari Ben-Menashe's *Profits of War: Inside the Secret U.S.-Israeli Arms Network*, 1992, which claimed to prove Ronald Reagan's 1980 "October Surprise," a theory according to which the Reagan-Bush presidential campaign engineered President Carter's demise by negotiating a secret deal with Iranian Shiite fundamentalists for the release of American hostages. The theory was debunked by a 1992 Congressional investigation.

144 This was a good harvest considering *JFK* was up against Jonathan Demme's *The Silence of the Lambs* and James Cameron's *Terminator 2*, and was one of the most controversial films of the genre in recent history.

145 Lambert, xvi.

146 See James Riordan: *Stone: The Controversies, Excesses, and Exploits of a Radical Filmmaker* (1996), and Toplin (1996).

147 Lambert, 213. Lambert is alluding to Jefferson Smith, the main character in Frank Capra's 1939 film *Mr. Smith Goes to Washington*, a political satire in which Mr. Smith, the good-natured leader of a Boy Rangers brigade, is appointed to replace a deceased US Senator and gets picked apart by powerful Washington insiders. See also Kenneth Turan: "'JFK': Conspiracy in the Cross Hairs: Oliver Stone's Riveting, Controversial Saga of the Kennedy Assassination," *Los Angeles Times*, December 20, 1991; Lardner (1991); and Carpenter (2017).

148 Gary Crowdus: "Clarifying the Conspiracy: An Interview with Oliver Stone," *Cineaste*, Vol. 19, No. 1, 1992, reprinted in Charles L.P. Silet, ed.: *Oliver Stone: Interviews (Conversations with Filmmakers)* (2001), 98.

149 Oliver Stone: "Making the Movie J.F.K.," Speech delivered to the National Press Club, January 15, 1992, *C-SPAN*.

150 See titles by Jean Hill (1992), James Earl Files (1994, 2007), Fletcher Prouty (1995), and Ed Hoffman (1997).

151 Max Holland: "Much Ado about Nothing," *The Weekly Standard*, December 12, 2017.

152 This was not the view of the vast majority of the ARRB's staff. Holland: "Much Ado about Nothing". On Horne's belief that the Zapruder film is a forgery, see Chapter 17. See also Douglas P. Horne: *Inside the Assassination Records Review Board: The U.S. Government's Final Attempt to Reconcile the Conflicting Medical Evidence in the Assassination of JFK* (self-published, 2009), and Horne's two essays: "Evidence of a Government Cover-up: Two Different Brain Specimens in President Kennedy's Autopsy," and "Interviews with Former NIPC Employees: The Zapruder Film in November 1963," in Fetzer (2000). Horne is also the focus of several low-budget online interviews and lectures such as "Altered History: Exposing Deceit and Deception in the JFK Assassination Medical Evidence" (2014), *The Future of Freedom Foundation*.

153 In 2018, President Trump, who frequently showed sympathy for the conspiracist cause, accepted to push the final deadline to 2021. His stated purpose was to protect the identity and families of former CIA assets. Ian Shapira: "Trump Delays Full Release of Some JFK Assassination Files until 2021, Bowing to National Security Concerns," *The Washington Post*, April 26, 2018.

154 Kay, 41–51. To his credit, Stone never publicly claimed that the 9/11 attacks and the Kennedy assassination were connected. See, for example, Anthony D'Alessandro: "Oliver Stone Remembers 9/11: What the U.S. Government Knew & How We Could Have Prevented That Tragic Day—TIFF," *Deadline Hollywood*, September 11, 2016.

155 Molly Hennessy-Fiske: "Eclectic Crowds Flock to Dallas' Dealey Plaza," *Los Angeles Times*, November 22, 2013; Jon Herskovitz and Marice Richter: "On 50th Anniversary of JFK Death—Tears, Memories, Suspicion," *Reuters*, November 22, 2013.

156 Fetzer, "'Smoking Guns' in the Death of JFK," *Murder in Dealey Plaza*, 1; Holland: "Much Ado about Nothing".

157 Russo and Molton, chap. 10; Shenon, 1–13, 520–63. See also David Robarge: "Angleton Unrevealed," *Washington Decoded*, October 15, 2017, a review of Morley's *The Ghost*, with responses by Morley and rejoinders by Robarge.

158 Rory Carroll: "Who Killed JFK? Fifty Years on, Slew of New Books Add Fuel to Conspiracy Fire," *The Guardian*, November 15, 2013.

159 Fetzer: "'Smoking Guns'…".

160 Fetzer also cofounded Scholars for 9/11 Truth. He furthermore claimed that the Apollo moon missions were faked, that no passenger plane hit the Pentagon on September

11, 2001, that the 2012 Sandy Hook school shooting was staged by the Israeli Mossad (for which he was sued for defamation), that Senator Paul Wellstone's 2002 plane crash was a government-sponsored murder, and that the Holocaust may not have happened. Jon Tevlin: "Northfield Pub Puts Free Speech Limits to the Test," Minneapolis *Star Tribune*, January 21, 2015. See also Fetzer's website (www.assassinationscience.com) and contributions to *Black Op Radio* (www.blackopradio.com). Videos of the 2003 JFK Symposium held at the University of Minnesota, Duluth, can be found on *YouTube*.

161 Barkun defines this term as "conspiratorial constructs in which multiple conspiracies are believed to be linked together hierarchically [and] nested within one another. At the summit of the conspiratorial hierarchy is a distant but all powerful evil force manipulating lesser conspiratorial actors," Barkun, 6.

162 Kay, 45, 50.

163 Barkun, 26–9. See also Chapter 1 of this book.

164 See Fetzer: "Thinking about 'Conspiracy Theories': 9/11 and JFK," and Scott: "JFK and 9/11: Insights Gained from Understanding Both," in Fetzer, ed.: *The 9/11 Conspiracy: The Scamming of America* (2007). See also Scott: "America's 'Deep State': From the JFK Assassination to 9/11," *Global Research*, June 20, 2014.

165 Kay, 49–51.

166 Carroll: "Who Killed JFK? …"

167 An earlier incarnation of this book, titled *Mary, Ferrie & the Monkey Virus: The Story of an Underground Medical Laboratory* (1995), appears to be the inspiration behind Vary Baker's outlandish love story. See John McAdams: "Lee Oswald's Girlfriend in New Orleans? Secret CIA Bioweapons Researcher? Should We Believe Judyth Baker?" (n.d.), *The Kennedy Assassination*.

PART II

Motive

"Like Caesar, he is surrounded by enemies…"

5

THE ANTI-CIVIL RIGHTS MOVEMENT

Right-wing racists, Nixon, and the FBI

5.1 Who wants to be an assassin?

One of the reasons JFK is widely believed to have been murdered by a group of powerful conspirators is the large number of known and alleged political opponents he made on his way to the White House and during his three years in office. These presumed mortal enemies are sometimes identified as rivals of his father and family, as opponents of his Catholic faith, or as victims of his electoral tactics, but mostly they tend to be picked from a long list of organized criminals, right-wing ideologues, and powerful bureaucrats staunchly opposed to JFK's policies on Civil Rights, Cuba, Vietnam, or détente with the Soviet Union. The most popular conspiracy suspects are Chicago mob boss Sam Giancana, New Orleans kingpin Carlos Marcello, Florida crime lord Santo Trafficante, Jr., and mob-affiliated labor unionist Jimmy Hoffa; future US Presidents Lyndon Johnson and Richard Nixon; FBI Director J. Edgar Hoover; active and former high-ranking CIA officials—namely Allen Dulles, Charles Cabell, Richard Bissell, and Richard Helms; members of the Joint Chiefs of Staff—including Generals Maxwell Taylor and Curtis Lemay; and an array of rich industrialists, like Texas oilmen Clint Murchison and H.L. Hunt. These last three groups (the CIA, the Pentagon, and private contractors) often get lumped together into a large warmongering consortium alternately nicknamed the "military industrial complex," the "Secret Team," the "Oligarchy," or some similar catchall. Political and judicial investigators of the assassination, namely the members of the Warren Commission (e.g., Earl Warren, Gerald Ford, and John J. McCloy), and leading figures in the Attorney General's office (e.g., Nicholas Katzenbach and Ramsey Clark) are frequently lumped into this stew of malefactors.

Conspiracists also often incriminate a secondary group of clandestine operatives whom they claim carried out the assassination, helped set up Oswald as a patsy,

DOI: 10.4324/9781003222460-7

and covered up evidence of their involvement. These co-conspirators are usually described as lower ranking members of the mafia or CIA—such as James Angleton, Win Scott, or George Joannides—or possibly mercenaries working for them. In most instances, conspiracists do not delve too deeply into the possible identities of these faceless "mechanics".[1] The few names on offer include US Air Force Brigadier-General Edward Lansdale and CIA henchmen E. Howard Hunt and Frank Sturgis.[2]

The large number of suspects whose names appear in the conspiracist literature is too vast to be exhaustively dealt with here. This and the following chapters will therefore only examine the most prominent suspects (individuals and groups) fingered by the conspiracists and consider whether they had a clear motive to murder Kennedy. If none of the leading figures demonstrates a strong enough motive to kill the president, it is reasonable to assume that the many secondary suspects—those whom only a small number of conspiracists find suspicious—are even less likely to have been involved.

The rest of this chapter will consider whether Kennedy might have been killed for reasons of anti-Catholic bigotry or racism to halt the civil rights movement. This section of chapters will end with an assessment of Lee Harvey Oswald's probable motive and consider whether the conspiracy press offers compelling enough evidence to puncture a hole in the lone assassin theory.

5.2 Race, oil, and taxes

In the hours that followed Kennedy's death, the most natural assumption many Americans made was that Southern racists had murdered the president to protest his civil rights platform. It is "THEY" whom Mrs. Kennedy had in mind that afternoon when she chose a plural pronoun to describe her husband's unidentified killer(s). This was also the gut reaction of Chief Justice Warren, of much of Kennedy's White House staff and entourage, and of thousands of other Americans who saw Dallas as a hotbed of right-wing radicalism. Such assumptions were not unfounded. That city was, after all, home to many Birchers, Klansmen, racists, anti-Catholics, and influential radical conservatives like the segregationist former Army General Edwin Walker and the oilman and media tycoon Haroldson Lafayette "H.L." Hunt, Jr. (more on them below). This is why one of the first acts posed by the FBI following the assassination was to locate and question any known right-wing subversives in the area.[3]

It is unlikely that such a conspiracy, if true, could have been in the works very long. Although civil rights were a hot issue since the mid-1950s, Kennedy was not closely connected to the movement until a few months before his death. In fact, JFK was rather slow to endorse the civil rights movement, and even slower to propose legislation. He said nothing about it in his January 1961 inauguration speech and continued to show caution during the following 29 months.[4] Indeed, his first two years in office were marked urging moderation and performing piecemeal damage control, hoping thus to prevent a violent racist backlash. Kennedy's

caution was finally discarded on June 11, 1963, the day Alabama Governor George
Wallace famously stood in the door of the University of Alabama at Tuscaloosa to
prevent two African American students from registering. The President forthwith
dispatched to Alabama Deputy Attorney General Nicholas Katzenbach, along with
some federalized National Guardsmen to compel Governor Wallace to stand down.
That very evening, Kennedy proposed the creation of a civil rights bill on live
television. Warmly welcomed by advocates of desegregation, the bill was met by
opponents with a spree of violence that included the bombing of churches and the
murders of civil rights activists.[5] Racial hatred was thus a reasonable explanation
for Kennedy's death, at least initially. But once Lee Oswald's identity became better
known, the widespread belief that right-wing radicals were to blame became harder
to sustain. It would soon be eclipsed by the growing belief that the Soviets and/or
Cubans had done it—at least until the Warren Commission argued such rumors
were unfounded (see Chapter 9). But not everyone agreed that Southern racists
should be acquitted so easily.

Two of the major conspiracy suspects in this group of right-wing reactionaries
are Texas oilmen H.L. Hunt, Jr. and Clinton Williams "Clint" Murchison (given his
alleged connection to Lyndon Johnson, we will discuss Murchison in Chapter 9).
Hunt was an eccentric and rabid anti-communist who was active politically through
print media and radio. Yet he had no direct association with the John Birch Society
(JBS)—a cult-like hyper-conservative organization founded by grape juice magnate
Robert W. Welch, Jr.—or any other right-wing group. He was not outrightly racist
either, though he espoused strong anti-Catholic views.[6] Conspiracists Gary Shaw
and Larry Harris, among others, nevertheless identify Hunt as a principal suspect
because of Kennedy's plans to reduce capital gains tax exemptions to oil companies,
as well as his "liberal views" and his "bleeding heart actions".[7] This is plausibly the
reason for which Hunt and his son, Nelson "Bunker" Hunt, helped finance a full-
page anti-Kennedy newspaper ad titled "Welcome Mr. Kennedy to Dallas," which
appeared in the *Dallas Morning News* on the day of JFK's visit (see Figure 3.2). But
were capital gains tax exemptions enough of a reason to want Kennedy dead? A few
careful considerations make this theory a long shot. First, to take out a full-page
ad attacking the president on the same day one plans to kill him is tantamount to
shooting a cop at a policeman's ball: it's a suicide mission reserved for a madman,
not a billionaire oil tycoon wed to his fortune. The second is that Kennedy's tax
exemption bill had already been defeated in Congress, bled dry by the powerful
oil lobby and its minions in Washington.[8] There was no need to kill this bill with
bullets since money, backroom politics, and good old fashion lobbying had already
succeeded and could do so again legally, cleanly, and more cheaply than any professional death squad and massive cover-up could. And so, H.L. Hunt is an easy target
for those who have it in for big business, but not a very convincing one.

Another group of right-wing suspects is the Dallas Police Department (DPD).
Left-wing conspiracists like Mark Lane and Thomas Buchanan have depicted the
DPD as the shock troops of the conservative state of Texas, working in concert
with other right-wing radicals to undermine the civil liberties of liberals and leftists,

including those of Lee Oswald by manufacturing false evidence: a planted Italian rifle, fake fingerprints, a deliberately misapplied paraffin test, doctored photographs, etc.[9] Little attempt is usually made to scrutinize the beliefs and affiliations of individual Dallas policemen to prove their connection to right-wing extremists or racial bigotry. The simple fact that such men were employed by the DPD—and hence the conservative Texas establishment—is considered enough to indict the entire department. (For this reason, we will respond to such claims in Chapter 12 when we consider the physical evidence used against Oswald.)

Two other right-wing conspiracy suspects are retired US Army General Edwin Walker and freelance radical activist Joseph Milteer. Usually discussed in the context of a failed assassination attempt on him by Lee Harvey Oswald (which conspiracists dispute, if they discuss it at all), Walker is considered by some researchers as a leading suspect due to his brash public opposition to the man's civil rights bill and negotiations with communist states, to his affiliations with right-wing groups like the JBS and White Citizens' Council of America, to his 1961 demotion by the Kennedy administration "for making derogatory public statements about prominent Americans,"[10] and to his failed attempt to become Governor of Texas—an election he lost in the primaries to John Connally, the collateral victim of JFK's murder.[11] Walker's fiery dislike of Kennedy, civil rights, liberalism, and nuclear arms treaties is acknowledged universally. However, the evidence connecting him to JFK's murder is as thin as gulag soup. One of the few reasons offered to link the retired General to the assassination is that Walker reportedly flew the American flag upside down outside his house the morning of Kennedy's visit. He then flew it full mast following his murder.[12] Another is that Walker had a friendship with Robert A. Surrey, the author of the "Wanted for Treason" handbill that circulated in Dallas prior to Kennedy's arrival (see Figure 3.1), and that Bernard Weissman, one of the men behind the "Welcome Mr. President" newspaper ad, once served in the Army under Walker.[13] But like H.L. Hunt's connection to that same ad, there is no logical reason for us to believe that publishing a defamatory handbill against a person is proof of their intention to kill them in broad daylight. If anything, it could only have served to incriminate him. Walker was smart enough to understand this, and this why most conspiracists do not give this theory much credit.[14]

A larger group of researchers holds that Southern racist Joseph Milteer was involved in the assassination. This claim is almost entirely based on a private conversation between Milteer and a fellow criminal (William Somersett), which, taken out of context and interpreted loosely, has led many to claim Milteer had advanced insider knowledge of Kennedy's death.[15] Milteer was an independently wealthy Georgian active in radical right-wing groups like the National States Rights Party, the White Citizens' Council, the Constitutional American Party and the Dixie Klan. On November 9, 1963, Somersett secretly recorded Milteer while acting as an informant for the Miami police. Their exchange involved discussing a possible murder attempt against Kennedy. A sniper could target the President during one of his motorcades, he suggested, "from a high office building with a high-powered rifle," a scenario not unlike the one that took place thirteen days later in Dallas. That being said, the topic was introduced by the informant, not Milteer, who—the FBI, Secret Service, Church Committee, and House Select Committee on Assassinations (HSCA) all concluded—was merely offering his gullible listener some vainglorious talk.[16] In the same conversation, Milteer suggested this hit would likely take place in Miami or Washington during the warmer months and be performed by angry Cuban ex-pats or Dixie Klan Imperial Wizard Jack Brown. He also claimed that Kennedy had over 15 lookalikes moving around the country, serving as decoys. Most of this information is of course false, which is probably why conspiracists tend to ignore these incongruent claims to focus exclusively on the "high office building with a high-powered rifle" part of the exchange. Milteer's recorded words said nothing of Dallas, of Dealey Plaza, of Lee Harvey Oswald, nor of any of the specifics of the actual assassination, nor did it explain how a Marxist lone nut might be framed to take the fall. Thus, Milteer's alleged "insider knowledge" is discordant with both the future "official story" and alternative tales that selectively cherry-pick his words. An honest examination of the data suggests Milteer was merely a smug armchair pundit shooting the breeze about a possible future, the same way Secret Service agent Forrest Sorrels, Kennedy's special assistant Kenneth O'Donnell, and JFK himself quipped over the following days.[17] Yet many conspiracists found this low-lying fruit too hard to resist.

Milteer was interviewed by the FBI on November 27, 1963. They found no reason to suspect him any further.[18] This did not prevent photographic "expert" Robert Groden to look for Milteer in hundreds of pictures and films of Dealey Plaza (the conspiracists' answer to *Where's Waldo?*) and find him hiding in a crowd of bystanders on Houston Street.[19] What sinister purpose might it have served Milteer to stand there, arms crossed, looking somberly at the president? Groden does not explain. His claims would nonetheless later be investigated by the HSCA's forensic anthropologists, who concluded that the height, hairline, and facial features of the man on the picture had not much in common with the actual Milteer, suggesting that those who take part in such photographic excavations see pretty much what they want to see.[20]

Those who continue to claim that radical right-wing figures were directly involved in Kennedy's murder have little to show for it. Worse, they suggest that these suspects were willing to kill Kennedy to halt his civil rights legislation when JFK's two most likely successors—Lyndon Johnson and Bobby Kennedy—had both publicly expressed stronger support for the movement than JFK ever did. In other words, killing Kennedy was bound to *accelerate*, not halt, the adoption of federal civil rights legislation—which is exactly what happened once Lyndon Baines Johnson (LBJ) took office.[21] Right-wing zealots would have done better using legal propaganda methods to support the campaign of Republican contender Barry Goldwater, a notorious opponent of civil rights, than to try squashing that movement using live rounds. Furthermore, the only one of these suspects who had any connection to Lee Harvey Oswald was General Walker, whom the FBI, Warren Commission, HSCA, and most other skeptics agree was the near-victim of Oswald's rifle, not the puppet master who framed him. There would have been little reason for Chief Justice Warren and his Commission staff, almost all of whom were liberal-minded supporters of Kennedy's civil rights bill, to sit on this sort of information if it held any truth. Indeed, it would have bolstered a cause they held dear.[22]

In conclusion, for a cover-up to succeed, right-wing assassins would have had to keep their involvement unseen to this day with the help of a large contingent of collaborators inside the White House, Congress, FBI, Dallas Police, and six different government panels, committees, and commissions, which is a very ambitious task to say the least.

5.3 Tricky Dick takes a powder

As the first President born in the twentieth century, favorably disposed toward desegregation at home and détente with the Soviets, Kennedy made a connection with young voters, African Americans, and the white working class despite his elite origins. His age and optimistic speeches also inspired an electorate ready for change. But it was the media, and some controversial assistance from Illinois labor unions, that earned him a photo-finish victory against the veteran statesman Richard Nixon in what is still considered one of the closest elections in US history.

Nixon and Kennedy had both agreed to take part in the first ever nationally televised presidential election debates. The gambit worked in Kennedy's favor. He had the looks and charisma that gave him the appearance of a confident young visionary compared to his older, paler opponent. Nixon, with his unshaven face and refusal to wear stage makeup, looked sweaty and sickly next to the tanned Kennedy, who recently had been campaigning throughout the South. Despite his experience, confidence, and poise, Nixon saw his numbers fall in the weeks that followed the debates, especially among those who followed them on TV instead of the radio. The electronic age had entered Washington politics, and Nixon was its first victim.

Kennedy also proved his mettle as a shrewd debater and tactician by making Nixon look passive against the recent communist revolution in Cuba. As a member of the National Security Council, Vice President Nixon was aware of (but could not discuss publicly) the plans that President Eisenhower put in motion to help CIA-trained anti-Castro Cubans invade the island and depose its government. As a member of the Senate Foreign Affairs Committee, Kennedy was privy to know about this, and he used it against his opponent by repeatedly asking him to explain why his administration did nothing about Castro's nationalization of foreign businesses. Since Nixon was sworn to secrecy, he could do little but offer vague promises to support "the free people of Cuba".[23] Electoral tricks like this one led Nixon to harbor long-lasting resentment toward the Kennedy clan.[24]

Yet, ironically, Kennedy and Nixon had been friendly during the previous decade, more so than Kennedy and Lyndon Johnson ever were nor would be. As journalist Alan Peppard noted, from the time the two men arrived in Washington in 1947 until Kennedy's death, "their collegial relationship occasionally veered toward something approaching warmth. [...] Even during the 1960 presidential contest when both men felt evident mutual contempt, it was tempered with mutual respect".[25] Many biographers have also highlighted the fact that Nixon and Kennedy's economic and foreign policies differed only by degrees and that JFK was on the conservative wing of the Democratic Party while Nixon was a centrist Republican. Nixon also had little to gain politically from the assassination. With Vice President Lyndon Johnson waiting his turn and John Kennedy's two younger brothers in tow, it was possible to foresee that one martyred Kennedy might lead to sixteen more years of Kennedy Democrats in the White House. This is why conspiracy theorists tend to narrowly focus on Nixon's rumored jealousies of the privileged Kennedys and his resentment of their sexual indiscretions while ignoring the many ideological similarities shared by the two men.[26] In any event, it became clear by 1962 that Nixon's real enemy, the one he blamed for "giving him the shaft" during the 1960 presidential election and the California gubernatorial election of 1962, was not the Kennedy family but the media. As he told a crew of journalists, his tone deeply acerbic, the evening of that difficult second defeat:

> I leave you gentlemen now and you now write it. You will interpret it. That's your right. But as I leave you I want you to know—just think how much you're going to be missing. You won't have Nixon to kick around anymore. […] I believe in reading what my opponents say and I hope that what I have said today will at least make television, radio, the press, first recognize the great responsibility they have to report all the news and, second, recognize that they have a right and a responsibility, if they're against a candidate, give him the shaft, but also recognize if they give him the shaft, put one lonely reporter on the campaign who will report what the candidate says now and then.[27]

Although Nixon's paranoia and willingness to engage in dirty politics would become well-known following the Watergate Affair, there is little evidence that Nixon had any intention to harm Kennedy personally, nor that he had any significant relation to the numerous other conspiracy suspects.

Some conspiracists find Nixon's presence in Dallas on the eve and morning of the assassination too convenient to be accidental, that it suggests he was somehow involved in Kennedy's murder.[28] After all, why would Kennedy's defeated 1960 rival and future successor cross paths with him only hours before he was murdered? Oliver Stone's film *Nixon* even suggests Nixon had attended a secret meeting the previous day with anti-Kennedy oil tycoons so that he might be vetted as a possible 1964 presidential candidate.[29]

But Nixon, now a high-profile New York corporate attorney representing the Pepsi Cola Company, had a legitimate and non-sinister reason for being in Dallas: to attend the annual meeting of the American Bottlers of Carbonated Beverages, which happened to take place in Dallas that year (unless, of course, that was all part of the plot!). Nixon's attendance at the conference was noted by multiple eyewitnesses, including the time at which Stone's film has him visiting Kennedy's shadowy killers.[30] Most sources, conspiracist and otherwise, agree that Nixon left

Dallas hastily on the morning of November 22, just as the Kennedy welcome wagon gathered at Love Field airport. While some might view this as suspicious, it can equally be reasoned that an antiquated politician like Nixon would have little desire to stick around to celebrate the man who recently quashed his political dreams. While conspiracists probe the inconsistent record of where Nixon was when he first heard about JFK's murder—suggesting he lied about it, not that journalists sometimes make mistakes—all reputable sources agree that this happened back in New York and that the former Vice President was visibly devastated.[31] Having lost two brothers to tuberculosis, Nixon saw the assassination not just as a national tragedy but as a personal one for the Kennedy family who had now lost two sons. That same evening, Nixon wrote a condolence letter to Jacqueline Kennedy whom he met on several occasions and admired, while she was still in Bethesda Naval Hospital awaiting the end of the autopsy and embalming procedures.[32] In any event, conspiracists offer no verifiable evidence to support their claims that Nixon had foreknowledge of the assassination, only speculation that his rivalry with JFK and his "suspicious" visit to Dallas made his involvement likely. This is a circular reasoning fallacy, which rests on the belief that since Nixon would later sponsor criminal acts (two break-ins, illegal wiretaps, evidence tampering, secret bombings in Cambodia, a *coup d'état* in Chile, and possibly others), that the murder of a political rival was not beyond his capacities.[33]

5.4   Hoover? Damn!

As the founder and longest serving director of the FBI, John Edgar Hoover was already deeply entrenched in the Washington bureaucracy when John Kennedy came to power. As the country's second-highest ranking law enforcement official (reporting to a revolving door of Attorney General), Hoover served eight different presidential administrations between 1924 and his death in 1972, becoming nothing less than a national institution. A hard-nosed hunter of communists, he was particularly ruthless in his tactics to uproot, intimidate, and vilify suspected enemies of the state, which included pretty much anyone with socialist sympathies.[34] His Counterintelligence Program (COINTELPRO), for example, allowed FBI agents to secretly circumvent civil liberties in their intelligence-gathering activities and to intimidate real and perceived subversives, whether these were members of the Communist Party, civil rights activists like Martin Luther King, Jr., or merely actors and athletes with strong leftist views.

In sharp contrast to his new boss, Robert F. Kennedy (RFK), who was anxious about the growth of organized crime syndicates, Hoover believed that Soviet agents and communist agitators remained America's most pressing menace. This helps explain why he resisted RFK's efforts to focus the Justice Department's resources on prosecuting homegrown Italian gangsters "with a resolve and weaponry far beyond what had been brought to previous attempts".[35] Moreover, the two men had little affection for one another and had little in common in terms of their family backgrounds, moral convictions, and personalities. Bobby was far from holding Hoover's admiration. He also transgressed the man's conservative professional standards on several occasions. He nevertheless held enough power to push the aging director into preemptive retirement. It has also been suggested, by both conspiracist and non-conspiracist authors, that Hoover had a gambling addiction and a sordid sexual secret that left him open to blackmail by criminal networks. But such allegations have yet to be substantiated and are ridiculed by those who knew Hoover best.[36]

In addition to his icy relationship with RFK, Hoover was quick to conclude that Lee Oswald acted alone in murdering President Kennedy. He also helped President Johnson—with whom he had a longtime friendship—select the Warren Commission's members.[37] Hence, many conspiracy theorists place Hoover at the center of the conspiracy.[38] After all, the argument goes, Hoover thought the Kennedys were soft on communism and saw them as a threat to his job and extra-legal intelligence network. Since Hoover had the power to influence the Dallas Police, FBI investigations, and through these the Warren Commission, and because Hoover was allegedly fearful that mobsters or other assassins might expose his sexual misdeeds should they be prosecuted, it is assumed that he was willing (and able) to use his power to cover up the crime and thereby help his good friend Lyndon Johnson take power.

But this argument is not historically plausible. It also assumes that Hoover wielded more power than he actually did. For instance, while he did advise Johnson in the selection of Warren Commission members, he remained opposed to the creation of a civilian inquiry, preferring to let the FBI produce its own definitive report on the President's death.[39] Furthermore, though Hoover's G-Men had been lackadaisical in investigating mafia operations in the 1940s and 1950s, preferring to focus on communist activists, they had already stepped up their monitoring of organized crime as early as 1957, during the Eisenhower administration, due to political pressure over reports of a mafia "convention" taking place in Appalachian, New York. In fact, it was through such monitoring operations, which included illegal bug-planting and wiretaps of the offices of mafia kingpins, that Hoover learned of Joe Kennedy's electoral deal with Chicago mob boss Sam Giancana in 1960 (see Chapter 6).[40] But since the wiretaps were illegal, the FBI boss could not reveal this information to the public without exposing his own illegal activities, and Hoover was not the sort of man to leak Bureau intelligence to the media. Nevertheless, this information proved a powerful tool for Hoover to remind President Kennedy how important it was that the two men collaborate. These extralegal surveillance methods also revealed some disturbing sexual trysts between JFK and women with mafia and Soviet connections. This led the old-fashioned FBI boss to suspect that the President's extracurricular activities might become a greater threat to national security than the criminal rackets that Bobby was trying to shut down.

Such information was precious to Hoover, who kept a separate filing system for his most sensitive data. According to Kennedy biographer Laurence Leamer, Hoover "held a treasure trove of information on policymakers and presidents that had helped to ensure his continued tenure".[41] Kennedy had certainly not helped his cause by leaving behind him a trail of compromising mistresses. Hoover made calculated use of this embarrassing information, for instance, by sending the President a memo concerning his private meetings and phone calls with Judith Campbell, a consort of mobsters Sam Giancana and Johnny Roselli. "It was a cunning move on Hoover's part," writes Leamer, "to pass on even the most questionable of tales, proving his loyalty and indispensability, while reminding the Kennedys that if he were a teller of tales, what tales he could tell".[42] Historian Mel Ayton adds:

> This is an excellent example of how Hoover operated. Hoover could not use his subtle blackmailing techniques by referring to his agents' reports. The Kennedys would have been outraged that the FBI director had been snooping on them. However, if scandalous material had been disseminated through other organs, Hoover could righteously say that he was bringing the offending material to their attention and "protecting" them.[43]

One might rightly wonder whether assassinating his boss would have been an intelligent way for Hoover to maintain his position in Washington when a few private memos and embarrassing photos might more easily have done the trick.[44]

Bobby Kennedy and Director Hoover's professional relationship was also far less corrosive than conspiracists suggest. While the two certainly had offsetting priorities, their objectives, methods, and general political views were in many ways similar. Both felt that communists and criminals had to be dealt with harshly and, if necessary, outside the bounds of legality. Both feared the civil rights movement could escalate into a national crisis. Both had a hatred of Communist Cuba. They also respected each other enough not to encroach on their respective jurisdictions. Hoover was always careful to respect the chain of command, and Bobby signed off on many of Hoover's legally questionable surveillance requests, including wiretapping the phones of civil rights leader Martin Luther King, Jr.[45] The two were also equally dedicated to protecting the President's reputation—one from filial piety, the other out of patriotic duty. They also agreed that organized crime was a problem, they just didn't agree on what role the *federal* authorities should play in combatting it.[46] It is therefore hard to believe that Hoover's best interests lay in murdering President Kennedy. Certainly, he had more to gain by serving Kennedy faithfully (or subtly blackmailing him) than taking a chance with a more scrupulous administration, one that might have an inkling to fire or investigate him. Despite Hoover's friendship with LBJ, there is no reason to believe that Johnson's election in 1964 was assured. Indeed, killing JFK could reasonably have propelled RFK to run for the job (which he did, four years later). Such considerations certainly would have made Hoover's position far more precarious than if JFK lived to see another election.[47] Conspiracists need be reminded that even the shrewdest of criminals can't read the future.

Painting Hoover as a modern-day Brutus is even more problematic if we consider that John Kennedy (as well as his father, who had good relations with Hoover) expressed only satisfaction with the Director in both public and private communications.[48] There also exists no direct evidence that Kennedy planned to force Hoover into retirement. In fact, Hoover's reappointment was virtually assured, so long as Kennedy managed to win the next election.[49] On the other hand, it is true that Hoover's behavior in the days and months following the assassination can be described as a "rush to judgment" and an attempt to cover up Oswald's prior contacts with the Bureau. Indeed, Hoover's rapid identification of Oswald as a lone assassin (within 48 hours of the crime), his apparent lack of interest in assessing the killer's motive, his resistance to sharing classified information with the Warren Commission, and the suspension of several FBI agents who handled the Oswald file prior to the assassination have led conspiracists to speculate that the FBI director was covering up a major crime.

On this point, conspiracists like Mark Lane and Jim Marrs often start with a reasonable premise (i.e., that Hoover was intentionally hiding information from the public and from the Warren Commission) but are themselves guilty of rushing to an invalid conclusion by alleging that Hoover was thereby covering up a right-wing coup d'état. There are many possible explanations for Hoover's post-assassination behavior, from his own addiction to secrecy and dislike of criticism to his embarrassing realization that the FBI's half-hearted vetting of Oswald—a known defector to the USSR and vocal supporter of Communist Cuba—had indirectly helped the assassin pull off his caper. Such a revelation would certainly sully Hoover's reputation and that of the Bureau. It might even be cause for Hoover' dismissal, just as the failed Bay of Pigs invasion had recently cost former CIA Director Allen Dulles his job (see Chapter 7). As Historian Kathryn Olmsted argues, Hoover had professional reasons for quickly closing the case on Oswald:

> if Oswald was *not* a lone nut—if there had in fact been a plot to kill the president—the people might think that the FBI should have uncovered and stopped it. Ergo, Hoover quickly decided, there was no conspiracy. […] A thorough investigation could lead to conclusions that no one wanted to hear.[50]

Far from being an FBI asset, Lee Oswald was in fact a black eye to the organization. Hence, the secret that Hoover wanted to hide was not that the FBI was in cahoots with the killer, but that it could have, and failed, to stop him.

5.5 Right guy, wrong address

Lee Harvey Oswald first became a person of interest to the FBI in May 1962 upon his return to America following an aborted defection and short stay in Russia. This simply means that the Bureau opened a file to maintain a record of Oswald's whereabouts should he ever happen to engage in subversive activities. Many conspiracists find it hard to believe that Oswald was readmitted into the United States and allowed to reclaim his citizenship. It is important to note that he never officially

renounced it while in the USSR, that he was only one of several defectors to successfully come back that year, and that he was just one of 350 Americans who went
to live in the Soviet Union between the years 1958 and 1964 (many of whom also
returned).[51]

Oswald kept a low profile during his first year back home, during which time he
did not interact with other Marxists save for writing letters to left-wing newspapers.
He also remained quite poor and incapable of holding down a steady job. Hence,
he quickly lost standing on the FBI's long list of suspected subversives. Indeed, the
Bureau perceived Oswald as a negligible threat (wrongly, it turned out) compared
to high-profile socialists like Bayard Rustin and A. Philip Randolph, both of whom
were deeply involved in the civil rights movement.[52] It is therefore not surprising
that the FBI lost interest in him until he reemerged as a person of interest in August
1963 when, having left Dallas for New Orleans, he was photographed distributing pro-Castro leaflets in public. His file was subsequently transferred to the New
Orleans FBI office, who interviewed him following his arrest for taking part in a
sidewalk scuffle with some anti-Castro Cubans.[53] In the wake of this event, Oswald
enjoyed a moment of fame by appearing on local radio and TV as the spokesman
of the New Orleans chapter of the Fair Play for Cuba Committee—of which he
turned out to be its only member. Oswald returned to Texas in the fall of 1963,
where he once again fell off the FBI's radar.

Apart from J. Edgar Hoover, conspiracists generally blame two FBI men, Guy
Banister and James Hosty, as complicit in Kennedy's murder, along with two questionable pieces of evidence. The first is a stamped address—544 Camp Street—that
appeared on some of the *Fair Play for Cuba* leaflets distributed by Oswald in New
Orleans.[54] A private investigator named Guy Banister worked in the same building
as the Camp Street address (aka: the Newman Building) though his office had
a different entrance and address (i.e., 531 Lafayette). Banister raises conspiracist
eyebrows because he was a retired FBI agent, a former Assistant Superintendent
of the New Orleans Police Department, an active JBS member, a staunch segregationist, and an anti-communist activist. He was also an alcoholic with money
problems.[55] The peculiar proximity of these addresses is the sum total of the evidence offered by conspiracists Jim Garrison, Jim Marrs, and Oliver Stone to argue
that Oswald was an FBI asset working for the intelligence community in New
Orleans, and only parading as a Marxist loner. This evidence is problematic because
there is no tangible proof that Oswald and Banister ever met, nor that Oswald ever
set foot inside that building.[56]

The reason Oswald chose the Camp Street address to stamp on some of his
leaflets died with him. According to conspiracists, our only conclusion must be that
he was using Banister's office as a headquarters for manufacturing his false Marxist
persona. But Gerald Posner offers a simpler explanation:

> When Oswald worked at Reily, he was only a block away from 544 Camp
> Street and his weekly visits to the unemployment commission [on foot;
> Oswald didn't drive] took him directly past the address. He easily could have

seen the FOR RENT signs at the small corner building [...] $30 a month, too much for Oswald on his minimal income [...] It is possible that Oswald, who had used phony addresses on dozens of applications and forms, had decided when settling on a false address for his imaginary Fair Play chapter that it should embarrass his nemesis, the extreme right-wing and the city's anti-Castro militants.[57]

Posner is referring to the right-wing Cuban Revolutionary Council, which Oswald knew had previously rented that space and which, unbeknownst to Oswald, had regular dealings with Guy Banister. While speculative, this explanation is corroborated by known facts about Oswald's time in New Orleans and his frequent use of false addresses and pseudonyms, many of which would have served no practical purpose except in the eyes of a paranoid leftist worried that government agents were on his tail. And so, while the apparent connection between Oswald's leaflets and Banister's address seems too good to be true, it is not altogether surprising if one examines the finer historical context, such as the fact that both men—one a communist and the other an anti-communist—had an interest in the local anti-Castro community. In a city like New Orleans in 1963, it would not have been too hard to infer several spurious connections between the pro-Castro Oswald and a dozen or more anti-Castro activists like Guy Banister, Carlos Bringuier, and David Ferrie, or government agencies like the CIA, the FBI, and the Office of Naval Intelligence (ONI), all of which had regional offices in that city. The 544 Camp Street "evidence" is thus another example of circular reasoning—a random factoid that is cherry-picked to support the researcher's conviction that Oswald had a "connection" to government agents. A further problem with this supposed evidence of an Oswald-Banister axis is the fact that while the Camp Street and Lafayette Street addresses do lead into the same building, they are distinct and separate commercial spaces with no adjoining doors or spaces except for the sidewalk outside. No other evidence connects Banister to a plot to kill Kennedy, which is why the Secret Service and Warren Commission, as well as the HSCA 15 years later, threw out the 544 Camp Street theory as a meaningless distraction.[58]

The second piece of conspiracy "evidence" linking Oswald to the FBI is the widely accepted fact that less than two weeks before the assassination, Oswald walked into the Dallas FBI field office located near the Texas School Book Depository where he then worked, to deliver an envelope addressed to FBI Special Agent James Hosty (whose name Oswald misspelled as "Hasty"). The unsealed envelope included a handwritten note. The event is corroborated by several witnesses, including Hosty's secretary and fellow agents.[59]

Oliver Stone's *JFK* depicts Hosty as Oswald's FBI "handler," another sinister agent who helped maneuver the patsy, perhaps by making Oswald believe he was helping the FBI expose the would-be assassins while he was unwittingly being framed for the crime. Stone, Marrs, and Garrison speculate that Oswald, an undercover FBI informer, was in fact delivering a warning to Hosty—perhaps of a plot to kill Kennedy—which the FBI agent dutifully ignored. There is no evidence to support this theory, though many questions can still be legitimately raised concerning the Oswald note's purpose and contents. This is because Hosty later acknowledged that he intentionally destroyed it following Jack Ruby's murder of Oswald, allegedly to spare the Bureau a good deal of embarrassment. In fact, Hosty did not speak of the note to the Warren Commission; it remained an FBI secret until it was outed in 1975 during the Church Committee hearings, feeding the post-Watergate angst of many JFK buffs. Oswald had also apparently written Hosty's phone and car license plate numbers in his address book, information that was also withheld from the Warren Commission. Garrison and Stone, among others, therefore concluded that Oswald was an FBI asset, and that this information was kept secret to eliminate proof of the FBI's complicity in the affair.

However, these conspiracists choose to ignore a great deal of evidence concerning the FBI's interest in Oswald prior to JFK's assassination and their stated reasons for destroying this proof of Oswald's state of mind. As discussed previously, Oswald had been a low-ranking FBI person of interest since his return from Russia. He was interviewed by the Bureau upon his return to America and in New Orleans following his arrest. Oswald's file at that time was no more disturbing than those of hundreds of other left-wing activists and would have probably grown dusty had the CIA not informed the FBI in October 1963 that it had recently spotted a Lee Harvey Oswald in Mexico City, visiting the Soviet and Cuban embassies.[60]

When the FBI office in New Orleans looked for Oswald again, it discovered he had recently moved back to Dallas. The file made its way back to Hosty, who struggled to locate and interview the young man. Hosty first tracked down Marina Oswald, now living in the suburb of Irving with her friend Ruth Paine. On November 1, 1963—three weeks before Kennedy's trip to Dallas—Hosty learned from Mrs. Paine that Lee only came by on weekends, and that he resided in a rooming house during the rest of the week near his new job at the Texas School Book Depository. Unable to locate the boarding house (because Oswald was registered there under the false name O.H. Lee), Hosty visited the Paine household again on November 5, when he spoke again with Ruth and Marina and gathered some more information on Oswald. (He would not meet Lee in person until after his arrest on November 22.) News of Hosty's visits greatly irritated Lee, who saw himself and his family as being harassed by the Feds. On Hosty's second visit, Marina snuck out the back door and took down his license plate number, as Lee had asked her to do if he returned. Here lies the non-suspicious reason for which Lee Oswald had Hosty's license plate number in his address book and for his visit to the FBI office on the next business day—to threaten Hosty never to come near his wife while he wasn't at home.[61]

Hosty was not the only one to see the note. Those at the Dallas FBI office who read it do not agree on its exact contents, but all agree that it contained a veiled threat against Hosty to leave the author's family alone, and that it certainly did not inform him of any impending hit or conspiracy.[62] When asked in 1975 why he did not immediately tell his superiors, Hosty responded that since the note was unsigned, and because this sort of threat was not uncommon, he put it aside and forgot about it until the two men met for the first time at the DPD on November 22, during Oswald's interrogation. When Hosty introduced himself to the suspect, Oswald broke out of his otherwise calm demeanor and got angry at him. This is when Hosty says he realized the note came from Oswald. He subsequently informed his superior, Special Agent in Charge J. Gordon Shanklin. When asked why he destroyed the note, Hosty told the Church Committee that he was ordered to do so by Shanklin, who feared it would embarrass the Bureau. This happened following Jack Ruby's assassination of Oswald, when the note had lost all forensic value as evidence in Oswald's trial, and before the Warren Commission had been set up. After investigating this cover-up, the HSCA concluded that the Oswald note, had it not been destroyed, would probably not have changed the conclusions of the Warren Commission.[63]

Hosty and 17 other agents who handled the Oswald file were discretely reprimanded and suspended without pay by order of J. Edgar Hoover, who accused them of "gross incompetency" for failing to assess Oswald as a threat and for failing to place him on a security watch list.[64] Hosty never gained anything from his connection to Oswald except lost pay and a setback in his career and reputation. Hoover had little to gain personally by suspending his agents in secret, nor could it serve as a public relations exercise. One can also reasonably conclude that these punitive measures against Hosty and other agents would not prevent any of them from speaking out to the Warren Commission, the Church Committee, the HSCA, or any of a thousand American or foreign journalists, either before or after their retirement, had they suspected that Oswald was anything else than an antisocial lone Marxist. But like so many other lone gunmen who have performed similar acts, Oswald had just seemed too insignificant to attract the sustained attention of federal agents. Their error was not to engage in a conspiracy to murder the president but to lack vigilance in performing their menial duties.

5.6   The Brave New World Order

In closing this chapter, a few words should be said about superconspiracies[65] and their relation to JFK myths. The authors of superconspiracies typically postulate that an imminent global takeover is nearing its climax with the formation of a one-world tyranny ruled by Jewish bankers, greedy corporatists, white supremacists, amoral socialists, extraterrestrial lizards, or some other amoral group with worldwide ambitions and infinite resources. Daniel Pipes, the author of *Conspiracy: How the Paranoid Style Flourishes and Where It Comes From* (1997), describes such theories as fear-driven global scenarios obsessed with invisible hierarchies. Their long list of conspirators frequently include the fearsome and undetectable "Illuminati" as well as real but mostly innocuous think tanks like the Council on Foreign Relations, the Trilateral Commission, and the Bilderberg group.[66] Because such theories often originate in the United States from the imaginations of right-wing extremists, religious millennialists, radical libertarians, and anarchistic antifascists,[67] such theories tend to obsess over the alleged widescale infiltration of American institutions, from the White House down to local school boards, by a network of faceless power brokers often referred to as the "deep state".[68] All violent, tragic, or unexplained phenomena can serve as fodder to fuel this highly seductive form of paranoia, from the assassinations of Austrian Archduke Franz Ferdinand in 1914 to the slaying of counterculture musician John Lennon in 1980, from the supposed "false flag" operations that caused the explosion of the USS Maine in 1898 to the "faked" terrorist attacks of September 11, 2001, from suspicious plane crashes to reports of strange lights in the sky.[69]

While authors like Fletcher Prouty, Peter Dale Scott, Jim Marrs, and James Fetzer stand out as prominent Kennedy buffs with superconspiracist tendencies (see Chapter 4), the vast majority of veteran JFK theorists tend to steer clear of esoteric themes like the occult, extraterrestrial visitors, ancient mysteries, Flat Earth theories, and overt Anti-Semitism. Inversely, the authors of superconspiracies are generally more interested in the "bigger picture," caring little more about the minutia of JFK's murder than the finer details of the other theories they selectively scavenge. Superconspiracists are intellectual hoarders, building grandiose collages and flowcharts fleshed out from the works of disparate others. Their interest lies not in *proving* that JFK was killed by a massive conspiracy—they take this as a given—but in trying to build a unified theory of why the world is as it is, even if this requires them to misquote their sources, including their fellow conspiracists. A good example of this is found in the works of Milton William Cooper, whose writings freely mix Kennedy lore with wild speculations about secret societies, think tanks, religious and racial minorities, gun control, the Vatican, Luciferian plots, and extraterrestrials. Cooper's explanation for Kennedy's death—which conflicts not just with the Warren Report but also with most popular JFK myths—is that Secret Service agent Bill Greer, the President's limousine driver, killed his boss on behalf of the Illuminati to stop him from exposing a fascistic interstellar arrangement between former Republican President Dwight Eisenhower and space aliens from the Pleiades star cluster.[70]

Because superconspiracies are by their very nature inclusive, syncretic, and perpetually evolving, they are more likely to contain a variety of "weird" elements not typically found in leading JFK conspiracy books, such as New Age beliefs about mystical energy or interdimensional travel, futuristic mind control technologies, vaccine dangers and "chemtrails," Unexplained Aerial Phenomena (aka: UFOs), shape-shifting aliens, and ancient astronauts.[71] Nevertheless, JFK buffs have had a marked influence on those who traffic in superconspiracies, first because JFK myths, many of which propound a massive coup d'état, offer superconspiracists a narrative that is easy to appropriate. Without much alteration or additions, the average Kennedy conspiracy book can serve as a springboard for any number of anti-statist, anti-fascist, anti-capitalist, anti-internationalist, anti-socialist, or anti-Semitic (etc.) agenda. If one begins with the assumption that JFK was a victim of his own government, it can be easily inferred that his death was no singular event but one of many attempts by a "deep state" (whichever way that concept is defined) to consolidate its power globally. Second, being for decades one of the most prolific set of conspiracy theories, the JFK literature is easy to find, skim through, and cherry-pick for useful opinions or pieces of "evidence" that serve another theory, for example, by connecting his murder to similar killings (Gandhi, RFK, King, Lennon, etc.) or pairing Kennedy's troubles with Vietnam and Cuba with other world conflicts (Panama, Bosnia, Iraq, Afghanistan, etc.).

According to Daniel Pipes, many superconspiracies—such as the anti-Semitic belief that a "Zionist Occupational Government" is controlling Washington—are the children of the 1950s' Red Scare, during which anti-communist statesmen like Senator Joseph McCarthy bandied long lists of alleged Soviet spies lining the halls of the State Department. With the emergence of intercontinental ballistic missiles during the 1960s and shifting popular fears from communist traitors to nuclear war, superconspiracies about Soviet infiltrators were abandoned by the mainstream but appropriated by small fringe groups who traded McCarthy's faceless communist spooks for whatever group they feared more than Russians, be they Jews, fascists, liberals, or weapons manufacturers.[72]

"Deep state" conspiracy theories have recently grown more popular, especially following the 2016 election of President Donald Trump and the increased visibility of militant right-wing groups (aka: the "alt-right" or "white nationalists") in political protests and internet social networks, along with their vocal left-wing opponents (Occupy, "Antifa," Anonymous, etc.).[73] Superconspiracies are a powerful medium for militant protestors who have discovered new applications for traditional conspiracy narratives, adapting them to reflect their own values and mission to "speak truth to power". Such theories get amplified by popular media pundits like the alt-right-libertarian shock jock Alex Jones—who appears to believe that E. Howard Hunt killed Kennedy—and the left-leaning New Age guru David Icke—who believes Kennedy's murderers came from the Draco star system—each of whom further adapts them to suit the beliefs of their target audience.[74]

Some of the most influential peddlers of superconspiracies to also wade into the Kennedy pool are Trump associates Roger Stone and Jerome Corsi.[75] A longtime confidant and supporter of the New York real estate tycoon, Stone is a self-confessed "libertarian and libertine" who sports a huge back tattoo of President Richard Nixon. He is a flamboyant political consultant and right-wing pundit who made his living from character assassinations and conspiracy-mongering. He is also the author of *The Man Who Killed Kennedy: The Case against LBJ* (2013). Corsi is a Harvard-educated conservative author and contributor to conspiracist websites like Alex Jones' *Infowars* and Joseph Farrah's *World Net Daily*. His books on President Barack Obama, Senator (and future Secretary of State) John Kerry, NAFTA, and the "deep state" have been called "political hit jobs" and shameless attempts to rewrite history.[76] He is also the author of *Who Really Killed Kennedy?* (2013), a rehash of multiple theories that fingers hundreds of suspects, a book that led him to befriend Stone, hop on the Trump electoral bandwagon, and earn a spot near Trump's ear. From that point on, the two men played an important role shaping the man's paranoid discourse, from claims that Barack Obama faked his birth certificate to "proofs" that the Clintons are murderous criminals. Other by-products of this relationship include Trump's repeated claims that the "deep state" is conspiring to frame him, that the father of Senator Ted Cruz, Trump's 2016 Republican rival, was in fact an accomplice of Lee Harvey Oswald, and that declassifying all remaining Kennedy-related materials (against the advice of his intelligence advisors) may unearth proofs of a massive conspiracy.[77]

It is hard to tell whether President Trump fully bought into the conspiracy stories fed to him by Stone and Corsi, or whether he used them merely to score points with his electoral base. What this episode teaches us is that more than a half century later, JFK conspiracy lore can still mobilize mass attention and serve as a powerful tool to produce fear and mistrust in the country's so-called establishment. But popularity, of course, is not a measure of truth, whatever populist politicians might claim. As journalist Adam Gopnik suggested,

> What we should fear is not a deep state but a state robbed of its depth. […] There is no 'deep state' that exists beyond the scrutiny of responsible citizens; there is a cynical paranoia that always acts, and is meant to, as a pathogen to public trust.[78]

Notes

1 L. Fletcher Prouty, with Richard E. Sprague: "The Guns of Dallas," *Gallery*, October 1975.
2 Fletcher Prouty and Oliver Stone popularized the theory that Lansdale engineered the assassination under the orders of the CIA and/or Joint Chiefs of Staff. Hunt was an ex-CIA agent who served as President Richard Nixon's White House security advisor. He oversaw the infamous 1972 Watergate burglary for which he was indicted and incarcerated. Sturgis was a freelance anti-Communist who had dealings with, but never officially worked for, the CIA. Because of this, and because the two men looked similar to unidentified tramps photographed in Dealey Plaza shortly after Kennedy's murder, Hunt and Sturgis were accused by conspiracy researchers of being part of a team of assassins. *Rockefeller Commission Report* (1975), chapter 19.
3 Vincent Bugliosi: *Reclaiming History* (2007), 1265.
4 Ibid., 1260–1.
5 McWhorter, chaps. 20–27. Four hours after Kennedy's speech, Mississippi NAACP field secretary Medgar Evers was murdered by a gunman using a high-powered rifle and scope. A racist connection with Kennedy's assassination was thereby easy to make. The gunman, Ku Klux Klan member Byron De La Beckwith, would not be convicted of the crime until 1994. Bugliosi, endnotes, 720–4.
6 Bugliosi, 1265–6.
7 Gary Shaw with Larry R. Harris: *Cover Up: The Governmental Conspiracy to Conceal the Facts about the Public Execution of John Kennedy* (1976, self-published), 166–71.
8 Bugliosi, 1267.
9 Thomas G. Buchanan: *Who Killed Kennedy?* (1964); Lane: *Rush to Judgment* (1966).
10 Walker was relieved of his command by JFK's Defense Secretary Robert McNamara over a news article that said Walker radicalized his troops with right-wing propaganda. An Army inquiry later confirmed some of the charges. Walker resigned later that year, foregoing his pension and calling the JFK administration "little men". Eric Pace:

"Gen. Edwin Walker, 83, Is Dead; Promoted Rightist Causes in 60's," *New York Times*, November 2, 1993.

11 Shaw and Harris, 166–7. See also Livingstone: *The Radical Right and the Murder of John F. Kennedy: Stunning Evidence in the Assassination of the President* (2006), and Jeffrey H Caufield: *General Walker and the Murder of President Kennedy* (2015).

12 Joachim Joesten: *Oswald: Assassin or Fall Guy?* (1964), 148–50, cited in Shaw and Harris, 167.

13 Bugliosi, 1264, footnote.

14 Longtime conspiracist and Jim Garrison fan Jim DiEugenio calls Caufield's +1000 page brick a "pretentious, bombastic, overlong and tedious dud" and "the worst book on the JFK case since [Waldron and Hartmann's] *Ultimate Sacrifice*". Jim DiEugenio: "Jeffrey H. Caufield, M.D., General Walker and the Murder of President Kennedy," *Kennedys and King*, March 4, 2016 (accessed 2018).

15 Jim Marrs: *Crossfire: The Plot the Killed Kennedy* (1989), 265; Anthony Summers: *Conspiracy* (1980), 404, cited in John McAdams: "Joseph Milteer: Miami Prophet, or Quitman Crackpot?" (n.d.), *The Kennedy Assassination*. See also Hurt: *Reasonable Doubt* (1985) and Groden and Livingstone: *High Treason* (1989).

16 McAdams: "Joseph Milteer…"

17 Testimony of Kenneth P. O'Donnell, WC VII; Shenon, 358–9; Manchester, 121; Bugliosi, 1269.

18 The FBI also considered Somersett's secondhand reports unreliable. Communications between FBI and Secret Service, National Archives file number 180-10091-10212, 124-10008-10267, 124-10012-10306, and 180-10123-10039, cited in McAdams: "Joseph Milteer…"

19 Groden: *The Killing of a President* (1994), 196, cited in McAdams: "Joseph Milteer…"

20 HSCA, Vol. VI, 242–57.

21 Bugliosi, 1262–3.

22 Shenon, *passim*; Bugliosi, 1272.

23 "October 7, 1960, Debate Transcript," *Commission on Presidential Debates*, 2012.

24 See Christopher Matthews: *Kennedy & Nixon: The Rivalry That Shaped Postwar America* (1996).

25 Alan Peppard: "Kennedy Rival Nixon Left Dallas as JFK Arrived in November 1963," *Dallas Morning News*, November 2, 2013.

26 A good example of this can be seen in Oliver Stone's film *Nixon* (1995).

27 "Remarks of Richard Nixon, Beverly Hilton, November 7, 1962," *Richard Nixon Presidential Library*, PDF.

28 Fletcher Prouty: "Nixon's Three Stories of Where He Was on November 22, 1963," June 1978, *The Col. L. Fletcher Prouty Reference Site*.

29 "Jack Jones," the film's fictional oil tycoon played by actor Larry Hagman—famous for playing corrupt oilman J.R. Ewing in the Eighties TV series Dallas—was a thinly disguised parody of Texas oilman H.L. Hunt.

30 Peppard, "Kennedy Rival Nixon Left Dallas…"

31 Ibid.

32 Ibid.

33 Sometimes this takes the form of a *post hoc ergo propter hoc* fallacy ("after this, therefore before this") whenever conspiracists claim that an event's consequence (e.g., that Kennedy's death made it easier for Nixon to return to the White House) is a proof of its cause (e.g., that Nixon was involved in killing Kennedy *in order to* make it easier for him to become president).

34 Mel Ayton: "The Truth about J. Edgar Hoover," *Crime Magazine*, July 19, 2005.

35 Leamer, 598.

36 Kenneth D. Ackerman: "Five Myths about J. Edgar Hoover," *The Washington Post*, November 9, 2011. Authors like Anthony Summers and Seymour Hersh speculate that Hoover's longtime close friendship with Assistant FBI Director Clyde Tolson was a thinly disguised homosexual partnership. See Summers: *Official and Confidential: The Secret Life of J Edgar Hoover* (1993) and Hersh: *The Dark Side of Camelot* (1997), 148–9. But such reports usually rely on anecdotal evidence and unsubstantiated assumptions, as Hoover was very protective of his private life. Sources close to Hoover and Tolson, including future FBI Assistant Director and Watergate informant Mark Felt (aka: "Deep Throat"), described it as a brotherly relationship between life-long bachelors. Felt and O'Connor: *A G-Man's Life: The FBI, Being 'Deep Throat,' and the Struggle for Honor in Washington* (2006). FBI Assistant Director Cartha DeLoach, who for many years worked closely with Hoover and Tolson, stated:

> No one who knew Hoover and Tolson well in the FBI has ever even hinted at such a charge. You can't work side by side with two men for the better part of 20 years and fail to recognize signs of such affections.
>
> *(Cited in Ayton: "The Truth about J. Edgar Hoover,"*
> *see also Bugliosi, 1154–5)*

According to Andrew and Mitrokhin (*The Sword and the Shield: The Mitrokhin Archive and the Secret History of the KGB* (1999)), many rumors alleging Hoover's homosexuality were fomented by false letters written by the KGB. Joseph E. Persico: "Secrets from the Lubyanka," *New York Times*, October 31, 1999.

37 November 29, 1963, phone conversation between Hoover and Johnson, quoted in "Walkthrough: Formation of the Warren Commission," (n.d.), *Mary Ferrell Foundation* (accessed 2018).

38 See, for example, "The Top G-Man," in Marrs, 213–26—but only if you have the patience to scale a pile of red herrings, unjustified suppositions, "suspicious connections," and suffer a serious bout of chronological vertigo.

39 Posner, 405–7.

40 Leamer, 599.

41 Ibid., 596. See also Ackerman: "Five Myths about J. Edgar Hoover".

42 Ibid., 600. Judith Campbell (later Campbell-Exner) was introduced to Kennedy by singer Frank Sinatra, who moved freely between political and mafia circles. Leamer, 604.

43 Ayton: "The Truth about J. Edgar Hoover".

44 Conspiracists who claim that Hoover must have participated in Kennedy's murder because he was not compelled to retire by subsequent presidents are guilty of a *post hoc* fallacy. Hoover could have, in theory, blackmailed all these men—including Kennedy—to maintain his job at the FBI. No clear reason has been offered to explain why Hoover had to kill Kennedy, but not Johnson or Nixon, to accomplish this. Of the three, JFK was the most morally compromised given his numerous mistresses and indirect ties to the mob. See Chapter 6.

45 Leamer, 600–1. See also "From 'Runt of The Litter' to 'Liberal Icon,' The Story of Robert Kennedy," An interview with RFK biographer Larry Tye on "Fresh Air," *National Public Radio*, July 5, 2016.

46 Since organized crime did not pose an imminent danger to national security, Hoover felt that prosecuting mobsters was better left to state and local law enforcement. As he explained in a 1964 interview:

I am inclined toward being a states' righter in matters involving law enforcement. That is, I fully respect the sovereignty of state and local authorities. I consider the local police officer to be our first line of defense against crime, and I am opposed to a national police force.

U.S. News & World Report, *December 21, 1964, cited in Ayton: "The Truth about J. Edgar Hoover"*

47 There is little evidence to connect Hoover to Sirhan B. Sirhan, RFK's convicted assassin. See Dan Moldea: *The Killing of Robert F. Kennedy* (2006). Besides, using one conspiracy theory to prove another is a circular argument.

48 Hersh, 149.

49 Ibid., 152.

50 Olmsted, 114.

51 "The Defector Study," *Staff Report of the Select Committee on Assassinations, U.S. House of Representatives*, (HSCA), March 1979.

52 McWhorter, 105–6.

53 Oliver Stone's *JFK* depicts the altercation as a staged event to set up Oswald as a fake communist. Gerald Posner responds that the event demonstrates Oswald's delusional self-importance as a lone revolutionary. Posner, chap. 8. No evidence has emerged that Oswald was a double agent working for an anti-Castro organization.

54 While conspiracists focus almost exclusively on this one, Oswald had in fact stamped *three* different fake addresses on his leaflets, which Posner suggests does not evoke a well thought-out plan. Posner, 136.

55 David Reitzes: "Who Was Guy Banister?" *JFK Online: The JFK 100*, 2001.

56 The purported witnesses used by Garrison, Marrs, and Stone to argue that Oswald had worked for Banister—namely Delphine Roberts and Jack Martin (aka: Edward Stuart Suggs)—had wildly inconsistent testimonies that evolved over time, were contradicted by verified facts (such as Oswald's actual whereabouts), and had lifestyles and reputations that make them questionable witnesses. Posner, 138–40.

57 Posner, 123. Oswald worked at the William B. Reily Coffee Company as a machinery greaser from May until July, 1963, when he was fired for lack of effort. *Warren Report*, 403–4.

58 See "544 Camp Street and Related Events," HSCA Volume X, chap. XIII, 123–36, par. 468 and 473. While the HSCA did believe that Oswald and Banister might be acquainted, their evidence relied almost entirely on the testimony of unreliable witnesses Jack Martin and Delphine Roberts (see earlier note).

59 Accounts differ as to which day Oswald did this. Hosty's secretary remained firm that it was the first business day after the Veterans Day holiday, which would make it Tuesday, November 12, 1963.

60 Many conspiracists allege that Oswald was not in Mexico City. Many conspiracists allege that Oswald was not in Mexico City. See Chapter 2, Section 2.4 (footnote 45). But most of the Mexico witnesses were either American civilians or employees of the Cuban and Soviet governments, who could not have easily been working for, or manipulated by, the CIA. Posner, chap. 9. On the other hand, the possibility that Oswald might be a Soviet agent was very real in 1963, especially to President Johnson and members of the Warren Commission. See Chapter 9 of this book.

61 Bugliosi, 111–3, 123–6, 157–9. See also David Reitzes: "Oswald's Note to FBI Agent Hosty," *JFK Online: The JFK 100*, 2001.

62 For a detailed summary and critique of conspiracist claims involving Hosty, see Posner, 206–17. See also Billy Cox: "FBI Agent Kept Tabs on Lee Harvey Oswald," *Dallas Herald-Tribune*, June 13, 2011.

63 *HSCA Report*, 196. See also Posner, 215 and Bugliosi, 302–3.

64 Handwritten note on an FBI memo from Gale to Tolson, dated December 10, 1963. Cited in Olmsted, 119.

65 Barkun, 6. See also Chapter 4, Sections 4.6 and 4.9.

66 Daniel Pipes: *Conspiracy* (1997), 115–7.

67 Influential examples include Pat Robertson (*The New World Order*, 1991), Milton William Cooper (*Behold a Pale Horse*, 1991), and Jim Keith (*Black Helicopters over America: Strikeforce of the New World Order*, 1997).

68 David Aaronovitch: "The Deep State," *BBC Radio 4*, 19 August 2018. Variations of the "deep state" conspiracy myth are widespread throughout the world, especially in the Middle East and Eastern Europe where levels of corruption and government secrecy are rather high and popular trust in public institutions is, understandably, often quite low. See also Uscinski (2019), *passim*.

69 Pipes, 14–9. See also Canadian Security and Intelligence Service: "Who Said What? The Security Challenges of Modern Disinformation," chap. 1, *Government of Canada*, 22 February 2018.

70 Cooper: *Behold a Pale Horse* (1991), 215. See also Barkun, 60–3 and 261 (note #28), and Mark Jacobson: "Who Was William Cooper? The Man Behind One of the Most Controversial Books of Our Time," *Publisher's Weekly*, September 21, 2018. Cooper's work inspired many other superconspiracists, including radio talk show host Alex Jones and the convicted perpetrator of the 1995 Oklahoma City bombing, Timothy McVeigh.

71 See works by Pipes (1997), Kay (2011), and Barkun (2013). An example of the marriage between the two genres can be found in the post-*Crossfire* writings of Jim Marrs, such as *Alien Agenda* (1997), *Rule by Secrecy* (2000), and *The Illuminati* (2017).

72 Pipes, 115–8.

73 One of the most popular recent "deep state" theories is the pro-Trump, anti-Establishment QAnon theory. See Justin Caffier: "A Guide to QAnon, the New King of Right-Wing Conspiracy Theories," *Vice*, 13 June 2018 and Brandy Zadrozny and Ben Collins: "How Three Conspiracy Theorists Took 'Q' and Sparked Qanon," *NBC News*, August 14, 2018.

74 On Jones: Barkun, 191–2, Jon Ronson: "Alex in Wonderland," *This American Life*, WBEZ Chicago, March 15, 2019, and "The Assassination of JFK: Alex Jones Conspiracies," *YouTube*. On Icke: Barkun, 104–10.

75 Jeffrey Toobin: "Roger Stone and Jerome Corsi's Time in the Barrel," *The New Yorker*, February 1, 2019, par. 8.

76 Ibid., par. 20.

77 Nolan J. McAskill: "Trump Accuses Cruz's Father of Helping JFK's Assassin," *Politico*, May 3, 2016; Dan Spinelli: "Trump Revives Rumor Linking Cruz's Father to JFK Assassination," *Politico*, July 22, 2016; Roger Stone: "Why I Urged Trump to Release JFK Assassination Files," *Infowars*, October 23, 2017.

78 Adam Gopnik: "The J.F.K. Files, Trump, and the Deep State," *The New Yorker*, October 29, 2017.

6

"DOUBLE-CROSS! DOUBLE-CROSS!"

The mafia and Jack Ruby

6.1 This is our thing

The word mafia (or mob) is a general term used to describe organized criminals, usually united by blood ties, language, culture, or other historical bonds. Today, it is frequently used to depict any criminal racket united by ethnic identity (e.g., the Russian or Korean mafia) but most often, and especially in the United States, it refers to criminal groups whose membership is determined by Italian, and more specifically Sicilian, lineage.[1] Sicilian crime syndicates in the United States usually refer to themselves as *La Cosa Nostra* ("our thing"). They have historical roots dating back to the Middle Ages when Sicily was controlled by successive waves of invaders, leading the local population to develop a clandestine self-help network based on ethnic and family ties, promises of mutual protection, vigilante justice, and a rigid code of silence (*omertà*). The main purpose of this arrangement was to coordinate actions against invaders and arbitrate disputes between family groups.[2]

When large numbers of southern Italians migrated to the new world during the late nineteenth and early twentieth centuries, largely to serve as poor factory labor, the mafia culture was imported with them. In multiple North American cities, unscrupulous family networks accelerated their upward mobility with criminal schemes that included gambling, loan-sharking, protection rackets, prostitution, and the production and sale of illegal products, like alcohol during Prohibition (1920–33). In later years, infiltrating labor unions became an efficient way to influence workers and sales, extort money and favors from managers, and manipulate voting behavior. American crime families were mostly independent of each other but operated under the aegis of a New York-based "Commission," an informal coordinating body that dealt with encroachments, turf wars, and disloyal members.

DOI: 10.4324/9781003222460-8

Until the late 1950s, Sicilian crime syndicates enjoyed a great deal of freedom in the United States. This was due to several reasons: their secretive nature, the difficulty for the authorities to gauge their size and power, the fact that, being virulently anti-communist, these organizations posed no obvious threat to national security, and because *mafiosi* usually only murdered each other—at least, that was the standard in North America. But that all began to change in 1957 when the New York police discovered a secret *Cosa Nostra* summit taking place in Apalachin, New York, which revealed for the first time the depth and extent of the network across the country. This watershed event would lead Congress, the FBI, the Justice Department, and state and local law enforcement to monitor and prosecute organized crime more intensely. Such efforts included the Senate Select Committee on Improper Activities in Labor and Management (aka: the McClellan or "Rackets" Committee) in which Senator John Kennedy and his brother Robert, who served as lead counsel, faced off with Sam Giancana, Jimmy Hoffa, and other notorious mobsters. This marked the beginning of the end of the golden age of organized crime in America, a period immortalized in Hollywood films like *The Godfather* and *The Untouchables*. It also led to several ideological conflicts at the federal and state levels concerning whose job was to prosecute these cartels, a conflict personified during the early 1960s by FBI Director J. Edgar Hoover and Attorney General Robert Kennedy (see Chapter 5).

Numerous conspiracy theorists claim that the mafia was involved in JFK's murder, either alone or as part of a wider conspiracy. Such authors highlight the alleged confessions of various members of organized crime—mostly fringe operatives, self-confessed contract assassins, mob outsiders who claim to have overheard suspicious talk about Kennedy or, in several cases, confirmed lunatics and charlatans seeking attention and money. The most frequently evoked example of these disclosures was the 1983 "prison confession" of Carlos Marcello, the New Orleans don who bore a personal grudge against Bobby Kennedy, partly for having Marcello deported to Guatemala in 1961, the country of origin listed on his fake birth records.[3] Another reason offered by several conspiracists is the claim that Chicago mob boss Sam Giancana felt double-crossed by JFK for helping him win the 1960 election only to later be prosecuted by his administration. Others identify Florida capo Santo Trafficante, Jr. or corrupt union leader Jimmy Hoffa for harboring a murderous grudge against the Kennedy brothers, either over Bobby Kennedy (RFK)'s crackdown on organized crime or JFK's failure to liberate Cuba.

"Mob hit" conspiracists offer an ambitious list of "connections" between mobsters and Kennedy, grandiose webs of intrigue that usually amount to a series of guilt-by-association fallacies or the faulty assumption (i.e., false dilemma) that wanting to see someone dead is proof enough of their having killed him. To avoid getting lost in endless speculations, we will restrict our focus to Giancana and Marcello, the primary suspects of the "mob hit" narratives. We will then respond to theories that argue that Lee Harvey Oswald and Jack Ruby had ties to members of the *Cosa Nostra* who coaxed, duped, or helped them commit murder.

6.2 My father's godfather is not my friend

More controversial than John Kennedy's extramarital affairs and the deceitful tactics he used to win the 1960 presidential debates were the backdoor negotiations that helped his father, Joseph Kennedy, Sr., strike a deal with Chicago trade unions to have them support his son's presidential bid, which he orchestrated through a network controlled by mafia kingpin Sam Giancana. According to Seymour Hersh,

> The deal included an assurance that Giancana's men would get out the Kennedy vote among the rank and file in the mob-controlled unions in Chicago and elsewhere, and a commitment for campaign contributions from the corrupt Teamsters Union pension fund.[4]

This, he argues, allowed Kennedy to win Illinois with "a margin nearly four times as great as his final plurality in the nation as a whole," enough to secure the presidency with a thin majority of Electoral College votes.[5] While this was not clearly illegal (and worse things have occurred in Chicago[6]) it smacked of old-school corruption, something that could embarrass the new president should it ever go public.

It was also at Joe Kennedy's urging that JFK nominated his younger brother and campaign manager to the post of Attorney General. Bobby Kennedy had cut his teeth in the Justice Department during the 1950s working for various congressional committees, positions obtained largely thanks to his father's connections. This included the Senate Permanent Subcommittee on Investigations, through which Bobby became friends with Senator Joseph McCarthy and developed a hatred of Marxists and mobsters.[7] Bobby's nomination was a surprising choice, since he had never prosecuted a single case in court. Hersh argues that this appointment was made to ensure that no allegations of electoral fraud reached a courtroom while Kennedy was in office.[8] The irony was not lost on John Kennedy's aides, but such was Joe Kennedy's influence over his sons and the ties that bound their family. Bobby soon asserted himself as the President's most ruthless henchman and stepped-up federal prosecutions of organized crime. "It undoubtedly looked like double-cross to the mob chieftains," wrote conspiracy author Jim Marrs, "and in the underworld, the only solution for a double-crosser is elimination—a 'hit'".[9]

The Kennedy-mafia collaboration seems counterintuitive to anyone familiar with the intense acrimony that existed between RFK and *mafiosi* like Hoffa, Marcello, and Giancana.[10] Yet, Hersh argues, the mob had remained favorable to getting JFK elected because, unlike Kennedy, neither Nixon nor Johnson had shown much interest in overturning the communist Cuban regime, which would allow them to resume their lucrative casino and brothel operations in Havana.[11] Mob leaders therefore saw Kennedy, warts and all, as the candidate most likely to assist their cause. Even though Giancana would rage that he got "double-crossed" when Bobby was named Attorney General (this was recorded by FBI wiretaps), and although authors like Marrs claim this was enough of a reason for the mob to kill Kennedy,[12] Hersh does not believe they had sufficient motive to murder the

President, even as late as 1963. In fact, Giancana, Marcello, and Florida crime boss Santo Trafficante, Jr. (the former don of Havana, Cuba) were privy to a juicy state secret that would only be exposed in 1975 by the Church Committee and fully declassified in 2007. This secret was that President Kennedy had already approved a secret CIA plan to assassinate Castro—a plan that required the mafia's assistance, and more specifically that of Johnny Rosselli, a Las Vegas mobster close to Giancana.[13] This gave the heads of the *Cosa Nostra* enough incentive to want to keep JFK in office despite Bobby's crackdown on organized crime. As Hersh put it, "Why kill the goose that's going to lay the golden egg?"[14]

Furthermore, November 1963 was a good time for US crime lords to lay low and not engage in what JFK buffs describe as the most complex mob hit in history. Indeed, convicted mobster and murderer Joseph Valachi had just broken the mafia's code of silence by agreeing to testify in front of a televised Senate commission, which aired live in October 1963. In it Valachi gave a detailed history of the *Cosa Nostra*, of his 30 years in the mob and told all about its leaders, inner workings, and rule of *omertà*. Valachi's public testimony aided federal law enforcement to connect multiple crimes to a single, large-scale criminal conspiracy. Assassinating President Kennedy—or, more appropriately, his brother Robert—would have been more useful *before* Valachi's earth-shattering confession, not after. More importantly, if the mob had had the will and resources to murder Kennedy and then Oswald, it should have had no problem killing Valachi as well. And yet, the rat sang like a canary as they watched and did nothing. Valachi lived into the following decade and died of natural causes.[15]

Conspiracists often appeal to the informal confessions of various mobsters as proof of the mafia's involvement in Kennedy's murder.[16] One of these is the alleged 1962 confession of Carlos Marcello to Edward Becker, a California private investigator and friend of Johnny Roselli who once worked for murdered Las Vegas casino manager Gus Greenbaum. As first reported in Ed Reid's 1969 book, *The Grim Reapers: The Anatomy of Organized Crime in America*,[17] Becker said he visited Carlos Marcello's New Orleans home with some friends in September 1962, hoping to pitch an investment opportunity. While the two men were alone, Becker says, he brought up Marcello's troubles with Bobby Kennedy, to which the mobster reportedly answered: "the dog will keep biting you if you only cut off its tail"—implying, Becker explained, that Marcello put an order out to murder the president to get RFK off his back—and that he planned to "get a nut to do it". Marcello then added in his Sicilian dialect that it was time for him to "take the stone out of my shoe" ("*Livarsi 'na pietra di la scarpa!*").[18]

The first problem with this "confession," excluding the fact that it is mired in innuendos, is that it is unfalsifiable: no one can prove it ever happened because it has no corroborating evidence. Furthermore, given that the alleged discussion took place over a year before the assassination and not long after Marcello's embarrassing exile to Guatemala, it is entirely possible that Marcello, if he did say this to Becker, was merely venting his anger, not confessing a capital crime. When we consider that the two men never met before, that Becker was not an active member of the syndicate and therefore not sworn to *omertà*, that Marcello was a discrete man with a history of engaging in financial rackets, not murder, and the fact that Becker survived ratting out a mafia kingpin to Ed Reid, we can safely assume that Becker's story is not likely true. Certainly, it would hold little water in a court of law. In any event, the FBI and House Select Committee on Assassinations (HSCA) both investigated Becker, and although they confirmed that the meeting probably happened, they also believed, based on Becker's history and Marcello's habits, that this story was not believable.[19] FBI wiretap recordings taken in 1979 (after the publication of the HSCA's final report) and later released by the Assassination Records Review Board revealed no evidence that Marcello was involved in JFK's death.[20]

It is of course rational to deduce that if someone is of sound mind is confessing a crime, that there is a strong chance they did it. But making such assumptions is problematic, especially when it comes to mobster confessions. For instance, most of these alleged confessions were not made under oath. They were confirmed only through second- and third-hand sources—what we call anecdotal evidence—or under conditions that might have elicited a false confession, such as the desire to plea bargain for a reduced sentence. Mobsters also live by a different moral code than the average person. While most law-abiding citizens (including the average conspiracist) would not dare confess to a murder they did not commit—especially that of a president—the world of organized crime is one built on notoriety, hubris, and fearmongering. So it should not be surprising that in 1985, 22 years after the assassination, an aging, ailing, and incarcerated Carlos Marcello "confessed" to a fellow inmate (who turned out to be an FBI informant) of having met with Lee Harvey Oswald in 1963 and ordered him to murder Kennedy. This may simply have been a ploy by Marcello to earn his cellmate's respect and not be harassed by the other prisoners. It could also have been the ramblings of a senile old gangster, which is what the FBI and Marcello's prosecutor concluded.[21]

Over the past 50 years, many attention-seeking charlatans such as James Files, Charles Harrelson, Roscoe White, and Chauncey Holt "confessed" that they shot at Kennedy in Dealey Plaza.[22] As later chapters will show, there is little evidence of a second shooter in Dallas, even less that *all* of these men could have been involved. Conspiracists also cite the confessions of several other alleged witnesses whose mental health, truth-telling record, or personal credibility are so questionable, and whose testimonies are so full of holes and factual errors, that they would never be taken seriously by objective historians or prosecutors. Such individuals include Robert Easterling (Henry Hurt: *Reasonable Doubt*, 1985) Jack Martin, Richard Case Naggell and Rose Cherami (Jim Garrison: *On the Trail of the Assassins*, 1988), Gordon Arnold and Ed Hoffman (Nigel Turner: *The Men Who Killed Kennedy*, 1988), and Loy Factor (Sample and Collum: *The Men on the Sixth Floor*, 1995).

No alleged collaborator has yet come forward with a clearly *self-incriminating* confession, the sort that demonstrates genuine remorse *and* is supported by clear evidence. To see what real confessions look like, and how to elicit them convincingly, one need look no further than the 1972–74 Watergate Affair and how it was quickly exposed, namely through the meticulous process of legal depositions.

It bears repeating that confessions, like all other lone witness reports, are never damning *per se*, either legally or logically, without clear evidence to corroborate them. Indeed, many witnesses lie, forget, remember wrongly, or misinterpret what they experienced. Inversely, confessions can be dismissed when they are either self-contradicting, inconsistent with verified facts, or when the "confessor" has much to gain by incriminating themselves. Narcissism, revenge, and greed are powerful motivators to lie. Poor mental health and dementia also affect one's recall. Yet, JFK assassination confessions are often publicized with no supporting proof, only vague claims made many years after the fact, and often through second-hand testimony. They are also often made in exchange for money, a high-profile interview, a lucrative book deal, or other forms of media attention.[23] This is not altogether surprising. Considering the ongoing popularity and profitability of scandalous gossip, who wouldn't want to confess being part of the crime of the century when the worst consequence one might face is just being ignored?

6.3   Jack be nimble, Jack be quick

The main way conspiracists link the mob to Kennedy's murder is by claiming that Oswald's assassin Jack Ruby was a mafia hit man following orders from Sam Giancana, Carlos Marcello, or another crime lord. According to former HSCA staffers G. Robert Blakey and Richard Billings, who subsequently co-authored *The Plot to Kill the President* (1981), "The murder of Oswald by Jack Ruby had all the earmarks of an organised-crime hit, an action to silence the assassin, so he could not reveal the conspiracy".[24] Mob hit theories have also been promoted by Anthony Summers (*Conspiracy*, 1980), Henry Hurt (*Reasonable Doubt*, 1985), David Scheim (*Contract on America*, 1983), and Lamar Waldron (*Legacy of Secrecy*, 2006) to name but a few. According to these authors—and to those who claim that the mob and CIA jointly killed JFK—Ruby was a long-standing mafia asset who was compelled to silence Lee Oswald, another mafia accomplice. Invariably, such books rest on the unproven assumption that because Ruby's killing of Oswald *looked like* a mob hit, it necessarily was one. But was it really that similar? As former prosecutor Vincent Bugliosi points out, the similarities are not that strong. There is no prior example, for instance, of an uninitiated mafia assassin shooting a man through the stomach in broad daylight inside a police station without a getaway plan. The only actual similarity between Ruby's murder of Oswald and a typical mafia hit, argues Bugliosi, is that Ruby used a handgun.[25] To be fair, he was also wearing a hat.

These theories rest on long chains of unproven "connections" between Ruby, Oswald, and the mob,[26] and also many red herrings (irrelevant side stories). In two brief paragraphs, Henry Hurt offers us a typical example of the chronically vague and speculative language used by these authors:

> Jack Ruby *seems* to have maintained *business associations* that kept him in touch with *important mobsters of the sixties*. He was *linked* to men who, in turn, were *dealing with* much diverse figures as Fidel Castro and President Kennedy,

in addition to the crime syndicates of New Orleans, Chicago and Havana. Indeed, *some* of the *connections* had *links* to the CIA. *Just how closely Jack Ruby was involved is debatable*, but he clearly had *contacts* with *elements* of the mob that were *dealing* with *powerful entities*. […]

There is *every reason to believe* that the criminal *ties* Ruby established as a youthful street brawler in Chicago *controlled* him at the moment he murdered Oswald in 1963. It is *equally likely* that those same *clawlike fingers* kept their grip on him through thirty-seven months of custody. A *force* powerful enough to make him murder *would certainly be strong enough* to seal his lips. Except for the most minor slips, Ruby kept his silence until a blood clot and cancer took his last breath at Parkland Hospital on January 3, 1967.[27]

Such ambiguous claims offer no tangible evidence of Ruby's involvement in mafia affairs: no names, no eyewitness testimonies, and no verifiable leads. The only clear admissions are those that might prove the theory wrong: Ruby's mafia connections are "debatable," he made no prison confession, he died of natural causes, etc. Like many of his fellow researchers, Hurt leaves it up to his paranoid readers to fill in the blanks with their favorite suspicions.

Most conspiracists concede that Jack Ruby had only superficial connections to organized crime, that he intentionally murdered Oswald, and that he obsessively hung around the Dallas police station where Oswald was incarcerated for three days. They also agree that Ruby died while in prison of an undiagnosed cancer that spread to his lungs and brain. Lone gunman theorists agree to all this. The sinister parts of these "mob hit" theories are therefore to be found in the tentative "links" that string these known facts together—suspicious connections that are only convincing to ready believers and those who remain unfamiliar with the facts of Ruby's life story, his professional activities, his personality, and his state of mind. Conspiracists also bolster their claims by quoting each other, or spotting smoking guns in missing evidence or ambiguous data.

A good example is found in their inspection of Ruby's phone records, especially his calls to New Orleans during the weeks before the assassination. Hurt writes:

There is no question that Ruby was having serious trouble with the entertainment union to which his strippers belonged […] and it is entirely possible that his New Orleans activities were strictly related to trying to acquire strippers from outside the local circuit. *On the other hand, it is not unreasonable to wonder if Ruby had reached out to New Orleans for some other reason.*[28]

After offering us the simplest, most rational, and best supported explanation (that Ruby was engaging in innocuous business calls), Hurt offers up an ambitious, hypothetical, and unsupported (but far more tantalizing) explanation that fits his narrative. Such conjectures are regular fare in this literature. When it is not possible to extrapolate a sinister explanation from anodyne factoids, they either ignore the historical record or flag it as proof of "coordinated perjury".[29]

Conspiracists perceive many suspicious connections between Ruby and Oswald. Several of their favorite "witnesses" also claim to have seen Ruby in Dealey Plaza before or during the assassination. We will consider some of these in the following chapters. Let us for now consider the evidence of Ruby's motive, and his reasons for being in the Dallas police headquarters before and during his shooting of Oswald.

Jack Ruby's alleged connections to the mob were investigated at length by the Warren Commission (1964) and HSCA (1979), as well as by Gerald Posner (1993) and Vincent Bugliosi (2007) who found no solid proof that Ruby was anything more than a socially awkward nightclub owner who lived in a morally gray zone between legitimate business and petty vice. The claim that Ruby was a hit man is also logically problematic. Rather than discourage conspiracy chatter, the murder of Oswald made millions of people believe that the mob had a hand in the president's murder—a rather strange way for the mafia to cover their tracks. It would have been better, for instance, for such assassins to stage a fake suicide.

This theory is also an insult to the intelligence of the mafia dons who allegedly ordered the hit, because it indirectly implies they let Oswald be questioned three days before Ruby decided to shoot him. Indeed, it is well-documented (and recorded on video) that Ruby was in and out of the police station that weekend, including the night Oswald was arrested, at which time he came within three feet of Oswald, armed with a revolver.[30] Ruby could have thus finished the job several times before Sunday morning, by which time he could have spilled every secret he knew. And so, the idea that Ruby was the mob's best available method for silencing Oswald—as opposed to picking him up at the Book Depository or at his boarding house minutes after the crime to make him disappear—makes kingpins like Carlos Marcello look like buffoons.

In the interest of being thorough, let us nonetheless consider some of the "proofs" connecting Ruby to organized crime, including the calls he allegedly made to mobsters before the assassination.[31]

The Warren Commission wrote off Ruby as a deranged loner. Most of the "mob hit" theorists shed little more light on his motive or state of mind. Such books take us instead on long, meandering stories about the mafia's inner workings and its leaders' hatred of Kennedy—much of it second-hand gossip. They also tend to ignore one of Ruby's deepest aversions, anti-Semitism, which caused him to drum up his own paranoid theory about Kennedy's murder.

Before settling down as a nightclub owner in Dallas, Jack Ruby (born Jacob Rubenstein) was a peddler of small merchandise from Chicago. His childhood was marked by parental neglect: a drunk and violent father who abandoned him and his seven younger siblings when he was only ten, a mother who was committed on several occasions to psychiatric hospitals, and a brawling and volatile temperament that grew from his having to fend for himself in the streets of Chicago. A patron of nightclubs and boxing lounges, Jack was a squat, colorful, and mouthy youth who regularly got into fights. He was also a social butterfly who strove to impress anyone who listened. He could be extremely jovial and in the next moment fly into a rage. He was a largely unreligious Jew who was especially sensitive to anti-Semitic remarks and other forms of discrimination—which would later feed his admiration of Kennedy, the country's first Catholic president. After working various jobs as a waiter, newspaper salesman, union organizer and recruit in the Army Air Force, Ruby joined his sister Eva in Dallas to invest in the nightclub industry. After several business failures, Ruby enjoyed moderate success running the Carousel Club, an exotic show bar, though he remained financially strained until his arrest on November 24, 1963. While conspiracists claim that his debt was the hook the mafia used to control him, the truth is that most of this money was owed to his brother Earl, sister Eva, a few local friends, and the Internal Revenue Service (IRS), to whom he owed $45,000 in back taxes.[32]

Those who knew him best depicted Ruby not as a mobster but as an attention-seeking hustler always trying to make a quick buck by handing out vouchers and business cards, promoting local boxers, or peddling diet pills and cheap merchandise. Ruby did have numerous "connections" to organized crime, which is to say that he knew, did business with, and befriended many people with ties to the mob, drug trade, and prostitution. This should surprise no one given his past occupations as a bookmaker and union organizer, and his ownership of bars and strip clubs. His union connections, investigated by the FBI in 1940, revealed no direct link to a crime ring.[33] Even more telling, Ruby had approached the FBI in 1959 hoping to serve them as an informant. They found his help "essentially useless," and his FBI file was closed.[34] Ruby also maintained cordial relations with Dallas policemen, for whom he often expressed admiration.[35]

As the owner of a popular strip club, Ruby couldn't avoid befriending local criminals any more than he could avoid mingling with reporters, policemen, and other high-profile figures.[36] Though he was arrested nine times—on charges of disturbing the peace, carrying a concealed weapon, serving liquor after hours, and running obscene stage shows—none of the charges betrayed his vocation as a provider of adult entertainment.[37] He was also known for his violent outbursts against his showgirls, employees, and troublesome patrons. Rumors did circulate that he was a closeted homosexual and that he was disturbingly fond of his dogs, though this is hard to substantiate.

Using some rather peculiar logic, Henry Hurt sees Ruby's hot temperament and spotlight-hogging lifestyle as evidence that he was "an ideal pawn in the hands [...] of mobsters".[38] Those who knew him well, however, did not see Ruby as mafia material. Not only was he not Italian, he was excessively chatty, unpredictable, and greedy for attention. According to Chicago FBI agent Bill Roemer, who investigated Ruby's connections to Sam Giancana,

> Ruby was absolutely nothing in terms of the Chicago mob. We had thousands and thousands of hours of tape recordings of the top mobsters in Chicago, including Sam Giancana, and Ruby just didn't exist as far as they were concerned. [...] He was not a front for them in Dallas.[39]

Dallas Assistant District Attorney Bill Alexander, who prosecuted Ruby for Oswald's murder, offered similar remarks.[40] *Dallas Morning News* columnist Tony Zoppi, a friend of Ruby, also said: "You have to be crazy to think anybody would have trusted Ruby to be part of the mob. He couldn't keep a secret for five minutes. He was just a hanger-on".[41] Ruby's brothers Earl and Hyman, his sister Eva, and his Rabbi Hillel Silverman, all dismissed these mafia links as absurd.[42]

Ruby was known throughout Dallas but had few close friends. Indeed, many saw him as a benign nuisance who kept popping up at popular nightclubs and restaurants, boxing matches, football games, barbershops, and pool halls, even accidents and fires. As Vincent Bugliosi remarked, he was curious and desperate for attention:

> Ruby never saw a crowd that he didn't want to be a part of. […] It was Ruby's need to be in the middle of things that proved to be the catalyst, the one necessary ingredient in his makeup that made the shooting of Oswald when and where it happened a reality.[43]

The Dallas police station was only one of the many bustling places Ruby often frequented. Others included the local newspapers and radio stations. He bought drinks and food for cops and journalists, attended their funerals, and chatted them up in their workplace. Ruby practiced old-fashioned public relations, presented himself as the face of his businesses, genuinely believing he was making friends in the process. It served his purpose as a businessman and a narcissist to schmooze with whoever caught his attention. His befriending of policemen was also a business tactic: it helped keep unsavory characters out of his bars. This would indeed have made him a poor ally for organized criminals. "People in Dallas, in those circles, knew Ruby was a snitch," added Tony Zoppi, "the word on the street was that you couldn't trust him because he was telling the cops everything".[44]

Conspiracists often bring up the long-distance calls Ruby placed to Chicago, New Orleans, and Florida during the weeks leading up to Kennedy's murder, claiming that he was receiving instructions from Giancana, Marcello, and/or Trafficante.[45] Most of these have turned out to be spurious, especially considering that most of them happened prior to public announcements of Kennedy's trip to Dallas.[46] The small number of phone calls that remained suspicious to the Warren Commission and HSCA—made to mob-connected persons after Kennedy's trip to Dallas was confirmed—can be attributed to a business conflict that Ruby was having all through 1963 with a competing nightclub that hired amateur (i.e., non-unionized) strippers. Seeing himself as a victim of unfair competition, Ruby spent several months phoning and meeting members of the American Guild of Variety Artists (AGVA), a labor union that catered to exotic dancers and was, unsurprisingly, infiltrated by the mafia. This is the reason Ruby's long-distance phone activity increased significantly during the months before the assassination. The HSCA was able to confirm that Ruby had placed several calls to mob-connected unionists like Irwin Weiner, a Chicago bail bondsman who was an old friend of his brother Earl, and Robert "Barney" Baker, an associate of Jimmy Hoffa whom Ruby knew had experience with business disputes. The HSCA investigated Ruby's AGVA story and found it plausible and consistent, which did not prevent Scheim from impeaching their evidence: "Lying is second nature for mobsters, […] in particular, the main cover-story about Ruby's 'AGVA' problem. […] This coordinated perjury is a prima facie demonstration of mob conspiracy after the fact".[47] According to Scheim, then, the fact that everyone's story coheres—including those of non-mobsters involved— is an added reason to be suspicious. Sadly for Ruby, he had little success getting these men to pressure the AGVA on his behalf, which shows how little pull he actually had with the mob.

Despite numerous claims that Ruby appeared in various places in clandestine fashion during the weekend of the assassination—including an alleged 100-mile-per-hour drive to Houston and back—FBI reports, Warren Commission depositions, and HSCA interviews with Ruby's co-workers, sister, roommate, and other acquaintances account for the near totality of his movements during those three hectic days.[48] Their collective verdict is that Ruby had no verifiable contacts with organized criminals during that period, nor did his erratic behavior resemble that of a hit man under orders. Indeed, because his sister was convalescing from a surgery, Ruby had to manage two nightclubs at once (the Carousel and the Vegas) during the week of Kennedy's visit, which he found emotionally straining, especially once news of the President's murder was publicized. In respect for the President and his family, Ruby decided to close both bars for the weekend. He was outraged to discover that his competitors—including those that hired illegal strippers—elected to stay open.

All those who saw Ruby between the assassination and the time he shot Oswald attest to his worsening despair, repeated crying, and obsessive reading of newspapers whilst he bemoaned the fate of Mrs. Kennedy and her children. Family members and co-workers who talked with him on November 22–24 claimed he had suffered some kind of "emotional collapse," that he slept very little, and that he was talking and acting incoherently. He even began to make plans to fly to Chicago to visit his sister Eileen, who talked him out of it over the phone.[49] But Ruby was not only under financial and emotional stress, he was physically and psychologically strained. He had recently dealt with a work conflict over "Jada" (aka: Janet Conforto), one of his star dancers whose stage antics threatened to get him in legal trouble. He had recently been abusive toward members of his staff, some of whom quit or threatened to do so. A possible aggravating factor was that Ruby had started consuming Preludin, an appetite suppressant that was later banned.[50]

Ruby also flew into a rage at the sight of anti-Kennedy ads that appeared in the papers and local billboards in advance of Kennedy's visit. Ruby was particularly disturbed by a defamatory full-page ad in the *Dallas Morning News* titled "Welcome Mr. Kennedy to Dallas…" (see Figure 3.1), signed by a certain Bernard Weissman. Ruby complained about the ad to many people that weekend, and about a roadside billboard that read: "Save Our Republic: Impeach Earl Warren" (i.e., for his forced desegregation of schools in the South). Ruby took Polaroid pictures of the sign and still had them in his possession when he shot Oswald. At once patriotic and politically ignorant (he wasn't quite sure who Chief Justice Warren was), Ruby believed that these ads were the work of the right-wing John Birch Society and *also* of communists, and that "Bernard Weissman" was a false name used by racist assassins to blame Kennedy's murder on Jews.[51]

At Dallas police headquarters on the evening of the assassination, Ruby rubbed elbows with the policemen he knew and mingled with dozens of journalists. He lent himself as a guide and gofer to out-of-town reporters and local radio stations, helping them score interviews with various officials. This was Ruby's moment of fame, and he visibly relished it. His close brush with Lee Harvey Oswald, whom he believed had been smiling smugly during his brief exchange with the press, threw Ruby off-kilter.[52] He spent much of the rest of the night in the offices of the *Dallas Times Herald* and *KLIF*, a local radio station, delivering refreshments to newsmen and chatting with them about what he witnessed at the police station. It was on his way home at dawn on the morning of November 23 that he noticed the "Impeach Earl Warren" billboard. He returned later with two employees to help him photograph it. Later that day, Ruby returned to the police station where he offered his help to reporters inside an NBC news van (for which they named him "the creep"[53]). There is no doubt that during the two days before Oswald's murder, Jack Ruby was more or less stalking the man, ensconced in the media circus within the police station. This does not mean, however, that he had already decided to kill him. Ruby's decision to murder Oswald, Posner suggests, percolated over two days, stoked by the many conversation he had with friends and journalists, and by his peculiar idiosyncrasies. Certainly, his behavior of the morning of November 24 suggests that his "hit" on Oswald was nothing if not spontaneous.

That morning, Oswald was slated to be transferred to the nearby county jail at 10 a.m. At that same time, Ruby was still lingering in his apartment, pacing and mumbling, still in his underwear. This was confirmed to the Dallas police, and later the Warren Commission, by Ruby's roommate George Senator.[54] At 10:19 a.m., Ruby received a phone call from Karen Carlin (aka: "Little Lyn"), one of his strippers who lived in Fort Worth. She was requesting a cash advance to pay her rent. Ruby agreed to wire her some money through the local Western Union office, which was located a few hundred feet from the Dallas Police Department.[55] Driving past, Ruby spotted a crowd of reporters but did not join them. He instead methodically went to the money wiring service and waited his turn in line. His Western Union receipt was stamped 11:17 a.m.: over an hour *after* Oswald's scheduled transfer. Ruby then exited, left his dog in his car, and walked to the police department to investigate the commotion. He had no way of knowing that Oswald's transfer had been delayed—not once but three times—first due to an unscheduled interrogation by postal inspector Harry Holmes, then to problems mobilizing an armored vehicle for the transfer, and finally by Oswald himself requesting a change of clothing. Had the man simply not asked to put on a clean sweater Ruby would have completely missed him when he snuck into the parking garage at 11:20 am.[56] Less than a minute later, in the brief time it took to escort the prisoner from the elevator to the police vehicle parked nearby, Ruby discharged his pistol into Oswald's abdomen on live television, in full view of dozens of policemen and reporters. The single shot punctured a half-dozen organs. Oswald died shortly thereafter.

Ruby was immediately tackled, arrested, and taken away to be interrogated. While the rest of the world was in shock, Ruby was exultant. He appeared to believe he did his country a favor that he had saved Dallas from the stigma of racists (whom he believed were behind the president's murder) and heroically done what every cop in the city was dying to do.

> I hope I killed the son of a bitch, he exclaimed shortly after, surrounded by witnesses, "I'll save everybody a lot of trouble. […] Do you think I'm going to let the man who shot our president get away with it? […] Somebody had to do it. You all couldn't".[57]

He later told police detective Barnard Clardy: "If I had planned this, I couldn't have had my timing better. […] It was one chance in a million".[58] He further told Secret Service agent Forrest Sorrels that he had done it for Mrs. Kennedy, to spare her from having to come back to Dallas to testify, and "to show the world that a Jew has guts".[59]

But rather than celebrate Ruby's murderous act, the media and local authorities soon cast him as a pathetic nutcase. They were perhaps partly right. Several months later, Ruby would be diagnosed with an advanced-stage terminal cancer that had spread to his brain, and which had possibly begun to affect him in November 1963. Certainly, his peculiar behavior and the paranoid responses he gave to the Warren Commission only six months later (see next) suggest that the man was suffering delusions caused by extreme mental stress.[60] For this reason, Ruby's high-profile lawyer recommended that he plead insanity. This would unfortunately backfire on him.[61]

Considered sane by the jury, Ruby was charged with premeditated murder and was sentenced to death in March 1964. He was deposed by the Warren Commission in June, at which time his paranoia was obvious. Many conspiracists point to the fact that Ruby requested no less than nine times to be transferred to Washington because he believed his life was in danger. This is proof, wrote Henry Hurt, that Ruby saw himself as a "pawn in a conspiracy" and was about to be silenced just as Oswald had been.[62] But such claims take little account of the true nature of Ruby's paranoia; that he saw himself, with Kennedy, as the target of an anti-Semitic conspiracy. In his deposition and communications with family Ruby repeatedly claimed that anti-Semites were trying to kill him, that 25 million Jews were being systematically tortured and murdered on the lower floors of his prison, and that a conspiracy was underfoot to blame the Jewish people for Kennedy's murder and to peg him as a member of this evil confederacy. In the few years he had left to live, Ruby kept a picture of Kennedy in his cell, tried to commit suicide several times, and gave his siblings the impression he was deranged. He died of a pulmonary embolism on January 3, 1967, the result of the cancer spreading into his lungs.[63]

6.4 Well I'll be a monkey's uncle!

If tying Ruby to the mafia requires a great deal of speculation and cherry-picked facts, connecting Lee Oswald to the mafia requires no less than the wholesale rewriting of history. The proponents of the "mob hit" theory generally claim that Oswald (or someone who looked like him) took part in the shooting of Kennedy, and did so on behalf of the mafia. He therefore was either not a true Marxist or was so simple-minded that he did not realize the mob was pulling his strings. Either way, the Oswald-mafia connection rests on dishonest research and fallacious logic.

According to Henry Hurt, who throws in the additional twist that anti-Castro Cubans helped orchestrate the plot, "evidence is overwhelming that Lee Harvey Oswald was someone's tool in a conspiracy. [...] But just how and with whom is one of the great mysteries of the century".[64] But searching for such evidence in government files, Hurt explains, is likely not to produce satisfactory results because the government was not directly involved in the crime and therefore does not know the full story either. What evidence it might once have had of a plot hatched under its nose has likely been filed away, destroyed, or misplaced as a result of "bureaucratic ineptitude," resistance to change, and loyalty to each agency's own interests.[65] There is no clear evidence connecting Oswald to the mafia he concedes, nor to anyone else, except that it fits his hypothesis—but not without, we should add, his having to bend, cut, or ignore the puzzle's different pieces until they more or less serve his thesis. This is another example of circular reasoning.

Who exactly was Lee Harvey Oswald? Hurt's best guess, based on what he calls "a preponderance of common sense evidence," is that the man was likely a government agent sent to New Orleans to infiltrate the Cuban exile community and report back on the schemes of anti-Castro extremists. Hurt claims he was then kidnapped and smuggled out of New Orleans by a band of mafia-funded anti-Castro mercenaries, assisted by Guy Banister, David Ferrie, and Jack Ruby. These men then replaced Lee with a lookalike named "Carlo," who shot Kennedy from the sixth floor of the Texas School Book Depository and disappeared out a window on a rope ladder, leaving the real Oswald there to be picked up by the Dallas Police.[66] A breath-taking story!

And what are Hurt's sources for this remarkable tale? A single man named Robert Easterling whose own "confession" of having been part of this plot includes a never-identified Cuban colleague named "Manuel Rivera," whom he said had test-fired Mannlicher-Carcano bullets at coconuts to be planted in Dallas as false evidence. Easterling also told stories of Lee Oswald getting into bar fights and drinking until he vomited,[67] and of Kennedy's grassy knoll killer using a 7-millimeter "Czechoslovakian rifle" with a "catch box," with bullets "designed to disintegrate," so that he might leave no trace of his handiwork. Hurt even describes his star witness as "a multiple felon, an ex-convict, a raging alcoholic, a diagnosed psychotic and schizophrenic," a violent man with several assault, burglary, and bootlegging charges, several stays in mental institutions, "grandiose delusions" (he claimed he was close friends with J. Edgar Hoover) and several unproven murders to his account.[68] Despite all this, Hurt finds it remarkable that neither the FBI nor the Secret Service took Easterling seriously.[69]

Other conspiracists are a tad more sensible. According to Blakey, Billings, and Scheim, Oswald was a genuine Marxist but could not have avoided assimilating some of the mores of organized criminals growing up in mob-infested New Orleans. Oswald's marksmanship and thirst for blood, they further argue, came to the mafia's attention through his uncle Charles "Dutz" Murret—whom Scheim describes as a "criminal operative in the empire of New Orleans mafia boss Marcello" and "Oswald's surrogate father [who] had a lifelong influence on his nephew".[70] The decision to recruit Oswald as a hit man-*cum*-patsy was made, they allege, when Marina Oswald informed Uncle Dutz of Lee's failed attempt to kill General Walker a few weeks before they moved to New Orleans. Scheim does not tell us how the news might have travelled from Murret to Marcello, nor what compelled the pro-Castro Oswald to collaborate with right-wing crooks, only that Lee was the "nut" whom Marcello had chosen to fulfill his Sicilian oath to Edward Becker to "take the stone out of my shoe".[71] An additional "proof" for this theory comes in the form of a liquor storeowner named Emile Bruneau, who bailed Lee out of jail on the night of August 9, 1963, after his arrest for fighting in public with anti-Castro activist Carlos Bringuier.[72] Bruneau, Scheim tells us, was an "associate" of Nofia Pecora, who was himself an "associate" of Carlos Marcello: case closed.

There are obvious problems with this account in addition to being a fine example of the guilt-by-association fallacy. First, Marina Oswald told the Warren Commission she never spoke to anyone about the Walker shooting, not even Ruth Paine with whom she was closest, until after Lee died, and that her purpose for pushing Lee to move to New Orleans in the spring of 1963 was to get her husband away from General Walker and the temptation to use his rifle again. Telling Uncle Dutz about the Walker shooting runs against to everything else Marina has said about the Walker incident.[73] It also betrays the fact that Marina spoke little English (Lee did not want her to learn it), and that the Murrets spoke no Russian—a frustration that Dutz brought up several times in his exchanges with Lee.[74]

Second, Dutz Murret was far from being a "surrogate father" to Oswald. Not only did Oswald find the Murrets too religious and too "bourgeois" for his taste,[75] it is also brutally obvious throughout Murret's Warren Commission testimony that he never had much affection for his nephew and sister-in-law:

Mr. JENNER - What kind of a boy was Lee Harvey Oswald?
Mr. MURRET - Well, I'll tell you; I didn't take that much interest in him. [...] He liked to read, and he stuck by himself pretty much in the apartment the way I understand it.
Mr. JENNER - Did you and Marguerite get along all right?
Mr. MURRET - Not too well.
Mr. JENNER - Not too well?
Mr. MURRET - No. [...]
Mr. JENNER - Did there come a time then when they left New Orleans?

Mr. MURRET – Yes.

Mr. JENNER – Where did they go?

Mr. MURRET – I don't know.

Mr. JENNER – To Texas?

Mr. MURRET – I imagine so, but I don't know where they went.

Mr. JENNER – But they did leave your house?

Mr. MURRET – Yes; they sure did.

Mr. JENNER – And you didn't hear from them for a while, is that right?

Mr. MURRET – Well, my wife might have heard from them, and she might even have told me, but I didn't take any interest in that after they left.[76]

A surrogate father, indeed! Nevertheless, the Murrets were Lee's only family in New Orleans, and he was closer to Murret's wife Lillian (Marguerite Oswald's sister) than to his uncle, whom he telephoned in April 1963 upon his return to New Orleans, asking her for shelter. Though he had been back from Russia nearly a year, the Murrets had no knowledge of it until that day. In fact, they had not spoken to him in nearly six years.[77] The Murrets took Lee in for two weeks while he looked for a job and a place for his family to live. The Oswalds visited the Murrets' occasionally until Lee was arrested in August. When he reached out to them again for assistance, none of the Murrets were available to bail him out except his cousin Joyce, who refused to help him. Lillian, who was in the hospital with an ear infection while Dutz was away at a Catholic retreat, called her husband's friend Emile Bruneau to ask him to front the money to Oswald, which he did without ever meeting with him. (Dutz had to repay Bruneau himself.) Uncle Dutz paid the Oswalds a visit the next day. It was his first time visiting the Oswalds' home since they moved in earlier that spring. Dutz was angry at the news of Oswald's arrest and even more at the state of their home, Lee's inability to provide for his family's needs, and his photos of Castro. The little affinity that existed between Murret and Oswald withered and never returned.[78]

Finally, Charles Murret was far from being either a "criminal operative" or friend of Carlos Marcello. After investigating Oswald's relationship with the Murrets, the HSCA concluded that Dutz probably never met Marcello and had only worked as a bookmaker during the 1940s for a man named Sam Saia, a gambling club owner with financial ties to Marcello. The extent of Marcello's connection to Dutz—a devout Catholic with no criminal record and a Jesuit priest for a son—was indeed slim. All that the HSCA could uncover was that during his employment as a bookie for Saia, Murret had used Marcello's wire service to receive information on racing results—a far cry from being a criminal mastermind.[79]

Although allegations of the mafia's involvement figure prominently in JFK conspiracy theories, most of the "evidence" used to support them is anecdotal, vague, spurious, incorrect, or fallacious. After researching the dark side of Camelot for five years—including Bobby Kennedy's attempts to find out if the mob killed his brother—Seymour Hersh said he found nothing that would change the basic conclusions of the Warren Commission.[80] FBI agent Bill Roemer, a major figure in the Bureau's investigations of organized crime in Chicago, stated that although Giancana's office was secretly bugged from 1959 to 1965, and that the FBI closely monitored his and other mafia leaders' conversations during that period, no mention was ever made of their involvement in the assassination.[81] Wiretaps on Carlos Marcello's phone in the late 1970s, following the HSCA's "revelations" that a second gunman, one possibly linked to both Oswald and the mob, also revealed nothing.

In short, if the mafia did participate in Kennedy's murder, either by hiring Oswald or having him silenced, we must assume that the law of *omertà* is stronger than the undying human propensity to blab. The 1963 testimony of Joseph Valachi suggests that the latter is stronger.

Notes

1 Italian crime syndicates in the United States were never strictly Sicilian and sometimes even included prominent Jewish members such as Meyer Lansky and Moe Dalitz. Bugliosi, 1145–6.
2 John Lawrence Reynolds: *Shadow People: Inside History's Most Notorious Secret Societies* (2006), chap. 8.
3 George Lardner, Jr.: "U.S. vs. Marcello," *The Washington Post*, February 19, 1980.
4 Hersh, 131. The deal between Joe Kennedy and Giancana was apparently struck through mob attorney Robert J. McDonnell, who confessed this to Hersh. Tina Sinatra also claims to have heard of this deal through her father, singer Frank Sinatra, who was close to Giancana and the Kennedy family and who helped facilitate these meetings. Hersh, 135–8.
5 Ibid., 132. Some authors challenge the importance of the Illinois turnout, but not that the deal with the unions did not occur. Paul von Hippel: "Here's a Voter Fraud Myth: Richard Daley 'Stole' Illinois for John Kennedy in the 1960 Election," *The Washington Post*, August 8, 2017.
6 See "Illinois Has Long Legacy of Public Corruption," *NBC News*, 12/9/2008.
7 "From 'Runt of the Litter' to 'Liberal Icon,' the Story of Robert Kennedy," An interview with RFK biographer Larry Tye on "Fresh Air," *National Public Radio*, July 5, 2016.
8 Hersh, 153–4.
9 Marrs, 178.
10 Hoffa had a deep and widely known hatred of Bobby Kennedy. He even proffered the wish to see him dead. The HSCA thus considered him a suspect but found no evidence linking him to JFK's death. It is also unclear how shooting the President instead of the Attorney General could have helped Hoffa get RFK off his back. Posner, 457.
11 "Allan Gregg: Journalist Seymour Hersh on the Truth Behind JFK," *TVO*, December 8, 2010.
12 This claim is not only a hasty generalization—only Giancana is known to have raised funds, garnered votes, and shared lovers with John Kennedy (Bugliosi, 1159 and endnote)—it is also a false dilemma as there is no reason to assume that mob bosses are subject to standard operating procedures that require them to treat presidents the same way they treat low-ranking snitches.
13 This declassified CIA memo, titled "the Family Jewels," is available on the CIA's website.
14 Gregg (2010).
15 Bugliosi, 1157.

16 By "informal confession" I mean admissions that, unlike Valachi's testimony, were neither written, recorded firsthand, nor made under oath. Noel Twyman (*Bloody Treason*, 1997, 285) and James Fetzer (*Murder in Dealey Plaza*, 2000, 14–5), list several people whom they say admitted their involvement in, or overheard colleagues discuss, a plot to kill JFK. These include Carlos Marcello, Santo Trafficante, Jr., Johnny Roselli, Sam Giancana, CIA agents David Atlee Phillips and E. Howard Hunt, and even President Johnson. There are no firsthand records of any of these confessions (except perhaps for E. Howard Hunt's so-called deathbed confession—see below). Many of these "confessions" also contradict each other, or other theories that the CIA and Pentagon were involved. Yet Twyman and Fetzer don't appear bothered by this. Fetzer further assumes that the mafia and CIA's collaboration to murder Castro proves they also joined forces to murder Kennedy, a clear example of the hasty generalization fallacy.

17 After "confessing" to Reid, Becker was later deposed by the HSCA. He then repeated the story in a book he co-authored with Charles Rappleye in 1991 (*All-American Mafioso: The Johnny Rosselli Story*) and on television in 1992 ("JFK, Hoffa and the Mob," *PBS: Frontline*, November 17, 1992). HSCA Volume IX: chap. III: "Carlos Marcello," 81–4; George Lardner, Jr.: "Investigator Detailed Mafia Leaders' Threat against Kennedy," *Washington Post*, July 21, 1979; Bugliosi, 1167–73.

18 Cited in Posner, 458.

19 HSCA Report, 169–72.

20 FBI Record 124-10164-10166, April 23, 1980, cited in Bugliosi, 1173–5.

21 According to declassified FBI memos, the informant, Jack Van Laningham, was deemed a credible witness. Nevertheless, Marcello himself was considered too ill and erratic for this uncorroborated claim to be taken seriously. This was the opinion of Van Laningham's FBI contact Agent Thomas Kimmel, Jr., and Marcello's prosecuting attorney Ron Sievert. Even mob-hit conspiracist Anthony Summers agrees. See "The Claims that Mafia Bosses Trafficante and Marcello Admitted Involvement in Assassinating President Kennedy," (n.d.), *Anthony Summers & Robbyn Swan*. The theory that Marcello ordered the hit on JFK is presented in Waldron and Hartmann, *Legacy of Secrets* (2008), 754–5, 773–4. See also Marcella S. Kreiter: "The Issue: The Kennedy Assassination—Did the Mob Do It?" *United Press International*, November 17, 2013.

22 "The Assassin from Blockbuster Video: The James Files 'Confession'," (n.d.), "The Three Tramps," (n.d.), and David B. Perry: "A Few Words from an 'Amateur Sleuth'," *Fourth Decade*, November 1996, at John McAdams: *The JFK Assassination*. James Fetzer, among others, continued to cite such "confessions" despite the many contradictions in their stories. Fetzer, 14–5.

23 See, for example, the interview of Saint John Hunt by George Knapp (*Coast to Coast A.M. with George Noory*, July 21, 2013), about his father's (ex-CIA agent E. Howard Hunt) alleged deathbed confession. First, listening to this "confession" will set you back a few dollars. It also got largely ignored by all credible news publications. E. Howard Hunt's so-called deathbed confession may have been a case of dementia, a false confession, or an example of a chronic liar who finally came to believe his own lies. For a conspiracist view, see Larry Chin: "Hunt's Deathbed Confession Reveals JFK Killers: The Last Confession of E. Howard Hunt-US Government/CIA Team Murdered JFK," April 4, 2007, *Jeff Rense Homepage*. For a skeptical view see McAdams with Magen Knuth: "E. Howard Hunt and Frank Sturgis: Were Watergate Conspirators Also JFK Assassins?" (n.d.), *The Kennedy Assassination*.

24 Blakey and Billings: *The Plot to Kill the President* (1981), 339. Blakey served as HSCA lead counsel. Billings edited its Final Report. The rest of the Committee was not convinced that either Ruby or Oswald had pertinent ties to the mafia.

25 Bugliosi, 1163.
26 Three individuals often used to connect Ruby to the mafia are Joseph Locurto (aka: Joe Bonds), his former nightclub-owning partner, professional gambler Lewis McWillie, and New Orleans nightclub owner Harold Tannenbaum, with whom Ruby traded exotic dancers. Henry Hurt: *Reasonable Doubt* (1985), chap. 8. To which Posner replies: "there is no firm evidence that [Ruby] did anything more than socialize with some people involved in those vices". Posner, 360.
27 Hurt, 176 and 172. Emphasis added.
28 Ibid., 181. Emphasis added.
29 See, for example, Scheim: *Contract on America* (1988), 270–1.
30 Ruby admitted to the FBI that he had his .38 caliber revolver on him inside the precinct on that Friday evening. Warren Commission document CD1259.9, cited in Posner, 378.
31 The following discussion is drawn largely from Posner, 350–401, which cites FBI reports, Warren Commission, and HSCA depositions and exhibits, and interviews by the author with those who were close to Ruby. See also Bugliosi, 1078–97. For a conspiracist view, see Scheim, chap. 9; Hurt, chap. 8; and Waldron and Hartmann, chap. 18.
32 Bugliosi, 1092–6.
33 Posner, 352.
34 FBI memo, November 6, 1959, discussed in Posner, 359 (footnote).
35 Bugliosi, 1097–100.
36 One of these friends was future Dallas kingpin Joe Campisi. Ruby was a frequent patron of his restaurant, the Egyptian Lounge. Despite Scheim's allegations that Campisi was Ruby's mob "handler" in Dallas, it is unlikely that Campisi would have wanted to incriminate himself by visiting Ruby in prison soon after he killed Oswald—which Campisi did. Posner, 367 (footnote) and 397 (footnote).
37 Posner, 361.
38 Hurt, 175.
39 Cited in Posner, 354.
40 Ibid., 354.
41 Ibid., 361.
42 Posner, 350–64. All of the above-cited individuals considered Ruby's actions to be those of an emotionally wrought and ill-informed man visiting "Texas Justice" on a communist and (presumed) bigot. One exception is former Dallas journalist Seth Kantor (*The Ruby Cover-Up*, 1978), who was briefly acquainted with Ruby prior to 1962. See Bugliosi, 1133–44.
43 Bugliosi, 1120.
44 Cited in Posner, 361.
45 These allegations, made by Scheim (121–2), are dispelled by Posner (362–4) and Bugliosi (1103–8).
46 The same can be said about a "suspicious" trip to Cuba Ruby took with his friends Tony Zoppi and Lewis McWillie in September 1959 (*over a year before JFK was elected!*) which some conspiracists claim proves he worked for Trafficante. The actual purpose of this trip was for Zoppi and McWillie to promote the Tropicana Night Club casino in Havana. Ruby accompanied them for leisure and to try to promote his own business ventures. In any event, Santo Trafficante had just been released from prison two weeks prior to Ruby's Havana visit and stayed in Florida that whole time. Bugliosi, 1110–1.
47 HSCA Volume IX: V, E "Labor Difficulties with the American Guild of Variety Artists, Early 1960's," 196–201; Scheim, 270–1.
48 Local authorities investigated several false sightings of Oswald and Ruby. The alleged trip to Houston is described in Scheim, 261 (cited in Posner, 366).

49 See Testimony of Eileen Kaminsky, WC XV.

50 Posner, 374. Preludin (aka: phenmetrazine) is an addictive substitute amphetamine and nervous system stimulant.

51 Weissman did exist. He was a conservative 26-year-old discharged soldier who lent his name to the ad's actual sponsor, billionaire oil tycoon Bunker Hunt. See Chapter 5 and Posner, 369–71, 380–2.

52 Posner, 378–9. Many speculate (e.g., Hurt, 186; Stone's *JFK*) that Ruby demonstrated insider knowledge of Oswald's personal history when he corrected District Attorney Henry Wade during a press conference. Wade mistakenly stated that while in New Orleans, Oswald had been a member of the Free Cuba Committee (a right-wing organization) rather than the left-wing and pro-Castro Fair Play for Cuba Committee. However, such information had already been published the previous summer in New Orleans newspapers and had been circulating several hours among journalists in Dallas, seeking information on Oswald. Having spent several hours in their company and also reading and watching the news, it was not unusual that Ruby, in his self-appointed role as police "interpreter," to publicly correct Wade, who had not been following the news as closely.

53 Ibid., 385.

54 Testimony of George Senator, WC XIV.

55 Unbefitting a mafia hit man expecting to be arrested, Ruby took his favorite dog with him and left her in the car before entering the police station. Phil Rogers: "Jack Ruby 'Thought He Was Going to Be a Hero,' Niece Says," *NBC 5 Chicago*, November 20, 2013.

56 Much speculation exists about how Ruby got into the parking garage. No credible witness said they saw him enter. Conspiracists Mark Lane and Henry Hurt claim that Ruby was let in by someone inside the station, suggesting that policemen were in on it. Skeptics (including the Warren Commission and Ruby himself, during a polygraph test) say he snuck in through a briefly unguarded entrance ramp. Early statements Ruby made to the police demonstrate his familiarity with the comings and goings of the policemen posted outside the building. According to Gary Mack, the late curator of the Sixth Floor Museum at Dealey Plaza, Ruby could equally have been let in by a friendly policeman or reporter with no sinister motives, someone Ruby chose not to incriminate, and then have penetrated through a fire escape staircase that accessed the parking garage. See David Von Pein: "How Did Jack Ruby Get into the Police Basement?" (n.d.), *DVP's JFK Archive*.

57 CE 2002: Interview of W.J. Harrison, and Testimony of DPD detective Lewis D. Miller, WC XII, cited in Swanson, 236–7.

58 Testimony of Barnard Clardy, WC XII.

59 Testimony of Forrest Sorrels, WC XIII.

60 Posner, 401.

61 Ruby's brother Earl hired Melvin Belli, a flamboyant high-profile San Francisco lawyer, to defend Jack. But rather than resort to a "murder without malice" plea (Texas' equivalent of an unpremeditated manslaughter charge) that could have earned Ruby a five-year conviction, Belli convinced Ruby to plead insanity on the basis of his mother's psychiatric illnesses and his difficult childhood. See Posner, 398–401.

62 Hurt, 189.

63 Posner, 399–401. A deleted scene from Oliver Stone's *JFK*, based on Jim Marrs' *Crossfire*, falsely depicted Ruby forcefully receiving a "cancer injection" from a hospital doctor. See David Reitzes: "The JFK 100: Jack Ruby Injected with Cancer," *JFK Online*, 2001.

64 Hurt, 109, 430–1.

65 Ibid., 430.

66 Ibid., 254, 360–79.
67 Oswald drank little and was reportedly home every evening at that time. Posner, 122 (footnote).
68 Hurt, 346.
69 Ibid., 39–350.
70 Scheim, 42–3, 167. See also Blakey and Billings, 343–4, 364.
71 Ibid., 57. See the discussion above on Edward Becker.
72 Posner, 150–3.
73 Testimony of Mrs. Lee Harvey Oswald, WC I.
74 Testimony of Mrs. Lillian Murret, WC VIII.
75 Testimony of Mrs. Lee Harvey Oswald, WC I.
76 Testimony of Charles Murret, WC VIII.
77 Testimony of Mrs. Lillian Murret, WC VIII. See also Posner, 121–7.
78 Posner, 155–7, 167.
79 Bugliosi, 1177–9.
80 Hersh, 451.
81 Giancana never realized he and his colleagues were being listened to, proved by the fact that they shared a great deal of information on other crimes that led to arrests and indictments. Posner, 461–2.

7

SPOOKS AND NUKES

The CIA and its war on Cuba

7.1   Ike's dirty little secret

President Kennedy's predecessor, Dwight D. "Ike" Eisenhower, was a decorated five-star US Army General who served as Supreme Commander of the Allied forces during World War II. Under his authority, the United States, Britain, and Commonwealth allies liberated North Africa and Western Europe from Nazi Germany. Having overseen the sudden and rapid expansion of the US armed forces, along with a vast military bureaucracy and private weapons industry, the new Republican president was deeply concerned that this "military industrial complex" might, left unchecked, develop an "unwarranted influence, whether sought or unsought" over democratic institutions and US foreign policy.[1] Cold War tensions against the Soviet Union during the 1940s and 1950s, and the desire to curtail communist expansion in Africa, South America, and East Asia, had encouraged US policymakers to further enlarge the military, including a nuclear arsenal large enough to kill millions in seconds. For this reason, and because the Soviet Union now also possessed atomic and hydrogen weapons—which could trigger a worldwide cataclysm if a direct armed conflict broke out—Eisenhower delegated all "peace-time operations" (a euphemism for clandestine acts of war, better known to conspiracists as "covert operations" or "black ops") to the CIA.[2]

Conspiracists frequently describe the CIA as a fourth branch of the US military.[3] Such a claim is technically false but is based on the unofficial reality that in its 75-year history, the CIA has often behaved less like a spy agency and more like a small army. It was founded in 1947 by President Harry Truman out of the defunct Office of Strategic Services (OSS), a wartime intelligence agency created to spy on the Axis powers and coordinate subversive activities behind enemy lines. Headed by a combination of military men and Ivy League intellectuals, the Agency was

DOI: 10.4324/9781003222460-9

still a small civilian intelligence-gathering service when Eisenhower took office in 1953. It was also still searching for an identity between the three fields in which it operated: the foreign diplomatic service, the military, and the amoral world of international espionage.

From its inception, the CIA was designed to circumvent the military chain of command by reporting directly to the president. This allowed it to maintain discretion and efficiency. In contrast to the Truman administration, which favored a defensive foreign policy focused on the containment of communism—with the CIA serving primarily as an intelligence-gathering tool—Secretary of State John Foster Dulles pushed President Eisenhower to adopt a more aggressive policy of "rollback".[4] This entailed using the CIA to perform deniable small-scale military operations against foreign governments and revolutionaries. The CIA's transition to this new role was facilitated by Allen Dulles, John Foster's brother and former Switzerland director of the OSS, who was appointed DCI in 1953. The Dulles brothers used the CIA throughout Eisenhower's presidency (1953–61) to perform covert operations in Iran, Guatemala, Indonesia, Indochina, and the Congo to help foreign allies put down communist insurgents or trigger regime change through assassinations, disinformation campaigns, and anti-communist counterrevolutions.[5]

Thus, in the hope of countering Soviet expansion, averting nuclear war, and limiting the growth of the ballooning federal budget (these were Republicans, after all), the Eisenhower administration transformed the CIA from a simple spy agency into a paramilitary organization that mostly operated outside the supervision of Congress and the Pentagon.[6] As Eisenhower reached the end of his second mandate, the CIA became deeply embroiled in communist Cuba. Its final and unfinished task, as Kennedy entered the White House in January 1961, was to execute a finalized plan for the "liberation" of Cuba using volunteer Cuban expatriates, supported by an airstrike by unmarked US warplanes. The change of administration would throw a wrench into the CIA's plans.

7.2   Caribbean kerfuffle

After gaining its independence from Spain in 1898, Cuba lived under the thumb of US corporate colonialism, unscrupulous politicians, mischief tourism, and organized crime. Fidel Castro, an idealistic young lawyer with a fondness for Marxist theory and emotional speeches, led a revolution in 1959 that successfully deposed corrupt president Fulgencio Batista. Soon after taking power, Castro declared Cuba a communist republic and allied himself with the Soviet Union. With a potential Soviet nuclear launch pad, a hundred miles off American shores, the Eisenhower White House discretely set out to incite a counterrevolution. The CIA was commissioned in March 1960 to train a small army of anti-communist Cuban expatriates in secluded training camps in Guatemala and Mexico, using military hardware and personnel borrowed from, but not controlled by, the Pentagon. The plan called for an amphibious invasion of Cuba during the spring of 1961, one which would have no obvious US assistance (deniability was quickly becoming a CIA watchword). It was bolstered by the assumption that this invasion would trigger a popular uprising against the Castro regime.

Although Senator John Kennedy was not privy to all the details of this project until his inauguration in January 1961, he was informed of the general plan right after his election in November 1960. There was a general agreement in the Kennedy electoral camp that Castro was a threat to US national security and a catalyst for communist movements in Latin America. Contrary to many conspiracists' claims, Kennedy expressed his approval for this operation quite early on.[7] On numerous occasions, including his televised debates with Nixon in October, Kennedy manifested the will to isolate Cuba and restore its democratic regime, with force if needed.[8] He soon learned that the CIA had in fact already begun organizing an invasion. The new president thus had no time to develop his own plan of action. Upon entering the White House in January, Kennedy would inherit two international Pandora's boxes. The first was Cuba and the blowback that a failed CIA-sponsored invasion would cause. The second would be Vietnam (see Chapter 8).

Despite Kennedy's call in his inaugural address to "let every nation know, whether it wishes us well or ill, that we shall pay any price, bear any burden, meet any hardship, support any friend, oppose any foe, in order to assure the survival and the success of liberty,"[9] the new president had not come prepared to develop a new strategy to counter the global expansion of communism. But that does not mean it was not a heartfelt priority. As Congressman and Senator, Kennedy supported hard-line Cold War policies. He had also warned voters during his presidential campaign (wrongly, it turned out) that America lagged behind the USSR in terms of a nuclear "Missile Gap".[10] Once elected, Kennedy remained a staunch cold warrior, along with most of his cabinet. "He fully subscribed to the policy of containment," wrote Vietnam historian and journalist Stanley Karnow, "arguing that the line had to be held against 'the relentless pressure of the Chinese Communists'".[11] Faithful to the domino theory propounded by his predecessors—the belief that communism must be countered with force in all parts of the globe lest one successful revolution cause many others—JFK said, "No other challenge is more deserving of our every effort and energy... [Otherwise] our security may be lost piece by piece, country by country".[12] Conspiracists tend to downplay the hawkish nature of Kennedy's foreign policy or dismiss quotes such as these as disingenuous talk used purely to win the White House. In a popular variation, James Douglass argues that JFK did come to the White House as a hawk, but that he experienced a radical shift toward pacifism following the 1962 Cuban Missile Crisis (see Section 4).[13] Whether or not Kennedy's speeches reflect his true beliefs, one cannot deny that they informed his aggressive foreign policy toward communism in Germany, Cuba, Vietnam, and Soviet-supported "wars of national liberation".

JFK was thus quite willing, at least initially, to maintain the course set by Eisenhower and the Dulles brothers to use the CIA's covert warfare programs to destabilize communist regimes and insurgents.[14] While many conspiracists depict Kennedy as a political dove, historians generally agree that Kennedy's policy of détente was an evolving philosophy that emerged later in his mandate, and which was influenced by the failures of his early attempts to roll back communism and doomsday fears produced by the 1962 Cuban Missile Crisis that brought the two superpowers to the brink of nuclear war.[15] In any event, Kennedy quickly endorsed the CIA's plan to overturn Castro, which went ahead as planned on April 17, 1961.

While some conspiracists rightly argue that JFK opposed the CIA's last-minute request for US Air Force assistance, this was not because he disapproved of the invasion *per se*, but rather because such an airstrike would implicate the United States directly. In fact, both JFK and his Secretary of State Dean Rusk feared that a *second* airstrike (they did green light a first one, with disappointing results) could lead to open conflict with Russia and therefore chose the safer option of letting the Cuban mercenaries go it alone.[16] In contrast to those who claim that the CIA deceived Kennedy over Cuba, even scuttled the invasion to embarrass him, the failure of the invasion was in fact due to a collective bureaucratic blunder caused by poor planning, competing agendas, and overstretched resources.[17]

Indeed, the operation was a humiliating fiasco. The invading force—nicknamed "Brigade 2506"—was quickly outnumbered ten to one by Cuban armed forces and local militias. Word of the impending invasion had been intercepted by Cuban intelligence when some eager exiles gave their families advance notice of their return. Other contributing factors include a poorly executed first airstrike that left the Cuban air force largely intact, unexpected foul weather, and a poor location to set up a beachhead—a secluded inlet surrounded by dense vegetation and swampland. The Brigade's transport vessels, unprotected and easily detectable, were routinely destroyed from the skies.[18] Munitions ran out. Hundreds died. Over a thousand were captured. No popular uprising happened. Within three days, Castro proclaimed his victory over the "Yankee imperialists".[19]

Kennedy accepted responsibility for the failure but privately blamed the CIA for conducting a covert operation that they could not keep covert and poisoned his relations with the Soviets.[20] He then fired DCI Allen Dulles and his two lieutenants, Charles Cabell and Richard Bissell, who had criticized Kennedy for refusing the second airstrike. Oliver Stone's *JFK* presents the firing of these men as the catalyst for a murderous conspiracy. But this is based on an erroneous oversimplification of JFK's position on Cuba and his relationship with the CIA. Kennedy was in fact more upset with the operation's shoddy planning than with its ultimate purpose. This is evidenced by the fact that he instructed his new DCI John McCone[21] to initiate a more discreet, but no less draconian, program to get rid of Castro.

Another popular conspiracist argument holds that JFK's National Security Advisor McGeorge Bundy purposefully sabotaged the Bay of Pigs invasion by canceling the second airstrike (the first one usually gets ignored) to make it look like Kennedy did so.[22] If true, it served as a rather paltry attack on Kennedy, who subsequently fired Dulles—Bundy's benefactor—and doubled his efforts to remove Castro (see Section 3). Bundy is another victim of the guilt-by-association fallacy due to his connections with his brother William (a former CIA analyst and future member of the Council on Foreign Relations) and his membership in Yale

University's Skull and Bones society, a popular pool of intrigue. If conspiracists are correct, then it is hard to explain why Kennedy chose to take personal responsibility for the failed invasion, and why he did not sack McGeorge Bundy along with the CIA's "three sacred cows".[23]

7.3   The mongoose is loose

Under McCone, the CIA embarked on a second attempt to overthrow "the Beard," only this time the Cuban Project was to be closely supervised by the White House, Pentagon, and especially by Attorney General Robert Kennedy.[24] This ambitious new operation—code-named Mongoose—engaged multiple agencies fighting on multiple fronts. Its primary aim was to destabilize the Cuban regime through sabotage and propaganda performed by US intelligence agents, Cuban exiles, and friendly locals. The operation was run from an abandoned naval air station south of Miami, Florida, but was directed from the Pentagon by US Air Force (USAF) Brigadier General Edward G. Lansdale. Lansdale was a CIA-connected military intelligence officer with years of prior experience in advertising, who had recently spent two decades in Southeast Asia conducting covert operations (see Chapter 8). Intrigued by the man's expertise in psychological warfare, the Kennedy brothers thought Lansdale's avant-garde brand of "psyops" would prove more successful than Dulles' traditional military tactics to remove Castro from power.

Lansdale had an arsenal of strange and unorthodox ideas, many of which he had tested, with varying levels of success, against communists in Indonesia, the Philippines, and South Vietnam. A fervent amateur anthropologist, Lansdale believed that manipulating popular culture rather than using brute force was the key to produce an effective counterrevolution. Hence, "psyops" used against Castro had to adapt to Cuban realities. One of the zaniest tactics Lansdale would propose, revealing his sense of theatrics and Madison avenue training, was to try to convince the island's large Roman Catholic population that Jesus Christ's return to earth was imminent, but that this would only occur if they got rid of Fidel and brought in more pious leaders. This plan could be achieved, he proposed, by using an American submarine to fire star shells over Havana on All Souls' Day while spreading rumors that Christ was avoiding Cuba because of the communists still in power. He called it "Elimination by Illumination". "Once Mongoose got under way," writes journalist and historian Max Boot, "the flow of far-fetched ideas turned into a deluge".[25] Other half-baked ideas concocted by Lansdale's staff included airdropping real one-way plane tickets to Mexico, faked photographs of the Generalissimo in compromising situations, and toilet paper with an imprint of Castro's face. Some less whimsical suggestions proposed by an Air Force contingency mill (which thankfully died in the think tank) included faking a Cuban attack on the Guantanamo Bay US naval base, crashing American passenger planes into Cuba and making it look like they were shot down, and organizing fake Cuban terrorist attacks on American cities.[26]

Lansdale—who is nicknamed "General Y" in Oliver Stone's *JFK*—is portrayed in the film as a rogue agent under the orders of his former colleague Allen Dulles, who orders "Y" to organize Kennedy's assassination. This storyline is based almost entirely on anecdotal evidence reported by Colonel L. Fletcher Prouty, a former Pentagon colleague of Lansdale's who reinvented himself as a conspiracy "expert" (see Chapter 4). Prouty, who served as a creative consultant to Oliver Stone, is portrayed in the film as "Mr. X," a Deep-Throat-type whistleblower who informs the film's protagonist, a fast and loose adaptation of New Orleans District Attorney Jim Garrison (see Chapter 4), that "General Y" had Kennedy murdered on behalf of the CIA and Joint Chiefs of Staff. Both Prouty's writings and Stone's film make the bold assertion that the CIA initiated Operation Mongoose without White House approval, and that Kennedy's attempt to shut it down precipitated his assassination.[27]

Sadly, these and other authors completely disregard the close collaboration that took place between Bobby Kennedy and Ed Lansdale,[28] and the fact that the Kennedy brothers were among Lansdale's biggest fans in Washington at a time when his "James Bond" appeal, created by a novel both brothers had loved (*The Ugly American*, 1958), had begun to grow stale at the Pentagon and CIA.[29] Contrary to Prouty's assertions, Lansdale was Robert F. Kennedy (RFK)'s *homme de confiance* in the intelligence community. "Bobby was enamored with the mythic Lansdale," writes Laurence Leamer, "a sterling proponent of a passionate plan to have the Cubans fight their own battles, a plan that resonated perfectly with Bobby's own thinking".[30] Indeed, Bobby frequently disregarded the advice of his other advisors, who in turn feared that Lansdale was setting up another Cuban fiasco.[31] Bobby's admiration for Lansdale was equally shared by the President. "JFK loved new and faddish military ideas," explains historian Jonathan Nashel, "especially ones that offered alternatives to increased bombing campaigns and more American soldiers […]. 'It was as if Brigadier General Edward Lansdale had been invented with the Kennedy Administration in mind'".[32] Ironically, the Cuban operation relied on the same kinds of terrorist tactics—infiltration, subversion, and intimidation—for which President Kennedy had publicly condemned Latin American communists.[33] But this hypocrisy went unnoticed by most Americans, who for another decade remained largely ignorant of Kennedy's secret war on Castro.

Operation Mongoose quickly became "the largest covert project in history, involving close to five hundred full-time CIA operatives, part-time agents, Defense Department, State Department, and USIA personnel, and several thousand Cubans as well".[34] It was for most of its life an RFK–Lansdale collaboration. But the two men made inflated assumptions of pro-American sentiment in Cuba, unlike DCI McCone who proved far more pessimistic concerning the chance of a Cuban counterrevolution.[35] McCone's misgivings, however, would fall on deaf ears. Supported by Bobby, Ed Lansdale "showed no awareness that Castro might have been a popular leader and arrogantly assumed that most Cubans would welcome this new 'revolution' imposed by the hated gringos".[36] Hence, "Bobby's Project" failed to succeed; the Castro regime was far too resilient, and popular, to dislodge with propaganda and fireworks.

In the end, infiltration and intimidation proved no more effective than invasion, even with this unprecedented mobilization of resources. It did, however, foment a growing indignation among Castro supporters—which included an obscure ex-Marine, defector, and pro-Castro Marxist named Lee Harvey Oswald, who spent much of this time reading communist newspapers that frequently discussed US-sponsored attacks in Cuba.

7.4 My enemy's enemy is my friend

As late as September 4, 1962, President Kennedy remained determined to meet any Cuban hostilities against the United States or its allies with any means, including military action:

> It continues to be the policy of the United States that the Castro regime will not be allowed to export its aggressive purposes by force or the threat of force. It will be prevented by whatever means may be necessary from taking action against any part of the Western Hemisphere. The United States, in conjunction with other Hemisphere countries, will make sure that while increased Cuban armaments will be a heavy burden to the unhappy people of Cuba themselves, they will be nothing more.[37]

But things changed less than six weeks later when it became obvious that this policy could goad the Soviets into a thermonuclear war. On October 14, 1962, a U-2 spy plane photographed Soviet nuclear missiles sitting in Cuba, ready to be deployed. Kennedy, who until then had balked at appeasing Castro, considered calling an airstrike. He quickly realized that killing Soviet troops who were stationed on the island, as well as the possibility of not destroying all targets, could trigger an immediate nuclear retaliation. The 13-day crisis that followed brought the two superpowers to the brink of war, forcing the Kennedy administration to give up the option of ever again invading Cuba. It was a hard sell with the Joint Chiefs of Staff—particularly Generals Maxwell Taylor and Curtis Lemay—who had pushed for a massive airstrike and land invasion.[38] But the administration's lack of certainty concerning the readiness of these missiles, and the likelihood that the Soviets would likely help their ally against a US attack, compelled the President to order "quarantine" (naval blockade) of the island instead of an airstrike, while Bobby pursued third-party negotiations with Soviet premier Nikita Khrushchev.

A tense naval cat-and-mouse game ensued, with American vessels shadowing Soviet transports and submarines, trying to prevent them from reaching the Cuban coast.[39] Naval maneuvers were monitored closely and directed from the White House. Because it was an essentially defensive strategy, the quarantine forced the Soviets to decide whether or not to shoot first. This gave the President's actions added legitimacy under international law. In the end, Soviet First Secretary Khrushchev withdrew the nuclear arsenal, but not without a formal guarantee that the United States would never again invade Cuba. The President acquiesced.

He also agreed—secretly, unbeknownst to his military staff—to dismantle outdated Jupiter missiles in Turkey.[40] Although relations between the Kennedy White House and the Joint Chiefs were soured by this crisis, few could deny that the Kennedy brothers had successfully brokered a peace without shame. Many historians believe this was Kennedy's finest achievement, though one could equally argue that the whole affair was provoked by JFK's Cuban Project.

The Cuban Missile Crisis of October 1962 forced the Kennedys to develop a more targeted strategy for bringing down Castro, one that involved cold-blooded murder. Conspiracists often claim that concessions made to Castro and Khrushchev prove JFK wanted to normalize relations with Cuba and bring an end to the Cold War, leading the Joint Chiefs, the CIA, and the "military industrial complex" to murder him. Indeed, a popular example is the black and white Washington backroom scene in Oliver Stone's *JFK*, in which the Joint Chiefs, Defense bureaucrats, and Vice President Johnson hatch a conspiracy amidst swirling cigar smoke and free-flowing liquor. Again, such theorists deliberately ignore all the Kennedy-sanctioned plots against Castro that continued until his assassination, or else they insist these were part of a rogue CIA program. "Horrified by the specter of nuclear annihilation," writes conspiracist peace activist and Catholic mystic James Douglass,

> Kennedy gradually turned away from his long-held Cold Warrior beliefs and toward a policy of lasting peace. But to the military and intelligence agencies in the United States, who were committed to winning the Cold War at any cost, Kennedy's change of heart was a direct threat to their power and influence. Once these dark 'Unspeakable' forces recognized that Kennedy's interests were in direct opposition to their own, they tagged him as a dangerous traitor, plotted his assassination, and orchestrated the subsequent cover-up.[41]

Few would contest that Kennedy exercised more caution than his military advisors during the Missile Crisis. But the logical leap made by Douglass and others, who assume that disagreeing with the President's tactics implies planning to murder him, is not historically factual. Indeed, JFK did express concern at the Joint Chiefs' confidence in destroying all Cuban missiles in a single airstrike, but in this, he was not alone. Many of Kennedy's advisors expressed far more caution than JFK or his brother. These included White House special counsel Ted Sorensen, Ambassador to the United Nations Adlai Stevenson, and Secretary of Defense Robert McNamara.[42] It would therefore be more accurate to say that the hawkish and dovish arms of the Kennedy administration were at odds, with the President trying to forge a consensus between the two. In the end, he opted for the strongest *defensive* response, which was a naval blockade. Indeed, even Bobby Kennedy was reluctantly compelled to temper his own position, which was initially closely aligned with the hawks.[43]

James Douglass, Oliver Stone, and Fletcher Prouty, among others, frequently cite Kennedy's June 10, 1963, Commencement Address at American University as evidence of a change in worldview. Conspiracists even quote it as proof that JFK was now endorsing pacifism:

> What kind of peace do I mean? What kind of peace do we seek? Not a Pax Americana enforced on the world by American weapons of war. Not the peace of the grave or the security of the slave. I am talking about genuine peace, the kind of peace that makes life on earth worth living, the kind that enables men and nations to grow and to hope and to build a better life for their children—not merely peace for Americans but peace for all men and women—not merely peace in our time but peace for all time.[44]

It was indeed a memorable speech, one in which he called for greater collaboration between Americans and Soviets in reducing their nuclear stockpiles and consider their shared humanity, insofar as they "share the same planet," "breathe the same air," and "cherish our children's future". This was certainly one of Kennedy's most inspiring moments, and it does, to an extent, demonstrate his deepening aversion to nuclear war and hope for better international relations. However, it is far from being the romantic utopian mission statement many conspiracists—as well as many apologists of the Camelot myth—imagine it to be. As Kennedy himself stated in passages that are too often ignored:

> I am not referring to the absolute, infinite concept of peace and good will of which some fantasies and fanatics dream. I do not deny the value of hopes and dreams but we merely invite discouragement and incredulity by making that our only and immediate goal.
>
> Let us focus instead on *a more practical, more attainable peace*—based not on a sudden revolution in human nature but on *a gradual evolution in human institutions*—on *a series of concrete actions and effective agreements which are in the interest of all concerned.* There is no single, simple key to this peace—no grand or magic formula to be adopted by one or two powers. Genuine peace must be the product of many nations, the sum of many acts. It must be dynamic, not static, changing to meet the challenge of each new generation. *For peace is a process—a way of solving problems.*
>
> With such a peace, there will still be quarrels and conflicting interests, as there are within families and nations. World peace, like community peace, does not require that each man love his neighbor—it requires only that they live together in mutual tolerance, submitting their disputes to a just and peaceful settlement. [...]
>
> As Americans, *we find communism profoundly repugnant as a negation of personal freedom and dignity.* [...] The Communist drive to impose their political and economic system on others is the primary cause of world tension today. [...] Our commitment to defend Western Europe and West Berlin, for example, stands undiminished because of the identity of our vital interests. *The United States will make no deal with the Soviet Union at the expense of other nations and*

other peoples, not merely because they are our partners, but also because their interests and ours converge.[45]

Considered a whole, this speech is less indicative of Kennedy having experienced a life-changing paradigm shift and more in line with his continuing pragmatic form of Cold War liberalism, which ran through all his speeches since his days in Congress. According to this philosophy, it is more effective to appeal to an enemy's rational self-interest and highlight each other's shared values than force their compliance with saber-rattling tactics and belligerent rhetoric, even if one finds their political system "profoundly repugnant". Indeed, it is rarely acknowledged by conspiracists that Kennedy's June 10, 1963, speech made zero moral concessions to communism as a worldview, form of government, or economic system. One must therefore be cautious not to cherry-pick only those parts of a speech that, wrenched from its context, appears to support one's beliefs. Doing so is an exercise in circular reasoning. What JFK was proposing in this speech was not a Soviet-American peace treaty, and even less to usher in a secular messianic age, but a "process," a "way of solving problems," in other words, a practical method, for nuclear powers to manage their future crises peacefully.

A central reason for which countless conspiracists (and nostalgic idealists) misinterpret this speech is due to their inattention to its historical context and purpose, which Kennedy explicitly states near the end of the Address: to set the mood for an upcoming round of talks between the superpowers and their allies to negotiate a Limited Nuclear Test Ban Treaty against all future atmospheric, space, and underwater atomic detonations, the fallout of which had already begun to affect the world's oceans and food sources.[46] This treaty would serve as a first step in "a series of concrete actions and effective agreements," not to "make peace with the Soviets" but to make the world safer from nuclear weapons:

> The conclusion of such a treaty, so near and yet so far, would check the spiraling arms race in one of its most dangerous areas. It would place the nuclear powers in a position to deal more effectively with one of the greatest hazards which man faces in 1963, the further spread of nuclear arms. It would increase our security—it would decrease the prospects of war. Surely this goal is sufficiently important to require our steady pursuit, yielding neither to the temptation to give up the whole effort nor the temptation to give up our insistence on vital and responsible safeguards.[47]

The Test Ban Treaty was signed on August 5 and ratified by Congress in September. It was the culmination of *eight years* of negotiations involving the United Nations, the United Kingdom, Canada, France, the Soviet Union, and the United States, dating back to Eisenhower's first term, a process which Kennedy supported since his days in the Senate—more evidence that this speech and the Treaty it promoted represented continuity, not a sudden change, in JFK's foreign policy goals.[48] If anyone suffered a paradigm shift as a result of the Cuban Missile

Crisis, it was Soviet Premier Nikita Khrushchev who, for the first time, since the Test Ban Treaty negotiations began in 1955, had finally become conciliatory.

Was this enough reason to have Kennedy murdered? When we consider that all subsequent Cold War presidents from Johnson to Bush signed bilateral and multilateral accords with enemy nations to limit nuclear arms, Douglass' thesis becomes unspeakably vacuous.

Kennedy biographers generally agree that the most reluctant people in Washington to relinquish the right to liberate Cuba were the Kennedy brothers, who continued after the Missile Crisis to fixate on bringing down Castro's regime despite JFK's promise never to invade the island again.[49] Nor did either brother consider that promise to mean they could not get rid of Castro in other ways. Indeed, they both returned to it like boys taunting a badger. "There was probably no one more determined," writes Leamer, "no one more willful in his resolve, no one more obsessed with Castro, and no one more committed to his downfall than the president's own brother".[50] Months after the missile Crisis, President Kennedy restated his resolve to "move on Cuba if it should be in our national interest [...] and to be ready to move with all possible speed".[51]

Operation Mongoose would therefore continue after October 1962 and endure until the end of the President's tenure. However, it grew frustratingly apparent to the Kennedy White House that to be truly effective, Mongoose would eventually require direct US military involvement, which would likely provoke another crisis with the USSR. The secret war on Cuba was also beginning to degenerate into a public relations time bomb when Cuban émigrés and local mercenaries with ties to the Mongoose project began operating on their own initiative, fomenting "international vigilantism in the waters off Florida" against Cuban and Soviet merchant shipping. One such altercation, which occurred in March 1963, forced the administration to tighten its control over these unruly civilian military "contractors".[52]

Conspiracists have argued that the Kennedys and anti-Castro militias were at odds with each other, leading the latter to murder the former. One of their alleged "proofs" that Kennedy was trying to shut down Mongoose, which the CIA was allegedly running without White House approval, is an FBI raid, ordered by RFK in July 1963, of a paramilitary training camp on Lake Pontchartrain, Louisiana.[53] Such evidence—and the very existence of the training camp—is based on a mistaken juxtaposition of unrelated police operations and second-hand reports collected by Jim Garrison from interviews he conducted alone with Jack Martin, a known drunk and spinner of yarns who worked for detective Guy Banister during the early 1960s (see Chapters 4 and 5). The House Select Committee on Assassinations (HSCA) investigated these claims in the late 1970s and conclude not only that Martin was unreliable but also that no evidence has emerged that Martin or Banister ever had any direct involvement in Operation Mongoose.[54] On the contrary, Attorney General Robert Kennedy had close relations with several high-profile anti-Castro volunteers, including Rafael "Chi-Chi" Quintero and Pepe San Roman. "Bobby was the great patron of the anti-Castro Cubans," explains Laurence Leamer, descending on them for secret visits, relishing their dangerous exploits, celebrating their courage. […] It did not matter that so many of their actions were hurting the innocent as well as their acknowledged enemies and did little more than stiffen the vigilance of Cuban Communists. They were on a sacred quest.[55]

Bobby was indeed at odds with DCI McCone over the Cuban operation, but this was concerning method, not purpose. While Bobby was rubbing elbows with exiled Cuban reactionaries, the CIA director was busy conspiring with mafia henchmen to eliminate Castro (see Chapter 6). These attempts involved trying to murder the strongman with gadgets, like exploding cigars, poison-laced wet suits, booby-trapped conch shells, and hypodermic needles disguised as pens, and enlist double agents from Castro's entourage, including Dr. Rolando Cubela Secades. Members of organized crime, who had more contacts and influence in Cuba, acted as go-betweens. DCI McCone believed that Bobby was impeding these efforts by publicly supporting Quintero and San Roman, thereby publicizing and privatizing the project.[56] McCone therefore encouraged Bobby to reduce his support of the exile brigades. The Attorney General was fully cognizant that the CIA had co-opted organized crime lords to help them kill Castro, and had even approved it, but he personally preferred to work with an army of patriots than with nefarious mobsters.[57] In early 1963, the situation in Vietnam began to grow tense, drawing the President's attention away from Cuba and toward Southeast Asia. But this was not the case for Bobby, who remained fully committed to the war against Castro.[58]

In a historical twist of irony, CIA agents in Paris were delivering a poisoned pen to a prospective Castro assassin the same day a Castro sympathizer murdered the president in Dallas. Had Kennedy lived a while longer, it is reasonable to believe that his plan to topple or murder Castro would have succeeded (though one might also ask at what cost?). Instead, Kennedy's death brought "Bobby's Project" to a close when President Johnson, who had never been very fond of these Cuban capers (see Chapter 9), shut down Operation Mongoose and decided to focus his efforts on rolling back communism in South Vietnam.[59] It is not altogether surprising that no one was more remorseful than Bobby when JFK was killed, who had every reason to believe that his own plots against Castro had hastened his brother's death.

7.5 A thousand paper cuts

How is all this significant? Conspiracists highlight the numerous disagreements that existed between the Kennedy brothers, the CIA, and Joint Chiefs of Staff concerning their dealings with communist Cuba and use this as proof that the President was killed by members of his own entourage. The problem with this sort of claim is that all governments are subject to internal tensions, the worst of which are seldom resolved by the murder of a democratically elected head of state. Indeed, such acts are almost always perpetrated by powerless and frustrated outsiders, not members of the executive. The Kennedy administration was indeed strained by ideological, methodological, and generational rifts. It was perhaps inevitably destined to suffer numerous conflicts between its pragmatists and idealists, internationalists and jaded cold warriors, aging bureaucrats and inexperienced go-getters—many of whom would continue working together in the subsequent Johnson administration. Rather than replacing a single man, entrenched bureaucratic conspirators would have needed to conduct a vast purge of JFK's like-minded colleagues to ensure that the new administration was fully supportive of this violent regime change and willing to betray the man who had brought them to Washington. Among those who refused to serve under Jonson, nothing prevented them from speaking out publicly or anonymously if they suspected foul play.

Far from being seduced by the wonders of pacifism, the Cuban experience reveals that Kennedy was determined to topple the Castro regime even if it meant breaking some laws. In fact, he showed greater resolve to end communism in Cuba than any of his successors, including Johnson and Nixon, whom most conspiracists paint as rabid anti-communists. But neither Johnson, nor Nixon, nor the CIA, nor the Joint Chiefs of Staff, nor the mob, nor angry anti-Castro Cubans would have had much to gain over Cuba by ridding themselves of Kennedy. JFK's promise to never again invade Cuba was not be erased with a bullet, nor was his promise an impediment to future military actions since even Kennedy was ready to violate it should the security of the United States be at stake. He had approved of the CIA's plans to assassinate Castro and had left the Agency largely in charge of rolling back communism in Latin America. Far from benefitting his alleged enemies, Kennedy's assassination allowed the Cuban regime to survive peacefully until the present day by cooling the fervor of hotheads in Washington and allowing the Castro regime to find stability in isolation.

Many conspiracists claim that Kennedy promised to "splinter the CIA into a thousand pieces". This phrase has become a cliché of conspiracist literature.[60] According to Fletcher Prouty, Kennedy was at the time of his death preparing to turn over all CIA covert operations to the Joint Chiefs of Staff, putting an end to the CIA's non-intelligence-gathering activities. This evidence, he claims, can be found in Kennedy's National Security Action Memorandum (NSAM) No.55, 56, and 57.[61] However, NSAM No.57, which was signed soon after the failed Bay of Pigs invasion (and not in 1963), does nothing of the sort:

> Under this principle, the Department of Defense will normally receive responsibility for *overt* paramilitary operations. *Where such an operation is to be wholly covert or disavowable, it may be assigned to CIA,* provided that it is within the normal capabilities of the agency.[62]

In other words, Kennedy feared that the CIA lacked the resources and manpower to perform complex military operations, like an amphibious invasion of Cuba or secret U-2 spy flights, while at the same time maintain "plausible deniability".[63] If Kennedy really did want to "splinter the CIA"—a claim based on a single allegation leaked to a journalist by an anonymous White House staffer—there is little proof that he fostered long-lasting hate for the Agency. Certainly, no evidence exists to suggest that he set out to downsize the CIA once he replaced Dulles with McCone, who was in office over two years by the time Kennedy died.

If simple revenge was the CIA's or the Joint Chiefs' intent, then having Kennedy murdered in a crowd of civilians seems rather risky, and not particularly imaginative for experts of covert warfare like Edward Lansdale. Its short and long-term effects on foreign policy would have been hard to predict. It would also have the foreseeable effect of turning the victim into a national hero. Having him fall from grace through a well-orchestrated *character* assassination, such as by publicizing evidence of his sexual misdeeds with enemies of the state,[64] or exacerbating the anger of white Southern Democrats against his civil rights plan, might have provoked the election of a more conservative president in 1964, such as Senator Barry Goldwater, the Southwestern Republican presidential candidate waiting in the wings. Conspiracists who ignore the Goldwater campaign are either poorly informed or intentionally ignorant of the political context of the period and the precarious political position Kennedy found himself in nearing the end of his term, especially in the South. It was the very reason for which he agreed to put on a series of public relations exercises, which included a certain trip to Texas.

Notes

1 *Why We Fight*, dir. Eugene Jarecki, Sony Pictures, 2005. Quotes were transcribed from "Eisenhower's Farewell Address to the Nation, January 17, 1961," posted on John McAdams, ed.: *The Kennedy Assassination.*

2 Clinton D. Laurie: "A New President, a Better CIA, and an Old War: Eisenhower and Intelligence Reporting on Korea, 1953," *Studies in Intelligence*, Vol.54, No.4, December 2010, *Central Intelligence Agency.*

3 See, for example, L. Fletcher Prouty: "The Fourth Force," *Gallery*, December 1975, *Rat Haus Reality.*

4 "Kennan and Containment, 1947," and "Foreign Policy under President Eisenhower," (n.d.), *U.S. Department of State, Office of the Historian.*

5 Olmsted, 122–3. See also Chalmers Johnson: *Blowback: The Cost and Consequences of American Empire*, 2nd Ed. (2004), *The Sorrows of Empire: Militarism, Secrecy, and the End of the Republic* (2004), and *Nemesis: The Last Days of the American Republic* (2007).

6 CIA History Staff: "Fifteen DCIs' First 100 Days," (n.d.), *Central Intelligence Agency.*

7 "The Bay of Pigs," (n.d.), *John F. Kennedy Presidential Library and Museum.*

8 "October 21, 1960 Debate Transcript," *Commission on Presidential Debates.*

9 "Address by John F. Kennedy, 1961," *Joint Congressional Committee on Inaugural Ceremonies.*

10 See, for example, "Remarks of Senator John F. Kennedy, American Legion Convention, Miami, Florida, October 18, 1960". *John F. Kennedy Presidential Library and Museum.*

11 Stanley Karnow: *Vietnam: A History* (1983), 247, citing Kennedy's State of the Union Address, January 30, 1961.

12 Kennedy Address to the Society of Newspaper Editors, April 20, 1961, cited in Karnow, 247.

13 James Douglass: *JFK and the Unspeakable*, 2008 (preface and introduction, *passim.*). A Catholic nuclear peace activist who paints JFK in messianic colors, Douglass claims

JFK was killed by a caste of warmongers willing to do the "unspeakable" (a term he never clearly defines) to gain world domination.

14 "A Short History of the Department of State: Kennedy's Foreign Policy," (n.d.), *U.S. Department of State, Office of the Historian.*

15 Journalist Arne Hoffman argues that Kennedy's shift toward détente was influenced by German statesman Willy Brant, then mayor of West Berlin, during the latter part of JFK's mandate. See Hoffman: *The Emergence of Détente in Europe: Brandt, Kennedy and the Formation of Ostpolitik* (2007).

16 According to Russo and Molton, Cuban and Soviet intelligence were already aware of an impending invasion following the first—and only partly successful—air raid on Cuban airfields two nights before the invasion (on April 15, 1961). The first air raid was approved by Kennedy. A second raid, requested by CIA Deputy directors Charles Cabell and Richard Bissell, "would point straight back to Washington, thus imperilling the [upcoming] Khrushchev summit and Jack's chance for an early foreign policy bonanza. [...] Politics prevailed". Russo and Molton, 117–9. See also "The Bay of Pigs," *John F. Kennedy Presidential Library and Museum,* and Brian VanDeMark: *The Road to Disaster: A New History of America's Descent into Vietnam* (2018).

17 "The Bay of Pigs," *John F. Kennedy Presidential Library and Museum.* See also Michael Voss: "Bay of Pigs: The 'perfect failure' of Cuba invasion," *BBC News,* 14 April 2011.

18 Despite refusing a second airstrike, Kennedy approved the use of unmarked fighter planes to protect the counterrevolutionaries' aging B-26 bombers based in Nicaragua. But these US-based fighters proved useless as the bombers arrived late due to not having factored in the time zone difference between Nicaragua and Miami. "The Bay of Pigs," *John F. Kennedy Presidential Library and Museum.*

19 Voss: "Bay of Pigs: The 'perfect failure' of Cuba invasion".

20 Russo and Molton, 118.

21 McCone was an engineer and former businessman who previously served as chairman of the US Atomic Energy Commission. While a Republican, he shared Kennedy's concerns about nuclear proliferation and was a devout Catholic.

22 E.g., Fletcher Prouty: "The Bay of Pigs: The Pivotal Operation of the JFK Era," (n.d.), *The Col. L. Fletcher Prouty Reference Site.*

23 *JFK,* dir. Oliver Stone (1991).

24 Bobby Kennedy's hatred of Castro and participation in the Cuban Project is well documented. See Hersh (1997), Leamer (2001), and Russo and Molton (2008).

25 Max Boot: "Operation Mongoose: The Story of America's Efforts to Overthrow Castro," *The Atlantic,* January 5, 2018.

26 These were part of Operation Northwoods, an offshoot of Robert Kennedy's Cuban Project overseen by USAF General Lyman Lemnitzer. A perverse side effect of this aborted project, which was declassified between 1998 and 2001, was that it convinced many conspiracists that the US government perpetrated similar "false flag" attacks on US citizens in the Gulf of Tonkin in August 1964 and on September 11, 2001. The role that the Kennedys played in the creation of such contingency plans is rarely acknowledged by conspiracists. See, for example, Michael Rupert: *Crossing the Rubicon: The Decline of the American Empire at the End of the Age of Oil* (2004).

27 See Prouty's Interview by Dave Ratcliffe: "Gen. Ed Lansdale in Dealey Plaza," (n.d.), *The Colonel L. Fletcher Prouty Reference Site.*

28 Leamer, 562–6; Jonathan Nashel: *Edward Lansdale's Cold War* (2005), 71–5.

29 Eugene Burdick and William Lederer's *The Ugly American* depicted the failure of US diplomats to reverse the growth of communism in Southeast Asia. The novel includes a

character named "Colonel Hillandale," an expert in counterrevolutionary operations, a thinly disguised representation of Lansdale (see Chapter 8). The novel not only inspired Kennedy to appoint Lansdale to Mongoose, but it also inspired him to create the Peace Corps. John Hellmann: "Vietnam as Symbolic Landscape: The Ugly American and the New Frontier," *Peace & Change*, Vol.9, No.2–3, July 1983.

30 Leamer, 563.

31 Ibid., 564, 609–13.

32 Nashel, 14–15 (quoting David Halberstam's *The Best and the Brightest* (1972), 124).

33 John F. Kennedy: "The President and the Press," speech given to the American Newspaper Publishers Association at the Waldorf-Astoria Hotel, April 27, 1961, *John F. Kennedy Presidential Library and Museum*.

34 Leamer, 611. The United States Information Agency (USIA), dissolved in 1999, was a government-sponsored public relations agency that promoted American viewpoints and interests abroad to counter those of communist regimes.

35 Ibid., 566.

36 Ibid., 565.

37 "Statement By President John F. Kennedy On Cuba," US Department of State, *Bulletin*, Vol.XLVII, No.1213, September 24, 1962, 450, read to news correspondents on September 4 by White House Press Secretary Pierre Salinger. *Foreign Relations of the United States, 1961–1963, Volume X, Cuba: Document 411*, January 1961–September 1962. *U.S. Department of State: Office of the Historian.*

38 Leamer, 654–5.

39 Graham T. Allison: *Essence of Decision: Explaining the Cuban Missile Crisis* (1971), *passim*.

40 The Jupiter missiles were already slated to be decommissioned. See Robert Kennedy: *Thirteen Days, A Memoir of the Cuban Missile Crisis* (1969), 95, cited in Allison, 101.

41 Douglass, ix and back cover.

42 Allison, chaps. 4 and 6.

43 Leamer, 658.

44 "Commencement Address at American University, June 10, 1963," *John F. Kennedy Presidential Library and Museum.*

45 Ibid.

46 "Nuclear Test Ban Treaty," (2016), *John F. Kennedy Presidential Library and Museum.*

47 "Commencement Address…"

48 "James N. Giglio: Hail to The Chiefs: John F. Kennedy," Kansas City Public Library, Truman Library Institute, and Missouri State University, March 20, 2012, *The Kansas City Public Library*.

49 Leamer, 653; Russo and Molton, 220–1.

50 Ibid., 662–3.

51 "Notes of President Kennedy's Remarks at the 508th Meeting of the National Security Council," January 22, 1963, *Foreign Relations of the United States, 1961–1963, Volume XI: Cuban Missile Crisis and Aftermath, Document 271. U.S. Department of State: Office of the Historian.*

52 Leamer, 673.

53 *JFK*, dir. Oliver Stone (1991); Jim Garrison: *On the Trail of the Assassins* (1988), 37–43; Ray and Mary La Fontaine: *Oswald Talked: The New Evidence in the JFK Assassination* (1996), 182.

54 David Reitzes: "Garrison Ripples: The La Fontaines and Big Jim," in John McAdams, ed.: *The Kennedy Assassination* (n.d.); and HSCA, Volume X, chap. XII.

55 Leamer, 678.

56 Ibid., 679.
57 Ibid., 675.
58 Karnow, 248.
59 Leo Janos, "The Last Days of the President: LBJ in Retirement," *The Atlantic Monthly*, July 1973.
60 The phrase originates from an anonymous White House source citing a private discussion he had with Kennedy shortly after the failed Bay of Pigs invasion. "CIA: Marker of Policy or Tool?," *New York Times*, April 25, 1966. See also Craig Frizzell and Magen Knuth: "Mortal Enemies? Did President Kennedy Plan on Splintering the CIA?," in McAdams, ed.: *The Kennedy Assassination* (n.d.).
61 Prouty: "Lyndon B. Johnson, John F. Kennedy and the Great American Coup D'Etat," (n.d.), *The Col. L. Fletcher Prouty Reference Site*.
62 "National Security Action Memorandum No. 57: Responsibility for Paramilitary Operations, 06/28/1961" (Emphasis added), *U.S. National Archives*.
63 Kennedy re-assigned the U-2 spy flights to the US Air Force on account of the crash of Francis Gary Powers' U-2 plane over the Soviet Union in May 1960. According to journalist Max Holland, citing a declassified 1998 CIA publication (Pedlow and Welzenbach: "The CIA and the U-2 Program, 1954–1974," 207–9):

> Because the administration was anxious to preserve 'plausible deniability' in case of an incident, responsibility for the U-2 mission was shifted from the CIA to the Strategic Air Command. A cover story involving a regular air force pilot was deemed marginally more credible and signified how dread of another U-2 incident was still greater than any concern about new reports of SSMs [i.e.: Surface-to-surface missiles, in Cuba].
>
> *Holland: "The 'Photo Gap' that Delayed Discovery of Missiles,"* Studies in Intelligence, *Vol. 49, No. 4, 2009, (note 79),* Central Intelligence Agency.

64 Inge Arvad, a Danish journalist and former love interest of Adolf Hitler, and Ellen Rometsch, a suspected East German communist party member who was believed by the FBI to be a Stasi informant, were two of Kennedy's mistresses—not to mention Judith Campbell Exner, a consort of Chicago mobster Sam Giancana (see Chapter 6).

8

DOMINOES AND DICTATORS

The Pentagon and the war in Vietnam

8.1 War, war, what is it good for?

One cannot put the topic of motive to rest without addressing a central conspiracist argument: that Kennedy died for trying to withdraw US troops from Vietnam.[1] This claim stands in stark opposition to authoritative historical documents suggesting that Vietnam, unlike Cuba or West Berlin, remained a peripheral concern of the Kennedy White House until its final weeks. According to Jack Valenti, special advisor to President Lyndon B. Johnson (LBJ) during the months that followed the assassination, "Vietnam at the time was a cloud no bigger than a man's fist on the horizon. We hardly discussed it because it wasn't worth discussing".[2] As we will see, the conspiracists' overblown emphasis on Vietnam as the fulcrum of JFK's murder is largely due to their personal anxieties about the war and less to the historical evidence.

The Vietnam War, or Second Indochina War to be more precise, did not officially begin until the August 1964 Gulf of Tonkin incident, a naval skirmish between US warships and North Vietnamese torpedo boats that provoked LBJ to escalate US military operations in South Vietnam—events that gave rise to many conspiracy claims, some of which turned out to be partly right.[3] The fact that Johnson committed over two million troops to that war effort, that it was structured as a defensive "police action" with unclear objectives, and that 58,000 American deaths resulted from it, in addition to two million Vietnamese killed, would make it the most unpopular war in American history.[4] Many future JFK buffs were deeply affected by this conflict. Some had been former military officers (Colonel L. Fletcher Prouty), disgruntled veterans (Oliver Stone, James Fetzer), or left-wing civil libertarians outraged by the draft and US-inflicted atrocities (Mark Lane, James Douglass). However, the Vietnam War angle was slow to emerge in JFK conspiracy lore, largely because the growing unpopularity of the war led many of

DOI: 10.4324/9781003222460-10

its opponents to speculate only toward the end of the conflict (during the early to mid-1970s) that the conflict might have ended much sooner, or not happened at all, had Kennedy remained in office.[5] The problem with this line of reasoning, in addition to its largely speculative nature, is that it tends to ignore, bend, or completely distort major historical facts about Kennedy's Vietnam policy.

According to L. Fletcher Prouty, the CIA—more loyal to the Pentagon than Kennedy—planned and carried out his assassination because he was planning a full withdrawal of US troops from Vietnam, thereby shutting down a multibillion dollar warmongering racket run by the Joint Chiefs of Staff on behalf of private weapons contractors.[6] Due to his status as a decorated veteran, a first-hand observer of covert operations, and his personal acquaintances with high-ranking military and CIA figures during the Kennedy years, Prouty is not easy to dismiss as a figure of authority, at least not at first glance. His detailed descriptions of classified documents and secret operations also make him a fascinating storyteller. He is, in a way, the closest thing to a whistleblower the JFK buffs have on their side.

Unfortunately, Prouty's trove of classified secrets has allowed him to make many unsubstantiated claims that turned out to be false.[7] His tendency to cite private conversations that cannot be verified requires his readers to accept his many claims on faith. Many of Prouty's opponents attack his credibility as a friend of right-wing cranks and racists, often resorting to the guilt-by-association fallacy.[8] This chapter will instead focus on assessing the credibility of three of Prouty's major claims: (a) that Kennedy planned to withdraw all military personnel from that country in his second term, thereby ending the conflict; (b) that US involvement in Vietnam had been secretly planned nearly *20 years* prior to Kennedy's assassination; and (c) that had Kennedy not been killed the Vietnam War would never have happened. To do so, we must first consider the historical context.

8.2 The heat is on in Saigon

From 1885 to 1954, Vietnam was a province of French Indochina, a colony rich in natural resources, especially rubber. The French authorities were temporarily expelled during World War II by the Imperial Japanese forces, who were themselves opposed by the Viet Minh, a nationalistic communist militia founded and led by Ho Chi Minh. When France reasserted its authority over its lost Asian colonies following the end of the war, it became the new target of the Viet Minh and was defeated in a historic battle at Dien Bien Phu. In 1954, the two sides signed a peace treaty in Geneva that granted independence to Vietnam, Laos, and Cambodia as separate states and separated Vietnam into a northern communist state friendly to China and a southern capitalist state supported by France (and then increasingly by the United States). These agreements, which did not include the United States as a signatory, called for a national election to be held in 1956 to establish a single unified Vietnam.[9]

Until then, southern Vietnam had been largely agrarian and Buddhist. It was flooded following the Geneva Accords with over a million northern migrants—more than three quarters of whom were Catholic Christians hostile to the Marxist regime in Hanoi.[10] The pro-French emperor Bao Dai, a corrupt and inefficient despot more interested in gambling and women than politics, was ousted in 1955 by Ngo Dinh Diem, a zealous Catholic nationalist. Diem's rise to power was engineered with the help of American intelligence operatives, namely Edward Lansdale (see Chapter 7), and an eyebrow-raising 98% majority in a manipulated referendum. Diem quickly proved no less autocratic than the ex-emperor and jealously guarded his power by delegating positions of power through nepotism. He and his brother Ngo Dinh Nhu (Diem's chief of intelligence) alienated the Buddhist peasantry by harassing and torturing suspected communist radicals—who called themselves the National Liberation Front of South Vietnam, but which Diem contemptuously nicknamed the "Viet Cong"—and herding thousands of peasants into *agrovilles* (later called "strategic hamlets"). Designated as safe zones from communist infiltrators, *agrovilles* were in reality cloistered work camps that disrupted long-standing cultural traditions like ancestor worship and land tenure customs.[11] Inversely, Diem initiated no significant social reforms and resisted American pressures to fight government corruption. "He channeled the bulk of U.S. Aid into his own priority, South Vietnam's military and police machinery, leaving only a small fraction for economic development," writes Stanley Karnow, "and he was less interested in building an army to fight Vietcong guerillas than in forming conventional units that would protect him against his rivals in Saigon".[12] Diem's methods invited several assassination attempts by anti-communist rivals. To his American allies, Diem was a friendly but unpredictable tyrant, "a puppet who pulled his own strings".[13]

The gradual replacement of the French presence by the Americans was not altogether sinister, given recent communist revolutions in North Korea (1945) and China (1949) and to the "domino theory" popular among all political factions in Washington at the time.[14] For these reasons, the United States saw itself compelled to support French colonial authorities before 1954 and the Diem regime afterward. This came in the form of financial aid, intelligence gathering, weaponry, and "military advisors"—an ambiguous phrase that suggested a noncombat role for US military personnel who, by the time Kennedy came to office, were frequently taking part in armed incursions against the Viet Cong in violation of the Geneva Accords.[15]

Despite Diem's verbal support for democracy, the election decreed by the Geneva Accords never took place. This was, first, because Diem refused to recognize the Viet Cong, Viet Minh, and North Vietnamese government as legitimate entities, and second, because he feared (with good reason) that the rising popularity of communism among the southern peasantry and working class might lead to a unified and democratically legitimated communist state. Diem's intransigence pleased President Eisenhower and his Secretary of State John Foster Dulles, who in the wake of an unsuccessful attempt to push communists out of Korea had pledged support to Diem's regime as the bulwark of democracy in the region. But in doing this, they knowingly turned a blind eye to the corrupt machinations of the Ngo oligarchy and the growing opposition to Diem, including among anti-communists.

When Kennedy took office, Eisenhower warned him to watch out for Laos, a potential powder keg, believing South Vietnam was stable.[16] This was echoed by members of Kennedy's administration, including Secretary of Defense Robert McNamara, Secretary of State Dean Rusk, and high-ranking Pentagon officials such as Generals Maxwell Taylor and Paul Harkins, who through a militaristic lens saw Vietnam as an anti-communist success story. This was also the view of General Lansdale, whom the Kennedy brothers trusted. This skewed optimism toward South Vietnam's political situation shaped US foreign policy in the region for the first two years of the Kennedy administration, leading many to believe that a short but significant injection of money, troops, and materiel would lead Vietnam to become a stable American-like republic before the end of the 1960s. As Karnow observed, Kennedy's cabinet and advisors, "like industrial managers," were already planning a timetable for reduced American assistance as early as 1962. "The word 'victory' now popped up in many utterances made by prominent American military and civilian officials".[17] Talk of withdrawing US troops from Vietnam must therefore be put in perspective. Such plans were discussed in conjunction with a *massive, short-term influx* of US military assistance, based on the belief that an aggressive counter-insurgency program would ensure a quick and decisive victory over the Viet Cong. "JFK was a strong believer in guerilla and counterinsurgency warfare," write Miller and Wainstock, "and found in General Maxwell Taylor a military advisor and leader who thought along the same lines".[18] But Kennedy's optimism would wane during his third year in office.

During the late 1950s, Senator John Kennedy had been a vocal proponent of both the domino theory and the Diem regime. Diem's Catholic-inspired anti-communism, and Brigadier General Lansdale's advocacy on his behalf, made Diem politically endearing to Senator Kennedy.[19] Once in office, however, he began to see Diem's nepotism and intransigence as an impediment to the survival of the South Vietnamese republic. He wasn't alone. A growing number of civilian advisors within the State Department and CIA, as well as Henry Cabot Lodge, Kennedy's recently appointed ambassador in Saigon, and Senate majority leader Mike Mansfield, his former colleague, expressed increasing pessimism about Diem. Such individuals advised Kennedy to cut off support for Diem, who had so alienated his own population and military leaders that supporting him any longer could only increase support for the Viet Cong.[20] According to these critics of Diem, the war in Vietnam was primarily cultural. Winning it requires a long-term strategy that combined government reforms and social policies aimed at winning the hearts and minds of the South Vietnamese to lessen the appeal of revolutionary Marxism. Opinions within the Kennedy administration were thus divided between two factions: a group of optimists, largely within the Defense Department and Pentagon, who saw Diem's regime and increased military strength as a recipe for rapid success, and a group of pessimists, largely in the White House and State Department, who favored a change in leadership and a thorough reform of the state apparatus.[21] It was a complex debate with no unifying solution, writes Karnow, "both sides realized that it was a mixture, but they disagreed over emphasis".[22] "In this crisis," Leamer adds,

"Kennedy [...] was overseeing a petty, preening bureaucratic warfare in which egos and personal ambitions outweighed the crucial issues that his administration faced".[23]

As he did with Cuba, Kennedy wavered between two entrenched positions dividing his advisors. Senator Mike Mansfield's change of heart following a 1962 fact-finding mission gave JFK much cause to rethink his optimism. Mansfield had previously been a strong Diem supporter and had a major influence on Kennedy's views on Vietnam. Now Mansfield told him that only a costly full-scale war would keep the communists from winning. Mansfield's crisis of faith in Diem was, according to Miller and Wainstock, "the equivalent of a kiss of death".[24]

The decision to maintain or cut off support to Diem haunted Kennedy until the end. He did not want to respond too weakly to the spread of communism but he also did not want to broaden the conflict by engaging North Vietnam directly, which might lead to an unstoppable escalation of force that could trigger a revolution in South Vietnam (or worse). Increasingly, Kennedy moved toward Diem's pessimistic opponents. The problem was compounded by the fact that Diem had no likely successor able to outcharm the Viet Cong.

As long as the ARVN (Army of the Republic of [South] Viet Nam) continued to function with minimal US assistance, Kennedy preferred not to tinker with the Saigon power structure. The President's ambivalence was palpable in a September 2, 1963, TV interview he gave to anchorman Walter Cronkite. "I don't think that unless a greater effort is made by the [Vietnamese] government to win popular support that the war can be won out there," he told the journalist who, less than three months later, would announce his death to the nation. "In the final analysis, it is their war. They are the ones who have to win it or lose it". This excerpt appears in Oliver Stone's *JFK*, suggesting (within the context of the rest of the film) that Kennedy was planning a full withdrawal of troops. However, the film misleadingly fails to include what Kennedy went on to say: "We can help them, we can give them equipment, we can send our men out there as advisors, but they have to win it". Kennedy later added, "I don't agree with those who say we should withdraw. That would be a grave mistake [...] this is a very important struggle even though it is far away".[25] What the Cronkite interview demonstrates, as did other speeches and interviews given by Kennedy around that time, is that the President was in a tight place over Vietnam. Not only was he trying to appeal to moderate conservatives in preparation for the next election, but he was also well aware that voices inside his government were divided, and that political unrest in Saigon was forcing him to decide whether to cut Diem loose through a US-approved coup d'état, or whether this might push South Vietnam into a civil war and a subsequent communist takeover.[26]

The decision to have Diem removed was essentially made for him over the summer of 1963, when urban youths and Buddhist monks took to the streets to protest the Diem regime's brutal crackdowns—with some monks setting themselves on fire. The images captured by the media left Kennedy deeply troubled.[27] It did not help Diem's case that his fiery sister-in-law Tran Le Xuan (better known as Madame Nhu, wife to Diem's ruthless henchman brother) made barbecue jokes to the media: "Let them burn," she said, "and we shall clap our hands!"[28] A group of South Vietnamese generals subsequently approached the CIA to test the American mood for regime change. For the latter half of 1963, Lieutenant Colonel Lucien Conein, a French-born CIA agent, acted as the liaison between the Kennedy administration and these conspiring generals. Getting wind that the tide was turning, the Ngo brothers tried to broker a secret deal with the North. This increased calls from the US State Department to break relations with Diem.[29] Ambassador Lodge, who was given authority by JFK to handle the situation, made it his priority to facilitate the coup, which took place on November 3, 1963, with the tacit approval (but not official endorsement) of President Kennedy.[30] According to historian James Galbraith, the whole operation was symptomatic of a White House that was "fractious, disorganized, preoccupied with American politics, [and] ignorant of the forces it faced in Vietnam".[31] Many of Kennedy's advisors believed that by allowing this coup, public support for democracy in Vietnam would increase and the flow of new Viet Cong recruits would dry up. Ambassador Lodge cabled Kennedy a few days later, stating: "The prospects now are for a shorter war".[32] He could not have been more wrong. Kennedy himself seemed to have regretted the coup almost immediately.[33]

In retrospect, the coup did little to improve the efficiency, transparency, or popularity of the Saigon regime. If anything, it turned an unpopular Catholic oligarchy into an unstable military dictatorship. Since Kennedy was killed less than three weeks later, it is hard to assess how he might have dealt with a post-Diem Vietnam, but it should be clear to anyone with a firm grasp of the historical context that President Johnson's policies, which led to a rapid escalation of America's military involvement in Vietnam, were largely informed by a different context than those of his predecessor. Conspiracists chronically ignore the importance of Diem's demise in shaping the chain of events that followed. "Inefficient as Diem had been," explains Karnow, "his successors were worse. They squabbled among themselves, and the chronic turmoil in Saigon dashed America's hopes for progress on the battlefield. [...] The U.S. commitment inexorably deepened. Diem's demise, then, marked a fresh phase in the conflict".[34]

The overthrow of Diem's regime, writes C.M. Ricklefs, represented an important watershed in Vietnam-US relations, first by putting an end to all semblance of democracy in South Vietnam and turning the Saigon regime into an overtly right-wing dictatorship, further feeding support for the Viet Cong. Second, it caused the Saigon regime to grow increasingly more dependent on the United States, militarily and otherwise, which played into the hands of Viet Cong propaganda, which proclaimed that the Americans, like the French before them, had come to stay. Internecine conflicts between ARVN generals would further mine the regime's ability to roll back the insurgents, triggering calls in both Vietnam and Washington for a large scale mobilization of US combat troops to stem the communist tide—a deepening quagmire caused by the power vacuum left behind by Diem and Kennedy's half-hearted decision to try something new.[35]

8.3   Withdrawal anxiety

There has been much controversy surrounding Kennedy's reluctance to mobilize combat troops in Vietnam. Withdrawing troops (or sending more) was a recurring topic of conversation among his Southeast Asia strategists, but it must be understood within the context of Diem's problematic leadership. To base our judgments of JFK's policies on what happened *after* Diem was removed from power is to misread history anachronistically. Withdrawing a contingent of 1,000 military "advisors" (from a total of nearly 17,000 American personnel),[36] as National Security Action Memorandum (NSAM) No.263 called for on October 11, 1963 (see later), is not equivalent to withdrawing *all* military support for the regime.[37] Besides, the greatest advocates of troop withdrawal in 1963 were the militarists in the Pentagon, the very people whom Oliver Stone and Fletcher Prouty claim were rabid opponents of withdrawal and the president's assassins.[38] As discussed earlier, these believed that victory in Vietnam was imminent and that Diem could finish the job on his own once the bulk of the work was achieved with US assistance. In reality, the situation in Vietnam was worsening, but the data was unclear and misused to serve competing agendas in Washington. Indeed, during much of 1963, the war against the Viet Cong was some days being won and some days being lost depending on whose reports first reached the President's desk: the optimistic militarists or the pessimistic politicos. Kennedy himself was torn because, as he admitted publicly, he was committed to both defeating the communists in South Vietnam and limiting American involvement and casualties.[39] He also believed that the Vietnamese communists were benefitting from spinning the conflict as a war of national liberation against foreign invaders, and that the more American troops stood on the front lines, the easier it was for the enemy to cast themselves as the victims of imperial aggression.[40]

A broad consensus has emerged among leading historians that Kennedy was dedicated to the escalation of force in Vietnam *if and only if* it was required to prevent the communists from taking power.[41] Conspiracists, on the other hand, usually parrot the minority view that JFK intended a full withdrawal of troops from Vietnam during his second term. This is a central premise of many conspiracy theories, one that requires careful scrutiny. It is based partly on the memoirs of Kennedy's advisors—namely Kenneth O'Donnell, Ted Sorensen, and Arthur Schlesinger, Jr.—who claim that in private conversations Kennedy often expressed the desire to withdraw from Vietnam.[42] However, such claims are usually based on unverifiable statements reported a decade or more after the fact (aka: anecdotal evidence), when the Vietnam War had long fallen into disrepute. Conspiracists generally take such reports at face value without considering the possibility that JFK was merely exclaiming his frustration, just as he did when he allegedly claimed that he would "splinter the CIA into a thousand pieces" (see Chapter 7). It is important to note that such reports also represent a minority view among Kennedy's former advisors. Those who were directly involved in setting Vietnam policy, namely Dean Rusk, Robert McNamara, Walt Rostow, McGeorge Bundy, General Maxwell Taylor, Henry Cabot

Lodge, and even Bobby Kennedy, all stated that at the time of his death, JFK was not seriously considering any major withdrawal of troops from Vietnam, not without victory first being assured.[43] The conspiracists' claims are also contradicted by confidential memos and Vietnam reports that would later be leaked with the *Pentagon Papers*[44] and by Kennedy's official communications and personal records.[45]

Several conspiracists claim that Kennedy spoke openly of commitment whilst secretly planning a withdrawal. There is little evidence of this. Historian Marc Selverstone writes:

> If Kennedy was indeed so committed to withdrawal that he was prepared to phase out U.S. troops regardless of the military situation, then we should expect to find him communicating the finality of that commitment to Secretary of Defense McNamara—presumably the key person in on the charade—particularly in a situation where the two of them could speak about it privately. That is not, however, what appears in the documentary record. In fact, given the opportunity to express such resolve to McNamara in private, Kennedy did just the opposite. [...] If there is any "smoking gun" here, it is pointing not at the notion of a back-channel operation, in which Kennedy concealed his policy leanings from his most senior national security advisers, but to genuinely held concerns about the timing and even advisability of a U.S. troop withdrawal.[46]

If Kennedy was, in fact, secretly planning a full withdrawal from Vietnam, it would make it one of the greatest and most successful examples of an American statesman lying to the public. This should, in turn, compel his admirers to seriously question the moral integrity of a man willing to let untold numbers of Americans and Vietnamese die needlessly so that he might secure his reelection. As a political science professor Bruce Loebs argues:

> Had JFK withdrawn U.S. forces in the spring of 1963, [...] the U.S. might not have become deeply involved in the Vietnam War [and] Lyndon Johnson, who correctly believed he was following his predecessor's policy in Southeast Asia, probably would not have reintroduced military forces after Kennedy had removed all U.S. troops. [...] If the Schlesinger-Stone thesis is correct, Kennedy is responsible for the death of more than 58,000 Americans and millions of Southeast Asians. [...] If Schlesinger is right the President willfully sacrificed American lives for political profit. [...] The unavoidable conclusion from this tale is grotesque.[47]

The fitting conclusion to conspiracist allegations that Kennedy had a secret plan to withdraw all US troops from Vietnam—but only during his second term—would be that he wasn't a hero of peace, but a callous opportunist unconcerned by the deaths of thousands. One would further have to wonder why Kennedy was murdered for trying to pull out a paltry one thousand troops when President Nixon would, a mere six years later, begin pulling out a half million. As Loebs points out, "if [Oliver] Stone's premise is true—that the military industrial complex would murder presidents to prevent them from withdrawing US forces from Vietnam—these assassins killed the wrong president".[48]

8.4   Memorandum, Shmemorandum

The ultimate "proof," according to Prouty and Stone, that Kennedy planned a full withdrawal is found in comparing two 1963 Vietnam policy documents: NSAM No.263, drafted on October 11 by the Kennedy administration, and its follow-up resolution, NSAM No.273, drafted by the Kennedy White House but signed by Johnson on November 26, four days after Kennedy's death. According to Prouty, the first document demonstrates Kennedy's commitment to withdraw a thousand advisors by Christmas 1963 and the rest by 1965, while by signing NSAM No.273, Johnson "essentially reversed Kennedy's new withdrawal policy," committing more troops to South Vietnam and covert operations against the North with the intention of goading North Vietnam into a war. "In that document," states Oliver Stone's Mr. X, "lay the Vietnam War".[49] But a closer reading of these documents (and of documents they refer to) reveals that the Prouty-Stone thesis is both historically incorrect and deceiving by omitting information.[50]

NSAM No.263 was a basic presidential approval of the recommendations made in a report authored by Defense Secretary McNamara and General Maxwell Taylor, chairman of the Joint Chiefs of Staff.[51] In this report, dated October 2, the two optimists explain that the situation in Vietnam is improving, that there is no solid evidence of an impending coup against Diem, and that—coupled with US pressure on the South Vietnam government to fight corruption and enact reforms—a complete transition of military operations to the ARVN could be effected in 1965. It explained that the Government of South Vietnam's military program

> has made great progress in the last year and a half, and that this progress
> has continued at a fairly steady rate in the past six months even through
> the period of greatest political unrest in Saigon. The tactics and techniques
> employed by the Vietnamese under U.S. monitorship are sound and give
> promise of ultimate victory.[52]

For this reason, McNamara and Taylor suggested withdrawing a token number of 1,000 "advisors" by Christmas 1963. This phasing out of American troops was not a withdrawal of US support but "an initial step in a long-term program to replace U.S. personnel with trained Vietnamese without impairment of the war effort".[53] This withdrawal would be accompanied by renewed support for the strategic hamlet program and continued use of US military advisors in a supporting role in the war against the Viet Cong.

The McNamara-Taylor report was problematic for Kennedy. According to Karnow, "what Kennedy wanted from McNamara and Taylor was a negative assessment of the military situation, so that he could justify the pressures being exerted on the Saigon regime".[54] He was, after all, receiving a very different message from the State Department and Ambassador Lodge, who believed Diem would oppose all reforms and that a coup against him was imminent.[55] Kennedy therefore approved the McNamara-Taylor recommendations, but with caution. That same day (October 2), the President accepted plans for withdrawing a thousand troops but stipulated that

> the political situation in South Viet-Nam remains deeply serious. The United States has made clear its continuing opposition to any repressive actions in South Viet-Nam. While such actions have not yet significantly affected the military effort, they could do so in the future.[56]

On October 5, Kennedy met again with his advisors to further frame the McNamara-Taylor recommendation for a partial withdrawal. This led to the signing of NSAM 263 (on October 11) which stipulated that "*no formal announcement be made* of the implementation of plans to withdraw 1,000 U.S. military personnel by the end of 1963".[57] In other words, the Pentagon was ready to celebrate victory in South Vietnam and begin the transition to a support-only role in Vietnam. Kennedy, informed by the more pessimistic diplomatic corps, was unwilling to commit to a withdrawal without some confirmation that Diem—or whoever might replace him—was winning the war against the Viet Cong. There is no indication here, in what were then classified memoranda and therefore not a public relations stunt, that Kennedy was pushing for a major withdrawal. On the contrary, he was trying to rein in the optimistic militarists already galloping off to another conflict. In any event, Kennedy's timid endorsement of the coup against Diem is evidence of his preference for a pragmatic long-term strategy. Had he not cared about the outcome of the struggle between the South Vietnam oligarchs and the Northern communists, there would have been no need to worry about Diem's removal. An early pullout, in fact, could have left him solely responsible for the collapse of his regime.

As vice president, Lyndon Johnson shared a closer relationship with the optimists in the Pentagon. This is why he did not hesitate once he became president to endorse the entirety of the October 2 McNamara-Taylor report, *including its call for a withdrawal of a thousand military personnel* by the end of 1963.[58] If the idea for withdrawal had truly been imposed by Kennedy, and if Johnson had been involved in the plot to assassinate him, as Stone and Prouty suggest, then one would expect to see this being reflected in Johnson's Vietnam policies. But this is not the case. Kennedy had been perceived by Southern conservatives as being too soft on communism, which made him show caution toward any serious talk of troop withdrawal, even as a symbolic gesture. But this was not Johnson's problem, who was less afraid of committing himself to this token withdrawal and more trusting of the Joint Chiefs' perspective on Vietnam.[59] Johnson's decision was reinforced by Ambassador Lodge in Saigon, now convinced in the wake of the coup against Diem that South Vietnam could defeat the communists without direct US involvement. This would soon be proven false, but in late November 1963, Washington strategists—distracted by domestic events—could all hope for the best.

The event that would truly lead conspiracists to see Vietnam as the cause of JFK's murder occurred almost a year later, in the months leading up to the next presidential election.[60] Following skirmishes between US navy ships and North Vietnamese torpedo boats in August 1964, the Johnson administration backtracked from its initial expectations of an imminent victory in South Vietnam and pushed for a new escalation. Whether the Gulf of Tonkin incident was partly fabricated by the Johnson administration to gain Congressional approval to engage the Viet Minh directly is irrelevant to the false claim that NSAM No.273 represented a reversal of Kennedy's Vietnam policy. Attempts by conspiracists to reverse engineer JFK's "real" Vietnam policy from the controversial Gulf of Tonkin Resolution (passed August 10, 1964) is both historically irrelevant and another example of the *post hoc* fallacy.

8.5   Elementary, my dear Colonel

The other pillars of Prouty's argument are similarly riddled with logical problems. A good example is his claim that a "high cabal" orchestrated the war in Vietnam to generate enormous profits. Based on a 1945 conversation he allegedly had with an unnamed harbormaster in Okinawa, Japan, Prouty insists that a huge shipment of weapons was secretly sent to Indochina to bolster the Viet Minh's efforts to fight off the French, preparing the way for future US involvement in the region:

> With the early surrender of Japan, this massive invasion did not occur, and the use of this enormous stockpile of military equipment was not necessary. Almost immediately, U.S. Navy Transport vessels began to show up in Naha Harbor, Okinawa. This vast load of war material was reloaded onto those ships. I was on Okinawa at that time and during some business in the harbor area I asked the Harbormaster if all that new materiel was being returned to the States. His response was direct and surprising, "Hell No! They ain't never goin' to see it again. One half of this stuff, enough to equip and support at least 150,000 men, is going to Korea and the other half is going to Indochina".
>
> In 1945, none of us had any idea that the first battles of the Cold War were going to be fought by U.S. Military units in those two regions beginning in 1950 and 1965, yet that is precisely what had been planned and it is precisely what happened. Who made that decision back in 1943–1945? Who selected Syngman Rhee and Ho Chi Minh to be our new allies as early as mid-1945? This is another one of those windows that permits us to see that some decision had to have been made in some detail [by] a power elite; yet there is absolutely no record of who made the decisions and for what purpose.[61]

Not only is this "historical" passage unverifiable and speculative, but it also alleges that a simple harbormaster can have insider knowledge into the secret workings of the US intelligence community and of a global "power elite". Prouty also suggests that this group is so powerful, united, and clairvoyant that it can plan military conflicts with precision decades before they occur. It makes for a simple explanation of the Korean and Vietnam wars, but it ignores the many forces and haphazard events that give rise to and shape such conflicts.

No serious historian could find this account convincing. It elicits instead numerous questions and red flags. For instance, if the members of this elite are gifted with such superior insight, how did they not foresee that Japan would agree to an "early surrender"? How would Kim Il Sung, the *communist* North Korean dictator, have known to invade South Korea in 1950 in accordance with this *capitalist* elite's agenda? How did the elite foresee the surprise French defeat at Dien Bien Phu, or the negotiated 1954 Geneva Accords? How could they know that Diem and the South Vietnam army would bungle the job so badly that US military assistance would be approved by Congress for *four* successive administrations (or did they manipulate Congress as well)? Is Prouty's "high cabal" so insightful that it caused the South Vietnamese generals to plot the fall of Diem expressly so that the war could drag on but were unable to stop the fall of Saigon in 1975? And why was this alleged special shipment of American weapons not used by Vietnamese communists against the French before 1954, and why is Prouty its sole whistleblower? Each of these questions, investigated carefully, defies such a deterministic and simplistic view of the Vietnam conflict. The December 1946 Battle of Hanoi, for instance, was fought by the Viet Minh with an assortment of outdated weapons, including "a hodge-podge of ancient French muskets, old American Remington rifles, British Bren automatics, Japanese carbines, and spears, swords, and machetes as well as homemade [...] grenades".[62] Why then did they wait until 1954 to oust the French when, if Prouty is correct, the Viet Minh had the resources to do so in 1946? The truth, of course, is that by 1954 the Viet Minh was supported by Communist China, which ensured their victory at Dien Bien Phu without the need for American weaponry.

Like so many other conspiracists, Prouty's view of human history is teleological (dictated by necessity), depicting the world's greatest conflicts and tragedies as the product of a single, all-powerful, greedy, and invisible oligarchy that can control the outcome of any event.[63] It also flirts dangerously close with the *Protocols of the Elders of Zion* and other anti-Semitic conspiracy theories that blame rich Jewish bankers for fomenting and profiteering from all major international conflicts.[64] Prouty has merely replaced the traditional Jewish financial consortium (e.g., the Rothschild family) with a faceless Wall Street bureaucracy.[65]

Yet, to be fair, Prouty's argument is not entirely based on falsehoods. Many details of the military bureaucracy he describes are based on first-hand knowledge. And it is true that the United States did lend support to the Viet Minh in the early 1940s, but this was during its war against Imperial Japan, with whom the United States was also at war. It should also be noted that this short-lived collaboration had been solicited by the communist Ho Chi Minh, not decreed by some capitalist power elite. "From an official U.S. perspective," explains Karnow, "[Ho] was then merely a useful expedient, as were so many other local partisans at the time".[66] Such military assistance is reminiscent of the aid Soviet Russia and Marxists in the French resistance received from Western democracies to help them fight the Nazis and is therefore not proof of a conspiracy to draw the United States into a conflict with them two decades later.

Finally, the central underlying assumption of the Prouty-Stone argument is that Kennedy was killed by greedy weapons contractors trying to turn Vietnam into a lucrative war racket. As Stone's "Mr. X" explains it:

> Don't underestimate the budget cuts that Kennedy called for in March of 1963. Nearly 52 military installations in 25 states. Twenty-one overseas bases. Big money. You know how many helicopters have been lost in Vietnam? Nearly 3,000 so far. Who makes them? Bell Helicopter. Who owns Bell? Bell was nearly bankrupt when First National Bank of Boston approached the CIA about developing a helicopter for Indochina usage. How about the F-111 fighter? General Dynamics of Fort Worth, Texas. Who owns that? Find out the defense budget since the war began. $75 going on $100 billion. Nearly $200 billion will be spent before it's over. In 1949, it was $10 billion. No war ... no money.[67]

According to Stone's *JFK*, which here simply regurgitates Prouty's writings, proof that the Vietnam War was triggered by a corporate conspiracy is the fact that weapons contractors made money off it. Of course, the same could be said of the two World Wars and just about every other armed conflict in modern history. This is a very seductive and misleading argument that will enrage any cash-strapped tax-paying proletarian, because it distracts the reader's attention away from the probable *causes* of an event to the more infuriating issue of *who benefits* from it.[68] But what *proves* that weapons manufacturers had Kennedy murdered? Let us consider this argument in standard form[69]:

P1: If JFK had **not** been **A**ssassinated, he would have **W**ithdrawn from Vietnam.

P2: If JFK had **W**ithdrawn from Vietnam, weapons contractors would **not** have made **B**illions in profit.

————

C1: Hence, if JFK had **not** been **A**ssassinated, weapons contractors would **not** have made **B**illions from that war.

P3: But weapons contractors did make **B**illions from the Vietnam War.

————

C2: Therefore weapons contractors **A**ssassinated JFK.

According to Stone and Prouty, it is the fact that contractors got rich from this unpopular war that proves JFK planned to withdraw from Vietnam. But how do we know that the contractors are behind the assassination? Apparently, it is the fact that they would not have gotten rich from the war had Kennedy lived.

Though valid (i.e., the logic follows to an indisputable conclusion), this argument is clearly unsound for several reasons. First, nothing in the reasons offered entails that, to get rich, it was *necessary* for weapons manufacturers to get rich *in Vietnam* (P2), nor is there any reason compelling these weapons producers to *have to* kill JFK to get rich (C1). For instance, they could have sold their expensive technology to someone else, or in some non-weaponized form. They were not obliged to *only* sell weapons of war nor to sell this technology *solely* to the US military. The United States is not North Korea.

Also, the first premise (P1) is not factually acceptable as it is contested by the most authoritative historians (as seen earlier) and rests on the assumption that the final conclusion (C2) is true. This is a circular reasoning fallacy. Moreover, premise 3 (P3) also forces us into a false dilemma, suggesting that had Kennedy pulled out from Vietnam, weapons manufacturers would have necessarily gone bankrupt, and this is clearly not true. Even if that were the case for Bell Helicopter, the claim contains a hasty generalization, as Stone and Prouty do not accuse only the owners of Bell Helicopter of murdering JFK, but the entire "military industrial complex". Bell's financial status is not representative of the financial health of other weapons makers (General Dynamics, Lockheed, etc.) and therefore does not apply to the argument as a whole, which makes it a pointless distraction (a red herring). Finally, nothing in this argument, even if all else were true, proves that the "military industrial complex" is responsible for Kennedy's death. In effect, one can imagine a scenario in which all of these premises are true while, at the same time, an angry lone nut murdered the president. In such a case, the weapons makers merely got lucky. The problem with such a conclusion, of course, is that conspiracists leave little room in their theories for good or bad luck, precisely because luck does not sit well in the conspiracy blame game.

And so, when studied carefully, one can see that this entire argument is rife with logical traps and deceptions that are hard to perceive when one is watching a nail-biting thriller or reading a heart-pumping narrative. One who wishes to evaluate its claims carefully is required to pause the film or put the book down and untangle its claims in an orderly fashion, the way one might unspool a knotted ball of yarn. But most of us don't take the time to reflect carefully on claims we accept to be true. This can be a dangerous mistake.

By assuming that Kennedy would have prevented the Vietnam War had he not been killed in Dealey Plaza, conspiracists live in a hypothetical world where their hopes and fears, not chaotic events or heated policy debates, determine the flow of human events. In doing so, Prouty, Stone, and numerous others take part in rewriting and mythologizing the past. Theirs is not just a case of oversimplification; it is a delusional scavenger hunt, selectively drumming up clues to prove a foregone conclusion. For the sake of argument, let us finish this chapter with two thought experiments that envision a world in which JFK was not murdered.

First, there was no guarantee on the day Kennedy died that he would win the 1964 presidential election. Although Lyndon Johnson would defeat Barry Goldwater handily, LBJ benefitted from the aura of his dead predecessor, transformed into a civil rights martyr by Jackie Kennedy and the media. This beatified vision of

Kennedy prevented Senator Goldwater from overtly attacking Kennedy's moral transgressions and political record, or exploiting the civil rights crisis to his full advantage (e.g., by harnessing anti-Kennedy sentiment throughout the South). On the other hand, Johnson had the background, experience, and public image to successfully spar with the Southwestern populist, while Kennedy's youthful, rich, East Coast Ivy league persona might not have helped him as much against Goldwater as it had against Nixon. As with Ronald Reagan's rout of Jimmy Carter in 1980, or Donald Trump's surprise victory over Hilary Clinton in 2016, one could still envisage on the morning of November 22, 1963, the possibility of a conservative backlash and Republican victory in 1964, followed by an escalation of US involvement in Asia. Meanwhile, a relatively healthy but politically spent John Kennedy would begin typing his memoirs, seated comfortably in his family home on Nantucket Sound, when the first nuclear bomb hit Hanoi.

Second, when Barack Obama became president in 2008, many Americans greeted him as a savior. Indeed, Obama and Kennedy shared many similarities in their ideas and personalities. Both were polarizing youthful figures espousing minority rights, multilateral diplomacy, pragmatic liberalism, and less rigid party partisanship. More than any other statesman since Kennedy, Obama seemed poised to lead the country into a prosperous future or become the victim of a terrible act of violence. Yet neither of these two scenarios happened. Instead, Obama became somewhat of a "normal" if not underwhelming commander in chief, not unlike his recent predecessors. One could even argue that the greatest cause of Obama's descent from national hero to federal caretaker was the fact that he was *not* assassinated but rather worn down by a tough economic recession, an uncooperative Congress, an unwinnable war in the Middle East, and the sort of tensions and frustrations faced by most two-term presidents. If anything, Obama can be commended for the small number of scandals he generated while in office, the most important of which were falsely concocted by conspiracists (including his successor) who claimed he was a secret Muslim born in Kenya.

A similar fate could have awaited John Kennedy had he lived and won a second mandate—though that may be optimistic given that many of his private actions and executive decisions laid him wide open to scandals. In other words, Kennedy might have spent his last years in office not making the world more peaceful, but reacting to scandals, fighting impeachment procedures, and desperately trying to win an unwinnable war in Southeast Asia, while frustrated young leftists took to the streets to condemn *his* Vietnam War. What the world might resemble today had Kennedy not been assassinated is anyone's guess. But it is far from certain that he would have inaugurated the idyllic future conspiracists imagine or been able to avoid sinking deeper into the Vietnam quagmire.

Notes

1 For example, L. Fletcher Prouty: *JFK: The CIA, Vietnam, and the Plot to Assassinate John F. Kennedy* (1995); *JFK*, dir. Oliver Stone (1991); by Peter Dale Scott: *The War Conspiracy*, 1972; etc.

2 Cited in Stanley Karnow: *Vietnam: A History* (1983), 322–3.

3 *The Vietnam War*, dir. Ken Burns and Lynn Novick, *PBS*, 2017; David Coleman and Marc Selverstone: "The Tonkin Gulf," *The Miller Center at the University of Virginia* (2018); Lt. Comm. Pat Paterson, US Navy: "The Truth About Tonkin," *Naval History Magazine*, Vol. 22, No. 1, February 2008, *U.S. Naval Institute*.

4 "Vietnam War, 1954–1975," *Encyclopaedia Britannica*.

5 To reach such conclusions is a slippery slope fallacy: assuming that one event (JFK not dying) would necessarily lead to a particular chain of events (his reelection, peace in Vietnam, peace with Russia, an end to the Cold War, etc.).

6 See Prouty: *The Secret Team* (1973); *JFK: The CIA...* (1992); "Gen. Ed Lansdale in Dealey Plaza," an Interview with Dave Ratcliffe, *The Col. L. Fletcher Prouty Reference Site*; and "The Guns of Dallas," *Gallery*, October 1975. See also Jeff Steinberg: "Interview with 'Mr. X' Col Prouty," November 11, 1992, *The Larouche Connection/Larouche PAC Video Archive, YouTube*, and Chapter 4 of this book and Stone's *JFK*'s scenes featuring "Mr. X" (a Pentagon insider modeled on Prouty).

7 McAdams: "L. Fletcher Prouty: Fearless Truth Teller, or Crackpot?," *The Kennedy Assassination*. See also the critical reviews of Prouty's two books (linked to that page) by military historian David Fuhrmann. See also Lawrence Wright: "The Church of Scientology, Fact-Checked," Interview with Terri Gross on *Fresh Air*, WHYY Philadelphia, *National Public Radio*, February 8, 2011, about Prouty's false claims concerning Scientology founder L. Ron Hubbard's military service records.

8 For example, Bugliosi, 1359–60. On Prouty's background, see Chapter 4.

9 Ricklefs, M. C., et al.: *A New History of Southeast Asia* (2010), 318–21, 346–60. See also Karnow, Chapter 5.

10 United Nations High Commissioner for Refugees: "Chapter 4: Flight from Indochina," *The State of the World's Refugees* (2000), PDF, 80.

11 Miller and Wainstock: *Indochina and Vietnam: The Thirty-Five-Year War—1940–1975* (2014), 119–36. Other reasons for Diem's unpopularity include banning polygamous marriages, making children of second and third wives illegitimate under the law, and using the guillotine to execute revolutionaries.

12 Karnow, 235. See also 256–9.

13 Ibid., 235.

14 See Chapter 7; Nevins et al.: *A Pocket History of the United States* (1992), 564; *The Fog of War*, dir. Errol Morris (2003); and Kennedy's "Address Before the American Society of Newspaper Editors," April 20, 1961, *John F. Kennedy Presidential Library and Museum*.

15 While the number of "advisers" never rose above 800 during the Eisenhower administration, it grew during JFK's tenure to an astounding 13,000 by May 1963. Miller and Wainstock, 141, 146, and 151.

16 Miller and Wainstock, 143; Karnow, 247.

17 Karnow, 267–8.

18 Miller and Wainstock, 146.

19 Leamer, 328–9; Miller and Wainstock, 127.

20 Miller and Wainstock, 148–9; Karnow, chap. 8. A good example is Colonel Pham Ngoc Thao, one of the officers who helped plan the successful 1963 coup d'état against Diem. Thao hailed from an upper-class Catholic background but became a double agent for the North during Diem's rule. It was later discovered that he purposefully mismanaged the strategic hamlet program to help the Viet Cong.

21 Karnow, 255.

22 Ibid., 262–3; Miller and Wainstock, 156.

23 Leamer, 720.

24 Miller and Wainstock, 149.
25 "Transcript of CBS broadcast with Walter Cronkite, 2 September 1963". Kennedy repeated largely the same argument in a September 9, 1963, *NBC* interview with David Brinkley. Both transcripts are posted at the *John F. Kennedy Presidential Library and Museum*. According to Karnow, Kennedy was reciting Ambassador Lodge's last report almost verbatim. Karnow, 290. Lodge was a Republican and Nixon's former running mate in the 1960 election, as well as a Republican candidate in the 1964 primaries.
26 Leamer, 720–1.
27 Zi Jun Toong: "Overthrown by the Press: The US Media's Role in the Fall of Diem," *Australasian Journal of American Studies*, Vol.27, No.1, July 2008.
28 Cited in Karnow, 281.
29 Ibid., 292; Miller and Wainstock, 156.
30 Ibid., 295. Diem and Nhu were both violently murdered. This troubled the Kennedy brothers, who had not given much thought to helping them go into exile. See Karnow, chap. 8, and Leamer, 722–3. Fletcher Prouty's anecdotal account of the coup (with no references) is in flagrant conflict with Karnow's carefully referenced account. See Prouty, *JFK: The CIA…*, chap. 17, and Karnow, 309–10.
31 James K. Galbraith: "Exit Strategy," *Boston Review*, October/November 2003.
32 Cited in Karnow, 311.
33 In a Dictaphone recording dated November 4, 1963 (two days after the coup), Kennedy expressed his misgivings regarding the coup and its intended effects. Leamer, 726–8.
34 Karnow, 278.
35 Ricklefs et al., 353.
36 Galbraith: "Exit Strategy".
37 Kennedy's call for the withdrawal of 1,000 military advisors by December 1963, which President Johnson approved once in office, was, according to Karnow, "a bureaucratic accounting exercise". Karnow, 268.
38 Marc J. Selverstone: "It's a Date: Kennedy and the Timetable for a Vietnam Troop Withdrawal," *Diplomatic History*, Vol.34, No.3, June 2010, 490–3.
39 "Transcript of CBS broadcast with Walter Cronkite, 2 September 1963".
40 This was also Edward Lansdale's belief, which influenced JFK's perspective on Vietnam. See Max Boot: *The Road Not Taken: Edward Lansdale and the American Tragedy in Vietnam* (2018).
41 Selverstone: "It's a Date"; Miller and Wainstock, 151. Some, echoing James Galbraith, argue that JFK was seeking total withdrawal. See Galbraith: "Exit Strategy".
42 Bruce Loebs: "Kennedy, Vietnam, and Oliver Stone's Big Lie," *USA Today Magazine*, May 1993, Vol.121, No.2576.
43 Ibid.
44 Officially titled *United States–Vietnam Relations, 1945–1967: A Study Prepared by the Department of Defense*, The *Pentagon Papers* were leaked to the press in 1971 by Daniel Ellsberg, a military analyst at the Rand Corporation, a subcontractor for the Pentagon. Selverstone, 487.
45 Selverstone: "Kennedy Vietnam Tapes," *CSPAN*, October 16, 2013.
46 Selverstone: "It's a Date," 493–4.
47 Loebs: "Kennedy, Vietnam, and Oliver Stone's Big Lie".
48 Ibid.
49 *JFK*, dir. Oliver Stone (1991).
50 See NSAM No.263, NSAM No.273, "Report of McNamara-Taylor Mission to South Vietnam" (October 2, 1963), and "U.S. Policy On Viet-Nam: White House Statement"

(October 2, 1963), available at *John F. Kennedy Presidential Library and Museum, Office of the Historian of the U.S. State Department*, and/or *The Pentagon Papers*.

51 Prouty states that the report was actually "Kennedy's own production," written by Prouty's superior General Victor Krulak under JFK's guidance and passed off as McNamara and Taylor's own work (Prouty: *JFK...*, chap. 17). While the report could have been drafted by a third party, it is unlikely in the light of other historical data that McNamara and Taylor did not contribute to its contents nor agree with its recommendations. Again, Prouty's unsupported allegations conflict with Karnow's detailed and documented account.

52 "Report of McNamara-Taylor Mission to South Vietnam," Section II,B.

53 "Report of McNamara-Taylor Mission to South Vietnam," Section I,B, Article 3.

54 Karnow, 293.

55 Ibid., 267–9.

56 "U.S. Policy On Viet-Nam: White House Statement," item 4.

57 NSAM No.263, October 11, 1963. Emphasis added.

58 NSAM No.273.

59 Miller and Wainstock, 159–60.

60 As stated in Chapter 7, one of the most neglected historical figures in JFK conspiracy theories is the 1964 Republican presidential candidate Barry Goldwater. The Senator from Arizona had for several months been advocating a tougher stance against civil rights agitators and communists in Asia, to the point of promoting the nuclear option in a first-strike capacity. Though Johnson easily beat Goldwater, it was largely by taking a tough stance against communism in Asia and painting Goldwater as an unstable extremist. Rick Perlstein: *Before the Storm* (2002).

61 Prouty: *JFK...* chap. 1 (n.p.). Len Osanic, ed.: *The Collected Works of Col. L. Fletcher Prouty*, [CDROM] (n.d.).

62 Karnow, 157; Selverstone: "Kennedy Vietnam Tapes"; Dan McLaughlin: "American Arms to the Vietminh: Prouty's Unfounded Allegation," April 6, 1998, in John McAdams, ed.: *The Kennedy Assassination*.

63 See Pipes, 22.

64 Richard S. Levy, Introduction to Binjamin W. Segel: *A Lie and a Libel: The History of the Protocols of the Elders of Zion* (1996).

65 Prouty defines this group as "the great financial powers of the Western World aided by their omnipotent Wall Street lawyers". Prouty: *JFK...*, chap. 1 and Epilogue; Steinberg: "Interview with 'Mr. X' Col Prouty". See Chapter 4 of this book.

66 Karnow, 135–40. See also McLaughlin: "American Arms to the Vietminh".

67 *JFK,* dir. Oliver Stone (1991). Careful readers will notice the anachronism in this scene as Mr. X claims knowledge of future events by predicting how much money will be spent "before the war is over".

68 This is another example of *Post Hoc Ergo Propter Hoc* reasoning ("after this, therefore before this"). Benefitting from an event (e.g., earning a promotion following the death of a colleague) does not imply that one caused their death.

69 See Appendix 2. This argument takes the shape of a hypothetical syllogism ("If (not A) then (W); if (W) then (not B); Therefore, if (not A) then (not B)"), followed by a *modus tollens* or "negation of the predicate" ("If (not A) then (not B); (B); Therefore (A)").

9

"A DAMNED MURDER, INC.!"

LBJ and the Warren Commission

9.1 Lyndon B. Satan

A final and central figure in the conspiracists' long list of suspects is JFK's Vice President and successor, Lyndon Baines Johnson (LBJ). Conspiracists frequently cast Johnson as one of "The Men Who Killed Kennedy," though the nature and extent of his alleged involvement evolved over time and varies from author to author.

Mark Lane's *Rush to Judgment* (1966), one of the most influential early conspiracist manifestos, levels no specific accusation at Johnson, either for planning or covering up the crime, saves indirectly for creating the Warren Commission.[1] Indeed, the reasons for which Johnson became a conspiracy suspect have less to do with his actions in Dallas or immediately after than with his later track record as president. Although LBJ passed some of the most progressive domestic legislation in the US history—the Civil Rights Act, the Voting Rights Act, Medicare, Medicaid, and the Freedom of Information Act (FOIA)—he would become a pariah to many young liberals by the late 1960s, a constituency that should have been among his strongest supporters. This is largely due to the unpopular Vietnam War, growingly perceived as "Johnson's War" and not, as the previous chapter argued, a problem inherited from his predecessors.[2] The American war effort in Vietnam transformed LBJ's image from that of a wily Texas progressive to a stooge of the Pentagon and Wall Street, especially in the eyes of the idealistic young socialists of the New Left movement, a breeding ground for JFK buffs.[3]

Between 1967 and 1969, spurred by highly mediatized Clay Shaw trial (see Chapter 4), a growing contingent of Kennedy buffs began blaming LBJ for Kennedy's murder, the man who appeared to have most benefitted from his death.[4] As journalist Max Holland explains, "Garrison represented a watershed in

DOI: 10.4324/9781003222460-11

conspiracy thinking. Prior to his arrival on the scene in February 1967, not even the Warren Commission's worst critics dared allege that *the federal government itself was complicit in the assassination"*. Garrison's allegations of federal government treachery, and the growing unpopularity of the Vietnam War, ensured that Johnson would be seen from now on as a leading conspirator, albeit as an "accessory after the fact".[5] Both verbally and in print, Garrison depicted Johnson as a CIA puppet and as a power-hungry opportunist.[6] Reiterating Garrison's "memoirs," Oliver Stone's *JFK* depicts a scene in which newly sworn-in President Johnson signs National Security Action Memorandum No.273 that, the film alleges, reverses Kennedy's order to withdraw all US troops from Vietnam (see Chapter 8). LBJ then tells his military leaders: "You just get me elected, and I'll give you your damned war".[7]

Fletcher Prouty resurrected this theory a few years after Garrison's failed prosecution of Clay Shaw. Initially unaware of the plot, he argued, Johnson's position in the Dallas motorcade—where he would hear bullets pass over his head—was carefully orchestrated to ensure his cooperation in the subsequent cover-up.

> The man they had killed was no longer a problem and they had made certain that his successor, Lyndon Johnson, heard and remembered the sound of those guns. It is the sound of those guns in Dallas, and their ever-present threat, which is the real mechanism of control over the American government. [...] He never forgot that sound and its significance. He had been educated at Dealey Plaza.[8]

For Prouty, then, it was "they" (a vaguely defined "Secret Team") who caused Vice President Johnson to ride a few cars' lengths behind JFK in a second open-top limousine—in direct violation, he asserts, of all Secret Service protocols—to send him the very important message that he could either cooperate with their conspiracy or die.[9] Apparently, "they" couldn't just give him a phone call.

Johnson's alleged role in the conspiracy grew more sinister by the late 1980s. Jim Marrs' *Crossfire*—the book that provided much of the backstory for Oliver Stone's *JFK*—describes Johnson as a corrupt politician with a long history of misdeeds that include fraud, graft, vote-rigging, bribing public officials, secret prostitution rings, and contract killings:

> While this ambitiously driven man from Texas most probably did not initiate a death plot against Kennedy, everything known about the man—from the deaths and coverups of Texas scandals, to his continued prosecution on [sic] the unpopular Vietnam War—indicates that Johnson may have had the willingness to join in a conspiracy that would place him in the White House. [...] Johnson certainly had the ability to erase or mask all evidence that might lead to the truth of the assassination. [...] And there can be no question that Johnson, above all others, clearly benefitted the most from Kennedy's death.[10]

Subsequent conspiracists[11] laid the blame squarely on Johnson's shoulders, whom they depict as the architect, ringmaster, and principal benefactor of the crime: "JFK was not killed because of Vietnam, or by the Mob, or the military, or the anti-Castro Cubans, but by politics," argues Scottish conspiracist Robin Ramsay, "The Kennedy brothers backed LBJ and his gang, his financial backers and supporters into a corner".[12] Their collective demonization of LBJ, with narrative variations, goes something like this:

Vice President Johnson was about to be dropped as JFK's 1964 running mate because he was embroiled in two scandals dating back to his days in the Senate, transgressions that threatened to have him arrested and thereby undermine Kennedy's re-election. On one hand, these authors claim, Johnson had partnered with Billy Sol Estes, a corrupt Texas businessman and Democratic Party fundraiser, to perform fraud, distribute bribes, and commit murder (including the killing of Henry Marshall, a Department of Agriculture agent investigating Estes for fraud[13]) to conceal various financial crimes. At the same time, they argue, Johnson had a criminal association with Bobby Baker, a corrupt Senate secretary who ran a clandestine graft and prostitution ring for US Senators on behalf of various lobby groups. Because of this, and because he was likely to be indicted by Congress and Bobby's Department of Justice, Johnson chose to eliminate President Kennedy, take his place in the Oval Office, cut Bobby loose, and shut down federal investigations of Baker and Estes that threatened to ruin his career.

In order to pull this off, Johnson is said to have enlisted a former staffer's protégé, a convicted murderer named Malcolm "Mac" Wallace,[14] who put together an assassination team made up of Jack Ruby, Lee Harvey Oswald, an unidentified young Latina woman named Ruth Ann, and a World War II veteran named Loy Factor—a Chickasaw Indian with a metal plate in his head who was deemed incompetent by the Veterans Administration. The plan called for Wallace, Oswald, and Factor to simultaneously shoot at the President from the sixth floor of the Texas School Book Depository (TSBD), guided by the hand signals of Ruth Ann to make it appear that a single person was shooting at Kennedy. They then left in haste—all except Oswald, who was tricked into getting captured, charged, and then "silenced" by Ruby. LBJ used his connections with the Dallas Police, the FBI, the Secret Service, Congress, and Chief Justice Earl Warren to publicly crucify Oswald, smother the evidence of this conspiracy, and cover up his crooked dealings with Estes and Baker.[15]

There are many inconsistencies in this story, especially compared to the ballistic evidence and witness testimonies describing what happened in Dealey Plaza.[16] It also ignores the fact that Wallace was known to be with his son in Anaheim, California, at the time of the assassination.[17] Indeed, the basic "facts" of this story not only clash with the Warren Commission's and House Select Committee on Assassinations (HSCA)'s findings but also with the claims of many conspiracy theorists who have dismissed the Johnson-Wallace theory as nonsense.[18] The evidence offered by this theory's proponents is also incredibly vague and open to interpretation. These include an unidentified palm print left on a box in the TSBD; the fact that Mac Wallace previously received a suspended sentence for a murder he clearly committed; several "suspicious" accidents (including Wallace's 1971 death in a car crash); and the unsolved "suicide" of Henry Marshall. It also elicits further questions, such as: why would Ruby or Oswald even agree to take part in such a scheme? Why did Bobby Kennedy do nothing about this (or LBJ's other crimes) while he remained in his job at the Justice Department for almost a year after John's murder, when he himself *chose* to resign to run for the Senate? Why did none of the hundreds of witnesses inside and outside the TSBD corroborate any part of this story to the Dallas Police, the Texas Sherriff's office, the FBI, the Warren Commission, or the media? And why did it take over twenty years for this story to be told?

It is worth noting that these sordid murder accusations laid against LBJ only emerged in the mid-1980s when Billie Sol Estes, upon being released from prison a second time, testified before a Texas grand jury that Johnson murdered several of the men Estes himself was suspected of killing, and that LBJ had Kennedy killed with Mac Wallace's help. Estes, who was known by state and federal authorities to be a Ponzi schemer and scam artist, convicted for mail fraud, conspiracy to defraud, and concealing assets from the Internal Revenue Service, told this story in court in 1984 in exchange for immunity from future prosecutions.[19] The prosecutor found no evidence to corroborate Estes' statements, nor was any of Estes' suspects still alive at the time, making his claims unfalsifiable. A 2007 search for Estes-Johnson letters by the LBJ Presidential Library in Austin revealed only a sporadic correspondence between the two men—most of which occurred nearly a decade before the assassination. None involved any discussion of crimes or cover-ups.[20] In effect, little compelling evidence has been produced by conspiracists, including Estes, to prove that Johnson had a close relationship with either him or Wallace. Claims that such evidence, which has never been seen, was hidden or destroyed are examples of arguing from ignorance.

The entire story of Johnson hiring Wallace to murder JFK essentially rests on the credibility of Billie Sol Estes, a convicted pathological liar and con man. Sadly, the court's failure to confirm any of Estes' wild accusations would not prevent him from popularizing this theory by selling it for 100,000$ to French conspiracist William Reymond (*JFK: Le dernier témoin*, 2003), and retelling it in his own memoirs (*Billie Sol Estes: A Texas Legend*, 2004). Estes' fibs were then recycled by Johnson-hating conspiracists like Republican zealot and former Nixon and Trump apparatchik Roger Stone to power his anti-Democrat rumor mill.[21]

Estes'"confession" produced other misshapen offspring. One of the most popular is *The Men on the Sixth Floor* (1995), the self-published work of amateur researchers Sample and Collom—a sign shop owner and real estate agent—who reported Estes' allegations filtered through another self-serving "confession," that of the aging and ailing Loy Factor whom Collom had met while in prison. A brain-damaged man with hepatitis, diabetes, a wooden leg, and a life sentence for killing his wife, Factor regurgitated Estes' cockamamie story to these two authors, inserting himself and the still-unidentified "Ruth Ann" into the narrative without any witness to corroborate his story or any supporting evidence, except for inaccurate recollections of the interior of the TSBD. This would not prevent subsequent researchers like Robin Ramsay from swallowing Sample and Collom's theory whole, calling it "closer to proof than anything which has been discovered before" and concluding that their book "solved the case" of JFK's murder.[22]

The least fictional aspect of this theory is the unsavory relationship between Bobby Baker and Lyndon Johnson during his time as Senate majority leader (1955–60). Presidential historians Larry Sabato and Robert Dallek agree that Johnson, who once called Baker his protégé and surrogate son, had been too close to him not to know about, and probably benefit from, Baker's illegal graft and pimping activities. It is also likely that Baker's unethical actions—and Johnson abetting them—would have been exposed by a 1963 Senate investigation had it not been smothered by the commotion surrounding JFK's death and the Senate Democratic majority's interest to avoid airing the party's dirty laundry in public. In the end, Baker resigned his position as Senate secretary—which merely postponed his conviction for tax evasion, theft, and fraud until 1967—while Johnson dodged a potentially embarrassing inquest.[23] However, none of this serves as evidence that LBJ was involved in Kennedy's murder. As Johnson and Kennedy biographer Robert Dallek explains, Robert Kennedy (who had little love for Johnson) kept a close eye on the Baker investigation and wished to use it as a reason for Jack to dump LBJ from the 1964 presidential ticket. Indeed, the Kennedy brothers did consider various options for replacing Johnson should he be forced to resign over his friendship with Baker, but these were contingency plans, not firm intentions. JFK was also convinced that sacking Johnson without a just motive would likely hinder his upcoming campaign. As Dallek observes, JFK made numerous public and private remarks in the weeks just before his death to the effect that he needed Johnson to carry Texas and Georgia in the upcoming election.[24]

Kennedy Historian Larry Sabato insists even more strongly that JFK had no immediate plans to get rid of Johnson for one important reason. Although Johnson would likely be sullied by an investigation of Baker, dropping him from the ticket over this scandal-in-waiting could explode in Kennedy's face. The President had, it turns out, also benefitted from Baker's favors while in the Senate and as recently as the previous spring when he began an affair with Ellen Rometsch, a high-class call girl being pimped out by Baker to "Washington's best and brightest". Worse, the East-German-born Rometsch was suspected by FBI director J. Edgar Hoover of being a communist spy, a piece of information Hoover shared with the Kennedys and shrewdly promised to keep under wraps—signifying, by extension, that he was keeping an eye on the President's sexual trysts.[25] And so, even if JFK wanted to change running mates in 1964, doing so was likely to cause Johnson, Hoover, Baker, or any other LBJ friend to tell the press of his own indiscretions. We can therefore legitimately wonder whether an assassination attempt on JFK would have been prudent or even useful for Johnson to save his career when blackmailing him would have been easier, safer, and cheaper.

For all these reasons (and more listed later), the far-fetched Johnson-Wallace scenario is not very convincing, which explains its minority status within the JFK literature. The rest of this chapter will therefore focus on more moderate "proofs" that Johnson killed Kennedy, and especially eight allegations popularized by Jim Marrs.

9.2   Missiles from Marrs

A Texas libertarian with a clear dislike for the progressive Johnson, Jim Marrs claims LBJ was roped into the conspiracy through his friendship with FBI chief J. Edgar Hoover and his financial ties to Texas oil barons Clint Murchison and H. L. Hunt, as well as Brown & Root, a construction company that grew wealthy through Vietnam War government contracts (another *post hoc* fallacy). In addition to indicting Johnson based on his character and reputation (an *ad hominem* fallacy), Marrs identifies eight distinct "proofs" of Johnson's complicity. These claims have been widely repeated by other conspiracists. They therefore merit special attention.

9.2.1   In the line of fire

First, Marrs states that Johnson and Kennedy should never have been in the same motorcade: "It was against established security practice for the president and the vice president to be together in public".[26] He is suggesting here that the motorcade arrangement is itself evidence of a sinister plot directed not just by the mob, anti-Castro Cubans, or the military, but from inside the White House.

If true, one should wonder why a secret cabal capable of killing a president and getting away with it would have been so negligent as to produce such a glaring proof of insider malfeasance. Of course, had Marrs acknowledged the reasons for LBJ being in Dallas that day, he might have found himself having to blame the dead president for this conspiracy.

There were in fact numerous good reasons for Johnson to be in that motorcade. He was a lifelong Texas politician with the connections and traction to help an East Coast Ivy league liberal appeal to a conservative Southern electorate. This was, after all, the main reason for which Johnson was drafted as JFK's running mate in 1960, even though the two men were political rivals. And it was also why Kennedy needed him by his side again in November 1963: to woo the Dallas electorate and local party financiers. Moreover, Johnson was not the only other public figure taking part in this public relations exercise. JFK's popular wife Jacqueline, Johnson's wife Lady Bird, Texas Governor John Connally, his wife Nellie, and Texas Senator Ralph Yarborough all took part in the Dallas motorcade, as well as in Houston, San Antonio, and Fort Worth during the previous days. All things considered, it would have been surprising, and evidence of a rift inside the Kennedy White House, for the Johnsons *not* to take part in the Dallas procession.

It was also neither illegal nor unprecedented for a vice president to appear in public with the president. Indeed, they still stand together today at every State of the Union address and many public functions. According to Donald Ritchie of the Senate Historical Office and Thomas Mann of the Brookings Institution, "the

Secret Service, which is charged with protecting the president and vice president, does not have an official written rule mandating that the two travel separately".[27] There is also no obligation for the Secret Service to prevent the two figures from appearing together in public, neither today nor in 1963. Such decisions are taken on a case-by-case basis, and Kennedy was known to flout security precautions when these threatened his image as a man of the people.[28] Marr's premise also rests on the assumption that the vice president is the only heir to power when a president dies in office. There are in fact legal provisions for a long line of potential successors to take power in times of crisis, a list that includes the Speaker of the House, the Secretary of State, and the Attorney General, none of whom were present in Dallas that day.[29]

9.2.2   No ticket for you!

Second, Marrs alleges that Johnson was going to be dropped as JFK's running mate in 1964 due to his connections to Estes and Baker (see above mentioned details) and was therefore motivated to kill him to prevent this from happening. Marrs' uncited source appears to be a 1965 memoir by Evelyn Lincoln, Kennedy's former secretary, who wrote that JFK expressed his desire to replace LBJ with Governor Terry Sanford of North Carolina, a more like-minded Southern Democrat. Kennedy allegedly said this to her for the first and only time on November 19, 1963—three days before his death.[30] Given that Lincoln was allegedly told this in private and did not report it until two years later, it is unlikely that this conversation was leaked to Johnson, who would have had *only three days* to plan and carry out the whole affair. Lincoln could perhaps have informed Johnson herself, but then, she profoundly disliked the Vice President and "never hid the disdain she felt for her idol's successor".[31] She might also have misconstrued one of Kennedy's frustrated outbursts, as when he expressed the desire to undo the CIA (see Chapter 7) or withdraw troops from Vietnam (see Chapter 8), neither of which he followed up on. In any event, the credibility of Lincoln's claim has been hotly criticized by former JFK confidants, including Arthur Schlesinger, Jr. and Robert Kennedy, who would have been privy to any serious discussion of sacking Johnson.[32]

Lincoln's assertion is also problematic, given Kennedy's unpopularity throughout the South. Johnson's name on the ballot had been a key element in JFK's narrow 1960 victory and was the key to win the next contest. The divisiveness of the civil rights movement within the Democratic Party must be kept in mind here. Kennedy could not permit himself to become less popular south of the Mason-Dixon line, not just to win the election but also to avoid further escalations of violence against his civil rights bill.[33] It is possible that JFK would have preferred working with Sanford, but it is far from certain that trading LBJ for him would have helped Kennedy win more votes. Dropping Johnson from the 1964 ticket was therefore more risky than beneficial and would likely have only occurred if Johnson was indicted.

Marrs observes that many in JFK's entourage were not favorable to the idea of a future Johnson presidency. This may be true. But this possibility was still remote when they arrived in Dallas. Indeed, many months before Lincoln's memoir appeared, Kennedy's widow gave a series of oral history interviews to her husband's former advisor and friend Arthur Schlesinger, Jr., now a history professor. In these tapes, created for the Kennedy archives and only made public in 2011, Mrs. Kennedy explains that her husband and Bobby had discussed ways to prevent LBJ from running for president in 1968, after Jack's *second* term (perhaps so that Bobby could run). But she also said Jack made no plans to drop Johnson from the 1964 ticket.[34] Marrs' second allegation, while not necessarily false, is based on no compelling evidence that gives LBJ the motive to kill Kennedy.

9.2.3 Cui bono?

Third, Marrs claims Johnson stood to benefit most from Kennedy's death, establishing him as a primary murder suspect. It is true that Johnson might never have sat in the president's chair had JFK won a second term or been defeated by a Republican, and that LBJ's health worsened significantly during his five years in office, a major reason for which he did not run in 1968. And so, 1964 might have been the only time LBJ could run for president and win.

But this is hardly compelling logic. The critical thinker's response should therefore be "so what?" Using this kind of reasoning, Richard Nixon is the primary suspect in causing Johnson's heart attacks and Bobby Kennedy's murder, and Gerald Ford is guilty of orchestrating the Watergate break-in *and* its discovery by a hotel security guard, *and* pushing through the tax evasion indictment and resignation of Spiro Agnew, Nixon's first VP, all of which had to happen for Ford to take Nixon's position. Indeed, following Marrs' reasoning, anyone who inherits a fortune should be arrested for murdering their parents.

This is not to say that political crimes never occur nor that they can't be successful. But while criminals often do benefit from their crimes, one cannot assume as Marrs does that benefitting from a crime makes one a criminal. Proof of foul play should elicit suspicions, but unproven suspicions prove nothing. As Jonathan Kay remarked, "the death of any public figure (JFK is a good example) always produces hundreds of indirect beneficiaries".[35] If LBJ did conspire to kill Kennedy, the fact that he replaced him in the Oval Office is not proof of guilt. He was, after all, Kennedy's legally vested successor who would have replaced him whether he was assassinated, committed suicide, or choked on a tuna fish sandwich.

9.2.4 Now you see it, now you don't!

Fourth, Marrs claims that by ordering the cleaning and refurbishing of SS-100-X,[36] the presidential limousine, "within seventy-two hours of Kennedy's death," and ordering Governor John Connally's suit cleaned of its gory stains, Johnson exposed his involvement in the conspiracy. "In any other case," he writes:

> this would have been destruction of evidence, since bullet marks on the windshield and blood traces could have provided essential clues as to the

number and direction of shots [...while] Governor Connally's clothing [...] was useless for study as evidence.[37]

Without clearly listing his sources, Marrs makes it difficult for us to verify that these actions occurred as described. But according to the Benson Ford Research Center, which hold the historical archives of the Ford Motor Company:

> The [president's limousine] was impounded for evidence in the weeks following the assassination on November 22, 1963. Soon after plans were made to modify the car in Cincinnati, Ohio and then return it to Washington D.C. [...] Following the assassination of President Kennedy, a committee was formed (originally comprised of thirty people) of six people representing the Secret Service, Army Materials Research Center, Hess & Eisenhardt and Pittsburgh Plate Glass Company. The White House approved a plan for a revamp of the X-100 around December 12, 1963. Work was completed May 1, 1964 and extensive testing was performed in Cincinnati, Ohio and Dearborn, Michigan before the car was delivered to the White House in June. Costs have been estimated to exceed $500,000 and were shared by Ford Motor Company, some Ford suppliers and the federal government.[38]

In stark contrast to Marrs' simple scenario, a conspiracy to destroy evidence in this case is unlikely, given a large number of civilians involved in inspecting, cleaning, fixing, testing, and assessing the costs of the vehicle.

But let us assume that Johnson did issue such a directive and that no one questioned its legality. Does this indicate foul play on his part? While there was some initial questioning by the President's entourage as to whether the Kennedy shooting was part of a wider attack, the FBI had come to a rapid conclusion that Lee Oswald acted alone. Once dead, Oswald could not face trial and the criminal case against him was closed in every practical sense. This does not prove that the FBI did not frame Oswald or participate in a conspiracy,[39] but it is hard to see how this alleged "destruction of evidence" incriminates the new President. With a confirmation from the FBI and Dallas Police that Oswald, now dead, was their only suspect, and the fact that the limousine was no longer being held as evidence for a trial, Johnson was free to have it cleaned of the gore of the murder. With a lengthy FBI report summarizing the evidence that led to Oswald, his rifle, and his prints in the TSBD, as well as a full photographic report on the limousine completed by the Secret Service on November 23—a report that outlined all of the damage sustained by the car, as well as the bullet and bone fragments found inside it—Johnson was legally free to have the limousine refurbished for use by his administration.[40]

As for Connally's suit and shirt, having them cleaned of blood and brain splatter did not render them "useless," because it was the *bullet holes*, not the blood spatter, that allowed the Warren Commission to conclude that Connally's wounds were caused by a single bullet coming from behind, which pierced the back, chest, right sleeve, and left pant leg of his clothing (see Chapters 2 and 13).[41] Marrs is thus guilty of circular reasoning: the limousine and Connally's blood-splattered clothes are only "destroyed evidence" if one first assumes that Oswald did not act alone. Only a convinced conspiracist would see this premise as proof of conspiracy. Forensic experts would not. That is not to say that Johnson did not believe in a conspiracy—in fact he did (see later)—but it does not establish that he was involved in one.

9.2.5   Texas confession: the case of Leo Janos

Fifth, Marrs argues that Johnson confessed to a reporter in 1973 that the CIA had "something to do with" the Kennedy assassination. Marrs takes this to mean that the Agency murdered JFK and that LBJ's knowledge of this proves he was involved. This claim is derived from a frequently misquoted *Atlantic Monthly* magazine article written by Leo Janos, who conducted a series of interviews with the retired President shortly before he died of a heart attack at the age of 64. The part of the interview that Marrs cites is the following:

> During coffee, the talk turned to President Kennedy, and Johnson expressed his belief that the assassination in Dallas had been part of a conspiracy. "I never believed that Oswald acted alone, although I can accept that he pulled the trigger." Johnson said that when he had taken office he found that "we had been operating a damned Murder Inc. in the Caribbean." A year or so before Kennedy's death a CIA-backed assassination team had been picked up in Havana. Johnson speculated that Dallas had been a retaliation for this thwarted attempt, although he couldn't prove it. "After the Warren Commission reported in, I asked [Assistant Attorney General] Ramsey Clark to quietly look into the whole thing. Only two weeks later he reported back that he couldn't find anything new." Disgust tinged Johnson's voice as the conversation came to an end. "I thought I had appointed Tom Clark's son—I was wrong."[42]

As Janos suggests, Kennedy's successor died believing JFK's murder was the result of a possible conspiracy. Many historians accept this as true.[43] But we should also consider *what sort* of conspiracy Johnson had in mind.

Conspiracists often use this interview as proof that the CIA killed Kennedy. Marrs asks rhetorically, "Was Johnson well-aware of such a plot and only mentioned it in later years so that future historians would not classify him as dense and unaware?"[44] Fletcher Prouty calls the "Murder, Inc." passage (now a favorite conspiracist catchphrase) "a statement that had the megaton force of a full size hydrogen bomb".[45] But a major problem with such claims is that the passage is cherry-picked out of context.

First, the alleged Johnson "confession" is cited here in its entirety. This short excerpt of Janos' lengthy interview is the only portion of the article discussing Kennedy's murder and Johnson "confessing" his and the CIA's involvement. The passage is also ambiguous and represents a digression from the rest of the exchange. We should also take note that the interview was published posthumously. If Janos misquoted him, Johnson had no chance to elaborate on what he really meant or correct the record.

Nevertheless, this passage makes it clear that Johnson believed in a *communist Cuban* conspiracy—an act of retaliation against JFK for his attempts to murder Castro using the CIA and mafia (hence the "Murder, Inc." idiom, an oblique reference to a best-selling 1951 history of mafia murders[46])—and not, as Marrs and others believe, a CIA, mob, military, or racist hit on the President, and even less one commanded by LBJ. Indeed, Johnson had been informed long before the Warren Commission and the American public that the CIA had identified a suspicious man in Mexico City named Lee Harvey Oswald, visiting and phoning the Cuban and Soviet embassies a few weeks prior to JFK's trip to Dallas.[47] The evidence gathered by the FBI and CIA did not reveal that Oswald received any order there to murder Kennedy, but neither could they assure the new president that he had not.[48]

The Janos article also demonstrates that while he believed in a Cuban conspiracy, LBJ continued to think, a decade later, that Oswald pulled the trigger, which contradicts Marrs' theory that Oswald was a government agent and unwitting "patsy". If Johnson was actually confessing his sins to Janos, it is unclear why he would place the blame on the CIA and continue to lie about Oswald's "real" credentials. LBJ's so-called confession is thus inconsistent with the scenario Marrs and his colleagues are trying to prove. While this glaring distortion of Janos' article can be imputed to poor reading skills, it appears more like a deliberate attempt to mislead his readers.

9.2.6 Texas hangover: the case of Madeleine Brown

Sixth, Marrs claims that Johnson was overheard plotting against Kennedy on the eve of the assassination by his mistress, Madeleine Duncan Brown. Brown first made this revelation in 1982, over a decade after Johnson died and nearly twenty years after the shooting in Dallas.[49] This conversation, she claims, occurred on November 21, 1963, at a restricted party at the north Dallas home of Texas multimillionaire Clint Murchison, a party to which she allegedly accompanied Vice President Johnson.

> It was a party, she said, attended not only by LBJ, but FBI Director J. Edgar Hoover, former Vice President Richard Nixon, the late oil tycoons H.L. Hunt and Sid Richardson, and a handful of other rich and famous men.[50]

Johnson emerged from a private discussion with these men and, according to Brown, told her: "After tomorrow, those goddamn Kennedys will never embarrass me again. That's no threat. That's a promise".[51] In several talk show interviews and her 1997 memoir *Texas in the Morning*, Brown added other conspiracy-laden allegations, namely that she witnessed a meeting between Jack Ruby and Lee Oswald in Ruby's Carousel Club during which Oswald gloated of having shot at Colonel Edwin Walker. If true, this clashes with Marrs' own claim that Oswald was framed for the killings of both Kennedy and Tippit *and* the attempted murder of Walker.[52]

In recent decades, Brown has become a seductive insider to many conspiracists, but her credibility is weak. Although Johnson was known to have had several mistresses, including in his home state of Texas, and may even have had some dalliance with Brown, he nonetheless had a solid alibi for the time Brown said he was with her at Clint Murchison's home. Johnson's movements on the eve of the assassination are not only accounted for by the media, he was also photographed in different venues alongside Kennedy or with his wife Lady Bird. Similarly, Clint Murchison, whom Brown said had hosted the plotters' reception, had not been living in Dallas for nearly four years.[53] Hoover and Nixon were also seen elsewhere: Nixon was at a downtown Dallas hotel surrounded by Bottlers Convention attendees, while Hoover remained in Washington right through the weekend of Kennedy's murder and funeral.[54]

Since Brown made many disproven claims concerning this alleged party, about the night she allegedly met Johnson in 1949, regarding Johnson's alleged paternity of her son Steven, and given that she was found guilty of fraud in 1988, it is safe to conclude that Brown's ground-shaking testimony, which rests on little more than her memory and honesty, is about as reliable as a long-range Texas weather forecast.[55]

9.2.7 The Warren Kangaroo Court

Marrs' seventh premise and most important impeachment of Johnson is one that is repeated widely. It holds that LBJ appointed the Warren Commission to misinform the public and cover up important facts about the assassination. In this respect, writes historian Kathryn Olmsted, the conspiracists "had the advantage of being partly right".[56] However, their final assessment—that the CIA and government killed JFK—turns out to be wrong. The evidence that Johnson wished to hide, explains Olmsted, had nothing to do with the murder itself but with Oswald's possible motive.

The Warren Commission was created by newly sworn-in President Johnson a week after JFK's death to explain to the confused public the details of Kennedy's and Oswald's murders.[57] Its mandate was not to identify the president's killer—that was already done by the FBI and Dallas Police—but to dispel counter-theories about Oswald, namely that he was a Soviet assassin and claims that Jack Ruby was hired by the mob. These concerns were shared by FBI director J. Edgar Hoover, who feared that multiple public investigations of Oswald were likely to dig up compromising information on state and FBI secrets and get the Bureau blamed for ineptitude.[58]

Many conspiracists claim the Warren Commission was set up by Johnson and Hoover on the orders of a shadowy group of conspirators. Historical evidence proves otherwise. It was the pressures of Congressmen and acting Attorney General Nicholas Katzenbach, Bobby Kennedy's right-hand man, that pushed Johnson to set up a federal inquiry. Fearful that Lee Oswald, a communist defector and supporter of Castro, might turn out to be a contract assassin, LBJ was easily convinced to keep the investigation in Washington, and on a short leash.[59] No proof of a Castro-Oswald relationship has surfaced in nearly six decades, despite the research of the Warren Commission, HSCA, Assassination Records Review Board (ARRB), and investigative journalists like Gus Russo and Philip Shenon. Nevertheless, President Johnson was certainly willing in late 1963 to entertain the possibility that such a relationship did exist, and that exposing it to the public might lock him into a course of action that everyone would regret. The Kennedy White House had, after all, spent nearly three years trying to secretly get rid of Castro. These plots, which were "common knowledge in Havana," had led Fidel Castro to utter a thinly veiled threat of revenge in September 1963, which was reported in many US newspapers, including the New Orleans *Times-Picayune*, which Oswald read frequently.[60] If a public investigation revealed that Oswald was a foreign communist agent who had visited enemy embassies in Mexico shortly before the assassination (possibly to receive his orders), the pressure would certainly mount on the Johnson White House to take immediate military action against Oswald's sponsors—a slippery slope toward nuclear war. It was therefore important that the men overseeing the inquiry be the type that could be coaxed not to expose this explosive evidence.

The Commission would be overseen by a bipartisan group of trusted Washington insiders whose discretion and devotion to the nation's best interests could be assumed (see Chapter 2). Despite conspiracist claims that these men deliberately covered up evidence of the "real" assassins, the appointed commissioners did not oversee the vast majority of the proceedings. The bulk of the work was performed by 14 lawyers and 12 investigators directed by former US Solicitor General J. Lee Rankin. The depositions of witnesses were performed in private but never kept secret, and none were recorded anonymously, under gag order, or without a stenographer present—at Chief Justice Earl Warren's insistence. As Gerald Posner points out, "the staff could call any witness it wanted, and none of its more than 400 requests were ever denied by the commissioners".[61] Many of the Warren Commission's staffers, a majority of whom were pro-Kennedy liberals, even set out with the assumption that they would uncover some kind of plot and became disappointed when they could not. These included David Belin, Burt Griffin, Leon Hubert, and William Coleman. "We thought we would be national heroes," Griffin explained.[62]

Nevertheless, the Warren Commission also had several failings. Most of these are understandable and non-sinister bureaucratic mistakes. Others, at best, can be seen as misguided attempts to save the country from war and, at worst, a conspiracy of silence to cover up the vilest moral transgressions of the Kennedy administration, such as its secret war on Castro. Johnson gave the Commission a tight schedule to dispel popular fears of Soviet and mafia conspiracies before they could become an issue in the coming election. In that respect, LBJ won his gamble: he handily defeated Republican Senator Barry Goldwater without looking weak against communism. However, the rushed deadline forced the Commission to cut several corners, including publishing their 26 volumes of depositions and thus exhibits without an index. This has led many conspiracists to claim that this was done deliberately to make it harder for researchers to pick out the proofs of a cover-up.[63]

Compelled to rely largely on evidence drawn from FBI, Secret Service, and Dallas Police reports, the Commission was handed a pre-established conclusion: that Oswald single-handedly perpetrated the crime, and that Jack Ruby was an unstable misfit whose love of JFK and hatred of communists pushed him over the edge. In working with limited channels, the Commission nevertheless thoroughly profiled the lives of these men, along with their possible links to Southern racists, the mob, and communist Cuba, conducting hundreds of additional witness depositions.[64]

The Commission was also highly dependent on the FBI, the CIA, and the Attorney General's office, all three of whom (including Bobby Kennedy) were especially tight-lipped on what lead counsel Rankin called "tender spots"—information that might incriminate or damage them.[65] This is where Commission staffers were most shortchanged. Without evidence of Kennedy's secret war on Castro or details of Oswald's dealings in Mexico City, it was almost impossible to place the murder into its appropriate Cold War context. As Warren Commission junior counsel Burt Griffin later explained, knowledge of the Castro plots

> might have allowed us to say something reasonably definitive about Oswald's motive. It would have put a new dimension on his Cuban activities and opened new areas of exploration. The fact that we could not come up with a motive for Oswald was a great weakness of the report.[66]

Without a clear context on which to pin Oswald's motive, the Warren Report ended up casting him as an antisocial oddball and his crime as a random act of folly. This may have spared the FBI, CIA, and White House—including J. Edgar Hoover and Bobby Kennedy—much public embarrassment and a few Congressional investigations, but it shortchanged the public, who filled the gaps and contradictions in the Report with whatever rumors best fit their beliefs.

JFK buffs have also criticized Johnson's choice of commissioners, namely his appointments of John J. McCloy (because, as a former Wall Street lawyer, chairman of the Chase Manhattan Bank, and president of the World Bank, he represented private financial interests and those of the "military industrial complex"), Gerald Ford (because he would later, as newly sworn President, pardon Richard Nixon for the Watergate scandal), and Allen Dulles (who as DCI was fired by JFK after the Bay of Pigs fiasco). The first two are clear examples of guilt-by-association and *post hoc* fallacies (respectively). The presence of Dulles on the Commission, however, is legitimately questionable for those without a good understanding of what the Warren Commission was set up not to divulge (see later). Chief Justice Earl Warren also receives criticism for limiting the Commission's suspects to Lee Harvey Oswald, for being overly cautious not to embarrass the Kennedys, and for his unwillingness to fully investigate Oswald's trip to Mexico City and ties to other Marxists.[67]

When Warren was asked by President Johnson to preside over this Commission, the Supreme Court Judge was at first reluctant. But LBJ was a shrewd negotiator, and he brought the man to tears evoking scenarios of a global nuclear holocaust should evidence of the Castro plots be publicized and lead to open conflict with the Soviet Union.[68] Warren was thus made aware from the very beginning that his mandate was not to pursue every possible lead but to paint a general portrait of both assassins and list the evidence that proved their guilt. This helps explain some of Warren's most controversial decisions, such as not divulging the doubts expressed by his fellow commissioners toward the Single Bullet Theory, his refusal to publish JFK's autopsy pictures, and his reluctance to force Jackie and Bobby to testify.[69]

Allen Dulles's presence on the Commission is damning in the eyes of hard-boiled conspiracists. "I knew Allen Dulles very well, I briefed him many a time in his house," laments Oliver Stone's Mr. X, "But for the life of me I still can't figure out why Dulles was appointed to investigate Kennedy's death, the man who had fired him!"[70] Former DCI Dulles' appointment does seem suspicious, like the case of a fox guarding a henhouse, if we fail to consider that he was selected by Johnson because he had insider knowledge of the CIA's covert operations in Cuba and could therefore keep an eye on any embarrassing evidence the Commission might find. Furthermore, appointing Dulles had not been Johnson's idea. This nomination was made at Robert Kennedy (RFK)'s urging[71] largely because, even though JFK had fired Dulles—for public relations reasons more than any personal conflict[72]—the veteran spymaster was a discrete insider whom Bobby Kennedy trusted, one who believed in the necessity of covert operations and the absolute secrecy these required.

Throughout his time on the Commission, Dulles never divulged what he knew about Kennedy's Cuban Project, leaving his colleagues to speculate wildly concerning Lee Oswald's motive. By most insider accounts, this was not due to the man's acumen so much as his rapidly declining health. Dulles' behavior on the Commission was often disjointed, inattentive, and inconsistent and was likened by some to a "doddering schoolmaster" and senile old "nit," not a shrewd master spy managing a black op.[73]

Robert Kennedy's position is hard to decipher because he wavered between several theories to explain his brother's murder. Though he initially confronted DCI McCone about it, and also considered the mob's involvement, Bobby finally came to believe, much like LBJ had, that Jack had been killed in revenge by the Cubans.[74] In drawing this conclusion, RFK saw himself as partly responsible for his brother's death. This helps explain why he openly praised the Warren Report but privately criticized it. It also helps explain why he requested the presence of Allen Dulles on the Commission. By protecting the CIA's reputation, Dulles was also protecting the Kennedy legacy.[75]

There is little doubt that the Warren Commission was from the outset intended to serve as a public relations exercise, and that several of its members—especially

Earl Warren and Allen Dulles—withheld information from the public. Many conspiracists forget, however, that in the tense Cold War climate that followed the Cuban Missile Crisis, the most likely target of American paranoia was the Soviet Union. Early conspiracy theories held by President Johnson, Bobby Kennedy, Nicholas Katzenbach, and high-ranking members of the CIA—namely Deputy Director (and future DCI) Richard Helms, chief of counterintelligence James Angleton, and Mexico City station chief Win Scott—believed that the Soviets and/or Cubans had pushed Oswald to murder Kennedy.[76] In trying to defuse growing speculations that foreign communist regimes were to blame, Johnson and the Warren Commission unintentionally sowed the seeds of a different breed of conspiracism, one that made the American government the villain and leftists its victims. As Olmsted explains, "These leaders were not trying to protect the 'real killers'. Instead, they were statists trying to maintain Americans' trust in their system of governance. Ironically, their lies would shatter that trust".[77]

9.2.8 "Not in your lifetime"

Finally, Marrs suggests that Johnson's order to keep "an immense amount of assassination evidence and documents" classified until the year 2039 is glaring proof of his guilt. "It was this act, more than any other which has caused so much speculation about a possible role by Johnson in the assassination".[78]

It is true that twenty percent of the Warren Commission's records (some 25,000 pages) became classified and thus kept from public view. An additional fifteen percent of its correspondences, working papers, and internal memoranda were also restricted, as well as six pages of testimony (including Jackie Kennedy's description of JFK's wounds) and nearly half the transcripts of its executive sessions.[79] The "sealing" of these records into the next century (a date which Earl Warren nebulously identified as "not in your lifetime"), and the uncertain nature of their contents, elicited questions from conspiracists and skeptics alike.[80] But this is not evidence of foul play, nor is it proof of Johnson's involvement in a conspiracy. In fact, conspiracists often ignore two central facts concerning these records.

First, the 75-year rule was not a decision taken by President Johnson or Chief Justice Warren. It was a consequence of archiving official documents under the Federal Records Act of 1950, documents that included previously classified files. This so-called deception was explained to the public by Dr. Robert Bahmer, Archivist of the United States, in September 1964, three months before the Commission bequeathed its records to the National Archives. While the Warren Commission made no provisions for when these files would be released, Bahmer explained that at least some of them, given their already classified status, would likely not be released until A.D. 2039. As journalist David Wise noted in 1968, "Bahmer had *not* said the Warren files would be closed that long, but subsequent news stories stressed the 75-year rule".[81] Because the Warren Commission disbanded after archiving its files, the National Archives was left with the task of handling these materials, which it could not legally release for up to 75 years without the consent of all affected parties. Thus, whoever claims that the Kennedy files were deviously "locked away" by the Johnson government is guilty of grossly distorting the truth and spinning scandals out of mundane bureaucratic procedures.

The second fact that is largely ignored by conspiracists is that the same president who allegedly sealed the Commission's records for 75 years also gave his assent to the FOIA in 1966—the very law that allowed thousands of curious conspiracists to request, often successfully, the release of classified documents that no longer threatened national security. Under the FOIA provision, journalist David Wise managed to have numerous documents released as early as 1968, including the deliberations of the commissioners and a 185-page *List of Basic Source Materials* identifying the classified documents.[82] Since then, many more revelations have come to light concerning the classified parts of the Warren Commission archive, whether it was through the 1975 Rockefeller Commission and Church Committee or the 1976–79 HSCA, all of which, by the time Marrs wrote his book, had found no clear evidence of a conspiracy to murder Kennedy either by Lyndon Johnson, the FBI, the CIA, the Joint Chiefs of Staff, the mafia, the Cubans (both pro- and anti-Castro), or the Soviets. After Marrs published *Crossfire* (1989) and Oliver Stone's *JFK* (1991) further popularized his defaming attack on Johnson, the majority of the remaining classified documents were released via the 1994–98 ARRB in response to the public outcry provoked by Stone's film (see Chapter 4).

Conspiracists continue to comb through these declassified records looking for proofs of a conspiracy, but such "proofs" usually require an influx of faith. A new trove of Kennedy-related documents was declassified in 2017 and 2018, some of which would have proved embarrassing to the FBI, CIA, White House, and Kennedy family had they been released in 1964, but no one has yet managed to find in these papers clear and verifiable proof of a plot to murder Kennedy.[83] "I've already seen those records," said former ARRB Executive Director and General Counsel Jeremy Gunn in 2013, "there's nothing in there that I can identify [as evidence of a conspiracy]. The story of what is available in federal government records is for all practical purposes revealed".[84]

Though no evidence has yet surfaced to inculpate Lyndon Johnson in a conspiracy to kill his predecessor, LBJ has, ironically, been partly responsible for his own bad press. His relationships, no matter how tenuous, with scoundrels and crooks like Bobby Baker and Billie Sol Estes, his rightly deserved reputation as a shrewd political nipple-twister, his extramarital affairs, his attempt to manipulate the Warren Commission's conclusions (even if it was to avoid a nuclear war), his repeated efforts to win an unwinnable war on the other side of the globe causing hundreds of thousands of deaths, his enactment of the draft lottery… All of these actions fueled mistrust against him, generating countless conspiracy theories about his possible role in the murder of Kennedy. Johnson's major crime, in the end, may not have been graft, fraud, lies, or conspiracy, but the fact that in spite of his outspoken love for humanity, he never was very fond of people.

Notes

1 Lane: *Rush to Judgment*, 2nd Edition (1992), 23, and chap. 29 ("The Commission"). In a footnote, Lane expresses suspicions concerning a 1965 bill signed by LBJ, which maintained federal government ownership of Oswald's rifle, though this leads to no specific premise. Lane, 128. Some early conspiracists, including Joachim Joesten (*Oswald: Assassin or Fall Guy*, 1964) and Penn Jones (*Forgive My Grief*, 1966) do claim that Johnson was involved, but such sources had only a mild influence on the rest of the movement. Max Holland: "The British JFK Producer Who Brought Shame on the History Channel," (n.d.), John McAdams, ed.: *The Kennedy Assassination*.

2 Brian VanDeMark: *The Road to Disaster: A New History of America's Descent into Vietnam* (2018).

3 See Chapter 4 and David Coleman and Marc Selverstone: "Lyndon B. Johnson and the Vietnam War," (n.d.), *Presidential Recordings*, Miller Center, University of Virginia.

4 The Latin phrase "cui bono?" (who benefits?) is a popular catchphrase frequently used by conspiracists to establish a suspect's guilt on the simple fact that they benefited from the event. While illicit gain can serve as a *circumstantial* proof of guilt, it is fallacious to assume, as many conspiracists do, that those who prosper from crimes *necessarily* are criminals, while those who don't are *necessarily* innocent (this is a false dilemma).

5 Holland: "The British JFK Producer..." (Emphasis in original); David Belin: "Earl Warren's Assassins," *New York Times*, March 7, 1992.

6 Ibid., 282–3.

7 *JFK*, dir. Oliver Stone (1991).

8 Prouty: "The Guns of August," *Gallery*, October 1975; Prouty: "Lyndon B. Johnson, John F. Kennedy and the Great American Coup D'État," (n.d.), *The Colonel L. Fletcher Prouty Reference Site*. In a 1990 letter to Garrison, Prouty explained:

> The first question LBJ asked his old '19 year' neighbor in DC [FBI chief J. Edgar Hoover] was 'Were THEY shooting at me?' LBJ thought that THEY had been shooting at him also as they shot at his friend John Connally. Note that he asked, 'Were THEY shooting at me?' LBJ knew there were several hitmen. That's the ultimate clue... THEY.
>
> *Prouty letter to Garrison, March 6, 1990,*
> *The Colonel L. Fletcher Prouty Reference Site.*

9 On the claim that this violated Secret Service protocols, see Section 9.2.1 and Chapter 14.

10 Marrs, 298–300. Notice the "*cui bono?*" *post hoc* fallacy in the last sentence.

11 For example, Glen Sample and Mark Collom (*The Men on the Sixth Floor*, 1995); Robin Ramsay (*Who Shot JFK?*, 2002); Nigel Turner ("The Men Who Killed Kennedy: The Guilty Men," *History Channel*, 2003); Roger Stone (*The Man Who Killed Kennedy: The Case Against LBJ*, 2013); Joan Mellen (*Faustian Bargains: Lyndon Johnson and Mac Wallace in the Robber Baron Culture of Texas*, 2016).

12 Ramsay, 112.

13 Estes was accused of selling nonexistent fertilizer tanks. Marshall was found dead of carbon monoxide poisoning. His head was bludgeoned and his body was shot (post-mortem?) through the chest five times by a single-shot bolt-action rifle. The case was initially filed as a suicide and changed to homicide following exhumation. No one was charged for the murder, though Estes remained a suspect. Robert McFadden: "Billie Sol Estes, Texas Con Man Whose Fall Shook Up Washington, Dies at 88," *The New York Times*, May 14, 2013.

14 Wallace was the nephew of Henry Wallace, former President Franklin D. Roosevelt's second Vice President (1941–45). He was charged and convicted in 1952 of the murder

"with malice" of John Douglas Kinser—his estranged wife's lover. He only received a suspended sentence, possibly because the court considered it a crime of passion. Joel Kirkpatrick: "Mac Wallace Gets Suspended Sentence," *The Daily Texan*, February 28, 1952. Conspiracists claim this suspended sentence was earned by Johnson's machinations and was the reason for which Wallace, owing Johnson a life debt, accepted to murder John Kennedy.

15 Ramsay, chap. 5; Bugliosi, 919–21; "The Men Who Killed Kennedy: The Guilty Men," dir. Nigel Turner.

16 See Chapters 11–13.

17 Dennis McLellan: "Researcher Disputes O.C. Author's Conclusions," *LA Times*, January 16, 1996; John McAdams: "Looking for Faust in Texas," *Washington Decoded*, February 11, 2017.

18 McAdams: "Looking for Faust…"

19 Just a few months following his 1984 grand jury "confession," Estes, still on parole, was arrested and charged for sexual assault on his housekeeper (on the same day she was hired!). "Billie Sol Estes arrested for Sexual Assault," *UPI*, August 14, 1985.

20 "Billie Sol Estes dies at 88; notorious Texas con man in 1960s scandal," *Los Angeles Times*, May 16, 2013.

21 Bud Kennedy: "Even for Texas, Billie Sol Estes was a big talker, a big dealer and a big storyteller," *Fort Worth Star-Telegram*, May 15, 2013; "Billie Sol Estes dies at 88; notorious Texas con man in 1960s scandal," *Los Angeles Times*, May 16, 2013; McFadden: "Billie Sol Estes…"; Holland: "The British JFK Producer…"; Bill Sanderson: "Roger Stone's New Book Says L.B.J. Killed Kennedy," *The Observer*, November 21, 2013.

22 McLellan: "Researcher Disputes…"; Ramsay, 98–112; Bugliosi, 919–21.

23 John Thurber: "Bobby Baker, protégé of Lyndon Johnson felled by influence-peddling scandal, dies at 89," *The Washington Post*, November 17, 2017.

24 Robert Dallek: *Lyndon B. Johnson: Portrait of a President* (2005), 142–3.

25 Larry Sabato: "John F. Kennedy's Final Days Reveal a Man Who Craved Excitement," *Forbes*, October 16, 2013; Leamer, 691–2.

26 Marrs, 296.

27 Juliet Lapidos: "Do Obama and Biden Always Fly in Separate Planes?" *Slate*, April 13, 2010.

28 Gerald Blaine and Lisa McCubbin: *The Kennedy Detail* (2010), Chapter 12.

29 This provision was in force in 1963 as per the Presidential Succession Law of 1947.

30 Evelyn Lincoln: *Kennedy and Johnson* (1968), 204–5.

31 Robert McGill Thomas, Jr.: "Evelyn Lincoln, Secretary to Kennedy, Is Dead at 85," *The New York Times*, May 13, 1995.

32 Thurston Clarke: "'It Will Not Be Lyndon': Why JFK Wanted to Drop LBJ for Reelection," *The Daily Beast*, November 18, 2013.

33 McWorther (2001) and Perlstein (2001), *passim*.

34 Rick Klein: "Jacqueline Kennedy Reveals That JFK Feared an LBJ Presidency," *ABC News*, Sept. 8, 2011.

35 Kay, 87–8.

36 The limousine was a refurbished Lincoln Continental, leased from the Ford Motor Company and administered by the Secret Service. It was sometimes also referred to as X-100. Christopher Wynn: "Would a bubble-top have saved Kennedy? More answers from the strange story of JFK's Lincoln limo," *Dallas Morning News*, November 19, 2018.

37 Marrs, 297.

38 "Kennedy Presidential Limousine," (n.d.), *The Henry Ford*.

39 On the FBI's investigation of Oswald, see Chapter 5.

40 FBI ballistics expert Robert Frazier also conducted an investigation of the vehicle on November 22–24, 1963, and submitted a separate report. "The JFK Assassination: Former Agent Recalls His Role in the Investigation" (documentary film), *Federal Bureau of Investigation*, November 22, 2013. A photograph of Frazier's original drawings is posted at: http://mcadams.posc.mu.edu/limoexam.jpg.

41 Connally's clothes are on display at the Texas State Library and Archives in Austin Texas. See "Governor Connally's Suit," *Texas Investigates: The Assassination of President John F. Kennedy and Wounding of Governor John B. Connally*, Dec. 2, 2013. An illustrated report titled "Details of Governor Connally's Damaged Clothing," can be found at *Texas State Library and Archives Commission*.

42 Leo Janos, "The Last Days of the President: LBJ in Retirement," *The Atlantic Monthly*, July 1973.

43 For example, Olmsted, Chapter 4.

44 Marrs, 298.

45 Prouty: "Lyndon B. Johnson…".

46 Burton B. Turkus and Sid Feder: *Murder, Inc.: The Story Of 'The Syndicate'* (1951). See also Chapter 7.

47 "Who Was Lee Harvey Oswald," *PBS Frontline*, November 19, 2013. See Chapters 2 and 5.

48 Russo and Molton, chap. 10; Shenon, Prologue, chaps. 55–58, and Author's Note. Both Shenon and Russo & Molton rely heavily on Warren Commission and HSCA documents to piece together Oswald's time in Mexico City. Much of the rest is based on second-hand anecdotes. See Chapter 1, Section 1.4 (footnote).

49 Hugh Aynesworth: "'One-man truth squad' still debunking JFK conspiracy theories," *Dallas Morning News*, November 17, 2012.

50 Ibid.

51 Ibid.; "The Men Who Killed Kennedy: The Guilty Men," dir. Nigel Turner.

52 Marrs, 255–63. Compare this to Posner, chap. 6.

53 Murchison's presence at his East Texas ranch on the evening of November 21, 1963, was verified by his own employees. Aynesworth: "'One-man truth squad'…"

54 Aynesworth: "'One-man truth squad'…"

55 Brown claimed in 1987 that Johnson fathered her son Steven Mark Brown, who tried (unsuccessfully) to sue the Johnson estate for paternity—but only after he first sued (also unsuccessfully) Jerome Ragsdale, a Dallas lawyer, in 1980. This, and the fact that she said nothing of Johnson's paternity until after the suit against Ragsdale was lost, suggests, at best, that she was not certain of her paternity allegations. At worst, she was digging for gold. Brown was arrested in 1988 for forging the will of a dead relative: "She was sentenced to 10 years in prison, but the conviction was later reversed on a technicality [because] she had not personally signed the original will but had induced a lawyer friend to do so," Aynesworth: "'One-man truth squad'…"; David Perry: "Texas in the Morning Imagination," October 26, 2002, http://dperry1943.com/browns.html.

56 Olmsted, 112.

57 See Chapter 2.

58 Olmsted, 114. See also Chapter 5 of this book.

59 See Chapter 2.

60 "Castro Warns U.S. on Meddling with Cuba," *Los Angeles Times*, September 9, 1963; Olmsted, 126; Shenon, 153.

61 Posner, 405.

62 Quoted in Shenon, 122–126.

63 For example, Garrison, 14–23. This is a clear example of centrality, "the belief that the paranoid himself is the target of malevolent intent". Robins and Post, 9–10 (see Chapter 1).

64 *Warren Report*, chap. 5 ("Detention and Death of Oswald") and Appendix 16 ("Biography of Jack Ruby"), *National Archives: JFK Assassination Records*.

65 Posner, 405–6.

66 Interview of Burt Griffin, January 23, 1992, cited in Posner, 407.

67 Shenon, 264–5, 308–12, 328–9. Garrison also accuses Senator Richard Russell of acting as a military front man on account of his membership on the Senate Armed Forces Committee. Garrison, 14.

68 Olmsted, 118.

69 Jackie Kennedy was interviewed in her home. The goriest parts of her description of JFK's wounds were later redacted from her deposition. Bobby only offered a written statement and was not formally interviewed by the Commission, preventing him, among other things, from speaking about the plots against Castro. Shenon (2015), 331–2, 356–64, and Shenon: "Botched Investigation Fuels Kennedy Conspiracy Theories," An Interview with Dave Davies on *Fresh Air* (WHYY Philadelphia), *National Public Radio,* October 28, 2013.

70 *JFK,* dir. Oliver Stone (1991). See Chapters 7, 8, and 11.

71 Memorandum to President Johnson from Walter Jenkins (on behalf of AAG Nicholas Katzenbach and AG Robert Kennedy), November 29, 1963, Special File on the Assassination of John F. Kennedy, Box #2, *Lyndon B. Johnson Library and Museum*. PDF.

72 "Remarks upon presenting the National Security Medal to Allen W. Dulles, 28 November 1961," JFKWHA-058-003, *John F. Kennedy Presidential Library and Museum*; Evan Burgos: "An inside job: CIA a suspect for some in JFK's killing," *NBC News*, November 20, 2013; Kyle Whelton: "Was Allen Dulles' Appointment to the Warren Commission Part of a Cover-Up?," (n.d.), John McAdams, ed.: *The Kennedy Assassination*.

73 Shenon, 105–6, 326–7.

74 Hersh, 450–3; Olmsted, 126–7.

75 Burgos: "An inside job…"

76 Olmsted, 113; Shenon, 543–8.

77 Ibid., 118–9.

78 Marrs, 297. Marrs erroneously identifies this act as Executive Order 11652—which was signed by Nixon in 1972.

79 David Wise: "Secret Evidence on the Kennedy Assassination," *Saturday Evening Post,* April 6, 1968.

80 Shenon, 220.

81 Wise: "Secret Evidence…"

82 Ibid.

83 Michael E. Miller: "Strippers, surveillance and assassination plots: The wildest JFK Files," *The Washington Post*, October 27, 2017.

84 T. Jeremy Gunn: "Seeking the Truth in the Kennedy Assassination," lecture delivered at the University of New England's Center for Global Humanities, November 22, 2013, *YouTube*; Marcus D. Rosenbaum: "Inconsistencies Haunt Official Record of Kennedy's Death," November 10, 2013, *The Kennedy Assassination, 50 Years Later, National Public Radio*.

10

"I'M JUST A PATSY!"

Lee Harvey Oswald's life and motive

10.1   I led three lives

Most JFK buffs are offended, even scandalized, by claims that Lee Harvey Oswald caused President John F. Kennedy's death. This indignation extends to the conclusions of the 1976–79 House Select Committee on Assassinations (HSCA), which stated in its final report that Oswald was a willful participant in a small-scale conspiracy of undetermined size and nature. One of the reasons for this widespread reaction (see Chapter 4) is that blaming a self-professed Marxist for Kennedy's murder indirectly lays blame at the feet of all leftists, whose political ideology, it could be argued, provoked the assassin's murderous streak, and who might have themselves done the same under similar circumstances. Early JFK buffs, many of whom were political leftists, convinced themselves that Kennedy could have ended racism, the Vietnam War, the Cold War, and even organized crime had he only survived the ambush in Dallas. And so they took offense at the Warren Report, which appeared to suggest that socialism had informed Oswald's sociopathy, and was therefore the cause and not the solution of the problems they faced in a post-Kennedy world. Thinking of Lee Harvey Oswald as a "patsy" or scapegoat helped them channel their outrage against a warmongering state that failed to reflect their progressive ideals. In their understanding, the American government was the tool of a small group of oligarchs, faceless bureaucrats, and war profiteers, a repressive power structure, the visible face of which was that of Presidents Johnson, Nixon, and Ford. This outrage would endure for decades, drawing many new converts to their cause—including this author—who shared the convictions of the early Buffs that right-wing militarists, neocolonialists, and various political criminals had taken control of their world.

Many of those who turned to conspiracist explanations did so because the Lone Gunman Theory (LGT) simply robbed Kennedy's death of existential meaning.

DOI: 10.4324/9781003222460-12

The thought that an "angry lone nut" could kill such an inspiring leader (as he was remembered after his death) without a clearly established motive prevented them from deriving a deeper significance from the event. It suggested instead that history is driven by incompetent agents, careless middle managers, petty political squabbles, alienated malcontents, mental illness, and other chaotic forces. It also left them with inadequate tools to understand the events that followed. As seen in Chapter 3, the way many addressed this confusion was to adopt a saintly myth of John Kennedy, whether or not this agreed with the facts. For others, the Camelot myth could not on its own expiate despair. Some weight was missing to tip the scale. Lee Oswald also required a myth.

All those who knew him agree that Oswald was a tight-lipped and enigmatic figure who rarely shared his own thoughts, even with those closest to him. He embraced secrecy for its own sake and displayed many symptoms of political paranoia, including the twin convictions that he was an exceptional individual and a victim of state suppression.[1] For these reasons, Oswald's life and behavior are for many researchers a sort of Rorschach test: a fuzzy ink blot that is interpreted subjectively in accordance with the researcher's expectations. That said, a good deal of evidence concerning Oswald's personality, inner thoughts, and intentions can be deduced from his known movements and actions, from the opinions of those who knew him best—available in the form of legal depositions, personal memoirs, and biographies—and from Oswald's own writings and occasional media appearances. The purpose of this chapter is to reconstruct as clear an image as possible of the historical Oswald compared to the distorted portrait produced by careless researchers. In other words, we will consider whether Oswald was a patsy, an angry lone nut, or a more nuanced figure with a rational motive for murdering Kennedy.

10.2   Harvey and Lee

An objective novice JFK researcher would be surprised to discover how little attention Lee Oswald receives in the vast body of conspiracist literature. For authors like David Scheim, briefly establishing a murky connection between Oswald and the New Orleans mob—usually via his uncle Charles Murret (see Chapter 6)—is considered sufficient to prove a mafia-related conspiracy. More ambitious authors, like David Lifton, whose theories implicate the Secret Service, CIA, and other parts of the federal government, reason backward from suspicious factoids, incongruent testimonies, or convenient "what ifs…?" that suggest Oswald *could have been* a government agent who *might have been* framed for the crime. Having established this tenuous possibility, they proceed to dismiss all inconvenient facts about Oswald as irrelevant noise or malicious disinformation. To wit, Lifton's 747-page 1980 edition of *Best Evidence* devotes less than seven pages to Oswald—only one of which addresses the murder of Dallas patrolman J.D. Tippit, while none discusses the murder attempt on General Walker.[2] Filmmaker Oliver Stone claims that any discussion of Oswald's personal background is a distraction that has no bearing on the real evidence of the case.[3] Some have even produced wild fantasies about

Oswald's secret life. A curious example is Judyth Vary Baker, who spins an out-landish tale drawn from a mixture of other conspiracy books (she shows no famil-iarity with the "official" investigations), thriller and romance novels, and her own lovelorn imagination, suggesting that she and Oswald had a passionate love affair in New Orleans during the summer of 1963, at which time she was co-opted by David Ferrie to engineer a bioweapon for the CIA to use against Castro—which her lover Oswald delivered to Mexico City, never to return again.[4] No corrobor-ating witnesses or verifiable evidence is offered by Baker to support this account, only her tears and undying devotion to "Lee".

The most popular method conspiracists use to harmonize known facts about Lee Oswald's life—his difficult childhood, troubled family relations, service in the Marines, defection to Russia, pro-Cuban activism, alleged assassination of Kennedy, etc.—with what they believe must also be true—his being a government agent, his "fake" pro-Castro identity, his alleged attempt to warn the FBI, his wrongful "exe-cution," etc.—is what has come to be called the Two Oswalds Theory. Its general thesis is that there were two different men (possibly more) using the name Lee Harvey Oswald during the weeks, months, and years that preceded JFK's death, who navigated within the same circles in Fort Worth, Japan, Russia, New Orleans, Mexico City, and Dallas. The "real" Lee was a patriotic Southern-born US Marine and faithful intelligence agent. The other was an impostor and look-alike, instructed to produce a trail of false evidence that could later be used to incriminate Lee as an angry, violent, and antisocial lone communist.

The earliest proponent of this theory was Lee's own mother, Marguerite Oswald, who told the FBI on several occasions that her son was not a defector or assassin but a patriotic soldier and government agent, and that he had been impersonated by an impostor.[5] Some early JFK buffs took Marguerite at her word, topping her story with their own suspicions. These included Léo Sauvage (*The Oswald Affair*, 1964), Richard Popkin (*The Second Oswald*, 1966), and Michael Eddowes (*The Oswald File*, 1977), who claimed that the man who defected to Russia in 1959 was not the one who returned to the United States in 1962. After years of pressuring Oswald's widow Marina and brother Robert, Eddowes had Lee's body exhumed in 1981 to prove that the "real" Lee's body had never been there or was switched with that of the impostor, the one killed by Jack Ruby. A full scientific inquiry revealed that the body "showed no evidence of mutilation other than post-mortem disintegra-tion" and was indeed that of Lee Oswald.[6] Alas, this did not prevent Eddowes from describing this study—which he himself funded and commissioned—as further proof of a government cover-up.[7]

The Two Oswalds Theory was further developed by Jim Garrison (*On the Trail of the Assassins*, 1988) and filmmaker Oliver Stone (*JFK*, 1991). But its most popular and ambitious version comes from John Armstrong (*Harvey and Lee*, 2003), who argues that a deceptive body-double conspiracy had been in operation since Lee was a boy, long before JFK set his sights on the presidency. Armstrong's tale also featured two Marguerite Oswalds: a young, attractive, and intellectually well-balanced one, and the paranoid crazy old coot that appears in the works of many conspiracy skeptics.[8] Armstrong's account also involves a teenaged second Oswald living in North Dakota in 1953 while the "fake" one described by the Warren Report was skipping school and wandering the streets of New York. There was also a fake Russian Oswald (whom he nicknames "Harvey"), and several fake Lees mis-behaving all over Texas and Louisiana, whose mission it was to make the real Lee, a pure-minded and pacific Marxist, look like a stark lunatic. Armstrong's evidence consists largely of burying the reader under a pile of unverifiable, contradictory, vague, and not clearly pertinent second- and third-hand accounts that look like complete fabrications, unsubstantiated gossip, or mere examples of bad memory. And yet, the sheer ludicrousness of Armstrong's story does not prevent willing believers like Robin Ramsay from accepting it wholesale, exactly because it is con-trarian and esoteric:

> From the viewpoint of—say—the academic historian, Armstrong's thesis about such an intelligence operation [involving two Oswalds] is fantastic because implausible, preposterous. Inside the world of JFK buffs, it is fantastic because it is such a beautiful and elegant idea. [It] makes a kind of imme-diate sense when you consider the wildly contrasting behaviour and beliefs attributed to Oswald. [...] Because it explains a great deal, this is a good hypothesis.[9]

An exhaustive analysis of all "fake Oswald" sightings would take up too much space. Fortunately, it is not necessary to study each case to establish that such claims are simply not credible. For example, many of Armstrong's alleged sightings of "Harvey" offer no information that might incriminate "Lee" (or is it the other way around?). Their only utility appears to be that they help suspicious researchers expose an ambitious, poorly conceived, ineptly orchestrated, and unnecessary plot.[10] Conspiracy skeptics like Vincent Bugliosi nonetheless offer a long list of counterevidence to disprove several alleged fake Oswald sightings.[11] The most popular of these, made famous by Warren Commission gadfly Mark Lane, was his claim that the real Oswald was photographed standing *outside* the Texas School Book Depository (TSBD) during the assassination (i.e., the man who appears to be leaning out of the TSBD entrance in Figure 13.3). Ergo, argues Lane, Oswald was not on the sixth floor shooting down at the President. Several investigators, including the Warren Commission's Burt Griffin, and also Lee Oswald's brother Robert, investigated this allegation and discovered that the picture in question, taken by Associated Press photographer James Altgens, had actually captured Billy Lovelady, another TSBD employee who looked similar to Lee from a distance but not up close.[12]

Unlike the erroneous but somewhat forgivable "Lovelady sighting," many fake Oswald sightings held up by Jim Garrison, Anthony Summers, Robert Groden, John Armstrong, and Robin Ramsay (to name but a few) predate the events that would, according to their own theories, have turned Kennedy into a target: his alleged decision to withdraw from Vietnam, his first televised civil rights speech, the Bay of Pigs invasion, his crackdown on organized crime, his inauguration, and even his decision to run for the presidency at a time when Oswald, still living in the Soviet Union, had no reason or way to return to America. One must wonder what was the purpose of all these fake Oswald sightings when there was yet no meaningful reason to produce a trail of fake Oswalds. If the CIA or other nefarious group happened to have a long-standing program of clone assassins that they could be mobilized in a pinch, then this is its only ever witnessed example. Certainly, no evidence has ever surfaced to prove that the CIA makes a habit of training assassin doubles. This relegates most "fake Oswald" claims to the realm of the *ad hoc* rescue fallacy.[13]

Other popular second Oswald sightings include Lee allegedly trying to hire a getaway plane at Dallas' Redbird Airport in July 1963 (when the real Lee lived in New Orleans); a reckless joyride at a car dealership in Dallas on November 9, 1963, by a man who allegedly claimed to be Oswald and left behind no paperwork (while the real Lee was seen at the TSBD); a couple appearances at a Dallas firing range on September 28, 1963 (when the real Oswald was seen in Mexico City) and on November 24, 1963, the morning Lee spent in the Dallas Police Department before he was shot by Jack Ruby.[14] As Bugliosi explains, Lee's real whereabouts are known for almost every fake Oswald sighting, making the alleged conspiracy easy to debunk.[15] The existence of strong counterevidence against these fake-Oswald sightings and the unclear reasons for which this type of subterfuge needed to be performed (because, in any case, no "official" investigation relied on such sightings to build their case against Oswald) suggests that they are more likely cases of bad memory, poor judgment, or hoaxes.

10.3   Square pegs in round holes

Theories like the previous one motivate conspiracy-minded researchers to systematically cherry-pick any fact or assumption that supports their beliefs and toss out those that don't. Any information that threatens to make their theory inconsistent—like evidence that Oswald suffered illusions of grandeur, beat his wife, shot at Walker, idolized Castro, carried a rifle to work, shot JFK, lied to the police, etc.—can be rejected as disinformation or the work of a *doppelgänger*. Likewise, any eyewitness report, no matter how outlandish, vague, or unreliable, can be used to confirm any hypothesis as if it were blue-ribbon science. This encapsulates the widespread conspiracist practice to misconstrue incompatible information—what social scientists call "errant" and "fortuitous" data.

Errant data consists of information that is unaccounted for by, or stands in contradiction to, a widely accepted or "official" theory of events.[16] Conspiracists habitually traffic in errant data, picking and choosing evidence depending on what suits their needs, then basing their complicated theories on the *possibility* of their claims being true—not their *probability* and *simplicity*. An example of errant data is the fact that Jack Ruby's unimpeded entrance into the Dallas Police parking garage on November 24, 1963, seemed rather unlikely (but not impossible) given the level of security that had been set up to keep people like him from entering. No eyewitness claims they saw Ruby entering the parking garage via the Main Street entrance ramp, despite his own repeated claims that he snuck in alone and unhindered.[17] While some think it unlikely that this happened as Ruby described it, critical thinkers should be cautious not to accept (or reject) any claim simply because it coheres (or not) with their assumptions of what *should* have happened. Instead, one should test pieces of errant data against the larger body of verified evidence. This should be done cautiously, with the view that one's initial assumptions were possibly wrong. Indeed, many events are statistically unlikely—such as winning the lottery or being pooped on by a bird—yet such things occur every day. Hence, the combination of multiple *possible* claims should make us wary, especially when simpler explanations exist. Sometimes errant data fits no single scenario cleanly.[18] This is when we must tolerate a certain level of uncertainty.[19] "No story explains everything," state Uscinski and Parent, "but official stories should explain as much as possible. [...] All theories have anomalies because all theories simplify complexity. Errant data do not prove much on their own".[20]

Fortuitous data are the inverse. They consist of evidence that supports the "official" theory but seem simply too good to be true. Naturally, conspiracists (and others) tend to dismiss these as disinformation or what is popularly known as "fake news". The problem lies in how we assess what is fake. Exercising a certain amount of skepticism is healthy to avoid being duped by hoaxes and false alarms, but if we rashly conclude that *all* claims and *all* evidence that contradict our beliefs are necessarily fake, we are likely to retreat—as many conspiracists have—into echo chambers of like-minded thinkers, convinced that everyone but those who flatter our egos are liars. "Such a standard creates an impasse," write Uscinski and Parent, "if we reject stories because evidence supports them, then we will never be able to support *any* story".[21] For these reasons, critical thinkers must remain objective, impartial, and prudent in the face of compelling new evidence. Hoaxes do happen and well-meaning experts do make mistakes, but we also sometimes get lucky and find what we need in the first place we look. A good example of fortuitous data is the case of Yuri Nosenko, a Soviet KGB officer who defected to the United States in January 1964, a few weeks after Kennedy's assassination. As luck would have it, Nosenko had studied Lee Oswald's KGB file a few years earlier and assured CIA agents, who were detaining him in a safe house, that Oswald was no Soviet agent, that he had not given the Russians any useful secrets, and that the KGB had considered him a suicide-prone malcontent too unstable to serve as a Soviet asset. The information offered by Nosenko could have put to rest many conspiracy theories swirling through the Johnson White House, CIA, and Warren Commission during the months that followed. The only problem was that almost no one was disposed to believe Nosenko, including CIA Director of Counterintelligence James Angleton, who remained convinced that Nosenko was a false defector, and that his information on Oswald was Soviet disinformation. It would take three years of solitary confinement, forced deprivations, and mild torture before Nosenko was finally considered a truthful defector and allowed to remain in the United States. In this case, the fortuitous data was entirely true, but the paranoia of the CIA interrogators made it unnecessarily suspect. This, sadly, is the attitude of many conspiracists.[22]

A third type of problematic data is outliers. An outlier is a discordant piece of data that deviates wildly from statistical expectations. In simpler language, it is a parcel of information that cannot be made to fit *any* theory, conspiracist or otherwise. It is, in other words, a fact that leaves everyone baffled. The most noteworthy example of an outlier in the JFK conspiracy literature is the Warren Commission testimony of Sylvia Odio, a young Cuban woman living in exile in the United States who claimed that Lee Oswald came by her Dallas apartment in late September 1963 accompanied by two anti-Castro Cubans, none of whom she had previously known. The three men, she claimed, had come by to seek funds to buy weapons to help them fight Castro. This was not entirely far-fetched as Odio was the daughter of a rich Cuban businessman and counterrevolutionary who was at that time imprisoned in Cuba. What was unusual was that Oswald, whom she said was introduced to her as "Leon Oswald," a US Marine sympathetic to the anti-communist cause and whom she described as dirty with facial hair, had recently been recruited by "Leopoldo," the group's leader, who presented himself as an acquaintance of Sylvia's father. The three men were turned down and left. Odio also reported that "Leopoldo" phoned her the following day, again seeking financial support, and confessing to her that "Leon" was "kind of nuts," that he thought the Cubans "don't have any guts" because they failed to assassinate Kennedy after the failed Bay of Pigs invasion.[23] A few weeks later, when Odio saw on the news the man who was arrested for murdering Kennedy, she had an emotional breakdown and was hospitalized. Her sister Annie told FBI agent James Hosty—the one who had been charged with locating Oswald after his return from Mexico City—that Sylvia's meeting with the three men happened as she described it. Odio's psychiatrist Burton Einspruch also confirmed that Sylvia told him about these strange visitors before the assassination took place.[24]

Many conspiracists treat the Odio sighting as a Rosetta Stone of the JFK assassination. Anthony Summers, Sylvia Meagher, Robert Groden, and Oliver Stone, among others, claim that Odio's story proves there were really two Oswalds, one of whom was a fake traveling through Texas trying to incriminate the "real" one. But if this is true, why would a fake Oswald be showing himself in the company of *anti-Castro* Cubans, when the entire point of the plot, according to the conspiracists, was to make Oswald look like a *leftist* crackpot? The other problem is chronological. Odio claimed that the three men came to her door on September 26 or 27, 1963, when the real Lee Oswald was seen in Mexico, which makes the plotters, once again, look ruggedly incompetent.

Anyone who believes that Odio did meet Oswald is faced with several problems. Her physical description of Oswald as dirty and hairy, for instance, does not concord with any photograph or eyewitness report of Oswald during the days just before or after she said she saw him. Odio's credibility is also impeached by authors, like Gerald Posner, who point out that, had the real Oswald been fraternizing with anti-Castro Cubans—perhaps by infiltrating their group under false pretenses as he previously had in New Orleans (see Chapter 5)—the real Oswald would likely have used a *nom-de-guerre* such as "Alik Hidell," like his companion "Leopoldo," which was a typical tactic used by anti-Castro militiamen to avoid being identified by Cuban spies. Or, possibly, "Leon Oswald" was just such a name used by a man who, like Billy Lovelady, shared a slight resemblance with Oswald, but whose name only accidentally sounded like that of the president's assassin. In any event, explains Posner, Odio had a history of emotional and relationship problems that made her highly suggestible, anxious, and prone to exaggeration, including personality traits described by her psychiatrist and family. Because of all this, Odio was believed to be truthful by FBI agent James Hosty—insofar as she *believed* her own story was true— but not especially credible. After initially believing her story, Warren Commission investigators David Slawson and Wesley Liebeler concluded, after several follow-ups, that Hosty was probably right.[25] "If one is inclined to take witness testimony at face value," wrote John McAdams, "Odio is as good a person as any to take at face value". The problem is that scores of other Oswald sightings were reported in the wake of the assassination, the vast majority coming from witnesses who were honestly convinced they had seen and interacted with the real Lee Oswald—even though they could not have done so. Most likely, Odio was just another of these honestly mistaken witnesses.[26]

Other conspiracy skeptics, including Jean Davison (*Oswald's Game*, 1983) and Vincent Bugliosi (*Reclaiming History*, 2007), as well as conspiracist and former HSCA investigator Gaeton Fonzi, believe that Odio probably did meet Oswald but was likely mistaken about the date of his visit.[27] This is because no one is certain of Oswald's whereabouts on September 25, 1963, while he was in transit from New Orleans to Houston where, on September 26, he boarded a bus bound for Mexico City. Oswald's probable presence in Texas that day, along with his unknown location, suggests that there is a chance, however minute, that he took a side trip to Dallas to infiltrate an anti-Castro militia (albeit without trying to contact his family there) possibly to impress the Cuban authorities when he applied for a visa to Cuba a couple of days later. If this is the case, Oswald's visit to Odio's apartment becomes more probable and compatible with the LGT in virtue of Oswald's several other attempts to outfox or kill "fascists". Even so, responds McAdams, this scenario is nearly impossible given that Oswald is known to have made some local phone calls on the night of September 25, 1963, to the Houston home of Socialist Labor Party member Horace Twiford. This, along with the 240 miles that separate Houston and Dallas, makes it highly unlikely that he could have traveled to Dallas and back in less than 24 hours.[28]

In the final analysis, conspiracists and skeptics can each interpret the Odio sighting in whatever way seems appropriate to them because it can be spun in any number of ways, and no one is any wiser about what actually happened.

10.4   The mysterious Mister O

And so, we now ask, who exactly was Lee Harvey Oswald? Was he a government agent? An imposter? A patsy? A clone? Or was he a likely candidate for single-handedly murdering a president? In his testimony to the Warren Commission, Oswald's older half-brother John Pic offered the following reflection:

> ever since he was born and I was old enough to remember, I always had a feeling that some great tragedy was going to strike Lee in some way or another, and when this happened I figured this was it. In fact, on the very day of the assassination I was thinking about it when I was getting ready to go to work, [...] and I figured when he defected [to the USSR in 1959] and came back [in 1962]—that was his big tragedy. I found out it wasn't. [...] I think he resented the fact that he never really had a father, especially after he lost Mr. Ekdahl [their mother's third husband] and his one and only chance to get what he was looking for. Maybe that is why he looked to Robert and I like he did. [...]
>
> *I believe that Lee Oswald did the crime that he is accused of.* I think that anything he may have done was aided with a little extra push from his mother in the living conditions that she presented to him. I also think that his reason for leaving the Marine Corps is not true and accurate. I mean I don't think he cared to get out of the Marine Corps to help his mother. He probably used this as an excuse to get out and go to his defection. I know myself I wouldn't have gotten out of the service because of her, and I am sure Robert wouldn't either, and this makes me believe that Lee wouldn't have.[29]

Pic was convinced at the time, and remained so thereafter, that his youngest brother was an angry, lonely, and emotionally unstable man, that he had longed for a father who never came, that he was perpetually trying to shake off the grip of a soul-crushing mother, that he became pro-Cuban after he grew disillusioned with the USSR, that he was guilty of murdering President Kennedy for political and personal reasons, and that he most likely did it alone. Lee's other brother, Robert Oswald, expressed similar views:

> Lee's lifelong enjoyment of intrigue, his use of false names, his mysterious behavior even when he had nothing to hide, all have helped keep alive the rumors of his supposed connections with the FBI and the CIA. [...] Lee added to that impression because he enjoyed toying with people who interrogated him. He felt contempt toward almost anyone in authority. [...] I doubt that he would ever have confessed his guilt. [...] While I am ready at any time to be convinced that the Warren Commission was wrong, *I have not yet read or heard or seen any evidence that has shaken my conviction that Lee and Lee alone fired the shots that wounded Governor Connally and killed the President of the United States.*[30]

Their mother Marguerite Oswald, on the other hand, became a media star in the days and months that followed JFK's death, claiming to all who would listen (including several tawdry publications) that Lee was a US government secret agent who got double-crossed by his superiors.[31] To this Pic responded:

> It is my own opinion that she is out right now to make as much money as she can on her relationship with Lee Harvey Oswald. […] I don't really believe she really believes he is innocent. I think she is out to make money than if [sic] she has to say he is guilty. I think she is a phony in the whole deal.[32]

Lee Oswald's Russian-born widow, Marina Prusakova (aka: Marina Oswald Porter; she later remarried), has had an evolving opinion of Lee's role in the assassination. Initially, in agreement with the Warren Commission's conclusions, she came to accept many conspiracist claims that describe Lee as a government agent and patsy.[33] However, Marina never claimed to have witnessed any direct evidence of this herself.[34] The two daughters she had with Lee, June and Rachel Oswald Porter, have kept a low profile throughout their lives. In their few media appearances, they both expressed ambivalence as to whether or not their natural father had been part of a wider conspiracy.[35] In other words, even those closest to Oswald have struggled to understand him and disagree concerning his ultimate motive and implication. This led historian Mel Ayton, co-author of *Beyond Reasonable Doubt: The Warren Report and Lee Harvey Oswald's Guilt and Motive 50 Years On* (2014), to conclude that Oswald

> lived most of his adult life hiding behind a mask of normality. […] What lay beneath the surface was Oswald's fatally crippled personality. He had a defensive and surly character that no-one could penetrate, not even his wife Marina. […] To those who knew him well Oswald was secretive, aggressive and arrogant—to a degree almost paranoid.[36]

For these reasons, Oswald's motive for assassinating Kennedy, if one accepts that he did it, remains murky. He was a discrete man who left no note or explanation for his crime. Some argue that he intended to make his cause known during the court case that would surely follow had Jack Ruby's revolver not made that impossible.[37] We will survey the physical evidence in subsequent chapters along with the conspiracists' claims that Oswald could not have pulled off this caper alone, or that the physical evidence proves he wasn't guilty at all. Let us for now only consider his possible motive.

10.5   Komrad Oswaldkovitch

Widely respected journalists and authors have scrutinized the details of Lee Oswald's life and character. These include Priscilla Johnson McMillan, Norman Mailer, Mel Ayton, Peter Savodnik, Gerald Posner, and Vincent Bugliosi, to name but a few. These individuals interviewed Oswald's family members, friends, and acquaintances, including his wife Marina, his brothers John and Robert, his mother

Marguerite, his uncle and aunt in New Orleans, Russian friends in the USSR and America, Marina's Quaker friends Ruth and Michael Paine, Lee's former fellow Marines, various co-workers, anti-Castro activist Carlos Bringuier with whom Lee had a public dispute and radio debate in 1963, as well as some Russian and Cuban sources who had unique insights about Oswald (e.g., ex-KGB agent Yuri Nosenko and Cuban embassy secretary Silvia Durán).[38] Information about Lee Oswald's life, personality, and beliefs can also be gleaned from the published volumes of the Warren Commission and HSCA, who deposed many witnesses and studied a surfeit of official documents relating to his comings and goings for much of his short life, including his school, medical, and military records, his immigration documents, his FBI file, his contacts with known communists, his 1963 New Orleans arrest records, his interviews in the New Orleans media, the CIA's observation of his presence in Mexico City, and testimonies of those who attended his two days of questioning by the Dallas Police, the FBI, and the US Postal Service, before he was killed by Jack Ruby. Oswald also kept a personal journal while in Russia, which he called his "Historic Diary" and which he hoped to publish.[39] The document, Posner argues, "showed not only his fickle nature, but his deepening hatred of both the Soviet and American political systems".[40]

All of these investigations confirm that Lee Harvey Oswald was a melancholic, uptight, and frustrated young man with a troubled family background. His mother had been neglectful, flighty, manipulative, and emotionally distant. His two older brothers, whom he aspired to imitate, were placed in an orphanage for a few years while Lee, the youngest, stayed with his mother, often sharing one bed. His mother's third marriage[41] to New England-born engineer Edwin Ekdahl, the closest thing Lee ever had to a father, suffered a string of disputes and separations (Ekdahl frequently cheated on her) and ultimately fell apart.[42] As Robert Oswald remembered:

> It was a treat for us to have a stepfather who paid attention to us. [...] I think Lee loved him most of all. [...] Lee had never known a normal family life. [...Our mother] never had time to enjoy us. Other parents, it seemed to me, enjoyed their children. I just knew that we learned very early that we were a burden to her. [...] Lee was a lot more sensitive than any of us realized at the time. He kept his feelings to himself and didn't show how much he worried over the danger of losing the only father he had ever known. [...] The divorce was a blow to Lee. It meant the end of the only father-son relationship he would ever know.[43]

Ekdahl's departure, coupled with John and Robert's going away to military school and, again later, enlistment in the military, filled Lee with an enduring sense of abandonment and alienation.

The teenaged Lee and his mother changed addresses often. They briefly moved to New York where they squatted in John Pic's and his wife's small flat until tight living arrangements, personality clashes, and Lee's increasingly volatile temper forced them to leave.[44] This caused enduring bad blood between Lee and his oldest brother. It was at about the same time that Lee first heard of the execution of Julius and Ethel Rosenberg, which led him to develop an interest in communism.[45] Young Lee and his mother subsequently moved to the Bronx, where he increasingly suffered from an undiagnosed learning disability, displayed hostility toward authority figures, and often skipped school.[46]

In 1953, a judge declared Lee an unmanageable truant and had him committed to a youth detention center for a psychiatric evaluation. He was diagnosed at this time as having "personality pattern disturbance with schizoid features and passive-aggressive tendencies". The evaluator's report further described him as "an emotionally, quite disturbed youngster who suffers under the impact of really existing emotional isolation and deprivation, lack of affection, absence of family life and rejection by a self-involved and conflicted mother".[47] As Mel Ayton explains,

> Oswald was a bitter and angry young man. As a youth his mother had little or no control over him and, indeed, conspired with him in his rebellion. […] Prison files are full of case histories like his. He learned very early in life to hate the world, learned early that he had to sink or swim on his own resources. He also learned that he had to develop his life unsustained by a mother who could never give true maternal warmth.[48]

Like his brother Robert, Lee joined the Marines at 17—as soon as he was eligible—largely to escape his mother. John had previously joined the Coast Guard and would later enlist in the Air Force.[49] But Lee did not find the Marines fulfilling.[50] Nevertheless, he learned to shoot a rifle rather well in the Marines.[51] He also taught himself passable Russian, for which he was mocked by his fellow soldiers. He was stationed a short while in Japan where he worked in a radar station. In 1959, after earning a discharge to visit his mother in Texas, he traveled to Finland where he obtained a visa to visit the Soviet Union. Once in Moscow, Lee tried using the general knowledge he acquired in Japan about US spy plane missions to convince the Soviets to let him stay. But as ex-KGB agent Yuri Nosenko explained, "we had better information already coming from KGB sources than he could ever give us".[52] With his Soviet visa expiring, Lee attempted suicide in his Moscow hotel. The Soviets subsequently let him defect, partly to avoid a diplomatic scandal. It was at this time that Priscilla Johnson (later McMillan), a journalist and former translator for the US embassy in Moscow, first met and interviewed Oswald. "He seemed lonely," she later recounted, "He seemed very, very young. He seemed lost in a situation that was beyond [him]".[53]

Oswald remained in the USSR for over two years. Rather than serve as he hoped in the Soviet government, he was shipped to Minsk, Belarus, where he received a menial job in a radio factory. There he lived a normal Soviet life, befriending and dating local young adults who nicknamed him "Alik" (one of his later aliases). It was there that he met and married Marina Nikolayevna Prusakova, a young woman with her own troubled past.[54] But Lee soon grew disillusioned with what he had imagined would be a workers' paradise. Not having rescinded his US citizenship, he petitioned the government to let him return to the United States with his pregnant wife. Soviet authorities allowed Lee to emigrate as he was deemed to be more of a problem to them by remaining in Russia. Some authors speculate that, to allow her to leave, the KGB secretly ordered Marina to serve as a sleeper agent in her new country.[55] If this were true and the KGB and/or CIA held evidence to prove this Soviet-Oswald connection, it would explain their historical unwillingness to release all they knew concerning the Oswalds. It would also explain why Marina kept a low profile over the following decades. However, no clear evidence has surfaced to prove this. Its truth would also discredit the conspiracy theories alleging that Oswald was a CIA asset rather than a Soviet assassin. Russian journalist Peter Savodnik, the author of a biography of Oswald's time in Russia (*The Interloper: Lee Harvey Oswald Inside the Soviet Union*, 2013), found no suspicious thread linking the American defector to either the KGB or US intelligence:

> There's a real dearth of discussion of Oswald because he is constantly thought of […] as a cog in someone else's detective story. […] We never really know Oswald, I think, because we insist on not knowing him. We like the idea of him as a mystery. […] In fact, it's much less mysterious than we might have thought. Oswald was very complicated. He had many demons preying on him but he could be understood, like all people. And when you pay close attention to the Soviet period, when you examine that, a lot of these complexities are laid bare.[56]

Back in the United States, Lee and Marina had a poor and unstable life. They moved from house to house for over a year, through Fort Worth, Dallas, and New Orleans, sometimes living with friends or family members, sometimes in cockroach-infested apartments, never showing evidence of receiving financial aid from any government agency, except modest unemployment benefits. Most of Lee's employers found him lazy and entitled, spending too much time in conversation with other workers or pursuing his own interests instead of working. He lied on several applications and was quickly let go from the jobs he did get. His home life was chaotic. He became increasingly violent with his wife, who often disparaged him in front of others.[57] According to Robert Oswald, Marina's callous speech reminded Lee too much of his mother. Still, despite his lack of means, Lee maintained a clean appearance, did not take to drinking or smoking, and spent much of his time at home reading newspapers or writing to Marxist newspapers. He had few friends and few career prospects, yet he maintained the belief that he was destined for greatness. According to McMillan, "Lee told Marina that, in 20 years, he would be president or prime minister".[58]

In the last few months of his life, Lee grew fixated on Cuba and entertained the desire to move there, "like Hemingway".[59] The USSR and United States had revealed themselves to be decadent imperialist states and he saw Cuba as the last bastion of fair and open socialism.[60] By September 1963, when he applied for a visa to travel to Cuba, the Oswalds were effectively separated.[61] The needs of their two infant children and lack of income led Marina to move in with Ruth Paine, a Russian-speaking Quaker housewife who lived in the suburbs of Dallas and who was also separated. Having failed to obtain passage to Cuba, Lee returned to Dallas disheartened, taking up residence at a boarding house until the day of the assassination. Lee was resentful of the attention and support Marina was receiving from others and preferred not to depend on it himself. It was "a constant reminder to him of his failure".[62]

10.6   A downhill run

When the Cuban embassy in Mexico City rejected his visa application, Lee had little hope for the future. "Oswald hated the American way of life," explains Ayton,

> Years earlier he had come to detest his beloved Russia. And now his entry to his brave new world was barred. Failure seemed to follow him everywhere. He had nowhere to turn except inwards to his embittered and disillusioned self.[63]

Oswald had a self-righteous attitude, a passive-aggressive personality with paranoid tendencies, an aversion to teamwork, and a dislike of authority. This was not the sort of temperament one finds in a government agent. On the other hand, Lee shared many psychological traits one finds among conspiracy buffs. He saw himself as highly important and poorly respected, a victim surrounded by enemies. He mistook disagreements for hostility, and he responded in kind. He lacked a sense of humor, especially about himself. "If you disagreed with him, you weren't a friend," explains Ruth Paine.[64] "Lee always had spun fantasies," adds McMillan, "Marina had noticed it in Russia, when there were reasons for people to be secretive; even then, she realized that Lee liked secrecy for its own sake, and spun webs when there was no reason to".[65] Back in the United States, he used aliases to purchase a mail-order rifle, rent post office boxes, subscribe to communist newsletters, and rent his last place of residence—a tiny room with bed, nightstand, and little else. He had also failed, if only barely, to assassinate the ultraconservative General Walker in April 1963, whom Oswald perceived as an American Hitler. Though the police did not identify Walker's shooter until Oswald died, Marina confirmed Lee's guilt to the Warren Commission. Photographs of Walker's home were found among Lee's belongings and the ballistic evidence of the failed murder was compatible with Oswald's rifle.[66] Oswald had also posed for a series of pictures depicting him as a "hunter of fascists" on March 31, 1963—less than two weeks before the Walker shooting—in his Neely Street backyard in Dallas.[67]

Lee Oswald had thus experienced a succession of failures: failure to find a country where he felt at home; failure to be greeted as a returning hero; failure to make something of himself professionally; failure to set up a viable Marxist organization in New Orleans; failure to earn notoriety as a countercultural revolutionary; failure to visit Cuba; failure to obtain his wife's admiration; failure to provide for her and their children; failure to be like his brothers; failure to become a successful hunter of fascists. "He keeps trying to get up and make it at some level," explained Robert Oswald, "but he's not succeeding. He's failing at almost every level. He's failing in his marriage and in his attempts to do whatever he wants to do. He's on a downhill run".[68] McMillan highlights one particular occasion when Marina caught Lee in an uncharacteristic show of despair:

> There was a night in the summer of 1963 when Lee had lost his job. He seemed quite downcast. Marina found him in the kitchen with his legs wrapped around the back of a kitchen chair and his head on the back of the chair. He was sobbing, and he told her he didn't know what to do with himself.[69]

Had it not been for the chance conjunction of paths between Lee Oswald and President Kennedy on November 22, 1963, most of us would never have heard of Lee Harvey Oswald. It was Ruth Paine, upon the advice of her neighbor Linnie Mae Randle (whose brother, Wesley Buell Frazier, worked at the TSBD), who encouraged Lee to apply for a job there in mid-October.[70] If Oswald had been placed there by his "handlers"—whoever these might be—they would have had to be able to read the future to know that the TSBD had any strategic value.

There is also nothing evoking a massive conspiracy in the manner that Oswald came to the suburb of Irving the night before to visit his family at Ruth Paine's household. It was, on the other hand, unprecedented for Oswald to do so on a weeknight, and an awkward surprise for Marina:

> He asked her on three separate occasions to join him in Dallas—he would get an apartment the next day. After her third refusal, they had dinner with Ruth. The next morning, he nearly slept through the alarm clock, and he got up reluctantly. He got dressed, and then he came over to her and he said, "Don't bother to make breakfast for me," which was unusual, because she never did. Then he said, "I've left some money on the bureau. Be sure and buy shoes for Junie and Rachel." Then he said he would not be coming home for the weekend, because it wasn't good for Ruth to have him there too much. When she saw how much money he had left, she had never seen so much. She said to herself, "That must be everything he had." It was $170. Later that night, she found something else—her wedding ring, his wedding ring, in a cup that her grandmother had given her, on the bureau.[71]

When the police came by that afternoon, Marina showed them the rolled-up blanket in Ruth Paine's garage where she believed Lee was still storing his rifle. But it was gone. Earlier that morning, when he bummed a ride into the city with his co-worker Wesley Buell Frazier, Ruth's neighbor, Lee was carrying a long paper package which, he told Frazier, contained curtain rods for his apartment. The empty bag was later found in the Book Depository, not far from Oswald's mail-order rifle. No curtain rods were ever found, nor were any needed in his boarding house room.

Oswald's behavior in the 24 hours before the assassination is telling. It reveals his awareness that something important was going to happen, something he was willing not to pursue should his wife give their relationship another try. This suggests he was still undecided, at least until that moment when he left his wedding ring inside that cup. As he headed to work one last time, Oswald was no doubt reminded of those famous words by Karl Marx, whose writings he read frequently: "Philosophers have hitherto only interpreted the world in various ways; the point is to change it".[72] McMillan agrees:

> He concluded that the most he or anyone could do to alter the capitalist system was to strike it a blow at the very top, to decapitate it. He wrote this before he shot at General Walker. He seemed to have it in mind the rest of his life.[73]

10.7 Nuts to you

For nearly six decades, many have struggled to explain Lee Oswald's peculiar personality and erratic behavior, sometimes resorting to outlandish scenarios. This is partly due to the Warren Commission's failure to ascribe a clear motive to Kennedy's assassin. But that does not mean he had none. In fact, there were several opinions circulating among the Commission's staff, two of which offer us a good deal of insight.

The first theory was defended most strongly by Wesley Liebeler, the Commission's junior counsel investigating Oswald's personal life. Liebeler argued in a draft chapter of the Warren Report, which was ultimately rejected by the commissioners, that Oswald's decision to shoot Kennedy was a last-minute affair, one he formulated in the two or three days before it happened. This decision was swayed by his Marxist beliefs, his hatred of the United States, his Cuban patriotism, and his desire to prove to the Castro regime, the one that had shunned him, that he could be an important figure in the struggle against capitalist imperialism. Liebeler also argued that although Oswald's target was politically motivated, it was his troubled youth, his repeated failures, and his delusional personality that had served as fuel to ignite his murderous passions. "Lee Harvey Oswald was a man profoundly alienated from the world," Liebeler wrote, "His life was characterized by isolation, frustration, suspicion, failure at almost everything he ever tried to do, and increasingly, by a system of delusion and fantasy designed to protect himself from his own failure and impotence".[74] In other words, Oswald was an angry, lone, *politicized* nut, radicalized by his feelings of alienation—a central tenet in Marxist literature. This, in essence, made JFK a victim of the Cold War.

The reason this argument was rejected by the Commission—despite the fact that it is the dominant view among non-conspiracist Kennedy experts—was that it had the fearsome potential, at least in mid-1964, to stir public opinion in favor of a conflict with Cuba and a possible nuclear war with the Soviets—a scenario that President Johnson, Chief Justice Warren, Bobby Kennedy, and other Washington mandarins wished at all costs to avoid (see Chapters 7 and 9) even if that required lying to the public. The strongest available argument to account for Lee Oswald's actions—that he killed the President to protest his treatment of Cuba—could also be one that, made public, could lead to the unthinkable. The Commission thus chose to keep the whole matter of Lee Oswald's motive nebulous.

Congressman, Commissioner, and future President Gerald Ford, on the other hand, believed that Oswald's motive was essentially psychological (some might say Freudian) and that the answers lay largely in his *Historic Journal* which was a "vivid self-portrait of a young man, who, when he couldn't have his own way, resorted to melodramatic and rash actions to call attention to himself".[75] He was a classic teenage runaway—except that in his case, instead of taking a bus across town or hiding in a tree house, Lee Oswald fled to Russia. His impulses were juvenile, said Ford, like those of a small boy. His politics were too sophomoric to push him to murder. Ford therefore believed that Oswald was primarily motivated not by philosophy or international relations, but by his desperate thirst for attention—the sort he never received from his self-centered mother, his estranged stepfather, his two older brothers, and disparaging wife who frequently mocked his sexual incompetence (and possible impotence) in front of their friends. "He was like a child who, failing to gain the attention he wants, finds that smashing a toy or making a mess is the easiest way to obtain recognition".[76] Shenon adds, "Marina's mocking of his sexual performance had left him so humiliated that he set out to prove his masculinity with a rifle".[77]

A third theory, voiced by Warren Commission lead counsel J. Lee Rankin, which he based on Marina Oswald's testimony, was that her insignificant husband simply wanted to become famous.[78] Other non-conspiracist explanations have included mental illness, symbolic parricide, brute nihilism, and even demon possession. Similarities could no doubt be drawn between Oswald and other famous assassins, but none would likely be any stronger than the reasons discussed earlier, nor could we drum up enough facts to make these any more plausible. "In the end," concludes a resigned James Swanson, "perhaps the reason is much simpler and more fundamental and lies beyond rational human understanding: Lee Harvey Oswald was evil".[79]

That said, Oswald's guilt needs not to be established from a determined motive. His behavior following the murder—fleeing the crime scene, packing a revolver, shooting a policeman, resisting arrest while attempting to shoot another, lying to the police about easily discoverable personal facts, changing his story during his interrogation, showing little concern for the victims—say more about his state of mind, argues Swanson, than his psychological profile or political statements. Guilty people act guilty, and Lee Harvey Oswald certainly did that.[80] "He toyed with the interrogators down at the Dallas police station all that weekend," adds Robert Oswald, "It was a game to him. He knew something they didn't know, and he would keep it to himself. He was in control".[81]

The unlikelihood that Oswald participated in a conspiracy, right wing or otherwise, is evidenced by the way he crossed paths with Kennedy. There is nothing sinister in the way he was hired at the TSBD. He applied for that job on a scoop he received from a family friend because it was one of the few he could get with his low education and inability to drive a vehicle. Oswald did not have that job when he visited the Cuban and Soviet embassies in Mexico City in late September, and Ruth Paine and her neighbor had no verifiable connection to radical Marxists, the CIA, or organized crime. The parade route through Dallas was not finalized until November 15 (and only became official on November 18) a few days before the assassination, when Oswald had already been hired by the Book Depository.[82] Any theorist who disregards these facts is either poorly informed or deliberately sinning against logic.

Asking why Oswald specifically targeted President Kennedy is a question that is not easy to answer, but that may be the wrong question to ask. It may be more enlightening to ask why Oswald chose to assassinate the first important American statesman who happened to drive past his workplace at a time in his life when he had nothing to lose. As Mel Ayton suggests, "If Lee Oswald had not assassinated President Kennedy he would inevitably have committed a different kind of violent political act".[83] The violence Oswald displayed toward his wife, and the deep resentment he harbored toward his mother, his oldest brother, "fascists" like Walker and Bringuier, the Soviet Union, the American government, the FBI agents who appeared to be hounding him (though less than he imagined), and now Cuban immigration officials … all of this turned Oswald into a ticking time bomb. He might perhaps have shot somebody else. President Kennedy just happened to be the best available target. This is what Robert Oswald believed:

> At that moment, Lee was not shooting at a human being but at a prominent political figure who was receiving the applause of the crowd. This was his final protest at a world that had ignored him, sometimes mocked him, always failed to acknowledge his superiority. […] I am convinced that Lee could easily have chosen as his victim someone entirely different politically from John F. Kennedy. […] It is entirely possible that he would have tried to kill Nixon if he had been given the opportunity. […] The whole pattern of failure through most of his twenty-three years led to the outbursts of violence in April and the final tragedy in November 1963.[84]

Lee Oswald's motive may never be certain, but former prosecutor Vincent Bugliosi reminds us that to convict a suspect of murder in an American court, we need not establish their motive beyond a reasonable doubt, only that he or she had the intent to use deadly force. "Motive is the reason that prompts a person to act (or fail to act)," he writes, while "intent is the state of mind with which the act is done".[85] Did Lee Oswald intentionally fire shots at JFK's car with the intention to harm? If so, he can be found guilty even without a known motive. Indeed, even Oswald might not have been able to "convey all the psychic and subconscious dynamics swirling about in his fevered mind that led up to his monstrous act of murder".[86]

There remain many mysteries concerning Oswald's innermost thoughts. What the abundant literature on him tells us, however, is that despite the fact that Kennedy's murder made little sense to most people, it made perfect sense to Lee Oswald. As Norman Mailer suggests, "Oswald was a secret agent. There is no doubt about that. The only matter unsettled is whether he was working for any service larger than the power centers in the privacy of his mind".[87]

Our discussion of motive has drawn to a close. We now move on to ask whether Oswald had the skills and ability to perpetrate this crime on his own, and if not, whether he might have done so with some assistance. Is there evidence of other shooters, handlers, or planners? Was evidence tampered with or willfully destroyed, perhaps to make an innocent man *look* guilty? Or are we being deceived by our faulty assumptions? Questions relating to means and opportunity, and to our perceptions of these events, will be dealt with in the following sections.

Notes

1 On Oswald's hatred of the FBI, see Posner: *Case Closed* (2003), *passim*. On the seven elements of political paranoia, see Robins and Post: *Political Paranoia* (1997), chap. 1. See also Chapter 1 of this book.
2 Bugliosi, 1957–1970. See also Chapter 2.
3 "Oliver Stone on 50th Anniversary of JFK Assassination & *The Untold History of the United States*," Interview with Amy Goodman on *Democracy Now*, November 5, 2013.
4 "The Men Who Killed Kennedy," Episode 8: "The Love Affair," Nigel Tuner Productions, *History Channel*, 2003; Baker: *Me & Lee: How I Came to Know, Love and Lose Lee Harvey Oswald* (2011).
5 Bugliosi, 1025; June 3, 1960 memorandum by J. Edgar Hoover, Warren Commission FBI item 14. See also Chapter 4 of this book.
6 L.E. Norton et al.: "The Exhumation and Identification of Lee Harvey Oswald," *Journal of Forensic Science, JFSCA*, Vol.29, No.1, January 1984, 19–38. PDF.
7 Bugliosi, 1039–44.
8 Donald Jeffries: "John Armstrong's 'Harvey and Lee'," (n.d.), *Keeping It Unreal*. For detailed descriptions of this "crazy old Marguerite," see works by Posner, Bugliosi, and Shenon.
9 Ramsay, 127, 129, 135.
10 Bugliosi, 1024.
11 Ibid., 1021–56. See also McAdams: "Theories of Two Lee Harvey Oswalds: Seeing Oswald Double," (n.d.), *The Kennedy Assassination*.
12 Shenon, 199; Robert Oswald: *Lee: A Portrait of Lee Harvey Oswald by His Brother* (1967), 196–7.
13 A one-time exceptional explanation that defies trends, predictability, or the rules of logical consistency.
14 Bugliosi, 1030–9.
15 The one glaring exception, writes Bugliosi, is the Sylvia Odio case. See later.
16 Uscinski and Parent, 50–1.
17 Ruby repeated the story during a polygraph examination, which he passed successfully. Shenon, 368–73, 421–2; Bugliosi, 297–8.

18 For example, there were other ways for Ruby to enter the parking garage. It is also pos-sible that someone let Ruby inside for completely innocuous reasons. See Chapters 2 and 6, and David Von Pein: "How Did Jack Ruby Get into the Police Basement?" (n.d.), *DVP's JFK Archive*.

19 Another example is the number of Dealey Plaza witnesses who claimed they heard more or less than three gunshots being fired at Kennedy (see Chapters 11–13).

20 Uscinski and Parent, 50.

21 Ibid., 51.

22 On Nosenko, see Posner, chap. 3, and Shenon, 205–7.

23 *Warren Report*, chap. 4, "Background of Lee Harvey Oswald," 322.

24 Testimony of Sylvia Odio, WC XI; Shenon, 212–5; Posner, 175–81; Bugliosi, 1295–335; McAdams: "Odio: The Mother of All Oswald Sightings," (n.d.), *The Kennedy Assassination*.

25 Shenon, 445.

26 McAdams: "Odio: The Mother of All Oswald Sightings."

27 See "The Odio Incident and Anti-Castro Cuban Exiles," in Bugliosi, 1295–335.

28 Ibid.

29 Testimony of John Edward Pic, WC XI. Emphasis added. Almost a decade older than his youngest brother, John Pic and Lee Oswald had different fathers. Robert Oswald, the middle brother, was closer in age to John but, having the same father as Lee, shared a closer bond and had more frequent interactions with Marguerite Oswald's youngest son. For this reason, and because he was a resident of nearby Denton (Pic lived in distant San Antonio), Robert would be the one to take care of Lee's funeral arrangements following his murder by Jack Ruby. Though the three brothers were close in their youth, John and Lee had little contact for almost a decade by the time of JFK's assassination, largely on account of their age difference, their travels, military postings, and Lee's self-exile to the Soviet Union. In fact, John met Lee only once after the latter became an adult (at a Thanksgiving dinner at Robert's home in November 1962).

30 Oswald, 216–7, 224. Emphasis added. Robert Oswald has maintained a consistent opinion concerning Lee's motive and guilt. Testimony of Robert Edward Lee Oswald, WC I (1964); "Who Was Lee Harvey Oswald," *PBS Frontline*, November 19, 2013.

31 For example, Malcolm Abrams: "Why I Believe Lee Was a CIA Agent," an interview with Marguerite Oswald, *Midnight*, September 27, 1976. PDF.

32 Testimony of John Edward Pic, WC XI. Marguerite Oswald, who went through two divorces and had stormy relations with her three children for decades—including neglect and financial and emotional manipulation—was described by her sons (and many others) as a conniving and vindictive attention-seeker. Marguerite Oswald remained estranged from her two surviving sons after Lee's assassination, as well as from Lee's widow Marina and her grandchildren.

33 "Marina Oswald," an interview with Marina Oswald Porter by Barry Nolan, *Hard Copy*, November 19, 1990, *YouTube*.

34 Tom Brokaw: "Now: An Interview with Marina Porter," *NBC*, August 1993, *YouTube*; "A Conversation with Marina," in Bugliosi, 1485–8.

35 Steve Salerno: "June Oswald, Lee Harvey's Oldest," an interview with June Oswald Porter, *The New York Times Magazine*, April 30, 1995; Keith Kachtick: "Lee Harvey's Legacy," an interview with Rachel Oswald Porter, *Texas Monthly*, March 1995; See also TV interviews given by Rachel and June Oswald Porter (in the mid-1990s) for *Hard Copy* and *NBC Today*, available on *YouTube*.

36 Mel Ayton: "Lee Harvey Oswald's Motives," (n.d.), John McAdams, ed.: *The Kennedy Assassination*.

37 Robert Oswald visited Lee while he was in police custody, at which time Lee asked him to contact John Abt, a lawyer for the American Communist Party. Oswald made the same request to Marina and Ruth Payne. "Who Was Lee Harvey Oswald? Interview: Robert Oswald," (1993) *PBS Frontline*, November 19, 2013; "Who Was Lee Harvey Oswald? Interview: Priscilla Johnson McMillan," (1993) *PBS Frontline*; Ayton: "Lee Harvey Oswald's Motives". According to Ayton, Oswald saw himself as a left-wing hero in the tradition of Julius and Ethel Rosenberg, the American Marxist couple who were arrested and executed in 1953 for leaking nuclear secrets to the Soviets: "In attempting to contact Abt Oswald was revealing something about himself—he was already preparing for his appearance on the political stage, emulating the Rosenbergs by becoming a 'cause célèbre'".

38 See Priscilla Johnson McMillan: *Marina and Lee* (1977); Norman Mailer: *Oswald's Tale: An American Mystery* (1995); Oswald (1967); Peter Savodnik: *The Interloper: Lee Harvey Oswald Inside the Soviet Union* (2013); Mel Ayton and David Von Pein: *Beyond Reasonable Doubt: The Warren Report and Lee Harvey Oswald's Guilt and Motive 50 Years On* (2014); Posner: *Case Closed* (1993); Bugliosi: *Reclaiming History* (2007); "Oswald in the Soviet Union: An Investigation of Yuri Nosenko," *Staff Report of the Select Committee on Assassinations U.S. House of Representatives* (HSCA), March 1979.

39 Paul Gregory: "Lee Harvey Oswald Was My Friend," *The New York Times Magazine*, November 7, 2013.

40 Posner: "Oswald in Russia," illustrated supplement (n.p.), *Case Closed*.

41 Lee and Robert's father—Robert Edward Lee Oswald, Sr.—was Marguerite's second husband. He died of a heart attack before Lee was born. John Pic said he was a temperamental and violent man who "doled out whippings". Hector Saldana: "Oswald's brother was in S.A. in '63'," *San Antonio Express-News*, November 21, 2013.

42 Robert Oswald notes that Edwin Ekdahl's first name was shared by the man Lee tried to murder in April 1963, and his birthplace and "Yankee accent" were like those of the young president whom Lee murdered. He also speculates that symbolic parricide was a possible motive, conscious or not, for both of these shootings. Oswald, 34–5.

43 Ibid., 36, 39.

44 Testimony of John Edward Pic, WC XI.

45 The arrest, trial, and execution (in June 1953) of Julius and Ethel Rosenberg for trading scientific secrets to the Soviets was, according to McMillan, a key instigator of Oswald's Marxism. "Who Was Lee Harvey Oswald? Interview: Priscilla Johnson McMillan".

46 His writings suggest he had dyslexia. Posner, 24 (footnote).

47 Renatus Hartogs, M.D., Ph.D.: "Youth House Psychiatrist's Report, Case No. 26996, 5/7/53"; McAdams: "Lee Harvey Oswald: Troubled Youth," *The Kennedy Assassination*; Posner, 11–4.

48 Ayton: "Lee Harvey Oswald's Motives".

49 John was stationed in Japan when he heard of Lee's defection to the USSR. He was an Air Force laboratory technician in San Antonio, Texas, when the Kennedy assassination occurred.

50 Robert Oswald believed Lee was jealous of his successes in military school, the Marines, career, and marriage, including the fact that Robert had a son and Lee only had daughters. Oswald, 230–3.

51 Dr. John K. Lattimer (*Kennedy and Lincoln: Medical & Ballistic Comparisons of Their Assassinations*, 1980), interviewed in "Peter Jennings Reporting: The Kennedy Assassination—Beyond Conspiracy," *ABC News*, 2003. Lattimer points out that Oswald received the grade of marksman while in the Marines, scoring a 48/50 in a 200-yard rapid-fire test (i.e., over twice the distance than the one from which he allegedly shot

Kennedy). According to Marina Oswald, Lee frequently practiced his shooting and aim (without ammunition) in their home during the months before the assassination. Testimony of Mrs. Lee Harvey Oswald, WC I. Robert Oswald has stated that Lee was a rather good shot with targets, but much less at hunting prey.

52 Yuri Nosenko, Interview with Gerald Posner, September 1, 1992, quoted in Posner, 48.

53 "Who Was Lee Harvey Oswald? Interview: Priscilla Johnson McMillan".

54 According to her daughter June, Marina was born out of wedlock and had been sent to Minsk to live with distant relatives. Steve Salerno: "June Oswald, Lee Harvey's Oldest".

55 For example, Russo and Molton, 163–4.

56 Heather Maher: "Why Lee Harvey Oswald Fled to the Soviet Union," *The Atlantic*, November 20, 2013.

57 This was corroborated by Marina as well as her daughter June and family friend George de Mohrenschildt. Salerno, op. cit.; Testimony of Mrs. Lee Harvey Oswald, WC I; Oswald, 127; and Shenon, 322–5.

58 "Who Was Lee Harvey Oswald? Interview: Priscilla Johnson McMillan"; Paul Gregory: "Lee Harvey Oswald Was My Friend".

59 "Who Was Lee Harvey Oswald? Interview: Robert Oswald".

60 Posner, chaps. 1–10.

61 On his Cuban visa application, completed on September 27, 1963, Oswald wrote the date of September 30, 1963, as his intended arrival in Cuba. This gave no time to his family to join him. Oswald does not seem to have sought visas for the rest of his family. See JFK Exhibit F-408, HSCA, Volume III, 129.

62 Oswald, 125–6.

63 Ayton: "Lee Harvey Oswald's Motives".

64 Interview of Ruth Paine by *The Press Democrat*, September 10, 2013, *YouTube*.

65 "Who Was Lee Harvey Oswald? Interview: Priscilla Johnson McMillan".

66 In the early 1990s, Marina Oswald Porter again confirmed that Lee tried to murder the "fascist" Walker. "Marina Oswald," an interview with Marina Oswald Porter by Barry Nolan, *Hard Copy*, November 19, 1990.

67 Family friend George de Mohrenschildt was given a copy of one of the pictures, on the back of which was an epitaph, written in Russian, which read: "this is the hunter of fascists! Ha! Ha! Ha!" In an unpublished memoir released by the HSCA in 1978, de Mohrenschildt wrote, "Here Marina was again making fun of her husband, jeering Lee's very serious anti–fascist feelings". George de Mohrenschildt: *I Am a Patsy!* (chap. 22: "A Message from Lee"), *22 November 1963: An Introduction to the JFK Assassination*.

68 "Who Was Lee Harvey Oswald? Interview: Robert Oswald".

69 "Who Was Lee Harvey Oswald? Interview: Priscilla Johnson McMillan".

70 Testimony of Linnie Mae Randle, WC II.

71 "Who Was Lee Harvey Oswald? Interview: Priscilla Johnson McMillan".

72 Karl Marx: "Eleventh Thesis on Feuerbach," *The German Ideology*, 1846. When interviewed by radio journalist William Stuckey on August 27, 1963, and again on WDSU TV in New Orleans, Oswald presented himself as a Marxist and student of Marxist philosophy (and not as a communist in the Soviet tradition). Both interviews are available on *YouTube*.

73 "Who Was Lee Harvey Oswald? Interview: Priscilla Johnson McMillan".

74 Wesley Liebeler: "Possible Personal Motives," draft chapter of final Commission Report, June 23, 1964, staff files, Warren Commission, NARA, cited in Shenon, 410.

75 Gerald R. Ford and John R. Styles: *Portrait of the Assassin* (1965), 53–60, and "Oral History Interview by Vicki Daitch," July 18, 2003, *John F. Kennedy Presidential Library and Museum*, 9–10, cited in Shenon, 471.

76 Cited in Shenon, 471.

77 Ibid., 471.
78 Ibid., 174, 415.
79 Swanson, 297.
80 Ibid., 67, 208–12, 228.
81 "Who Was Lee Harvey Oswald? Interview: Robert Oswald".
82 McAdams: "Changed Motorcade Route in Dallas?" (n.d.), *The Kennedy Assassination*.
83 Ayton: "Lee Harvey Oswald's Motives".
84 Oswald, 214, 219, 240.
85 Bugliosi, 935–6.
86 Ibid., 935–6.
87 Mailer, 352.

PART III

Means

"It's gonna be a turkey shoot!"

11

THE SHOOTING GALLERY

The motorcade and Dealey Plaza

11.1 Snipers, snipers, everywhere!

The previous chapter showed that Lee Oswald had as good a motive to kill Kennedy as any other suspect blamed by conspiracy theorists. It also established that his formative life events, from his early childhood to his employment at the Texas School Book Depository (TSBD), were less sinister than is often alleged. However, this does not prove he killed JFK, nor does it prove he was not part of a wider conspiracy. While Oswald's behavior and character do place him atop a long list of suspects, it is necessary that we also examine the physical evidence of the assassination to respond to the theories that depict him as a Cuban or Soviet operative, a double-agent in some kind of right-wing plot, a puppet of organized crime, or a victim of the CIA and "military industrial complex". To establish that Oswald was none of these things we need to prove he was present at the TSBD's sixth-floor window and that he had the tools and skills to murder the president. Simply put, we need to prove he had the means to do it.[1] This will be the subject of the following two chapters. But first, we must consider whether Oswald was part of a larger operation, wittingly or otherwise. To do this, we will carefully examine the evidence offered by JFK buffs that allegedly prove the existence of other assassins and plotters lurking in Dallas and Dealey Plaza.

One of the most succinct and comprehensive conspiracist descriptions of what happened on November 22, 1963, is found in Oliver Stone's 1991 *JFK*, a creative reconstruction of New Orleans District Attorney (DA) Jim Garrison's prosecution of businessman Clay Shaw for conspiring to kill Kennedy (see Chapter 4), which streamlines multiple theories into a single, more or less coherent narrative. In one highly charged courtroom scene, Garrison tells the jury:

DOI: 10.4324/9781003222460-14

Once you conclude the magic bullet could not create all seven of those wounds [to Kennedy and Connally], you'd have to conclude that there was a fourth shot and a second rifle. And if there was a second rifleman, then, by definition, there had to be a conspiracy.[2]

A long and tense philippic follows, detailing the DA's assumptions of what may have happened that day—a speech that combines some of the real claims made by the historical Garrison, and some that emerged in later decades. Many of the real Garrison's claims—those that turned out to be risible—are largely left out of the scene, which mimics all of the standard TV courtroom clichés. The narrative includes the following suspicious "facts":

- An anonymous man fakes an epileptic seizure to distract the crowd from the assassins moving into place. The "epileptic" later vanishes.
- A team of assassins moves into the TSBD, let in by "unknown workmen" refurbishing floors on the sixth floor. Another team moves into the Dal-Tex building across the street.
- A communications team takes position throughout Dealey Plaza, using a variety of radio equipment.
- A third team of assassins moves into the railyard behind the picket fence, atop the "grassy knoll". They are spotted by railroad worker Lee Bowers sitting in a control tower.
- Fake police officers take position in the railyard and TSBD parking lot to turn away curious onlookers.
- Bursts of triangulated gunfire simultaneously strike Kennedy on a coordinated signal, making it look like the work of a single sniper:

  Three teams. Three shooters. The triangulation of fire that Clay Shaw and David Ferrie discussed two months before. They have walked the plaza. They know every inch. They have calibrated their sight. They have practiced on moving targets. They are ready. Kennedy's motorcade makes the turn from Main onto Houston. It's gonna be a turkey shoot! *They don't shoot him coming up Houston*, which is the easiest shot for a single shot from the Book Depository. They wait. They wait until he gets in the killing zone, between three rifles.[3]

The DA then scrutinizes the Zapruder film, firing off more damning "proofs" about the sequence of shots:

- The president's limousine rolls past at an unusual 11 miles-per-hour crawl.
- The first shot misses the limousine (possibly to distract onlookers).
- Kennedy is hit in the throat *from the front*.
- A *third* shot hits Kennedy in the back.
- A *fourth* shot misses him and strikes Connally, still holding his Stetson hat.

- A *fifth* shot misses again, striking bystander James Tague.
- The limousine driver steps on the brakes.
- A *sixth* shot strikes Kennedy in the front-right side of the head:

> This is the key shot. The President going *back and to his left*. Shot from the front and right. Totally inconsistent with the shot from the Depository. […] What happens then? Pandemonium. The shooters quickly disassemble their various weapons, all except the Oswald rifle.[4]

Central to Stone's argument is his suggestion that Oswald did not—indeed *could not*—have perpetrated this crime on his own. *JFK* does not present its argument in standard form (what Hollywood film ever does?), but we can safely summarize the essence of Stone's material defense of Lee Oswald as the following:

P1: The evidence indicates that at least six shots were fired at President Kennedy.
P2: Either Lee Harvey Oswald fired more than three shots, or else he fired a "magic bullet".
P3: Oswald could not have fired a magic bullet.

C1: Hence, Oswald had to have fired more than three shots.
P4: But the evidence indicates that Oswald could not have fired more than three shots.

C2: Therefore, there were multiple shooters and, by logical necessity, a conspiracy to kill Kennedy.[5]

Needless to say, Stone's version breaks entirely with the narrative offered by the vast majority of government, academic, and journalistic investigations of Kennedy's murder (see Chapters 2 and 4). One leading conspiracy skeptic, former Deputy DA Vincent Bugliosi, went so far as to state that except for the date, location, and victim, Stone's film got almost everything wrong about Kennedy's murder.[6]

So what exactly happened in Dealey Plaza? An exhaustive inspection of all, or even most, conspiracist claims would require thousands of pages. Indeed, the community of JFK buffs has over the decades constructed a massive labyrinth of speculations and counter-theories concerning what *might* have happened in Dallas on November 22, 1963. Many of these scenarios are mutually inconsistent, despite Stone's impressive efforts to weave them into a single plotline. Some are self-contradicting. Some rely almost entirely on a single, incongruent piece of data—such as the House Select Committee on Assassinations (HSCA)'s conclusion, based on controversial acoustic evidence, that an anonymous second shooter at the "grassy knoll", who left no trace of his existence, fired a single shot that failed to hit anything. Some are downright nutty, based on little more than a grainy black-and-white photo or blurry home movie blown up in size or watched frame-by-frame.

One stark example, which we will not waste the reader's time studying in detail, is the theory that JFK was killed by his limousine driver, Secret Service agent Bill Greer, who supposedly turned around and shot his own boss with a pistol without anyone noticing.[7] Some also claim that Secret Service agent George Hickey, who sat in the follow-up car tailing the president's limo, accidentally shot JFK with an AR-15 assault rifle (whose bullet bypassed the driver and windshield that sat between Hickey and Kennedy).[8]

Given this profusion of "evidence" that comes in the form of rhetorical questions, suspicious "connections," inconsequential factoids, unprovable thought experiments, and wild goose chases, let us focus our efforts on the most popular claims found in the literature—namely those stated in Stone's *JFK* (see above), and the 16 "smoking guns"[9] offered by James Fetzer in the prologue of his book *Murder in Dealey Plaza* (2000)[10]:

1. A throat shot from the back is impossible since it would have impacted bony structures.
2. The headshot trajectory is inconsistent with the position of JFK's head at the time of the shot.
3. The suspect's weapon was not a high-velocity rifle and could not have fired the fatal headshot.
4. The bullets linked to Oswald's rifle could not have caused the explosive damage observed on JFK's head.
5. Bullet fragments in JFK's head are consistent with a shot that entered the area of his right temple.
6. The official autopsy report was contradicted by more than 40 eyewitnesses.
7. The autopsy X-rays were fabricated.
8. JFK's brain disappeared and was replaced with a fake brain.
9. Inconsistencies between witness reports and autopsy photographs prove these were altered.
10. Inconsistencies between witness reports and the Zapruder film prove it was altered.
11. Early TV and radio broadcasts reported shots from the front.
12. Eyewitness reports were discounted on the basis of altered X-rays, films, and photographs.[11]
13. The motorcade route was changed at the last minute to bring the limousine closer to the Book Depository.
14. Secret Servicemen violated their own policies for the protection of the President in Dealey Plaza.
15. Neither the mafia, Cubans, nor the KGB could have perpetrated such a massive cover-up after the fact.
16. Many individuals (namely organized crime figures) confessed they took part in the assassination.[12]

This long list of claims reveals that, while the details of Lee Oswald's life are too often ignored by conspiracists, the physical layout, material evidence, and minutia of the murder sequence receive the opposite treatment: they are stringently scrutinized, albeit selectively, with a quasi-cultish zeal. We should therefore study them carefully.

Dealey Plaza is an open public square on the western edge of downtown Dallas, bordered by tall buildings on three sides and an elevated railroad overpass on its western flank (see Figures 2.1, 11.1, and 11.2). It is also where three major boulevards (Commerce, Main, and Elm) converge under the overpass to either merge with the north-south Stemmons Freeway or continue westward as a single road (Commerce Street). While it is obvious to proponents of the Lone Gunman Theory that JFK had to be shot on a street near Oswald's workplace, conspiracists require a more ambitious and convoluted explanation.

To kill Kennedy, it is claimed, an open space was needed so that the assassins might catch him in a "triangulation of crossfire" (shots from three different angles) lowering his chance of survival to zero. It is not clear how Dealey Plaza served this purpose better than other parts of the city; hundreds of windows and dozens of rooftops surrounded the President's car minutes earlier, where his chance of escaping through heavy crowds of panicked pedestrians would have been lower.[13] Perhaps, as some argue, Dealey Plaza offered a better chance for the shooters to disappear, or perhaps no better place could be found where they could set up the scapegoat. In any event, such considerations make the triangulation theory weaker.

Assuming that these special teams of assassins existed, they would have been located, according to our theorists, (a) in one of the upper floors of the TSBD, (b) on the second floor of the Dal-Tex building located on the north-east corner of Houston and Elm, beside the TSBD (see Figure 2.1), and (c) in the parking lot and railyard above the hill (the so-called grassy knoll) on the north side of Elm Street, west of the north Pergola (the rounded monument beside the TSBD).[14] Some claim a fourth team fired shots from within a storm drain.[15] Rather than inflict two to four wounds on JFK, the sheer number of shooters proposed by conspiracist authors should have turned him into Swiss cheese. Apparently, it never occurred to the plotters (or to the conspiracists) that planting a bomb on the motorcade route would have been much easier to orchestrate and harder to investigate. In any event, no material evidence of these assassins—for example, bullet casings, foreign cigarettes, photos, matching footprints—was ever collected at these locations by proper authorities, unwitting civilians, or insightful conspiracists. Their entire existence must be deduced from the ballistic evidence, or the memories of a few questionable witnesses, or simply assumed because the theory demands it.

11.2   A henchman behind every bush

Conspiracists perceive many suspicious characters lining the motorcade route in hundreds of photos and film frames of Dealey Plaza. These include a man holding an open umbrella, which, they claim, served as a signal for the shooters to start

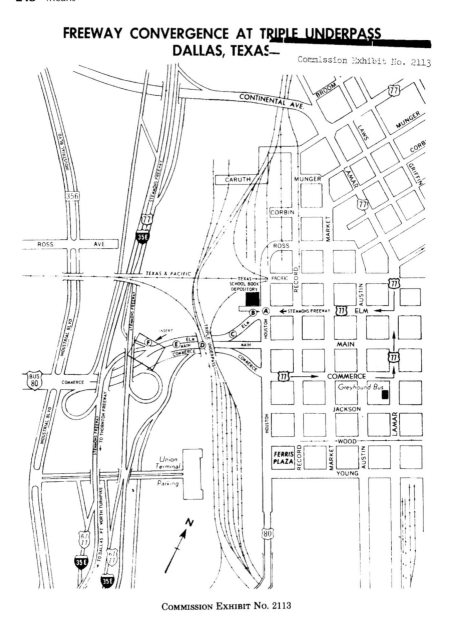

FREEWAY CONVERGENCE AT TRIPLE UNDERPASS DALLAS, TEXAS—

Commission Exhibit No. 2113

COMMISSION EXHIBIT NO. 2113

FIGURE 11.1 Map of freeway convergence in Dallas

Source: Warren Commission Exhibit 2113, National Archives and Records Administration.

FIGURE 11.2 View of Dealey Plaza from Texas School Book Depository (TSBD)
Source: HSCA JFK Exhibit F-339, National Archives and Records Administration.

firing,[16] as well as a man sitting on the Elm Street curb holding a bulky (and outdated) two-way radio, presumably to communicate with the shooters. Some authors see both, irrespective of the logical and logistical problem of having two separate signalers serve the same purpose.[17]

The existence and intentions of this "Communications Man" is deduced solely from grainy pictures of a swarthy skinned "Cuban" and a stocky blond-haired Caucasian sitting on the Elm Street roadside moments after the shooting.[18] Various Cuban mercenaries and CIA agents have been offered as possible matches, with little agreement among researchers. Fletcher Prouty claims that the stocky Caucasian is a CIA agent named James Hicks.[19] The real Hicks, however, was nothing of the sort. He was a surveyor from Arkansas and a charlatan who later testified for Jim Garrison in front of a New Orleans grand jury in exchange for the DA's promise to help him beat a drunk-driving rap in Oklahoma.[20] Hicks' January 1968 grand jury testimony was not only inconsistent with established facts, it also makes us wonder why a man who was supposedly in a covert assassination team would risk blowing his cover— indeed the whole conspiracy—by testifying publicly in a highly mediatized court case.[21] Hicks' explosive testimony, if true, would have made him a star witness. Yet Garrison chose not to use it in the Shaw trial.

As for the "Umbrella Man," that argument was debunked by the HSCA in 1978 when it was discovered that this man was just an eccentric protestor named Louie

Steven Witt. Witt had used the umbrella as a symbol to protest Joe Kennedy, Sr.'s pre–World War II support of British Prime Minister Neville Chamberlain—the original "umbrella man"—whose policies of appeasement allowed Hitler's armies to invade Czechoslovakia and Poland. By holding up an umbrella under a sunny blue sky, Witt told the HSCA, he was warning Kennedy not to appease the Soviets like his father, the former Ambassador to the Court of St-James, did the Nazis. Responding to this revelation, Josiah Thompson, a rare JFK buff with a sense of humor, mused: "You can never, on your own, think up all the non-sinister perfectly valid explanations for [such a] fact … A cautionary tale!"[22]

The theory of the vanishing epileptic was debunked long before Jim Garrison and Oliver Stone used it as evidence of a plot. This man was no sinister operative. He was Jerry Belknap, a Dallas resident whose epilepsy was diagnosed and who was investigated by the FBI and considered of no significance. As Gerald Posner explains, Belknap was a lifelong epileptic who was taken to Parkland hospital in an ambulance minutes before Kennedy's motorcade entered Dealey Plaza. No record of his treatment was found because "he felt better when given water and an aspirin, and there was such a rush of people at the emergency room [due to the subsequent assassination], he realized he was not going to be quickly treated".[23]

Stone's film also refers to three anonymous "tramps" photographed in Dealey Plaza minutes after the assassination by journalists who thought the Dallas police had captured important suspects.[24] The photographs show the men being escorted to the nearby Sheriff's office by uniformed policemen with shotguns (Figure 11.3). Conspiracists have had a field day identifying these men as various CIA operatives, mafia thugs, or right-wing mercenaries,[25] or describing the policemen as actors in costumes with discrete listening devices tucked in their ears.[26] This is a peculiar allegation since the two officers in the photos were correctly identified by the Warren Commission as Dallas policemen Marvin Wise and Billy Bass.[27] Sargent D.V. Harkness, a third policeman who does not appear on the photographs, did explain to the Commission that three transients found in a nearby railcar were detained, questioned, and later released. But because their arrest records were accidentally misplaced (they were only located in 1989 by conspiracy researcher Mary La Fontaine), questions have abounded on the identity of these suspected assassins long after the HSCA's forensic anthropologists studied their pictures closely and found no matching features between the tramps and leading conspiracy suspects. In the end, the tramps turned out to be exactly what Sargent Harkness told the Warren Commission: tramps! They were tracked down in the early 1990s by a tabloid TV program and identified as Harold Doyle, John Forrester Gedney, and Gus W. Abrams, unemployed men who had fallen on hard times. As John McAdams explained,

> Suspicious of authority and fearful of being blamed, they remained quiet about their identities until the surviving two were tracked down almost 30 years later. Never objectively 'mysterious' they only seemed that way because the absence of information left room for wild speculation.[28]

FIGURE 11.3 Three tramps being escorted past the TSBD
Source: *Fort Worth Star-Telegram*, University of Texas at Arlington Libraries.

In addition to falsely identifying the three tramps as CIA assassins, Fletcher Prouty initiated the now-widely disseminated claim that one of the tramp photographs shows that Edward Lansdale, the military spymaster who advised Vietnam's Ngo Dinh Diem and oversaw Operation Mongoose (see Chapters 7 and 8), was present in Dealey Plaza during the shooting. This proves Lansdale's complicity, Prouty wrote to fellow retired officer Lieutenant General Victor H. Krulak in 1984–85, and also to Jim Garrison in 1990.[29] Prouty had by then begun to target Lansdale (who died in 1987) as a key conspirator.[30] This in turn led Oliver Stone to depict Lansdale as "General Y" in the film *JFK*.

The man in the photo whose face is not visible (see Figure 11.3) and whom Prouty claimed was Lansdale (Figure 11.4) is walking past the three tramps along the south wall of the TSBD, heading for the rear parking lot. He is wearing a suit, has a slight stoop, and what Prouty called a "large class ring" on his left ring finger. All this, he claims, is proof that his former superior officer helped plan the assassination. That is *all* the evidence he offers to prove it. Prouty's "Lansdale sighting" is based on the concurrent claim that the tramps and policemen on the picture were all "actors" also involved in the conspiracy, which would be untenable if Prouty had revealed these policemen's real names—which he in fact did in a previously published essay![31] This sort of strategic forgetfulness is rampant throughout Prouty's writings and interviews. To anyone without an ulterior motive to place him at the scene of the crime, the "Lansdale" in the picture could equally be just a "simple, uncomplicated pedestrian," to use Prouty's own words, trying to get to

FIGURE 11.4 Major General Edward Lansdale
Source: US Air Force Photograph.[32]

his car.[33] Indeed, the TSBD parking lot was full of cars "that day and every day," said Marilyn Sitzman, Abraham Zapruder's assistant, who worked in the Dal-Tex building across the street.[34] This is perhaps why Oliver Stone carefully avoided mentioning Lansdale's name in his film and cutting out scenes that directly appealed to this "proof".[35]

The letters to Krulak and Garrison make it clear that Prouty had an axe to grind with Lansdale. A major reason for this is found in a 1988 biography of Lansdale by military historian Cecil B. Currey, who cited Lansdale as saying:

> I continue to be surprised [...] to find Fletcher Prouty quoted as an authority. He was my 'cross to bear' before [the *Pentagon Papers* whistleblower] Dan Ellsberg came along. [...] He was a good pilot of prop-driven aircraft, but had such a heavy dose of paranoia about CIA when he was on my staff that I kicked him back to the Air Force. He was one of those who thought I was secretly running the Agency from the Pentagon, despite all the proof otherwise.[36]

Incensed by these words, Prouty told Garrison that Lansdale was a "classic chameleon," that Currey's book was "bullshit," and that it was probably written by CIA agents.[37]

In addition, Prouty's claim that Lansdale planned JFK's murder runs into logical problems. First, we should ask why an accomplished CIA mastermind (as Prouty describes him) would expose himself in broad daylight 50 yards from the crime scene, with no other purpose than to give reassuring winks[38] to genuine tramps and policemen. How does Prouty's entire account of the tramps picture make any sense except as a proof of paranoia, dementia, or dishonesty? It is indeed difficult not to agree with Cecil Currey's Lansdale that Prouty's imagination has outgunned his credentials.

It is true that Ed Lansdale was a discrete man who knew more about clandestine operations than he let on publicly. Nevertheless, what historians do know about him made him a poor choice to organize JFK's murder. His views on foreign policy, for instance, were more in line with those of the Kennedy brothers during this time than with the military brass or CIA, who according to Stone and Prouty hired "General Y" to plan out the murder. This clash of opinions was in fact a principal reason for Lansdale's forced retirement just a few weeks before Kennedy landed in Dallas.[39] Despite its widespread popularity, Prouty's entire "Lansdale in Dallas" theory ends up being no more than a red herring fallacy. But instead of being seen for what it is—a malicious settling of accounts with a dead man, reminiscent of the final plot twist in Christopher Nolan's *Memento* (see Chapter 1)—Prouty's lurking Lansdale allowed many conspiracists to finally put a face on the evil machinery of war they called the "military industrial complex": a secretive and morally ambiguous figure who represented another America, a man who, with some imaginative simplification, could serve as a usable devil. "It can be tempting to engage in this kind of speculation," writes Jonathan Nashel, "but what such conspiracy scripts chiefly testify to is the self-propelling power of Lansdale mystique". For many JFK buffs, "the mysteries of Lansdale's persona as a CIA agent and his celebrity makes him the ubiquitous linchpin of their conspiracy networks".[40]

Finally, many conspiracists, including "patient zero" Mark Lane and Dealey Plaza witness Jean Hill,[41] claim that fake Secret Service agents stood in the TSBD parking lot—located behind the "grassy knoll" area, between the TSBD and triple underpass—preventing real policemen and curious civilians from pursuing the assassin(s) while he/they made his/their escape (accounts vary). Lane described this alleged fraud (again) in a 2014 interview:

> The police officer named Smith [was] probably the single most important witness to the assassination. [...] He was in the motorcade. When he heard the [last] shot, he knew it came from the area near the wooden fence on the grassy knoll to the right front of the president's limousine. He took his motor bike and drove up [...]. A man emerged from behind the fence. He thought he had caught the assassin. Actually, he had caught the assassin. But the man took out his credentials and said, 'United States Secret Service.' And he did have those credentials. *And they had been issued by the Central Intelligence Agency.* And so he was allowed to leave because he had these credentials. Later on, when the Secret Service was compelled to tell where its agents were, they said nobody was walking, nobody was on the ground; they were all in the motorcade. So who was that guy who had CIA-created credentials? Well, we still don't know. [...] When Smith tried to tell this to the Warren Commission [...], Wesley Liebler [sic] said, 'Is there anything you saw that day which seemed suspicious or out of the way?' [LAUGHTER] Other than the fact that you caught the assassin? [LAUGHTER] [...] That was it. And, of course,

that guy disappeared. *And Smith disappeared.* This is the single most important witness that day because he caught the assassin and had a gun pointed at him. *His name does not appear in the Warren Commission report.*[42]

While there is little doubt that many bystanders, journalists, and policemen rushed up the grassy knoll after the president was shot, their purpose for doing so is not clear, nor did a single, cause push them to do so. Conspiracists who believe there was a shooter behind the picket fence often assume that the crowd immediately ran up the hill to investigate the area from which they thought shots had been fired. Some witnesses may have done so, but if was the case, we should reasonably expect that some frightened bystanders would *run away* from a rifle discharge, not toward it. Yet that is not what occurred. Home videos taken by Marie Muchmore and Orville Nix—the best available film records of the assassination after the Zapruder film—prove there were very few people standing on the north side of Elm (the "grassy knoll" area) at the time of the fatal headshot. The only two individuals who can clearly be seen on the north side of Elm as the limousine passes are running up the concrete staircase, *toward the fence.* They are simultaneously *looking backwards* (away from the fence and toward the limousine carrying the fatally wounded president). This shows that their focus was on the president's car, not on the fence they were rushing toward.[43] This suggests that the earliest "grassy knoll runners" were trying to get away from the motorcade and Elm Street, probably to steer clear of subsequent shots that might be directed at the president's car and therefore also toward them. This is a natural reaction during a shooting, but it requires some effort by the contemporary viewer to consider these acts in their proper context. After all, no one could know at the time that the shooting was over.

Once the rest of the motorcade disappeared down Elm Street (this took several minutes), a crowd gathered near the grassy knoll and climbed up its slope. But the latter part of the Nix film shows us that before this happened, the crowd pursued the president's car along Elm Street (westward) before several onlookers began to climb the knoll (northwards), perhaps trying to catch a glimpse of the president's limousine, which had disappeared from view when it drove up an on-ramp and sped away northwards on the Stemmons Freeway to reach the nearest hospital (see Figure 11.1). Running up the grassy knoll would have offered curious onlookers the possibility to catch a last glimpse of the president's car driving away, another non-sinister and perfectly valid explanation that conspiracists never seem to consider. Many, like NBC reporter and future *PBS Newshour* anchorman Robert MacNeil, admitted they ran up the knoll just to follow the crowd, which he assumed had seen something noteworthy. "Several people gathered at the fence," he later reminisced, "A policeman went over the fence so I went over the fence too. And there was nothing in there but railroad tracks and a few trains parked a short distance away".[44]

One of the first people to enter the TSBD parking lot was Dallas motorcycle policeman Joseph "Joe" Marshall Smith, whose Warren Commission testimony appears to be the birthplace of the "fake Secret Service agent" theory. Smith, who left the motorcade to investigate the fence area, told the Warren Commission he nervously drew his pistol upon crossing the fence but did not see a shooter. He was then approached by a man in plainclothes who showed him what looked like Secret Service credentials: "He saw me coming with my pistol," Smith explained, "and right away he showed me who he was".[45] Smith did not explain whether the man identified himself as a Secret Service agent or whether Smith just assumed his badge was that of the Secret Service. Smith's testimony is also unclear concerning the distance that separated them. What is quite clear is that Smith only saw one man shows him a badge, and that the interaction was brief. He made no suggestion that the man interfered with him or prevented him from investigating the parking lot area. In fact, Smith's testimony suggests that the anonymous "Secret Service" agent assisted him in checking cars for a suspect or weapon. It is also obvious from his testimony, contrary to what Lane suggests, that there was nothing noteworthy or suspicious about this "agent":

> Mr. SMITH: I started up toward this Book Depository after I heard the shots, and *I didn't know where the shots came from.* I had no idea, because it was such a ricochet.
>
> Mr. LIEBELER: An echo effect?
>
> Mr. SMITH: Yes, sir; and this woman came up to me and she was just in hysterics. She told me, "They are shooting the President from the bushes." So I immediately proceeded up here. […]
>
> Mr. LIEBELER: There is a parking lot in behind this grassy area back from Elm Street toward the railroad tracks, and you went down to the parking lot and looked around?
>
> Mr. SMITH: Yes, sir; *I checked all the cars. I looked into all the cars and checked around the bushes. Of course, I wasn't alone. There was some deputy sheriff with me, and I believe one Secret Service man when I got there.* I got to make this statement, too. I felt awfully silly, but after the shot and this woman, I pulled my pistol from my holster, and I thought, this is silly, I don't know who I am looking for, and I put it back. Just as I did, he showed me that he was a Secret Service agent. […] he saw me coming with my pistol and right away *he showed me who he was.*
>
> Mr. LIEBELER: Do you remember who it was?
>
> Mr. SMITH: No, sir; I don't—because then we started checking the cars. In fact, I was checking the bushes, and I went through the cars […].
>
> Mr. LIEBELER: Did you have any basis for believing where the shots came from, or where to look for somebody, other than what the lady told you?
>
> Mr. SMITH: No, sir; except that maybe it was a power of suggestion. But it sounded to me like they may have came [sic] from this vicinity here.[46]

The controversy emerged from the fact that a Secret Service spokesman confirmed later that day that no agents were present in Dealey Plaza between 12:30 and 1 p.m. (when patrolman Smith met the "fake agent"), and because neither the Warren Commission nor the HSCA could identify this person.[47] Smith's testimony therefore gave rise to claims of conspirators posing as fake Secret Service agents. Many other witnesses claimed they saw one or more Secret Servicemen in the grassy knoll area within minutes of the assassination, but Smith was the only witness who told the authorities he was *shown* a Secret Service badge. Others (like Jean Hill) who later claimed they saw such credentials made their statements several years later, often contradicting earlier statements made to the Dallas Police, FBI, or Warren Commission. After further investigation, the HSCA concluded that most of these "sightings" were the product of faulty assumptions: "Significantly, most of the witnesses who made identifications of Secret Service personnel stated that they had surmised that any plain clothed individual in the company of uniformed police officers must have been a Secret Service agent".[48]

The Dallas Police had numerous plainclothes detectives on duty that day. Dealey Plaza was also surrounded by government offices from which many agents and functionaries had emerged during their lunch hour to watch Kennedy's motorcade.[49] The local county sheriff's office, for instance, was located on the southeastern corner of Houston and Elm, diagonally across from the Book Depository, which explains why many Sheriff's deputies were on site within minutes. This also explains why several civilians thought they saw a Secret Service agent (or two) where none were present.

Despite these reports, it is important to note that no contemporaneous witness ever claimed that a team of fake agents was hustling the crowd. Such claims emerged years later. We can reasonably assume then that these multiple sightings could have been caused by a very small number of plainclothes "government agents" aiding the local police out of a sense of duty. This leads us to the unlikely scenario that the conspirators stationed far too few "fake agents" at the grassy knoll to be able to fend off a throng of civilians, journalists, and policemen, who in fact did manage to snoop about freely. Apart from making authors like Lane more suspicions, one should wonder what purpose this fraud could have possibly served.

How then could Officer Smith have been mistaken? There is no definitive answer, but two possible reasons are simpler that Lane's. First, according to Posner, it would have been easy for Smith to mistake several agency badges for that of the Secret Service, particularly if the man merely flashed it, and there is no evidence in Smith's testimony that the man *stated* he worked for the Secret Service.[50] Second, the HSCA investigated several leads concerning the agent in question and learned that military intelligence officers were assigned to security detail in Dallas, at least one of whom was present in Dealey Plaza. The Committee also discovered that it was standard protocol at the time for plainclothes military agents to identify themselves as members of another agency (such as the Secret Service) when dealing with civilians, for the purpose of remaining inconspicuous.[51] While the "fake Secret Servicemen" theory cannot be fully resolved, the simplest explanation is that it is a false rumor resulting from what Carl von Clausewitz called the "fog of war," the confusion that permeates a crisis that makes witnesses see and remember things out of context.[52]

11.3   The "changed" motorcade route

Another theory holds that the motorcade route was changed at the last minute to bring Kennedy's car closer to the TSBD.[53] The purpose of this furtive operation, it is argued, was to facilitate the "triangulation of crossfire" and/or to frame Oswald more easily. In his 1988 book *On the Trail of the Assassins*, Jim Garrison recounts how he allegedly made this discovery in 1967, during his investigation of Clay Shaw:

> One morning I was in my office reading and rereading a newspaper. [...] "I have never seen you so preoccupied," said Frank [Klein]. [...]
>
> "This is the front page of the Dallas Morning News for November 22, 1963." [...] I gestured to the large diagram on the paper's front page indicating the route of the presidential parade. [...] *It covered almost five-sixths of the front page.* [...] "This diagram indicates that the President's parade was supposed to continue on Main Street through the center of Dealey Plaza— without even leaving Main."
>
> He stared at it in disbelief. [...] the motorcade route *continuing on Main through the center of Dealey Plaza as it headed for the Stemmons Freeway.* [...] "Are you telling me that at the last moment they just moved the President of the United States off of his scheduled route to here where the Depository is?" [...]
>
> "Of course," I replied, "you can't tell me it's possible to hijack the President—with the whole world watching—unless there's *some kind of cooperation* between the city administration and the federal government." [...] I pulled open my middle desk drawer and took out a copy of the Dallas Morning News front page that had been introduced as a Commission exhibit. I handed it to Frank [...].
>
> "Those bastards! *They just removed the entire motorcade route from the front page!*" [...]
>
> On five sixth of the Dallas Morning News page where the diagram of the motorcade route was supposed to be was nothing but a large square of solid grey. [...] "This is what you call," I replied, "a coup d'etat."[54]

The "kind of cooperation" required to change the parade route, Garrison claims, brought together Dallas Mayor Earle Cabell and his brother US Air Force (USAF) General Charles Cabell, along with fellow former CIA Deputy Director Richard Bissell and former DCI Allen Dulles, seeking revenge for Kennedy firing them following the failed Bay of Pigs invasion.[55] This sinister claim is repeated by many conspiracists even though it rests on no more than a set of guilt-by-association fallacies. Furthermore, this conversation described in Garrison's book not only demonstrates his flair for paranoid hyperbole, it is also almost completely false.

Although the *Dallas Morning News* did print a map of the motorcade route on November 22, 1963, the actual map was approximately 4 × 3 inches large: less than *one-twentieth* of the whole page, raising questions about Garrison's memory, honesty, or whether he ever saw it at all.[56] While he is correct that the map did not show the motorcade's turns on Houston and Elm, this was essentially due to the small scale of the diagram, not to some evil scheme. Details of the parade route (the one Kennedy did follow) had in fact already been printed *three days* earlier, on November 19, *in the same paper*, with a verbal description of the entire route, including the turns on Houston and Elm.[57] On the same day (November 19) a rival paper, the *Dallas Times Herald*, published a similar description of the motorcade route, including the "suspicious" Main-Houston-Elm detour.[58] And like the *Dallas Morning News*, the *Times Herald* also printed a diagram of the motorcade route on its front page on the eve of Kennedy's visit (November 21). This one was more than double the size of the one described by Garrison and did show the Main-Houston-Elm detour.

There is some humor in this. Had Garrison studied a map of Dallas closely, he might have noticed that it was not only illegal and dangerous but almost physically impossible for a motorcade composed of motorcycles, limousines, and buses to continue down Main Street and turn north onto the Stemmons Freeway (to get to the Dallas Trade Mart, the President's ultimate destination). The only alternatives from the actual motorcade route were (a) to turn away from Main and take Elm several blocks earlier (a riskier turn through the downtown core, surrounded by hundreds of windows, high buildings, and heavy crowds); (b) to avoid Main Street altogether and drive down Elm Street through the whole downtown stretch (a less commercial thoroughfare and a poorer choice for a parade whose purpose was to make Kennedy *more*, not less, visible); or (c) the route proposed by Garrison, which implies veering off Main street and taking the Stemmons Freeway onramp *by driving across the grassy Plaza over curbstones and concrete dividers!*—a sure way to cause thousands of dollars of damage to the vehicles and city infrastructure, and cause a possible multicar pile up. The "suspicious" turn onto Houston and Elm streets, then, was the safest and most intelligent route available to get the President's motorcade from Downtown Dallas to the Trade Mart without risking an embarrassing act of stupidity. And this is exactly what Texas Governor John Connolly, Kennedy's special assistant Kenny O'Donnell, Special Agent Winston G. Lawson (the White House's Secret Service advance agent), and Agent Forrest V. Sorrels (the Special Agent in charge of the Dallas Secret Service office) made sure to avoid when they met to discuss the motorcade plans during the preceding weeks. As the Warren Report explained:

> Elm Street, parallel to Main Street and one block north, was not used for the main portion of the downtown part of the motorcade because Main Street offered better vantage points for spectators. To reach the Trade Mart from Main Street the agents decided to use the Stemmons Freeway (Route No. 77), the most direct route. *The only practical way for westbound traffic on Main Street to reach the northbound lanes of the Stemmons Freeway is via Elm Street*, which Route No. 77 traffic is instructed to follow in this part of the city.[59]

There thus never was a "last minute change". The route was set and made public on November 18 for the first and only time.

11.4 Why not shoot him on Houston?

According to Stone's *JFK*, a lone gunman in the TSBD's sixth-floor window would have taken aim sooner, when the President's car first turned right on Houston: "the easiest shot for a single shot from the Book Depository".[60] This, however, was not the view of skilled marksmen who studied the evidence and tried to replicate it.[61] First, taking aim at Kennedy coming up Houston would have unnecessarily exposed Oswald (who was a right-handed shooter) to the crowd below and people in the motorcade, running the risk of alerting the Secret Service and President before he could get a shot off (see Figure 11.5). Second, evidence suggests that Oswald took aim in a sitting position, leaning on a box and/or windowsill to improve his rifle's stability, which an experienced marksman would have known would yield better results. Indeed, the arrangement of boxes that were found stacked around and beneath the sixth-floor window—the so-called sniper's nest—would not have allowed the shooter to take multiple accurate shots at an approaching target on Houston Street. Rather, these were arranged to help the shooter take aim at a target on Elm Street (see Figure 11.6). With the limousine driving down Elm Street away from his lair, and the police and crowd's attention focused on it, Oswald could fire several shots before he would be located.

In addition to maintaining the element of surprise, this configuration would require the shooter to make the fewest adjustments to score a series of accurate shots. This is especially true when we factor in the declination of Elm Street between the TSBD and the triple underpass, an angle that replicates the "flat, low trajectory" many conspiracists claim was necessary. According to the late Dr. John Lattimer, a professor of medicine and expert in forensic ballistics who conducted several academic studies of the Mannlicher-Carcano rifle: "This shift, while real, was small and did not prove to be any great problem, since the automobile was going downhill and away from Oswald's high perch, thus shifting very little in his field of vision".[62] All this makes it evident that a series of shots down Elm Street promised better results than shooting the target face-front on Houston. Oswald had enough rifle-shooting experience to know that.

We should also consider that the shooter needed several seconds to locate his target—a distant figure whom he never saw in person before—and whose position in the motorcade he did not know in advance. There are countless other reasons for not having shot Kennedy earlier (nerves, coughing, sweaty palms, etc.), allowing us to conclude that this premise is a false dilemma.

11.5 No security detail in Dealey Plaza?

In his 1975 essay "The Guns of Dallas," and again in his 1992 book *JFK: The CIA, Vietnam, and the Plot to Assassinate John F. Kennedy*, Fletcher Prouty states that

COMMISSION EXHIBIT 875—Continued

FIGURE 11.5 View of Houston Street from sniper's nest

Source: Warren Commission Exhibit 875, National Archives and Records Administration.

FIGURE 11.6 View of Elm Street from sniper's nest

Source: *Fort Worth Star-Telegram*, University of Texas at Arlington Libraries.

security measures in Dealey Plaza were deliberately reduced to help the snipers perform their job. As an example, he claims that specific military units from Fort Sam
Houston, who should have been called on to help protect the motorcade, were told
to "stand down" and were never replaced by other units. "How simple and how
correct it would have been," he writes,

> for Secret Service men, aided by all of the Armed Forces required, to have
> checked those buildings, to have sealed any unused floors (such as that famous
> deserted sixth floor), and then to have shut all of the front windows[63]

This dereliction of duty is further proven, he claims, by the fact that manholes along
the motorcade route were left unsealed and by the absence of Dallas policemen and
military intelligence units to protect the president's motorcade.

This argument has been repeated by numerous conspiracists, citing him as an
informed insider.[64] It also figures prominently in Oliver Stone's *JFK*. We will deal
with most accusations made against the Secret Service in Part IV of this book.
Let us now respond to the claim that JFK was deliberately left unprotected in
Dealey Plaza.

First, there was no less police presence in Dealey Plaza than there was along
the rest of the motorcade route. Dealey Plaza was also the finishing point of the
motorcade: the President's car would be speeding up by the time it reached the
triple underpass to get to the Dallas Trade Mart for a scheduled luncheon. This
explains why the crowds were thinner along Elm Street than they were along Main

or Houston, and why fewer policemen were needed on Elm to keep civilians from rushing the motorcade. A police cordon was also set up near Houston and Main that prevented most pedestrians from walking onto the wide-open Plaza. In addition to providing a motorcycle escort and crowd control throughout the motorcade route, Dallas policemen were stationed at strategic points all around Dealey Plaza— including atop the triple underpass and on the more distant Stemmons Freeway overpass—to prevent cars from stopping, trains from crossing, and pedestrians from standing over the motorcade route during its passage.[65] Motorcycle policeman Joe Smith (see above) acknowledged that a sheriff's deputy was in the TSBD parking lot when he came by to search the area.[66] Three other police officers were stationed at the corner of Houston and Elm to perform crowd control.[67] Many other police, sheriff, and other government officials were on the scene. Even Chief of Police Jesse Curry and Dallas County Sheriff J.E. "Bill" Decker were present, riding in the lead car just ahead of Kennedy's limousine.

What no one was apparently ordered to do was to keep a constant vigil watching all of the windows overlooking the route. As the Warren Report explained:

> No arrangements were made for police or building custodians to inspect buildings along the motorcade route *since the Secret Service did not normally request or make such a check*. Under standard procedures, the responsibility for watching the windows of buildings was shared by local police stationed along the route and Secret Service agents riding in the motorcade.[68]

While Prouty and Stone see this as sinister, the Warren Commission and HSCA attributed it to flawed standard operating procedures (SOPs) and to a failure in communications between the Secret Service and local police.[69] Furthermore, there were over *2,000* windows overlooking the entire motorcade route.[70] Watching or sealing all of them would have prevented the local police from performing its many other functions, such as protecting the President at the Dallas Trade Mart, a convention and business center that raised far more security concerns than the motorcade did.[71] To be sure, Prouty's scenario would have required such an unprecedented military presence throughout the city that it would have defeated the very purpose Kennedy's motorcades were meant to serve: to present him as an approachable populist, not a Northern carpetbagger or banana republic dictator. Failing to seal *only* the windows in Dealey Plaza, as Prouty suggests, would have required the Secret Service and Dallas police to know in advance that the President was going to be shot at that exact location. This not only displays more circular reasoning, it also ignores the brute fact that no windows were *ever* sealed anywhere on the Dallas motorcade route, nor in any of Kennedy's other public processions in the United States and abroad (see Figures 11.7 and 11.8).

In any event, the Secret Service was not at that time in the business of sealing windows or manholes (which, it turns out, were inspected in advance by the Dallas Police Department [DPD] and Secret Service) but of keeping the crowds from

FIGURE 11.7 Kennedy in open-top motorcade, Berlin, West Germany, 26 June 1963
Source: Robert Knudsen/JFK Library.[72]

getting too close to the President, protecting him with their bodies from acts of aggression, and rushing him out of danger as quickly as possible.[73] Prouty's obsession with the windows in Dealey Plaza is therefore a red herring, a distraction fallacy. Of course, the obvious solution to this whole problem of open windows was not to henceforth seal every window along a president's itinerary, but simply to never let them travel in open-top cars.

As for the absence of military units, Prouty makes two errors in judgment. The first is that Dallas was not Da Nang or Beirut, it was not a hostile war zone to be secured with tactical teams and military snipers but a peaceful American city filled with voters whom Kennedy wanted to woo. It ran counter to JFK's political style to surround himself with soldiers and Secret Service agents. As former JFK Secret Service agent Gerald Blaine remarked: "It was common knowledge among the

FIGURE 11.8 Kennedy in open-top motorcade, Cork, Ireland, 28 June 1963
Source: Robert Knudsen/JFK Library.[74]

majority of the White House Detail agents that President John F. Kennedy, on several occasions, had asked that agents not ride on the rear steps of the presidential limousine".[75] Indeed, JFK was a charismatic figure whose brand was largely based on his youth, visibility, and attentiveness to popular opinion. This is why the Secret Service was kept from walking or riding alongside his car through all of JFK's motorcades, and why he made it a habit of driving through large crowds in open-top vehicles.[76]

Second, military intelligence agents were in fact present in Dallas that day, though not to fulfill the functions Prouty describes. Fifteen years later, the HSCA examined Prouty's claims and found no evidence of a stand-down order given to military intelligence units. Indeed, the Committee interviewed Colonel Robert E. Jones, who was Operations Officer of the 112th Military Intelligence Group between June 1963 and January 1965. Jones confirmed that the 112th *did* provide a small force of agents to help protect the President, both in San Antonio and Dallas.[77] However, these agents were not responsible for sealing open windows or posting snipers on rooftops, but to identify possible human threats from lists of known subversives. But the FBI had not yet identified Oswald as a person of interest, nor had the other intelligence services much reason to look for him that day. Hence, there is no reason to believe that the 112th Military Intelligence Group would have been able to prevent a well-hidden sniper from firing at Kennedy, nor would it have known to look for an employee of the Texas School Book Depository watching the parade from a window in his own workplace.

Notes

1 To avoid confusion, I will reserve the word "opportunity" to our discussion of a possible cover-up (see Part IV of this book), that is, the opportunity for conspirators to get away with the crime.

2 *JFK*, dir. Oliver Stone (1991).

3 Ibid. Emphasis added.

4 Ibid.

5 This argument is structured as a *reductio ad absurdum*—an argument that aims to show that a certain claim is false (e.g., "Oswald shot Kennedy") because it leads to an impossibility (i.e., a "magic bullet"). This argument combines a disjunctive syllogism (P2 to C1) and a modus tollens (C1 to C2). See Appendix 2 and Kaye, chap. 3.

6 Vincent Bugliosi, interview with Michael Enright: "The Enright Files: John F. Kennedy," *CBC Ideas*, November 4, 2013.

7 No serious publisher has yet produced a book devoted to this theory, but the internet contains several websites that do using looped, poor-quality segments of the Zapruder film. For example, "Kennedy Assassin Cohort Bill Greer Spews Lies Until His Death," *NODISINFO*, 15 November 2013. This website's author, Cassim K. Igram, is a former osteopath who lost his license for "unprofessional, unethical and dishonorable conduct". "Chicago-Area Conspiracy Theorist Targets Sandy Hook Family," *Chicago Tribune*, May 28, 2013.

8 Bonar Menninger: *Mortal Error: The Shot that Killed Kennedy* (1992). The theories that claim Hickey and Greer shot Kennedy are debunked in Blaine and McCubbin: *The Kennedy Detail* (2010), chap. 22.

9 James H. Fetzer: "Prologue: Smoking Guns in the Death of JFK," Murder in Dealey Plaza (2000), 1–16.

10 To facilitate cohesion and avoid repetition, we will consider these claims by theme rather than sequentially, both in this and the following chapters.

11 Smoking Guns #12 and 15 implicitly contain the fallacy of circular reasoning by assuming that a cover-up necessarily occurred. Hence, these are not acceptable pieces of verifiable evidence, they are secondary premises based on the assumption that the other fourteen "smoking guns" are true.

12 Smoking Gun #16 has already been dealt with in the previous section (namely in Chapter 6).

13 One would have to assume that a professional military-grade ambush, as Stone's film describes it, would trap its target where no escape was possible. Such locations did exist, but the portion of Elm Street in Dealey Plaza was not one of them. Elm Street led to an onramp onto the Stemmons Freeway, which offered the president's driver a quick and easy getaway route, better than any other point in the motorcade. Conspiracists never discuss this logistical problem.

14 Marrs, 9–17; Garrison, 154 and footnote; Groden: "Comments on the Panel's Report by Robert Groden…" HSCA, Vol. VI, 306–8; Prouty: "The Guns of Dallas"; Stone: *JFK*.

15 This strange and impossible claim was popularized by Penn Jones (see Chapter 4) and Tom Wilson, a retired steel engineer and self-appointed photography and film expert. "The Men Who Killed Kennedy, Episode 6: The Truth Shall Set You Free," dir. Nigel Tuner.

16 Highly imaginative authors suggest it was a secret weapon, rigged to fire deadly "flechettes". Robert Cutler and Richard Sprague: "The Umbrella System: Prelude to an Assassination," *Gallery*, June 1978, reposted at McAdams: "The Umbrella Man Shooting Darts in Dealey Plaza," (n.d.), *The Kennedy Assassination*.

17 For example, Prouty: "The Guns of Dallas". Prouty later endorsed Sprague and Cutler's outlandish "flechette" theory (see previous note). Consider also the "convenient" size of the communications man's radio, facilitating its detection by conspiracists, compared to the tiny and imperceptible earpieces worn, according to Prouty, by fake policemen in Dealey Plaza (see below), who claimed that these were too small to be seen in the photos. Both of these are examples of the *ad hoc* rescue fallacy.

18 For example, Richard Bothun photo #4, public domain; Prouty: "The Guns of Dallas," Photo #24 (origin unknown).

19 Prouty: "The Guns of Dallas".

20 Thomas Bethell Diary, September 14, 1967, in McAdams, ed.: *The Kennedy Assassination.*

21 "Orleans Parish Grand Jury Special Investigation: Jim Hicks, Jan. 11, 1968," PDF, posted on *Assassination Archives and Research Center.* Some inconsistencies in Hicks' deposition included him standing in the parking lot beside the Book Depository, seeing a shooter kneeling inside the trunk of a light-colored Pontiac backed up to the grassy knoll fence, hearing bullets fly over his head, and hearing a bullet hit a street sign—a sign he said was removed within 30 minutes of the assassination. He also claimed he was threatened and attacked by two men who threw him out of a plate glass window to pressure him not to talk. The deposition shows Garrison feeding Hicks answers consistent with his theory of triangulated crossfire, but inconsistent with other eyewitness reports, including those of Marilyn Sitzman and Bill and Gail Newman, who stood near the spot where Hicks claims he was standing.

22 Errol Morris: "The Umbrella Man," (an interview with Josiah Thompson), Fourth Floor Projections, 2011, *New York Times.*

23 Posner, 231, citing Warren Commission Document CD1245. Unlike diabetic seizures, epileptic seizures are temporary and many who suffer them return to their normal activities within hours, even minutes.

24 These pictures were taken by William Allen, a *Dallas Times Herald* staff photographer, as well as George Smith of the *Fort Worth Star Telegram* (Figure 11.3), and Jack Beers of the *Dallas Morning News.*

25 Frank Sturgis and Howard Hunt are two conspiracist favorites. See Chapter 5.

26 Prouty: "The Guns of Dallas"; Prouty: "Ed Lansdale in Dealey Plaza Nov 22 1963" (video), *The Col. L. Fletcher Prouty Reference Site.*

27 Prouty even named them in his 1975 essay "The Guns of Dallas" but then seems to have forgotten who they were in later decades (see note #29).

28 McAdams: "JFK Assassination a Hobo Hit? The Three Tramps," (n.d.), *The Kennedy Assassination.*

29 "Career and Personal Documents from Lieutenant [sic] General Victor Krulak," *The Collected Works of Col. L. Fletcher Prouty,* [CDROM] edited by Len Osanic (n.d.), and Letter from L. Fletcher Prouty to Jim Garrison, March 6, 1990, *Colonel L. Fletcher Prouty Reference Site.* In a letter to Prouty dated March 15, 1985, Krulak responded with a list of his own suspicious clues concerning the "tramps picture" (most of which have been debunked), and the following comment: "That is indeed a picture of Ed Lansdale. The haircut, the stoop, the twisted left hand, the large class ring. It's Lansdale. What in the world was he doing there?" Prouty made similar remarks to Mark Lane, who used them in *Plausible Denial: Was the CIA Involved in the Assassination of JFK?* (1991). But when historian Jonathan Nashel contacted Prouty in 1992 to ask him for more evidence of Lansdale's complicity, Prouty "categorically denied" making such allegations. He then told Nashel he had "unnamed sources" linking Lansdale to JFK's murder. It seems Prouty was proactive in spreading the rumor, but wary to publish such claims himself. (It must be remembered that Prouty's allegations could be dismissed—until the widespread use

of internet—as private conversations not subject to libel). Nashel, 19–20, 201–3, 225–6 (note #54), and 263–4 (note #48).

30 No prior mention of Lansdale being the logistics commander of the assassination appears in any of Prouty's *published* conspiracy theories.

31 Prouty: "The Guns of Dallas" (1975).

32 https://en.wikipedia.org/wiki/Edward_Lansdale#/media/File:Major-general-lansdale. jpg

33 Prouty: Letter to Krulak, May 26, 1985, in Osanic, ed.: *Collected Works…*

34 Marilyn Sitzman interview with Josiah Thompson, November 29, 1966. *The Kennedy Assassination.*

35 An early version of the script made a larger issue of this. Lansdale's name still appears in the film, but only on a (partly obscured) desk plate. On Stone, Prouty, "Mr. X," Lansdale, and "General Y," see Nashel, 202, and David Reitzes: "General Y," *The JFK 100*, (n.d.), *JFK Online.*

36 Cecil B. Currey: *Edward Lansdale: The Unquiet American* (1988), 384.

37 Letter from Prouty to Garrison, March 6, 1990.

38 "Ed Lansdale in Dealey Plaza Nov 22 1963" (video), *The Col. L. Fletcher Prouty Reference Site.*

39 Edward Geary Lansdale, interview with Stanley Karnow, January 31, 1979, "Vietnam: A Television History," *America's Mandarin (1954–1963), WGBH: Open Vault;* Karnow (1983); Leamer (2001); Max Boot: *The Road Not Taken: Edward Lansdale and the American Tragedy in Vietnam* (2018).

40 Nashel, 203.

41 Jean Hill and Bill Sloan: *JFK: The Last Dissenting Witness* (1992), 26. Hill, who appears on the Zapruder film as the woman in the red raincoat (see Figure 13.2), plays a central role in many conspiracist accounts of the assassination, including Stone's film. On the credibility of the "fake Secret Service agent" witnesses, see Chapter 13.

42 "Mark Lane: Did the Secret Service Help Kill JFK?" [Transcript], *The Lew Rockwell Show,* Episode 385, December 25, 2014, *LewRockwell.com.* Emphasis added. DPD Officer J.M. "Joe" Smith was deposed in Dallas by Warren Commission assistant counsel Wesley J. Liebeler on July 23, 1964. His account was reinvestigated by the HSCA. Lane's description varies wildly from these two accounts and is peppered with speculations, inconsistencies, and false claims. See Testimony of Joe Marshall Smith, WC VII (excerpted below). Lane died in 2016.

43 The Muchmore home video shows three figures on that concrete staircase. Their identities remain disputed. One of them, wearing a red shirt or coat, is identifiable in the Nix film. Two of these bystanders are visibly startled and begin turning away from the motorcade, keeping their eyes fixed on it. The Nix and Muchmore home videos are available on *YouTube* and other websites.

44 MacNeil appeared to be speaking of motorcycle patrolman Clyde Haygood, who was one of the first persons to head up the grassy knoll, about a minute after the fatal shot. Robert MacNeil, interview with Judy Woodruff, in Rachel Wellford: "Robert MacNeil Remembers the 1963 Gunshots that Killed President Kennedy," *PBS Newshour: The Rundown,* November 20, 2013; Testimony of Clyde A. Haygood, WC VI; Jerry Organ: "'Smoke' on the Grassy Knoll," (n.d.), in John McAdams, ed.: *The Kennedy Assassination.*

45 Testimony of Joe Marshall Smith, WC VII.

46 Ibid., WC VII. Emphasis added.

47 *HSCA Report*, 183–4:

only one agent had left the motorcade at any time prior to the arrival at Parkland Hospital. This agent, Thomas "Lem" Johns, had been riding in Vice President Johnson's follow-up car. [...] he had left the car at the sound of shots and was momentarily on his own in Dealey Plaza, though he was picked up almost immediately and taken to Parkland Hospital. [...] Except for Dallas Agent-in-Charge [Forrest] Sorrels, who helped police search the Texas School Book Depository, no agent was in the vicinity of the stockade fence or inside the book depository on the day of the assassination.

48 Ibid., 184.
49 "They included Alcohol, Tobacco and Firearms (ATF) agents, postal inspectors, officers from the Special Service Bureau of the Dallas Police, county Sheriffs, IRS agents, and even an Army Intelligence agent". Posner, 267–8.
50 Ibid., 268. See previous note for examples.
51 Based on the testimony of Lieutenant-Colonel Robert E. Jones (ret.), commander of military intelligence for Texas region, *HSCA Report*, 184.
52 "War is the realm of uncertainty; three quarters of the factors on which action in war is based are wrapped in a fog of greater or lesser uncertainty". qtd. in "Fog of War," *The Oxford Dictionary of Phrase and Fable*, 2006, *Encyclopedia.com*.
53 For example, Prouty: "Guns of Dallas"; Garrison, 101–3; Stone: *JFK*; Fetzer, 13.
54 Garrison, 101–3. Emphasis added.
55 Garrison never produced any evidence to incriminate Earl Cabell, who by then was a retired congressman. New Orleans journalist Iris Kelso said this idea came to Garrison in 1971, not 1967, possibly to replace Clay Shaw who had now been exonerated of Garrison's charges (see Chapter 4). Kelso: "Garrison Planned to Link General to JFK Slaying," *Washington Post*, September 16, 1973.
56 Garrison seems to have borrowed the idea from Joachim Joesten's *Oswald: Assassin or Fall Guy?* (1964), whose conspiracy claims the Warren Commission made many efforts to debunk. McAdams: "Changed Motorcade Route in Dallas?" (n.d.), *The Kennedy Assassination*.
57 *Dallas Morning News*, November 19, 1963; McAdams: "Changed Motorcade..."
58 *Dallas Times Herald*, November 19, 1963; McAdams: "Changed Motorcade..."
59 *Warren Report*, chap. 2: "The Assassination: Planning the Texas Trip," 28–32, emphasis added; Commission Exhibit No. 2113, 34. See Figure 11.1.
60 *JFK*, dir. Oliver Stone (1991).
61 For example, "JFK: The Lost Bullet," *National Geographic Channel* (2011), in which retired Secret Serviceman John Joe Howlett, with the aid of an expert Marine sniper and laser technology, replicates the known and possible actions of the shooter in the sixth-floor window.
62 John K. Lattimer, et al.: "Could Oswald Have Shot President Kennedy? Further Ballistic Studies," *Bulletin of the New York Academy of Medicine*, Vol.48, No.3, April 1972, 520, *National Center for Biotechnology Information*.
63 Prouty: "The Guns of Dallas"; Prouty: *JFK...*, 291–4.
64 For example, Ramsay, Chapter 1.
65 Testimony of J.W. Foster, WC VI; Testimony of J.C. White, WC VI; Testimony of Joe E. Murphy, WC VI.
66 Testimony of Joe Marshall Smith, WC VII.
67 *Warren Report*, chap. 8, 448–9.
68 Ibid., chap. 2, 39. Emphasis added.
69 SOPs are:

rules of thumb [that] permit concerted action by large numbers of individuals, each responding to basic cues. [...] Since procedures are 'standard' they do not change quickly or easily. Without such standard procedures, it would not be possible to perform certain concerted tasks. But because of them, organizational behavior in particular instances appears unduly formalized, sluggish, and often inappropriate.

Allison, 83

70 Manchester, 32–3.
71 "Presidential Parade Detail," Report by Dallas Assistant Chief of Police Charles Batchelor, Warren Commission Document 81.1, AG Texas, November 30, 1963, *Mary Ferrell Foundation*.
72 www.jfklibrary.org/asset-viewer/archives/JFKWHP
73 Blaine and McCubbin, 206–7.
74 www.jfklibrary.org/asset-viewer/archives/JFKWHP
75 Ibid., 362, referring to "Confidential Statement of Special Agent John 'Jack' Ready, April 22, 1964, to the Warren Commission" (declassified in 1992).
76 Ibid., 197–210, 360–4. Kennedy rode in open-top motorcades in Hawaii, Houston, Tampa, Chicago, and San Diego, with his security detail riding in tow in a follow-up car. Photographs can be seen at David Von Pein: "Henry Rybka, Don Lawton, and Secret Service Confusion at Love Field," September 2016, *DVP's JFK Archive*.
77 *Hearings before the Subcommittee on the Assassination of John F. Kennedy of the Select Committee on Assassinations, House of Representatives,* Executive Session, Washington, DC, April 20, 1978, 1–14, cited in McAdams: "L. Fletcher Prouty: Fearless Truth Teller, or Crackpot?" (n.d.), *The Kennedy Assassination*.

12

THE MAN IN THE HIGH WINDOW

The evidentiary case against Lee Harvey Oswald

12.1   The unknown unknowns

The most widespread allegation made by JFK conspiracy theorists is that Lee Harvey Oswald could not have single-handedly shot Kennedy (if at all). This argument is usually composed of several premises that, for simplicity's sake, can be reduced to the following three:

   P1: Oswald's shooting skills were insufficient to strike JFK twice from the sixth-floor window.
   P2: Oswald was not physically present on the sixth floor of the TSBD when the shots were fired.
   P3: The rifle, handgun, and/or ammunition allegedly used by Oswald could not have produced the evidence collected by the authorities (or, inversely, that the alleged evidence, while pointing to Oswald, was fabricated, planted, or otherwise manipulated to incriminate him).

   ──────

   C: Therefore, Oswald did not kill President Kennedy.[1]

The first and second premises are fairly easy to debunk (see later). The third premise is a bit trickier to disprove due to the incomplete evidence record. In other words, there are far too many unknowns to dismiss this claim categorically. That being said, it is not unusual for a crime of this nature to be difficult to reconstruct with a high level of certainty—a crime that involved long-range weaponry, projectiles traveling at undetectable speeds, multiple moving vehicles, a public crime scene contaminated by hundreds of participant observers, and the unpredictable fragmentation of bullets and bones. This problem is compounded by the historical quirks that hampered various investigations, such as the political, bureaucratic, and

DOI: 10.4324/9781003222460-15

legal pressures that compelled leading authorities (Secret Service, Dallas Police, FBI, autopsy doctors, White House, Warren Commission, etc.) to disregard established protocols.[2] It is further compounded by the complicated nature of forensic ballistics (the study of projectiles and firearms used in crimes) and forensic pathology (the study of the causes of death resulting from a crime).[3] The chances of reaching false conclusions are therefore high, especially considering that most authors who write about the Kennedy assassination (including this one) lack specialized training to interpret the evidence fully and accurately and are therefore liable to trust their false expectations. It is understandable, then, that unanswered questions relating to the ballistics evidence of JFK's murder gave birth to endless speculations concerning the rifle that was allegedly used, the bullet cartridges it contained, the wounds suffered by Kennedy and Connally, the two men's peculiar physical reactions, and the damages sustained by the bullets. All of these factors have led conspiracy believers to proclaim that the Lone Gunman Theory is physically impossible. This chapter will therefore assess the main "proofs" offered by Oliver Stone, James Fetzer, and others that Oswald did not shoot Kennedy.

The belief that a government conspiracy *had* to occur whatever the evidence suggests is an example of circular reasoning, reverse engineering one's premises to reach a preordained conclusion. Another problem with the third premise listed earlier is that it contains a false dilemma by claiming that *either* (a) the evidence proves there was a government conspiracy *or* (b) the evidence has been planted to hide the conspiracy. Either option leads to the faulty conclusion that Oswald was necessarily innocent when other explanations exist. For example, Oswald could have willingly participated in a conspiracy but, because his wife or some other close friend was involved, decided to keep his mouth shut to avoid incriminating them. Fallacious logic is not always easy to detect, especially when it bolsters our biases. It discretely creeps into the reasoning process of authors and readers who are so convinced they are right that they will cherry-pick or ignore evidence to ensure that they win the debate.

Moreover, conspiracists often resort to categorical language to refer to physical evidence, using words like "necessary" and "impossible," "never" and "always," which belong to the realm of deductive logic and theoretical mathematics. Qualified crime scene investigators understand that it is rarely appropriate to invoke certainty or impossibility when assessing bullet fragments and wounds. Projectiles often behave unpredictably. Their trajectories can be influenced by the shooter's slight and involuntary twitches, microscopic irregularities in the weapon, the composition, shape, and quality of the bullet itself, and environmental factors that cannot be known or replicated, such as the wind's exact direction and speed. We should also keep in mind that properties of the target—such as JFK's posture, physical structure, movements, and clothing—can also affect how a bullet behaves. We should therefore prioritize objectivity and humility when analyzing physical evidence, even at the cost of remaining uncertain, to avoid jumping to false conclusions. It is always difficult to prove a conclusion beyond *all* reasonable doubt, more so when based on 60-year old evidence, some of which no longer exists in physical form.

Conspiracist Sylvia Meagher made the oft-repeated claim that the old Italian Mannlicher-Carcano rifle that was allegedly used to kill JFK has such a high rate of failure it should be deemed a "humanitarian" weapon.[4] Hence, it could not have possibly scored a direct hit to Kennedy's head. Inversely, many weapons experts state that bolt-action rifles—including the Carcano—are quite dependable and accurate on long-range targets, up to 500 or 600 yards.[5] This is nearly *six times* the distance that separated the sixth-floor window from JFK's limousine (265 feet or 88 yards). According to weapons experts Frank de Haas and Wayne van Zwoll:

> Despite wide criticism levelled against it, the Carcano is a well-designed and rugged action for military use since, presumably, the Italians did not have any major trouble with it or they would have changed the design. [...] The 6.5 military round [...] was a good military cartridge, comparing favorably with other 6.5 military loads.[6]

It takes a keen eye, accurate measuring tools, and familiarity with the characteristics of a specific weapon—in other words, expertise—to fully understand what ballistic evidence does and does not prove, no matter how straightforward such evidence might appear to nonexperts.

The study of the ballistic evidence of the JFK assassination has produced a constantly evolving scenario, even among those who defend the Lone Gunman Theory. The more we know about the science of ballistics and the more accurate our measuring tools become, the more our understanding of what happened on November 22, 1963, will require adjustments. As we will see, both the Warren Commission's and the House Select Committee on Assassinations (HSCA)'s findings were flawed, but subsequent investigations by weapons experts, forensic pathologists, and other professionals demonstrate that these findings were far less flawed than conspiracy theorists would have us believe.

12.2 To be or not to be in the TSBD

According to Jim Garrison and Oliver Stone, Lee Harvey Oswald was a terrible shooter who often got "Maggie's drawers" (a no-hit flag) at the military firing range.[7] No mention is made of the officers who oversaw his training and awarded Oswald his shooting credentials. Instead, this claim seems to originate from Nelson Delgado, one of Oswald's former fellow Marines,[8] and the jeers Lee received from friends in Russia while on a hunting excursion after he failed to shoot a rabbit with a shotgun. On the other hand, Lee's brother Robert, who had often gone hunting with him using bolt-action rifles, stated that Lee was an able shooter who rarely missed his target.[9]

Oswald's military records seem to support his brother's opinion. While in the Marines, Lee received training with the M1 Garand rifle, similar to the Carcano except for the manual bolt-action loader. He received a grade of sharpshooter (the second highest grade) in 1956. With less motivation and practice, he managed to qualify as a marksman (the third highest grade) in 1959, still "above average for a Marine" according to his examiner.[10] Dr. John Lattimer performed peer-reviewed analyses of the Carcano, studied Oswald's Marine shooting scorecards, and confirmed his ability to shoot consistently into a target 600 feet away at rapid fire without a telescope.[11] This does not invalidate the claims that Oswald sometimes shot poorly, but it must be kept in mind that he may have simply lacked effort, practice, or familiarity with the weapons he used on those other occasions. According to Marina Oswald, Lee frequently "dry fired" his rifle during the previous summer, and he had only barely missed killing General Walker with the same weapon earlier that year.[12] Hence, there is no reason to believe that Oswald could not have shot Kennedy with a Mannlicher-Carcano rifle from the sixth floor of the Texas School Book Depository (TSBD).

As for Oswald's presence on the sixth floor before and during the assassination, Stone's film is also gravely misleading. In his closing statement of the Clay Shaw trial, the film's Jim Garrison makes a passing reference to a man named Bonnie Ray Williams, a TSBD employee who is said to have been eating his lunch on the Depository's sixth floor shortly before the assassination, and that Williams failed to see anyone there, including Oswald.[13] The film simultaneously depicts a whole team of gunmen (in "ACME Air Conditioning" overalls, no less) playing the role of the "unknown workers" Garrison claims were on the sixth floor serving as one of the assassination teams shooting at Kennedy and setting up Oswald.

But Williams' testimony to the Warren Commission, corroborated by his fellow employees, dispels all these claims.[14] First, there were no "unknown workers" in the TSBD that day. A group of workers was indeed laying down new plywood flooring in the sixth-floor warehouse, just as they had the previous weeks on the fifth floor. All of these workers, which included Williams—a 20-year old who had been employed there slightly longer than Oswald—are named in his deposition.[15] As the men broke for lunch around 11:45, they saw Oswald, who worked as an order filler, stay behind. One of them, Charles Givens, returned briefly to the sixth floor to fetch his cigarettes and saw Oswald standing near the window from where the shots later came. Givens told the Warren Commission:

> Well, it was about a quarter till 12, we were on our way downstairs, and we passed him, and he was standing at the gate on the fifth floor. I came downstairs, and I discovered I left my cigarettes in my jacket pocket upstairs, and I took the elevator back upstairs to get my jacket with my cigarettes in it. When I got back upstairs, *he was on the sixth floor in that vicinity, coming from that way [...] toward the window up front where the shots were fired from.*[16]

Ten to fifteen minutes later, Williams returned to the sixth floor with his lunch to watch the motorcade from a window. He sat for five to twelve minutes and left when no other employees joined him. Williams claims he saw and heard no one during this time. This makes it unlikely that an entire team of shooters was setting up an operation and planting false evidence. However, because of the re-flooring

FIGURE 12.1 Boxes on the sixth floor of the TSBD (south central window)

Source: DPD/Dallas Municipal Archives, University of North Texas Libraries.[17]

work, boxes of books had been stacked to the ceiling on the east side of the warehouse where Oswald is said to have been, and around the windows where Williams was sitting (see Figure 12.1).[18] A single assassin could have been hiding nearby, watching the street or quietly assembling his weapon. Williams' absence from 11:45 to noon had given Oswald fifteen minutes to set up the "sniper's nest" (see Figure 12.2) and retrieve his rifle from wherever he stashed it that morning. The Warren Commission also assessed that the Carcano could be assembled in a few minutes with a screwdriver or even a dime.[19] In any event, no one saw Oswald between the time Givens saw him on the sixth floor (shortly before noon) and two minutes after the shooting, when patrolman Baker and TSBD manager Roy Truly, looking for an intruder, passed him by on the second floor. Later that evening, during his interrogation, Oswald told Captain Fritz he had been sitting in the first-floor lunchroom the entire time. No witnesses saw him there either.[20]

Although none of this proves Oswald was the shooter in the sixth-floor window, the circumstantial evidence that he was on the sixth floor is strong, and it points to no other suspects, especially not to a *team* of assassins. Oswald was inside the building and was last seen on the sixth floor. No one but Carolyn Arnold—15 years later and not under oath—claimed to have seen Oswald during the lunch hour. But this was in the *second-floor* lunchroom, not in the first-floor "domino room" where

FIGURE 12.2 Southeast corner of the sixth floor of the TSBD

Source: DPD/Dallas Municipal Archives, University of North Texas Libraries.[21]

he said he had been.[22] On November 24, after nearly two days of interrogations, Oswald changed his story, claiming he had indeed been alone on the upper floors (and not on the first floor) when he heard "the commotion surrounding the assassination," after which he came downstairs, destroying his earlier alibi.[23] His prints were found on the boxes that made up the "sniper's nest". His rifle was found nearby. So was the paper bag he carried to work that morning, the one he said contained curtain rods for his room. The bag was found empty, with traces of oil— presumably from the rifle—and lint from the blanket in which it had been stored in the Paines' garage. No curtain rods ever surfaced. Oswald's discarded clipboard, with shipment orders from that morning, was discovered weeks later on the sixth floor by TSBD employees, suggesting that proofs of his presence were not deliberately planted. Several witnesses standing outside, including Howard Brennan, saw a man with Oswald's likeness and stature—or the barrel of a rifle, depending on where they were standing—in the easternmost sixth-floor window before and during the shooting.[24] Bonnie Ray Williams and fellow employees Harold Norman and James Jarman, Jr. were sitting at the southeastern window of the fifth floor watching the motorcade pass when they heard shots being fired above them. The three men heard windows rattle and were sprinkled with dust from the ceiling. Norman said he heard two or more slugs hit the floor. They then all ran downstairs, frightened.[25]

With all of this evidence, it is hard to argue that Oswald was not inside the building, that he was definitely not on the sixth floor, and that he was not in some way involved in the assassination.

12.3 Carbine conspiracy

Retired philosophy professor James Fetzer has spent the last few decades trying to prove that the physical evidence stacked against Oswald—the bullets, the autopsy X-rays, the backyard photographs, and the Zapruder film—is almost all fake.[26] If Fetzer is correct, Oswald didn't only *not* shoot Kennedy, the alleged murder weapon (the 6.5-millimeter Mannlicher-Carcano that was retrieved from the TSBD shortly after the crime) was *incapable* of causing the President's wounds. The Carcano is not in fact a rifle, he insists, and therefore lacked the necessary firepower to cause the "explosive damage" suffered by the President's head.[27]

The Mannlicher-Carcano is a military-grade bolt-action rifle—or carbine, depending on which expert you ask—that fires 160-grain, round-tipped, full copper-jacketed bullets loaded individually as single rounds or using a six-cartridge clip.[28] In accordance with the Geneva conventions, this very hard type of bullet is designed to *pierce* rather than mutilate its victims. According to forensic scientist Luke Haag, it is also remarkably stable. The Carcano was widely used by Italian, Finnish, and other European militaries during the first half of the twentieth century until semi-automatic rifles, which can fire multiple rounds without the hassle of reloading each cartridge, supplanted its use.[29] Being foreign and unpopular in America, the aging Carcano was marketed at a cheap price during the early 1960s, which helps explain why Oswald, who had little money but sufficient experience with military-grade rifles, chose to purchase this model. In fact, he would have been one of the few civilians reading that magazine ad to know that its price was a bargain.[30]

The Carcano was listed as a "36-inch 6.5 Italian Carbine" rather than a "rifle" in the Klein's Sporting Goods ad from which the order coupon was obtained.[31] Because of this, Fetzer concludes that it was incapable of inflicting the damage and wounds typical of a high-velocity rifle, invalidating the Warren Commission's conclusions.[32] But Fetzer is guilty of playing with semantics. Most weapons experts who studied the recovered Carcano identified it either as a "rifle" or a "short rifle," not a carbine. Indeed, a carbine is not an altogether different weapon. It is usually just a smaller version of an existing rifle with a shorter and sometimes thinner barrel.[33] But the definition of "carbine" (from the French *carabine,* which, ironically, also means "rifle") is not universal. The Mannlicher-Carcano was originally conceived as a short rifle modeled on the German Mauser. It was only later produced in a longer format with a larger caliber. Hence, both terms can be used to describe the weapon in question, as the recovered Carcano's 6.5-millimeter bullets were smaller than those of the larger 7.35-millimeter Carcano rifle but were almost identical in shape and length with more popular bolt-action rifles, such as the 7.65-millimeter German Mauser.[34]

Identifying a firearm as a carbine may indicate a slower shooting velocity compared to its larger counterpart—which is why Fetzer makes the distinction—but it does not by definition make it a low-velocity weapon.[35] According to de Haas and van Zwoll, the 6.5-millimeter Carcano has a muzzle velocity of 2,000–2,300 feet per second (fps), making Oswald's 6.5-millimeter "carbine" a *high-velocity* weapon, with "ample power to take deer-sized game to about 200 yards".[36] Again, that's over twice the distance required for a Carcano-wielding assassin to shoot Kennedy from the sixth floor of the TSBD. In fact, a large number of test-firings using Oswald's Carcano and similar models were conducted for the Warren Commission by the FBI and the US Army's Ballistic Research Laboratory. Both agencies concluded that the Carcano was able to cause the damage and wounds observed by the forensic investigators.[37] The HSCA firearms panel ran similar tests in 1978 and reaffirmed the Warren Commission's findings.[38] Many other tests were performed by civilian weapons experts under verifiable conditions.[39] All of these concluded that the 6.5-millimeter Carcano could cause the wounds suffered by Kennedy and Connally. In fact, both the Lattimer (1972) and Haag (2013) studies found the Carcano surprisingly reliable, powerful, and efficient when used appropriately on distant targets.[40]

Fetzer also commits the fallacy of equivocation when he argues that Carcano bullets, being of military-grade and full-metal-jacketed, could not have caused the "explosive damage" suffered by JFK's skull. "This kind of ammunition," he argues "is not intended to maim but, *absent its impact with hard bodily features*, to pass through a body. It does not explode".[41] Fetzer's description of the design and purpose of the Carcano bullet is correct, but he misinforms his readers by claiming that the shrapnel trail in JFK's skull X-rays (which, exceptionally, happens to *not* have been faked) belongs to an *exploding* projectile, which the 6.5-millimeter Carcano bullet was not. But none of the forensic investigators ever suggested that *a bullet* exploded inside Kennedy's skull, but rather that *the skull itself* exploded under the impact and pressure wave caused by a solid projectile striking "hard bodily features" (i.e., the hard, dense occipital bone at the back of Kennedy's head).[42] Simply put, the bullet *fragmented* on impact, it did not "explode". Instead, Fetzer would have us believe that the Carcano bullet should have remained intact as it passed through the President's hard skull at maximum velocity, which would, of course, defy the laws of physics.

Inversely, Garrison and Stone have argued that the so-called pristine bullet recovered on a gurney at Parkland Hospital—the alleged "single bullet" that the Warren Commission labeled CE399 that bore through Kennedy's neck and Connally's chest, wrist, and thigh—could not have possibly been fired by a weapon as powerful as the Carcano because it would have been significantly deformed after shattering Connally's wrist.[43] The apparent inconsistent effects suffered by each bullet will be assessed in Chapter 13, but we should point out here that the conspiracists are caught in a serious contradiction. They cannot simultaneously argue that a 6.5-millimeter full-metal-jacketed bullet, traveling at maximum velocity, would penetrate and emerge from a human skull without suffering major damage, while a similar bullet would emerge utterly mangled after it bore through a man's throat and, traveling at a significantly slower speed, traversed another man's chest and wrist. One of these two claims could be right, but they are scientifically and logically inconsistent.

12.4 Rifle me this, rifle me that

Other conspiracists impeach the Mannlicher-Carcano rifle for different reasons. Mark Lane and Jim Marrs, for instance, offer the following "proofs" of Oswald's innocence: (a) that there is no evidence connecting Oswald to "Alek J. Hidell," the name used to mail order the alleged murder weapon from a Chicago sporting goods store; (b) that Oswald's fingerprints were not on the rifle; (c) that Oswald failed a police-administered paraffin test, which proves he did not fire a weapon that day; (d) that the (planted) Mannlicher-Carcano was defective and could not have been used to shoot Kennedy; and (e) that the *real* murder weapon recovered by the Dallas Police was a 7.65-millimeter German Mauser.[44]

12.4.1 Oswald's alias

The name Alek James Hidell was a fake name used on several occasions by Oswald (which he spelled different ways), namely to open a post office box in Dallas and produce a variety of fake documents such as a bogus Selective Service System Notice of Classification card, a fake US Marines Certificate of Service card, a fake smallpox vaccination certificate (issued to Lee Oswald by a nonexistent "Dr. A.J. Hidell"), and membership cards for the New Orleans chapter of the Fair Play for Cuba Committee, which his wife Marina testified having forged at Lee's urging. The name also appears on the Klein's Sporting Goods and Seaport Traders, Inc. mail-order forms used to purchase Oswald's Mannlicher-Carcano rifle and the .38 Smith & Wesson pistol he had when arrested, and which he allegedly used to kill officer J.D. Tippit.[45] No living person with that name could be identified by the Warren Commission. While some conspiracists claim these fake IDs were produced by unknown conspirators to scapegoat Oswald, which does not explain why his wife would testify to having participated in forging them, nor why Oswald had them on him when arrested. The FBI, the Warren Commission, and the HSCA's handwriting experts confirmed that most of these documents were clearly signed by Oswald.[46] As Gerald Posner explains, "Oswald feared the FBI had him under surveillance, but he felt safe using Hidell and the supporting documents whenever he thought his own name might attract government scrutiny that he wished to avoid".[47] Those who claim that the A.J. Hidell alias proves Oswald was an undercover intelligence agent cannot explain why he would keep spelling the name differently or why he would be so foolish as to record his real and fake names together on the same documents, such as his Dallas post office box application and vaccination certificate, thereby exposing his true identity to any amateur sleuth.

12.4.2   Oswald's handprints

The issue of Oswald's fingerprints is a slightly more complicated matter. His finger and palm prints were indeed lifted by the Dallas Police from several boxes that made up the sniper's nest. Conspiracists argue (correctly) that this only proves Oswald handled the boxes earlier, but not immediately before the assassination took place. Furthermore, they allege, no fingerprints could be found on the rifle itself, proving that Oswald had not touched it.

This claim is misleading. Shortly after the assassination, Lieutenant J.C. Day of the Dallas Police Identification Bureau did lift (i.e., with a piece of tape) a palm print belonging to Oswald from the rifle's barrel, which unlike much of the stock is made of metal. This is why the same print was not visible to the FBI's forensic research team in Washington later that night, leading conspiracists like Mark Lane to claim that the palm print was faked by the Dallas Police Department (DPD).[48] Admittedly, no recoverable prints were found at that time on the weapon itself, though the FBI did identify some "faint ridge formations" that may have been Oswald's but lacked sufficient detail to make sure they were his.[49] Conspiracists have been quick to claim that since the rifle had no clearly identifiable fingerprints, this proves Oswald was innocent.

This is an argument from ignorance fallacy that fails to consider the science of fingerprint gathering. As John McAdams explains:

> While the presence of fingerprints on a weapon clearly inculpates a suspect, the lack of such prints doesn't let him off the hook. It's entirely normal and routine for guilty suspects not to have left usable prints on a weapon.[50]

Indeed, several conditions are necessary for a fingerprint to be identifiable, from the cleanliness and humidity of the suspect's hands to the type of surface that was manipulated.[51] Despite what we see on television, rifles and handguns are notoriously poor surfaces for collecting prints. A 1997 peer-reviewed article by fingerprint specialists Clive A. Barnum and Darrell R. Klasey of the San Francisco Laboratory Center of the Bureau of Alcohol, Tobacco, and Firearms (ATF) explained that usable prints are in fact recoverable from firearms only 10% of the time.[52] Hence, finding no prints on the Carcano, especially using 1963 technology, would not have been out of the ordinary. Surprisingly, Lane's book cites the Warren Commission testimony of FBI Agent Sebastian F. Latona, the FBI fingerprint expert who examined the Carcano in Washington on the evening of November 22, 1963, as proof of this missing and subsequently falsified evidence.[53] Lane appears to have read this text selectively, as Latona later offers the following remarks:

> Representative BOGGS: A weapon of this type, in your examination, do you find a lot of other prints on it as well? You do not?

> Mr. LATONA: No. First of all the weapon itself is a cheap one as you can see. [...] The wood is to the point where it won't take a good print to begin with hardly. The metal isn't of the best, and not readily susceptible to a latent print.[54]

Like an unscrupulous defense attorney, Lane never concedes that the lack of recoverable prints on the weapon is unsurprising, nor that it does not serve as proof of Oswald's innocence. On the contrary, Lane goes on for several pages asking rhetorical questions, suggesting that Dallas Police Lieutenant Day deceptively, if unconvincingly, manufactured a fake Oswald palm print.

12.4.3 The paraffin test

Another popular claim is that a paraffin test administered to Oswald by the Dallas Police, the results of which were inconclusive, proves he did not shoot a rifle that day. A paraffin (or dermal nitrate) test involves making a cast of the hands and cheek of a shooting suspect using paraffin wax, which is then treated with a solution to verify if these were tainted with gunpowder residue. Lane concedes that paraffin tests are often inconclusive as they are subject to contamination by foreign agents (read: chemicals, not spies). He also concedes that nitrates were found on Oswald's hands but not on his cheeks. However, as with fingerprinting, an uncorrupted paraffin test only inculpates a suspect when it is positive. It does not prove he is innocent when the test comes up negative. The inconclusive test would therefore indicate that, barring a false positive, Oswald fired a handgun that day (e.g., to shoot Officer Tippit) but not necessarily a rifle.[55]

Weapons experts familiar with bolt-action rifles, such as FBI Special Agent Cortlandt Cunningham, were not surprised at the test results and explained to the Warren Commission why a false negative could result after firing a bolt-action rifle:

> I personally wouldn't expect to find any residues on a person's right cheek after firing a rifle due to the fact that by the very principles and the manufacture and the action, the cartridge itself is sealed into the chamber by the bolt being closed behind it, and upon firing the case, the cartridge case expands into the chamber filling it up and sealing it off from the gases, so none will come back in your face, and so by its very nature, I would not expect to find residue on the right cheek of a shooter.[56]

But rather than concede this much, Lane argues that "a positive response on both hands and a negative response on the face is consistent with innocence [...] indicating that the nitrates present were caused by some activity other than the use of a firearm".[57] Oswald's hands, he argues, had probably been tainted by the paint from the new plywood floorboards being laid down on the TSBD's sixth floor that day—even though none of the other workers, including Oswald himself, ever claimed he helped them in any way put down new flooring. In fact, Bonnie Ray Williams stated that Oswald was usually off on his own filling orders and interacted little with other workers.[58] Lane thereby goes on to accuse the Warren Commission of tossing aside evidence that would exonerate Oswald: "Confronted with but one legitimate interpretation—that the paraffin test results were consistent with innocence—the Commission concluded that the test, formerly presented as a cornerstone in the case against Oswald, was 'completely unreliable.'"[59]

But the paraffin test was never a "cornerstone in the case against Oswald," except perhaps in the hours during which he was being interrogated. Indeed, paraffin tests were already known by the FBI and most criminologists to be unreliable more than a decade *before* the Kennedy assassination,[60] and the Dallas Police investigators knew that as well. Why then administer a paraffin test? Given the information available to Lane as early as 1966 when *Rush to Judgment* was first published, he should have been honest enough to recognize that, like the modern polygraph (the so-called lie detector test), a paraffin test could, even with no forensic value, be a useful psychological tool in a police interrogator's arsenal. Interrogators often administered this test so that they might use a positive match, coupled with the suspect's ignorance of the test's unreliability, as an incentive to confess. This is exactly what Special Agent Cunningham told the Warren Commission:

> What they do is they ask, say, 'we are going to run a paraffin test on you, you might as well confess now. […] It is definitely not reliable as to determining whether or not a person has fired a weapon.[61]

There was therefore no way for the Dallas Police to be certain that Oswald had fired a rifle that day, or that the Mannlicher-Carcano had not been fired by somebody else. But as long as Oswald was alive and did not know that such tests were unlikely to mean much in court, the Dallas Police was free to use it as a pressure tactic until either the suspect confessed or was incriminated by other evidence—which were still being processed at the time of Oswald's interrogation. While the paraffin test was unlikely to have had much power on its own to convict Oswald, it was blown out of context by Lane to prove something it simply could not: that Oswald was innocent.

12.4.4   A "defective" scope?

Conspiracists further claim that the Mannlicher-Carcano found on the sixth floor of the TSBD was not in operating condition, namely because its scope was badly misaligned. Because of this, it is claimed, no assassin could have used it to shoot Kennedy with sufficient precision to score two of three hits.[62] However, it is important to note that although the scope was misaligned at the time that the FBI inspected it later that evening (after it was transported to Washington), this does not mean it was dysfunctional when the shots were fired at noon in Dallas. In fact, it was quickly determined by the FBI's forensic investigators that the rifle, which was found lying between stacks of boxes with a "rather severe scrape" on its scope, had been tossed aside without care. This is consistent with the Lone Gunman scenario according to which Oswald, to be seen on the second floor two minutes later, would have had to rush away from the sixth floor after taking the shots. The scope could thus have been knocked askew when it was tossed aside or fell to the floor.[63] Lattimer also explains that, having been mounted with only two screws, the scope could easily have been wrenched out of alignment if knocked or dropped.[64]

This said, the FBI did concede that the scope could not be perfectly realigned without inserting thin metal wedges (called "shims") under its mount, causing it to aim high and slightly to the right. Although no shims were found on the sixth floor, no one ever looked for some either. It is possible—though unlikely—that Oswald had inserted one or more shims under the scope mount to correct its alignment and these were knocked loose when the rifle was dropped by the shooter or manipulated by law enforcement. Another possibility is that Oswald was aware that the scope was misaligned and compensated for it by aiming off-center. Yet even without shims, Bugliosi explains, the scope was not as useless as conspiracists claim, since

> the defect would have actually assisted the assassin in his aiming at a target moving away from him [...] so that if you aimed with this weapon as it actually was received at the laboratory, it would be necessary to take no lead whatsoever in order to hit the intended object. The scope would accomplish the lead for you.[65]

Indeed, the shots did land to the right side of Kennedy's head and neck, which is consistent with the claim that Oswald's scope was misaligned and he was aiming at JFK's heart or the center of his head.

There is also no reason for us to assume that Oswald *did* use the scope, because it was possible for him to fire the Carcano at a slow-moving target less than 300 feet away using only the rifle's iron sights. It may even have made the job easier since this would have required fewer head movements and less time to adjust between shots. This is precisely what sharpshooter Monty Lutz of the Regional Crime Laboratory of Wisconsin State concluded after serving on the HSCA firearms panel: "The ability to grasp the rifle and put it into the shoulder and recover after each firing is considerably easier using just the iron sights".[66] We may never know whether the man who shot JFK used a rifle scope or iron sightings to target his prey. But given the fact that Oswald had successfully done both in the Marines, and that the latter was easier to do and more likely to prove successful, the entire issue of whether or not the scope was defective is a red herring.

12.4.5 A German Mauser?

Finally, Mark Lane claimed that the weapon that was actually discovered by Dallas policemen on the sixth floor of the TSBD was not Oswald's Mannlicher-Carcano but a 7.65-millimeter German Mauser that was later switched for an Italian Carcano when the conspirators realized they planted the wrong weapon. For this to occur, a large number of Dallas policemen, sheriff's deputies, and FBI weapons analysts who saw or handled the murder weapon in the TSBD or later, as well as the Dallas district attorney, much of his staff, and many members of the Secret Service, FBI, Warren Commission, HSCA, and Assassination Records Review Board who studied the evidence, not to mention all of the amateur gunmen who are familiar with both weapons and who have studied images of the assassination evidence, would have to be involved in this hoax. Yet Lane and those who parrot his claim have produced no proof of this corruption either in the form of secret orders, suspicious communications, or proof of evidence tampering. Indeed, the sheer size of this alleged conspiracy, and the complex logistics required to plant, eliminate, or alter the evidence successfully, is hardly factored into this theory. What is offered instead is a small number of contradictory statements made by law enforcement officials during the twenty-four hours that followed Kennedy's death, and the reminiscences of a single, undependable whistleblower named Roger Craig (see later). Even so, this claim continues decades later to be bandied as a damning proof of a setup.[67]

Like most "proofs" of a conspiracy, this claim was not pulled out of thin air but was born out of an oversimplification and misunderstanding of the facts, in this case of the early statements made by Dallas law enforcement officials, including Sheriff's Deputies Seymour Weitzman and Eugene Boone who initially misidentified the rifle as a Mauser in front of journalists while they were in lockdown in the TSBD. Admittedly, the Mannlicher-Carcano closely resembles the more popular German Mauser. It was, in fact, modeled on it. This is why even Sheriff Deputy Weitzman, who had previously run a sporting goods store and was familiar with exotic firearms, incorrectly identified it as a German bolt-action rifle. This erroneous claim was passed on and repeated by other officials (including District Attorney Henry Wade) and members of the media, who falsely identified it as an Argentine 6.5-millimeter Mauser, a British .303 Lee-Enfield rifle, or a .25 caliber Japanese World War II rifle.[68]

It is important to point out that neither Weitzman nor Boone ever touched the rifle and, by their own admission, only inspected it "at a glance".[69] A correction was made by Lieutenant J.C. Day of the DPD Identification Bureau and Police Captain Will Fritz, who were the first to inspect the weapon closely and notice that it was some type of 6.5-millimeter Italian rifle. Only this much could be determined from a visual inspection at the scene of the crime. It was only later that evening that the rifle was correctly identified as a Mannlicher-Carcano—not a popular weapon in Texas—but not before Weitzman and Boone had already signed a sworn affidavit attesting that they had discovered a Mauser. The Carcano was shipped that same evening to the FBI laboratory in Washington for further inspection. Thus, the misidentification was a case of two policemen making a hasty judgment and reporters trying to get their story published as quickly as possible. Although Weitzman and Boone later admitted their mistake, and although video evidence taken by WFAA-TV cameraman Tom Alyea[70] shows that the recovered rifle was in fact a 6.5-millimeter Mannlicher-Carcano, serial number C2766, the rumor mill had been churned and continues to churn in conspiracist media.

No evidence of 7.65-millimeter bullets, casings, or fragments was ever found anywhere in the TSBD or Dealey Plaza. This includes the many fragments retrieved from Kennedy and Connally's bodies and from the limousine. That simple fact suggests that a 7.65 Mauser was not used to shoot Kennedy and the issue should have been laid to rest when CBS's Dan Rather debunked it in 1967.[71] Yet, Mark Lane revived it in 1976 with his documentary film *Two Men in Dallas*.[72] Lane's star witness in this video was former Dallas deputy sheriff Roger Craig, who is quoted in *Rush to Judgment* as having heard a "shrill whistle" about 15 minutes after the shooting and then seeing Oswald run out of the TSBD and jump into a green Nash Rambler station wagon driven by an unidentified black man. The Warren Commission dismissed Craig as an unreliable witness, given that Oswald was spotted at the same time by several witnesses riding a bus and a taxi to his boarding house in the suburb of Oak Cliff.[73] Lane nevertheless argued that Craig had first-hand knowledge of a conspiracy and the Warren Commission doctored his 1964 testimony to quash the explosive evidence he had revealed to them.

And what was this damning evidence? Craig explained in *Two Men in Dallas* that in the hour that followed the shooting, while he was on the sixth floor of the Book Depository, he joined deputy sheriff Boone who had just located what appeared to be the murder weapon. Craig inspected it closely with Boone, Weitzman, Day, and Fritz and saw a stamp on the rifle's barrel marking it as a "7.65 Mauser". He also said it was Weitzman who first noticed and pointed the stamp out to him. Craig is the only one of these men who claimed he saw such a stamp. Weitzman only claimed that the weapon *looked* like a Mauser and later recanted, embarrassed, when Day showed him his error. Curiously, Craig made no claims of having seen such a stamp in his Warren Commission testimony (which Lane claimed was redacted). More curious is the fact that Lane made no reference to Craig having seen a Mauser in his 1966 book *Rush to Judgment*, even though the Mauser switcheroo story figures prominently in it and Craig was already on the conspiracist bandwagon with his erroneous "green Rambler" story. Craig's German Mauser story, which emerged over a decade after he first started sharing his "memories" of the assassination, seems therefore largely contrived. This conclusion is further corroborated by a 1968 interview Craig gave to the *Los Angeles Free Press*:

FREE PRESS: Did you handle that rifle?
ROGER CRAIG: Yes, I did. *I couldn't give its name because I don't know foreign rifles*, I know it was foreign made [...] but *there was another rifle, a Mauser, found up on the roof of the Depository* that afternoon.
FREE PRESS: A Mauser up on the roof? Who found it?
ROGER CRAIG: I don't know who found it, but I do know that a police officer verified its existence.[74]

In addition to getting the getaway car story wrong and having inconsistent memories of what happened that day,[75] Craig's account of the disappearing Mauser should be taken with a large grain of salt. By the time *Two Men in Dallas* first aired,

Craig had recently died of a self-inflicted rifle wound. He had been suffering from depression and chronic pain, caused by a work-related gunshot wound and a car accident, for which he was consuming heavy doses of painkillers and alcohol. He had also gone through a divorce and, unable to perform his duties as a deputy sheriff, was unemployed and living with his father.[76] All told, Craig's story is the sad account of a depressive man at the end of his rope making up stories to garner attention and money.[77] Those, like Mark Lane, who claim his death was suspicious need to explain why Craig was only "silenced" a decade after he began speaking out about Kennedy's death and only *after* he recorded this interview, which is still available to all. They also need to explain why Mark Lane—the man who success-fully publicized Craig's story to the whole world—was not also silenced but died of natural causes four decades later at the ripe old age of 89. It is still unclear whether Craig had a bad memory, a troubled mind, or intentionally concocted these tales, but it is clear that his story evolved over time and was wildly at odds with those of his colleagues and the evidence pointing to Oswald.

Given all this, one can hardly argue that the 6.5-millimeter Mannlicher-Carcano, which was identified as Oswald's rifle by the Dallas Police, the FBI, the Warren Commission, and the HSCA, and which Oswald's wife and his friend George de Mohrenschildt saw in his possession, could not be used to kill President Kennedy. On the contrary, the Carcano had idiosyncratic signatures that could not be mistaken for those of any other weapon or bullet. We therefore now turn to one of the most crucial questions in the conspiracy literature: Did the bullets shot at Kennedy come strictly from Oswald's rifle, or does the evidence show other weapons were used?

Notes

1 This is an inductive argument (see Appendix 2) that reaches a highly probable—but not logically necessary—conclusion *if we assume that all its premises are in fact true*. But notice that even if all premises were true, the conclusion could still be false as Oswald could (logically) have killed JFK in a manner that diverges from the "official story" (e.g., he could have been the "grassy knoll shooter").

2 See Part IV of this book.

3 Interview with Luke Haag, forensic Investigator for Albuquerque Police Department—Major Crime Scene Team, *CBS This Morning*, November 11, 2013.

4 Sylvia Meagher: *Accessories After the Fact: The Warren Commission, the Authorities, and the Report* (1967), 101, cited in McAdams: "Firearms Factoids: the Humanitarian Rifle," (n.d.), *The Kennedy Assassination*. Meagher's claim is based on a June 1964 letter to the editor published in the science fiction journal *Analog: Science Fact/Science Fiction*. The letter's author (John P. Conlon of Newark, OH, a former serviceman and gun enthusiast whose credentials are listed in a May 1962 letter to *Guns* magazine) actually *discounts* the claim that the Carcano was inaccurate. He argues instead that it was as precise as any other rifle within 200 yards.

5 Chuck Wills and Berman Museum of World History: *The Illustrated Encyclopedia of Weaponry* (2012), 259. See also J.K. Lattimer et al.: "Could Oswald Have Shot President Kennedy? Further Ballistic Studies," *Bulletin of the New York Academy of Medicine*, Vol. 48, No. 3, April 1972.

6 de Haas and van Zwoll: *Bolt Action Rifles* (2003), 65, 70.

7 *JFK,* dir. Oliver Stone (1991); Garrison, 99.

8 Testimony of Nelson Delgado, WC VIII: "It was a pretty big joke, because he got a lot of 'Maggie's drawers,' you know, a lot of misses, but he didn't give a darn". See also Posner, 20–1 (footnote), who argues that Delgado only knew Oswald toward the end of Lee's service, when he was disenchanted and had stopped training seriously.

9 Testimony of Robert Oswald, WC I; Posner, 66–7 (footnote).

10 Oswald scored a 212 in 1956. The rank of sharpshooter meant he could hit a 10-inch bull's eye at a minimum of 200 yards (600 feet) eight out of ten times in the standing position. Kennedy sat approximately 265 feet away from the sniper's nest at the time of the head shot. Considering that Oswald's scores were better while sitting, and that he is believed to have shot at Kennedy from this position, this makes him capable of shooting Kennedy with an M1. With enough practice at working with the bolt, writes John Lattimer, one could learn to perform just as well with the Carcano. Oswald scored a 191 in 1959, which according to his Marine marksmanship officer James Zahm was above average for a Marine and excellent for a civilian. Testimony of Sgt. James A. Zahm, WC XI; Testimony of Lt. Col. Allison Folsom, WC VIII; Lattimer, 521–2; Posner, 20–1.

11 Lattimer, 520.

12 Testimony of Mrs. Lee Harvey Oswald, WC I. The Carcano bullets purchased by Lee were not a conclusive match with the fragments collected from Walker's home but were consistent with that type of weapon and bullet. Posner, 112–7.

13 Garrison's *Trail* completely ignores Williams and his Warren Commission testimony, even though he was the only other known person to have been on the sixth floor in the half hour before the assassination.

14 Testimony of Bonnie Ray Williams, WC III; Posner, 223–8.

15 These were Bill Shelley, Charles Givens, Danny Arce, Harold Norman, and Billy Lovelady. They were all TSBD employees who were all accounted for by the Dallas Police in the half hour that followed the shooting. Testimony of Bonnie Ray Williams, WC III.

16 Testimony of Charles Douglas Givens, WC VI. Emphasis added.

17 https://texashistory.unt.edu/ark:/67531/metapth337742/ (Dallas Police Department (22/11/63), Item: DSMA_91-001-1119001-4036)

18 CE 484, a picture taken by DPD on November 22, 1963, shows the location where Williams ate his lunch (his lunch bag and pop bottle, which the police originally mistook as belonging to the assassin, are visible). The area is surrounded by boxes stacked over 8 feet high.

19 In fact, the rifle had not been fully assembled. Only two screws had been used to mount the scope, which allowed it to be functional, but accounts for why it was misaligned when discovered. Lattimer, 515.

20 Swanson, 228.

21 https://texashistory.unt.edu/ark:/67531/metapth339412/ Dallas Police Department (22/11/63), Item: DSMA_91-001-1114002-4030)

22 The second-floor lunchroom was typically used by office personnel. Warehouse employees generally ate in the first floor "domino room". Arnold reportedly made this claim to Anthony Summers in 1978 (*Conspiracy,* 1980), contradicting the signed statement she made to the Dallas Police on November 22, 1963, declaring that she had not seen Oswald. Other co-workers gave statements supporting Arnold's 1963, not the one made to Summers. Posner, 226.

23 CE2064: "Memorandum of Interview by Postal Inspector H. D. Holmes," December 17, 1963, 6–7, cited in Swanson, 228.

24 Conspiracists have exploited some confusion between witnesses who said they saw dark-skinned men on the *sixth* floor and some who saw a shooter on the *fifth*. The dark-skinned men were proven to be Williams, Norman, and Jarman watching from the *fifth* floor. Amos Lee Euins, a young man standing across the street, correctly identified the shooter and "a piece of pipe" in "the last window of the floor below the ledge," which was wrongly reported as the fifth floor but is unmistakably the sixth. *Dallas Times Herald* photographer Robert Jackson took snapshots that corroborate these testimonies. *Warren Report*, chap. 3, 64.

25 Testimonies of Bonnie Ray Williams, Harold Norman, and James Jarman, Jr., WC III; *Warren Report*, chap. 3, 70.

26 Fetzer, ed.: *Assassination Science: Experts Speak Out on the Death of JFK* (1988), *Murder in Dealey Plaza* (2000), *The Great Zapruder Film Hoax* (2003), and *The 9/11 Conspiracy: The Scamming of America* (2007).

27 Fetzer: *Murder in Dealey Plaza*, 6.

28 Jim Garrison argues (wrongly) that there was no clip to be found with the rifle. It therefore could not have been used to fire three shots in just a few seconds. Garrison, 98–9. On the contrary, several news photos exist of Lt. J.C. Day holding the Carcano at the Depository, with the ammunition clip still in it (and one unfired bullet loaded in the chamber). McAdams: "Firearms Factoids…".

29 Wills et al., 259.

30 Forensic scientists Luke Haag and Mike Haag, interviewed in "Cold Case JFK," *PBS: NOVA*, November 13, 2013, and *CBS This Morning*, November 11, 2013.

31 Categorizing the Carcano as either a rifle or carbine is complicated. The one Oswald owned (serial #C2766) was 40 inches long, not 36 inches like the one he ordered, but the serial number matches Klein's internal shipping paperwork. This is sinister in the eyes of conspiracists but can be explained by the fact that Klein's stopped advertising the 36-inch model in March 1963 and began advertising the 40-inch model (both of which used 6.5-millimeter caliber bullets) in April, after Oswald's purchase. Since "A.J. Hidell" purchased the Carcano with an order coupon from the March 1963 issue of *The American Rifleman* magazine, this suggests that Klein's simply ran out of the advertised model and decided to send Lee one of the newer ones. According to William J. Waldman, vice president of Klein's Sporting Goods, Inc. in 1963:

> the weapons were of the same general design, but as I say, there were details that were different. We originally had ordered one style of Carcano rifle, one that was known as the Model 91TS. As time went on, we changed to another model known as the Model 91/38EFF, this on April 13, 1962.
>
> *Testimony of William J. Waldman, WC VII*

32 Fetzer: *Murder in Dealey Plaza*, 5.

33 Carbines were originally designed for cavalrymen, for whom carrying a longer and bulkier rifle slung over the shoulder was impractical. Over time, the term came to apply to any rifle with a shortened barrel. Richard C. Rattenbury: "Rifle" and "Carbine," *Encyclopædia Britannica Online*, 2015.

34 Apart from using smaller ammunition, the 6.5 Carcano (including Oswald's) has a shorter barrel and a bent bolt. De Haas and von Zwoll, 66. This makes both Klein's ad and Fetzer's claim that Oswald's weapon was a "carbine" acceptable, although Fetzer's distinction is a red herring that leads to an invalid conclusion.

35 Velocity is classified as low when the muzzle velocity is under 1,000 feet per second (fps), medium between 1,000 and 2,000 fps, and high when above 2,000 fps. Edward C. Klatt MD: "Firearms Tutorial: Ballistics," *The Internet Pathology Laboratory for Medical Education*, The University of Utah Eccles Health Sciences Library.

36 de Haas and van Zwoll, 70.
37 Testimonies of Robert A. Frazier (FBI Special Agent and Firearms Identification Specialist) and Ronald Simmons (Chief of the Infantry Weapons Evaluation Branch of the Ballistics Research Laboratory of the Department of the US Army), WC III.
38 *HSCA Report,* 50–1.
39 In 1967 CBS News ran a series of tests using the same Carcano model and ammunition at White Ballistics Laboratory in Maryland and concluded that the Mannlicher-Carcano was stable, dependable, and powerful enough to be the murder weapon. "CBS News Inquiry: The Warren Report," *CBS Television,* 25th June, 1967. Dr. John K. Lattimer's 1972 peer-reviewed study of Oswald's Carcano agreed (Lattimer et al.: "Could Oswald Have Shot President Kennedy?"), as did Luke and Mike Haag's 2013 *NOVA* experiments ("NOVA: Cold Case JFK").
40 Lattimer (1972); "NOVA: Cold Case JFK" (2013). Lattimer's group fired hundreds of rounds using four similar Carcano rifles and ammunition from the same production lots as those found in Dealey Plaza. Unlike the 1967 CBS study, they experienced no failures to fire.
41 Fetzer: *Murder in Dealey Plaza,* 6. Emphasis added.
42 Interviews with Peter Cummings (forensic pathologist at Boston University School of Medicine) and Larry Sturdivan (former wound ballistics researcher for the US Army Biophysics Lab and author of *The JFK Myths: A Scientific Investigation of the Kennedy Assassination,* 2005) in "NOVA: JFK Cold Case".
43 Garrison, 241.
44 Lane: *Rush to Judgment* (1992), 114–58; Marrs: *Crossfire* (1989), 435–58.
45 McAdams: *JFK Assassination Logic* (2011), 158–160; Dale Myers: "Oswald's Mail-Order Revolver Purchase; Critical Allegations Prove False," August 5, 2010, *Secrets of a Homicide.*
46 Ibid., 158. Oswald forged or amended other identifications, changed the expiry date of his Uniformed Services Identification and Privilege card, and supplied fake names or addresses on several occasions. Posner, 91–2 (footnote).
47 Posner, 91.
48 McAdams: *JFK Assassination Logic,* 160; Lane: *Rush to Judgment,* 154.
49 Ibid., 160–1. Thirty years later, a PBS *Frontline* investigation asked former HSCA fingerprint expert Vincent Scalice to review this evidence with new technology. Scalice identified several points of identity linking different partial prints together and confirmed that these were Oswald's fingerprints. William Cran and Ben Loeterman: "Who Was Lee Harvey Oswald?" (1993) *PBS: Frontline,* November 19, 2013.
50 McAdams: "Firearms Factoids…".
51 Clive A. Barnum and Darrell R. Klasey: "Factors Affecting the Recovery of Latent Prints on Firearms," *Journal of Forensic Identification,* Vol.47, No.2, April, 1997, 140–8. Cited in McAdams: "Firearms Factoids…"
52 Barnum and Klasey: "Factors…"
53 Lane: *Rush to Judgment,* 154.
54 Testimony of FBI Agent Sebastian F. Latona, Supervisor of Latent Fingerprint Section, WC IV.
55 *Warren Report,* 180; McAdams: *JFK Assassination Logic,* 206.
56 Testimony of FBI Special Agent Cortlandt Cunningham, WC III.
57 Lane: *Rush to Judgment,* 149–50. See also Marrs: *Crossfire,* 442–3. Lane assumes that Oswald would have shot Tippit with a single hand rather than two—which is possible but not verifiable. He also assumes that Oswald could not get nitrates on his other hand

by manipulating or reloading his pistol. According to Cunningham, "Even with the mere handling of this weapon I could pick up residues. One could not testify that a person has fired a weapon because he had residues on his hands". Testimony of FBI Special Agent Cortlandt Cunningham, WC III.

58 Testimony of Bonnie Ray Williams, WC III

59 Lane: *Rush to Judgment*, 151.

60 Henry W. Turkel and Jerome Lipman: "Unreliability of Dermal Nitrate Test for Gunpower," *Journal of Criminal Law and Criminology*, Vol.46, No.2, 1955, PDF, *Northwestern University School of Law Scholarly Commons*; McAdams: *JFK Assassination Logic*, 206–7.

61 Testimony of FBI Special Agent Cortlandt Cunningham, WC III.

62 Lane: *Rush to Judgment*, 123; Garrison, 99. There was also some concern by the Warren Commission that Oswald's Carcano was defective because its investigators could not properly load a single round in the chamber and because the empty clip had not been ejected. Lattimer investigated these concerns using rifles of the same model and found these to be typical Carcano quirks that did not affect loading and shooting using the rifle clip. Lattimer, 516–7.

63 Bugliosi, 491.

64 Lattimer, 522.

65 Bugliosi, 491, citing the testimony of Robert A. Frazier, WC III.

66 "Testimony of Firearms Panel: Monty C. Lutz, Donald E. Champagne, John S. Bates, Jr., and Andrew M. Newquist," HSCA Hearings, Volume I; Bugliosi, 490–1 (and footnote).

67 For example, Robert Groden: *The Killing of a President* (1994), 66; Ray and Mary La Fontaine: *Oswald Talked* (1996), 374; Len Osanic: "50 Reasons for 50 Years: Episode 17," (n.d.), *Black Op Radio*, *YouTube*; Steven Hager: "The Disappearing Mauser is a Key to the JFK Assassination," December 12, 2016, *The Tin Whistle*.

68 Newsreel of the hours and days following the assassination, excerpted in Osanic: "50 Reasons for 50 Years". Instead of adding the 7.65-millimeter Mauser to the list of "false positives," Osanic holds on to the Mauser story while dismissing the media fog that elicited other contradictory claims.

69 Seymour Weitzman: interview with Dan Rather in "CBS News Inquiry: The Warren Report"; Testimony of Seymour Weitzman, WC VII.

70 Alyea was one of the few reporters who managed to get inside the TSBD before it was sealed by police. Alyea's film roll was then tossed out a window to fellow reporters who rushed it to a local TV studio. The video aired at 3:30 p.m., local time, before Day and Fritz could confirm the model of the rifle. The unedited Alyea film is available on *YouTube*.

71 "CBS News Inquiry: The Warren Report".

72 "Two Men in Dallas," dir., Lincoln Carle (1976).

73 Oswald had the bus transfer in his pocket when arrested. McAdams: "Roger Craig: The Rambler Man," (n.d.), *The Kennedy Assassination*.

74 "Texas Editor, Former Dallas Sheriff Tell FP Amazing New Information," *Los Angeles Free Press*, March 1, 1968, cited in McAdams: *Kennedy Assassination Logic*, 67. Emphasis added.

75 These include having seen three 7.65-millimeter rifle cartridges lined up perfectly under the sixth-floor window, against the claims of all other witnesses and against the photographic evidence (see Figure 13.5). Another is Craig's claim of having been present during Oswald's interrogation and hearing him say that Ruth Paine owned a green

Nash Rambler (Paine's car was of a different color and make). "Two Men in Dallas"; McAdams: "Roger Craig: The Rambler Man".

76 Magen Knuth: "Roger Craig: Mysterious Death?" in McAdams, ed.: *The Kennedy Assassination* (n.d.). The article includes a link to the autopsy report.

77 In 2008, Craig's daughter Michelle Palmer (née Deanna Craig) sent an email to conspiracist John Simkin in which she said her father suffered from paranoia and, she suspected, bipolar depression and/or borderline personality disorder. David Reitzes: "The JFK 100: Lee Harvey Oswald in Custody," footnote #33, *JFK Online*.

13

GOING BALLISTIC

Of missing and magic bullets

13.1 The ghosts on the grassy knoll

How many shots were fired at Kennedy? This is the crucial question that leads most conspiracists to conclude there were at least two shooters in Dealey Plaza and that the Warren Commission deliberately covered this up. The Commission's conclusion relied on the fact that the police recovered three 6.5-millimeter shell casings[1] near the sixth-floor window of the Texas School Book Depository (TSBD) where witnesses standing outside spotted someone who looked and was dressed like Lee Oswald, and on "the consensus among the witnesses at the scene […] that three shots were fired".[2] It also concluded, based on the footage of Abraham Zapruder's 8-millimeter camera and the testimony of weapons experts, that these shots had to be fired within a span of little more than six seconds—enough time for someone experienced with a bolt-action rifle to fire three shots but not four, and probably not with the utmost accuracy. Given these parameters, and taking into account Oswald's marksmanship and familiarity with the bolt-action Carcano, it was within the realm of possibility—even if some Commission members and countless others thought it unlikely—for him to score two out of three hits in six seconds.[3]

Conspiracists claim it was impossible for Oswald to strike Kennedy two out of three times in that brief period. More importantly, they claim that any evidence of a fourth shot (or more) would necessarily involve a second shooter, and hence a conspiracy. Most conspiracists spend much of their time arguing for the existence of such proof by scrutinizing the ballistic evidence, autopsy photographs, X-rays, and witness reports. They also allege JFK was shot from several directions, including a shot from the Elm Street "grassy knoll" located at the front-right of the president's limousine. This argument is usually based on the locations of the gunshot wounds suffered by the two victims, the bullet fragments extracted from them and, most importantly, the so-called "pristine" or "magic" bullet that was recovered on (or

DOI: 10.4324/9781003222460-16

near) Governor Connally's stretcher in Parkland Hospital, the one labeled CE399 by the Warren Commission.

One of the conspiracists' principal witnesses of a second shooter is Jean Hill, the woman in the red raincoat who appears on the south side of Elm Street in the Zapruder film (see Figure 13.2). She is standing beside her friend Mary Moorman, who is taking Polaroid pictures of the motorcade. In her Warren Commission testimony, Hill claimed that more than three shots rang out:

> Mrs. HILL: […] We were standing on the curb and I jumped to the edge of the street and yelled, "Hey, we want to take your picture," to him and he was looking down in the seat—he and Mrs. Kennedy and their heads were turned toward the middle of the car looking down at something in the seat, which later turned out to be the roses, and I was so afraid he was going to look the other way because there were a lot of people across the street and we were, as far as I know, we were the only people down there in that area, and just as I yelled, "Hey," to him, he started to bring his head up to look at me and just as he did the shot rang out. Mary took the picture and fell on the ground and of course there were more shots.
>
> Mr. SPECTER: How many shots were there altogether?
>
> Mrs. HILL: I have always said there were some four to six shots. There were three shots—one right after the other, and a distinct pause, or just a moment's pause, and then I heard more.[4]

Hill's proximity to the President when the fatal headshot occurred makes her an important witness to the assassination. Her divergent testimony has also made her a darling of TV talk shows and conspiracy researchers, including Oliver Stone.[5] Although she was clearly uncertain of the total number of shots she heard, she was adamant that she heard more than three. On that point, her testimony has been relatively consistent from the day of the assassination until she died in 2000, despite being ridiculed by her husband and friends for making such claims publicly.[6] But Hill's later claims became far more ambitious than the "four to six shots" she described to the Warren Commission, especially in her book *JFK: The Last Dissenting Witness* (1992), published in the wake of the worldwide sensation caused by Stone's 1991 film. For instance, she now claimed that after the fatal headshot, she saw a gunman atop the grassy knoll standing behind the wooden fence, whom she noticed, she said, after seeing a muzzle flash and puff of smoke in that location.[7] She said he wore a policeman's uniform and a badge. (Conspiracists henceforth began calling this elusive assassin "Badge Man".) She then allegedly darted through the motorcade vehicles that followed after JFK's car and rushed up the knoll toward this assassin. But as she rushed to intercept him (how an unarmed grade-school teacher hoped to apprehend an armed assassin, she does not explain) another man who "flashed a badge of some kind" and claimed to be with the Secret Service, gripped her and forcefully led her, along with another plain-clothed agent, toward a third-floor interview room in the Dallas County Criminal Courts Building. Once there, two other anonymous agents gave her grim warnings: "If you know what's good for you, you'll keep quiet about it. It would be very foolish of you to ever repeat what you're saying outside this room". They then compelled her to sign a blank sheet of paper, she said, on which they later forged a false statement.[8]

Unsurprisingly, Hill's signed—and allegedly forged—affidavit of November 22, 1963, tells a different story.[9] There is no mention in it of any shooters on the grassy knoll, of puffs of smoke, or muzzle flashes. Apart from stating she heard more than three shots, her only unusual claim is of having sighted an unidentified man running from the Book Depository toward the train yards behind the grassy knoll which made her curious enough to go visit the area.[10] She returned empty-handed a few minutes later to her friend Mary Moorman, who had remained in the Plaza. In addition, there were several mistaken observations in Jean Hill's original affidavit, such as claiming she saw a small dog nestled between the Kennedys (there were bunches of flowers there, but certainly no dog) and that she saw "some men in plain clothes shooting back" at the assassin, which absolutely no one else saw or heard. The affidavit then discusses a journalist called "Mr. Featherstone" [sic], who approached Mary Moorman while Jean was scouting the parking lot, with an interest to publish their Polaroid pictures. It was this man who escorted Mary and Jean to the press room of the nearby Sherriff's office, where they were held for questioning.

Although Hill later dismissed this account as a malicious forgery, its easily disprovable errors and exceptional claims make it a rather unconvincing hoax. On the other hand, the many mundane parts of her affidavit—parts that evolved into sensational claims in later years—were confirmed by Mary Moorman and journalist Jim Featherston, both of whom agreed that it was he, and not "government agents," who escorted the ladies to the Sheriff's office after the shooting.[11] In her 1964 Warren Commission testimony, Hill said "I never saw a weapon during the whole time, in anyone's hand," which contradicts her 1992 book. She had also exonerated anyone at the Sheriff's department from coercing or intimidating her, except for journalist Jim Featherston, whom she found pushy and who seemed more interested in Moorman's pictures than what Hill had to tell him.[12] She later alleged that her Warren Commission testimony was also doctored. Stone's film makes the same sullen claim. What they do not acknowledge is that Hill was interviewed by a radio station and two television stations (WBAP-TV and WFAA-TV) on the day of the assassination, and again in the months that followed. In all of these media appearances Hill told a story similar to the one that appears in her November 22, 1963, affidavit. It then began to evolve by the time she was deposed by the Warren Commission and morphed into an altogether different account by the time she published her 1992 book and appeared in several 1990s talk shows.[13] Obviously, it is much harder to falsify multiple live TV broadcasts than a few written statements. All things considered, it is highly unlikely that Hill's signed 1963 affidavit, as well as her Warren Commission testimony, were rewritten against her will.

Despite her exceptional proximity to the fatally wounded president, Hill turns out to be one of the least reliable witnesses of the assassination. Her early statements not only contain provably wrong observations, she also failed to notice key parts of the assassination sequence, such as the First Lady climbing onto the back of the limousine.[14] Hill also spent several months telling her friends that the running man who had caught her attention was none other than Jack Ruby—even though it is well-established that Ruby was inside the *Dallas Morning News* offices at that time, purchasing ads for his nightclubs.[15] Numerous photographs were taken during the minutes that followed, along with the Nix, Muchmore, and Zapruder home videos, also show inconsistencies in Hill's claims. For example, the photographic evidence shows that JFK was not looking toward her just before he was hit. She also said she was close enough to the limousine to touch its front fender, yet she can clearly be seen standing several feet away, on the grass.[16] Hill said she was watching the President during the fatal headshot, but the Zapruder film has her watching the follow-up car. She further claimed that the limousine stopped in front of her. The Nix film shows it slows down (briefly), but no film suggests it stopped. Hill said she ran to the grassy knoll immediately after Kennedy's car passed her by, but photographs have her standing or sitting on the south curb of Elm Street until the press buses—the last vehicles in the motorcade—drive past.

Several other parts of Hill's book are provably false—such as her claim that her then boyfriend, motorcycle patrolman "J.B. Marshall" (Hill says they were having an affair at the time), told her the parade route was changed at the last minute. Not only is this claim provably wrong (see Chapter 11), there was also no Dallas patrolman by that name.[17] For John McAdams, Hill's changed-parade-route claim is "a classic 'gotcha'. While quite impressive to people who have read a conspiracy book or two, it's the poison pill that makes the testimony impossible to swallow for anybody who's well informed".[18] By ascribing an oft repeated but easily debunked falsehood to a deceased Dallas policeman, perhaps to make her story sound more authoritative, Hill and fellow author Bill Sloan have exposed their story as a manufactured hoax. Worse still, the sort of bolt-action rifle Hill claimed was used by the "Badge Man" does not emit smoke (unless he was using a vintage colonial musket!), whereas revving motorcycles and car exhaust pipes—not to mention cigarettes—do produce clouds of smoke, all of which abounded in Elm Street and around the grassy knoll during the moments that followed the shooting.

The most revealing element of Hill's testimony, however, is not that she got so many things wrong but that she kept adapting her "experiences" to the most popular conspiracist interpretations. This may not have been deliberate: conspiracy authors Mark Lane and David Lifton approached Hill early in this process and convinced her to change her views.[19] She soon stopped claiming she saw a small dog in the limousine, a grassy knoll shoot-out, and a runaway Jack Ruby (though she clearly believed all these claims when she first proffered them) and gradually incorporated more mainstream conspiracy tenets, like the House Select Committee on Assassinations (HSCA)'s theory of a grassy knoll shooter, the claim that the back of Kennedy's head was blown out,[20] and allegations that people were trying to kill her.[21] Her most blatant distortion of history was reserved for *Dallas Morning News* journalist Jim Featherston, who was first depicted by Hill as a pushy reporter trying to wrangle exclusive photographs, then as a robber and intimidator, and finally as an anonymous Secret Service henchman trying to destroy evidence. This account is contradicted by the fact that Moorman's Polaroid picture (Figure 13.1), which Hill and other conspiracists claim captured the "Badge Man" shooting at Kennedy, got published the same day. It was also later returned to Moorman, who was able to sell its publishing rights for a profit.[22] No one who rubbed shoulders with Jean Hill that day, including Moorman and Featherston, ever endorsed her fanciful account. "Mrs. Hill told her story over and over again for television and radio," Featherston later wrote,

> Each time, she would embellish it a bit until her version began to sound like Dodge City at high noon. [...] At one point I told Mrs. Hill she shouldn't be saying some of the things she was telling television and radio reporters. I was merely trying to save her later embarrassment but she apparently attached intrigue to my warning.[23]

As for Hill's claims that she was manhandled by government agents, that the Polaroids were stolen, and that she and Moorman were told never to speak of what they saw, Moorman said they're all false.[24]

As for the grainy black and white Polaroid taken by Moorman which some allege captured the "Badge Man" shooting at Kennedy (see Figure 13.1), it requires

FIGURE 13.1 Polaroid photo of Kennedy limousine taken by Mary Ann Moorman
Source: Moorman.[25]

FIGURE 13.2 Frame 298 of Zapruder film featuring Jean Hill and Mary Moorman
Source: Zapruder Film ©1967 (Renewed 1995) the Sixth Floor Museum at Dealey Plaza.

a great deal of squinting and faith to see something there that remotely looks like a gunman. No one—not even Jean Hill—claimed that the picture contained such a proof until conspiracy researchers Jack White and Gary Mack presented this theory in the 1988 *History Channel* documentary "The Men Who Killed Kennedy".[26] In fact, the two men claimed they saw *three* figures lurking in the shadows behind the concrete abutment. They identified these as "Badge Man," his accomplice "Hard Hat Man," and a self-identified bystander named Gordon Arnold, who claimed he was kicked and robbed of his camera by JFK's assassins.[27] This claim injected new inconsistencies into the grassy knoll shooter theory, such as moving the assassin to a different location than behind the picket fence where Lane, Stone, and others place him. This third (fourth?) sniper's nest stood a dozen paces east and south of the fence, behind a much lower cement retaining wall where the shooter would certainly have been spotted by nearby witnesses, including Marilyn Sitzman and Abraham Zapruder who, as seen on the Moorman polaroid, stood on an adjacent pillar.

Dr. Lenny Rudin, CEO of Cognitec, Inc., a firm specialized in forensic video processing software, conducted a digital contrast-enhancement study of the Moorman photograph, one of several that debunked this theory.[28] Rudin concluded that the area of the image identified by Mack and White as Badge Man, Hard Hat Man, and Gordon Arnold (none of whom were spotted by any witnesses), contains no more than a mixture of shadows and leaves, and the possible reflection of sunlight on a pop bottle.[29] Rudin further concluded that, when compared to the relative dimensions of other objects and people, White and Mack's three "silhouettes" would have had to be the size of decorative garden gnomes or suspended 20 feet in the air some 40 feet behind the retaining wall.

All this should lead us to seriously question Hill's testimony, including her certainty of having heard four to six shots. Still, that does not prove she deliberately lied. After all, even Moorman, who never believed in any grassy knoll shooter, claimed on November 22 to have heard "three or four shots in all".[30] And Hill and Moorman were not the only persons who claimed they heard more than three bangs. However, they are part of a small minority who claimed they heard more than three *shots*. Some took these other bangs to be shots, but most thought they were echoes, a tire blowout, a backfire, or even firecrackers.[31] Indeed, there was widespread confusion concerning the origin and total number of the shots. Conspiracists tend not to consider the impact of ambient noises on the memories of witnesses—a crowd of hundreds of cheering people, calling out to the President and First Lady, and the sound of the motorcade itself, which included V8 limousine engines and the loud rumbling of Harley Davidson motorcycles. This explains in part why the crowd was so slow to react to the sound of the shots and the uncertainty of many concerning how many shots they heard.[32] This confusion was a catalyst for the HSCA's study of the Dallas police Dictabelt and its erroneous conclusion that an unseen second shooter fired a fourth shot and vanished (see Chapter 4).

Another earwitness who originally claimed he heard a grassy knoll shot (and later recanted) was Secret Service agent Paul Landis. Landis, who stood on the right running board of the follow-up car, wrote on a November 27, 1963, statement that he heard a shot come from the front of the motorcade. Conspiracists have used Landis' statement as proof of a grassy knoll shooter, but given that Landis was the only person in the motorcade who made this observation, and given that he did not see anyone shooting at them from the front, Landis himself never bought into the theories of a grassy knoll shooter. Rather, he concluded that it was more likely that he was mistaken rather than everyone else.[33]

Those who rode in the motorcade were more likely to locate the shooter correctly compared to distant bystanders. This is because they were in a direct line of fire compared to onlookers who stood at a distance from this axis and were therefore more likely to hear simultaneous echoes as loudly as they heard the real shots.[34] After running numerous firing tests with the Carcano, Dr. John Lattimer concluded that

> the sound of each shot was very loud. […] If one stood even a little in front of the riffle muzzle […] the reports were so loud as to be nearly intolerable. […] If such a rifle had been discharged a few feet to the right rear of photographer Abraham Zapruder (as from the "grassy knoll", as alleged by some) Mr. Zapruder would have been acutely aware of a deafening explosion with each shot.[35]

Although Abraham Zapruder remained uncertain as to the number and origin of the shots, he certainly never claimed to have heard deafening sounds and conceded that it was hard to distinguish between real shots and echoes because "there was too much reverberation. There was an echo which gave me a sound all over".[36]

Zapruder had his back to the rounded concrete pergola. The TSBD stood to his back and left. A shot from the knoll would have rang out to his right, just a few yards from his ears. Though Zapruder is often identified as a "grassy knoll witness," his claims are inconsistent with that theory, which places the rifle a dozen to two dozen feet to his right. However, his claims are consistent with a more distant shot that echoed off the pergola behind him.[37] Nor did Zapruder's assistant Marilyn Sitzman—who stood on the pillar beside him, a few feet from the spot where Jean Hill claimed the "Badge Man" had stood—have any perception of a grassy knoll shooter. Conspiracy researcher Josiah Thompson asked Sitzman in a 1966 interview if she witnessed a grassy knoll shooter (i.e., on her right):

> As far as the sound of the shots go, the first one, as I said, sounded like a fire-cracker, and the second one that I heard sounded the same, because I recall no difference whatsoever in them. And I'm sure that if the second shot would have come from a different place—and the supposed theory is they would have been much closer to me and on the right side—I would have heard the sounding of the gun much closer. [...] The loudest thing I heard that after-noon was the siren.[38]

Unlike Zapruder, she remained firm that the shots came from farther away, in the direction of the School Book depository, to her left.[39]

The vast majority of conspiracists claim that four to six shots were fired that day. Some, like Fletcher Prouty and Robert Groden, have claimed there were more.[40] Inversely, nearly 95% of all witness statements claimed they heard three shots or fewer.[41] In trying to account for the small number of divergent testi-monies, the Warren Commission learned what ballistics experts already knew: that such rifles produce multiple sounds from a single shot. These include the muzzle blast of gunpowder and hot gases projecting the bullet forward, the report of the bullet breaking the sound barrier, and the sound of the bullet striking a hard sur-face like pavement, a tree branch, or a metal light post—all of which could have been struck by the shot that missed the limousine.[42] Add to these sound effects the quaint architectural layout of Dealey Plaza—a small, partly sunken, open green space surrounded by concrete structures—the result of which is a swirling bowl of echoes. "In a complicated geometry like Dealey Plaza," notes mechanical engineer and explosives expert Michael Hargather, "you could get multiple shot reflections. In that geometry, someone could hear multiple sounds from a single shot".[43] Indeed, some witnesses heard shots coming from unlikely places, such as the concrete Pergola between the Grassy Knoll and TSBD (behind which sits a road leading into the TSBD parking lot, with no space for shooters to hide) and from the triple underpass (where several policemen and railroad workers were standing, none of whom heard a nearby muzzle blast).[44] According to Lee Bowers, who worked in a signal tower in the train yards behind the TSBD parking lot, echoes were a typical feature of Dealey Plaza:

Mr. BOWERS: I heard three shots. One, then a slight pause, then two very close together. Also reverberation from the shots. […] The sounds came either from up against the School Depository Building or near the mouth of the triple underpass. […] I had worked this same tower for some 10 or 12 years, and was there during the time they were renovating the School Depository Building, and had noticed at that time the similarity of sounds occurring in either of those two locations.

Mr. BALL: Can you tell me now whether or not […] the three shots came from the direction of the Depository Building or the triple underpass?

Mr. BOWERS: No; I could not. […] *There is a similarity of sound, because there is a reverberation which takes place from either location.*

Mr. BALL: Had you heard sounds originating near the triple underpass before?

Mr. BOWERS: Yes; quite often. Because trucks backfire and various occurrences.[45]

Oddly enough, many researchers name Bowers as an eyewitness to a conspiracy, even though he said he heard only three gunshots and that all of them came from the TSBD. This is because his vantage point in the signal tower gave him an unobstructed view of the north side of the picket fence, a popular location for those who believe in a grassy knoll shooter.[46] But apart from seeing a few custodians, railyard workers, and parking lot attendants trying to get a glimpse of the motorcade, none of whom seemed particularly sinister to Bowers, his testimony reveals rather little. Yet, conspiracists like Mark Lane have given excessive attention to two anonymous men standing near the grassy knoll fence who briefly caught Bowers' attention. He described them as a heavy-set middle-aged man and a young man in a plaid shirt or coat. According to Bowers, they did not seem to be together nor to communicate with anyone else. Neither was armed, wearing a uniform, or equipped with a radio, and at least one of the two was still "milling around" after policemen and dozens of onlookers swarmed the scene. Bowers gives no account of a shooter or fake agents hanging around the parking lot before the shooting, and even less of a man in a police uniform sporting a rifle. Nor did he see anyone taking off in a hurry after the shots rang out, only people flooding *into* the area. Once again, the conspiracists seem to be clutching at straws.

The same goes for three vehicles Bowers saw circling the parking lot within the half hour before the assassination. Two of these were muddy and had out-of-state license plates and political or touristic bumper stickers: nothing that screamed out "assassin" or "getaway car". Conspiracists have nevertheless described these vehicles as part of a coordinated operation to mobilize, communicate with, or evacuate a team of assassins stationed behind the grassy knoll fence. The only available evidence—Bowers' imprecise memories—tells us that these were just as likely to be tourists or employees searching for an elusive parking spot.[47]

The only unusual part of Bowers' testimony is his claim of having seen "some commotion" take place near the fence around the time that the gunshots were fired:

Mr. BALL: When you said there was a commotion, what do you mean by that? [...]

Mr. BOWERS: I just am unable to describe rather than it was something out of the ordinary, a sort of milling around, but something occurred in this particular spot which was out of the ordinary, which attracted my eye for some reason, which I could not identify.[48]

What this commotion might have been, Bowers had no clear idea, but this should come as no surprise considering that his view of the motorcade was obstructed, and that he noticed the reaction of panicked onlookers before he could know that something had happened to Kennedy.[49] Bowers' testimony tells us nothing about a grassy-knoll shooter, but this did not deter Mark Lane from interviewing him in 1966 and concluding that someone had fired a rifle from behind that fence. In this interview, Bowers told Lane pretty much the same thing he told the Warren Commission, with one slight but important variation:

There was something which occurred which caught my eye in this immediate area on the embankment. Now what this was, I could not state at that time and at this time I could not identify it other than there was some unusual occurrence, *a flash of light or smoke or something* which caused me to realize something out of the ordinary had occurred there.[50]

Despite his palpable uncertainty and the many plausible and completely mundane reasons that could explain what Bowers saw in that moment (the sun reflecting off a metal cigarette case, for example), this vague statement was enough for Lane and a gaggle of other researchers to conclude that the grassy knoll shooter is a historical fact.[51] While Bowers' testimony does not rule out the possibility of a grassy knoll shooter, it lends almost no weight to it. Some fairy tales are based on more evidence than this. When Bowers died in a car crash three months after this interview, some conspiracists saw it as the work of a hit squad trying to silence him, even though Bowers' story was now in the open and Jean Hill and Sam Holland (who stood on the triple overpass and said he saw a puff of smoke at the knoll[52]) should probably also have been killed, and yet never were.

Stone's *JFK* makes the unsubstantiated claim that six bullets were fired at Kennedy—two of which (the first and fifth) missed the limousine entirely, one of which hit JFK in the throat from the front, another struck him in the back from behind, a fourth skewered Governor Connolly through the back, chest, wrist, and thigh, and a final shot hit Kennedy in the head from the front, presumably from the grassy knoll. Others add more shots, including one from the Dal-Tex building[53] that hit Kennedy in the back of the head to account for the multiple fractures suffered by JFK's skull which cannot be explained with a grassy knoll shot.[54] The problem with all this is that no evidence has been found to prove that more than two bullets ever hit Kennedy and Connally. Even if all of these shooters were wielding identical Mannlicher-Carcano rifles, were firing the same round-tipped 6.5-millimeter copper-jacketed military ammunition, and had a superhuman team of evidence manipulators to clean up after them, we are still left to wonder where all these other bullets went and why they left no trace of their existence. Indeed, we'd have to wonder whether all of these were magic bullets.

13.2 The missing bullet: resetting the clock of the assassination

JFK buffs make two major miscalculations in their analysis of the ballistic evidence. The first, ironically, is to trust the Warren Commission too much regarding the timeframe of the assassination. As we will see, JFK's shooter had almost twice as much time than both the Warren Commission and conspiracists claim. The second is to accept a popular but fallacious depiction of the Warren Commission's Single Bullet Theory—which they rebaptized the Magic Bullet Theory—to try to discredit it. The first error is more forgivable, as conspiracists were not the only ones who made the faulty assumption that the shooting occurred in six seconds or less. The second is caused by a mixture of shoddy research, willful blindness, and intellectual dishonesty.

Josiah Thompson titled his 1967 book *Six Seconds in Dallas* after the apparently powerful claim that Lee Oswald did not have enough time (i.e., a *maximum* of six seconds) to aim and fire three shots with a bolt-action rifle. This is based on a faulty reading of the Warren Report, which states:

> Exacting tests conducted for the Commission demonstrated that *it was possible to fire three shots from the rifle within 5.5 seconds.* It should be noted that the first loaded shell was already in the chamber ready for firing; Oswald had only to pull the trigger to fire the first shot and to work the bolt twice in order to fire the second and third shots. They testified that *if the second shot missed,* Oswald had between 4.8 and 5.6 seconds to fire the three shots. *If either the first or third shot missed, Oswald had in excess of 7 seconds to fire the three shots.*[55]

In other words, the expert marksmen hired by the Commission concluded that 5.5 seconds was within the *minimum* range of time Oswald would need to fire three shots and activate the bolt twice. It is important to note that the Commission was working from the assumption that Oswald's first shot—which they assumed would be the most accurate—struck Kennedy in the neck, that his second shot missed the car, and that approximately 6 seconds passed between the throat and headshots (based on Zapruder film frames that showed Kennedy getting hit). Based on these assumptions, the Commission estimated that a minimum timeframe of 4.8–5.6 seconds, though unlikely, was possible. Nevertheless, because the sequence of shots remained uncertain, it accepted the possibility that Oswald had upward of 7 seconds to take all three shots. 5.5 seconds was therefore a conservative estimate. Their mistake arose from having started the clock at the first *hit*. But that was not necessarily the first *shot*.

Recent investigations have concluded that Oswald actually had between eight[56] and eleven[57] seconds to fire three rounds. This longer timeframe would certainly give a shooter of his ability enough time to comfortably shoot, reload, adjust, take aim, and fire two more rounds.[58] Using laser-guided rifles and reconstructed computer models based on home videos of the assassination, journalist Max Holland and computer animator Dale Myers separately reached the conclusion that the Warren Commission falsely assumed that the Zapruder film had captured the whole shooting sequence. It had not.[59]

Zapruder's silent film, Holland explains, failed to record the first shot, the one that missed Kennedy's car and that many mistook for a firecracker. It has always been known that Zapruder stopped filming between the moment the advance motorcycles appeared on Elm Street and the moment at which the presidential limousine did the same, but the Warren Commission did not see this as problematic. By combining ear and eyewitness accounts with the reactions of individuals in the opening frames of Zapruder's last sequence, Holland makes a strong case that the first shot, which missed the motorcade, was fired before Zapruder started filming again. One witness attesting to this is Amos L. Euins, who stood at the corner of Elm and Houston and could locate the position of the president's car at the moment of the first shot. Visible reactions to this first shot captured on the Zapruder film (which began rolling again) include that of Governor Connally, who stops waving and turns to his right to look behind. Since the Texas Governor told the Warren Commission that he immediately recognized the first bang as a rifle shot (which he wrongly believed hit the President but not him[60]), it is reasonable to assume that the first shot occurred shortly before he turned to look, before Zapruder started filming the final sequence. Enhanced versions of the film also show that Secret Service agents riding in the follow-up car—namely John Ready and George Hickey—perked up and looked away from their assigned quadrants and toward the buildings behind them (see Figure 13.3),[61] while agent Glen Bennett, seated in the same car, watched the President get hit in the neck soon after hearing what sounded to him like a firecracker.[62] Alongside the motorcade, on the south side of Elm, a little girl named Rosemary Willis stops running after the president's car and looks back behind her, toward the TSBD. This is consistent with other earwitnesses who heard a loud crack or bang when Kennedy's car finished rounding the curb, moments *before* Zapruder began filming the president's car.

All this reveals that Oswald had plenty of time to fire three rounds. It does not, however, explain why the first shot would miss its target. There is no conclusive answer to this quandary, but two possibilities stand out as likely. First, the Warren Commission did not give much attention to the missing shot, preferring to focus its efforts on explaining how the other two shots struck and killed Kennedy. This has given conspiracists, as well as lone gunman theorists, much room to speculate about the fate of this bullet. Posner argues that Oswald's first shot hit a tree branch that caused it to fragment, sending small pieces in several directions. This theory was first proposed by FBI firearms expert Robert Frazier who told the Warren Commission:

FIGURE 13.3 Photograph of motorcade on Elm Street taken by James Altgens
Source: James Altgens, AP-The Canadian Press.

> I have seen bullets strike small twigs, small objects, and ricochet for no
> apparent reason, except they hit and all the pressure is on one side and it
> turns the bullet and then it goes off at an angle. [...] There may have been
> a shot which deflected from a limb or for some other reason and was never
> discovered.[63]

If so, writes Posner, this would explain why traces of lead and antimony, but not
copper, were identified on the damaged Elm Street curbstone. Posner speculates
that a piece of the bullet's core, wrenched free of its copper jacket, hit the curb
before it (or another fragment from the same bullet) struck James Tague in the
cheek. TSBD employee Virgie Rachley and five other witnesses attested to seeing
something ricochet off the curbstone.[64]

Max Holland believes that Oswald took his first shot when the president's car
was beneath his window, *before* his view of the car was obscured by the large oak
tree discussed by Posner (see Figure 11.6). The lost bullet, Holland argues, probably
struck a metal traffic mast that stood in the way (see Figure 13.4). Several pieces
of evidence make Holland's theory more plausible. First, it is consistent with the
timing of the first shot and the limousine's position described by those standing
at the corner of Houston and Elm. "About 1.4 seconds before Zapruder restarted
filming," Holland explains,

> a horizontal traffic mast extending over Elm Street temporarily obscured
> Oswald's view of his target. That mast was never examined during any of

FIGURE 13.4 View of Elm Street traffic mast from sniper's nest

Source: Warren Commission Exhibit 875, National Archives and Records Administration.

the official investigations. Yet if this mast deflected the first shot, that would surely explain why the bullet missed not only the president, but the whole limousine.[65]

A Secret Service film taken from the sniper's window on November 27, 1963, captures the position of the old traffic mast overhanging Elm Street, while Tina Towner's home video places Kennedy in a position consistent with a shot partly obscured by the traffic mast.[66] The deflection of the bullet off the hanging metal object would, like Posner's theory, explain why the projectile that struck the curb stone left no traces of copper (having fragmented against the traffic mast). But unlike Posner, it also explains why the first shot was mistaken for a firecracker by many earwitnesses, including some familiar with rifle fire.

The position of the recovered shell casings on the sixth floor also corroborates Holland's theory, as one of them was ejected in a different direction, and farther away, than the other two (see Figure 13.5). This suggests that Oswald took the first shot in a standing position, looking down on Elm Street, and crouched or sitting for the next two—which accounts for the longer pause many witnesses heard between the first and second shot. A meticulous reconstruction of this theory by the *National Geographic* channel in 2013 proved consistent with the position of the three shells.[67] It is also consistent with the statements given by bystander Howard Brennan to the Dallas Police and Warren Commission that he saw a man *standing up* in the

FIGURE 13.5 Sniper's nest with three spent 6.5-millimeter cartridges
Source: DPD/Dallas Municipal Archives, University of North Texas Libraries.[68]

sixth-floor window just before the shooting began.[69] Holland's theory of an early misfire is consistent with the known evidence and recollections of several witnesses. Unfortunately, it cannot be proven with certainty as the traffic signal that hung there in 1963 no longer exists and was never examined. In the end, it appears that the missing bullet just doesn't want to be found.

13.3   When conspiracists conspire: the Magic Bullet Theory

Even before the Warren Commission realized that bystander James Tague was stuck by a stray bullet fragment—proving that at one shot missed the car—its staff had already run into the problem that there was not enough time, as the Zapruder film showed, for a shooter wielding a bolt-action rifle to strike Kennedy, reload, and hit Connally separately. The evidence suggested that there were either two shooters or one single bullet that caused multiple wounds. Assistant counsel Arlen Specter proposed the latter, and James Tague's testimony convinced most of the Commissioners—not without a heated debate—that Kennedy and Connally were struck by the same projectile. Specter's Single Bullet Theory has been mocked by conspiracists since its inception. Oliver Stone's film even called it "one of the grossest lies ever forced on the American people". How could a bullet cause seven wounds to two men and emerge nearly undamaged on a hospital gurney, the film's protagonist asks, when similar rounds fired through wrists of cadavers were warped beyond recognition?[70] Unsurprisingly, this Magic Bullet Theory continues to be touted as proof of a government whitewash. Jim Garrison explained it thus:

> According to the government's account, the seven wounds were inflicted as follows: the bullet entered the President's back or neck (1) headed downward at an angle of 17 degrees. It then moved *upward* and departed from Kennedy's body out of the front of his neck (2). It continued into Connolly's body at the rear of his right armpit (3). <u>Inasmuch as Governor Connally had been sitting directly in front of President Kennedy,</u> it must be assumed that the bullet somehow moved over to the right far enough to head leftward into Connally. Now the bullet headed downward at an angle of 27 degrees, shattering Connally's fifth rib and departing from the right side of his chest (4). The bullet continued downward and then entered Connally's right wrist (5), shattering the radius bone. After coming out of the other side of the Governor's right wrist (6) it entered his left thigh (7) from which it later fell out.
>
> According to the official story, this bullet was later found in <u>almost perfect condition</u> in a corridor of Parkland Hospital, apparently having fallen from a cot. The bullet was <u>nearly flawless</u>, deformed slightly only at the base. Curiously, more fragments were found in Governor Connally's wrist than were found to be missing from bullet No.399.[71]

Stone's *JFK* goes even further. In its dramatic courtroom scene, the film's Jim Garrison explains that this "magic bullet" would have needed to change directions twice in midair as it traveled from Kennedy's neck into Connally's back, then stop and dramatically pause and, after traveling through Connally's chest, turn right to pass through his wrist, and make a final "dramatic U-turn" to embed itself backward into his thigh from which it later simply fell out. "The government says it can prove this with some fancy physics in a nuclear laboratory," Garrison tells the jury, "Of course they can! Theoretical physics can prove an elephant can hang from a cliff with its tail tied to a daisy, but use your eyes, your common sense…"[72]

"Magic" is too polite a term to describe this bullet, because even intelligent people are often taken in by well-crafted stage tricks. Indeed, this scene turns Arlen Specter's entire theory into a cartoonish lampoon. "Never in the history of gunfire," the Hollywood Garrison tells his jury, "has there been a bullet this ridiculous!" On that point, he is entirely correct—except for the fact that almost no part of this nonsensical story was ever proposed by the Warren Commission. Indeed, the Magic Bullet Theory presented by Garrison, Stone, Groden, and others was not a creation of the Warren Commission, but a straw man fallacy concocted by the conspiracists.

A close examination of the ballistic evidence demonstrates that a single bullet was able to cause all of Kennedy's and Connally's wounds, apart from those inflicted

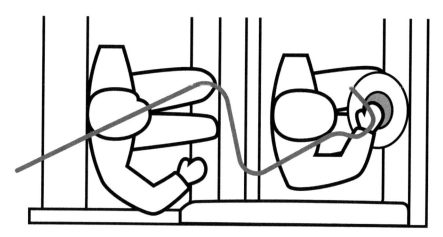

FIGURE 13.6 Diagram of Magic Bullet Theory according to conspiracists
Source: J.D. Lillo.

to JFK's head. In fact, no other evidence exists to suggest the two men were hit by different bullets, even less separate rifles. First, the conspiracists mistakenly describe the two men as sitting in perfect alignment, facing frontward, and at the same elevation, making the Single Bullet Theory scientifically impossible (see Figure 13.6). But this positioning is provably incorrect. Kennedy's limousine—a specially modified Lincoln Continental identified by the Secret Service as SS-100-X— had particular characteristics specifically designed for motorcades. This included a hydraulic lift that allowed the president's seat to be raised nearly a foot above those in the forward part of the car, and low-riding jump seats for additional passengers (e.g., Governor Connally and his wife) to ride along without eclipsing the president.[73] Although the rear seat was not fully raised on that day, due to Kennedy not wanting to make his wife uncomfortable, the President nonetheless sat three to four inches higher than Governor Connolly.[74] By the time of the second shot, the car was driving down an incline, increasing the alignment of the two men in respect to the TSBD's sixth-floor window. The position of the jump seat also placed Connally several inches inward, while Kennedy, whose arm is leaning over the side of the car, occupies a more rightward position (see Figure 13.7). All this is visible on the Zapruder film and in countless photographs of the Dallas motorcade. Connally's body is also rotated partly to his right, having just been startled by the first shot,[75] at the time Kennedy's arms shoot up toward his neck.[76] Connally reacts almost immediately afterward and slumps sideways into the arms of his wife before the final headshot strikes Kennedy. Many videos, photographic and computerized reconstructions, have been performed over the last six decades by the Secret Service, FBI, Warren Commission, HSCA, private news media, and documentary filmmakers. All who did not set out to prove a conspiracy concluded that the two men and all of their (nonlethal) wounds were in line with the TSBD sixth-floor window. With the development of three-dimensional laser scanning

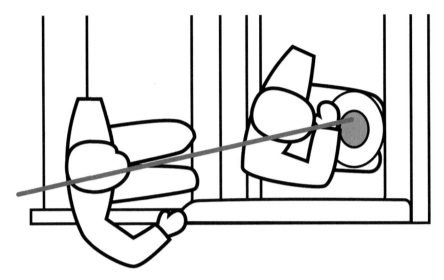

FIGURE 13.7 Diagram of Single Bullet Theory according to Warren Commission
Source: J.D. Lillo.

technology and computerized reconstructions, this scenario has been confirmed to the highest probability.[77]

13.4   Lining up the wounds

Having established that the Single Bullet Theory is scientifically plausible, let us consider the wounds that this single bullet (CE399) allegedly caused. We will then consider whether the extensive damage sustained by the President's head (Wound #9) was consistent or not with a shot from the TSBD's sixth-floor window.

13.4.1   Wound #1: Kennedy's right upper back

Conspiracists consider Kennedy's back wound to be controversial because it was not observed by the doctors and nurses at Parkland hospital. This is not surprising considering that the Parkland medical staff saw the body for no more than 20 minutes and were focused on keeping the President alive, not conducting his autopsy.[78] No forensic pathologist took part in these procedures. Out of respect for Mrs. Kennedy, who was standing nearby watching them fail to revive her husband,[79] and given the need to attend to Governor Connally, gravely wounded but still alive, no one at Parkland had time to conduct a thorough examination of JFK's gore-soaked body, especially to notice a discrete bullet wound in his upper back. For this reason, Parkland doctors never located the first wound produced by CE399. Instead, they wrongly assumed that Kennedy's throat wound (see Wound #2 below) was either a wound of entry or the result of a deflected fragment.[80]

The back wound was first examined later that night during the autopsy at Bethesda Naval Hospital. It was recognized as a wound of entry, though it was not dissected (as it should have if a full forensic autopsy had been performed). Still, probes were inserted and X-rays were taken. No bullet was found lodged in the chest or neck. The Bethesda pathologists identified the back wound as being located "fourteen centimeters below the tip of the right mastoid process, the bony prominence of the skull directly behind the earlobe". In other words, slightly to the right of the spine, beside the first thoracic vertebra.[81] This is significant because Garrison and Stone (among others) place this wound at the *third* thoracic vertebra, too low to respect the straight-line trajectory described by the Warren Commission. But in fact, this is an error that finds its "proof" in the approximate location of the bullet hole in JFK's clothes and the wound drawn on the autopsy face sheet, not on the *measurements* recorded on the face sheet and in the final autopsy report. Faced with a discrepancy between these documents, conspiracists have favored the less official and more approximate face sheet diagram. The HSCA's Forensic Pathology Panel investigated this allegation and found that the face sheet was never meant to be drawn to scale, but to act as an *aide-mémoire* for the pathologists to later write their report.[82] The face sheet even verbally identifies the distance from the wound to the tip of the right mastoid process as 14 centimeters, consistent with the autopsy report and the autopsy photographs certified as authentic by the HSCA. This suggests that neither Stone nor Garrison studied the evidence closely.[83]

13.4.2   Wound #2: Kennedy's throat

Inversely, Kennedy's throat wound *was* observed by the emergency doctors at Parkland Hospital but was not visible to the pathologists at Bethesda Naval Hospital. This is because it was dissected in Dallas to perform a tracheotomy to help the injured Kennedy breathe. The missing exit wound left the pathologists in Maryland confused. The problem was resolved the next day when Bethesda pathologist James Humes contacted Dr. Malcolm Perry in Dallas and concluded (correctly) that the tracheotomy had destroyed a wound of exit just under the President's Adam's apple. The Parkland doctors, not having seen the entry wound in Kennedy's upper back, and being unfamiliar with the rest of the evidence from Dealey Plaza, had assumed it was an entry wound because it was rather small ("a few millimeters in diameter") and the soft tissue in Kennedy's neck did not exhibit the telltale lacerations of a typical exit wound.

Again, conspiracists have been quick to assume that the Parkland emergency doctors were right and that the Bethesda pathologists engaged in a cover-up. However, the explanation is simple. The small size of the wound is explained by the pressure exercised on Kennedy's throat by his shirt collar and necktie which kept the exit wound tight and prevented his soft throat tissue from being blown outward.[84] According to the FBI, Kennedy's shirt collar displayed a "ragged, slit-like hole and the ends of the torn threads around the hole were bent outward. These characteristics are typical of an exit hole". JFK's necktie also displayed a "small elongated nick [that] may have been caused by the projectile after it passed through the front of the shirt".[85] A trail of muscle damage substantiated the likelihood that the bullet had traversed Kennedy's throat without striking bone.[86] Hence, Bethesda pathologists Humes, Boswell, and Finck concluded the bullet had "entered the right superior posterior thorax above the scapula and traversed the soft tissues of the supra-scapular and the supra-clavicular portions of the base of the right side of the neck".[87] In other words, CE399—a hard, round-tipped military-grade bullet— burrowed through the soft parts of Kennedy's neck without suffering much damage, leaving two small (entrance and exit) wounds. This, incidentally, is exactly what the "humanitarian rifle" had been designed to do: to pierce and not mutilate its victims.

13.4.3   Wounds #3 and #4: Connally's back and chest

Traversing Kennedy's neck had two effects on the bullet. It first began to slow down and lose some destructive power.[88] Second, and more importantly, it caused the round-tipped bullet to lose stability and begin to tumble or "yaw". In repeated firing tests using the Carcano and ammunition similar to that found in the rifle and TSBD, forensic firearms experts Luke and Mike Haag discovered that the 6.5-milli- meter Mannlicher-Carcano bullet, which is otherwise stable thanks to its heavy- weight and long cylindrical shape, has an inherent defect: it invariably begins to tumble after traversing soft media like blocks of glycerine soap and ballistic jelly, two substances used by forensic investigators to replicate the effects of gunshots through soft human tissues.[89] In other words, the bullet that exited Kennedy's throat would be expected to perform not just one, but *a continuous series* of what Oliver Stone called "dramatic U-turns"—rotations around its longitudinal axis. This is known to have happened because the wounds in Connally's back (near his right armpit), chest (near his right nipple) and right wrist, are etched permanently in the holes of his suit coat and shirt, all of which were oblong in shape, indicating that the bullet did not bore through him nose first (which would have produced circular holes) but tumbled through the air and through his chest, wrist, and thigh,[90] as it collapsed his lung and struck a "glancing blow"[91] on his fifth rib, which explains why CE399's tip was not flattened or crushed as conspiracists think it should be.

13.4.4   Wounds #5 and #6: Connally's right wrist

Now traveling less than half its original speed, the single bullet shattered the radius bone in Connally's wrist,[92] striking it sideways—as proven by the elongated slits in his shirt cuffs and jacket sleeves.[93] Lead fragments were recovered from the wounds in his chest, wrist, and thigh, suggesting that the slower moving bullet got flattened or bent as it punched through the wrist bone, causing some of the softer lead core to be squeezed out of the base of the bullet, like toothpaste out of a tube.

Many conspiracists argue that Connally could not have been shot in the wrist by CE399, because he kept hold of his Stetson hat. This is a strange claim considering that no one at Parkland doubted that the Governor's wrist was shattered, nor did

Connally, who lived to tell about it. This claim therefore implies that Connally's wrist was hit by another bullet that the one that punctured his back, lung, and thigh. It would also have had to strike him later, since Connolly had no previous memory of being hit in the wrist,[94] but before the car left Dealey Plaza, since the Zapruder film shows him slumping onto his wife as the car speeds away, his wrist hidden from view. A subsequent shot would therefore have had to be fired from inside the car (or perhaps from the sky!) to avoid injuring Agents Greer and Kellerman sitting in the front seat, Mrs. Connally, Jackie Kennedy, and Special Agent Clint Hill who climbed aboard seconds after the fatal headshot. But since there is no evidence of any other bullet hitting Connolly (or of assassins milling about in helicopters), it is safe to say that the whole issue of Connally holding his Stetson is a distraction that serves little purpose.

In any event, the Itek Corporation, a defense contractor that specialized in photographic analysis and camera systems for satellites, studied the Zapruder film in 1976. Its analysts noticed that Governor Connally's Stetson seemed to flip upward immediately after he was shot in the back, suggesting that he either did loosen his grip on the hat or held onto it with a floppy wrist.[95] In 1998, Nellie Connally told a reporter that her husband held on to that hat all the way to the hospital.[96] Whether or not this is true, there is no medical reason that compels us to believe that a man with a shattered wrist would necessarily drop what he's holding.[97]

13.4.5 Wound #7: Connally's thigh and the "pristine" bullet

Bullet CE399 ended its murderous journey by piercing John Connolly's left thigh with just enough velocity to break the skin and fall out into his clothing. It was discovered at Parkland Hospital after it fell off a stretcher, after the Governor was cut out of his clothes and transferred but before he underwent surgery, and therefore before Kennedy's body was fully examined that night in Bethesda. This is significant because if the bullet were planted for others to find, it would have had to be done without knowing what bullets or fragments Parkland and Bethesda doctors would retrieve from the two men, and before the inspection of the president's limousine could be completed,[98] thereby risking to expose their plot by planting more bullets than Oswald could fire.[99]

A further problem with this false bullet theory is that it is anachronistic. The Single Bullet Theory, as seen in Chapter 2, was a late creation of the Warren Commission to account for conflicting evidence caused by James Tague's deposition. Until late April 1964, the FBI, the Secret Service, and most members of the Warren Commission remained convinced that two separate bullets struck Kennedy and Connally and that the single bullet idea was preposterous. "How could anybody tamper with evidence to make it fit a theory that didn't even exist yet?" muses John McAdams.[100]

Besides, anyone who carefully observes bullet CE399 will see that it is certainly not "pristine". Since the bullet was tumbling and not traveling at full muzzle velocity, it did not suffer the kind of damage one might expect had it struck Connally

FIGURE 13.8 Bullet found on stretcher at Parkland Memorial Hospital (side view)

Source: Warren Commission Exhibit CE399, National Archives and Records Administration.

FIGURE 13.9 Bullet found on stretcher at Parkland Memorial Hospital (posterior view)

Source: Warren Commission Exhibit CE399, National Archives and Records Administration.

directly, without first traversing Kennedy's neck. Nevertheless, it was noticeably damaged (see Figures 13.8 and 13.9). As Dr. John Lattimer described it:

> This bullet, if seen only in a side view, which has been widely republished by critics of the Warren Commission report, appears to be deformed very little. In fact, its apparent lack of deformity permitted critics to describe it

inaccurately as a pristine bullet. […] When I actually picked up this bullet and inspected it, I found it to be flattened on its rear end to a significant degree, as if from a severe blow on one side. (Photographs taken from the side do not show this flattening.) It is also slightly bent, on its long axis.

The soft lead at the base of bullet 399 appeared to be scooped out slightly on one side, with fine transverse scratch marks across the base. […] That bullet 399 was fired from Oswald's rifle has been verified by tests done by the FBI laboratory staff, who found that *the rifling scratches on bullet 399 conformed exactly to the rifling scratches on the test bullets fired from the same gun.* No one appears to have contested this point.[101]

In other words, bullet CE399 was not only fired by a 6.5-millimeter Mannlicher-Carcano rifle, its striations (the spiraling grooves produced by the rifle barrel when fired) showed it to have been fired by *the very same rifle* that Oswald had purchased and which was found in the TSBD.

The fragments recovered in Connally's wounds also account for most of CE399's missing lead mass. After weighing a hundred identical bullets from the same lot as CE399, establishing that the average weight of a 6.5-millimeter Carcano bullet as 160.844 grains,[102] and compressing sample bullets until they were flattened like the one recovered at Parkland, Lattimer and his associates extracted an amount of lead weighing approximately 2.1 grains, which is remarkably close to the weight missing from CE399.[103] According to Parkland Hospital surgeon Dr. Charles Gregory and HSCA head pathologist Dr. Michael Baden, the four largest fragments extracted from Connally's body weighed a bit less than that.[104] Conspiracists who claim that more lead was extracted from Connolly than was missing from CE399 have either misread the evidence or are distorting the truth.

13.4.6   Wounds #8 and #9: the headshot

Many JFK buffs argue that the "back and to the left" movement of Kennedy's head proves he was shot from the right-front of the limousine, where the "grassy knoll" is located. It is also claimed that the blood and tissue that were blasted out of his head were projected backward, and that many individuals in Dallas witnessed a massive exit wound at the back of JFK's head where the Warren Commission says only a small wound of entry was found.[105] Let us examine these claims closely (in reverse order).

13.4.6.1   The head wounds

Nigel Turner's 1988 documentary "The Men Who Killed Kennedy" identifies three witnesses who reportedly saw a large exit wound at the back of JFK's head. These are Marilyn Willis, Beverly Oliver, and Virgil "Ed" Hoffman. The most obvious problem with these reports is that, whether or not one believes the Zapruder film is authentic (see Chapter 17), the vast majority of eyewitnesses separately testified that they saw the *top* or *right side* of Kennedy's head burst open, not the back. Witnesses standing on the north side of Elm Street were in the best position to see the upper right side of his head burst open, from the temple to the back of the ear.[106] No one riding behind the president's car, including JFK's special assistants and close friends Kenneth O'Donnell and David Powers, reported a blowout to the back of his head, nor did motorcycle patrolmen B.J. Martin and Bobby Hargis who rode just a few feet away. Secret Service agent Clint Hill, who stood over Kennedy and his wife while the limousine sped to Parkland Hospital, had a better vantage point than any witness. In fact, there exist no contemporaneous Dealey Plaza eyewitness reports of a blowout to the back of Kennedy's head. In contrast, accounts by Willis, Oliver, and Hoffman emerged several months or years later. They also evolved over time.[107] For example, Oliver, who was a Dallas nightclub showgirl, also claimed she saw Jack Ruby at the Carousel Club a few weeks before the assassination fraternizing with Oswald (whom she says identified himself to her as a CIA agent). Her claims were contradicted by several of the dancers she worked with. Oliver also claimed she took a film of the assassination that was then stolen by the authorities. She described the camera as a Yashica Super 8-millimeter zoom camera to conspiracy authors Jim Marrs and Gary Shaw. That model did not exist in 1963. When in 1994 the Assassination Records Review Board asked her for more information on this camera, Oliver said she never owned one.[108]

Parkland emergency doctors gave descriptions of the head wound that were consistent with a shot from the back and exit wound on the right side, but which convinced many that Kennedy was shot from the front. In an official statement made on November 22, 1963, Parkland hospital administrator J.C. Price said

> there was a great laceration on the right side of the head (temporal and *occipital*) causing a great defect in the skull plate so that there was herniation and laceration of great areas of the brain, even to the extent that *the cerebellum* had protruded from the wound.[109]

While Price's statement suggests that severe damage was inflicted to the President's skull, brain, and cerebellum in the occipital area (the lower rear part of his head), it is not clearly explained whether the attending medical staff saw this through a hole in the back of the skull (the occipital bone) or whether they could see the inside of the occipital area from a hole in the side of the head. Conspiracists tend to interpret such statements in the light of their assumption that there was a sizeable hole in the back of JFK's head, but this is not what Price said. The rear blowout theory can only be sustained by misinterpreting this statement and by simultaneously ignoring other statements and pieces of evidence that show the doctors witnessed a temporal and/or parietal exit wound (i.e., on the right side of the head), which everyone agreed was rather large (approximately 5 inches, or 13 centimeters, in diameter).[110]

In a signed November 22, 1963, statement, Dr. Kemp Clark described the head wound as a large wound in the right *occipito-parietal region*, from which profuse bleeding was occurring. […] There was considerable loss of scalp and bone tissue, both cerebral and cerebellar tissue were extruding from the wound. *Further examination was not possible* as cardiac arrest occurred at this point.[111]

Dr. Marion Jenkins, a Parkland anesthesiologist, also described the wound as temporal and occipital and believed he saw cerebellum, but nonetheless described the injury as a wound of exit, and concurred with the autopsy photographs shown to him by the HSCA in 1978 and the *PBS* program *NOVA* in 1988 that President Kennedy did not suffer a blowout at the back of the head.[112] Dr. Malcolm Perry, the first surgeon on the scene, was in the presence of Kennedy's body the longest. He described the head wound as "*a large avulsive wound* on the right posterior cranium,"[113] which is to say that some of the President's skull was broken and loosely attached to the scalp in the manner of a "flap". This flap of scalp and skull bone was attached to the rear occipital-parietal area and likely hung open for him to notice, giving the appearance that the wound continued into the occipital area, even though the center point of the wound was not at the back of the head but near or above the right ear.[114] Dr. Perry never examined the back of the head.[115]

The Warren Commission testimony of Dr. Robert McClelland is most elucidating:

Dr. McCLELLAND: As I took the position at the head of the table […] to help out with the tracheotomy, I was in such a position that I could very closely examine the head wound, and I noted that the right posterior portion of the skull had been extremely blasted. It had been shattered, apparently, by the force of the shot so that the parietal bone was protruded up through the scalp and seemed to be fractured almost along its right posterior half, as well as *some of the occipital bone* being fractured *in its lateral half*, and this sprung open the bones that I mentioned in such a way that *you could actually look down into the skull cavity itself* and see that probably a third or so, at least, of the brain tissue, posterior cerebral tissue and some of the cerebellar tissue had been blasted out. There was a large amount of bleeding which was occurring mainly from the large venous channels in the skull which had been blasted open. […]

Mr. SPECTER: n what position was President Kennedy maintained from the time you saw him until the pronouncement of death?

Dr. McCLELLAND: On his back on the cart. […]

Mr. SPECTER: Was he on the stretcher at all times?

Dr. McCLELLAND: Yes. […]

Mr. SPECTER: Did you observe the condition of the back of the President's head?

Dr. McCLELLAND: Well, partially; not, of course, as I say, *we did not lift his head up since it was so greatly damaged.* We attempted to avoid moving him any more than it was absolutely necessary, but I could see, of course, all the extent of the wound.

Mr. SPECTER: You saw a large opening which you have already described?
Dr. McCLELLAND: I saw the large opening which I have described.[116]

Like the others, McClelland saw a large wound on the right-rear portion of
Kennedy's head, but he saw this wound by *looking down into the skull*. Kennedy
was lying *on his back* the whole time McClelland was in the room. He was not
looking at the wound through a hole at the back of the head but from above.
Such statements receive little attention from conspiracists but they reveal a great
deal about the larger context. Most Parkland doctors stated that Kennedy's head
wound stretched from the side of his head (above the ear) toward the back, that
part of his cerebellum, or something that looked like it, was exposed (blown
inward, toward the temple), and that a piece of his skull hung open in an avulsive
(flap-like) manner.[117] Beyond that, they had little time to examine Kennedy's
wounds. There was no attempt to look for entry or exit wounds in his back, and
the body was left for pathologists to examine once the President was declared
dead some 20 minutes after being admitted. "Quite simply," concludes John
McAdams, the Parkland emergency doctors "could not have actually seen the
area near the External Occipital Protuberance that conspiracists think was blown
out. But then, everything behind the ears is 'posterior,' and also—depending on
your perspective—'back'".[118]

Some important circumstantial details must be kept in mind. The first is that
despite the apparent inconsistencies between these testimonies and the subsequent autopsy results, most of the Parkland medical team would later accept the
conclusions of the autopsy doctors once they read their report, including the claim
that the massive wound on the side of Kennedy's head was a wound of exit.[119] The
second is that Kennedy's head was awash with gore and was bleeding profusely
throughout the brief period that he was treated at Parkland, making it difficult for
these surgeons, who were hurriedly trying to save his life, to carefully assess the
particularities of his wounds. Their efforts were focused on stopping the bleeding,
helping him breathe, and performing cardiac resuscitation, not to mention having
to manage their stress as they struggled to do the impossible.

13.4.6.2 The gory ejecta

As the last shot rang out, many witnesses saw a red cloud of brain matter erupt
from the President's head. Some believed it was ejected backward, which could be
consistent with a grassy knoll shot. Conspiracists often highlight the fact that Jackie
Kennedy climbed onto the *back* of the limousine, presumably to retrieve a piece
of skull, and that motorcycle patrolmen B.J. Martin and Bobby Hargis—who rode
at the rear-left of the limousine—were sprayed with fine droplets of blood. Special
Agent Clint Hill, who was running to catch up to SS-100-X, and Special Agent
Sam Kinney, driving the Secret Service follow-up car, also said they were sprinkled
with ejecta. Common sense might suggest that brain matter was splattered in their
direction by a shot from the front-right.[120]

But what *seems* to have happened and what *actually* happened are not always consistent, particularly in situations that involve complex movement and flying particles. What conspiracy theorists often leave out is the fact that the front of the limousine was also awash with blood, bone fragments, and brain tissue. A forensic inspection of the vehicle also produced two large bullet fragments that matched the chemical composition of the smaller lead fragments later retrieved from the President's skull. These bullet fragments, listed by the Warren Commission as CE567 and CE569, represent mangled portions of a 6.5-millimeter Mannlicher-Carcano bullet's outer copper jacket, which also contained lead deposits matching the fragments in Kennedy's head.[121] "There was no lead from any third bullet," explains Dr. Lattimer.[122] The windshield was also damaged by a bullet or piece of flying skull bone, but only on the *inner* part of the double-layered glass,[123] while droplets of blood and gore found their way onto the *outer* side of the windshield.

Associated Press photographer James Altgens, who stood toward the front of the limousine (see Figure 13.3) and was also sprayed with ejecta, believed that the headshot came from the rear.[124] Indeed, enhanced versions of the Muchmore and Zapruder films, viewed slowly, clearly show the ejecta erupting upward and forward (see Figure 17.1). In other words, the motorcade was traveling *into the ejecta* so that those riding or running directly behind Kennedy's limousine were sprinkled by a drizzle of blood splatter that was precipitating, like a foggy mist, as they drove or ran through it. Many witnesses also observed that there was a strong breeze in Dealey Plaza that day. B.J. Martin told the Warren Commission it seemed to be blowing toward them (i.e., from the west) as they turned onto Elm Street,[125] suggesting that the ejecta was blown toward Martin, Hargis, Hill, and the Secret Service follow-up car as they followed the President. And so, unless all of these pieces of evidence were distorted, manufactured, or planted by a coordinated cover-up (see Chapters 14–17), the headshot had to originate from the rear.

13.4.6.3 The head snap

Finally, what does the evidence tell us concerning Kennedy's "back and to the left" motion? While it is undeniable that his head does snap back in the Zapruder film, there are several reasons for us not to take this as proof of a grassy knoll shooter.

First, had the bullet been fired from the front—whether it was from the picket fence, as Lane and Thompson agued, or from the concrete wall where Arnold and Hill placed the "Badge Man"—it would in all probability have left a large exit wound on the *left side* of JFK's head.[126] The vast majority of medical personnel who looked at the President's head that day concurred that much of the right side of his head and brain were damaged and blown *outward*, making it an *exit* wound. No medical professional reported anything remotely resembling a wound of exit on his left side. Had the shot come from the grassy knoll, bullet and skull fragments would have most likely damaged the rear seat of the limousine, showered bystanders on the south side of Elm, or struck Mrs. Kennedy who sat beside her husband in a direct line of fire from the knoll. But no evidence suggests this ever happened. Medical evidence shows that the left portion of Kennedy's brain remained largely intact, and that no part of the left side of his skull was damaged. Indeed, the rear-to-front pattern of skull fractures suffered by Kennedy's head led multiple wound ballistics experts to conclude that the fatal headshot came from a projectile that entered the back of JFK's head and caused the right side of his skull to explode outward.[127]

When James Altgens witnessed the fatal headshot, he said he saw the President's body moved forward before snapping backward.[128] By scrutinizing the published single frames of the headshot, researchers discovered as early as 1965 that the Zapruder film did record a brief forward lurch (at frames 312 and 313) before the head moved "back and to the left".[129] In other words, the force of the bullet propelled Kennedy's head forward a few inches before another force made it go back. There are multiple explanations for this double movement that don't require a shot from the front, including a neurophysiological spasm, the natural recoil of Kennedy's spine and neck muscles after being thrust forward, the constraining effect of the President's back brace (see Chapter 15) which impeded his upper body from slumping forward, or the "jet effect" produced by his exploding skull.[130] Whatever the reason, wound ballistics experts find no contradiction between the double head snap and a shot from behind. Former Dallas County medical examiner Dr. Charles S. Petty, who served on the HSCA Forensic Pathology Panel, explained in a 1986 mock trial of Lee Oswald that human heads are too heavy to be propelled backward by a rifle bullet in the manner alleged by JFK buffs:

> This was an automatic, involuntary reaction on the part of the President's nerves and muscles. There was a blast inside the head, the nerves were fired off, and the muscles were set into action. The muscles in the back are stronger than the muscles in the front and so therefore the head moved backward.[131]

Chemist and meteorologist Kenneth Rahn, a retired science professor and amateur JFK researcher, agrees: "The head does not snap backward rapidly the way it snapped forward," he explains,

> Rather the head starts moving backward slowly and gains momentum over several frames. [...] The rearward motion was of JFK's entire upper torso, with the head just moving along with the neck. [...] The available data strongly suggest that it was indeed a combination of effects, whose detailed contributions will probably never be known with certainty.[132]

It must be conceded that a thorough assessment of the assassination's ballistic evidence is no longer possible without relying on various probabilities and assumptions. Such a study also invariably produces newer uncertainties and interpretations that will require further investigation. Luckily, the advantage of studying forensic evidence, unlike eyewitness accounts, is that it can become clearer as technologies improve, provided the original evidence has not been lost or corrupted with time. The work of the National Archives, Texas-based libraries, and other public institutions in preserving these artifacts, from bullet fragments to John Connally's clothes, has been of inestimable worth to all researchers genuinely seeking the truth, but less so for those engaging in paranoid question begging.

The last three chapters have shown that, if we take the evidence at face value, it is simpler to believe that Lee Oswald shot Kennedy with a 6.5-millimeter Mannlicher-Carcano rifle from a sixth-floor window, and that he did so unaided, than it is to believe that he didn't. Those who attempt to remove Oswald and his rifle from the equation are stuck with the burden of proof and the duty to honestly disprove the evidence weighing against him. As John McAdams concluded,

> Any sane conspiracy theory has to include Oswald. And it's better if it includes Oswald pretty much the way the Warren Commission portrayed him. [...] This view has huge logical advantages, but it has a big psychological disadvantage: it requires throwing away a large number of juicy pieces of 'conspiracy evidence'.[133]

The fourth and final part of this book will therefore consider whether the evidence used to incriminate Oswald—the ballistic, medical, photographic, and film evidence that support the Lone Gunman scenario—could have been manufactured and planted by powerful groups trying to frame a patsy.

Notes

1 *Warren Report*, 79:

> Around 1 p.m. Deputy Sheriff Luke Mooney noticed a pile of cartons in front of the window in the southeast corner of the sixth floor [see Figure 12.2]. Searching that area he found at approximately 1:12 p.m. three empty cartridge cases on the floor near the window. [...] Captain J.W. Fritz, chief of the homicide bureau of the Dallas Police Department, issued instructions that nothing be moved or touched until technicians from the police crime laboratory could take photographs and check for fingerprints. Mooney stood guard to see that nothing was disturbed. A few minutes later, Lieutenant J. C. Day of the Dallas Police Department arrived and took photographs of the cartridge cases before anything had been moved.
>
> *(See Figure 13.5)*

2 The Commission did concede that "some heard only two shots, while others testified that they heard four and perhaps as many as five or six shots". *Warren Report*, 110.

3 *Warren Report*, 117. The Commission assumed the *second* shot missed the limousine but did say it was possible that the *first* shot missed. This would have given Oswald approximately eight seconds (according to the Commission) to fire all three bullets. Recent investigations suggest that the shooter had nearly 11 seconds to fire three shots. See "JFK: The Lost Bullet," *National Geographic Channel*, 2013.

4 Testimony of Mrs. Jean Lollis Hill, WC VI.

5 Hill served as an advisor for Stone's *JFK*. She also played a short cameo.

6 Testimony of Mrs. Jean Lollis Hill, WC VI.

7 Bill Sloan with Jean Hill: *JFK: The Last Dissenting Witness* (1992), 17–35.

8 Ibid., 22–35.

9 Voluntary Statement of Jean Hill, Sheriff's Department, County of Dallas, Texas, November 22, 1963, *Office of the City Secretary, Dallas Municipal Archives, John F. Kennedy/ Dallas Police Department Collection.*

10 Her Warren Commission testimony makes it clear that this was an unarmed man in plainclothes (not a shooter in a police uniform) running *toward* the railyard, not *away* from it as she later described the "Badge Man".

11 McAdams: *JFK Assassination Logic,* 57–8.

12 Testimony of Mrs. Jean Lollis Hill, WC VI.

13 McAdams: *JFK Assassination Logic,* 56. Many Hill interviews are available on *YouTube.* Compare those she and Moorman gave in 1963 with those Hill gave in the early 1990s (e.g., on the *Maury Povich Show* in 1991).

14 Moorman, who lay down on the grass at this point, does remember the event while Hill, who remained standing and often claimed there was some sort of pause, did not. Interview with Mary Moorman on WFAA/ABC TV, 11/22/63, available on *YouTube.* "It seemed like an eternity," Hill told the Warren Commission, "but I'm sure there was just a slight pause before things started moving again". Testimony of Mrs. Jean Lollis Hill, WC VI. It appears that Hill suffered some sort of emotional shock, possibly for several minutes, and then later tried to complete her missing memories with various assumptions or second-hand reports. This would account for a number of inconsistencies in her memories and her conviction of telling the truth.

15 *Warren Report,* chap. 6, 334–5.

16 She told Maury Povich in 1991 that she touched the limousine, which is discounted by her earlier statements and photographs. The Altgens AP photograph (Figure 13.3) reveals that there was a full street lane—and two police motorcycles—separating JFK's limousine from Hill and Moorman.

17 Hill appears to be speaking of B.J. Martin, a Dallas patrolman who rode to the left and rear of Kennedy's car. McAdams: *JFK Assassination Logic,* 55. Hill's reasons for using a false name are not explained. One could posit poor memory, another sensationalist fib, or an attempt to protect B.J. Martin's anonymity (which is unlikely, given she identified his exact position in the motorcade and that Martin had died by the time she published her book). Nor was it to protect her marriage, since Hill had been divorced for nearly 30 years when her book was published.

18 McAdams: *JFK Assassination Logic,* 59.

19 Peter R. Whitmey: "Jean Hill: The Lady in Red," 1999, Ken Rahn, ed.: *The Academic JFK Assassination Site.* Lane interviewed Hill before she even testified to the Warren Commission. In her WC testimony, she claims that Lane, who had written that Hill was manhandled by government agents, had distorted her account of Jim Featherston's "theft" of Moorman's pictures. By 1992, Hill was repeating Lane's version with no mention at all of Featherston.

20 In her Warren Commission testimony, Hill merely stated that JFK's hair "rippled up," which accords with the Zapruder film, which shows the right lateral side of his head (i.e., opposite Hill) burst open. Testimony of Mrs. Jean Lollis Hill, WC VI.

21 Hill died of natural causes at age 69. Her alleged death threats are unverified. Whitmey, 15–7.

22 The photograph was immediately circulated worldwide by wirephoto services. Hill acknowledged this in her Warren Commission testimony. Moorman's pictures were returned to her the next day, after which she sold nonexclusive reproduction rights to UPI. Moorman has kept the original picture in her possession and tried (unsuccessfully) to auction it off for $50,000 in 2013. Laura T. Coffey: "JFK 'grassy knoll' photo fails to sell

at auction," *Today News*, November 15, 2013, NBC; Josiah Thompson: "Mary Moorman and Her Polaroids," (n.d.), *Assassination Science*.

23 Jim Featherston: "I Was There," in Connie Kritzberg, ed.: *Secrets from the Sixth Floor Window* (1994), 31–3, cited in David Reitzes: "Jean Hill and Jim Featherston," 2000, *JFK Online*.

24 "Mary Moorman: The Silent JFK Witness Speaks," Interview with Gary Stover, May 24, 2011, *iAntique.com*.

25 https://en.wikipedia.org/wiki/Mary_Moorman#/media/File:Moorman_photo_of_ JFK_assassination.jpg

26 Mack later recanted. See Michael E. Young: "Gary Mack and the evolution of a JFK conspiracy theorist," *Dallas Morning News*, 2 March 2013. On White, see Chapter 17.

27 Arnold first shared this story to a Dallas journalist in 1978. Earl Golz: "SS 'imposters' spotted by JFK witness," *Dallas Morning News*, August 27, 1978, cited in David Reitzes: "Nowhere Man: The Strange Story of Gordon Arnold" (n.d.), *The Kennedy Assassination*. Arnold later appeared in Episode 2 of *The Men Who Killed Kennedy*.

28 "Unsolved History: JFK: Beyond the Magic Bullet" (Season 3, Episode 2), dir. Robert Erickson, *Discovery Channel*, 2004. British photographic expert Geoffrey Crawley, the only scientist put forward by *The Men Who Killed Kennedy* to support White's and Mack's theory, turned out to have rejected it. Dale K. Myers: "Badge Man: A Photogrammetric Analysis of Moorman Photograph No. 5 of the JFK Assassination," 2004, *Secrets of a Homicide*; David Reitzes: "Nowhere Man".

29 Marilyn Sitzman, who stood a few feet away on the concrete wall, recalled seeing a young couple sitting nearby holding coke bottles, which fell and broke during the shooting. Josiah Thompson: "Interview with Marilyn Sitzman," November 29, 1966, *The Kennedy Assassination*.

30 Voluntary Statement of Mary Ann Moorman, Sheriff's Department, County of Dallas, Texas, November 22, 1963, *Office of the City Secretary, Dallas Municipal Archives, John F. Kennedy/Dallas Police Department Collection*.

31 Secret Service Agent Bill Greer, who was driving the president's car, believed the limousine had suffered a blowout and pumped the brakes to test the car's stability. Blaine and McCubbin, 212. When he realized they were shots, Greer accelerated suddenly—which is noticeable in the Nix and Muchmore films, but less so in Zapruder's. This accounts for the car's sudden deceleration without implicating the Secret Service in a conspiracy. Some conspiracy-minded witnesses, like Jean Hill, were thus right to say they saw the limousine's break lights come on, but wrong to claim that the car came to a stop.

32 Interview of sound designer D.D. Stenehjem, "Unsolved History: JFK: Beyond the Magic Bullet".

33 Blaine and McCubbin, 352–3; Paula Schleis: "Cleveland-Area Man Who Was on JFK's Secret Service Detail Talks about Dallas," *Akron Beacon Journal*, November 16, 2013.

34 Governor Connally, an experienced hunter, was one of the only people to immediately identify the first shot as rifle fire and not firecrackers or a blowout: "This shot I heard came from back over my right shoulder, which was in the direction of the School Book Depository, no question about it. I heard no other". Testimony of Gov. John Bowden Connally, Jr. WC IV.

35 J.K. Lattimer et al.: "Could Oswald Have Shot President Kennedy?".

36 Testimony of Abraham Zapruder, WC VII.

37 Bystander Bill Newman, who stood with his family in front of Zapruder, also came to believe that the sight of Kennedy's explosive head wound influenced his interpretation of where the shots came from. His initial belief in a shot from the front, he said in later

interviews, had less to do with the sounds he heard than the location of Kennedy's head wound, which produced a powerful visual suggestion that the sounds came from somewhere behind him. Testimony of William Eugene Newman, "On Trial: Lee Harvey Oswald," dir. Ian Hamilton (1986), in which Newman does not identify the "garden" of his November 22, 1963, affidavit as being the grassy knoll (a claim which conspiracists often use as a "proof" of a grassy knoll shooter) but the *east side of the pergola* (i.e., behind and to his left) toward the TSBD. Like Zapruder, Newman could have heard the shots echo off the concrete pergola.

38 Josiah Thompson: "Interview with Marilyn Sitzman," November 29, 1966, *The Kennedy Assassination*.

39 Thompson: "Interview with Marilyn Sitzman," November 29, 1966.

40 Prouty: "The Guns of Dallas"; Groden: "Comments on the Panel's Report by Robert Groden…," 306–8. See also Groden's interview by Len Osanic: *Black Op Radio*, September 18, 2008.

41 John McAdams: "Dealey Plaza Earwitnesses" and "Earwitness Tabulation," (n.d.), *The Kennedy Assassination* (accessed 2018).

42 *Warren Report*, 110; "JFK: The Lost Bullet".

43 New Mexico Tech Research University Professor Michael Hargather, interviewed on "NOVA: Cold Case JFK," *PBS*, November 13, 2013.

44 Statement by J.C. Price, Decker Exhibit 5323 (19H492), cited in McAdams: *JFK Assassination Logic*, 15; Voluntary Statement of William Eugene Newman, Sheriff's Department, County of Dallas, Texas, November 22, 1963, *Office of the City Secretary, Dallas Municipal Archives, John F. Kennedy/Dallas Police Department Collection*; Testimony of Lee E. Bowers, Jr., WC VI.

45 Testimony of Lee E. Bowers, Jr., WC VI. Emphasis added.

46 A deaf-mute named Virgil "Ed" Hoffman gained notoriety by claiming he saw a rifle-wielding railyard worker (aka: "Train Man") run from the grassy knoll after the shooting. (How a deaf man could know when the shooting began, ended, or ever happened, Hoffman doesn't explain.) As recorded in Hoffman's 75-page conspiracy memoir *Eye Witness* (1997), "Train Man" disassembled the rifle in seconds (just like they do on TV?), handed it to a man in a suit (aka: "Suit Man"), and the two ran away down the tracks incognito. Three railroad workers standing nearby—Sam Holland, James Simmons, and Richard Dodd—as well as Lee Bowers, never noticed Hoffman at any time. Policemen stationed on the triple underpass and on the more distant Stemmons Freeway overpass never saw him either. Hoffman's claims (none of which were made under oath) are marked by so many contradictions, unlikely claims, and evolutionary changes that it is questionable whether he saw anything at all, save perhaps Kennedy's car speeding up the Stemmons onramp. Posner, 256–7; McAdams: *JFK Assassination Logic*, 14–5; M. Duke Lane: "Freeway Man" (2007), *The Kennedy Assassination*. Unsurprisingly, Hoffman collaborated with Jean Hill's "biographer" Bill Sloan for his book *JFK Breaking the Silence* (1993), four years before he published his own.

47 Thompson: "Interview with Marilyn Sitzman," November 29, 1966.

48 Testimony of Lee E. Bowers, Jr., WC VI.

49 Posner also discovered that Bowers, as part of his duties in supervising the movement of trains on 13 different tracks, had to turn on a signal right after the third shot was fired, which would have caused him to turn away from Dealey Plaza and miss part of this "commotion". Posner, 254 (footnote).

50 Lee Bowers interview by Mark Lane, 1966. Emphasis added. The interview is available on *YouTube*.

51 If true, Bowers' claim contradicts Hill's own "sighting" of the "Badge Man," who allegedly fired at JFK several dozen feet to the east—that is unless there was a *second* shooter on the grassy knoll!

52 Holland described the puff of smoke as having been caused by *the first of four shots*—which does not help conspiracists explain away the Single Bullet Theory (see below). Holland also misperceived the location of Jacqueline Kennedy in the limousine. See Voluntary Statement of S.M. Holland, Sherriff's Department, County of Dallas, Texas, November 22, 1963, *Office of the City Secretary, Dallas Municipal Archives, John F. Kennedy / Dallas Police Department Collection.*

53 One of the oldest of these comes from a 1966 *Triumph* magazine article written by Lawrence R. Brown ("The Kennedy Assassination: Let's Solve It") in which he claims the back shots are consistent with a low trajectory. Early proponents of this theory were Josiah Thompson (*Six Seconds in Dallas*, 1967, 132–3) and Jim Garrison (who parroted it in his 1967 *Playboy* interview), and later Robert Groden (*The Killing of a President*, 1993), who offered photographic "evidence" of a suspicious "dark-completed man" hanging out of a broom closet window. Jerry McLeer: "The Missed Shot: A Shot from the Dal-Tex Building?" (n.d.), *The Kennedy Assassination Research Page*. No contemporaneous witness ever claimed they heard a shot come from the Dal-Tex building. The only proof of this "Broom Closet Man" comes from a grainy blow-up of a black-and-white picture (see Figure 13.3) which took 30 years to be identified as evidence of another shooter—conveniently replacing Mack and White's debunked proof of the "Badge Man".

54 Sherwood Ross and James Fetzer: "Six JFK Shooters, Including Three Tied to CIA, Named by Assassination Authority," December 28, 2013, James Fetzer: *Exposing Falsehoods and Revealing Truths*. Ross and Fetzer's theory of a double headshot, developed further by Gary Aguilar in *Assassination Science* and *Murder in Dealey Plaza*, is based on the discredited Two Headshot Theory of Randolph Robertson ("Statement of Randolf H. Robertson, M.D. Before the Legislation and National Security Subcommittee of the Committee on Government Operations," US House of Representatives, November 17, 1993). Robertson's article was submitted to the journal *Radiology*, but his findings were found unsound by the peer-review panel. McAdams: "The Medical Evidence," (n.d.), *The Kennedy Assassination*.

55 *Warren Report*, Appendix 12, 645. Emphasis added.

56 Gerald Posner came to the more conservative conclusion that Oswald had about eight seconds to shoot, which is "enough time for even a mediocre shooter to aim and operate the bolt twice". Posner, 319–22. McAdams concurs. *JFK Assassination Logic*, 234–5.

57 Max Holland and Kenneth Scearce: "11 Seconds in Dallas Redux: Filmed Evidence," *Washington Decoded*, November 11, 2008.

58 As stated in Chapter 12, Oswald did not need the scope at this distance, giving him more time to aim. Lattimer also found that the Carcano has "little recoil" when fired in a sitting position using an improvised shoulder harness strap as a sling, like the one Oswald had fixed to his rifle. "If the interval between each shot was increased to five seconds (10 seconds total) aiming became quite easy". Lattimer et al., 516–7. See also Lattimer: *Kennedy and Lincoln: Medical and Ballistic Comparisons of Their Assassinations* (1980), 297, Figure 119.

59 "JFK: The Lost Bullet," *National Geographic* (2013); Max Holland and Johann Rush: "J.F.K.'s Death, Re-Framed," *The New York Times*, November 22, 2007; "The Kennedy Assassination: Beyond Conspiracy," *ABC News*, 2003; Dale K. Myers and Todd W. Vaughn: "Holland's Magic Bullet: A Forensic Ballistician Examines a Dubious Theory," November 22, 2016, *Secrets of a Homicide*.

60 See Chapter 2. The enhanced Zapruder film shows that Connally was hit less than a half-second after Kennedy. Posner, 328.

61 James Altgens' photograph (Figure 13.3) captured the Secret Service men looking toward the TSBD, while Kennedy, struck by the second shot, raises his hands to his throat.

62 Bennett wrote a brief note later that day detailing the sequence of (a) hearing a "fire-cracker" and (b) hearing and seeing the two hits strike "the boss," first in the back of the neck and then in the back of the head. "CE 2112 – Letter Dated May 14, 1964, from Secret Service to Commission, with Copy of Original Notes of Special Agent Glen Bennett," WC XXIV, 542–3. See also Holland and Scearce: "11 Seconds in Dallas Redux," op. cit.

63 Testimony of Robert A. Frazier (Resumed) WC V; Posner, 323.

64 Testimony of Mrs. Donald Baker, WC XV; Posner, 324.

65 Holland and Rush: "J.F.K.'s Death, Re-Framed".

66 "JFK: The Lost Bullet". The position of the limousine is also confirmed by Secret Service agent Clint Hill, who rode on the left running board of the follow-up car. Clint Hill and Lisa McCubbin: *Mrs. Kennedy and Me* (2012), 289.

67 "JFK: The Lost Bullet," *Warren Report*, 63–4.

68 https://texashistory.unt.edu/ark:/67531/metapth339287/ (Dallas Police Department (22/11/63), Item: DSMA_91-001-1133001-4051).

69 Testimony of Howard Leslie Brennan, WC III.

70 This is a reference to Warren Commission Exhibit CE856, a bullet from shooting tests conducted for the Warren Commission at the US Army Edgewood Arsenal in Maryland in 1964. Alfred G. Olivier and Arthur J. Dziemian: *Wound Ballistics of 6.5-mm Mannlicher–Carcano Ammunition*, CRDLR 3264, March 1965 (declassified in 1973), *Mary Ferrell Foundation*.

71 Garrison, 240–1. Italics in the original. Emphasis (underlined text) added. In a footnote, Garrison claims it was Jack Ruby who planted it there. Stone's film makes a similar visual claim. We should also highlight Garrison's use of misleading language, as his expressions "almost perfect" and "nearly flawless" imply, grammatically and logically, that the bullet was in fact damaged. See also Groden and Livingstone: *High Treason* (1989).

72 *JFK*, dir. Oliver Stone (1991).

73 Hill with McCubbin, 276.

74 Blaine and McCubbin, 202.

75 Testimony of Gov. John Bowden Connally, Jr., WC IV.

76 The speed at which Kennedy reacted, and the position of his arms and clenched fists, have led medical experts to conclude that he suffered an involuntary neuromuscular spasm and was not voluntarily clutching his throat. According to vascular surgeon Robert R. Artwohl, this reaction is explained by the bullet having passed close enough to Kennedy's spine to cause a sudden stimulation of his brachial plexus nerves. Conspiracists have thus rightly critiqued Posner and Lattimer for wrongly identifying this as a "Thorburn position". Robert Artwohl, M.D.: "JFK's Assassination: Conspiracy, Forensic Science, and Common Sense," *JAMA: The Journal of American Medical Association*, Vol. 269, No. 12, March 24, 1993, 1540–3; McAdams: "The Medical Evidence," (n.d.), *The Kennedy Assassination*.

77 "The Kennedy Assassination: Beyond Conspiracy," *ABC News*, 2003; "JFK: The Lost Bullet," *National Geographic Channel*, 2013; "NOVA: Cold Case JFK," *PBS*, November 13, 2013.

78 This involved resuscitation attempts, blood transfusions, performing a tracheotomy, and assisted respiration with oxygen. Press Conference at Parkland Memorial Hospital, Dallas, Texas, November 22, 1963, cited in McAdams: "Parkland Hospital Press Conference: Dallas Doctors First Statements," (n.d.), *The Kennedy Assassination*.

79 Hill and McCubbin, 294–5.

80 Press Conference at Parkland Memorial Hospital…; McAdams: *JFK Assassination Logic*, 223–4.

81 *Warren Report*, Appendix 9, "Autopsy Report and Supplemental Report" (Commission Exhibit No. 387), 3; McAdams: *JFK Assassination Logic*, 221.

82 The autopsy report was drafted on Saturday November 23 and handed to the Secret Service on Sunday November 24 so that funeral arrangements could be completed. The body was buried on Monday November 25.

83 McAdams: *JFK Assassination Logic*, 219–21.

84 Ibid., 223–4.

85 Letter to J. Lee Rankin from J. Edgar Hoover, March 23, 1964 (FBI 105-82555 Oswald HQ File, Section 111). Kennedy's blood-stained clothes are held at the National Archives. They can be viewed at: "NARA Evidence Photos: JFK Clothes," *Mary Ferrell Foundation*.

86 *Warren Report*, Appendix 9, "Autopsy Report and Supplemental Report," 4–5.

87 Ibid., 6; Interview of Dr. Chad Zimmerman, "Unsolved History: JFK: Beyond the Magic Bullet".

88 Posner, 337–8, citing the Warren Commission's wound ballistics experts and a 1992 American Bar Association mock trial of Lee Oswald.

89 "NOVA: Cold Case JFK".

90 "Details of Governor Connelly's Damaged Clothing," PDF, *Texas State Library and Archives*.

91 "Unsolved History: JFK: Beyond the Magic Bullet".

92 The radius is the thicker of two forearm bones. The thinner ulnar bone was not hit. Though Connally's radial nerve was damaged, the ulnar and median nerves, which affect the hand's ability to grip objects, were not torn, allowing him to keep gripping his hat. Dr. Charles Gregory: "Parkland Memorial Hospital Operative Record—Governor John Connally Orthopedic Surgery," November 22, 1963, Commission Exhibit No. 392, 18–9, *History Matters*.

93 "Details of Governor Connelly's Damaged Clothing".

94 Testimony of Gov. John Bowden Connally, Jr., WC IV.

95 Itek Corporation: "John Kennedy Assassination Film Analysis," May 2, 1976, 39, quoted in McAdams: "The Single Bullet Strikes John Connally," (n.d.), *The Kennedy Assassination*.

96 Joe Nick Patoski: "What They Saw Then," *Texas Monthly*, November 1998.

97 McAdams relays the example of Hawaii Senator Daniel K. Inouye, who lost an arm in World War II, which he noticed was still clutching a grenade after it was severed by German gunfire. Daniel K. Inouye with Lawrence Elliott: *Journey to Washington* (1967), 151–2, quoted in McAdams: "The Single Bullet Theory," (n.d.), *The Kennedy Assassination* (accessed 2018).

98 Conspirators could not yet know that bullet fragments of similar chemical composition as bullet CE399 would also be found in the limousine, as well as a dint in the windshield (CE350) caused by a bone or bullet fragment that struck it *from the inside* (only the inner layer of the windshield was damaged). *Warren Report*, 77.

99 Posner, 337.

100 McAdams: *JFK Assassination Logic*, 244.

101 Dr. John K. Lattimer: *Kennedy and Lincoln*, 285–8, excerpted in McAdams: *The Kennedy Assassination*; Lattimer et al.: "Differences in the Wounding Behavior of the Two Bullets that Struck President Kennedy; an Experimental Study," *Wound Ballistics Review*, Vol. 2, No. 2, 1995.

102 CE399 weighed 158.6 grains when found. It had lost between 1.2 and 2.9 grains. Lattimer: *Kennedy and Lincoln.*

103 Ibid.

104 Testimony of Dr. Charles Francis Gregory, WC IV; Testimony of Dr. Michael Baden, Pathologist and Chief Medical Examiner for the City of New York, HSCA I. Some fragments were left inside Connally's body; the exact weight of the fragments could thus only be estimated.

105 Ira David Wood III: "22 November 1963: A Chronology"; Gary Aguilar: "The Converging Medical Case for Conspiracy in the Death of JFK" in James Fetzer, ed.: *Murder in Dealey Plaza* (2000).

106 See police statements, Warren Commission testimonies, and media interviews of Abraham Zapruder, Marilyn Sitzman, and Bill and Gayle Newman, who stood nearby and had an unobstructed view of JFK's right side. Bystanders on the triple underpass (e.g., Sam Holland) who saw Kennedy face-front, thought they saw the top of his head blow out. Those to the left of Kennedy—his wife Jackie, Mary Moorman, and even Jean Hill (in 1963–64)—made statements corroborating a blowout from the top or nonvisible right side of JFK's head. David Stahl with John McAdams: "Dealey Plaza Headwound Witnesses," (n.d.), *The Kennedy Assassination.*

107 Stahl and McAdams: "Dealey Plaza Headwound Witnesses".

108 McAdams: "Beverly Oliver: Babushka Babe? Or Bamboozling the Buffs?" (n.d.), *The Kennedy Assassination.*

109 J.C. Price: "Statement Concerning Resuscitative Efforts for President John F. Kennedy," November 22, 1963, *Warren Report,* Appendix 8, 530. Emphasis added. Price, who did not observe these wounds himself, was reporting the observations of the attending physicians. The temporal bone is located at the side of the head, around and behind the ear. The occipital bone is in the rear lower part of the skull, behind which the cerebellum resides. The parietal bone is the larger portion of the top of the head that stretches from the temples to the top-rear. The frontal bone makes up the front-top portion, including the forehead.

110 *Warren Report,* Appendix 9, "Autopsy Report and Supplemental Report," 3.

111 Dr. Kemp Clark's Statement, CE392, *Warren Report,* Appendix 8. Emphasis added.

112 Testimony of Dr. Marion Thomas Jenkins, WC VI; "NOVA: Who Shot President Kennedy?" *PBS,* Season 16, Episode 8, 1988.

113 Testimony of Dr. Malcolm Oliver Perry, WC VI. Emphasis added.

114 Secret Service Agent Clint Hill, who could see the President's head wound during the ride from Dealey Plaza to Parkland Hospital, and again during the autopsy in Bethesda, confirmed the location of both the throat and head wounds (including the "flap") just as the Warren Commission described them. Hill and McCubbin, 287, 305.

115 Testimony of Dr. Malcolm Oliver Perry, WC VI.

116 Testimony of Dr. Robert Nelson McClelland, WC VI. Emphasis added.

117 The issue of the protruding cerebellum later became a point of contention. According to the autopsy report, the cerebellum was not significantly damaged. Most of the Parkland doctors, who conceded they never closely examined the brain, later retracted this comment. Posner, 306–13.

118 McAdams: "Could the Parkland Doctors Have Seen the Back of Kennedy's Head?" (n.d.), *The Kennedy Assassination.*

119 McAdams: "Parkland Doctors Confront the Autopsy Evidence" (n.d.), *The Kennedy Assassination.*

120 James Fetzer: "Who's Telling the Truth: Clint Hill or the Zapruder Film?" January 12, 2011, *James Fetzer: Exposing Falsehoods and Revealing Truths.*

121 Photos of these fragments (and other JFK ballistic evidence) can be seen at: "Photo Set: NARA Evidence Photos: Bullet Fragments," *Mary Ferrell Foundation*.

122 John K. Lattimer et al.: "Differences in the Wounding Behaviour…," 30 and 37 (end-note 2). A 6.5-millimeter Carcano bullet will fragment when striking dense bones (e.g., a human skull), especially when traveling at full muzzle-velocity. The HSCA linked the Carcano bullets using neutron activation analysis. Testimony of Dr. Vincent P. Guinn, HSCA I, which includes "A Report to the HSCA on the Subject of 1977 Neutron Activation Analysis Measurements on Bullet-Lead Specimens Involved in the 1963 Assassination of President John F. Kennedy," (JFK Exhibit F-331), September 8, 1978, 511.

123 *Warren Report*, chap. 3, 77.

124 Testimony of James W. Altgens, WC VII.

125 Testimony of B.J. Martin, WC VI.

126 Lattimer et al.: "Differences in the Wounding Behaviour of the Two Bullets…," 29–36.

127 "Report of the Forensic Pathology Panel," *HSCA Appendix to Hearings*, Vol. VII, Sec. V; Dr. Peter Cummings, Forensic pathologist at Boston University School of Medicine, and Larry Sturdivan, US Army Biophysics Lab, interviewed in "NOVA: Cold Case JFK," *PBS*, November 13, 2013. Sturdivan adds that there is no reason to believe that the bullet had to progress in a straight line once it hit hard skull. Once it penetrated the skull, the bullet fragmented as it began to yaw, and followed a curved trajectory through soft brain matter from the back of the skull to the upper right side. Rather than being pierced by the bullet, the right side of the skull burst open due to the transfer of energy from the bullet into the gelatinous brain tissue. It erupted outward at a point where the skull bones were weakest.

128 Testimony of James W. Altgens, WC VII.

129 An animated image showing the forward movement of Kennedy's head can be seen at David Reitzes: "The Fifth Shot ('Back and to the Left')," (n.d.), *JFK Online*. See also Jerry Organ: "The Zapruder Film," (n.d.), *The Kennedy Assassination*.

130 Kenneth Rahn: "The Different Second Motion," (n.d.), *The Academic JFK Assassination Site*.

131 Testimony of Dr. Charles S. Petty, "On Trial: Lee Harvey Oswald".

132 Rahn: "The Different Second Motion".

133 McAdams: *JFK Assassination Logic*, 250–1.

PART IV

Opportunity

"We're through the looking glass here!"

14

THE SECRET CLEANING SERVICE

Did JFK's bodyguards cover up a conspiracy?

14.1   *Et tu, Brute?*

As a result of carefully assessing the historical context and physical evidence discussed in the previous chapters, we are faced with two options. The first is to admit that the evidence is overwhelmingly stacked against Lee Harvey Oswald as the most likely, if not the only, plausible suspect in John F. Kennedy's murder. The other is to conclude that much of this evidence must have been fabricated.

In choosing the first option, one can still believe in some sort of conspiracy, albeit one that would have to include Soviet or Cuban intelligence agents (like those stationed in Mexico City, prodding Oswald to show himself worthy to migrate to Cuba) instead of the suspects discussed in Part I.[1] Such a theory might also involve the complicity of people close to Oswald: his wife Marina, Russian expatriate friend George de Mohrenschildt, or some as-yet unidentified members of the American Communist Party or Fair Play for Cuba Committees.[2] But such a conspiracy would likely have had to be small, politically left-wing, and pro-Cuban. But that is not what most JFK buffs would like you to believe.

The second option, if it is to be logically consistent, requires believing in a massive plot to destroy and fabricate mountains of evidence, not only to frame Oswald but also to mislead the public. The conspirators would have needed to be on the scene within minutes of the shooting, have access to all the evidence that was collected, and know exactly what, where, and how to remove, replace, create, or destroy it. They would have to be able to infiltrate or manipulate the FBI, the Secret Service, the Dallas Police, the Dallas District Attorney's office, the Dallas County Sheriff, the 1964 Warren Commission, the 1968 Clark Panel, the 1975 Rockefeller Commission, the 1977–79 House Select Committee on Assassinations (HSCA), and the 1992–98 Assassination Records Review Board. They would have had to control or influence independent investigations by CBS, NBC, PBS, ABC, *Life*, and

DOI: 10.4324/9781003222460-18

the *Saturday Evening Post*, to name but a few. To accomplish all this, the conspirators would probably also require the collaboration of hundreds of individuals in the news media—from both sides of the political spectrum—as well as academics and scientists performing their research through scholarly journals and private firms like Kodak, Ford, Itek, Cognitec, and others.

However, unlikely this scenario may seem to skeptics, such a massive plot is what most JFK buffs claim did in fact happen. Yet, few of them have offered an exhaustive explanation for how all these coordinated cover-ups could be successfully carried out or provided compelling evidence of their having taken place. Instead, most JFK buffs focus their efforts on disproving the "official story" either by highlighting its apparent inconsistencies or by drawing hypothetical links between suspicious characters and speculative, ambiguous, or missing (and presumably destroyed) evidence. Others attempt to reverse engineer their conclusions from the alleged secret interests and motives of JFK's presumed enemies (see Part II of this book). With few exceptions, conspiracists begin with a false dilemma, assuming that any evidence they can interpret as proof that Oswald did not act alone (including damning evidence that was possibly fabricated) is necessarily a proof of a right-wing government cover-up.

Though they mostly agree on this general conclusion, JFK buffs are a loosely knit confederation of amateur sleuths, each focusing on a specific quadrant of this massive deception, citing each other's unproven suspicions in support of their own convictions. In this endeavor, argues Michael Barkun, conspiracists substitute direct evidence for repetition in their search for truth. The more a rumor is repeated by other researchers, the more likely it is to be accepted unquestioningly, a form of "pseudoconfirmation" that feeds and reinforces the crowd-sourced grand narrative of a massive inside job.[3] Their cast of villains is therefore extensive, with local operators tailored to fit each researcher's favorite bogeymen: Mark Lane prosecutes the Dallas Police, Jim Garrison arraigns the FBI and CIA, Fletcher Prouty court martials the Joint Chiefs of Staff, Anthony Summers and Henry Hurt denounce anti-Castro Cubans, David Mantik carves up the US Navy medical staff, Vincent Palamara and David Lifton take shots at the Secret Service, David Scheim and Lamar Waldron rat out organized crime, Jim Marrs and Roger Stone impeach President Johnson, Peter Dale Scott and Oliver Stone target the "military industrial complex," and the list goes on. Through a brilliant act of syncretism, conspiracists have convinced one another that each of their personal devils was equally part of the plot—a confederation of dozens, perhaps hundreds, of fellow conspirators bound by a secret covenant and assisted by thousands of minions and dupes.

An exhaustive study of every cover-up allegation would be impossible here. The record can nevertheless be set straight by assessing three of their most popular claims: (a) that the actions of the Secret Service before, during, and after the murder suggest that they helped murder the President, (b) that the Bethesda autopsy and its pictures and X-rays were fraudulent, and (c) that the Zapruder film and Oswald's infamous "backyard photographs" were doctored to frame him. The rest of this chapter will examine the first of these claims. The last two will be assessed in the following chapters.

According to James Fetzer, the Secret Service played a pivotal role in Kennedy's murder:

> Clint Hill was not the only agent to attempt to respond after shots rang out. Secret Service agent John Ready, who was on the right running board whereas Clint [Hill] was on the left, began to respond but was called back by Emory Roberts, Agent in Charge of the Presidential Protection Detail. This is [...] only one of more than fifteen indications that the Secret Service set up JFK for the hit, which include that two agents were left behind at Love Field, that the vehicles were in the wrong order, that the 112th Military Intelligence Unit was ordered to "stand down" rather than provide protection throughout the city, and that the motorcycle escort was reduced to four, who were instructed not to ride forward the rear wheels [sic]. Open windows were not covered and the crowd was allowed to spill out into the street.[4]

Fetzer further adds that the Secret Service violated its own protection directives by letting the speed of the motorcade drop to less than 10 miles per hour as it turned onto Elm Street; by making agents ride in the follow-up car instead of on, or running beside, the presidential limousine; by allowing the president's car to come to a halt in the middle of Elm Street; by being willfully unresponsive to the gunshots; by suspiciously making the president's doctor sit in the last car of the motorcade, far away from his patient; and by stripping and rebuilding the limousine by Monday morning, November 25, in violation of criminal laws pertaining to the destruction of evidence. We have already responded to some of these claims in the previous chapters (e.g., the presumed absence of the 112th Military Intelligence Unit, the open windows in Dealey Plaza, and the rebuilding of the limousine). Let us consider the other claims carefully.

14.2   A stand-down order?

The argument that a stand-down order was emitted to prevent an army unit from being mobilized in Dallas is a fantasy concocted by, among others, Fletcher Prouty.[5] As discussed in Chapter 11, no order calling for a military detachment, or to seal-up windows and post snipers on rooftops, was ever emitted or canceled that day, nor on any other part of Kennedy's Texas trip—which included other open-top motorcades through downtown Houston and San Antonio. This is because it was not a standard operating procedure in 1963 for the military to perform such tasks, nor did the Secret Service have any realistic compulsion, nor the necessary resources, to seal thousands of windows or scatter its agents on dozens of rooftops. Nor was it ever Prouty's task as a CIA–US Air Force liaison officer, as is alleged in the film *JFK*, to arrange for additional security to protect the president. Arrangements for presidential security was the sole prerogative of the Secret Service and White House staff in collaboration with local law enforcement, none of whom ever called for the sealing of windows on any of Kennedy's trips anywhere.[6] It was the Secret Service's responsibility to assess the safety of proposed motorcade routes and public venues, follow the president closely, observe and identify possible threats, whisk him to safety if necessary, and take a bullet for him if required.[7]

That being said, the Secret Service did request that the Dallas Police, the FBI, and a small detachment of military intelligence agents help them steward the motorcade and identify and detain known subversives (see Chapter 11), which at the time did not include Lee Oswald. He probably should have been listed. He was, after all, an avowed communist and pro-Castro activist with a criminal record and had recently been identified by the CIA visiting Soviet and Cuban embassies abroad. But lack of vigilance on the part of the Dallas FBI office, or the lack of communication between the CIA and local law enforcement, is not proof of conspiracy. While the New Orleans FBI office had recently flagged Oswald as a person of interest (one of many), the Dallas FBI office was still only dimly aware that he existed and was primarily concerned with right-wing extremists (see Chapter 5). While the HSCA did blame the Secret Service and FBI for failing to take sufficient precautions in Dallas, it did not find them *willfully* negligent in their duties but rather lacking the necessary resources, agents, and effective standard procedures to protect a politician of Kennedy's standing and campaigning style. As the HSCA Report observed:

> President Kennedy posed a problem for the Secret Service from the start. As a policymaker, he was liberal and innovative, startlingly so in comparison with the cautious approach of President Eisenhower. His personal style was known to cause agents assigned to him deep concern. He traveled more frequently than any of his predecessors, and he relished contact with crowds of well-wishers. *He scoffed at many of the measures designed to protect him and treated the danger of assault philosophically. If someone wanted to kill him, he reasoned, it would be very difficult to prevent.*[8]

An army presence in Dallas would have only made Kennedy look like a crowd-fearing third-world dictator, not a populist democrat. He liked to meet voters in crowds, shake hands, and engage in small talk.[9] It was his political currency in congressional and presidential campaigns, trips abroad to places like Germany and Ireland (see Figures 11.7 and 11.8), and his public appearances in the United States, including his previous trips to Hawaii, Chicago, Tampa, and San Antonio.[10]

For several decades after the assassination, explains former Secret Service agent Gerald Blaine, he and his fellow Kennedy detail agents were reticent to ascribe any blame to the late president for putting himself in danger, thereby breaking the honor code of their profession.

If ever asked whether JFK had ordered them off the back of his car, the answer was always, 'Oh, no. President Kennedy was wonderful. He was very easy to protect. No I don't remember him ever ordering agents off the back of his car.'[11]

But several agents—including Blaine, Clint Hill, and Floyd Boring—have confirmed what the HSCA made public in 1979, which is that Kennedy regularly flaunted security concerns if these stood in the way of making personal connections with his electorate, including discrete admonitions to the Secret Service to back off.

Conspiracy researcher Vincent Palamara disregards the HSCA's conclusion and rejects these agents' changing story as proof of the Secret Service's complicity in JFK's murder and a subsequent cover-up.[12] In response, Blaine evokes a confidential letter from Secret Service Chief James J. Rowley to Warren Commission lead counsel J. Lee Rankin, dated April 22, 1964, which was declassified in 1992. With corroborating statements from his fellow agents, Rowley therein confirms that

> on numerous occasions during motorcades where the pace was slow and crowds were fairly well-controlled by the police, but the agents were none the less in position around the presidential car, the President would either tell me to tell the agents, or he would attempt to tell the agents on his side of the car, to get back.[13]

Palamara, a self-proclaimed "leading expert" on JFK's Secret Service detail[14] appears unfamiliar with this document, over a decade after it was declassified.

It is therefore reasonable to conclude that Kennedy did ask the Secret Service to keep their distance during his motorcades and other public appearances. As Blaine explains, this unwritten ordinance included not standing on the side or back of the presidential vehicle or running beside it in slow traffic.[15] Whether this was made explicit in Dallas or was by then a standard procedure matters little. Either course of action explains why the Secret Service appeared to have "fallen back" in Dealey Plaza, at least to Palamara and his ilk, without it being a sign that they wished him dead. Former agent Clint Hill concurs:

> [Kennedy] wanted maximum exposure with no evidence there was anything between him and the people. People felt a connection to President Kennedy when they saw him in person. That's what had gotten him elected, and now he needed to get reelected.[16]

The extra distance placed between Kennedy and his agents probably did make him look more approachable, but it also had the ill effect of reducing their reaction time and effectiveness in Dealey Plaza. A similar request was extended to Dallas motorcycle patrolmen, who complied by riding behind Kennedy's limousine rather than beside it. Though his Secret Service detail made numerous efforts to keep a tight perimeter around the President, Kennedy had the final authority not to abide by their recommendations, and he exercised it regularly. As Blaine explained:

> The SAIC [Special Agent in Charge] of the detail can recommend and advise, but if the president has his own agenda and is willing to take the risk, then he can countermand the recommendation. The Secret Service must then establish a security strategy to cover the president's decision.[17]

This was made evident during the early stages of the Dallas motorcade when Kennedy had his driver stop the vehicle—along with the rest of the vehicles riding behind it—so he could shake hands with locals holding a placard that read: "PLEASE MR. PRESIDENT STOP AND SHAKE OUR HANDS!"

Unlike his predecessor Dwight Eisenhower, a decorated Army general who exercised prudence in public, Kennedy was fond of riding through crowds in open-top cars. The presidential limousine was a convertible. It could be covered over with its built-in soft roof, a rigid removable metal roof, or a clear Plexiglas "bubbletop". Kennedy usually chose the latter if the weather obliged it, but otherwise preferred that the crowds see him (and, on this occasion, his wife) unobstructed.[18] The decision to take the bubbletop off at Love Field that morning was not the Secret Service's prerogative, as Palamara implies. While it was executed by Special Agents Roy Kellerman and Win Lawson, the choice to remove it was made by Kennedy's special assistant Kenneth O'Donnell.[19] Nor would it have necessarily spared JFK's life had it been left on as it was neither bulletproof nor bullet resistant, despite what many conspiracists falsely repeat.[20]

Let us also consider the actions of Special Agent Clint Hill in response to Fetzer's and Palamara's accusations that the Kennedy detail was collectively (and thus intentionally) unresponsive. As soon as the bullets were fired, Hill made a dangerous running attempt to catch up to Kennedy's car while it was speeding away, risking his life to shield the President and First Lady from a possible fourth shot. In doing this, Hill nearly fell to be crushed by the follow-up (Secret Service) vehicle. Pushing the First Lady back inside the car, Hill then rode spread-eagled atop the limousine, barely holding on as it sped up the freeway to Parkland Hospital. Hill was later awarded a citation for exceptional bravery, though this came at a great personal cost. The graphic nature of the President's head wound, which he stared at during the interminable 6-minute car ride to Parkland, and his obligation to observe the President's gruesome autopsy, left him with deep emotional scars.[21] Hill spent the next thirty years suffering from depression and survivor's guilt. Nightmares and a nervous breakdown forced him to leave the Secret Service in 1975, by which time he had spoken to no one of the details of that day, save to the Warren Commission. He later appeared in a televised interview with Mike Wallace on *60 minutes*, during which he was still visibly shaken from this experience. Yet he remained adamant that only three shots were fired in Dallas, all of them coming from the direction of the Texas School Book Depository.[22] He then slumped into alcohol and pain-killer abuse for seven more years before seeking and finding healthier forms of therapy.[23] While this is not proof that the whole Secret Service should be exonerated, it makes it unlikely that Hill would have kept his mouth shut, or suffered quietly all this time, had he suspected his colleagues of being murderers. In short, Clint Hill does not in the least fit the profile of a conspirator.

Neither do the other Secret Service agents who were on the scene. Agent Bill Greer, Kennedy's driver, has also received his fair share of conspiracist flak. Jean Hill and a handful of other witnesses have suggested that Greer brought the car to a halt during the shooting to facilitate the work of the assassins.[24] Not only would this incriminate Greer before a crowd of hundreds of witnesses, there is also no video record, and few verbal testimonies, to suggest that this ever happened. On the other hand, it is known that until that point, the limousine was moving quite slowly, having completed a 120-degree turn onto Elm Street. It is also known that after the first shot rang out, Greer pumped the breaks, thinking the car had suffered a blowout, which corroborates Jean Hill's claim that the brake lights came on.[25] But nothing suggests the car came to a stop for any length of time. Had such a thing happened, it likely would have caused the motorcycle patrolmen and the Secret Service follow-up car that tailed Kennedy's limousine by no more than a few feet to come to a screeching halt or collide into it. To wit, a brief segment of the Charles Bronson home movie captured the speed of the limousine, the police motorcycles, and the Secret Service follow-up car at the time of the fatal head shot. The Bronson film shows better than other evidence the narrow distance separating the President's car from the police and Secret Service vehicles. It is simpler therefore to believe that Jean Hill was mistaken, particularly in the light of the rest of her shoddy account, than that the eyes (and many cameras) of almost everyone else were not functioning correctly that day.

As for agent John Ready whom Fetzer says was prevented from jumping off the Secret Service follow-up car by Agent in Charge Emory Roberts, a non-sinister explanation is readily available. Since the turn on Elm Street marked the official end of the motorcade, standing orders had already been emitted that all agents would fall back to their vehicles at this point while the cars accelerated toward the Stemmons Freeway onramp to head to the Dallas Trade Mart. Roberts' order to Special Agent Ready, which he emitted *after* the head shot, was made with the knowledge that the lead car was about to take off and prevent Ready from getting run over by other vehicles. Clint Hill, more preoccupied with the protection of Mrs. Kennedy, had already flaunted the President's orders several times that day, which is proven by the numerous photographs of Hill riding on the left rear step of SS-100-X (the presidential limousine) on several occasions when the car was forced to slow down in front of thick crowds. Hill's hypervigilance and maverick spirit in protecting the First Lady gave him a head start over Ready, if not enough time to save the President's life. It also nearly got him killed, adding weight to Agent Roberts' order for Ready not to step off, out of fear that the President's vehicle was now rolling too fast. "After SA Hill got on rear step of the President's car," Roberts wrote in a November 29, 1963, memo, "it appeared that SA John Ready was about to follow and go for the right rear step, however, I told him not to jump, as we had picked up speed, and I was afraid he could not make it".[26]

Taking all this into consideration, Fetzer and Palamara are obviously clutching at straws. Nor was the parade route changed at the last minute. As seen in Chapter 11, the slow turns onto Houston and Elm were the only way the motorcade could parade down Main Street and then access the Stemmons Freeway to reach the Trade Mart in time for Kennedy's scheduled appearance. However, slowly the vehicles took that last turn, it was a risk that the motorcade's organizers had all accepted (or neglected to consider). These included members of Kennedy's personal guard, but also his special assistants O'Donnell and Powers, as well as Governor Connelly, all of whom were to ride in the motorcade, which, if they were part of a plot, would have put them at risk of being collateral victims. Indeed, Governor Connally nearly died in the process. None of this would suggest that the slow turn on Elm was the fruit of conspiracy.[27]

14.3 Moving the pieces

Fetzer and Palamara have also popularized the claim that some Secret Service agent were deliberately "left behind" at Love Field, presumably to lower the level of presidential protection, or because these agents were not in on the conspiracy. This claim is based on a very loose interpretation of a silent black-and-white news clip taken that day, which depicts Secret Service agent Don Lawton joking around with his fellow agents as the motorcade heads out of Love Field.[28] Gerald Blaine explains:

> It showed the agents jogging alongside the presidential limousine and Emory Roberts standing up in the follow-up car motioning to Don Lawton—the shift agent who had been assigned to stay at Love Field. Lawton raised his arms and in typical Don Lawton fashion said something along the lines of "It's all yours now guys. I've done my job. Now get out of here so I can have some lunch." [...] Despite the incorrect identification of the agent [as Hank Rybka], the problem with the theory is that neither Rybka nor Lawton was scheduled to be on the motorcade. [...] The argument has no basis at all, yet people have been debating it back and forth on blogs and presenting the theory at conspiracy conferences for years.[29]

But "Secret Service expert" Vincent Palamara sees something more sinister happening here, namely that Assistant to the Special Agent in Charge (ATSAIC) Emory Roberts is selecting his team of pushover agents to make sure Kennedy does not survive the trip.[30] If that were true, one has to wonder why Clint Hill made it onto the motorcade while Rybka/Lawton was "effectively neutralized".[31] Unless one views this newsreel footage with the conviction that it must contain proof of a plot, the scene doesn't have much to tell us about Kennedy's death.[32] Even if Lawton's broad smile and body language indicate his perplexity and disgust at being prevented from protecting his boss (as Palamara suggests), we should wonder why Lawton made no attempt to speak up about this before he died 50 years later.

Fetzer also concludes that, had the Dallas motorcade not been a murderous project, one would expect Kennedy's personal physician, Vice Admiral George Burkley, to have been riding with or near him, not at the end of the motorcade. Fetzer is also convinced that the President's car was conspicuously out of place:

> The Presidential limousine was the lead vehicle in the motorcade […] which is completely absurd. A proper motorcade would have the lower-ranking dignitaries early on, then those in between, and finally the highest official, who would naturally be surrounded by the press, who were there, after all, to cover a political event! In this case, however, everything was wrong.[33]

According to Fetzer, this switch was operated so that the shooters, who were apparently too dimwitted to identify Kennedy's car in any other configuration, would not shoot at the wrong vehicle.

Both of these claims are immeasurably silly. Kennedy was young and in relatively good health (more on this later), good enough to get through an hour-long parade without the assistance of his doctor—who was in fact a physician, not a first responder. Burkley's job was to keep Kennedy healthy enough to get through a whirlwind of speeches and schmoozing, not keep him alive through a violent attack. We should also ask Professor Fetzer what Dr. Burkley could have possibly done to save Kennedy's life had he been riding closer. He might have perhaps been able to save him had Kennedy been, say, allergic to bees and the conspirators launched a hive into his car, but Admiral Burkley could have done precious little to stop a copper-jacketed military-grade bullet from killing the President or patch a massive head wound in the six minutes it took for Bill Greer to rush him to Parkland Hospital.[34] Burkley's location in the motorcade is thus inconsequential, a pointless red herring.

As for Fetzer's suspicions that the press buses were stationed too far behind the President's car to be able to photograph or film him during the motorcade, this is another red herring. Considering the large number of journalists and civilians with cameras who lined the streets of Dallas that day, including all those who captured some part of the assassination, one has to wonder what a few dozen journalists stuck in a bus half a mile back could have done to improve the President's chances of survival, or our knowledge of what happened to him. In fact, this entire argument is circular. The only thing making the locations of Burkley and the press buses sinister is Fetzer's assumption that they should be. As for the "absurd" order of the motorcade's vehicles, it would appear that Fetzer never examined the widely available photos of a dozen other "unnatural" motorcades Kennedy rode in or asked himself why they were consistently arranged in such an order. Indeed, the only vehicles that really matter in this equation are the first two: the President's car and that of his bodyguards whose job it was to protect him. As Kennedy had plainly requested, the Secret Service agents were to ride *behind* him, not alongside his vehicle, and they complied as closely as they could without climbing onto the President's car. Contrary to Fetzer's belief, however, the position of these two cars at the head of the procession proves in fact that the Secret Service was *not* trying to get him killed. Indeed, SS-100-X was always placed in the best possible position to avoid getting blocked in by traffic and be able to make a quick getaway in case of danger—which is at the very *front* of the parade. No other position in the motorcade would have given Bill Greer the ability to take off as fast as he did once he realized they were being shot at. Professor Fetzer might prefer the types of parades in which the guest of honor only turns up at the end, but such parades are usually reserved for Santa Claus or Mickey Mouse, not an American president.

14.4   This is the way we wash our car

Was the Secret Service complicit in simply covering up, rather than being directly involved in, a murderous conspiracy? Vincent Palamara and David Lifton are two of the researchers who claim that the Secret Service wantonly destroyed evidence that would have proved there were multiple shooters.[35]

To correctly assess what happened after Kennedy died (or any historical event), one must avoid falling prey to emotional reasoning and pay careful attention to the context in which it transpired. A useful thought experiment that critical thinkers can use to avoid being misled by faulty historical claims is to imagine themselves within the situation being described and limiting their knowledge solely to the facts that could have been known *at that time*. One should then consider whether simpler explanations can account for any "suspicious behavior" denounced by conspiracists. Conspiracy researchers often disregard the full context of the Secret Service's handling of the President's limousine after his murder, and their transportation of his corpse back to Washington, leading them to make faulty deductions.

Before Kennedy was declared dead, the Secret Service was faced with the responsibility to protect Vice President Johnson—who was also in Parkland Hospital—from any possible threat on his life. Because the identity of the assassin(s) was not yet known, and because there was a real possibility in their minds that the shots fired at Kennedy were part of a larger attack on the country, it was quickly decided by Agent in Charge Emory Roberts that Lyndon Johnson had to be flown to safety in Washington. It was the height of the Cold War after all, and relations with the Soviets and Cubans were tense. A year earlier, Kennedy and Khrushchev had flirted with nuclear war over the latter's decision to place missiles in Cuba. Threatening right-wing pamphlets had also been circulating in Dallas during the previous days. Evacuating the new acting president was therefore the Secret Service's most pressing concern once it became clear that Kennedy wasn't leaving Parkland alive. Johnson (to his credit) refused to leave the grieving and catatonic former First Lady behind. Jacqueline Kennedy, for her part, refused to leave her husband's body.[36] The Secret Service was therefore compelled to take all three back to Love Field and fly them to Washington. And if Kennedy's body was to undergo an autopsy in Washington rather than Texas, it was naturally assumed that the limousine should be examined there also—such as at the FBI's forensic laboratories.

Conspiracists are right to point out that evacuating Kennedy's body this way was illegal under Texas law and that Dallas County coroner Earl Forrest Rose was entirely right to protest that it should remain within the state's jurisdiction until an autopsy was duly performed. But this was also the late president of the United States, whose dignity and whose widow's and successor's safety were in doubt. Fearing another ambush—no one yet knew who or how many shooters had fired at Kennedy, or if they still posed a threat—the Secret Service opted for safety and decorum over what they thought were petty legal matters. Kennedy aids and close friends Kenny O'Donnell and David Powers were in total agreement with the Secret Service's decision to evacuate the Johnsons and Kennedys, and Dr. Rose did eventually bend to their stern exhortation to let the corpse go.[37] A decision that is interpreted by conspiracists as malicious can therefore be explained without speculation as an act of loyalty performed under stress and uncertainty.

In a series of pictures taken during this time in front of Parkland Hospital, Secret Service agents can be seen in the ambulance dock placing the "bubbletop" and soft retractable canopy over SS-100-X and cleaning it from some of its gore (see Figure 14.1). The pictures give us little context, and Secret Servicemen remained tight-lipped for decades concerning their actions and thoughts at this time. Conspiracists have been quick to conclude that they were trying to destroy evidence of foul play. The principal culprit, according to Palamara, is Secret Service driver agent Sam Kinney, who piloted the follow-up car (679-X) during the motorcade. In a November 22, 1963, statement, Kinney wrote:

FIGURE 14.1 Secret Servicemen washing SS-100-X presidential limousine at Parkland Memorial Hospital

Source: Cecil Stoughton/JFK Library.

The President's car and 679-X then proceeded to the hospital at a high rate of speed, taking approximately 6 min. Upon arrival I jumped from my car and ran to the right rear of the President's car, where I assisted in removing Gov. Connally and the President. After all had been removed from the President's car I opened the trunk of the car and put on the bubble-top and a canvas cover. This took approximately 20 to 30 min. I asked for a motorcycle to escort the President's car and 679-X back to Love Field. [...] On the way to the airport I called by radio to Maj. Nedbaugh, USAF to have C-130 crew at the plane with ramp down for loading of the two cars. [...] The plane departed Love Field at 3:35 pm. We arrived AAFB [Andrews Air Force Base], Md at 8:05 pm. We were met at AAFB by 4 or 5 agents from the Washington, Field Office and some 6 motorcycles. We were then escorted non-stop to the White House garage. After reaching the garage the cars were secured by an all night watch by White House Police and Secret Service agents, pending an investigation.[38]

Kinney (who was not deposed by the Warren Commission) mentions that he placed the plastic bubbletop and canvas roofs back on the car, and other witnesses have attested that Dallas policemen were keeping curious onlookers from approaching the vehicle or taking close-up pictures.[39] Kinney also makes no mention of washing the car—which Palamara finds suspicious because several hospital orderlies have confirmed being asked to lend the Secret Servicemen buckets, mops, and assistance.[40] This leaves us with the possibility that Kinney was busy removing important evidence from the car.

Perhaps, but again, the logic of Palamara's scenario just does not add up. In the first place, Kinney is allegedly destroying important evidence in broad daylight in front of a crowd of hundreds (Figure 14.2) that included many policemen, curious civilians, Parkland Hospital staff, and White House photographer Cecil Stoughton who took the famous "agent with bucket" picture that many conspiracists offer as proof of Secret Service malfeasance (Figure 14.1). At least some of the people watching the scene or assisting these agents would have expressed concern or signaled it to the police, the FBI, or the media—unless they were all co-opted into the conspiracy or were too dim-witted to see what was happening.[41]

Many witnesses have reported that the weather had turned quite warm by midday, which means that the gore that covered the limousine's interior was beginning to cook in the sun and smell. We should also take note that under this stressful situation, Kinney and his fellow agents, who were trained to take a bullet, not to investigate murders, were probably more concerned with treating Kennedy's remains with dignity than preserving forensic evidence. Besides, such evidence would more likely consist in their minds of bullet holes and fragments, not blood and brain matter. Just as Mrs. Kennedy's natural instinct had been, it appeared, to climb over the back of the limousine to recover a piece of her husband's skull[42] (or was she destroying evidence too?), we can safely conclude that, without any clear evidence to the contrary, these Secret Service agents were not acting maliciously by

FIGURE 14.2 Crowd waiting for news of Kennedy outside Parkland Memorial Hospital

Source: *Fort Worth Star-Telegram*, University of Texas at Arlington Library.

collecting pieces of brain and bone out of the car to place them with the President's body for transportation.

Kinney's alleged "washing away" of the evidence also happened before the Parkland medical staff had completed its surgeries on Governor Connally, before Kennedy's autopsy could occur, and at a time when the Dallas Police and FBI's investigations in Dealey Plaza had hardly even begun. The chances of Kinney destroying or planting evidence that could contradict these other parts of a cover-up and thus expose the plot were thus high, which makes it unlikely that altering or destroying evidence was his intention. Had Kinney wished to do so, he could have waited until he had driven the car out of sight. In any event, two sets of pictures of the inside of the limousine were taken the following day in the White House garage—one by the FBI, the other by the Secret Service. Both sets show that large pieces of gore and bloodstains, as well as some tattered flowers, were never removed. One can thus wonder how much of the limousine Kinney bothered to clean.[43] The question will probably never be answered to everyone's satisfaction, but unless one resorts to circular logic the conspiracists carry the burden of proof to show that Kinney took part in an act of deception.

Once it was returned to the White House garage, the examination of SS-100-X became the responsibility of the FBI, who recovered two large bullet fragments out of the *front* of the car. Three lead particles, the weight and composition of which matched the broken bullet, were also found. These matched the fragments removed from the President's head during his autopsy. The FBI also discovered two dints in the windshield—one on its chrome rim and a crack in the glass, high on the driver's side—that appeared to have been produced by small projectiles coming from *inside* the car. As the Warren Report explained, this evidence is consistent with a bullet that hit Kennedy's head from the rear and exited in fragmented form toward the front.[44] The windshield was then removed and processed as evidence. It was displayed to the Warren Commission in April 1964.[45] The rest of the car was sent away to Cincinnati in late December to be cleaned, fixed, and refurbished (with bulletproofing this time) so that it could be used by the Johnson administration.[46] By this time, Lee Oswald was long dead and no other suspect existed, which made the blood-stained SS-100-X no longer a piece of forensic evidence, only a morbid relic.

While both the Secret Service and FBI director J. Edgar Hoover figure prominently on the list of conspiracy suspects, it is not clear how the two organizations could have coordinated this cover-up without a third organization to mastermind it. Conspiracists are often silent on this matter, but anyone who has studied the way institutional bureaucracies behave—with their particular chains of command, methods of internal communication, and bureaucratic trappings[47]—might find it difficult to believe that a seamless conspiracy can be conducted by rival government agencies. It becomes even more questionable when we compound the number of agents and White House aides still faithful to Kennedy who maintained access to the evidence, and private subcontractors like the Ford Motor Company and Hess & Eisenhardt who participated in the refurbishing of SS-100-X. While conspiracists like Palamara and Fetzer remain convinced that the windshield shown to the Warren Commission was a fake, the "evidence" they use to prove this is carefully pruned of its context and logically circular, based on a selective reading of former Secret Service agents' recollections—whom we are told is in every other case lying to us, except here.[48] There is perhaps no proper way to debate this with someone whose mind is closed off to fair inquiry, but to objective critical thinkers; it should be clear which account is more believable.

14.5 This is the way we patch the skull

David Lifton blames the Secret Service for letting an anonymous team of surgeons alter the President's corpse during the flight back from Dallas to Washington. Hence, even if the Bethesda pathologists were not willful participants in a conspiracy, they would still have falsely reported that Kennedy was shot from behind by a single gunman.[49]

Lifton claims that the body was deliberately left unattended aboard Air Force One for a period of about *14 minutes*, at which time someone altered Kennedy's wounds while nobody was watching. Alternately, he suggests, the body could have been placed in another casket prior to takeoff and secretly transferred into Air Force Two (the Vice President's plane), or possibly a third unidentified "supersonic jet," where its wounds were altered in flight. This second scenario would have given the body snatchers as much as three hours to alter the President's wounds, but it would also imply that the conspirators rushed the body by helicopter from Andrews Air Force Base to Bethesda Naval Hospital, where it was allegedly taken in through a back door, before Mrs. Kennedy, Admiral Burkley, and the rest of their retinue could discover the subterfuge. Whichever of these two scenarios is true, argues Lifton, none of the autopsy evidence can be accepted as true because it was all corrupted before the autopsy even began. The only reliable evidence, then, are the claims of the doctors at Parkland, which, according to Lifton, prove JFK was shot one or more times from the front.

To support his theory, Lifton lists several inconsistencies between the official autopsy results and an FBI report by Francis O'Neill, Jr. and James W. Sibert, two FBI special agents who attended the autopsy to observe the procedure, send a report to chief Hoover, and collect any bullets or fragments than could serve as evidence.[50] The most important of these discrepancies was O'Neill and Sibert's claim that when the autopsy doctors removed Kennedy's body from its casket (the original bronze one, presumably after it was switched back) and Dr. Humes, upon witnessing the size of the head wound, said it must have undergone "surgery" back in Dallas. Yet this was not recorded on Hume's final autopsy report. The emergency doctors in Dallas had, of course, no time to perform any surgical work on the body after Kennedy was declared dead and the Secret Service evacuated everyone back to Love Field. According to Lifton, the best explanation for this claim made by two untrained observers is that Kennedy's wounds were secretly altered before the body's arrival in Washington.

Another "proof" offered by Lifton is found in the recollections of a Bethesda Hospital morgue technician named Paul O'Connor, who many years later told Lifton that he saw the President's body arrive at the hospital in a gray shipping casket (not the expensive and heavy bronze one that had been loaded on Air Force One) with its brain cavity emptied of its contents. O'Connor also claimed that the body arrived inside a body bag, whereas the doctors in Dallas claimed it had been wrapped in plastic liners and sheets.

There are of course many reasoning and factual flaws in both of Lifton's elaborate scenarios. Concerning the first, Lifton does not explain or even appear to consider how this intricate operation could be completed aboard Air Force One in less than 15 minutes—a procedure that he alleges fooled three trained pathologists, a radiologist, two autopsy photographers, morgue and lab technicians, a team of morticians, and several FBI, military, medical, and civilian observers. Nor does he take into consideration the noise, commotion, and mess such an operation would undoubtedly produce—an act of butchery that would have required bone saws, drills, and other tools of pathology *without being heard or leaving traces of blood and body parts in the surrounding airplane cabin*. Nor does he explain how no one aboard Air Force One failed to notice unfamiliar individuals carrying medical equipment into and out of the tail cabin, a high-traffic area. One should also consider the smell which on opening the casket would have produced in what many witnesses described as a very warm and stuffy environment.[51] Presumably, Lifton's 15-minute corpse alteration session would also require these clandestine surgeons to patch up the back of Kennedy's skull in such a way that no one on the autopsy team would notice a foreign substance like plaster or rubber covering up the massive exit wound conspiracists claim was witnessed by doctors at Parkland (see Chapter 13) and which does not appear in any autopsy photo or X-rays. In any event, as Gerald Posner discovered, the casket had been hermetically sealed before it left Parkland and strapped to the floor of the plane, making the chances of someone opening it without being detected virtually nil.[52]

Unsurprisingly, Lifton developed a second scenario that gives his conspirators more time to perform their handiwork. Unfortunately, even three hours might not have sufficed for them to do so. According to Cyril Wecht, another JFK buff who, unlike Lifton, happens to be an accomplished forensic pathologist, this caper simply could not be performed in the timeframe required: "I could assemble a whole team of the best surgeons in the country," Dr. Wecht told Posner, "and still not be able to accomplish in a day what Lifton says was done in a few hours".[53] Whether or not this is true, a greater problem is presented to Lifton by the fact that Air Force One had no trap door in its rear cargo hold, which he claims was used to transfer the body out of its original casket and into another plane without alerting the bustling crowd of political aides, Secret Service agents, and journalists crowding the cabin before takeoff.[54]

Concerning the report of FBI agents O'Neill and Sibert, which stated that, according to Dr. Humes, JFK's head had undergone surgery before it reached the autopsy room, a simpler explanation is offered by skeptic Vincent Bugliosi, who reminds us that Dr. Humes had not yet inspected Kennedy's matted and gore-covered head when he made this remark. Once the pathologists inspected the head closely they recognized that the sizeable wound was entirely due to a gunshot and not to surgery. For this reason, Humes' initial assumption—a mere thinking aloud that caught the attention of untrained observers—was quickly dismissed and forgotten and would have never been heard of again had O'Neill and Sibert not recorded it in their report. Arguing otherwise, says Bugliosi, would imply that the alleged alterations made to Kennedy's body were performed so poorly that the pathologist noticed the postmortem wounds right away, revealing the "smoking gun" evidence to everyone present, and then, for no apparent reason, remained quiet about it for the rest of his life, along with everyone else in the room—including O'Neill and Sibert, who made little of it.[55] Both O'Neill and Sibert, as well as Dr. Humes, confirmed that when Kennedy's body was taken out of the original bronze casket, it was wrapped in the same bloodied hospital sheets and plastic liners that the Parkland medical staff reported they wrapped the corpse in, and that his brain was only removed during the autopsy, mining the credibility of morgue technician Paul O'Connor's uncorroborated claims.[56]

The entirety of Lifton's theory rests on the assumption that JFK's body, while aboard Air Force One at Dallas Love Field Airport, was left unattended long enough for a body heist and/or massive postmortem surgery to occur. But was it ever actually left unattended? Lifton's argument is not only based on a selective reading of William Manchester's *Death of a President* (1967) and the inconsistent 15-year old memories of support staff in Bethesda, it is also contradicted by those who were inside Air Force One and inside the hearses that transported JFK's body in Dallas and Washington, and who attest that it was never left alone, either by Mrs. Kennedy, Admiral Burkley, Kennedy's military advisor Brigadier General Godfrey McHugh, Kennedy aide David Powers, or his brother Bobby after the plane landed in Washington. Clint Hill also attests that Secret Service agent Richard Johnsen was posted near the body during the entire flight back to Washington.[57] We can safely conclude, then, that Lifton's argument is little more than a flight of fancy. That said, he was correct to point out that Kennedy's body was placed in two different caskets, though the reasons for this were rather mundane. As Secret Service agent Clint Hill explains, the casket purchased in Dallas was too large to fit through the Air Force One doors: its handles had to be broken off for it to enter the plane.[58] In the interest of proper decorum, a new mahogany casket was purchased in Washington by Kennedy aides David Powers and Kenneth O'Donnell. The body was transferred into it after it was embalmed in Bethesda Naval Hospital during the early hours of November 23.[59] This version of events accounts for virtually all irregularities that inspired Lifton's wildly implausible story.

David Powers called Lifton's theory "the biggest pack of malarkey I ever heard in my life".[60] Dr. Michael Baden, the HSCA's chief forensic pathologist, simply called it "laughable".[61] Indeed, anyone trained in the science of pathology, including conspiracist Cyril Wecht, is likely to find Lifton's theory even harder to swallow because, in addition to its outlandish logic and *Mission: Impossible* timeline, this theory fails to consider some basic facts about autopsies, namely that post-mortem wounds (wounds inflicted on dead bodies), which are easily discernable from antemortem wounds (wounds suffered before death, when the heart is still pumping blood), would be readily noticeable by even the least qualified patholo-gist, making the entire attempt to fool the Bethesda doctors a huge waste of time and resources.[62]

In sum, explanations like those of Clint Hill, Gerald Posner, and Vincent Bugliosi are perhaps less impressive than Lifton's action-packed, Hollywood-worthy story of a secretive heist and dead body makeover. But then, reality usually is.

Notes

1 ARRB *Final Report*, 86–91; Russo and Molton (2008); Shenon (2015).
2 Posner makes a strong case for de Mohrenschildt being little more than a peculiar social butterfly—not a CIA operative, as Anthony Summers describes him in *Conspiracy* (1980). Posner, 85–8.
3 Barkun, 26–9.
4 Fetzer: "Who's Telling the Truth: Clint Hill or the Zapruder Film?" January 12, 2011, *James Fetzer: Exposing Falsehoods and Revealing Truths*; Fetzer: "Smoking Guns…" (Smoking Gun #14), 12–3.
5 Prouty: *JFK…*, Chapter Nineteen (n.p.), Osanic, ed.: *The Collected Works…* (n.d.).
6 Hill and McCubbin, 289.

7 This remained standard procedure for decades to come, exemplified by the March 30, 1981, assassination attempt on President Ronald Reagan, during which Secret Service agent Tim McCarthy was shot after placing himself in the assassin's line of fire. Almost 20 years after JFK's death, the Secret Service's primary job was still to act as human shields.

8 *HSCA Final Report*, Section I.D.: "Agencies and Departments…," 228. Emphasis added; Blaine and McCubbin, 398.

9 Hill and McCubbin, 275–87.

10 Ibid., 284.

11 Blaine and McCubbin, 352.

12 Vincent Palamara: "The Secret Service: On the Job in Dallas," in Fetzer, ed.: *Murder in Dealey Plaza*, 160.

13 "Letter from Chief of Secret Service James J. Rowley to J. Lee Rankin, General Counsel, Warren Commission," June 9, 1964, 2 (JFK Document 012719: "U.S. Secret Service—Protective Information Guidelines"), quoted in Blaine and McCubbin, 360–1.

14 Fetzer: *Murder in Dealey Plaza*, 467.

15 Hill and McCubbin, 270–1, 277.

16 Ibid., 284.

17 Blaine and McCubbin, 397.

18 Hill and McCubbin, 284.

19 Testimony of Special Agent Roy H. Kellerman, WC II. Kennedy was a long-time close friend of O'Donnell's, and his benefactor. It would defy facts and logic to accuse O'Donnell of being part of a plot to murder his boss.

20 The "bubbletop" might have deflected some types of bullets but probably not the hard copper-jacketed military-grade bullets that killed him. Nor was the bubbletop a single, solid piece covering the entire car. It was composed of several sections that covered only the rear seat so that the president could still stand and wave, leaving it possible for a shooter stationed above or in front of the limousine to get a clear shot. Christopher Wynn: "JFK's Limo Epitomized President's Fresh Style, but Was Woefully Unprotected," *Dallas Morning News*, May 4, 2013.

21 Being assigned to Mrs. Kennedy's protection, Hill was responsible to report back the autopsy details should she later have questions about it. Hill and McCubbin, 305. Hill continued to ensure the protection of Mrs. Kennedy and her children until the 1964 election and developed a strong bond with the surviving Kennedys. It is unlikely, given this relationship and Hill's subsequent life experiences, that he would have willfully kept any involvement on his part or insider knowledge of a conspiracy secret for half a century.

22 One of my students contacted Hill on Twitter in 2013. His opinions had clearly not changed: "There were three shots," he told her, "All from the Book Depository. I know. I was there".

23 Blaine and McCubbin, 379–94.

24 In her Voluntary Statement to the Sheriff's Department, signed November 22, 1963, Hill claimed that the car came to a full stop. The belief that this was part of a wider plot to kill JFK emerged later, possibly under the influence of her contacts with several conspiracists. On Hill's credibility, see Chapter 13.

25 Blaine and McCubbin, 355–6.

26 ATSAIC Emory P. Roberts: "Schedule of Events Prior to and after the Assassination of President John F. Kennedy in Dallas, Texas on Friday November 22, 1963," November 29, 1963, US Secret Service, *JFK Online*.

27 Many journalists reported rumors—later substantiated—that several Secret Service agents went out drinking in Fort Worth the night before the Dallas motorcade (a fireable

offense). While this led to severe reprimands by the Warren Commission and HSCA, neither body could establish that this unprofessional conduct prevented the agents from responding more quickly to the gunshots. Shenon, 137–8, 374–7; Memorandum of Inspector Gerard B. McCann, December 10, 1963, US Secret Service, Commission Exhibit 1020, WC XVIII, PDF, *History Matters*.

28 Interview with Blaine and Hill, "Q&A: 'Shrugging' Secret Service Agent at Love Field Is Identified," *C-SPAN*, September 30, 2012.

29 Blaine and McCubbin, 359. This passage is a response to Vincent Palamara, author of *The Third Alternative—Survivor's Guilt: The Secret Service and the JFK Murder* (1993).

30 Palamara: *The Secret Service…*, 167–8.

31 Ibid., 168.

32 You can nonetheless watch (and maybe enjoy) Palamara's long rant against Blaine's book: "JFK Assassination: Secret Service Standdown EXPLAINED—Kennedy Detail, Clint Hill," June 1, 2011, *YouTube*.

33 Fetzer: *Murder in Dealey Plaza*, 12–3.

34 Signed statement of Special Agent Samuel A. Kinney (who drove the follow-up car): "The Trip and Assassination of President Kennedy in Dallas, Texas, November 22, 1963," *JFK Online*.

35 David Lifton: *Best Evidence* (1981); Vincent Palamara: "Limo Clean-Up + Skull Fragments," October 13, 2013, in *Vince Palamara's Main SECRET SERVICE Blog: JFK, The Kennedy Detail, and More*.

36 Hill and McCubbin, 299–300.

37 Douglas Martin: "Earl Rose, Coroner When Kennedy Was Shot, Dies at 85," *New York Times*, May 2, 2012.

38 Signed statement of Special Agent Samuel A. Kinney: "The Trip and Assassination…"

39 Palamara: "Limo Clean-Up + Skull Fragments".

40 Ibid.

41 Palamara's own blog references Dallas Police officer Bobby Joe Dale (quoted in Larry Sneed: *No More Silence: An Oral History of the Assassination of President Kennedy* (1998), 135–6) who assisted Sam Kinney and later said,

> Blood and matter was everywhere inside the car including *a bone fragment* which was oblong shaped, probably an inch to an inch and a half long by three-quarters of an inch wide. As I turned it over and looked at it, I determined that it came from some part of the forehead because there was hair on it which appeared to be near the hairline. […] Other than that, *nobody messed with anything inside the car in any manner, shape, or form. Nobody said, 'Clean this up!' We then put the top up and secured it.*
>
> *(Emphasis added. Palamara does not explain this counterevidence.)*

42 Scott Pelley: "Agent Who Jumped on JFK's Limo Recounts Fateful Moments," October 26, 2017, *CBS News*.

43 These pictures can be viewed at the *JFK Lancer* website.

44 *Warren Report*, 76–7.

45 Bugliosi, 353.

46 Pete Bigelow: "50 Years after JFK Assassination, His Limo Tells a Story," November 5, 2013, *Autoblog*; Christopher Wynn: "JFK's Limo…"

47 Allison, chap. 3.

48 Driver Agent Bill Greer claimed not to have noticed the crack in the windshield until the next day. This is not surprising considering that Agent Kinney drove SS-100-X from Parkland to Love Field and then again from Andrews AFB to the White House

garage. Anyone who has experienced a crack in their windshield knows that a relatively small dint will grow in size over several hours or even days. Greer assured the Warren Commission no such crack had existed before the Dallas motorcade. Such a testimony disproves conspiracist claims that the windshield was hit by a shot from the front, which Greer would have certainly not missed given the crack was located in front of the driver's face. Warren Commission Exhibits CE349, 350, and 351; Testimony of William Robert Greer, WC II.

49 Lifton: *Best Evidence* (1984), chap. 31, 838–59; Posner, 294–301; Bugliosi, 1057–70.
50 "ARRB MD 44 – Sibert and O'Neill Report on the Autopsy (11/26/63)," *Mary Ferrell Foundation.*
51 On conditions aboard Air Force One, see Manchester, 66, 309–10, and chaps. 5 and 6, *passim.*
52 Posner, 294–300.
53 Interview of Cyril Wecht by Gerald Posner, February 2, 1992, cited in Posner, 296.
54 Bugliosi, 1062–5.
55 Ibid., 1060–1; "Section II—Performance of Autopsy," HSCA VII (footnote #63 of this document reads:

> In an affidavit to the committee, Sibert acknowledged that the statement that head surgery was performed was determined 'not to be correct following detailed inspection.
>> See *affidavit of James Sibert, Oct. 24, 1978, House Select Committee on Assassinations (JFK Document No. 012806).*

56 Posner, 300, footnote. See also "Section II—Performance of Autopsy," HSCA VII. On O'Connor, see chap. 15.
57 Manchester, chaps. 5 and 6, 289–388; Posner, 296; Joel Grant: "Body Snatchers at Love Field? David Lifton's Kennedy Assassination Body Snatching/Body Alteration Theory," (n.d.), *The Kennedy Assassination*; Hill and McCubbin, 301–3.
58 Hill and McCubbin, 301–2.
59 Ibid., 306.
60 Quoted in David Von Pein: "Book Review: *Best Evidence*," July 2009.
61 Interview of Michael Baden by Gerald Posner, January 28 and November 7, 1992, cited in Posner, 298.
62 Interview of Cyril Wecht by Vincent Bugliosi, December 14, 1999, cited in Bugliosi, 1061.

15

OF MISSING WOUNDS AND FAKE X-RAYS

Was JFK's autopsy a fraud?

15.1 Your lying eyes

Conspiracy researchers Gary Aguilar and David Mantik, both of whom have medical degrees and practice medicine, have led the charge in claiming that JFK's autopsy photographs and X-rays were faked to hide the existence of a massive exit wound at the back of his head, caused by a shot from the front.[1] Mantik concludes, for instance, that Kennedy's throat wound was caused by a broken windshield glass shard that struck him from the front, that his back wound was caused by a piece of flying shrapnel (he does not say from where) that ricocheted off the street and caused only a surface wound, and that the fatal shot came not from the grassy knoll but "from the storm drain on the north overpass," which left an "orange-sized hole" in the right rear of JFK's skull.[2] Their principal method to prove this is to identify apparent contradictions between the (presumably faked) autopsy evidence and the (presumably accurate) testimonies of Parkland Hospital doctors.[3] They also highlight many discrepancies between the Bethesda autopsy report and the memories of individuals who witnessed some part of the procedure or handled its evidence. Other alleged proofs of a rigged autopsy include the pathologists' autopsy notes, which Aguilar and Mantik claim are inconsistent with their final report, and also Kennedy's brain[4] which mysteriously went missing sometime before 1968, suggesting, they say, that the conspirators stole or destroyed it to conceal the existence of multiple shooters.

It would take more than one book to respond to all of Aguilar and Mantik's theories. Doing so would also force us to discuss complex medical procedures that might confuse the nonexpert and which this author does not have the medical training to debate in depth and detail.[5] But this does not prevent us from identifying the many errors in logic and research that make Aguilar and Mantik's theories refutable irrespective of their medical backgrounds.

DOI: 10.4324/9781003222460-19

Aguilar summarizes his argument thus:

> *Only two possibilities exist*: either 40+ witnesses from two different locations [Parkland and Bethesda] were wrong about JFK's rearward skull injury, or JFK's autopsy photographs have been falsified in some manner to mask the rearward skull damage that these credible witnesses described. Besides doubts that arise from conflicting witness accounts, the autopsy pictures are also under siege on multiple other fronts: from credible witnesses who deny they show JFK's real head injury; from all three of JFK's pathologists and both autopsy photographers, who insist images they took are missing; and from government photo technicians, who claim they saw images in 1963 are [sic] no longer in the current inventory.[6]

There are a few evident fallacies in this summation. First, it contains a false dilemma, suggesting that there are only two possible interpretations for the inconsistencies in Aguilar's data. In fact, Aguilar could have easily concluded a third and simpler possibility, the one defended in this chapter, which includes the following three premises: (a) that the autopsy photographs are authentic, (b) that the *apparent* contradictions between the testimonies of these 40-plus witnesses and the conclusions of the autopsy pathologists are due to misunderstandings, and (c) that Aguilar is reading the data incorrectly. Another logical fallacy in this brief summary is an argument from ignorance, by which the *absence* of evidence (i.e., missing photographs) is treated as proof of a government cover-up. One could easily imagine several plausible and nonsinister reasons for their disappearance. For instance, that someone close to Kennedy—someone with access to these materials—made the pictures disappear out of concern for JFK's legacy and his family's reputation. A detailed explanation will make this clear, but let us first consider the historical context that gets ignored by the conspiracists.

Kennedy's autopsy took place from 8 to 11 p.m. on the evening of November 22, 1963, in a medical classroom with rows of bleacher-type seats that could accommodate a few dozen witnesses (Bethesda was a Navy teaching hospital). It was performed by chief autopsy pathologist James J. Humes, with the assistance of chief of pathology J. Thornton "Jay" Boswell and forensic specialist Pierre Finck. The X-rays were handled by acting chief of radiology John H. Ebersole. John Stringer, a morgue photographer, along with several laboratory technicians, also took part in the procedures. Rear Admiral George Burkley, Kennedy's personal physician, was present throughout the autopsy serving as the Kennedy family's representative, along with several members of the military attached to the Naval Hospital or the current administration (such as Brigadier General Godfrey McHugh). A few Secret Service and FBI agents were also present, some of whom took notes of their observations (see Chapter 14).[7] Civilian employees of Gawler's Funeral Home were also on hand to perform embalming procedures, which followed the autopsy and lasted until approximately 4 a.m.[8]

Many researchers who studied the Kennedy autopsy, including many Lone Gunman proponents, acknowledge that the Bethesda doctors were not sufficiently trained in forensic pathology to perform this type of procedure.[9] This, along with the pressures of the Kennedy family who wished to get on with funeral preparations,[10] caused the Bethesda pathologists to be insufficiently thorough in their assessment. According to Dr. Humes,

> There was no question but we were being urged to expedite this examination as quickly as possible, that members of the President's family were in the building, that they had refused to leave the premises until the President's body was ready to be moved [...] Did it harass us and cause difficulty? Of course it did, how could it not?[11]

According to forensic pathologist Dr. Michael Baden, chairman of the House Select Committee on Assassinations (HSCA) Forensic Pathology Panel, the Bethesda autopsy team ended up cutting many corners. A proper examination of the victim's body should have taken two or three days, not three hours. This shortened schedule prevented the autopsy doctors from inspecting the spine, dissecting neck organs, tracing bullet tracks, and inspecting the clothing. They should also have shaved the head. None of this was done to save time.[12] In other words, Kennedy received a general autopsy, not a complete forensic examination. This informal compromise between the pathologists (who wished to conduct a full autopsy) and the Kennedy family (who requested they only extract projectiles from his body, as per an FBI request) is the principal cause of the unending debate over the incomplete autopsy records. It also led many JFK buffs to conclude, hastily, that the missing data were deliberately destroyed to suppress any proof of a massive conspiracy.

The fact that the autopsy descriptive sheet (also called a face sheet) was not accurate or duly completed, and that Dr. Humes destroyed his autopsy notes after submitting his final report, led many to question the professionalism and honesty of the pathologists. However, like the Secret Service's decision not to leave JFK's body in Dallas (see Chapter 14), these actions must be studied within their proper context, which in this case took several decades to be fully understood. Doing so will allow us to extend a certain level of charity to the autopsy doctors, and also to early conspiracists like Josiah Thompson and Edward Jay Epstein (see Chapter 4) who could not understand why so much secrecy had surrounded Kennedy's autopsy. However, new disclosures should have led Mantik, Aguilar, and like-minded others to reconsider their assumptions. Sadly, this has not been the case.

15.2 My legacy, right or wrong

It has long been known that the final decision to hold the autopsy at the National Naval Medical Center in Bethesda, Maryland, belonged to Jacqueline Kennedy and not to the Secret Service or anyone else on the conspiracists' long list of suspects.

Mrs. Kennedy did not initially want her husband to undergo any autopsy until Admiral Burkley convinced her it was necessary for forensic and legal reasons. Given several choices of institutions—including Walter Reed National Military Medical Center, which *was* equipped to conduct forensic autopsies and would better serve a Pentagon-sponsored cover-up—she opted instead for Bethesda Naval Hospital. It was her choice that the entire procedure, including the embalming of the body for burial, be performed by military doctors. However, her reasons for this remained obscure for several decades (see next). Since her husband was a decorated veteran of the Navy, Jacqueline Kennedy felt that Bethesda Naval Hospital provided a more appropriate venue than the nearer Walter Reed Army Hospital, and a more discrete one than any private establishment in the region.[13] She had recently witnessed the media circus at Parkland and was painfully aware that her husband's medical history, and his attempts to keep much of it secret, would tarnish his reputation should the autopsy findings be leaked to the media.

Kennedy's ailments were unknown to the public at the time, even to many in his inner circle, but they were significant. Historian Robert Dallek, author of *An Unfinished Life: John F. Kennedy, 1917–1963* (2003), was the first to gain access to JFK's full medical records. He discovered that John Kennedy had suffered multiple ailments that his family and closest aides made great efforts to keep secret. This is why Admiral Burkley, who always followed Kennedy closely, insisted on being present during the whole autopsy and embalming process.[14]

As a boy, John Kennedy suffered from spastic colitis, a gastrointestinal disorder that caused him abdominal pains and irregular bowel habits. In his youth, doctors treated him for this illness with antispasmodic medications and steroids. Though successful, these treatments caused him to develop a form of osteoporosis that left him with chronic back pain throughout his adult life and for which he was regularly medicated with cortisone and painkillers. Kennedy underwent back surgery in 1944 that had little positive impact. He underwent a second major back surgery while he was a Senator, a procedure that nearly cost him his life.[15] This is why Kennedy regularly wore a back brace under his clothes, which the doctors in Parkland were surprised to discover when they stripped off his clothing.[16] Kennedy also suffered of prostatitis (the swelling of the prostate), urethritis (inflammation of the penile duct), as well as Addison's disease, an illness of the adrenal glands that can cause very low blood pressure, fatigue, and coma if untreated. Because of this, JFK consumed a cocktail of medications and regular shots of testosterone, which, Dallek argues, accounts for his heightened libido and numerous affairs. There have also been guarded reports that JFK contracted "gonococcal infections" (venereal disease) from his sexual indiscretions.[17] As Dallek explained,

> medical files covering the last eight years of Kennedy's life, including X-rays and prescription records, show that he took painkillers, antianxiety agents, stimulants and sleeping pills, as well as hormones to keep him alive, with extra doses in times of stress. At times the president took as many as eight medications a day.[18]

Public disclosure of these ailments and of Kennedy's dependence on powerful drugs would no doubt have embarrassed his family and supporters, and was likely to tarnish his memory and name. It was certainly not something the Kennedy family (especially his wife and brother Robert, who jealously guarded these secrets) wished to have revealed in a public inquiry, and even less by the media. Coupled with their understandable apprehension of seeing JFK's mangled body displayed on the front pages of newspapers and magazines, the secrecy surrounding the autopsy and its materials, which was largely imposed by Kennedy's own entourage, becomes suddenly less sinister. This also explains why Admiral Burkley asked Humes not to dissect Kennedy's adrenals or discuss them in his report and provides context for why Captain John Stover, the Commander of Bethesda Medical School, made members of the hospital staff sign confidentiality agreements the following morning.[19]

With Admiral Burkley, Robert Kennedy, and other White House officials breathing down their necks, the errors for which the Bethesda pathologists are usually blamed also become understandable. According to Dr. Humes, there was a "hysterical situation" in the autopsy room, "considerable confusion. […] How we kept our wits about us as well as we did is amazing to me. I don't know how we managed to do it as poorly or as well as we did under the circumstances".[20] The fact that they were suddenly enlisted to take part in such a historic procedure also helps explain why the pathology team did what they were told with little protest, and why they handed all autopsy documents—including the photographs, negatives, X-rays, blood and tissue smears, and the dissected portion of the brain—back to Admiral Burkley, most of it on the same night, keeping only their notes to complete their report, and the undissected brain.

Burkley then handed the autopsy materials to Attorney General Robert Kennedy, who stored them at the White House until he resigned his position the following year. Out of deference to the Kennedy family, Dr. Humes destroyed his blood-stained autopsy notes and recopied the face sheet from the original (with some parts left blank) to avoid any blood-stained paraphernalia from becoming a museum trophy or a black market curio.[21] Humes also made a verbal agreement with Admiral Burkley never to discuss the state of Kennedy's adrenals until all living members of the Kennedy family died, a promise he allowed Dr. Boswell to break in 1992.[22] This is a major reason for which the autopsy team remained tight-lipped for decades, especially toward the long queue of conspiracy buffs seeking an interview.[23]

15.3   Seeing double: the "faked" autopsy photographs

A total of 52 photographs and 14 X-rays were taken of Kennedy's body that night, only a handful of which are now in circulation.[24] Most of these are yet to be seen by the public. They remain in the possession of the National Archives, which stores them on behalf of the Kennedy family and limits their viewing pending the family's approval.[25] Two partial sets of autopsy pictures were leaked to the press.

The first came from black and white doubles made in 1963 and held by Secret Service agent James K. Fox. Fox sold these to conspiracy researcher Mark Crouch in 1981, who distributed them to other researchers, including David Lifton who published them in a second edition of *Best Evidence*. Another set of color photos were copied without permission by conspiracy author Robert Groden, co-author of *High Treason*, while serving as a consultant to the HSCA. Groden sold these pictures to a tabloid magazine in 1991. As the autopsy evidence belongs to the Kennedy family and not to the government, it was not subject to declassification orders under the 1992 President John F. Kennedy Assassination Records Collection Act. However, since these images were taken by military personnel and never officially classified, they are part of the public domain, which is why some of them appear in this book.[26]

Although Chief Justice Earl Warren considered the autopsy pictures too gruesome to be shared with most of his Commission staff and officials (see Chapter 2), they were reexamined, along with Kennedy's clothes, by the Clark Panel in 1968, the Rockefeller Commission in 1975, and the HSCA in 1977–79. Relying on JFK's dental records, antemortem X-rays, and photographs displaying unique physical characteristics,[27] all of these committees considered them authentic and confirmed the Warren Commission's conclusion that Kennedy's wounds were all caused by two shots from behind.[28] The 1992–98 Assassination Records Review Board (ARRB) and several media investigations, such as PBS *NOVA* in 1988, also confirmed the authenticity of the autopsy photos.[29] When the ARRB showed the pictures from the National Archives to autopsy photographer John Stringer (the only person permitted to take pictures of the autopsy), he confirmed that these were his original work.[30]

The autopsy photos carry additional proofs of their authenticity. Some of the autopsy pictures, including the highly controversial back-of-the-head pictures (e.g., Figure 15.4) which conspiracists claim is the back of someone else's head (or a molded replica), are in fact stereo pairs: two or more pictures of the same wound taken from slightly different angles and seconds apart, showing subtle variations in shade, color, angle, and background. When viewed side by side in a stereoscope (a device like the View-Master children's toy or double images used to produce three-dimensional [3-D] movies today), stereo pairs create *a 3-D effect.* Identical images do not create such an effect, and the portions of photographs that would have been altered from the original would be readily identifiable in a stereoscope.[31] This is because stereo pairs were almost impossible to fake using 1963 technology, making it unlikely that such pictures could have been altered. The original pictures also carry other markings that helped experts—including John Stringer, who took them—certify their authenticity. These include the autopsy case number written on the rulers that appear in each photograph, code numbers on each picture that correspond to the code on the film holder, and an autopsy log that registered all salient details of each autopsy, including the number of pictures taken.[32]

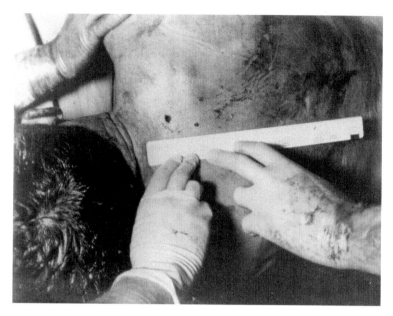

FIGURE 15.1 Autopsy photo of entry wound in JFK's back
Source: John Stringer/US Navy/National Archives and Records Administration.

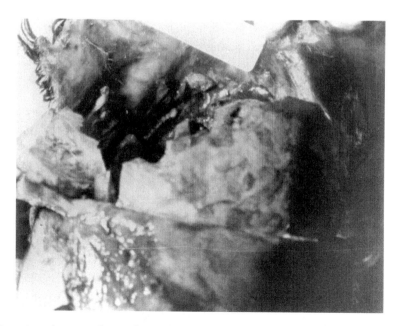

FIGURE 15.2 Autopsy photo of JFK's skull after reflection of scalp
Source: John Stringer/US Navy/National Archives and Records Administration.

15.4 Seeing red and white spots: the "fraudulent" autopsy report

If these teams of experts all agreed that the autopsy evidence was legitimate, and the pictures themselves carry markings of their authenticity, why do conspiracists continue to claim they were faked? The answer lies largely in their selective use of testimonies and their excessive preoccupation with subtle inconsistencies—some real, some imagined—between the autopsy report, pictures, and X-rays.

In addition to imposed time constraints, the Bethesda doctors ran into several problems that caused confusion in their findings. The first was that they could find no frontal exit wound that could be matched to the entrance wound in JFK's upper back. Rigor mortis[33] had rendered the body stiff by this time, so that the back wound could not be properly probed. Since there was no bullet found in the wound, Dr. Humes suspected that it had either fallen out from the same hole or exited through the throat. The latter was assumed to be the case due to some contusion suffered by the upper lobe of the right lung, but this was only confirmed the next day (November 23) when Dr. Humes, in a phone conversation with Dr. Perry in Dallas, was told that the doctors at Parkland witnessed a small wound in the throat before they performed a tracheotomy.[34] But the body had already been embalmed and transported to the White House, the neck could therefore not be dissected to verify. The HSCA would later confirm this trajectory after identifying in the X-rays a stress fracture to JFK's first thoracic vertebra, caused by the bullet passing near, but not striking, the spine.[35] Although Mantik and others have continued to claim that Kennedy's throat wound was a wound of entry, this theory has by now been discounted by numerous trained forensic pathologists.

A greater problem occurred during the HSCA hearings, during which the Bethesda pathologists were unable to locate the wound of entry at the back of Kennedy's skull on the autopsy photographs they were presented. These photographs (especially the color transparencies) do show a small reddish circle with a black abrasion collar high on the rear of the head near the "cowlick" (see Figure 15.4), which the HSCA's Forensic Pathology Panel identified as the probable wound of entrance.[36] However, the autopsy report places the entrance hole four inches lower; slightly above and to the right of the external occipital protuberance (EOP), the bony bump at the back of the head halfway between the two ears.[37] This discrepancy, with the ambivalence of Drs. Humes and Boswell to commit to a single entry wound in their ARRB depositions (30 years later) led Mantik and Aguilar to suspect that the circular reddish abrasion is a forgery. To confuse matters further, an irregular-shaped white spot near the subject's hairline, which receives no mention in the autopsy report (but can be seen on Figure 15.4), has led these authors to suspect this was the real entrance wound described by the pathologists in their report and not the suspicious reddish abrasion conspiracists argue was faked. Yet the "white spot" is clearly below the EOP and does not correspond with the autopsy report any more than the "red spot" does. Aguilar and Mantik therefore conclude that the head in the photograph is not Kennedy's because it is missing the massive exit wound they say should be located at the bottom right rear of the skull. So we now find ourselves with two different entry wounds and an invisible exit wound on a head that is said to be anyone else's but Kennedy's.

Confused? It seems everyone is. While Humes' and Boswell's original measurements of the entrance wound does not line up with either the red abrasion or the white spot, the Clark Panel (1968), the Rockefeller Commission (1975), and the HSCA (1977–79) all concluded that the red spot was the actual entry wound. All this confusion has led conspiracists to believe they caught the plotters red-handed defending two falsehoods. According to Mantik, this is as close as it gets to finding a "smoking gun".[38]

The confusion begins to clear when we realize that, having handed the photographs and X-rays to Admiral Burkley on the night of November 22, Humes drafted his autopsy report only the following evening, relying solely on his autopsy notes and Boswell's handwritten diagrams.[39] Humes was unable to double-check his face sheet measurements for possible errors. And since some of the markings on the face sheet (such as the entrance wounds on JFK's back and head) were diagrammed only approximately, these drawings could not help him correct any measurement errors. The lack of precision of the face sheet diagrams also caused mistakes to be made in the artist reproductions of the autopsy pictures published in the Warren Report—drawings which were based on Humes' autopsy report and were never intended to be exact representations of Kennedy's wounds—because the artist never saw them firsthand (see Figures 2.2–2.4). The Dox drawings (e.g., Figure 15.3), produced for the HSCA 13 years later, were far more precise than those made for the Warren Commission. Yet these also contained slight discrepancies from the original images taken by Stringer due to the artist's interpretation of details and reproduction of color transparencies into a black-and-white medium. Such differences have led conspiracists to dismiss the drawings, like the original photographs, as misleading forgeries.[40]

Mantik, Aguilar, and Fetzer spend a good deal of time impeaching the Warren Commission's drawings, but this is nothing more than a red herring. Indeed, it was the measurements on the autopsy report, not the faulty proportions of the drawings, that allowed the Warren Commission to establish the direction of the shots. The autopsy report clearly identified the back wound as being located "in the upper right posterior thorax […] just above the upper border of the scapula […] 14 cm below the tip of the right mastoid process [i.e., the bump behind the ear]".[41] In other words, the back wound is exactly where the autopsy photos place it and it is consistent with the single-bullet theory and an exit wound from the throat.

On the other hand, the fact that the Clark Panel, the Rockefeller Commission, and the HSCA's Forensic Pathology Panel all felt the need to correct the autopsy report's measurements of the head entrance wound could be construed as manipulation of evidence. Aguilar and Mantik see this and the "suspicious" 30-year silence of the Bethesda doctors as proof of a blunder by the conspirators, who apparently needed four additional government inquiries (if we include the ARRB) to correct this mistake. The simplest explanation, however, is that either Humes or Boswell

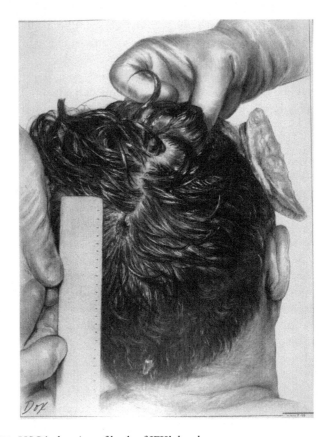

FIGURE 15.3 HSCA drawing of back of JFK's head

Source: JFK Exhibit F-48, Ida Dox/HSCA/National Archives and Records Administration.

misrecorded the entry wound's location on the face sheet. Not having the ability to double-check his notes against the body, pictures, or X-rays, Humes transcribed the erroneous measurement to his report. The X-rays and pictures both located the wound of entry high in the back of the head (at the cowlick), consistent with observations they made of the brain, of the trail of bullet fragments inside Kennedy's skull, and of the exit wound. The HSCA's Forensic Pathology Panel was also able to line-up the beveling marks[42] inside the skull with the exterior red abrasion and concluded that

> the upper scalp wound [i.e., the "red spot"], the location of which is identified by X-rays as approximately 10 centimeters (as measured on the X-ray) above the external occipital protuberance, is a typical entrance wound. [...] The skull defect, apart from its location, corresponds with the description within the autopsy report.[43]

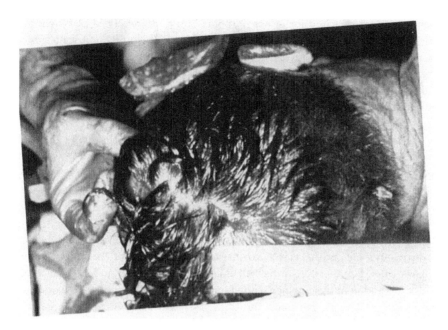

FIGURE 15.4 Autopsy photo (color transparency) of back of JFK's head

Source: John Stringer/US Navy/National Archives and Records Administration.

In other words, multiple images of the skull, when compared to each other, made it clear that the "red spot" (or something close to it) marked the original wound of entry. Given that Humes and Boswell would, after some hesitation, endorse the HSCA's positioning of the entry wound at the red abrasion, the simplest conclusion we can reach is that they made a mistake and either failed to notice or were too embarrassed to admit it. Dr. Humes, who did not see the autopsy photographs until 1966 and who was never shown enlargements of these pictures until 1977, came close to making such an admission: "When we catalogued the photographs and numbered them [...] I'll confess to possibly overlooking the area [of the red spot]".[44]

Can we account for this error with a simple and nonsinister explanation? I can only offer an educated guess, which is that Humes wrongly recorded the entry wound on his report as "2.5cm *to the right and slightly above* the external occipital protuberance (EOP)," instead of identifying it (rightly) as "2.5cm *above*, and *slightly to the right*, of the EOP". The difference between these phrases—transmitted verbally—is nearly imperceptible, but the difference would raise the reported entry wound closer to the red abrasion, which the HSCA's Forensic Pathology Panel only tentatively identified as the correct wound of entry since it could not examine JFK's skull and scalp firsthand, nor could it pinpoint with absolute certainty the exact location of Kennedy's EOP. If we also consider that Humes, Boswell, and Finck were hurried in their work by George Burkley and Robert Kennedy, that they were sleep-deprived for nearly 48 hours during the weekend of November 22–24, and that their proofing of the report was interrupted on Sunday afternoon by news of Lee Oswald's grisly death, it is not improbable that a small though not insignificant error like this would go unnoticed. Another possibility is that the pathologists failed to record the true location of the entry wound and mistook another recorded measurement—that of a skull laceration—as the location of the entry wound, which is what the HSCA's Forensic Pathology Panel later insinuated.

That said, several physicians, autopsy technicians, and pathologists who attended to JFK's body at Parkland and Bethesda, or who later studied the autopsy X-rays and bullet fragments (including Robert Grossman, Chester Boyers, Joseph Davis, Chad Zimmerman, Larry Sturdivan, and Peter Cummings) agree with Humes' initial description of the entrance wound being located near the EOP. One possible explanation for this is that JFK's scalp and skull had already been undermined (separated from each other) when photographer John Stringer snapped the color transparency used by the HSCA to establish the location of the entry wound (Figure 15.4). This means that the "red abrasion" in the photo no longer lined up with the location of the entrance wound in JFK's skull.[45] This appears to have been what Humes, Boswell, and Finck meant in 1967 when they were summoned to help catalog these photos for the National Archives: "Due to the fractures of the underlying bone and the elevation of the scalp by manual lifting (done to permit the wound to be photographed) the photographs show the wound to be slightly higher than its actually measured site".[46]

Mantik and Aguilar nonetheless maintain that the Parkland physicians correctly identified the President's throat wound as a wound of entry, and a massive, orange-sized wound at the back of Kennedy's head as the exit wound. We established in Chapter 12 that the Parkland doctors did not have much time to examine these wounds. Dr. Humes confirmed this in his November 23 phone call with Dr. Perry:

> I asked him, much to my amazement, had he or any other physician in attendance upon the President examined the back of the patient, his neck or his shoulder. They said no, the patient had never been moved from his back.[47]

Failure to examine JFK's upper back and the discrete wound in his throat led the Parkland emergency staff to wrongly describe the throat wound as a wound of entry. As far as the neck wound is concerned, the Bethesda pathologists got it right.

Mantik argues that the back wound, which he wrongly locates at the third thoracic vertebra, was too low to jibe with the single-bullet theory.[48] But the pathologists' report never made any mention of the third thoracic vertebra. Instead, they duly recorded its location from *visible* physical markers, namely the wound's distance (14 centimeter) from the tip of the right acromion process (the bony tip of the shoulder blade, above the shoulder joint) and 14 centimeter beneath the right mastoid process (the bump behind the ear), which places the shoulder wound at the *first* thoracic vertebra, consistent with the autopsy pictures and the single-bullet theory. Only researchers committed to trusting the earliest witnesses—as opposed to the most qualified ones—could honestly claim that the emergency room doctors in Dallas got this one right.

As to the extent of the damage suffered by Kennedy's head, there are numerous conflicting reports. Mantik finds it abhorrent that the Bethesda and HSCA pathologists contradicted the Parkland doctors: "The most critical piece of evidence for the HSCA's case—the red spot—was never reported by any witness, at either Parkland or Bethesda. The HSCA literally based its case on a piece of paper [i.e., the autopsy report]".[49] Mantik is arguing from ignorance here, claiming that because Parkland doctors did not report a "red spot" at the back of Kennedy's head, this proves such a wound did not exist. But then, the circular red abrasion would not have been visible to doctors at Parkland through the hair, gore, and stretcher that obscured the back of JFK's head. Mantik also fails to tell his readers that most Parkland physicians would later endorse the autopsy's findings. As Dr. Carrico told Gerald Posner:

> The president was lying on his back and shoulders, and you could see the hole, with scalp and brain tissue hanging back down his head, *and it covered most of the occipital portion of his head.* We saw a large hole *on the right side of the head.* I don't believe we saw any occipital bone. It was not there. *It was parietal bone.* And if we said otherwise, we were mistaken.[50]

Carrico's retraction was echoed by Drs. Giesecke, Peters, Baxter, Jones, and Perry, who remarked that the state of Kennedy's head made it next to impossible to assess his wounds properly without putting their hands inside the cranium and feeling around, which of course none of them did. "You must remember the President had a lot of hair," adds Dr. Perry, "and it was bloody and matted, and it was difficult to tell where that wound started or finished".[51]

One could surmise, as Mantik and others do, that the conspirators intimidated these witnesses to change their stories, but no evidence has been produced to suggest that these men were coerced. It is far more probable that, as medical experts who had spent just enough time with the victim to make a cursory diagnosis, these doctors were able to realize their hasty conclusions were wrong. On the other hand, two Parkland doctors—McClelland and Crenshaw—have continued to express doubts concerning the "official story" and are cited repeatedly by Mantik and Aguilar as witnesses of a cover-up. The only evidence they have to offer, however, are their memories of Kennedy's wounds, which clash with those of their former colleagues. The openly conspiracist views of McClelland and Crenshaw also prove that the Parkland doctors were not silenced. These two would otherwise not have been able to publicly endorse conspiracy theories or would have provided some account of how they were pressured not to speak out. They might also have "died in suspicious circumstances" as conspiracists often depict the deaths of their favorite "whistleblowers". But none of these things ever happened.

Aguilar and Mantik have deceptively included the recanting Parkland doctors on their list of over 40 witnesses of a right-rear exit wound.[52] Other witnesses on this list are well-established yarn spinners like Virgil "Ed" Hoffman and Beverly Oliver (see Chapters 11 and 13) and members of Parkland and Bethesda hospital staff who had even less time and medical training to observe JFK's wounds than the emergency doctors. One of these, a Bethesda morgue technician named Paul O'Connor, began claiming some 25 years later that he not only saw such a hole in the back of Kennedy's head, he also saw that his skull was empty when the body arrived at Bethesda, a claim that is refuted by all other Bethesda witnesses.[53] Curiously, Aguilar's list of rear-exit-wound witnesses includes the three pathologists at Bethesda and Secret Servicemen Roy Kellerman and Clint Hill, all staunch defenders of the Lone Gunman Theory, and even Mrs. Kennedy. It seems Aguilar's standard for vetting witnesses does not require them to believe anything they say.

Aguilar's favorite witness of the right-rear exit wound theory is Parkland doctor Robert McClelland, who unlike his former colleagues has remained an ardent defender of the grassy knoll shooter theory (see Chapter 13). But Aguilar only quotes parts of McClelland's Warren Commission testimony that discusses the alleged wound to JFK's cerebellum[54] and completely ignores McClelland's concession that Kennedy's head was never lifted nor the back of his head examined in Dallas. Aguilar is thus guilty of selection bias: cherry-picking only data that can support his theory. According to former Parkland doctor Marion "Pepper" Jenkins, a major reason for McClelland's ongoing conspiracist views is his enduring friendship with local conspiracy boffin Robert Groden, who helped turn McClelland into an underground hero.[55]

15.5   Believing is seeing: misreading the autopsy evidence

A further problem with the buffs' use of autopsy evidence is their tendency to engage in confirmation bias. "Confirmation bias occurs from the direct influence of desire on beliefs," writes behavior economist Shahram Heshmat,

> When people would like a certain idea [or] concept to be true, they end up believing it to be true. They are motivated by wishful thinking. This error leads the individual to stop gathering information when the evidence gathered so far confirms the views (prejudices) one would like to be true.[56]

That is to say, Aguilar, Mantik, and their fellow "assassination scientists" are reading the evidence incorrectly because they are bent on confirming existing beliefs. This leads them to observe photographs in the wrong orientation and fail to take note of the angle at which certain X-rays were taken. It is also due to their excessive and sometimes exclusive reliance on second- and third-generation copies, which tend to mute, accentuate, or otherwise distort salient features of the patient's body. It is also revealed in the way they misconstrue the testimonies of eyewitnesses or conclude that missing evidence is *de facto* proof of conspiracy.

15.5.1 Misreading the photographs

The first thing anyone should do before trying to interpret photographic evidence is to make sure they are viewing the images in the right orientation. Photos and drawings depicting the wounds in Kennedy's back and head (see Figures 15.1–15.4) are often presented incorrectly in conspiracy books and websites, with the victim's head at the top of the picture, as if he were sitting upright, rather than lying horizontally on a dissecting board—the true orientation of the body. While this makes the images easier to view, it distorts the historical context. Considering that rigor mortis did not permit the pathologists to bend the body into a sitting position, and taking note of objects in the background—the large autopsy table, the pathologists' hands, and the location of the photographer and his bulky tripod—we are compelled to see that the corpse is lying down on its back, or in some cases turned to its side.[57] Failing to see this can lead us to misconstrue the force of gravity and its impact on the victim's body—such as the way Kennedy's gore-matted hair (which was short at the sides and back, but longer on top) flops toward the left of the body, not toward the back (see Figure 15.4). This means that the back of the head could be viewed and photographed during the autopsy without it having been washed, which the pathologists stated they never did—and which has led Mantik to claim the picture is fake since the gore-matted hair should have covered the back of the head completely. The problem goes away when, viewed in its proper orientation, one sees that the gore-matted hair is simply hanging sideways, outside the frame of the picture. One will also notice that the pathologist's fingers are holding the scalp up to prevent it from sagging into the shattered skull.

Another misconstrued autopsy photo is a close-up of Kennedy's head wound identified as Fox #8 (or simply F8). It depicts a gaping wound in Kennedy's skull, with bone fragments flaring outwards (see Figure 15.2). This picture's scale, orientation, and contents have baffled conspiracists and skeptics for years. This is partly due to the lack of recognizable anatomical features and the fact that the pathologists did not clearly label its contents until 1966, when the photos were cataloged at the National Archives. At that time, they labeled the image as "missile wound over entrance in posterior skull, following reflection of the scalp".[58] They revised this description in 1968 for the Clark Panel, identifying it as the exit wound in the anterior lateral part of the head (i.e., near the temple above the ear).[59] Following this revised interpretation, Dr. Michael Baden, chairman of the HSCA Forensic Pathology Panel, described the photograph as showing

> the bullet exit area on the right side of the head […] the *front right part of the skull* of the President […]. This is a portion of a gunshot *wound of exit* as determined by the panel because of the beveling of the outer layer of bone visible in the photographs.[60]

Mantik, on the other hand, insists that it depicts a right-rear exit wound. In his published articles, he presents the image rotated 90 degrees clockwise (with the pathologist's ruler on the right side) and claims that the darker portion of the picture depicts the lower part of the occipital bone (the bottom-right back of the head, behind which sits the cerebellum).[61] This assessment is problematic, not least because the direction of the tunneling—assuming we are staring into the right occipital area, as Mantik suggests—forces us to conclude that the bullet entered the skull in the area of Kennedy's left eye. No one with a clear view of the assassination or of Kennedy's injured head has ever claimed they saw a gunshot wound there, or indeed anywhere on his face. Unless one ignores such inconsistencies in Mantik's "proof" of a massive lower-right-rear exit wound, we must conclude that F8 is certainly not depicting the lower back of the President's head.

Our best clues to assess the proper orientation of F8 are the secondary objects inside the picture. The size of the ruler and of the pathologists' fingers, for instance, allows us to compare the size of the head depicted in F8 to the other available photos (see Figures 15.1 and 15.4, for instance). This suggests that F8 is not an extreme close-up of an "orange-sized hole" at the back of Kennedy's head, but a wide view of *most of the skull*, and of a much larger wound than the one described by Mantik—a wound that takes up nearly a third of the size of the victim's cranium—larger even than the "13-centimeter defect" visible to the pathologists before "reflection of the scalp,"[62] that is, *before the scalp was lifted*. This seems counterintuitive at first because, based on other photos and eyewitness reports, one does not expect to see a wound this large in JFK's head. We must keep in mind, however, that the *visible* damage on the outside of the head was only a fraction of the damage sustained by the skull. Many of the witnesses in both Parkland and Bethesda who saw the President's head up close agreed that the *scalp* was largely intact outside the right-lateral part of his head, but that the *skull* underneath seemed to be been shattered.

Our most qualified and best positioned witness is John Stringer, the photographer who observed JFK's head wounds closely while he took these pictures. According to Stringer, who stood at the head of the autopsy table and took this shot looking down into the skull, this picture depicts the top-right of the head, with a large part of the scalp lifted and "peeled down" over the face (Kennedy's skinless forehead is in the center-right of the photo, the undermined scalp at the bottom) to expose the entire damaged area of the skull. The inside of the head is empty because the brain has by now been removed. According to Stringer, the "pristine" appearance of the back of Kennedy's head seen in other pictures (e.g., Figure 15.4) was only illusory.[63]

Thomas Evan Robinson, the mortician who reconstructed Kennedy's cranium and embalmed his body, observed the latter part of the autopsy. He agreed that Kennedy's skull above the occiput was severely damaged, that the scalp had been rolled back, and that the skull was further cut open to remove the brain.[64] Robinson also explained that, although a great deal of skull was broken or missing, much of Kennedy's scalp was undamaged, which allowed the embalmers to rebuild his head without performing major external alterations. Having made no clear distinction between the hard, brittle skull (which was shattered) and the soft malleable scalp (which was not significantly damaged, save near the exit wound, above the ear), conspiracists see a logical contradiction where there is, in fact, only a misunderstanding.[65]

Thus, the failure of the pathologists to properly label the picture in 1963 gave rise to irrelevant speculations, and confusion in how the picture was labeled (and relabeled) in 1966 and 1968. Although Stringer was present at the National Archives' 1966 cataloging meeting, he was not asked to comment on the contents or orientation of his pictures. Misconceptions about F8 would therefore continue for decades, even after Stringer's ARRB deposition set the record straight. In the end, F8 does not give us any clear proof of a second gunman. It tells us more about the people who obsess over it than about how Kennedy died. Indeed, excessive scrutiny of the few widely available autopsy pictures without a careful study of their context, and of the explanations of those who were there, can easily turn into a kind of Rorschach inkblot test in which one sees whatever they want to see. Considering that the human mind naturally seeks familiar patterns in chaotic information—a psychological phenomenon called pareidolia[66]—and that two-dimensional autopsy pictures can be hard to interpret, it is wise to exercise caution before reaching hasty conclusions.

While we could surmise that Mantik, Aguilar, and Fetzer have simply been short-sighted, a final example suggests they were purposefully duplicitous in trying to prove that the HSCA drawings of JFK's wounds are fraudulent. When comparing the Ida Dox drawing of the back of JFK's head (Figure 15.3) with the autopsy photographs, these authors refer to the wrong stereo pair (i.e., a black and white photo, not the color transparency shown in Figure 15.4) to claim that no red abrasion exists on the original photos,[67] a blatant example of evidence manipulation performed *by conspiracists*.

And what should we make of the notorious "white spot" that continues to spark conspiracist ire? Mantik claims it is the original (false) entry wound described in the (fraudulent) autopsy report which was then "corrected" by the HSCA to preserve the credibility of the cover-up. But neither the Bethesda pathologists nor the HSCA Forensic Pathology Panel ever made much of the "white spot". It receives no mention in the autopsy report and sits far below the EOP—too low to match Dr. Humes' location for the wound of entry. According to John Stringer, the white spot was merely a piece of bone stuck in Kennedy's hair.[68] The HSCA's Forensic Pathology Panel studied computer-enhanced photographs of the white spot and thought it was a piece of dried brain tissue.[69] Only conspiracists continue to claim it has any importance. The white spot is therefore another red herring, a vain attempt to spin the Lone Gunman Theory as inconsistent.

The exact location of the head entry wound may never be established definitively, unless Kennedy's skeleton is exhumed in some future investigation. All things considered, it remains possible to this author that the Bethesda and HSCA pathologists were both in fact discussing the same wound. It is logically consistent with the facts that the Bethesda pathologists, who never saw a "red spot" under the lighting conditions in which they were working, and who possibly erred in their measurements, witnessed the same wound as the HSCA Forensic Pathology Panel, who could only see the wound as it was photographed, a frozen moment in time, without the benefit of direct observation.

15.5.2 Misreading the X-rays

Mantik also appeals to Kennedy's X-rays, sometimes to claim that they agree with a version of Kennedy's wounds described by certain eyewitnesses but not the autopsy report, and sometimes to claim that the X-rays were doctored to frame Lee Oswald. Since the original autopsy X-rays remain the property of the Kennedy family, part of this problem is caused by the small number and poor quality of the copies now in circulation. The problem is exacerbated by the insufficient number of X-rays taken during the autopsy—too few, at least, to give us a complete set of data concerning the damages caused to Kennedy's skull.

X-rays are negative images that show a full range of densities. Because they reproduce the 3-D features of complex objects (e.g., a skull) onto a two-dimensional medium—usually a photographic film negative—they need to be interpreted by qualified radiologists trained to recognize the relative positions and distances of elements within the image. X-rays lose much information when they are reproduced as black and white prints, as published in the HSCA report, on a website, or books like this one (see Figures 15.5 and 15.6), because subtler shades of light and dark gray that appear on an X-ray can be lost when reproduced as photographs. Lack of understanding of how X-rays work has led many conspiracists—most of whom viewed only inferior copies of the originals—to perceive missing bones in the lower back area of Kennedy's head, or foreign objects (like bullet fragments) where they do not in fact appear.[70] Joe Durnavich explains how this might lead zealous conspiracists to misconstrue the autopsy data:

> An X-ray that has been copied and published in a book will have to sacrifice many of the gray levels that are in the original X-ray. Even a good quality photograph of an X-ray will not have a contrast ratio higher than about 63 to 1. A reproduction in a book will be even lower. These ratios are significantly less than the full range of gray levels contained in the original X-rays. This means that an X-ray reproduced to show good detail in the brighter areas, such as bones, will render darker areas, such as tissues, as all black. And if the publisher adjusts the gray levels so that both the brightest and the darkest areas reproduce, then detail will be lost in the middle gray levels. One will not be able to distinguish among the fine shades of gray visible on the original X-ray. Certain features will be undetectable. [...] Thus, one needs to be careful not to conclude that a large section of black in a published JFK X-ray necessarily means bone is missing from that section.[71]

Many photographs of JFK's postmortem X-rays were published in the HSCA's final report. Nonenhanced X-ray reproductions lack a great deal of detail. Enhanced X-rays contain more detail but tend to highlight features that are much

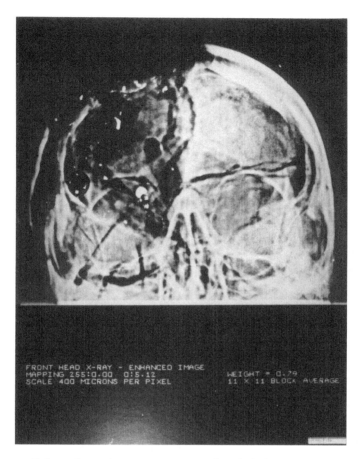

FIGURE 15.5 Enhanced anterior-posterior X-ray of JFK's skull

Source: John Ebersole/HSCA/National Archives and Records Administration.

more discrete on the originals, thereby adding unnecessary "noise" to the images. Depending on which version one studies, different features will be more salient. Unsurprisingly, disagreements occurred between the memories of the Bethesda autopsy team and the enhanced X-ray duplicates they were asked to interpret many years later. Misinterpretations are all the more likely when amateurs with little experience reading X-rays, who lack insight into the nature and details of Kennedy's wounds, and who lack objectivity, reach ambitious conclusions based on secondhand copies of the originals.

One bit of context that is often ignored is the fact that Kennedy's cranial X-rays were not taken directly face-front or exactly sideways due to rigor mortis and the nature of Kennedy's wounds, which prevented the radiologists from lifting and manipulating the head. This means that the X-rays were taken at a skewed projection angle that can lead ill-informed viewers to misalign various objects in the image.[72] Failing to recognize the proper angle of the X-ray can lead to seeing

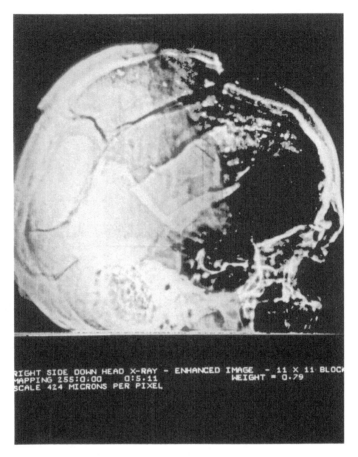

FIGURE 15.6 Enhanced lateral X-ray of JFK's skull

Source: John Ebersole/HSCA/National Archives and Records Administration.

fractures, missing bone, or bone and bullet fragments in the wrong parts of the skull. The size of objects can also be distorted depending on their distance from the X-ray tube.

Though a trained radiation oncologist, David Mantik reaches some peculiar conclusions about the contents of these X-rays. For instance, he claims that there is a round object, roughly 6.5 millimeter in diameter, on the anterior-posterior (AP) X-ray of Kennedy's head (Figure 15.5). Mantik is speaking of the circular white dot in the center-left of the picture, near the subject's right eye, which he says has the size and shape of a Mannlicher-Carcano bullet viewed head-on. This, he says, is proof that the X-rays were forged to incriminate Oswald. This was also done, he speculates, to hide evidence of a smaller bullet or fragment, or some other type of projectile on the X-ray.[73]

Even if such an "object" could be faked using 1963 technology (Mantik alleges it could), his argument can be discredited on numerous counts of bad logic. First, it was partly discredited by the HSCA when an expert radiologist, Dr. Gerald McDonnel of the Photographic Evidence Panel, examined the autopsy X-rays for evidence of alteration and found none. The panel's report thereby stated: "Except for two small areas of thermal damage and 'minor ... discoloration of the images due to incomplete processing of the film' Neither of these conditions affected the conclusion that the images were not altered".[74] In other words, the X-ray images contained two areas of discoloration caused by *heat damage*, not the presence of foreign objects, real or simulated.

This kind of discoloration is just one type of photographic pollution that radiologists call "artifacts". According to Murphy, Shetty, et al., "artifacts can [appear] in a variety of ways including abnormal shadow noted on a radiograph or degraded image quality and have been produced by artificial means from hardware failure, operator error and software (post-processing) artifacts".[75] Some major causes of artifacts are improper handling of the film and processing errors. Film radiography artifacts can take various shapes, including clear spots formed by air bubbles sticking to the film during processing, by fixer splashed on the film prior to developing, and dirt on the intensifying screen. One of the artifacts identified by the HSCA's Dr. McDonnel is the white circle that Mantik claims is a faked 6.5 millimeter Mannlicher-Carcano bullet. The other, smaller irregularity—an elongated 7×2-millimeter vertical spot located above and slightly to the left of the circular "object"—receives little attention from Mantik.

While the circular 6.5-millimeter "object" (or artifact) has elicited much conspiracist speculation, it seemed to have troubled none of the autopsy doctors. In fact, it was not even mentioned in their report. While this seems suspicious to Mantik, it is only so if one first assumes that the autopsy team had a hidden agenda. Indeed, neither the Warren Commission, nor the Rockefeller Commission, nor the HSCA (which, remember, was actively searching for a conspiracy) ever tried to argue that the white blob was a Mannlicher-Carcano bullet or fragment that proved Oswald's guilt. While the 1968 Clark Panel did believe the "object" was a bullet fragment, it did not attempt to use this to further incriminate Oswald. There was certainly enough evidence available to affirm the general conclusions of the Warren Commission without drumming-up a never-before-seen bullet fragment on a newly forged X-ray. If Mantik is correct, on the other hand, this would imply that the conspirators planted false evidence which they had no intention of using and whose only utility has been to help David Mantik expose them three decades later. This is an example of the furtive fallacy: the faulty assumption that nothing happens by accident, and that events are guided by some nefarious agent.

In 1997, the ARRB discovered during its deposition of Jerrol Custer, a Bethesda Hospital X-ray technician who was on duty that night, that Dr. Ebersole had indeed seen Mantik's alleged "6-millimeter object" during the autopsy—a "half circle that appears to be the lightest part of the film [...] in the right orbital superior"—after Custer pointed it out to him as a possible bullet fragment. This suggests that the "6.5-millimeter object" already appeared on the X-ray before the body was dissected and was not added later, as Mantik suggests.[76] Ebersole dismissed it offhand, telling Custer it was an artifact.[77] If Custer is right, Ebersole would presumably have said the same thing to the pathologists if they inquired, which explains why no mention of it was made in the autopsy report and why it was easily forgotten until the HSCA's Forensic Pathology Panel questioned them about it 15 years later. Like the "white spot" at the back of JFK's head, the "6.5-millimeter object" is little more than a distraction caused by circular logic. What is missing here is not just a motive, but also the signature hypercompetence of the JFK buffs' all-powerful enemy. Instead, Mantik offers us a one-time *ad hoc* explanation to suggest that, rather than being devilishly cunning, the men who killed Kennedy were in fact wildly incompetent.[78] We can therefore safely conclude that the "object" on the X-ray is just what many experts said it was, an artifact, and that Mantik is seeing monsters in his bedroom closet.

15.5.3 Misunderstanding the witnesses

We now arrive at the conspiracists' allegations that some of the autopsy evidence was stolen and possibly destroyed. This is said to include several X-rays and photographs as well as the major portion of Kennedy's brain. But even if this turns out to be true, we must be wary of the argument from ignorance fallacy; the absence of evidence does not in itself constitute proof of malfeasance. Evidence can be destroyed or misplaced in any number of ways, including accidents, negligence, or unrelated criminal causes. Such allegations also depend on uncorroborated eyewitness reports, many of which were recorded several years after the fact.

Claims of missing evidence are not particularly useful unless an official record of the missing evidence also exists to establish what is in fact missing. Fortunately, an official catalog of JFK's autopsy materials was produced in 1964 when these came into the guardianship of the National Archives in Washington. Some of these objects were not seen again, nor were the Clark Panel in 1968, the HSCA in 1977–79, and the ARRB in 1992–98, able to locate them. These include JFK's brain and tissue samples which will be discussed in the following section.

On the other hand, some eyewitnesses claimed they saw or heard of alternative autopsy photos and X-rays (presumed to be pre-doctored originals) or longer versions of the Zapruder film (see Chapter 17). If such evidence did once exist, it was never cataloged, and we are left with no other proof of their existence than what can be glean from the minds of such claimants. Unless multiple witnesses can independently corroborate the same information, which they rarely do, the hunt for all of this "hidden evidence" can easily turn into a wild goose chase.[79]

Critical thinkers should always consider the reliability of extraordinary witnesses and the logical consistency of their uncorroborated claims. If so, we should then seek some form of corroboration of their alleged experience to avoid being misled by false memories or deliberate fabrications, and to keep ourselves from falling prey, as conspiracists too often do, to researcher bias and circular reasoning. Considering how inaccurate eye and earwitness reports can be, uncorroborated testimonies should never be accepted as being true unless *several* credible eyewitnesses can produce clear and consistent memories of the alleged evidence: what it looked like, where it was being kept or produced, and when it went missing. Researchers who unquestionably believe uncorroborated memories are building their house on the shifting sands of anecdotal evidence, the lowest form of proof in both the legal and scientific professions. Unsubstantiated memories, which can be incomplete or mistaken, do not on their own prove much. Yet they can be tantalizing, particularly when they confirm our expectations.[80]

An interesting example of this occurred in the wake of the 1997 ARRB deposition of US Navy photographic technician Saundra Kay Spencer and her description of a set of photographs of JFK's body that she developed shortly after the autopsy. Aguilar and Mantik were quick to claim that Spencer's testimony is a smoking gun proving that JFK's autopsy was a sham. As Mantik explains,

> The images that Spencer saw are a key to the puzzle. There are too many odd features in her recollection—the photo collection was too limited, the images were on color negatives (instead of transparencies), and the wrong lab was used. The central clue lies in the nature of the images: they are almost bloodless, which is oddly similar to the extant views of the back of the head. Spencer's activity […] was probably an intermediary step in the alteration process. Although at least one photograph showed JFK's face, this view might have been included merely to misdirect Spencer into believing that the entire set of photographs that she saw was authentic. The fact that they were on color negatives is *prima facie* proof that they were not originals. That Spencer saw autopsy photographs only once is also evidence that this entire operation (of film alteration, in my view) was compartmentalized.[81]

Mantik's version of events seems indeed suspicious. But a closer look at the details shows him to be almost entirely wrong. In 1963, Saundra Spencer was a US Navy petty officer in charge of the White House Laboratory at the Naval Photographic Center (NPC) in Anacostia, DC. Unlike the official autopsy photographer John Stringer, she did not work at Bethesda Hospital. The NPC was the official processing lab for all White House photography, so Spencer's involvement in the manipulation and development of presidential photos is not intrinsically suspicious. In fact, her lab habitually handled photography jobs requested by the White House.[82] What was unusual about her functions that weekend is that she was requested to develop several pictures of Kennedy's corpse which had not been developed at Bethesda Naval Hospital on the night of the autopsy, photos that gave a different perspective on JFK's wounds.

Spencer told the ARRB that she received a request from the FBI or Secret Service[83] to process a set of 4 × 5-inch color photos that were brought to her workplace on Sunday November 24, which, she assumed at the time, were of Kennedy's autopsy. A few decades later, Spencer grew suspicious after seeing some published pictures of Kennedy's autopsy, which were different than those she developed in 1963.[84] Those pictures, she told the ARRB, showed Kennedy's corpse to be far less damaged than it appeared in the other autopsy pictures she saw in the media (i.e., those taken by Stringer):

> Q: Can you describe for me what you saw as best you can recollect?
> A: Briefly, they were very, what I consider pristine for an autopsy. *There was no blood or opening cavities*, opening or anything of that nature. It was quite reverent in how they handled it.
> Q: [...] Do you mean that the body appeared to be clean, had been washed? [...]
> A: Yes.
> Q: And that was different from what you had seen in other autopsy photographs, is that right?
> A: Yes. In other autopsies, they have the opening of the cavity and the removing of vital organs for weighing and stuff of this nature. The only organ that I had seen was a brain that was laid beside the body [...] but, *it didn't appear that the skull had been cut, peeled back and the brain removed*. None of that was shown.[85]

This testimony has led Mantik, Aguilar, and others to conclude that two sets of pictures were made of Kennedy's body—one legitimate and the other "extant" (read: fake)—and that the legitimate set was destroyed after the fake set was inserted with the postmortem evidence.[86] Spencer's description of JFK's body as reverent, clean, restful, and bloodless is certainly different from its appearance on Stringer's photos and every description given by those who attended the autopsy. There was no massive exit wound on the right side of JFK's head (as the autopsy report described it) nor at the right rear (as Mantik and Aguilar claim). All she remembered seeing was a small, ragged wound at the top-rear of the head measuring 1–2 inches in diameter, "just about where the rim [of a hat] would hit".[87] There was also a half-inch wound in Kennedy's neck that "appeared just indented. It was, again, clean, pristine, [...] it had some cleaning done to it or something".[88] There were also no measuring rulers, bloodied gloved hands, pathology tools, or other autopsy markers. All this should lead us to question whether these were autopsy pictures at all.

Conspiracists find it strange that Spencer was not interviewed by either the Warren Commission or HSCA, but this can be explained by the fact that she played no salient role in the investigation of JFK's murder until later reports of missing autopsy photos would make her a person of interest. In any event, Spencer confirms having signed a chain of evidence form for handling classified documents, which she assumed would have been kept in a file by the White House, the FBI, or the Secret Service.[89] Thus, Spencer never thought she had been drawn into a clandestine operation, only that the photographs she had developed were different from those that got published in subsequent decades. It should also be stated that Spencer, as she explains it, saw each of these prints very briefly during the development process, not much more than 10–15 seconds per image. Assuming that she was truthful and that her memories were not corrupted by time, Spencer's testimony still does not prove any foul play occurred. Certainly, the ARRB staff thought her a reliable witness, and they accepted her testimony as truthful in their report. But since the

ARRB's mandate was not to reinvestigate the assassination but only to find, catalog, and declassify all remaining evidence, they did not speculate as to the nature of these photographs.

It is reasonable to conclude, however, that the photographs Spencer developed in 1963 were a legitimate set of pictures, taken by Stringer or some other photographer *after* the autopsy procedures were over, during the latter stages of the embalming process. First, Kennedy's body as she described it matches the reconstructive efforts performed by the team of morticians that began fixing the body after Humes, Boswell, and Finck completed their work.[90] Even Douglas Horne, an ARRB staff member who endorses numerous conspiracist interpretations (see Chapter 17), was forced to admit that "[Spencer's] photography seemed to be of the body after reconstruction, but before it was clothed and put in the burial casket".[91] Remember also that the Kennedy family initially hoped to have an open casket funeral, and this necessarily required cleaning the body and fixing its wounds using wax, pieces of rubber, and some of Kennedy's own skin and hair. Thus, Spencer's memories of a peaceful body in a reverent pose are not surprising if what she developed were funerary pictures, taken a few hours after the bloody first set. The time line of events makes this scenario more than just possible. But since Kennedy's body was, in the end, not exposed for public viewing, few ever saw it in this condition save the morticians, Spencer's technical team at the White House photography lab, and a few others who witnessed the body in its final resting state. Since funerary pictures would not count as part of the autopsy record, it should not be surprising that they did not find their way into the National Archives. Inquisitive researchers can still legitimately wonder whether the Kennedy family (or someone else in JFK's administration) kept these pictures or had them destroyed. But this line of inquiry draws us away from conspiracy theories and toward the issue of property rights.

And what did Spencer herself believe? After looking through the color transparencies and black and white prints taken during the autopsy—pictures that have been stored at the National Archives since 1964 and which John Stringer confirmed were authentic—there was no doubt in her mind that both sets of photos were unaltered and genuine. She gave no sign of believing in any conspiracy, save maybe one involving the former First Lady:

> The only thing I can determine is that because of the pristine condition of the body and the reverence that the body was shown, that—this is speculation on my part—that perhaps the family had the second set shot and developed as possible releases if autopsy pictures were demanded, because at that time, Mrs. Kennedy was attempting to keep all sensationalism out of the funeral and maintain the President's dignity and name.[92]

15.6   Your brain in a vat

A final and major source of autopsy angst concerns Kennedy's brain, which went missing sometime before 1966, along with blood and tissue samples. Oliver Stone's

JFK and the writings of Fetzer, Mantik, and Aguilar present this as further proof of a joint government/CIA/military-industrial-complex attempt to suppress the existence of a grassy knoll shooter, despite the fact that this mystery was duly investigated by the HSCA's Forensic Pathology Panel who, following a trail of circumstantial evidence, arrived at a far less sinister explanation.

Because Kennedy's brain suffered significant damage and hemorrhaging, and because of the soft, gelatinous properties of this organ, it was removed during the autopsy and set to soak in a formalin solution (an embalming fluid containing formaldehyde) so that it could harden and be dissected. Hence, it was not replaced into the cranium before the morticians reconstructed JFK's head but remained at Bethesda Naval Hospital to be examined over the weekend. It was then placed in a "stainless steel bucket" and given to the Secret Service, along with some remaining tissue samples.[93] While some of the autopsy doctors assumed that these had been buried with Kennedy's body on Monday, a steel container holding the brain was identified at the National Archives in April 1965 after the transfer of autopsy evidence from the White House and placed with other Kennedy-related materials needing to be cataloged.[94] JFK's former secretary Evelyn Lincoln, now managing Kennedy's White House papers for the Archives, oversaw the transfer of these materials, all of which were contained in a secured "footlocker" (a locked storage trunk) whose key remained in Robert Kennedy's possession. When charged to record the footlocker's contents, Mrs. Lincoln observed that it contained a small box labeled "Item No.9" which included the aforementioned stainless steel container as well as tissue samples and blood smears. The locked footlocker remained in Mrs. Lincoln's National Archives office until November 1965.

Robert Kennedy phoned Mrs. Lincoln some months later to inform her that Angela Novello, his personal secretary, had been mandated to move the footlocker from Lincoln's office to another location in the same building.[95] The HSCA established that this occurred in November 1965 but could not determine the day or location where the footlocker was kept during this time. The archivists questioned by the HSCA believed it was placed in a vault or safe cabinet used by Robert Kennedy (RFK), though it could have been transported off the premises by Novello, RFK, or one of his representatives.[96] The former Attorney General was likely the only person with knowledge of the whereabouts of the autopsy documents until they were officially released by the Kennedy family and returned to the National Archives in 1966.

When the locker and its contents were cataloged in October 1966, it was discovered that "Item No.9" was now missing. So were several autopsy pictures, including a "full-view of the body from above".[97] In February 1968, Attorney General Ramsey Clark set up an investigative body (the Clark Panel) to look into the claims of New Orleans District Attorney Jim Garrison (see Chapter 4) concerning the autopsy evidence. Mrs. Lincoln and Admiral Burkley both told the Panel that the trunk remained locked and untouched until Novello moved it. Satisfied that the National Archives were not at fault for the missing objects, the Panel did not initiate further procedures to locate these items. It probably should have, but neither Attorney General Clark nor the pathologists in his committee could foresee that Robert Kennedy, now a US Senator and soon-to-be presidential candidate, would be assassinated four months later.

Many conspiracists see a connection between these events. The justification they typically use comes in the form of a *post hoc* fallacy in which the "proof" of the conspiracy is derived from the fact that two suspicious events follow each other in time—the disappearance of JFK's brain followed by RFK's murder—so that the first event is perceived as the cause of the second (i.e., that RFK was murdered *because* he knew about JFK's missing brain, which is assumed to have been caused by a massive conspiracy). For cautious critical thinkers, however, RFK's murder simply means that the primary witness and suspect in the case of JFK's missing brain could no longer be questioned.

When the Kennedy family's attorney Burke Marshall—RFK's former Assistant Attorney General—was questioned by the HSCA, he speculated that Bobby had probably taken or destroyed these materials since he alone had access to the footlocker's keys until October 1966, when the objects were first recorded missing.[98] The HSCA's Forensic Pathology Panel agreed with Marshall that RFK had likely retrieved those autopsy elements he found too gruesome or intimate to be seen by the public and returned the rest to the Archives.[99]

But why would Robert Kennedy risk being accused of destroying evidence of his own brother's murder? Conspiracists like David Talbot and James Douglass find it hard to weave RFK into their list of coconspirators because the rest of their narrative simply will not allow it. Bobby, they suggest, was planning on reopening the investigation of JFK's assassination once he became president.[100] Destroying evidence seems therefore counterproductive. But this is all based on speculation and does not take into account Bobby's remorse and his strong suspicions that he precipitated his brother's murder through either his dogged pursuit of organized crime or his secret war on Castro.[101] The simplest and least paranoid explanation, therefore, is that the disappearance of JFK's brain was merely another attempt on behalf of the Kennedys to impede the disclosure of JFK's ailments and to protect his family's legacy.[102] As a presidential contender, Bobby could not afford to have his family's secrets exposed on the campaign trail, particularly when he and Admiral Burkley had so closely conspired to keep his brother's ailments a secret.

John Kennedy was not the first historical figure to have body parts go missing. Einstein, Haydn, Lenin, Napoleon, and Galileo have all had parts of their corpses stolen—including some brains—either to be studied by curious phrenologists or sold and traded clandestinely as morbid showpieces.[103] This was the reason given by Doctor Humes for destroying his blood-spattered autopsy notes, and there is no reason for us to doubt that Robert Kennedy was equally fearful that his brother's body parts and naked autopsy pictures might turn up in some unpalatable publication or private collection. As Burke Marshall told the HSCA, Bobby was fearful that even the National Archives might someday expose these artifacts or donate them to a museum.[104]

Long before the emergence of Facebook, Robert Kennedy foresaw that once one of these artifacts appeared in the popular media, it was bound to stay there forever. Unless they were destroyed, there is no reason for us to believe that Kennedy's brain and tissue samples might not one day find their way back to the National Archives, much like Galileo's fingers and tooth found their way back to their resting place 357 years after they first went missing.[105]

Notes

1 Aguilar is an ophthalmologist specializing in plastic surgery. Mantik is a radiation oncologist. While their medical backgrounds make them legitimate investigators in this field (more so than, say, David Lifton), neither is trained in forensic pathology. Nor does their profession give them any advantage in analyzing eyewitness reports or avoiding circular reasoning. For a general summary of their theory see Gary Aguilar: "Medical Experts and the Kennedy Assassination," September 27, 2014, *C-SPAN*.

2 Mantik: "Paradoxes of the JFK Assassination: The Medical Evidence Decoded," in Fetzer, ed.: *Murder in Dealey Plaza* (2000), 290–1.

3 These include doctors Charles Carrico, Charles Baxter, Malcolm Perry, Adolph Giesecke, Marion Jenkins, Richard Dulaney, Paul Peters, Charles Crenshaw, and Robert McClelland. Some Parkland nurses and orderlies are also cited by these two authors.

4 According to the autopsy report, JFK's brain was removed to set in a formalin solution so it could later be dissected. The body was embalmed during the night of November 22–23, immediately following the autopsy. It was then sent to lie in state at the White House, and then at the Capitol, and was buried on Monday November 25. The extracted brain was therefore not buried with the rest of the body.

5 Interested readers are invited to examine the investigations of medical professionals who studied the Kennedy evidence and confirmed the essence of the Warren Commission's conclusions: John Lattimer (*Kennedy and Lincoln*, 1980), Larry Sturdivan (*The JFK Myths: A Scientific Investigation of the Kennedy Assassination*, 2005), Peter Cummings (*NOVA: Cold Case: JFK*, 2013), and the "Report of the Forensic Pathology Panel," *HSCA Appendix to Hearings*, Vol. VII, 1979.

6 Gary Aguilar: "The Converging Medical Case for Conspiracy in the Death of JFK," in Fetzer, ed.: *Murder in Dealey Plaza*, 189. Emphasis added.

7 In contrast to the scene depicted in Stone's *JFK*, there were no military representatives of the Joint Chiefs of Staff giving orders to the pathologists. Apart from the input of Admiral Burkley and of Robert Kennedy, Dr. Humes was in charge. Stone's film correctly states that an admiral was present in the room, but deceives the viewer by not stating that the admiral in question was Kennedy's personal physician, not a Pentagon official. Testimony of Captain James J. Humes, HSCA VII; "Section II—Performance of Autopsy," HSCA VII, 6–16; ARRB Testimony of John T. Stringer, 16 July 1996.

8 "Section II—Performance of Autopsy," 13.

9 Forensic pathology can be defined as the medical study of the criminal causes and circumstances of unnatural deaths, and the cataloging of such evidence for use in judicial proceedings. Most pathologists are trained only to identify causes of death, not the circumstances of a violent crime.

10 During the autopsy, Robert Kennedy was reportedly impatient that the procedures were taking too long and often inquired as to when they would finish. Manchester, 427. Jackie's initial desire to expose Jack in an open casket also meant that the body could not be dissected fully.

11 Testimony of Captain James J. Humes, HSCA VII; ARRB Testimony of John T. Stringer; Posner, 297–8, 302.

12 "Dr. Michael Baden, Interview with Gerald Posner, February 1, 1992," cited in Posner, 302. Autopsy photographer John Stringer added that close-up photographs of the entry wounds were not taken because of time constraints. ARRB Testimony of John T. Stringer.

13 Manchester, 398; Posner, 297–8. Mrs. Kennedy made this decision during the flight back to Washington. The alleged conspirators would thus have needed to have multiple teams of obsequious pathologists ready at Parkland in Dallas (including Dr. Earl Rose, a key figure in the HSCA Forensic Pathology Panel, who accepted the lone gunman theory) and at multiple hospitals in the Washington area. The decision to call upon doctors Boswell and Finck was taken by Dr. Humes shortly after he was called in by the hospital, around 5:15 p.m. EST, less than three hours before the autopsy began. Unless Humes can be shown to have collaborated with the alleged conspirators, it is difficult to see how the medical team at Bethesda could have been willing participants in a cover-up.

14 Robert Dallek, interview with Michael Enright, "CBC Ideas: The Enright Files – John F. Kennedy," *CBC Radio 1*, November 4, 2013; "George G. Burkley – Oral History Interview – 10/17/1967," conducted by William McHugh, *John F. Kennedy Library and Museum*.

15 James N. Giglio: "Hail to the Chiefs: John F. Kennedy," *Kansas City Public Library, Truman Library Institute, and Missouri State University*, Tuesday, March 20, 2012.

16 It was a thick corset-style brace with metal stays, a plastic pad, and several buckles. According to Dr. John Lattimer, its restricting effect may account for the double head snap that followed the fatal last shot and is likely the reason JFK remained erect after being shot through the back and throat. In other words, the brace made him an easier target. Cited in Bugliosi, 58–60 (and footnote).

17 Gus Russo: *Live by the Sword: The Secret War Against Castro and the Death of JFK* (1998), 326.

18 Dallek, cited in Lawrence K. Altman and Todd S. Purdum: "In J.F.K. File, Hidden Illness, Pain and Pills," *New York Times*, November 17, 2002; Dallek interview with Michael Enright.

19 ARRB Testimony of John T. Stringer.

20 Testimony of Dr. James J. Humes, HSCA VII.

21 Having seen some relics connected to Abraham Lincoln's assassination during a recent visit to Chicago (including Lincoln's death chair, which he said looked to be still stained with blood), Humes was sensitive to how the paraphernalia of Kennedy's autopsy might be used and decided to burn his blood-stained notes to prevent them from falling into the hands of "sensation seekers". Testimony of Dr. James J. Humes, HSCA VII.

22 Boswell was interviewed by Dr. D.L. Breo for an article titled: "JFK's Death—The Plain Truth from the MDs Who Did the Autopsy," *JAMA (Journal of the American Medical Association)*, May 27, 1992, Vol.267, No.20, 2794–803; ARRB Testimony of Dr. J. Thornton Boswell, 26 February 1996.

23 David Mantik's 1992 phone interview of former Bethesda radiologist Dr. John Ebersole, by then an elderly man suffering of cancer, justifies the pathologists' reservations. Not only does Mantik berate his witness, the published transcript (in Fetzer, ed.: *Murder in Dealey Plaza*, Appendix E, 438) is interspersed with Mantik's post-interview comments accusing the man of lying and extracting "proofs" of a grassy knoll shooter, despite Ebersole's overt disagreement with Mantik's theory: "Why this particular thing should become an obsession with people, I have no idea," he tells Mantik, "It was a nut who decided to kill a man, and you can do it".

24 Posner, 300. Official photos were taken by John Stringer, the Bethesda medical school's chief of photography, using a 4 × 5 graphic view camera mounted on a monorail and a

three-wheeled Salzman tripod. Some pictures were developed as color transparencies and some as black and white prints. Stringer estimates he took between 50 and 65 pictures. Deposition of John T. Stringer to the ARRB, 29–46, 126–8. Some pictures taken by Navy corpsman Floyd Riebe, a medical photography student who took wide shots of the autopsy room but did not have the requisite security clearance, were confiscated and overexposed by the Secret Service during the autopsy.

25 "JFK Assassination Evidence: Autopsy Photos and Xrays," 2013, *JFK Lancer*. IMPORTANT NOTE: A set of fake autopsy photographs is circulating on the internet which depict a naked full-body urethane JFK replica (with an empty cranium) produced for the Oliver Stone film *JFK* by special effects artist Gordon Smith. Carmen Albano: "Bodies of Work Series: Mr. Smith Goes to Hollywood," *Toronto Film Scene: Toronto's Online Film Magazine*, March 23, 2011.

26 A list of JFK's autopsy photos and X-rays, cataloged in 1966 for the National Archives, can be found at "Report of Inspection by Naval Medical Staff on November 1, 1966 at National Archives of X-Rays and Photographs of Autopsy of President John F. Kennedy" (MD 13), 11/10/66, "ARRB Master Set of Medical Exhibits," *History Matters*.

27 These include skin folds on his neck and various scars and skin markings. "Procedures Employed in Examining the Autopsy Photographs and X-Rays," HSCA, Vol. VII, 39; McAdams: *JFK Assassination Logic*, 179–80.

28 However, these bodies did not all agree with the Warren Commission and Bethesda autopsy team on the exact location of the head entrance wound. See next.

29 Two Parkland doctors (McClelland and Crenshaw) have supported the conspiracist view that Kennedy was shot from the front and that the autopsy pictures were altered. The five attending physicians who spent the most time with Kennedy's body, however, accept the autopsy evidence as legitimate. Posner, 307–12.

30 ARRB Testimony of John T. Stringer.

31 McAdams: *JFK Assassination Logic*, 163, 180; "Authentication of The Kennedy Autopsy Photographs and X-Rays," HSCA VI.

32 ARRB Testimony of John T. Stringer.

33 Rigor mortis (Latin for "stiffness of death") is caused by chemical changes inside the muscles when blood starts to settle after they cool and stop receiving oxygen.

34 James J. Humes: *Pathological Examination Report A63-272*, 2, Appendix IX of *Warren Report* (CE387).

35 Testimony of Michael Baden, HSCA I, cited in Posner, 305.

36 The circular reddish abrasion is discrete but clearly visible in large color prints. A ruler held by one of the pathologists suggests they were holding it there to measure the location and size of the red circle. A drawing of this picture made for the HSCA by artist Ida Dox (JFK Exhibit F-48) exaggerates the reddish abrasion, and the cowlick is moved to the center of the abrasion to make it more obvious (see Figure 15.3). Testimony of Ida Dox, Professional Medical Illustrator, HSCA I. While the drawing is indeed inaccurate, comparisons with the original do not suggest that the reddish abrasion was an invention of the artist, as claimed by Mantik and Aguilar. Fetzer, ed.: *Murder in Dealey Plaza*, 178, 221.

37 James J. Humes: *Pathological Examination Report A63-272*, 6.

38 Editorial note by David Mantik inserted in "Deposition of James J. Humes, M.D. Bethesda Naval Hospital Pathologist, Retired, to Assassination Records Review Board's Jeremy Gunn, 13 February, 1996," reprinted in Fetzer: *Murder in Dealey Plaza*, 450.

39 Posner, 306–7.

40 The relocation of the cowlick, made to line-up with the red circular abrasion, is the most obvious difference. Other differences are largely aesthetic.

41 James J. Humes: *Pathological Examination Report A63-272*, 3, 4, 6.

42 Beveling is a "funnel-shaped" opening, smallest at the point of entry and widening in the shape of a crater (i.e., toward the *inside* of JFK's skull). Beveling wounds help forensic pathologists identify the direction of a projectile.

43 "Part III: Observations and Conclusions Derived from the Examination of the Available Evidence," HSCA VII.

44 Testimony of Dr. James J. Humes to the HSCA.

45 This is supported by the fact that the pathologist's hand in the photo is pinching and stretching the scalp (see Figure 15.4).

46 MD 14: "Review of Autopsy Materials by Humes, Boswell and Finck," 1/26/67, 3, "ARRB Master Set of Medical Exhibits," *History Matters*; John Canal: "Were Key Autopsy Photographs Misinterpreted?," 2006 and "Historic Mix-Up by Top Forensic Experts Clouds JFK Case," 2015, McAdams, ed.: *The Kennedy Assassination*; Interviews with Cummings, Sturdivan, et al., "Cold Case JFK," 2013, *PBS: NOVA*.

47 Testimony of Dr. James J. Humes, HSCA VII; "ARRB Testimony of Charles Baxter, Ronald Coy Jones, Robert M. McClelland, Malcom Perry, Paul C. Peters, 27 Aug 1998," *Mary Ferrell Foundation*.

48 Mantik: "The Medical Evidence Decoded," 253. Mantik's measurement is based on the location of *the holes in Kennedy's jacket and shirt*, not on the autopsy report or photos. He does not consider the possibility that JFK's clothes (due to his back brace and posture) were bunched up at the neck. John Hurt, Jr.: "The Case for a Bunched Jacket," 1999; McAdams, ed.: *The Kennedy Assassination*.

49 Ibid., 239.

50 Charles Carrico, interview with Gerald Posner, March 8, 1992, cited in Posner, 309–10. Emphasis added.

51 Posner, 310–3, based on Posner's interviews with doctors Carrico, Giesecke, Jenkins, Perry, Baxter, Jones, and McClelland, March 3 to April 14, 1992.

52 Aguilar: "The Converging Medical Case for Conspiracy…," 199; McAdams: *JFK Assassination Logic*, 28–9.

53 Posner, 300. O'Connor failed to mention any of this to the HSCA in a testimony under oath, and only recalled it in the 1980s and 1990s for conspiracy authors Robert Groden and Harrison Livingstone (*High Treason*, 1989), Nigel Turner (*The Men Who Killed Kennedy*, 1988), and David Lifton (*Best Evidence: The Research Video*, 1990). O'Connor also stated that Kennedy's body arrived at Bethesda in a plain gray casket, his body wrapped in a body bag. This is contradicted by all major witnesses of the voyage to Washington and everyone in the autopsy room, who agree that the body was removed from *the damaged copper casket* purchased in Dallas, where it was wrapped in hospital bedsheets, gauze, and plastic bags. In 1986, prosecutor Vincent Bugliosi asked O'Connor during a televised mock trial of Lee Oswald why he did not share any of this with the HSCA in 1977. O'Connor said it was because no one asked him. "On Trial: Lee Harvey Oswald," dir., Ian Hamilton (1986).

54 According to the autopsy report and pictures, the cerebellum was intact. This was confirmed by the HSCA Forensic Pathology Panel. Testimony of Dr. Michael Baden, HSCA I.

55 Posner, 311.

56 Shahram Heshmat: "What Is Confirmation Bias?" *Psychology Today*, April 23, 2015.

57 This is corroborated by mortician Thomas Evan Robinson, who attended the latter part of the autopsy. Interview with Thomas Evan Robinson for the HSCA Forensic Pathology Panel by Donald A. "Andy" Purdy and Jim Conzelman, January 12, 1977, 7.

58 MD 12: "Draft of Military Inventory of Autopsy Photos and X-Rays (11/1/66)," 3, "ARRB Master Set of Medical Exhibits," *History Matters*.

59 "Photographs Nos. 17, 18, 44, and 45 show the other half of the margin of the exit wound; and also show the beveling of the bone characteristic of a wound of exit". This revision was made based on a semi-circular beveled notch in the skull (visible in this photo, slightly to the left of the center) that matched another semicircular beveled notch on a loose skull fragment (called "Harper Fragment") found in Dealey Plaza on November 23. "Review of Autopsy Materials by Humes, Boswell and Finck (1/26/67)" (MD 14), 4, "ARRB Master Set of Medical Exhibits," *History Matters*; McAdams: "The Harper Fragment: Evidence of a Shot from the Grassy Knoll?" (n.d.), *The Kennedy Assassination*.

60 Testimony of Dr. Michael Baden, HSCA I. Emphasis added.

61 Mantik: "The Medical Evidence Decoded," 292–5.

62 MD 12: "Draft of Military Inventory of Autopsy Photos and X-Rays (11/1/66)," 3.

63 ARRB Testimony of John T. Stringer.

64 Interview with Thomas Evan Robinson for the HSCA Forensic Pathology Panel, 1.

65 Ibid., 3. According to Robinson, the bones in Kennedy's face were also significantly fractured.

66 "Pareidolia: Why We See Faces in Hills, the Moon and Toasties," *BBC News*, May 31, 2013.

67 For example, Jim Fetzer: "JFK: Who's Telling the Truth: Clint Hill or the Zapruder Film?" January 12, 2011, James Fetzer: *Exposing Falsehoods and Revealing Truths*.

68 ARRB Testimony of John T. Stringer.

69 "Part III: Observations and Conclusions Derived from the Examination of the Available Evidence: Description of President Kennedy's Wounds," HSCA VII, 106.

70 See Mantik: "The Medical Evidence Decoded," 250–1.

71 Joe Durnavich: "Making Sense of the Head X-Rays," April 14, 2000, McAdams, ed.: *The Kennedy Assassination*.

72 The Anterior-Posterior (i.e.: frontal) X-ray (Figure 15.5) shows the skull rotated rearwards (i.e., chin-up) at a 30-degree angle, as if the viewer is looking up the patient's nose (this is called a "modified Waters projection"). Durnavich: "Making Sense of the Head X-Rays".

73 Mantik: "The Medical Evidence Decoded," 264–7. The "6.5-millimeter object" was first cataloged by the 1968 Clark Panel, who thought it was a fragment from Oswald's bullet. None of the pathologists remembered finding such a fragment when the Clark Panel interviewed them. This leads Mantik to claim that the "object" must have been forged between 1963 and 1968. Mantik never considers the chain of custody of the X-rays (see next), or the possibility that the radiologist and pathologists did see the "object" in 1963 but thought little of it (see next).

74 HSCA VI, "Section IV: Authenticity: Part II. Procedures Employed in Examining the Autopsy Photographs and X-Rays," 41.

75 Andrew Murphy, Dr. Aditya Shetty, et al.: "X-Ray Artifacts," (n.d.), *Radiopaedia.org*. Mantik admits that the 6.5-millimeter object looks "very transparent" on the original X-rays, more than any other apparent fragment, but rejects outright the possibility that it is an artifact. Mantik: "The Medical Evidence Decoded," 265–7.

76 If the two artifacts were metallic objects, they should both be plainly visible in the lateral X-ray of JFK's head. But that is not the case (see Figure 15.6). If the alleged bullet were intact, the lateral X-ray would certainly have captured it. If the bullet fragmented (as it should have) then it should not look anything like a perfect circle on the AP X-ray and would certainly not be identifiable as a 6.5-millimeter Carcano bullet.

77 "ARRB Testimony of Jerrol Francis Custer," 28 October 1997, 118.

78 An *ad hoc* rescue fallacy is an exceptional one-time explanation that, applied generally, would contradict the theory as a whole.

79 For instance, Mantik indulges in a five-page flight of fancy of photographic "what-ifs" in "The Medical Evidence Decoded," 273–9.

80 For example, Cary Aguilar: "Mystery of JFK's 'Second Brain'. Back and to the Left, Back and to the Left," *Consortium News*, January 7, 1999.

81 Mantik: "The Medical Evidence Decoded," 273–4. Italics in the original.

82 One of Spencer's other duties during the weekend of November 22–24, 1963, was to produce 10,000 "prayer cards" at the request of Jacqueline Kennedy. ARRB Testimony of Saundra Kay Spencer, 5 June 1997.

83 On this point Spencer's memory was fuzzy. The ARRB's Jeremy Gunn suggested the person in question was Secret Service agent James Fox, who is believed to have leaked some of the "official" autopsy pictures to the press, but Spencer remained uncertain. ARRB Testimony of Saundra Kay Spencer.

84 ARRB Testimony of Saundra Kay Spencer. Spencer said she developed 8–12 photographs. This was a "color negative C-22 process," which means they were not inter-negatives of color transparencies, the medium in which John Stringer took the "official" autopsy photographs.

85 ARRB Testimony of Saundra Kay Spencer. Emphasis added.

86 This scenario is logically inconsistent, as it requires the "extant" autopsy photographs (i.e., those taken by Stringer in Bethesda) to be developed *before* the "original" photographs were developed by Spencer, which then went missing.

87 ARRB Testimony of Saundra Kay Spencer.

88 Ibid.

89 Ibid.

90 Interview with mortician Thomas Evan Robinson for the HSCA Forensic Pathology Panel.

91 Horne made this remark on a Kennedy Forum discussion group. John Simkin, ed.: "Saundra Spencer," *Spartacus Educational: The Education Forum*, posted 19 July 2006.

92 ARRB Testimony of Saundra Kay Spencer.

93 "Chain of Custody of the Autopsy Materials," HSCA VII, Section 3, Part II.

94 This process was overseen by Admiral Burkley at the request of Robert Kennedy. "Subsequent History of the Materials," HSCA VII, Section 3, Part III.

95 The HSCA confirmed that Herman Kahn, the National Archives' Assistant Archivist for Presidential libraries, helped Novello perform this task at RFK's request. "Subsequent History of the Materials," 31.

96 Ibid., 30.

97 That is, a full-body picture of Kennedy's naked corpse. ARRB Testimony of John T. Stringer.

98 "Subsequent History of the Materials," 28.

99 Ibid., 33.

100 David Talbot: *Brothers* (2007); James Douglass: *JFK and the Unspeakable* (2008).

101 Hersh, 450–1.

102 Ermine Saner: "The President's Brain is Missing and Other Mysteriously Mislaid Body Parts," *The Guardian*, October 31, 2013; Lisa Scottoline: "Book Review: 'End of Days: The Assassination of John F. Kennedy' by James Swanson," *The Washington Post*, October 25, 2013.

103 Ibid., (n.p.).

104 "Subsequent History of the Materials," 28.

105 Saner (n.p.).

16

CROP MARKS ON MY FACE

Were Lee Oswald's backyard photos doctored?

16.1   That's my face but that's not me

There is an important scene in Oliver Stone's *JFK* in which the fictionalized New Orleans District Attorney (DA) Jim Garrison is seated in a restaurant with his assistant DAs and investigators. They are discussing some documents used by the Warren Commission to prove Oswald was guilty. One of these suspicious pieces of evidence is passed on to Garrison and critiqued by Assistant DA "Susie Cox".[1] It is a front cover of *Life* magazine featuring a full-page photograph of Lee Harvey Oswald, posing in the backyard of his rented apartment in Dallas.[2] This so-called backyard photograph shows Oswald dressed entirely in black in a kind of home-made revolutionary Marxist uniform, proudly exhibiting himself as a hunter of fascists (see Figure 16.1). He is holding a Mannlicher-Carcano rifle and two communist newspapers. On his hip sits a holstered revolver like the one he had in his possession during his arrest at the Texas Theater—the one he allegedly used to murder policeman J.D. Tippit. The film intermittently cuts to a scene depicting a pair of hands carefully cutting and pasting a picture of Oswald's head onto another man's body and pasting this composite "Oswald" onto a background resembling his backyard. "I even have doubts about this photo, boss," Susie tells Garrison, "It pretty much convicted Oswald in the public mind. Well, according to Captain Fritz, Oswald told him during his interrogation the photo was fake". The scene then cuts to a black-and-white flashback of Oswald's interrogation:

> OSWALD: That's not me.
> FRITZ: It came from Janet Williams' garage.[3]
> OSWALD: Well, I never saw that picture. It is my face, but my face has been super-imposed—the rest of the picture is not me at all. I've done a lot of photographic work, and that picture was made by someone else.[4]

DOI: 10.4324/9781003222460-20

The scene cuts back to Susie talking to Garrison's team:

> SUSIE: Oswald, who worked for Jaggars-Chiles-Stovall, did know spy photography pretty well. I took this picture to two experts. Look at the way the shadows on the nose fall in a straight line like it's high noon. But the shadow here on the ground reads like late afternoon or early morning. It's not the same time. Also look at the crop marks across the chin. It seems like his head is pasted on somebody else's body implicating him with this rifle and gun. And of the two newspapers in his hands, one is Leninist, the other Trotskyite. Any genuine Socialist would know they hate each other's politics![5]

Like much of Stone's film, this scene is based on the writings of Jim Garrison and Jim Marrs, who on this issue merely parrot Mark Lane, Robert Groden, and Jack White, all of whom claimed that this picture was fabricated to frame Oswald as a communist nut. In his 1988 memoir, Garrison says of the photos "found" by Dallas policemen in Ruth Paine's garage (see Figure 16.1):

> At first glance the photographs appeared to be of Lee Oswald. However, after study it was apparent that in each picture Oswald's face did not precisely fit the neck and body. Furthermore, the facial portrait of Oswald was exactly the same in each photograph, whereas the posture and the distance of the body from the camera differed. [...] For most people with common sense, including me, the combination of the brandished rifle and the communist newspaper raised more questions than it answered.[6]

Marrs offers his own long list of proofs that the backyard photos are fakes. In the interest of brevity, they are here paraphrased:

1. Oswald was knowledgeable enough about photography to know the photo was faked.
2. Oswald had no reason to lie about this.
3. Some of the backyard photos and negatives were suspiciously "suppressed" by Dallas Police.
4. Dallas Police had in their possession pictures of the Oswalds' empty backyard, which were then used to produce the background of the faked photos.
5. The camera that was allegedly used to take the pictures—the one submitted by Robert Oswald to the Warren Commission—was not Lee Oswald's.[7]
6. Marina's inconsistent testimony proves she was manipulated by the Warren Commission to falsely authenticate the backyard photos.
7. The photos are filled with evidence of cropping, compositing, inconsistent shadows, faulty proportions, and other proofs of falsification.
8. A single "graphics expert" (conspiracist author Jack White, famed for his theory of the "Badge Man", [see Chapter 13] and faked Zapruder film frames

FIGURE 16.1(a) Backyard photograph of Lee Harvey Oswald (CE133-A)

Source: DPD/Dallas Municipal Archives, University of North Texas Libraries (Warren Commission exhibits CE133-A, B, and C)[8]

[see Chapter 17]) are more credible than the entire House Select Committee on Assassinations (HSCA) photography panel.[9]

A central premise offered by Garrison, Marrs, and Stone to prove that these photos are fake is the fact that Oswald said so. But should we trust the presumed assassin to tell us what evidence was or was not fabricated? In addition to the fact that he, like any person suspected of a crime, is hardly an objective source on what constitutes legitimate evidence, we should also ask whether Oswald actually had, as Stone and Marrs suggest, the requisite knowledge and experience to know that a photo was doctored. Barring the obvious facts that Oswald, despite having received photography training in the military, was not an expert in "spy photography" (whatever that means) and he had only worked at Jaggars—a graphic arts company that specialized in advertising—for a few weeks in early 1963, an overwhelming amount of evidence exists to prove that Oswald deliberately lied to Fritz about these pictures.

While a Marine, Oswald served in a radar station in Japan, where he was trained to develop *aerial photography*. Upon his defection to the USSR, the Soviet KGB judged that his security clearance had been too low for him to have known major

FIGURE 16.1(b) Backyard photograph of Lee Harvey Oswald (CE133-B)

secrets concerning American U-2 spy flights. Even if he had, this would not make him any better at discerning fraudulent *portraits*. And while Jaggars did perform some printing of (almost entirely unclassified) maps for the government, Oswald never had the security clearance to work on US Army maps, nor were these developed at the Dallas location where he was employed. Garrison merely assumed that Oswald's employment at Jaggars' and company's cartography contracts for the US military were suspiciously connected, but this is yet another example of confirmation bias.[10] If he was in fact guilty of the assassination, Oswald would have had every reason to lie to Captain Fritz and claim that he had never seen these incriminating pictures before. Indeed, the number of known lies proffered by Oswald during his interrogations (e.g., concerning his ownership of a rifle, or his use of the aliases "O.H. Lee" and "A.J. Hidell"), and the subsequent evidence gathered by the Dallas Police, the Warren Commission, and the HSCA, make it highly unlikely that Oswald was truthful with Fritz.[11]

Stone's film is deliberately misleading in other ways. As stated earlier, the Dallas Police Department (DPD) found not one, but *three different photos* of Oswald sporting a Mannlicher-Carcano rifle. The Warren Commission entered two different snapshots of the backyard photos in evidence (labeled CE133-A and CE133-B) and a negative of the latter (labeled CE749, identified as "CE133-B (negative)"). For uncertain reasons, a third snapshot was not taken into evidence and remained in

FIGURE 16.1(c) Backyard photograph of Lee Harvey Oswald (CE133-C)

the possession of Dallas policeman Roscoe White, who preserved it for its historical and financial value. His widow, Geneva Dees, later produced it for the HSCA (who labeled it "133-C (Dees/White)"). According to Lee Oswald's mother Marguerite, a fourth backyard photograph of Lee holding the rifle above his head, with a note on the back dedicating the picture to his daughter June, was found by Marina on the night of the assassination. Having shown it to Marguerite, the two women talked about destroying it. Marguerite Oswald told the Warren Commission that Marina did so.[12]

The authenticity of these pictures was also confirmed by other witnesses and photography experts, supporting the Warren Commission's conclusion that Oswald thereby recorded his intention to perpetrate a political assassination. Jim Garrison disagrees, arguing that Oswald had no logical reason to incriminate himself this way:

> Had the photographs actually been the real Oswald posing prior to the assassination with a rifle in his hand, this would have been in conflict with human nature. It is very rare—if not unheard of—in the annals of assassination for the assassin-to-be to provide so much incriminating evidence against himself

in advance. It seemed plain enough to me that this was just another part of the process of setting up the patsy.[13]

Even if Garrison is being truthful, what he is offering here is a false dilemma, claiming that assassins always keep a low profile or else they are not assassins. But it should be evident to any informed critical thinker that when murder is performed as an act of *terrorism* (and that is what most political assassinations are), ideologically motivated assassins, many of whom are also emotionally if not psychologically deranged, routinely leave clues of their murderous intentions ahead of time. Many keep notebooks, pictures, letters, funerary videos, and other types of statements in their personal belongings. This was the case of Sirhan Sirhan, Robert Kennedy's murderer, and John Lennon's assassin Mark David Chapman. Countless examples of mass shooters, religious zealots, and political radicals advertising their hatred and prowess appear every year in the news and social media. The backyard photographs may not prove that Oswald was planning to murder the president, but they do suggest, if they are authentic and not some sort of joke, that he had the motive to promote Marxism violently. If we also consider that the snapshots were taken less than a month before the failed assassination attempt on General Edwin Walker, they further corroborate the authorities' conclusion that Oswald tried to kill Walker a few months before he shot Kennedy.

Conspiracists like Robert Groden and Peter Model (co-authors of *JFK: The Case for Conspiracy*, 1977) might be shown leniency for reaching a hasty conclusion based on limited evidence. But the fact that the HSCA conducted a thorough investigation (in 1979) of the backyard photographs, then published nearly 100 pages of photographic analysis by a panel of experts, makes subsequent conspiracy theorists carry a heavy burden of proof when they claim these pictures were faked. Many conspiracists have nonetheless ignored the HSCA's powerful evidence (and that of subsequent studies) showing that the backyard pictures are authentic. What follows is a summary of these findings.[14]

16.2   Hunter of fascists

According to Marina Oswald, Lee asked her sometime in late March or early April 1963 (it was a sunny Sunday afternoon, she recalled) to take pictures of him holding his rifle and newspapers. This took place in the backyard of their rented apartment, located at 214 Neely Street in Dallas, a few weeks before Lee tried and failed to assassinate retired General Edwin Walker. "He said that this was a very bad man," she told the Warren Commission,

> that he was a fascist, that he was the leader of a fascist organization, and when I said that even though all of that might be true, just the same he had no right to take his life, he said if someone had killed Hitler in time it would have saved many lives.[15]

At first, she thought it was a joke. She nevertheless complied, finding it all rather silly. Having little experience with a camera, Marina received instructions and assistance from Lee between taking each shot. However, her testimony was inconsistent as she claimed not to remember how many snapshots she took, stating sometimes she took only one, sometimes two, sometimes more. While conspiracists suggest that the Warren Commission coached her to make up this story from scratch, the inconsistencies in Marina's testimony could equally be ascribed to poor memory, stress, or the desire not to incriminate herself by admitting that she destroyed one or more pictures and negatives that she had found before the rest were discovered by the police.[16]

Three snapshots were discovered by Dallas Police on November 23, 1963, inside Ruth Paine's garage. Lee had been storing some possessions there since he had returned from New Orleans, including (until the previous morning) a Mannlicher-Carcano rifle. They also found a negative that matched one of the snapshots (CE133-B). The other negatives were never found. George de Mohrenschildt, an eccentric Russian expatriate and friend of the Oswalds, later gave the police an additional copy of CE133-A, which he said Oswald gave him in May 1963 before he left Dallas to go live in Haiti. This is the photograph that was published by *Life* in February 1964. On the back of de Mohrenschildt's copy was an inscription in Russian (possibly written by Marina[17]) that read: "Hunter of fascists—ha-ha-ha!" There was also an inscription written by Oswald's hand (confirmed by handwriting experts), which read: "To my friend George, from Lee Oswald, 5/IV/63". The date on the photograph and de Mohrenschildt's Warren Commission testimony both suggest that the photograph was developed a few days before Lee's failed murder attempt on General Walker, which occurred on April 10, 1963. Photography experts consulted by the Warren Commission confirmed that the angle of the sun and shadows and the state of the bushes in the background indicate that the pictures were taken in the early spring.[18] This means that the photographs, if authentic, were taken months before any presidential trip to Dallas was planned. If they are not authentic, it would suggest that a great deal of effort was expended to produce *a whole set* of incriminating pictures when a single one might have done the job and been harder to reveal as a fake.

FBI photography expert Lyndal Shaneyfelt examined the photographs and conducted test shots. He testified to the Warren Commission that the photos (especially CE133-B, the only one for which a negative could be examined) showed no signs of trickery and were indeed taken by Oswald's Imperial Reflex Duo Lens camera.[19] Four years later, *CBS* aired "A CBS News Inquiry: The Warren Report," a two-part investigative program hosted by Walter Cronkite. In it, photography expert Lawrence Schiller attempted to reshoot the backyard photos at the Neely Street address on a sunny late-March afternoon using a stand-in. He found that the same "inconsistent" shadows that appeared on Oswald's face in the original photos (a straight nose shadow, an angled body shadow, and shadows on both cheeks) occurred again, naturally, on their stand-in.

16.3   Autopsy of a portrait

The fact that Marina Oswald said she took the pictures herself and that the Warren Commission believed her did not convince early conspiracists. The HSCA, some of whose members *did* believe in a conspiracy, sponsored a significant investigation into the backyard photographs' authenticity. Here are their main conclusions, which help us see why the entire "fake backyard photos" theory is both logically faulty and evidentially false.

16.3.1   *The body in the photograph is distinctly Lee Oswald's*

The dimensions and size of the body in the backyard pictures relative to the size and distance of measurable objects in the background are identical to Oswald's. This includes his height, his build (in 1963), and his stance which, though somewhat unusual, was unmistakably Oswald's. Many earlier photographs reveal an idiosyncratic "Oswald lean," with his right leg locked upright and his left leg pointed forward.[20]

While conspiracists largely agree that the face in the pictures is Oswald's, they fail to consider that the number of photos of Oswald in circulation in 1963 would have been small (this was not the era of digital "selfies," after all). Oswald's haircut, weight, demeanor, and facial traits had also changed significantly over the previous years; his military and Soviet-era portraits would therefore have made him look far too young for a believable forgery. Hence, the conspirators would have needed a *recent* picture of the 23-year-old Oswald for the image to be convincing. They would have also needed an obscure photograph that could not be matched with some other original, one for which there were no other copies or negatives in circulation. This would eliminate family portraits, mug shots, ID badges, and old passport pictures as sources of false evidence. The HSCA also observed that Oswald's facial expressions changed from picture to picture. Most notably, his lips form a frown in CE133-B, while they form a smile in CE133-A. This means that the conspirators would have further and needlessly complicated their hoax by producing three different composite forgeries instead of just one.[21]

16.3.2   *The three images all came from different exposures*

Conspiracists such as Jim Marrs have claimed that the backgrounds of the three recovered backyard photos are identical. He also claims to have located and interviewed former Dallas Police and FBI photography processors who recall having seen, on the weekend of the assassination, similar photographic transparencies of the Oswalds' Neely Street backyard with no one standing in them. He therefore concludes that the background photos were composited using this original background.[22]

While Marrs' story does seem suspicious, the existence of such an image is consistent with the Warren Commission testimonies of FBI photography expert Lyndal

Shaneyfelt and Dallas Police Captain Will Fritz, who explained that once the location of the backyard photos was identified by Fritz and Special Agent Sorrels, it was examined and photographed (without Oswald standing in them, for obvious reasons) from different angles.[23] Some of these, which served as Warren Commission exhibits, feature a police detective standing in the approximate location and pose as Oswald.[24] If such pictures were used to make a fake portrait of Oswald, that means not only that the police had to be involved in the conspiracy but also they had just a few hours to fake, plant, and produce the false photographs.

The HSCA photography panel also identified slight variations between each of the three backyard photos. The movement of shadows, for instance, shows that as much as several minutes elapsed between each shot. The moving shadows also prove that the pictures were taken in reverse order (from C to B to A). This is corroborated by the fact that the photographer seems to have learned how to better position the camera from shot to shot and keep still while tripping the shutter to obtain a clearer and more centered portrait. This is consistent with Marina Oswald's claims of having had little previous experience using a camera. Studying these shots as stereopairs also helped the HSCA identify differences in parallax (the different positions of each point of view) between each snapshot and track the slight but gradual movement of the photographer toward the right before each picture was snapped.[25]

16.3.3   The photographs were all taken with the same low-quality camera

Each of the three photographs, as well as the lone surviving negative, contain recurring artifacts—scratches, areas of uneven focus, "pincushion distortion," and frame edge markings—produced by the inner apparatus of the camera while the original negative was being exposed. In other words, the camera left identical markings on every picture it took: a unique and random pattern of small imperfections that act as a sort of "photographic fingerprint".[26] Such artifacts are due to minute variations that affect each camera differently during the manufacturing process. They are a typical feature of inexpensive cameras that contain lower quality parts susceptible to bending, wear, and damage. The lower the quality of a camera's inner mechanism, the more readily identifiable its photographic fingerprint becomes. Since the edge markings are identical on each of the backyard pictures, this suggests that none of them was cropped or resized from a larger image and that they are all first-generation originals. On the other hand, this also suggests that if the backyard pictures were forged, they were produced with unsophisticated equipment, such as a worn and slightly damaged portable camera of the type Lee Oswald owned. If that were the case, however, any forgery would have been more apparent to photography experts. As the HSCA photography panel concluded:

> For this type of fakery to be successful, it would be necessary to use a large format camera with a good quality lens for the original photographs to

avoid introducing graininess, scratches, unsharpness, or distortion at this stage. Also, any alterations would have to be made on large photographs so that retouching or discrepancies could be concealed. Furthermore, the Oswald camera would have to be available to the person making the fake photographs and it would be necessary to calculate a calculation of supplementary lens focal length and original print size to obtain an in-focus image of the desired size with the fixed-focus camera. [...] Because such a process poses many technical problems, any one of which if not solved would lead to detection under close examination of the photographs, we do not believe such a procedure was used to produce the three backyard photographs of Oswald.[27]

The panel also identified unique scratches, graphite marks, and water stains on the pictures, suggesting that they were developed in a commercial outlet, not a professional studio. Since Oswald worked at Jaggars until late April 1963 and was familiar with the process of developing photographs, he may have developed the pictures himself, which explains why no one ever came forward to claim they developed that infamous *Life* magazine cover photo.

16.3.4   *The camera had to be Oswald's Imperial Reflex*

Conspirators would have had little time and opportunity to produce fake photographs, explained the HSCA photography panel:

> Aside from the obvious question of whether Oswald would place his signature on a fake picture, for the photograph to have been faked would have required access, within just a ten day period, to Oswald's backyard, his camera, his rifle (knowing that this would be the assassination weapon), and newspapers.[28]

The Dallas Police and FBI only recovered Lee Oswald's Imperial Reflex camera several months after the backyard pictures and the lone negative were discovered.[29] It was found in Ruth Paine's home by Robert Oswald on December 9, 1963, when he came by to collect the rest of his brother's belongings. He submitted it to Warren Commission investigators in February 1964 after they interviewed him in his Texas home, which is when he learned that the camera was being sought as evidence (the *Life* magazine cover photo had been published that week).[30] FBI investigators were soon able to establish that the backyard photographs were consistent with the type of film used for this camera. The HSCA Photography Panel was further able to match the frame edge markings and other artifacts found on the backyard photographs with those produced by Oswalds' Imperial Reflex on family pictures and subsequent test photographs.[31] Hence, conspirators would have had to have access to Oswald's camera, or to other pictures taken by that same camera, in order to meticulously forge every part of the camera's photographic fingerprint without also leaving any traces of having done so, such as inconsistent microscopic scratches. Considering the level of photographic technology this would require, and the limited time span available, the likelihood that this hoax could succeed is remote.

The FBI established in 1964 that the two Marxist newspapers held by Oswald, the dates of publication of which were identified, could not have reached his mailing address before March 27, 1963, and that the autographed picture given to George de Mohrenschildt did not come into his possession later than April 5.[32] The Warren Commission testimonies of Marina Oswald and George de Mohrenschildt placed these events in mid-spring, a few days or weeks before the failed shooting of General Walker, which occurred on the evening of April 10. Thus, the alleged conspirators would have had no more than a ten-day window of opportunity to pull off the whole operation at a time when Kennedy's trip to Dallas was on no one's radar and when Lee Oswald's chances of getting anywhere near JFK with a rifle were virtually nil.

16.3.5   There is no evidence of cropping, editing, or superimposing of images

The HSCA photography panel submitted the backyard pictures to several empirical tests. This included studying the grain pattern on large blowups, the comparison of stereopairs (to examine the depth of various objects), digital image processing, high-contrast analysis, and searching for inconsistent shadows, abruptly interrupted lines, scratches, contrasts, streaks, discolorations, or focus. Many conspiracists claim that the photographs were cropped, that Oswald's fingers seem unnaturally short, that his head and body are of inconsistent sizes, and that a line appears on his chin, proving that most of his head was cut and pasted onto the chin and body of a second man.

The fingers on Oswald's right hand—those holding the newspapers on CE133-A—do appear to have been cropped, especially on lower quality second-generation prints.[33] A closer look at his fingers, however (enlarged prints appear in the photography panel's report), shows them to be *curled* over the newspaper. It is useful to remember that while photographs are two-dimensional objects, the world they depict exists in three dimensions. As for the inconsistent sizes of Oswald's head and body, the panel responded that those who make such claims (namely Robert Groden) "failed to consider variations in posture and effect of tilt on the apparent length of a photographed image".[34] The panel's report includes photographic examples of a man standing erect and then slouching, whose body appears to have shrunk while the size of his head remains unchanged.

The HSCA concluded that there exists no evidence of any cropping, editing, or superimposing of different pictures. Such evidence would be easily seen, they explained, as cropped elements would look out of place when viewed in a stereoscope, appearing two-dimensional or incorrectly distanced from the rest of the body or background:

It is virtually impossible [using 1979 or older technology] to retouch one or both images in a stereo pair with enough skill to escape detection when viewed stereoscopically. [...] The falsification of stereo pairs would require extremely precise positioning of all points in one image relative to the points in the other. An error in the relative positions would be readily detected because, when the pair is viewed together, erroneously placed points would appear to lie either in front of or behind the plane in which they should be lying. It is unlikely that a sophisticated conspirator would attempt to falsify images by producing a stereo pair, since one picture would obviously be sufficient, easier to produce, and less susceptible to detection.[35]

16.3.6   The "inconsistent nose shadow" is caused by the movement of Oswald's head

In response to allegations made by Groden and Model in *The Case for Conspiracy* (1977), the HSCA ran test shots using manikins (dummies) to evaluate the shape, size, and orientation of shadows at different angles and under similar lighting conditions as those on Oswald's backyard pictures. What Groden—a self-professed photography expert—failed to do, they explained, was to account for the changing tilt *and* turn of Oswald's head and the movements of the sun and photographer between exposures. "The change in the position of the nose shadow produced by tilting the head can be nullified by rotating the head".[36] In other words, just because the shadow under the nose stayed (almost) the same, it does not mean that the head is the same from picture to picture. If Oswald's head turned to follow the camera, and if he tilted it slightly (as the photos suggest), this ensured that the shadow cast by his nose fell a similar way all three times. The HSCA report contains several test photographs that show how this process occurs.[37]

In 2009, Professor Hany Farid, director of the Neukom Institute for Computational Science at Dartmouth University, completed a three-dimensional computer modeling study of one of the backyard pictures (CE133-A) after being approached by several conspiracists.[38] Using the digital forensic tools used in the reconstruction of crime scenes, Farid noticed that a single light source (the sun) and the shadow patterns on and around Oswald were, in fact, consistent, despite the widespread assumption that they were not. "When I [first] looked at the photo," he explained,

> I didn't understand it. I didn't understand the shadows, and I do this for a living. [...] It turns out we're really bad at it. Even though our visual system is very, very good [...] we are really bad at judging shadows.[39]

Unsurprisingly, Farid's conclusions upset several conspiracists who, instead of trying to falsify his analysis, flung personal attacks at him or simply went on reporting disproven claims about the backyard pictures.[40]

16.3.7 The "chin line" is a distortion caused by second-generation prints

Finally, a major point of contention among JFK buffs is the apparent "chin line" on Oswald's face, which is most noticeable on CE133-A (Figure 16.1), and which conspiracists claim proves Oswald's face was cropped and pasted onto another body. Conspiracist publications and websites frequently replicate the version of this photo that was printed in *Life* magazine in February 1964, which happens to be a second-generation print (i.e., a picture of another picture) that lost some of its original sharpness and on which certain touch-ups were made by the magazine's editors (a softening of the shadows, for instance). While *Life* never claimed to have cropped or retouched Oswald's chin, the HSCA panel did notice that the so-called chin line is only clearly apparent in second- and third-generation images that have lost much of the original's intermediate levels of gray. What came to look like a chin line is in fact a more nuanced patchwork of shadows caused by lighting conditions and the particular shape of Oswald's lower face.

Though less obvious in other portraits, Oswald had a natural line running across his chin. It is readily evident in the mug shots taken of him on November 22, 1963.[41] Close examination also showed that part of the unusual shadow pattern was caused by a water spot that left mineral residue on the original negative. Similar water spots were observed on other parts of the same photograph.[42]

16.4 Keep it simple, stupid!

The entire theory of the faked backyard photos falls apart when investigated closely. Like a dead man on life support, the conspiracist view can only be maintained with a severe dose of paranoia and the willful ignorance of all the evidence stacked against it. This issue of doctored photographs is a clear example of how the principle of Ockham's Razor can help us remain grounded. By cutting away all unjustified assumptions and listening carefully to the insight of qualified experts, we are left with a coherent and supported demonstration that Oswald not only *was* the man in these pictures, but that he had the means, opportunity, and motive to take and process them himself (with some help from his wife).

Although conspiracists frequently claim that the backyard photographs, more than any other piece of evidence, confirmed Oswald's guilt in the eyes of the public, there is no reason for us to believe this. Public opinion is not what got Oswald killed, nor did it push the Dallas Police to arrest him. The public never plays more than a cursory role in a murder investigation, public pressure rarely sways judges' or juries' final decisions, and thus we should be thankful for this: the criminal justice system is designed to prevent public lynchings, not facilitate them. If anonymous right-wing forces removed Kennedy from office to start a war in Vietnam, initiate a draft, and conquer Southeast Asia (or any other reason offered by JFK buffs), popular opinion was most likely low on their list of priorities. And if the purpose of these pictures was to make Oswald a public scapegoat, then the conspirators gravely misunderstood their target audience.

In fact, the uninformed public has proved remarkably gullible from the beginning in accepting and spreading these unfounded claims of "fake evidence," and the backyard photographs have been used far more often as "proofs" of conspiracy than the opposite. The widely disseminated suspicions of Garrison, Groden, Marrs, Stone, and others indicate that such a fraud, if true, was so poorly orchestrated that any half-wit with a magnifying glass could solve the crime of the century in minutes, which speaks loudly of their irrational mistrust of epistemic authorities, if nothing else. On the other hand, researchers who most vocally argue that the backyard photos are genuine tend to be professional technicians and scientists who best understand the workings and limitations of the technology being discussed. If the backyard pictures are truly a hoax, then we should ask ourselves why so many experts in the science of photography were so easily duped by them, while so many amateur sleuths were able to see through this half-baked frame-up.

It is also important to realize that despite the contested authenticity of these photos, it was Oswald's *ownership* of the rifle and revolver used to kill Kennedy and Tippit that weighed against him most heavily, and there were sufficient other proofs that these were his, including purchase orders, mailbox receipts, multiple proofs of his use of aliases, and eyewitness accounts. Had Oswald survived long enough to see the inside of a courtroom, one can presume that individuals such as George de Mohrenschildt, Robert Oswald, and Michael and Ruth Paine, and maybe even Marina herself would have been convinced to testify against him or been compelled to do so and in the process confirm his ownership of these weapons, his violent tendencies, and his radical political views. Oswald could easily have been found guilty of murder without the help of "faked" photographs.

If by some unlikely chance these photographs were fakes, conspiracists still could not explain how a double of Oswald sporting a rifle and revolver could have sneaked into the Neely Street backyard undetected during a sunny spring afternoon in the company of one or more photographers—either by Oswald himself, or his house-bound wife and child, or his many neighbors. Neither can they explain where the "real" photograph of Lee Oswald's head came from. Not even Oswald himself, who claimed that the photo shown to him was fake, gave any indication of knowing where this picture came from. Such questions are largely ignored by conspiracists. Gullible readers might not take the time to consider such problems, but critical thinkers ought to.

If you're the sort of person who enjoys taking part in wild goose chases, you might find this a pretty wild one. As Garrison, Fetzer, and Marrs did, you might also conclude that the claims of self-appointed experts like Groden and White "make more sense" than mountains of evidence produced by hundreds of qualified experts, three government inquiries, and countless professional skeptics. You might even be tempted to agree with Jim Garrison who stated that

> in the absence of a rational explanation for such a suicidal picture-posing session on Oswald's part—and none was offered by either the Warren Commission or the House Committee—Groden's conclusion that the photos were fakes remains more persuasive to me.[43]

What Garrison failed to realize, and what a critical thinker must keep in mind, is that it is not the skeptic's duty to disprove every theory raised by conspiracists. Rather, it is the conspiracist's burden to prove that the reigning consensus is wrong. And in this case, the burden stacks high.

Notes

1 "Susie Cox" is a fictional character. The real Jim Garrison had no female assistant DA The film also fictionalizes other members of Garrison's team, including turncoat "Bill Broussard," loosely based on Garrison investigator William C. Wood (aka: Bill Boxley). David Reitzes: "Bill Broussard," *The JFK 100: One Hundred Errors of Fact and Judgment in Oliver Stone's JFK*, 2012, *JFK Online*.

2 The original *Life* magazine cover can be seen at: "Life Magazine for February 21, 1964, 'Lee Oswald with the Weapon He Used to Kill President Kennedy and Officer Tippit'," *The Henry Ford*.

3 "Janet and Bill Williams" are fictional names, used to refer to Ruth and Michael Paine. The reason for this change is unclear, but as with the character named "General Y," who is clearly intended to represent Brigadier General Edward G. Lansdale (see Chapters 7 and 8), this may have been done to avoid defamation lawsuits. The Paines never endorsed conspiracist views about Oswald and maintained their belief that he acted alone. Ruth and Michael Paine interviews: "Who Was Lee Harvey Oswald?" (1993), *PBS: Frontline*, November 19, 2013.

4 No notes were taken during the real interrogation. This dialogue is a selective reconstruction of Dallas Police Captain Fritz' testimony to the Warren Commission. Important parts of this testimony have been ignored by the film, namely Fritz' statement that three *different* backyard photos were found and the fact that the Dallas Police and Secret Service had to be told by Marina Oswald, who no longer lived at that address, where the picture was taken, making it less likely that the photos were forged. Testimony of J.W. Fritz, WC IV.

5 *JFK*, dir. Oliver Stone (1991). This distinction between Stalinists and Trotskyites is a silly false dilemma. There were many Marxist political associations in America and elsewhere during the 1960s that can be loosely defined as pro-Soviet (i.e., "Stalinist" or "Leninist") and anti-Soviet (i.e., "Trotskyite," "Internationalist," or "New-Left"). Yet, several examples exist of these groups collaborating, though not without friction, in civil rights protests and labor strikes during this period. Both groups were also pro-Castro, as was Oswald.

6 Jim Garrison: *On the Trail of the Assassins* (1991), 85–6.

7 Marrs is obliquely suggesting that Robert Oswald was also involved in the conspiracy to frame his brother.

8 https://texashistory.unt.edu/ark:/67531/metapth337200/ (Dallas Police Department (22/11/63), Item: DSMA_91-001-1224002-4118); https://texashistory.unt.edu/ark:/67531/metapth337630/ (Dallas Police Department (22/11/63), Item: DSMA_91-001-1203001-4084).

9 Jim Marrs: *Crossfire* (1989), 450–4. The reference made in Stone's film to two (unnamed) photography experts may refer to Major John Pickard of the photographic department of the Canadian Defense Department and retired Detective Superintendent Malcolm Thompson of the Institute of Incorporated Photographers of England, who separately claimed during the mid-1970s, after looking at *second-generation* images of these photos that they appeared to be forged. Marrs: *Crossfire*, 453. Marrs concedes that these two experts did not examine the original prints, but he does not inform the reader that

neither did anything more than a cursory examination of the images, and that both accepted the HSCA's conclusion that the original backyard photographs showed no sign of forgery. HSCA VI, Section IV-B: "Photograph Authentication," 177.

10 Posner, 89–90; Testimony of Robert L. Stovall, WC X.

11 Ibid., 22 8, 31–53.

12 Testimony of Marguerite Oswald, WC I; Testimony of Mrs. Lee Harvey Oswald, WC I; Priscilla Johnson McMillan: *Marina and Lee* (1977), 544–5, cited in Bugliosi, 179–80.

13 Garrison, 86.

14 HSCA VI, Section IV-B: "Photograph Authentication," 138–225; David Von Pein: "The Backyard Photographs," (Parts I and II) *DVP's JFK Archive*, 2015.

15 Testimony of Mrs. Lee Harvey Oswald, WC I.

16 Philip Shenon: *A Cruel and Shocking Act* (2015), chap. 18.

17 Marina could not recall whether this inscription was written by her, but she said it seemed like something she would have said. George Lardner, Jr.: "More Oswald Photo Evidence Said to Be Found," *The Washington Post*, September 15, 1978.

18 *Warren Report*, Appendix 10, "Expert Testimony: The Photographs," 592–7.

19 Ibid., 592–7.

20 David Von Pein: "The Backyard Photographs"; Peter Vronsky: "Lee – Marina Height Discrepancy Explained," (2004), *Lee Harvey Oswald in Russia*.

21 HSCA VI, Section IV-B: "Photograph Authentication," 174.

22 Marrs, 452–3.

23 This photo, titled "214 W. Neeley Back Yard," is found in *Commission Document 81.1 – AG Texas*, 228, *Mary Ferrell Foundation*. More can be viewed at *The Portal to Texas History: Dallas Municipal Archive*.

24 "B.G. Brown with Rifle in Back Yard at 214 W. Neely," *Commission Document 81.1 – AG Texas*, 240.

25 HSCA VI, Section IV-B: "Photograph Authentication," 175–6.

26 Ibid., 155.

27 HSCA VI, Section IVB1: "Addendum B: Report to the HSCA: The Oswald Backyard Photographs, by Dr. Leslie Stroebel, Mr. Andrew Davidhazy, and Dr. Ronald Francis," 214–5.

28 HSCA VI, Section IV-B: "Photograph Authentication," op. cit., 176–7.

29 Multiple searches of the Paine household uncovered photographic instruments belonging to Oswald, including a Minox-brand light meter that had belonged to Michael Paine and which was mistaken for a camera by Dallas policemen. McAdams: "Missing Minox or Major Mistakes?" (n.d.), *The Kennedy Assassination*.

30 CE2466: "FBI Report: March 16, 1964, of Interview of Robert Oswald at Denton, Tex. (CD 897, pp. 468–470)," WC XXV, 639.

31 HSCA VI, Section IV-B: "Photograph Authentication," 155–61.

32 Ibid., 176; Testimony of Lyndal L. Shaneyfelt, WC IV.

33 Robert Groden: *The Search for Lee Harvey Oswald* (1995), summarized in Fetzer and Marrs: "JFK Assassination—False Flag Attacks: How 'Patsies' are Framed: The Case of Lee Harvey Oswald," December 11, 2009, in Michel Chossudovsky, ed.: *Global Research*.

34 HSCA VI, Section IV-B: "Photograph Authentication," 175. See Figure IV-38.

35 Ibid., 146, 176.

36 Ibid., 196, caption to Figure RIT-11.

37 Ibid., 193–7 (par. 470–6).

38 Hany Farid: "The Lee Harvey Oswald Backyard Photos: Real or Fake?" *Perception*, 2009, Vol.38, PDF, *Dartmouth University*.

39 Quoted in Holly Ramer: "Hany Farid, Dartmouth Scientist, Says Controversial Oswald Rifle Photo Real," *Huffington Post* (Associated Press), November 5, 2009.

40 For example, Fetzer and Marrs: "JFK Assassination—False Flag Attacks: How 'Patsies' Are Framed…"; Fetzer: "Blowing the Whistle on Dartmouth: Hany Farid 'in the Nation's Service'," January 27, 2010, *James Fetzer: Exposing Falsehoods and Revealing Truths.*

41 HSCA VI, Section IV-B: "Photograph Authentication," 165.

42 Ibid., 164.

43 Garrison, 86. Students of logic may be able to detect an argument from ignorance and a circular reasoning fallacy in this short excerpt.

17

AMERICA'S BLOODIEST HOME VIDEO

Is the Zapruder film authentic?

17.1 A public nightmare, a private fortune

Abraham Zapruder captured one of the most watched, controversial, and blood-curdling historical events of the twentieth century on an 8-millimeter home movie. The Russian-born Dallas dressmaker, who worked in the Dal-Tex building across the street from the Texas School Book Depository (TSBD) (see Figure 2.1), brought his camera to Dealey Plaza on November 22, 1963, to film the President's motorcade.[1] Because Zapruder suffered vertigo, his administrative assistant Marilyn Sitzman agreed to stand with him atop a concrete abutment that offered a clear and unobstructed view overlooking Elm Street so that the two co-workers stood just a few dozen feet from the spot where JFK was shot. They were among the 10 or 20 witnesses closest to the event.[2]

The Zapruder film, as it soon became known, is a 26-second silent color film that captured much—but probably not all—of the assassination sequence.[3] Most notably, it captured the famous six-second sequence during which the President raises his fists to his throat and leans forward, Governor Connally grimaces and slumps into the arms of his wife, and Kennedy's head explodes graphically in a blast of brain tissue and blood.[4] Having learned from *Dallas Morning News* journalist Harry McCormack that Zapruder had filmed the scene, Special Agent Forrest Sorrels contacted him less than an hour after the assassination and requested to see the home movie.[5] Zapruder then accompanied McCormack to a local television station (WFAA-TV) to have it developed, only to learn they did not have the required technology. Zapruder nevertheless agreed to describe what he filmed during a live broadcast.[6] This is significant because no one, including Zapruder, had yet viewed the film; his televised interview was based solely on his memories of the event. Correspondence between Zapruder's hour-old memories and the undeveloped home movie is an important determinant of the film's authenticity.

DOI: 10.4324/9781003222460-21

It was then arranged for Zapruder to transport his film to the local Eastman Kodak laboratory to have it cut[7] and developed, and then to the Jamieson Film Company to produce three first-generation copies—two of which he gave to Special Agent Sorrels that very evening, after a private viewing in Zapruder's office. That same night, the Secret Service sent one copy to Washington and gave the other to the FBI. The FBI subsequently made second-generation copies. A major difference between first- and second-generation copies of the Zapruder film, apart from the latter's lower quality images, is that second-generation copies did not contain any part of the footage that appears in the sprocket hole area—the narrow, perforated strip on the left side of the original film that captured peripheral images that are not seen when projected onto a screen (see Figures 17.1 and 17.2). These images are another important factor in determining the authenticity of the existing film.

Throughout this time and into the next day, several media pressured Zapruder to sell them his film, but he was greatly disturbed by its graphic nature and the thought of it being exploited by sensationalist media.[8] He therefore requested sworn affidavits that no more copies be made without his approval, and that Kodak, Eastman, the FBI, and the Secret Service promise not to sell or give any copies to the media. In doing this, and in keeping the original copy of the film, Zapruder was retaining the publishing rights to his home movie.[9] Distraught by the sudden, intense, and unsolicited attention he was receiving, Zapruder struck an exclusive publishing rights deal with *Life* magazine editor Richard Stolley on the day after the assassination—a deal that would take the original film out of his hands under the proviso that its contents would never be shown in a graphic or morbid fashion. The two parties agreed to a substantial financial settlement (approximately $150,000) that was not disclosed at the time.[10] *Life* thus became the sole worldwide copyright owner of the original Zapruder film on November 23, 1963, and immediately set out publishing dozens of frames (except the most graphic ones).

The film was then hurriedly copied, spliced, resized, and edited to be printed as stills in the upcoming November 26 issue of *Life*.[11] Additional frames were later produced for the Warren Commission when the FBI's poorer quality second-generation copies were deemed inadequate. However, the original film was primarily viewed by the Warren Commission as a series of still photographs and published this way with the Commission's other exhibits. The original film remained in the possession of *Life* until 1968, when New Orleans District Attorney (DA) Jim Garrison subpoenaed and used it in the Clay Shaw trial. It was not seen by the wider public until 1975, when journalist Geraldo Rivera aired a bootleg copy on his talk show *Good Night America* (see Chapter 4).

This, at least, is what conspiracists call the "official story". Their own accounts of what happened to Zapruder's film are far more ambitious and sinister.

17.2 Reframing Zapruder: impeaching *Life*

The Zapruder film was controversial from the beginning. It was also exceptional: rarely have crimes been recorded this way before the advent of closed-circuit

TV and digital cameras. Many journalists, including future CBS anchorman Dan Rather, were sent to find Zapruder with the express order to buy or poach the film for an exclusive TV premiere. It was also considered unnaturally gory by the day's standards and many journalists, investigators, and civilians who viewed it that weekend expressed shock, dismay, and an unwillingness to have the late President immortalized this way. This explains why Zapruder was more than willing to let *Life* magazine, in his eyes a reputable news source, take sole responsibility for its use.

Despite the film's obvious forensic value for establishing a timeline for the assassination, early conspiracists like Mark Lane suspected it also contained proof of a second shooter, and that *Life*, the FBI, the Secret Service, and Warren Commission, by keeping the whole film from being viewed by the public, were jointly conspiring to hide more than just a gruesome historical relic. Indeed, such secrecy seemed to suggest that these groups were covering up their own duplicity. When Jim Garrison grew convinced that Lee Oswald was part of a CIA cell group operating in his New Orleans parish, he began repeating the claims of JFK buffs that the unseen Zapruder film surely contained something explosive. It might even have been cut and reframed—as Mark Lane convinced him it was—to frame Oswald more easily. Why else would *Life* keep it locked up in a vault all these years, Garrison asked.[12] This rhetorical question circulated like a virus until Oliver Stone's *JFK* gave it worldwide believability.

Richard Stolley, who negotiated the original deal between *Life* and Zapruder, has defended *Life*'s stranglehold on the film during those early years and corrected Stone's allegation of a 12-year long cover-up:

> *Life* did not bury the Zapruder film for 12 years, as Stone charges. All the relevant images were printed immediately except for frame 313 [See Figure 17.1]. We felt publishing that grisly picture would constitute an unnecessary affront to the Kennedy family and to the President's memory. Today, that may seem a strange, even foolish, decision. But this was 1963, a few years before Vietnam brought carnage into American living rooms. [...] *Life* published frame 313 in 1964 and several times later, and for years urged that the Kennedy investigation be reopened.[13]

Indeed, *Life* made the film available to all government commissions, many private media investigators, New Orleans DA Jim Garrison, and also private detective and conspiracist author Josiah Thompson (*Six Seconds in Dallas*, 1967), a former *Life* employee. It was during these exchanges that bootleg copies were made and distributed by conspiracists Mark Lane, Robert Groden, and others. Many conspiracists have nevertheless maintained that *Life* was a willing participant in a massive cover-up, if not in the assassination itself.

One of the "proofs" of conspiracy used by Garrison was the fact that two of the Zapruder film frames published by the Warren Commission were printed out of sequence. According to Garrison, these frames (314 and 315) had to have been *intentionally* switched to create the false impression of a "head snap"—that is, that Kennedy's head moved violently forward before it went backward—to reinforce the Lone Gunman Theory.[14] While this explanation is not impossible, FBI director J. Edgar Hoover had already explained this in 1965, two years before Garrison opened his investigation, stating that the switch was a printing error. Whether or not we accept Hoover's explanation, this simpler account is made stronger by the fact that other frames were also switched or missing from the Warren Commission's exhibits. These received less attention from conspiracists than did frames 314 and 315 because their contents were less controversial than the famous "head snap". Indeed, *Newsweek* investigated the issue in 1967 and, after interviewing former Warren Commission council Wesley Liebeler, concluded that this error occurred because the Commission was operating on a tight schedule that led it to miss the error.[15] The same year, the *New York Times* interviewed *Life's* managing editor George Hunt, who admitted that some frames were misplaced or destroyed by lab technicians while producing separate frames from the film. *Life* then published four of the "new" frames that were missing from the Warren Commission exhibits.[16] Regardless, the FBI had other undamaged second-generation copies that were viewed by Warren Commission staff. Hence, any frames that were switched or went missing while in *Life's* custody were not irremediably lost, and such errors were eventually identified and corrected. Unfortunately, these errors were now in the public domain, and popular opinion can't be easily swayed with a published retraction. These corrections also proved fruitless in preventing Lane, Garrison, Stone, and others from continuing to claim that the film was intentionally doctored.

We should question whether this re-sequencing of Zapruder film frames, intentional or not, would have given any more strength to Garrison's theory of a second shooter. After all, the Warren Commission did not base its conclusion that Oswald acted alone on a barely discernible head snap but on the ballistic evidence, the autopsy report, the testimonies of credible witnesses like Zapruder and Sitzman (who together shot the film), and all the evidence that connected Oswald to the recovered rifle, pistol, and bullets (see Chapters 11–13). Garrison's argument concerning re-sequenced film frames is therefore a red herring.

We should also take note that the head snap—real or faked—is barely perceptible when projected at the film's normal speed of 18.3 frames per second. Hence, the only dupes here would have been the few Commission staffers who studied individual frames but never watched the film through a projector. Given that *Life* did not own the only available version of the film but that other first- and second-generation copies were being held by the Secret Service, the FBI, the Zapruder family, and, later, the National Archives,[17] the conspiracist argument that *Life* helped cover up a conspiracy is another paradoxical example of hypercompetent assassins leaving an entirely unnecessary trail of incriminating and useless false evidence.

Despite claiming that the "head snap" was faked, Mark Lane and Jim Garrison simultaneously believed that the rest of the film was authentic enough for the whole world to see it. Multiple low-quality bootleg copies were thus produced and circulated by Lane in 1968 at the urging of Jim Garrison,[18] proving that the New Orleans DA was just as willing to break property rights laws and the chain of custody for state evidence as he accused the FBI and federal government of doing.

Groden did the same in the mid-1970s and was instrumental in getting the film played on national television (see Chapter 4). The Zapruder film thereby gained a certain mystique as an underground snuff film, a gateway drug into the shadowy world of conspiracy junkies, decades before the invention of *YouTube* and *Facebook*.

17.3   Reading between the frames: the archeology of paranoia

A new wave of Zapruder film denialism emerged during the late 1970s following a surge of widespread mistrust caused by the Watergate scandal, the House Select Committee on Assassinations (HSCA)'s lack of conclusive evidence to prove or disprove the existence of a grassy knoll shooter, the rapid growth of electronic media, and the rising public awareness of technological deceptions like subliminal messages in TV and magazine ads.[19] As amateur conspiracy sleuths pored over bootlegged Zapruder films, watching it slowly and repeatedly, frame-by-frame, or enlarged to reveal discrete "clues," a new cohort of Kennedy buffs came to believe that the film was, in its entirety, a finely crafted piece of propaganda. Some even wondered whether Zapruder himself was an agent of the faceless murderous cabal.

One influential Zapruder film denier was Jack White—the same who proposed, with Gary Mack, the "Badge Man" grassy knoll shooter theory (see Chapter 13). In a photographic essay titled "The Great Zapruder Film Hoax," White allegedly proves:

1.   That the Zapruder film, the Nix film, and other photos of the murder have all been altered;
2.   That the Zapruder film itself might not have been taken by Abraham Zapruder;
3.   That a handful of surviving and unaltered photographs provide proof of alteration;
4.   That in the Zapruder film as it exists today, people who were present at the time are no longer present; people who were not present at the time are present; the sun changes its position in the sky and casts false shadows; people remain mysteriously motionless when they should be moving; small people grow tall and tall people shrink; people make impossible rapid movements; signboards and lampposts reposition themselves; on and on—impressive evidence of alteration that emerges from the extant photographic record.[20]

Another is David Mantik, the radiation oncologist who extensively argued that the Kennedy autopsy evidence was faked (see Chapter 15). In a 1998 essay titled "Paradoxes of the JFK Assassination: The Zapruder Film Controversy," Mantik states:

> My own interpretation of all the evidence is that JFK was hit first in the head from the rear while slumped forward such as in Z[apruder frame]-312, then struck in the head for a second time (but from the front) while sitting erect. Such a posterior headshot has been strongly supported by the pathologists for

over 35 years but they persistently ignored evidence for the second headshot. Only the second headshot produced a spray of blood; not enough blood could have accumulated before the first shot to give rise to such a visible spray. The bloody spray now seen at Z-313 [see Figure 17.1] was probably imported from the image of the second headshot (which is no longer seen in the film).[21]

It can be tempting to dismiss such authors as either delusional or charlatans. Many have. The philosophical principle of charity should, however, lead us to assume that these arguments were made in good faith. Even if such claims seem far-fetched, Mantik, White, and many others believe them to be rational and provable. They therefore deserve a rebuttal. On the other hand, it could take a whole book and multiple expert studies—such as the ones performed by the HSCA on Oswald's backyard photos—to address each of their allegations. Let us therefore focus on four salient questions raised by these authors: (a) are the witnesses who claim to have seen an "unaltered" Zapruder film reliable? (b) Did the chain of custody of the Zapruder film allow it to be faked? (c) Did the eyewitnesses to the assassination see something different than what the "extant" film shows, and if so, can we trust their reports? (d) Did the technology used by Zapruder and the editing tools available to the FBI, Secret Service, and *Life* magazine (among others) allow them to fake the film?

17.3.1   Wet Brain Man

According to Mantik, the Zapruder film was secretly confiscated and heavily edited sometime between Friday, November 22, and Monday, November 25, 1963, after which it re-emerged as an altogether different "extant" film than the original that Zapruder pulled out of his camera. The evidence for this, Mantik argues, is that some eyewitnesses viewed and manipulated a different version of the film than the one the frames of which were shown to the public by *Life* and the Warren Commission. His main witness is Homer McMahon, a former employee of the National Photographic Interpretation Center (NPIC)—the CIA's and Department of Defense's joint aerial reconnaissance laboratory. McMahon told the Assassination Records Review Board (ARRB) in 1997 that he worked on a film in 1963 that was delivered to his Washington lab during the weekend of the assassination by a Secret Service agent who presented himself as "Bill Smith," who said he transported the film there from a Kodak laboratory in Rochester, New York, and who remains unidentified to this day. According to Mantik, this occurred sometime before Kennedy's funeral on Monday, November 25:

> McMahon recalls seeing the film projected at least 10 times that night [which night this was, Mantik does not say]. It was his opinion, based on this viewing, that JFK was shot 6 to 8 times from at least three directions, but the Secret Service agent told McMahon that there were just three shots, and that these

all came from the Book Depository. McMahon and his assistant were told to keep their work secret and were prohibited even from telling their supervisors (who were not present).[22]

Mantik identifies one of McMahon's assistants as Morgan Bennett "Ben" Hunter. Another co-worker remains anonymous. Former ARRB military analyst and conspiracist Douglas Horne states that McMahon refused to name this third person "because he is still current" (whatever that means).[23] Mantik gives us little more evidence than this to support his timeline of the original film's disappearance from Dallas for several hours (or days) on the weekend of November 22–24.

This brief account raises several questions. Uncertainty remains regarding which night these men allegedly saw the film that was delivered to them and regarding the identity of the enigmatic "Bill Smith" (so that McMahon's claims might be verified). Further questions ought to be asked regarding how the film could have been carried from Dallas to Rochester, then to Washington, where it was edited for several hours (or days), and finally returned to Dallas without Abraham Zapruder and early viewers of the film becoming aware of it having been altered or missing.[24]

Mantik is also making several misleading assumptions, namely that we should be surprised that CIA lab technicians trained to process spy plane photography were prohibited from speaking of their work outside the office; that lab supervisors might be absent from work in the middle of the night on a weekend; and that anybody, civilian or CIA, might be told not to discuss forensic evidence of a high-profile murder while the investigation is ongoing. As employees of the CIA and US Air Force, both McMahon and Hunter would already be subjects to various security and nondisclosure restrictions. This would no doubt apply to *any* work they performed at the NPIC, not just evil conspiracies.

McMahon also remarked in his 1997 ARRB deposition that he had not seen the video in over 35 years and that his memory was blurry. The name "Zapruder" also meant nothing to him. Indeed, he referred to it many times as the "Dal Kruder" film. Throughout his deposition, McMahon also gives no indication that he participated in altering *the contents* of the film, only that he helped produce a few dozen internegatives and color prints of various frames, enlarging them and enhancing their sharpness and "seeability" for Secret Service and FBI use.[25] Since McMahon claims that "Agent Bill Smith" first took the film to Rochester before flying it to the NPIC lab in Washington, conspiracists could suspect that the "real" editing happened there. But if that were so, McMahon would have seen the same "extant" film that was kept many years by *Life* magazine (or something close to it), which today proliferates everywhere on the internet, and not a different version in which Kennedy is "shot 6 to 8 times from at least three directions".[26] Simply put, Mantik is cherry-picking various factoids that, taken individually, seem suspicious enough, but once strung together create a nonsensical story.

And what about the credibility of Mantik's witnesses? According to the ARRB, Ben Hunter, McMahon's only named assistant, confirmed having worked on a home movie of Kennedy's death in the days that followed the assassination but cautioned his interviewers that his memory was "extremely fuzzy" and McMahon would no doubt remember the facts better than he did. This appears to be the case. There are some major discrepancies between the two men's testimonies. Rather than Secret Service Agent "Bill Smith," for instance, Hunter remembered a CIA agent called "Captain Sands" delivering the film to the NPIC lab and looking over their work, though he recalled few details. According to ARRB interview notes, Hunter said that

> the assigned task was to analyse (i.e.: locate on the film) where occupants of the limousine were wounded [...] and then produce color prints from appropriate frames [...]. His memories of film content were limited to seeing a skull explosion, bone fragments, and Jackie Kennedy crawling on the trunk of the car [...] but *he seemed convinced that it was the Zapruder film based on subsequent viewings of it over the years in documentaries.*[27]

Whatever Mantik might think Hunter was doing that night, it certainly doesn't seem to have been forging new evidence so much as the same sort of photographic analysis his lab was specialized to do and did regularly, only this time it concerned a home movie of the President's murder, not aerial photography.

Mantik's star witness is also highly questionable. McMahon's deposition is that of an aging man with a porous memory, a man straining to recall experiences he half-remembered and half-imagined decades later. While this may sound like a personal attack, McMahon described himself in his testimony as having a "wet brain" a claim Mantik might have been wise to pay closer attention to,

> [JEREMY] GUNN: Do you have any recollection now as to anything that was in the other part of the, the double 8 picture, the part that is not in the assassination sequence?
>
> MCMAHON: Ah, *I have senile dementia;* I, I can't remember, really—anything. Most of, of my reflections are, are, are what I have recalled and remembered after the fact. In other words, I did it once, and then I recalled it, and remembered it. I don't know how the mind works, but I do know that I—that I'm not—OK, *I'm a recovering drug addict and alcoholic.* Do you know what a "wet brain" is? You're looking at one. I damn near died, and *I'm not a competent witness,* because I don't have good recall [...].
>
> GUNN (21:41): With, with regard to the other events that you talked about, ah, what, what is your sense of how accurate your memory is of that?
>
> MCMAHON: I just told you, I don't, I don't have a full deck. Ah [chuckling], I don't know how, how accurate I am, I am presenting anything here. So, this is not—at the time I did it, I was not—I was not impaired, but I later became impaired. So, whether you're talking to a reliable witness or not is up to you to decide [chuckling].[28]

McMahon appears to be saying he had been diagnosed with Wernicke-Korsakoff syndrome, a medical disorder colloquially referred to as "wet brain" disease. According to the US National Library of Medicine, the condition is a combination of encephalopathy and psychosis brought on by a deficiency of thiamine (vitamin B1) to the brain, often brought on by severe alcoholism. The condition can cause irreversible brain damage and, untreated, can lead to death. "Some symptoms, *especially the loss of memory* and thinking skills, may be permanent".[29] Other symptoms include confusion, hallucinations, and confabulations. Needless to say, a person diagnosed with "wet brain" disease has a highly unreliable memory and McMahon is clearly extending a warning about his mental state to the ARRB staff—one of whom, Douglas Horne, has gone on to publicize McMahon's testimony as damning proof of a conspiracy (leaving out the whole part about his "wet brain").

It is, of course, logically *possible* that McMahon saw a different film than the one Abraham Zapruder sold to *Life*. Far more probably, he may have just misinterpreted what he first saw, so that "Agent Bill Smith" (whatever his real name might be) felt the need to rein in the man's imagination, much as *Dallas Morning News* journalist Jim Featherston tried (and failed) to do the previous day with Jean Hill while he stood with her in the Dallas County Sherriff's office (see Chapter 13). Given the lack of support for Mantik's and Horne's interpretation of McMahon's testimony, it may be simpler to believe McMahon himself, who admitted he wasn't at all sure what parts of his story were true and what parts he made up. In a case like this one, it's best not to jump to conclusions, especially when the only available witness is so clearly unreliable.

17.3.2   The chain of custody

Other than McMahon and Hunter, could someone else—at the NPIC or elsewhere—have doctored the Zapruder film? There is a significant weakness in Mantik's timeline that makes this close to impossible, which is that the Zapruder film's chain of custody is airtight. Given what we know of Zapruder's handling of the film, there was little opportunity for anyone to "borrow" and edit his film with or without his consent. If McMahon and Hunter did see a home movie of the assassination (and there is no reason to doubt that they did), it would most likely have been one of the copies Zapruder gave to Special Agent Sorrels, or a copy of one of these copies, especially if they handled it later than the night of November 22–23, because by the night of Saturday, November 23–24, the out-of-camera original—the one sold to *Life* by Zapruder—had already been flown to Chicago, where photo editors began preparing film frames for publication. The pictures hit the newsstands three days later, on Tuesday, November 26, giving the supposed conspirators less than a day to remove, transport, alter, and return the original film to Zapruder.[30]

Josiah Thompson, a philosophy professor turned private detective and JFK buff, explains in "Why the Zapruder Film is Authentic" (1998) that from the moment Zapruder recorded the film to the moment it was given to *Life*'s Richard Stolley on

November 23, the camera and original film never left Zapruder's eyesight or personal safe. Throughout those two hectic days, the camera was carried by Zapruder, the film was removed by Zapruder, it was handed by him to the Kodak lab technicians, and he remained present during the developing, copying, and viewing of the film by the Secret Service—viewings that contributed to his excessive stress and reported nightmares. This was done at the recommendation of Zapruder's lawyer to maintain his claim of ownership over the valuable document, and also of Agent Sorrels, who understood the forensic importance of an unbroken chain of evidence to prosecute the assassin. By keeping the film and Zapruder together, the chain of evidence was never broken. The Zapruder family also maintained ownership of a first-generation copy for the next three decades.[31] Even though Zapruder told the Warren Commission he had kept none, the existence of this additional copy was confirmed by the ARRB.[32] "At no time during this hectic weekend," Thompson explains, "did the original of the film ever leave the custody and control of Abraham Zapruder and *Life* magazine".[33]

Given the additional fact that Ben Hunter believed he had worked on a 16-millimeter and not an 8-millimeter sized film, that he had a "reasonably strong impression" that there were no images present in the sprocket holes of the film he examined, and that the film was "not high resolution,"[34] it is reasonable to conclude that Hunter and McMahon handled a second-generation copy of the film, not the original. Hunter also estimated that he and McMahon took between five and seven hours to produce a few dozen still frames, negatives, and test prints of the film they received. It is therefore hard to conceive how a major editing job, with all the complex changes Mantik and White claim were made to it, could have been performed clandestinely and returned in time *to be viewed for the first time* by Zapruder and the other civilians who watched the original film on or before November 23.

Jack White's argument takes us much deeper down the rabbit hole than Mantik's. He suggests that Zapruder's original film was most likely destroyed and replaced by a second film taken by an anonymous co-conspirator. This of course begs the question: who else could have taken a film of the assassination at the same time and from the same vantage point as Zapruder? Unless we posit that Zapruder's assistant Marilyn Sitzman was a co-conspirator, filming the scene unbeknownst to the man who stood right beside her and many other witnesses, such as journalist Harry McCormack who saw nobody standing near them, it is hard to conclude that more than one "Zapruder" original could exist. This line of reasoning is based largely on White's analysis of low-resolution blowups of pictures taken by bystanders Mary Moorman, James Altgens, Jim Towner, and Charles Bronson—all of whom stood *on the other side* of Elm Street. White argues, for instance, that stills taken from the Bronson home movie show Marilyn Sitzman standing *in front* of Zapruder during Kennedy's passage, blocking the view of Zapruder's camera from the Kennedy limousine. White therefore concludes that it was *impossible* for Zapruder to film that fatal scene in its entirety. Ergo: a whole other film has to exist.[35]

This argument is problematic for many reasons. Since White believes that *all* pictures and films taken in Dealey Plaza might have been doctored, it begs the question as to why we should consider anything Charles Bronson filmed as more authentic than Zapruder's. What counts as authentic for White turns out to be whatever best fits his foregone conclusion that Kennedy *had* to be shot by a man in the bushes. It must also be said that some colorizing, retouching, and editing work was performed by White to make his presumptions visible to his readers, a procedure he also performed on his pictures of "Badge Man" (see Chapter 13).

17.3.3   The reliability of eyewitnesses

According to Mantik, a surefire way to verify the authenticity of the Zapruder film is to compare it to the testimonies of Dealey Plaza eyewitnesses. Mantik argues that wherever eyewitness reports diverge from the Zapruder film or other films and photographs, one should always take the side of the eyewitnesses since their memories are not likely to be manipulated by conspirators the way images can. Based on "a careful review of the eyewitnesses," he writes, we can conclude that, *contra* Zapruder, Kennedy's limousine came to a *complete stop* while driving down Elm Street, during which time

> JFK most likely slumped forward twice, once after the throat shot, and then immediately after the fatal headshot (a motion not seen in the extant film). Between these two events, it is most likely that Jackie (slowly) lifted JFK to an erect position so that she could examine his head closely. [...] It seems likely that this upward movement, in a later version of the film (unnaturally accelerated by excised frames), has come to be seen as the head snap.[36]

Mantik reaches this conclusion by combining elements of eyewitness reports that appear to contradict the Zapruder film, namely those of bystanders Jean Hill, Mary Moorman, Bill Newman, and patrolmen Bobby Hargis and B.J. Martin. Of particular interest to him are claims that the limousine slowed down or stopped or claims that offer a conflicting account of the movement of JFK's body during the sequence.[37]

Rather than considering that these eyewitnesses might have misperceived, misinterpreted, or misremembered what happened, Mantik is convinced that their memories take precedence over all video footage and photographs that disconfirm their story. "When a simple and important event occurs," he argues, "humans can be quite remarkable for recalling it with consistency and with accuracy. In the heat of debate, it is precisely this fact that is forgotten".[38] A piece of evidence like the Zapruder film, which no one would dare contradict, he argues, must therefore have been altered to pre-emptively discredit the witnesses who saw or heard multiple shooters.[39] "Without the Zapruder film," he explains, "we would be forced to rely on the reports of eyewitnesses [...who] almost uniformly recalled a limousine stop (albeit a very brief one) in Dealey Plaza—in direct contradiction to the extant Zapruder film".[40] Thus, according to Mantik, because the Zapruder film does not capture any sign of this alleged limousine stop, it is necessarily a forgery. This is another example of the circular reasoning fallacy.

In his reading of eyewitness reports, Mantik commits many typical errors found in conspiracist literature. First, he makes selective use of testimonies (what statisticians call sampling bias). A cautious historian would first assess the similarities and differences in the testimonies of all available witnesses before determining which of them are most credible. It is rare that all witnesses to a public event will describe it the same. Hence, the memories shared by a majority are usually more reliable than those of a minority, particularly when the minority holds clashing accounts. Consider the reports of shots fired in Dealey Plaza (see Chapter 13). While several earwitnesses heard fewer or more than three shots, a majority reported three, and they did so before the media could tell them that three rifle slugs had been found near the TSBD's sixth-floor window. Mantik makes no reference to the overall number of witnesses at the scene (not even an approximation), nor to the proportion who said Kennedy's car either stopped, slowed, or drove past at the same speed.[41] He sometimes refers to "some" witnesses, more often to "many," and more than once to "*the* witnesses" as if they all shared his belief that the limousine stopped while JFK was shot from both sides.

In doing so, Mantik gives no consideration to the fact that some witnesses are more credible than others. Numerous conditions can influence one's reliability: mental health, sharper senses, emotional stability, a reputation for circumspection and truth-telling, an expertise in the subject matter (e.g., firearms, acoustics, engineering, etc.), proximity to the event, and the ability to focus and recall particular details. Mantik does not bear any of this in mind. Some of the witnesses on his short list—such as Jean Hill, Ed Hoffman, Beverly Oliver, and Gordon Arnold—are dubious at best.[42] Others—such as Abraham Zapruder, Marilyn Sitzman, Gail and Bill Newman, James Altgens, and Nellie Connally, all of whom said they saw the right side of Kennedy's head explode long before they saw the Zapruder film—are largely ignored by Mantik. And although many other witnesses believe they saw the limousine slow down, few described it as coming to a halt.[43]

Second, Mantik presents inaccurate overgeneralizations of witness reports. He claims, for instance, that the witnesses "speak with almost one voice,"[44] and makes little distinction between witnesses who (a) merely claimed the limousine slowed, (b) claimed that it *nearly* stopped but didn't, and (c) claimed it stopped for a second or longer. Very few witnesses ever claimed the latter, and certainly not contemporaneously and on the official record. A notable exception is Jean Hill (see Chapter 13), who not only claimed that the limousine stopped, she also said she had the impression that *everything* stopped, which might suggest that she was in shock. Many of Mantik's eyewitness reports are also anecdotal: second-hand accounts, the accuracy of which cannot be verified, often because the original source is deceased. Mantik cites several witness interviews conducted by fellow conspiracists decades after the fact that often contradict their earlier statements. There is little good reason to believe that later statements are more accurate than earlier ones, particularly when the earlier ones were sworn affidavits and later ones were not subject to perjury laws.

Third, Mantik makes use of faulty analogies[45] to argue that his short list of handpicked witnesses is more reliable than any film or photograph. Mantik suggests that, as a doctor, he has routinely relied on the medical histories of his patients to diagnose their ailments. These medical histories are usually given by the patient himself (or a close family member) and they tend to be reliable. "Almost always, by the time he has finished, the diagnosis is obvious".[46] Hence, he argues, people are generally trustworthy witnesses of their own experiences. But while this may be true of medical histories, first-hand accounts are quite different when they describe *sudden*, *brief*, and *shocking* events like those that happened in Dealey Plaza. While one may have faithful recall of a sequence of *recurring* symptoms, it is incorrect to assume that this same person would accurately remember a brief and singular external event like an assassination.

A second analogy offered by Mantik is a comparison between the eyewitness reports of a crime and those of a sport. After viewing a major sporting event only once, he explains, many sports fans remember with near exactitude a particular play or sequence of plays, sometimes many years later. "How is it possible that we could so easily agree on the central facts," he asks, "if eyewitnesses have such poor recall for events? The fact is that they don't, at least not for events that are reasonably simple and that are also significant in some way to the viewer".[47] What makes viewers of crimes and sporting events similar, Mantik suggests, is the fact that both types of events are "simple" and "significant". However, viewing a live sports game and viewing a crime unfolding close by have fundamentally different impacts on the viewer's recall. For example, they contain wildly different levels of predictability and danger. In any televised sports venue, there is often a shower of instant replays and play-by-play analysis. These reinforce the witness's memory by repeating the same information multiple times from different viewpoints. But anyone who has been to a live sporting event with no replays or announcers can attest to the general confusion a crowd can experience when an unexpected event occurs, such as a fumbled football or a deflected hockey puck. It also explains why live audiences are less likely to accept a controversial (but correct) referee's call compared to those who, viewing from the comfort of home, are offered multiple replays and the analysis of commentators. Sports fans are also equipped with a set of expectations drawn from their knowledge of the rules of the game and previous experience watching or playing the sport. In other words, they can *anticipate* familiar patterns, an ability that nonfans decidedly lack (which explains why my Irish-born wife finds ice hockey confusing). This ability to watch and predict the immediate future is reminiscent of expert chess players' ability to anticipate their opponent's next moves long before they occur, not as spontaneous events but as part of a limited set of possibilities.

The witnesses who viewed the Kennedy assassination, on the other hand, were far more likely to be confused by those rifle shots. Having been immersed in festive anticipation for dozens of minutes or longer, most witnesses would have needed several seconds or longer to adapt to unanticipated new circumstances. Unsurprisingly, a large proportion of Dealey Plaza witnesses mistook the first shot for a firecracker or backfire. Abraham Zapruder even testified that, after seeing Kennedy raise his arms to his throat, he believed that the President was joking around: "For a moment I thought it was, you know, like you say, 'Oh, he got me'".[48] Gail Newman made similar remarks in her WFAA-TV interview. This is not proof that the few witnesses who said the car stopped were mistaken, but it does suggest that, like everyone else, they were likely confused during the 6–12 seconds of the shooting. It was a very brief time span, bathed in confusion for all who looked on, with the sudden realization of danger threatening all those who stood near Kennedy's vehicle.

A third and final analogy in Mantik's essay compares his (undefined) group of conspiracy witnesses to the Marshall Experiment, a 1971 University of Michigan study that tested the recall capabilities of eyewitnesses after viewing a two-minute video, the purpose of which was to assess the ability of witnesses to recall complex events during a courtroom examination.[49] Mantik tells us that these witnesses "confronted with leading interrogation in a challenging atmosphere testified with approximately 83% accuracy and 84% coverage [of salient items]". He therefore concludes, "contrary to what adherents of [Zapruder] film authenticity have claimed, the Marshall experiment has shown convincingly that [...] a blanket statement of eyewitness unreliability is simple minded".[50] While this analogy seems more appropriate than the first two, Mantik is in fact misinterpreting the conclusions of this study. If witnesses of a crime can be considered reliable when testifying a short while later "in a challenging atmosphere," that may lend more credibility to the supporters of the Warren Commission than to conspiracists like Mantik who hold that the Warren Commission badgered and tricked its witnesses into promoting the "official story". Mantik also commits the fallacy of division[51] by assuming that the *overall* accuracy of witness reports implies that *individual* witnesses are equally trustworthy. In this case, Marshall et al. argued that courtroom witnesses *in general* are reliable. They did not attempt to prove that *individual* witnesses are necessarily reliable. Though their witnesses, *as a group*, recalled information accurately 83% of the time, but that does not mean that *all* witnesses were accurate 83% of the time. Rather, this figure suggests that 17% of witness claims are inaccurate, possibly wildly so. If we assume that some individuals in a sample group have excellent recall, which is often the case, we must accept that other witnesses in the same group score rather poorly to produce the *average* scores reported by Marshall. Hence, an 83% of accuracy ratio, if correct, does not prove that a specific witness (e.g., Jean Hill) is highly credible, nor even that ten witnesses out of several dozen (arbitrarily chosen by Mantik) should be considered reliable. On the contrary, the small group of divergent witnesses is more likely to have less accurate recall. Since Mantik has not assessed the total number of witnesses in Dealey Plaza who did not believe that the limousine actually stopped, this means that the claims of his ten arbitrarily plucked witnesses could all be unreliable.

Mantik also fails to point out that the Marshall study was not conducted on individuals under duress. The experiment's subjects were asked to view a two-minute video in a nonthreatening setting and asked to focus on its contents to report on them later. It lacked the element of surprise, the threat of danger, and the emotionally charged atmosphere that the assassination witnesses experienced. The film Marshall's subjects viewed was also two minutes long. That's 10 times longer than the maximum period it took for three shots to be fired at Kennedy (and 20 times longer than Mantik's preferred six-second scenario).

A more appropriate analogy can be drawn between the Dealey Plaza witnesses and what English professor Mary Karr replicated on numerous occasions in her graduate English seminar at Syracuse University.[52] In this recurring experiment, Karr staged an argument between herself and a colleague while her literature class was in session. The two professors would wander in and out of the classroom or speak over the phone, bickering intermittently over an extended period while the tone escalated. Karr eventually asked her students to write an account of what they had witnessed. What she discovered was that her students all tended to write a slightly different account, shaping the events through the lens of their own expectations, experiences, and values. What emerged from this experiment was a tapestry of disparate viewpoints—those of the feminist, the sexist, the member of a racial minority, the victim of abuse (etc.) who, while giving similar accounts of the sequence of the events, projected their personal concerns onto the story to help it make logical sense. While witnessing an assassination is no doubt different from watching one's teacher lock horns with a possible stalker or jilted lover, this experiment demonstrates that human brains are not objective recording devices. Rather, they are interpretation organs, acknowledging stimuli that are assumed to be meaningful and rejecting or reinterpreting those that make little sense. This, and the power of culture, rumors, fears, or conspiracy theories to shape our expectations, gives us insight into the production of false memories, or what psychiatrist Elizabeth Loftus, an expert in the formation of eyewitness memories, calls the misinformation effect:

> When people who witness an event are later exposed to new and misleading information about it, their recollections often become distorted. [...] Misinformation has the potential for invading our memories when we talk to other people, when we are suggestively interrogated or when we read or view media coverage about some event that we may have experienced ourselves.[53]

Finally, we can legitimately wonder why a small but disparate set of witnesses claimed they saw the President's car either slow down or stop. Dr. Mantik is not wrong to claim that the Zapruder film does not clearly capture Kennedy's limousine slow down significantly. However, his logic is faulty when he assumes that the only two possible explanations for this discrepancy are that (a) all eyewitnesses who saw the car either slow down or stop are mistaken, or that (b) the Zapruder film is a hoax. This is a false dilemma because a third and simpler explanation exists, one that accounts for all known evidence.

Other home movies taken that day, such as those of Marie Muchmore, Charles Bronson, and Orville Nix, captured at least some of the limousine's movement down Elm Street. All three of these films, unlike Zapruder's, record a slight deceleration of the limousine, followed by its sudden acceleration toward the triple underpass. It should be evident to anyone viewing these films that SS-110-X was traveling very slowly through Dealey Plaza from the time it turned onto Houston from Main Street until the shooting began. The car does not seem to pick up much speed until after Kennedy is shot in the head. This is not proof of a conspiracy: all major supporters of the Lone Gunman Theory accept that the car was moving this slowly. These films are also consistent with driver agent Bill Greer's statement that he pumped the brakes to check for a blowout moments before he realized the President was being shot at. After this, he accelerated quickly.[54] Thus, the sudden deceleration of the limousine, while not clearly captured by Zapruder, no doubt did happen. Any witness who claimed that the limousine slowed or *appeared* to stop is probably correct, depending on their position in Dealey Plaza. The few who claimed that the limousine actually *did* stop were probably mistaken, as it would not require a great stretch of their imagination to believe that the car stopped because its movement was already slow and the brake lights came on. Indeed, there is little difference between "deceleration from a slow crawl" and "a complete, if momentary, stop," especially when we consider the unexpected and shocking context in which the festive atmosphere was usurped by bursts of gunfire. But unless the many dozens of witnesses who did not see the car stop temporarily blacked out, and unless the Nix, Muchmore, and Bronson films have also been doctored (and one would have to seriously wonder how the conspirators might pull that off), we must conclude that at no time did SS-100-X ever actually stop, though it may have *appeared* to stop to a small number of witnesses. If this simpler interpretation is correct, how then can we explain why Zapruder's camera failed to capture the sudden deceleration of the limousine without agreeing with Mantik that the film was doctored?

The explanation is actually simple. Taken from the opposite (south) side of the street and from a greater distance than Zapruder stood from the car, the other three filmmakers did not need to pan their cameras much, if at all, to record the car riding down Elm Street. That is, they did not need to pivot the camera on a horizontal axis to follow the limousine's movement. By keeping their cameras stationary (or nearly), the limousine's relative position shifts *inside* the film's frame in accordance with its changing speed, making the slowdown and speedup more noticeable. Zapruder, on the other hand, was too close to Kennedy's car to keep his camera pointed in one direction. He had to pan a semi-circle from left to right to keep his camera pointed at the President's moving vehicle. In doing so, and in trying to keep the vehicle centered within his visual frame (Zapruder was an experienced amateur filmmaker, unlike some of the filmmakers named earlier), he adapted his movement to match the speed of the vehicle, slowing his own pivoting motion when the car slowed and panning faster when it took off, giving the car the *appearance* of a steady fluid progression. This also accounts for why the objects and people in the background of the film come into sharper focus in the frames during which the car slowed down and become blurry again during its final acceleration.

17.3.4 Oh! *The technology!*

Our final question raised by the "Zapruder film hoax" asks whether it was not only *possible*, as many conspiracists claim, but also *probable* that this film could be faked using the analog photographic technology that existed in 1963. The proponents of this theory—White, Mantik, Horne, Groden, Fetzer, etc.—use the film itself as proof of a hoax by highlighting "inconsistencies" and "oddities" in its various frames. No one has yet come forward with a verifiable copy of this true and undoctored original. Mantik, White, and Horne do report rumors that such films exist,[55] but no one has yet managed to get their hands on this holy grail, not even a low-quality bootleg copy or missing frame. In the same way that conspiracists obsessively excavate Warren Commission exhibits for reliable proofs of their own unreliability, their zeal to prove that the Zapruder film is a fake has led them to treat the "extant" film as both a piece of malicious disinformation and, at the same time, a reliable proof of what actually happened in Dallas—a sort of Rorschach inkblot test where every innocuous detail becomes a proof of deception.

Their most imaginative "proof" of falsification is their long list of discrepancies between the "Z-film," other images taken that day, and eyewitness memories of where they were standing during the shooting. The evidence of resizing and touch-ups that they present—people who appear shorter than parking meters, or half as tall as 14-foot light posts, or standing in different places in different films, or disappearing entirely—can seem convincing to the untrained eye. When looked at carefully, however, many of these suspicious discrepancies turn out to be optical illusions caused by the poor quality of the pictures, the viewer's forced perspective, the absence of context, or the poor memory of witnesses. Mantik, White, and Fetzer argue, for instance, that Mary Moorman and Jean Hill, whom the Zapruder film shows standing on the grassy part of the south side of Elm Street, actually stood in the street at the moment of the fatal head shot. This claim, which would require several other photos to have been faked (e.g., Figure 13.3), has been thoroughly researched and debunked by multiple authors, including Josiah Thompson and Gary Mack.[56]

A retired advertising executive, Jack White, built himself a second career scrutinizing the Zapruder film. It would require far too much space to debunk all Z-film "oddities" listed by White. It might also prove pointless as a good deal of the visual "proofs" he offers—an "Amoeba Man," a "Pickup Truck Man" a "Waltzing Zapruder," a lineup of cardboard-like "motionless people" who change colors and sizes from frame to frame, not to mention a number of "disappearing" windows and vehicles—were harvested from blurry and grainy images that are hard to make out before White traces their outlines and colors in shapes. Indeed, virtually all of White's photographic evidence requires so much interpretation that only committed believers will "see" what he wants them to see, another example of pareidolia.[57]

The fact that various home movies and photographs of the assassination show different bright and dark patches of colors and shadows can be explained by the different types of film and lenses, resolution, camera quality, level of exposure, and amount of lighting that textured each shot. For example, Orville Nix used a Type A indoor film for his Keystone Auto-Zoom Model K-810 8-millimeter movie camera, which explains why his film came out darker than Zapruder's and Muchmore's, and why certain dark areas appear to some researchers as if they were painted over.[58] Such an explanation is simpler, factually supported, and requires fewer assumptions than the claim that hundreds of photos and film frames were doctored to erase proofs of a grassy knoll shooter. On the other hand, if all of these images were secretly altered, we have to wonder why Mary Moorman's famous Polaroid picture (Figure 13.1)—the one that allegedly captured White's elusive "Badge Man" assassin and was published the next day in the *Dallas Morning News*—was not also retouched, stolen, or destroyed. Besides the Zapruder film, Moorman's Polaroid was one of the most coveted and publicized pieces of evidence of the assassination during the early days of the alleged cover-up. To accept White's claim that the conspirators doctored Orville Nix's home movie—which remained in private hands for several days—while they totally overlooked the Moorman Polaroid—which was outed minutes after the shooting—smacks of total incompetence on the part of an evil consortium with unlimited resources. In fact, Dallas, Texas, and federal authorities had no knowledge of the Nix film until it was voluntarily handed over by its owner in response to an FBI public request.[59] It is therefore hard to conceive why conspirators might have doctored Zapruder's film (instead of, say, making it disappear) when so many other potential home movies and photographs might serve to expose their fraud. As Josiah Thompson explained:

> The alteration of evidence in a criminal case is a desperate act. Would you take that chance if you knew that irrefutable evidence of the alteration might turn up somewhere else? [...] Let's take a photograph of a crime. First, you'd have to know exactly how you wanted to alter it. Secondly, you'd have to be sure no other copies—no negative hidden away, no second copy residing in someone else's possession—existed. Thirdly, you'd have to be sure that no other photographs taken by anyone else later would surface to expose the alteration. [...] Since the film in question was a movie, you might very well have to alter not just one frame, not just one sequence of frames, but many. Thirdly, *what about the other films?* At least thirty-eight people were taking pictures that day in Dealey Plaza. At the very least, the Muchmore and Nix films also would have to be altered. The Muchmore film was purchased by UPI on Monday, November 25th, and shown the following day on WNEW-TV in New York City. On Friday, November 29th, the Nix film was also purchased by UPI and shown the next week in theater newsreels. But the

critical problem for anyone thinking of altering the Zapruder film is not the Muchmore and Nix films. It is all the other films you don't know about. [...] Any one of these unknown films could expose your alteration.[60]

Another photographic oddity highlighted by White is the changing position from image to image of bystanders on the south side of Elm Street, some of whom, he alleges, disappear altogether. This can easily be explained by the fact that the people in the pictures are not standing shoulder-to-shoulder but at varying distances from the roadside, some of them in movement, which results in an optical illusion caused by the forced perspective of the viewer watching a three-dimensional scene through a two-dimensional medium. This effect explains many other "errors" that White and others offer as proof of forgery. Remember that the entire process of faking the Zapruder film would have had to occur before *Life* took possession of it on November 23, meaning that dozens of frames would have had to be altered in less than 24 hours without prior knowledge of the contents of the Muchmore, Nix, and Towner films, and an unknown number of still photographs. As with Oswald's backyard photos (see Chapter 16), we are at a loss to figure out how the conspirators could have manufactured a doctored film in so little time, one that could fool the country's leading film and photography experts for decades, but not a small group of amateur detectives. Would all this have been *possible*? Yes, perhaps, in a Walt Disney studio, using a small army of skilled animators working around the clock for many weeks, who will then keep silent for 60 years. But given the available technology and time constraints, and what we know about human nature, such a feat would have required supernatural assistance.

The problem with hoax-based conspiracy theories, whether they are about the Moon landing, the Holocaust, flat Earth, *Matrix*-type simulations, shape-shifting lizards, or massive evidence fraud (like this one), is that they too often rest on a blanket rejection of a myriad verifiable facts. Once one leaps onto the slippery slope of global skepticism as White, Mantik, and Fetzer have, claiming that all evidence that disproves their theories has surely been faked, because, well, it just *had* to be, no foundation remains on which to establish a reliable objective truth. When nothing is what it appears to be, the only truth left is in the eye of the believer and the whole enterprise of truth-telling becomes little more than an exercise in speculative metaphysics.

17.4   The ghosts in the machine

Fortunately, we can do more than merely estimate the probability that the Zapruder film is authentic. Several verifiable facts exist to help us rein in the conspiracists' imagination and demolish the entire "Zapruder film hoax" theory. While the conspiracists have gone to great lengths arguing that the film was touched up, blown up, cropped, re-sequenced, and partially destroyed, that Mary Moorman stood in the street and not on the grass (as the film shows), that Toni Foster was turned into a giant running woman, that assassins in pickup trucks were cropped out of the edge of the film (and so on),[61] one piece of evidence ought to have silenced them all, though most conspiracists ignore it. It is the fact that every frame of the Zapruder film contains a proof of its own authenticity in the form of ghost images.

In addition to purchasing the Zapruder home movie in 1997 and having it digitized, the National Archives and Records Administration (NARA) and the ARRB commissioned a scientific study of the film and the 8-millimeter Bell & Howell camera that produced it. This study was conducted by Roland J. Zavada, a retired chemist and 8-millimeter film expert from Eastman Kodak, seconded by James K. Toner, then Laboratory Head of Kodak's Imaging Science Resources Lab in Rochester, New York. According to the ARRB's Final Report, Zavada's mandate was neither to prove nor disprove the conspiracy theories about the film but "explain the relationship, if any, between the camera's operating characteristics and perceived 'anomalies' in the original film". This also included studying the chain of custody in November 1963, interviewing those who manipulated the original film and its earliest copies, and "studying manufacturer's edge print, processing lab edge print, and the physical characteristics of the optical printer believed to have been used to create the three first generation copies on November 22, 1963".[62]

Zavada was not requested to take any position on his findings. The Zavada Report, which was published in 1998 to accompany the ARRB's Final Report,

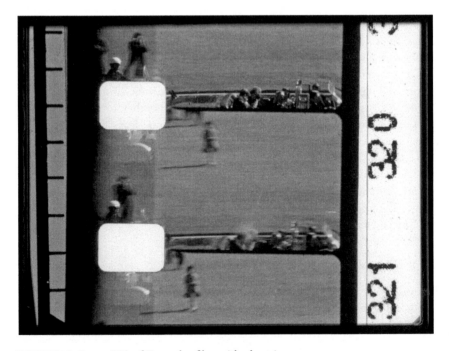

FIGURE 17.1 Frame 313 of Zapruder film with ghost images

Source: Zapruder Film ©1967 (Renewed 1995) The Sixth Floor Museum at Dealey Plaza (National Archives and Records Administration).

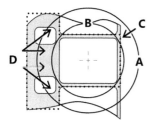

A = Maximum Lens Focal Length (Telephoto)
B = Minimum Lens Focal Length (Wide Angle)
C = Gate (portion of film exposed at each frame)
D = Sprocket holes and areas of double exposure
    (i.e.: "ghost images")

FIGURE 17.2 Approximate relationship between lens and gate on Zapruder's 414 PD B&H Zoomatic camera

Source: J.D. Lillo.

nevertheless offered damning proof against those who claim the Zapruder film was modified from its original. In subsequent communications with conspiracist Douglas Horne, Zavada clearly stated that any allegation that the Zapruder film as we have it was doctored is scientifically untenable.[63] Here is a summary of Zavada's findings.

Like most 8-millimeter portable cameras, Zapruder's device had a round lens, called the "Varamat lens exit window," that projects a *round* illuminated image onto an 8-millimeter film strip made of *rectangular* frames (Figure 17.2). In the case of Zapruder's 414 PD Bell & Howell Zoomatic camera, the 8-millimeter film strip is made up of two connected film strips that must be ejected and turned over to use the other half of the roll. The two strips are then separated during the developing process and connected end-to-end to produce a single reel. This is why sprocket holes only appear on the left side of the original film. To avoid creating a long series of double exposures during the filming process, the rounded edges of the larger illuminated image must be obscured so that each smaller rectangular frame is exposed only once. The apparatus that regulates this process is called the "gate," which quickly opens and shuts to expose each separate frame. The film scrolls down, intermittently pulled by an internal mechanism called the "claw". To prevent damage to the claw or film, the gate cannot be rectangular shaped. Hence, the gate of the 414 PD is shaped like a fattened sideways "T" (the dotted line in Figure 17.2). The claw pulls the film down using the sprocket holes, an area which, because of this process, gets exposed to the light of each frame.[64]

When shooting a film using the Wide Angle or Normal settings—as Zapruder did in parts of the film shot prior to filming the Kennedy motorcade—the images captured are mostly restricted to the area inside the smaller circle (B). But when the Telephoto (or "zoom") setting is used (A), as Zapruder did to film the motorcade (he confirmed this in his Warren Commission testimony), the rounded image bleeds into the sprocket hole area and images are transferred onto the perforated strip on the left side of the film (D). Since this portion of the film is not usually seen during projection, this peculiar effect goes unnoticed by those viewing the film using a standard 8-millimeter movie projector.

This has great importance in establishing the legitimacy of the Zapruder film. Given that the camera recorded images inside the sprocket hole area, and given the fact that the shape of the gate when using the Telephoto setting creates double exposures of the film in the spaces directly above and below each sprocket hole, it follows that the Zapruder film contains small and hazy "ghost images" on every single frame of the assassination sequence (see Figures 13.2 and 17.1), making the removal, rearrangement, resizing, or cropping of individual slides virtually impossible without creating a trail of inconsistent (or missing) ghost images. And so, like the edge markings on Oswald's backyard pictures (see Chapter 16), each frame of the Zapruder film contains a "fingerprint" of its own authenticity. This phenomenon is most evident when the two superimposed images show a significant contrast of dark and light features, allowing experts like Zavada and Toner (or anyone else with the requisite training and equipment) to track a "visual echo" stamped on each frame of the film. It is highly unlikely that any conspirator, no matter how well versed in faking photography, would have picked up on this unusual characteristic of Zapruder's camera. It is even more unlikely that they could have replicated these ghost images using the analog video technology that existed in 1963.

The response of conspiracists like David Lifton to Zavada's powerful counterevidence is sad but unsurprising: the ghost images must also be fake.[65] David Mantik has at least recognized that changes made to the real Zapruder film would be nearly impossible to pull off in a short period of time. He therefore assumes that the fake "extant" Zapruder film took several weeks or months to produce using a large number of qualified experts who, working in isolation and under strict orders not to discuss it with anyone, doctored a small set of slides without fully understanding what they were told to produce. The first problem with this theory is that Mantik can only speculate as to what exactly the folks at Kodak and the CIA could accomplish using 1960s era analog video technology. He reasons that since Disney was at the time producing a technological wonder called *Mary Poppins*, the CIA—no doubt benefitting from greater resources than any Hollywood studio— must have been decades ahead of the Mouse in its capacity to doctor films.[66] The thought of watching President Kennedy and Mary Moorman sing and dance with cartoon animals is certainly intriguing, but the analogy does not seem to prove anything. *Mary Poppins* does not contain realistic visual artwork, the sort that might make White and Mantik's theory plausible. His argument also fails to take heed of the well-established chain of possession of Zapruder's film.

This is why Mantik's conspiracist colleague Douglas Horne felt compelled to conclude that the Zapruder film hoax was achieved in less than three days.[67] Unfortunately for Horne, there just wasn't enough time for the conspirators to pull off this caper over a weekend. Such a rushed operation would require an even bigger staff of qualified experts than even Mantik suggests, and millions of dollars to execute and cover up, which would be bound to leave a trail of evidence in the form of covert government budgets, bank withdrawals, payout slips or checks, and the spontaneous wealth-getting of many individuals in the know. More money would be required to buy off everyone's eternal silence, to monitor them until they die, or, better yet, to make dozens of professional animators suddenly disappear, which would surely make law enforcement officials and journalists curious.

And so, where is the evidence for this massive hoax? Since none of the conspiracists has yet substantiated this theory with a single credible witness, or vestiges of a "true original" Zapruder film, or a trail of pertinent circumstantial evidence (like payment records or dead bodies), or rational explanations for all the unnecessary modifications that were allegedly made to the film like disappearing trucks, gigantic women, shrinking pedestrians, clothes-swapping and race-changing spectators, and Jack White's amazing "Amoeba Man," we have to conclude that these men are pulling hats out of rabbits.

All things considered, it is simpler to conclude that the Zapruder film is authentic. But rather than accept this and modify their theories, committed conspiracists prefer to believe that somewhere in the belly of a restricted government facility hides a technology so advanced and so secretive that it can be used to produce a new Shroud of Turin able to fool hundreds of experts and millions of ordinary civilians for over half a century, silence every possible whistleblower, and falsify all secondary pieces of evidence that might expose their scheme. This sinister plot is compounded by the cold-blooded nerve it would take for those who devised and orchestrated this hoax to take this secret with them to their grave.

In the final lines of an essay titled "'Smoking Guns' in the Death of JFK," James Fetzer, a leading proponent of the Zapruder film hoax theory, states, "anyone sincerely interested in this case who does not conclude that JFK was murdered as the result of a conspiracy is either unfamiliar with the evidence or cognitively impaired".[68] The more one considers the wealth of available evidence, and the more one carefully weighs the claims of JFK buffs using sound logic, the harder it is not to come to the conclusion that it is the JFK buffs who are either willfully lying or mentally troubled.

Notes

1 It was a 1962-model 414 PD Bell & Howell Zoomatic Director Series camera with a power zoom and a dual electric eye. The film numbered 486 frames of standard 8-millimeter Kodachrome II safety film, running at 18.3 frames per second. Richard B. Trask: *Photographic Memory: The Kennedy Assassination, November 22, 1963* (1996), 5.

2 Testimony of Abraham Zapruder, WC VII.

3 Max Holland and Johann Rush: "J.F.K.'s Death, Re-Framed," *The New York Times*, November 22, 2007. See Chapter 13.

4 Original, enhanced, stabilized, and slow-motion versions of the Zapruder film can be found on *YouTube*.

5 Sorrels was the Special Agent in charge of the Dallas district of the US Secret Service. McCormack accompanied Sorrels to Zapruder's office and was a witness of their discussion. "One of the Most Studied Home Movies in History, the Zapruder Film Shows the Assassination of JFK – in 26.6 Seconds on 486 Frames" (2015), *The Sixth Floor Museum at Dealey Plaza*.

6 Zapruder's November 22, 1963, interview on WFAA-TV can be found on *YouTube*.

7 Zapruder's camera used two-sided film. It had to be removed and reversed to record on the other half.

8 The experience profoundly disturbed Zapruder, who gave few interviews after that day. His testimony to the Warren Commission (six months later) was halted several times due to the witness crying. Testimony of Abraham Zapruder, WC VII; "Richard B. Stolley Remembers the Zapruder Film," *Entertainment Weekly*, January 17, 1992.

9 Josiah Thompson: "Why the Zapruder Film is Authentic," speech presented in Dallas on Friday, November 20, 1998, *JFK Assassination Research Materials*.

10 Ibid.; "Richard B. Stolley Remembers the Zapruder Film".

11 Ibid.

12 Garrison, 280.

13 "Richard B. Stolley Remembers the Zapruder Film".

14 Garrison, 280.

15 "Solved: Mystery of the Missing Frames," *Newsweek*, February 6, 1967.

16 "Life to Release Today Part of Kennedy Film," *New York Times*, January 30, 1967.

17 Zapruder died in 1970. Following the widespread dissemination of bootleg copies of his film, *Time-Life* returned the original film and publication rights to the Zapruder family for the sum of one dollar. The original film was placed in the National Archives in 1978, where it remains until this day. It was officially purchased by the US government in 1998 as part of the 1992 JFK Assassination Records Collection Act. The Zapruder family donated the film's copyrights to the Sixth Floor Museum in Dallas in 1999.

18 Garrison, 279 (footnote).

19 William M. O'Barr: "Subliminal Advertising," (Section 5: "The Rebirth of Subliminal Advertising"), The Johns Hopkins University Press, 2013, *Project Muse*.

20 Jack White: "The Great Zapruder Film Hoax" in James Fetzer, ed.: *Murder in Dealey Plaza* (2000), photographic insert, 1.

21 David Mantik: "Paradoxes of the JFK Assassination: The Zapruder Film Controversy," in Fetzer, 334.

22 Ibid., 331.

23 This could refer to a man Ben Hunter referred to as "Captain Sands," or Sands may just be the same person McMahon identified as "Agent Bill Smith" (trying to harmonize these accounts is a frustrating endeavor). See Dave Montague and Douglas Horne: Call Report, June 12, 1997, ARRB, in Fetzer, 312. This document says McMahon claimed viewing the film as a motion picture only four or five times, not ten.

24 There were two dozen or so early viewers of Zapruder's film, including *Life*'s Richard Stolley, *CBS'* Dan Rather, several AP and UPI journalists, and several government agents and civilian film technician. Thompson: "Why the Zapruder Film is Authentic".

25 Deposition of Homer A. McMahon to the ARRB, July 14, 1997 (transcript of recorded interview by Douglas P. Horne, May 2012), PDF, *Manuscript Service*.

26 Mantik: "Paradoxes…," 331.

27 D. Horne, J. Gunn, D. Montague, and M. Coombs: *Meeting Report*, June 18, 1997, ARRB, reprinted in Fetzer, 314–5. Emphasis added.

28 Deposition of Homer A. McMahon to the ARRB, op. cit. Emphasis added.

29 "Wernicke-Korsakoff Syndrome," 9/9/2015, *Medline Plus*.

30 Thompson: "Why the Zapruder Film is Authentic".

31 *ARRB Final Report*, chap. 6, Part II: "Clarifying the Federal Record on the Zapruder Film and the Medical and Ballistics Evidence," 1998, 125.

32 Michael E. Ruane: "As He Filmed, Abraham Zapruder Knew Instantly that President Kennedy Was Dead," *The Washington Post*, November 21, 2013. Zapruder also misled the

Warren Commission by saying he had been paid $25,000 for the film and given it all away to a police charity for officer Tippit's family. This was not technically a lie, because *Life* would pay Zapruder in annual installments of $25,000 and he had not yet received his second payment. Such behavior could be explained as the culturally inculcated caution of a Jewish man whose ancestors and kin had experienced Russian pogroms and Nazi repression. Zapruder was known as a cautious and discrete man.

33 Thompson: "Why the Zapruder Film is Authentic".

34 Horne et al.: Meeting Report, June 18, 1997, in Fetzer, 315.

35 Jack White: "The Great Zapruder Film Hoax," 2–3.

36 Mantik: "Paradoxes…," 332.

37 Mantik's premise that the car stopped—whether or not this is true—supports his thesis that the Zapruder film has been altered, but it has the secondary advantage (in the conspiracist view) of implicating Secret Service driver Bill Greer as a participant in the conspiracy and, by extension, the whole Secret Service Mantik gives no consideration to alternate explanations for why Greer hit the brakes (see Chapter 14) and how JFK's back brace restricted his movements (see Chapter 15 and Andrew King: "JFK and How a Tree-Planting at Rideau Hall Rippled through History," *Ottawa Citizen*, July 4, 2014).

38 Mantik: "Paradoxes…," 338.

39 Ibid., 331.

40 Ibid., 327.

41 Mantik does refer to the "ten closest witnesses," though his list is clearly arbitrary. It ignores important witnesses inside the limousine (Nellie Connally, Bill Greer, Jackie Kennedy), Secret Service Agent Clint Hill, photojournalist James Altgens, and Zapruder and Sitzman, all of whom were among the closest witnesses and believed that all shots came from the rear. Mantik's list of witnesses also includes Bill Newman (who originally thought the shots came from behind the pergola) but not Newman's wife Gail, who stood beside him and whose televised WFAA-TV testimony that same afternoon is consistent with the Lone Gunman Theory. This interview is available on *YouTube*. The Newmans were interviewed again at the Sixth Floor Museum on July 10, 2003. "Kennedy Assassination: Bill and Gayle Newman," *CSPAN*, 2009.

42 McAdams: "Beverly Oliver: Babushka Babe? Or Bamboozling the Buffs?" (n.d.), "Jean Hill: The Lady in Red," (n.d.), and David Reitzes: "Nowhere Man: The Strange Story of Gordon Arnold," (n.d.), on McAdams, ed.: *The Kennedy Assassination*. See also Chapter 13.

43 Bill Newman was one of the few to claim that the limousine stopped, though he felt it was more of a lurch than a halt: "It did seem to me that I recall seeing the taillights and for a very short moment it momentarily stopped," Newman recalled in 2003,

> And then they floor-boarded it and it went through the triple underpass. […] I never found confirmation of that. I don't know that the Zapruder film showed that and I've never had that confirmed, but I feel like that did occur. But in saying 'stop', I don't mean they stopped and ate a ham sandwich. It was a very short time span.
>
> *"Kennedy Assassination: Bill and Gayle Newman," Part 1*

44 Mantik: "Paradoxes…," 327.

45 An argument by analogy is an inductive argument based on the probability that two similar things will behave the same way (A is like B; A is an X; therefore B is probably also an X). Such arguments are strong only when the similarities between two elements are clear, pertinent, and lead to a high probability that they will behave similarly. A faulty analogy is a fallacy that makes an inappropriate inference between A and B's similarities, or one that does not clearly explain how the two are similar. See Appendix 2.

46 Mantik: "Paradoxes…," 338.

47 Ibid., 338.

48 Testimony of Abraham Zapruder, WC VII.

49 Marshall, Marquis, and Oskamp: "Effects of Kind of Question and Atmosphere of Interrogation on Accuracy and Completeness of Testimony," *Harvard Law Review*, Vol. 84, 1971, 1620, cited in Mantik: "Paradoxes…," 339–40.

50 Mantik: "Paradoxes…," 340.

51 The fallacy of division makes an inappropriate inference from the properties of a set to the properties of its constituent parts. For example, because a crowd at a sports game is booing the referee loudly, one might (falsely) assume that John, who is part of that crowd, is booing the referee loudly. Inversely, the fallacy of composition occurs when someone wrongly attributes some property of the constituent parts of a set to the set as a whole. An example would be to say that, because all the children in a given classroom have a single biological mother, all of these children (as a group) share a single biological mother.

52 "Mary Karr on Writing Memoirs: 'No Doubt I've Gotten a Million Things Wrong,'" Interview of Mary Karr by Terri Gross, *NPR: Fresh Air*, September 15, 2015.

53 Elizabeth F. Loftus: "Creating False Memories," *Scientific American*, Vol. 277, No. 3, September 1997.

54 Blaine and McCubbin, 207, 211–2, 355–6.

55 Such "witnesses" include former NPIC employees Dino Brugioni and Homer McMahon, a "purported former CIA agent" named Oswald LeWinter, and French conspiracy researcher William Reymond (Mantik, "Paradoxes…" 336–7). Here is a quick assessment of their credibility: (a) Brugioni's account is based on old memories and personal assumptions concerning the nature of the film he viewed and the stills he produced for CIA briefing boards on the night of November 22–23, 1963. His memories do not differ significantly from the "official" Zapruder film except for his memory of a larger mist of blood tissue emanating from Kennedy's head (Douglas Horne: "The Zapruder Film Mystery," 2014, *YouTube*). Considering that such frames were not published by *Life* to make the pictures more palatable to their readers, it is likely that Brugioni merely saw one of the uncut first-generation copies given by Zapruder to Special Agent Sorrels. (b) Homer McMahon, as discussed earlier, has suffered brain damage from alcoholism and drug abuse, leading him to question his own reliability. His timeline also clashes with Brugioni's. Nevertheless, Horne and Mantik take McMahon's account as reliable despite its numerous flaws and inconsistencies. (c) Oswald LeWinter was a former English professor-turned CIA impersonator who was arrested and convicted of fraud in 1998 for forging fake CIA documents that allegedly proved Princess Diana was murdered by British authorities (Vernon Loeb and Bill Miller: "Tinker, Tailor, Poet, Spy?" *The Washington Post*, February 15, 2001). Le Winter then attempted to make $15 million peddling these false documents to Diana's boyfriend's father, Mohammad Al Fayed. LeWinter spent over two years in prison for this crime. Unsurprisingly, Mantik leaves that out of his glowing account of the man. (d) William Reymond is a freelance French reporter who published sensationalist books on the mafia, Marilyn Monroe, and the Kennedy assassination (e.g., *JFK: Autopsie d'un crime d'état*, 1999). Reymond was in his late 1920s in the mid-1990s when, he alleges, he was shown the "uncut" Zapruder film, which he says once belonged to Howard Hunt, by an unnamed mercenary friend who claimed he participated in the JFK assassination. ("JFK Assassination: William Reymond Talks about an Unseen Film of the Assassination," (n.d.), interview with Jim Marrs,

YouTube). This friend also allegedly claimed he was one of three anonymous tramps photographed in Dealey Plaza—which is clearly false since the tramps have now all been identified (see Chapter 11). Reymond, a self-appointed expert, never produced any evidence of this "real" Z-film, nor does he reveal the identity of his sources. The film he allegedly saw included a wide limousine turn on Elm Street which was "cut out" of the extant film. If this is true, Reymond may have merely seen footage of another home movie—such as the one taken by Tina Towner who stood at the corner of Elm and Houston, which captured the limousine taking this turn, as did the Bell, Martin, and Hughes films. All things considered, these leading "witnesses" of the Zapruder film hoax proponents are clearly unreliable, in addition to the fact that no verifiable evidence exists to support their claims.

56 Thompson: "Moorman in the Street?" (n.d.), *JFK Lancer*; Mack and Thompson: "Moorman Line-of-Sight Tests: 25 November 2001," in McAdams: "Evidence of Fakery in the Zapruder Film: Was Mary Moorman Standing in Elm Street?" *The Kennedy Assassination*.

57 White: "The Great Zapruder Film Hoax" in Fetzer, ed.: *Murder in Dealey Plaza* (2000); White: "Mysteries of the JFK Assassination: The Photographic Evidence from A to Z" and "Was Mary Standing in the Street," in Fetzer, ed.: *The Great Zapruder Film Hoax* (2003); White: "The Great Zapruder Film Hoax," (n.d.), *YouTube*.

58 Gayle Nix Jackson: *Orville Nix: The Missing JFK Assassination Film* (2014); John Whitely: "Wanted: The 'Other' JFK Assassination Film," *USA Today*, June 12, 2014.

59 The film was returned to Nix three days later. He then sold it to United Press International for $5,000, who kept it until at least 1978, when it was loaned to the HSCA. The original film disappeared before copyrights and other copies of the film were returned to the Nix family in 1992. See Gayle Nix Jackson, op. cit. Although Orville Nix stated in a 1966 interview with Mark Lane that his film was returned to him with frames missing (which many conspiracists highlight), he also accepted the verdict that the shots came from the Book Depository, even though he originally believed, like many other witnesses, that they came from the knoll. (Part of this interview is posted on *YouTube*.) This can be explained by the fact that Nix stood in a position in which he was likely to hear echoes resounding off the pergola or overpass rather than only the shots from the TSBD.

60 Thompson: "Why the Zapruder Film is Authentic". Emphasis in the original.

61 White: "The Great Zapruder Film Hoax" (article and video); "Mysteries of the JFK Assassination: The Photographic Evidence from A to Z"; "Was Mary Standing in the Street"; Mantik: "Paradoxes…"

62 *Final Report of the Assassination Records Review Board*, 1998, 126; R.J. Zavada: "Analysis of Selected Motion Picture Evidence," *Kodak Technical Report 31842OP*, 9/25/98 (aka: the "Zavada Report"), Study 4, Part 3: "Recognized Image Anomalies in the Zapruder Original Film," 31–43, *Internet Archive*.

63 Letter from Zavada to Horne ("RE: Comments on Chapter 14: *The Zapruder Film Mystery*"), May 26, 2010, PDF, *JFK Assassination Research Materials*.

64 *Zavada Report*, Study 4, Part 2, Figures 4–15, 26, and Figures 4–23, 31.

65 Lifton's argument is based on the fact that the ghost images on the Zapruder film are larger than the ones Zavada replicated in the laboratory. Zavada's response was simple: "We simply didn't have enough studio light available". David Lifton: "The Pig on a Leash," in Fetzer, ed.: *The Great Zapruder Film Hoax* (2003); Rollie Zavada: "Zapruder Film Hoax Response" (2003), both cited in Clint Bradford: "Fetzer's New Book… His Third Miserable Attempt at Scholarly Work" (2003), *JFK Assassination Research Materials*.

66 Mantik: "Paradoxes...," 335. This is a shining example of the "myth of hypercompetence" discussed by conspiracy skeptics James Meigs (*Debunking 9/11 Myths*, 2006) and Jonathan Kay (*Among the Truthers*, 2011).

67 Douglas Horne: "The Zapruder Film Mystery," an interview summarizing his 2009 book, *Inside the ARRB* (Vol.IV), published on August 15, 2014, *YouTube*.

68 Fetzer, ed.: *Murder in Dealey Plaza*, 15.

18

CONCLUSION

Why conspiracists rewrite the past

18.1   Honey, I blew up the evidence!

During his 1996 deposition to the Assassination Records Review Board (ARRB), former Bethesda Hospital pathologist James Humes was asked to explain the inconsistencies between his different accounts of President Kennedy's autopsy X-rays over the previous three decades. Although conspiracists like Douglas Horne (who participated in this deposition) and David Mantik called Humes' conflicting account "sheer, unassailable nonsense" and proof of a cover up,[1] Humes offered his detractors this thought-provoking response:

> I'm still somewhat vague on the precise bottom line of all your efforts to do these things [...] But if you ask a person enough questions often enough, you're going to confuse themselves [sic] sooner or later and not say the same thing twice [...] so I'm concerned that we've got so much information put together that we—well, there's an expression in golf. You get paralysis of analysis. You know, you get more information than you can usefully put together.[2]

Frustration and confusion are palpable in Dr. Humes' deposition and in those of Drs. Boswell, Finck, and Ebersole, and in their subsequent (now published) exchanges with Horne and Mantik.[3] One could interpret their inconsistent recollections, as Mantik, Fetzer, and Horne do, as proof of a guilty conscience. But unless one starts with the assumption that Humes and his colleagues willfully took part in a conspiracy, their confused and erratic responses are not that suspicious.

To those who, like Humes, were briefly thrust into the center of history but not predisposed to the paranoid logic of the conspiracists, there was little reason for them to fastidiously cling to their memories of these events. After all, Humes

DOI: 10.4324/9781003222460-22

spent a mere three hours of his entire life performing an autopsy which, were it not for the identity of the victim and the pressure he was under to get it done quickly, would be a routine procedure. A neutral observer might even conclude that Humes fulfilled his duties rather well considering his lack of experience with gunshots wounds—which is why he sought the assistance of Dr. Pierre Finck, a colleague from nearby Walter Reed Army Medical Center who did have experience in wound ballistics and was available on short notice. Humes' incomplete autopsy report also attests to the strict deadline and restrictions imposed on him by the Kennedy family. Most importantly, he never had the opportunity to cross-check his autopsy notes against the X-rays and photographs of JFK's body. He then, for decades, maintained the professional discretion requested of him by Kennedy's physician Admiral Burkley, which explains why he burned his autopsy notes and never spoke of JFK's adrenals or other health problems until 1992, when these were revealed by Dr. Boswell in the *Journal of the American Medical Association*.[4] Humes then went on living his life much as he had before. In other words, it was his willingness to protect President Kennedy's medical secrets, not any desire to cause him, his family, or the country harm, that made Dr. Humes the punching bag of conspiracists.

Having been scrutinized, phoned, visited, and harangued for decades by hostile researchers, it is understandable that Humes lost patience against the stream of exacting questions and doubts put to him by Horne and the ARRB, and at their surprise over his faltering memory about the minutia of Kennedy's autopsy. He had, after all, written a full report of Kennedy's wounds and this should have, at least in theory, ended his involvement in the matter. But that report and his professional integrity were repeatedly brought into question by many who claimed that a conspiracy to falsify Kennedy's injuries occurred on his watch, and that he was a party to it. If this is what happened, as Mantik and Horne surmise, then Humes is one of the greatest liars of the twentieth century. But if it was not the case, then Humes would have of course paid little attention to those inconsequential details that the conspiracists interpret as proofs of a plot.

Remembering the past is a tricky thing, especially when it consists of routine events that coincided with others that seemed, at least at the time, more worthy of attention. Unless Humes is proven a liar, we must concede that he probably did not take notice of the many oddities that spark the imagination of those who, many years later, obsessively pore over the details of photos, written reports, and eyewitness testimonies. Humes may have committed several mistakes. Inaccurately recording the location of the entry wound on the back of Kennedy's head might have been the most consequential mistake he committed in his whole career. Perhaps he did recognize that mistake at some point but too late to do much about it and with no desire to incriminate himself with a teary confession. Or perhaps he remained genuinely confused, as many researchers continue to be, about the discrepancies between his report and the autopsy photos (see Chapter 15). On the other hand, rather than giving a man of Humes' standing and experience the benefit of the doubt, or conceding that this may be one of history's many unresolvable quandaries, the conspiracists have a tendency to weave grandiose storylines out of sheer possi-bilities, all because of a few inconsistent factoids.

Paranoid skepticism is the fuel that feeds conspiracy theories. It typically manifests itself in three ways: (a) an unwavering belief that reality is not what it seems and that all "suspicious" events are connected, (b) an obsessive scrutiny of small inconsist-encies and irrelevant details, and (c) the creation of ambitious scenarios that leave nothing to chance. The result is a Frankenstein monster composed of half-truths severed from their proper context and sown back together to fit a new script. It is then packaged for mass consumption in lucrative and sensationalist books, periodicals, "documentaries," websites, podcasts, and fictional movies and novels. These flood the popular culture with tantalizing pseudohistorical claims that, through repetition, become widely accepted as true and increase cynicism in the institutions, the job of which is to conduct responsible historical research: univer-sities, the media, government inquiries, educational publishing, and the like. Pretty soon, only the most dedicated and objective investigators can tell what counts as fact and what doesn't. I call this reckless obscuring of history the Oak Island Effect.

On the Atlantic coast of Nova Scotia, Canada, there exists a tiny island that has been the subject of intrigue for more than two centuries. Ever since a group of teenagers wandered onto the island in 1795 and discovered an abandoned tackle block hanging from a branch near a small, circular depression (what many skeptics conclude was a piece of rubbish left hanging near a natural sink hole[5]) someone has been excavating, planning to excavate, or preventing others from excavating, parts of this island in the hope of laying their hands on an ancient treasure. From flagstones to rotting logs, coconut husks, and mundane human artifacts—mostly nineteenth-century tools and, possibly, a scattering of old coins and discarded jew-elry—excavations have so far turned up little more than ambiguous clues that something else might be buried further down. Over the years, rumors began to abound that Oak Island hides Captain Kidd's treasure, the Knights Templars' lost gold, a Masonic secret vault, extraterrestrial technology or (why not?) the Biblical Ark of the Covenant. Various strange sightings, the death of several excavators, and the unexpected breakdown of heavy equipment have all been interpreted as proof that Oak Island is the resting place of an ancient and valuable prize.

What this elusive prize might be remains shrouded in speculation. A dozen or so major digs have been conducted over the last 200 years in several parts of Oak Island, mobilizing millions of dollars and much manpower, fuel, and complex machinery to bore 30 meters or more into the ground, creating piles of rock, dirt, human artifacts, garbage, and a good deal of deforestation. Excavation attempts have expanded in size and ambition over the last century so that a causeway now connects the largely uninhabited island to the mainland, allowing heavy construc-tion equipment to be driven in and out. There would have been even more digs had legal battles for ownership and drilling rights not stalled these efforts for decades, and had several excavation ventures not ended in the death of some workmen or, at other times, the total flooding and collapse of the pit due to the nearby Atlantic Ocean.[6]

Rumors persist that the island hides one of history's most valuable secrets despite the fact that the Woods Hole Oceanographic Institute (WHOI) in Massachusetts investigated the Oak Island "mystery" in 1995 and reported that little evidence exists to support any of the treasure seekers' theories.[7] One of the enduring myths that continues to draw serious believers and gold-digging adventurers to Oak Island is the recurring claims of ex-diggers and self-appointed experts that a series of booby traps have been carefully laid below ground over an intricate set of man-made tunnels that flood the hidden "treasure" every time someone with the wrong skill set or incorrect pedigree makes their way down the "Money Pit". Although sink holes and underground caverns are not foreign to the region, such explanations are usually dismissed by hardboiled believers.

It is not this book's purpose to determine whether an ancient treasure is, or ever was, buried on Oak Island. This tale is significant here because Oak Island offers a powerful visual analogy of what happens to historical evidence when it is mishandled and contaminated by cumulative waves of careless dreamers and adventurers trying to twist history to fit their personal ambitions. The area surrounding Oak Island's infamous "Money Pit," as well as other parts of the island deemed suspicious enough to excavate, have now been so disfigured that it may never again be possible to know with any certainty where the original depression discovered in 1795 actually stood. We may also never know if it ever contained anything that could not have been left there by nature, or whether the original pit served some far less exotic purpose to passing seafarers—perhaps as a latrine or an unfinished shelter. Many of the artifacts that have been retrieved from Oak Island by amateur archeologists are merely natural objects that can wind up in a sink hole after a storm or a flood (e.g., tree branches and logs), tools that were dropped during previous excavations (not all of which were recorded), or purposely planted false evidence to generate interest, drive up the value of the land, or inspire rich investors to fund more digs.[8] Apart from the somewhat surprising discovery of coconut fibers in various parts of the island, and the occasional trinket that would only convince a committed believer to keep digging, there is little evidence to suggest that anything of significant value is buried down there.

This is an important lesson for conspiracists (and mythmakers in general), because physical landmarks are not the only resource that can be warped beyond all recognition. Ideas and facts can be perverted as well. The events that transpired in Dealey Plaza on November 22, 1963, have evolved into a modern-day myth, much of which, as we have seen throughout this book, is a gross distortion of history. Conspiracists do not share the sole blame for this. The myth of Camelot was well developed before most JFK conspiracy theories emerged, and it was swallowed whole by much of the news media and public, both in the United States and abroad, during the weeks and years that followed JFK's death. It is also true that the Kennedy family, the Johnson White House, the Warren Commission, the FBI, and the CIA all tried to hide information about the slain president—from his personal health problems to his sexual misdeeds to his secret program to murder Castro. By doing so, they were all complicit in obscuring the truth, partly to protect JFK's legacy, partly to save face, and partly as a result of the dirty business of electoral politics and international relations. Kennedy certainly had many political enemies who would have loved to see him leave office, but as far as the bludgeoning of the historical record is concerned, his family, friends, colleagues, and admirers share a good deal of blame.

That said, the conspiracists discussed in this book—Lane, Garrison, Prouty, Groden, Lifton, Hurt, Scheim, Douglass, Marrs, Stone (Roger), Stone (Oliver), Fetzer, Palamara, Mantik, White, Horne, and many others—hold the lion's share of the guilt for misleading the public concerning Kennedy's personal life, his presidency, and especially his murder. Their collective sense of denial and careless historical revisionism has deceived millions of Americans, and much of the world, into believing a disheartening and cynical fantasy. I know this because, for the better part of 20 years, I was one of them.

America is still in many ways grieving the death of John Kennedy, but making sense of this horrible crime should not make us fall prey to the popular delusion that real life should be as neat and predictable as a Hollywood movie script, with its equal balance of good guys and bad guys and nicely resolvable plot lines. In real-life accidents do happen, mental illness exists, and pitiful loners do commit horrible crimes. In the real-world government, agencies do make mistakes, scandals are often exposed, investigations are sometimes botched unintentionally, and whistleblowers make revelations that are less clear-cut and explosive than first assumed.

As this book has shown, JFK buffs have severely muddied the waters of history—in many cases unintentionally, but almost always without sufficient respect for the concept of truth—by engaging in one of the clearest and longest-lasting examples of bandwagoning and circular reasoning. This is exemplified by their propensity to cherry-pick evidence, ignore crucial facts, appeal to evidence that does not exist, and ignore contradictions in their elaborate stories. One does not need to be a conspiracist to do that, but it too often ends up being a trick of the trade.

18.2   Fixing the blame: the scapegoating mechanism

To scapegoat is to arbitrarily ascribe blame to a person or group irrespective of any known proof of guilt. The term originates from English translations of the Bible and refers the ancient Hebrew custom of transferring the sins of the nation of Israel onto an actual goat that was then sent into the wilderness as a sign of God forgiving his people.[9] A scapegoat, then, is a substitute wrongdoer, taking upon its shoulders the punishment deserved by another person or group. Many ancient and modern religious traditions perform rituals of blame transference, the Christian ceremony of Eucharist, for example.[10] In secular culture, scapegoating occurs when someone is arbitrarily singled out and punished to satisfy a community's feelings of moral outrage and restore peace and order to their lives. Scapegoating is a utilitarian (consequence-based) form of punishment, not a deontological (rule-based) one. In simpler terms, it is the practice of blaming someone based on how much of a threat they are *perceived* to be, not what they *actually* did. In so doing, the "scapegoating mechanism" serves a dual purpose: (a) it allows the ones-passing-blame the satisfaction of putting a face on the source of some ill-defined "evil" that threatens their way of life, while (b) it lets them abdicate responsibility, individual or collective, for the crisis at hand and its causes.[11]

According to René Girard, the French-American literary critic and anthropologist who popularized the concept, the scapegoat's *actual* guilt matters less to the ones-passing-blame than their conviction that the scapegoat *deserves* to be punished. This psychological predisposition leaves no doubt in their minds that they have identified the cause of their distress because their judgment is not based on true and pertinent evidence so much as it is based on existential *coherence*. In other words, they perceive the scapegoat to be *necessarily* guilty because the deeply emotional story they hold to be true would make little sense otherwise.[12]

Consider the *Star Wars* science fiction saga. One of the main reasons the original trilogy inspired millions of youngsters during the 1970s and 1980s (including this author) was its poignant family drama about a reunited brother and sister—Luke Skywalker and Leia Organa—struggling not just to survive but to turn their long-lost father—the evil Sith Lord Darth Vader—away from his villainous ways. If Vader had turned out to be little more than a random psychopath and not a perversion of Anakin Skywalker, all of Luke's efforts to redeem his father would have been for naught and the *Star Wars* universe would lose much of its mythic appeal.[13] Likewise, if one gives up belief in the biblical Satan there cannot still be a deception of Eve or an end to Original Sin, only a vaguely defined state of nature subject to natural selection and an impersonal struggle for the survival of species. The story of Christ on the cross would then lose much of its meaning and value for Christians. Indeed, without an Adam and Eve and a Satan to trick them, the suffering Christ remains, at best, one of thousands of peace-loving gurus tragically killed in their prime. At worst, he becomes a failed revolutionary, a prince without a throne. In either case, the Christian story of the God-man would suddenly make little sense. Unsurprisingly then, the committed Christian believes in the power of Satan not because she has an empirical proof of his existence, but simply because the rest of the story compels her to do so.

According to Girard, scapegoating is a typical human reaction, the psychological by-product of unresolved feelings of anger and helplessness. Rather than face the humbling possibility that such feelings are caused by our failures, or that we need to change our beliefs, take responsibility for our predicament, make amends for past wrongs, or forgive our abusers, such feelings get purged through the easier path of blaming others, often at the cost of rejecting the truth. To put it another way, the ego protects itself by rejecting the unwanted truth because the alternative—perpetual uncertainty and insecurity—is too painful.[14] When faced with evidence that contradicts their beliefs, those who indulge in scapegoating often "double-down" on their false convictions instead of questioning them, thereby avoiding the embarrassment of being wrong.[15] A fundamental element of "successful" scapegoating, explained Girard, is that those who indulge in it remain oblivious to the possibility that the scapegoat is innocent: a substitute wrongdoer arbitrarily punished to quench their outrage. They could not otherwise maintain the narcissistic illusion that they, the ones-passing-blame, are the innocent victims of history and thereby avoid experiencing shame, helplessness, unsatisfied anger, inconsolable grief, and cognitive dissonance. This is why those who indulge in scapegoating see themselves as crusaders for justice and victims' rights, not self-righteous moral relativists as others often perceive them.

In many examples of scapegoating in both mythology and history—the exile of King Oedipus, the trial of his daughter Antigone, Romulus' murder of his brother Remus, the trial and execution of Socrates, the assassination of Julius Caesar, the crucifixion of Jesus, and the martyrdom of Joan of Arc, to name but a few—acts of group violence or ostracism against an individual or minority are often presented by those who perpetrate them as *necessary* abuses of justice in the pursuit of a greater good. The Roman statesman and philosopher Cicero, for instance, extolled the brutal murder of Julius Caesar to his friend Atticus: "The Ides of March are a consolation. Our heroes most splendidly and gloriously achieved everything that lay in their power". He then wrote to Gaius Trebonius that the murderers of Caesar made a "superhuman service [...] for the Republic". The Gospel of John has the Jewish high priest Caiaphas goading his colleagues to convict Jesus or else lose many freedoms they had obtained from Rome: "You do not realize that it is better for you that one man die for the people than that the whole nation perish [at the hands of the Romans]".[16] In America, acts of violent scapegoating occurred in colonial New England during the Salem witch trials, and until the mid-twentieth century in the South where the lynching of blacks was perceived by white mobs as a justified way to maintain their social hierarchy. Scapegoating occurred on a wider scale in Nazi Germany, where Jews were blamed for the German defeat in World War I and nearly eradicated, and in Communist Russia where purges and show trials were enacted by Stalin against all "enemies of the revolution".

Fortunately, malicious prosecutions are a miscarriage of justice in most Western democracies, largely because our justice systems are founded on the presumption of innocence and the burden of proof, not on the vagaries of public opinion. But this can only be true so long as scapegoating culture does not override existing norms of due process, respectful public discourse, and a shared belief in a single objective reality, which is far from assured in a "post-truth" era like ours.[17] The Oxford dictionary defines post-truth as "denoting circumstances in which objective facts are less influential in shaping public opinion than appeals to emotion and personal belief". Conspiracy theories are an affront to responsible historical research and rational discourse. But they are not the only form of scapegoating. One should not forget that the US Congress already participated in a massive red-baiting exercise during the 1940s and 1950s, an inquisition of left-wing ideologues under the aegis of the House Un-American Activities Committee (HUAC) and Joseph McCarthy's Permanent Subcommittee on Investigations of the US Senate. Ironically, it was these witch hunts, fueled by irrational conservative fears of scheming socialists, that led Lee Harvey Oswald to hate the American government enough to murder its highest official, and conspiracists like Mark

Lane, Thomas Buchanan, Harold Weisberg, Oliver Stone, and Zachary Sklar to view Oswald as a patsy and the Warren Commission as a government whitewash, filtered through the distorting lens of left-wing paranoia.[18] It should thus not be surprising to find the American government or large swaths of the public of any and all sociopolitical leaning to indulge once again in a fractious public inquisition, which tends to happen in periods of prolonged public mistrust, excessive pessimism, and widespread disinformation.

Everyone has the inborn tendency to indulge in scapegoating. It is part of the human condition. Conspiracy theorists have merely indulged in it more than the average person, perhaps because the typical peddler of conspiracy claims has a greater emotional need to do so. What matters most to the typical Kennedy buff is not that the objective truth will one day be revealed—assuming it hasn't already—but that some "higher truth,"[19] a romanticized and subjective version of the past that echoes their deepest convictions, will someday become the reigning consensus. This is one of the reasons why conspiracists are quick to endorse public opinion when it agrees with their views and to dismiss the majority as brainwashed when its opinions clash with their own. What JFK buffs call the "official story" cannot resolve their feelings of alienation and victimhood. Official government reports and media investigations that support the lone gunman theory will thus continue to be impeached, not because there is a dearth of evidence to prove Lee Oswald guilty, but because the "official story" can do nothing to push back the causes of evil perceived by most JFK buffs: predatory capitalism, war profiteering, government-corporate collusion, the erosion of civil liberties, social conservatism, and the political impotence of leftists and libertarians.

The campaign of the conspiracists to "expose the truth" of JFK's murder by winning the hearts and minds of Americans is a war of attrition that shows no sign of abating, save perhaps by the growing number of buffs who die of old age each year. A major reason for the longevity of JFK conspiracy theories is the nature of their scapegoat. The "military industrial complex" serves as a perfect patsy: tangible enough to be perceived as real, even by skeptics; dangerous enough to be blamed for countless deaths every year; greedy enough to sap public resources from the common weal; large and diffuse enough to be everywhere and nowhere at once; faceless enough to be ageless, deathless, and devoid of a human conscience; and elusive enough never to be brought to justice. It is never portrayed by conspiracists as what it truly is—a collection of flawed human beings who, like the rest of us, spend their days working, eating, sleeping, and striving to improve their place in the world—but as a Wellsian horde of Morlocks lurking in the dark and feasting on the innocent. Because it is so vaguely defined, such an enemy has become, in the words of historian Richard Levy, "infinitely adaptable".[20] It becomes, in other words, whatever boogeyman the theorist most fears: a war racket, Big Oil, a faceless bureaucracy, a fascist spy network, a criminal confederacy, a doomsday machine, or a coterie of homosexual thrill seekers. For the critical thinker, the question that ought to be asked is: "does such a monster even exist?" But to the orphans of Camelot—the conspiracists who feel that their country was stolen from them during the 1960s—asking this question affords them no hope, because the thought that the devil they fear might not even exist would inevitably lead them to see that they are the principal cause of their own anxieties.

In sum, conspiracists are not seeking facts but catharsis: a purging of anger and grief to attain a sort of spiritual renewal.[21] The act of scapegoating plays an important role in this process, allowing them to project their frustrations onto a visible target, thereby attaining a sense of purpose (to rid the world of injustice) and of belonging to a community of like-minded insurgents. "As soon as a victim can be found upon whom everybody will agree," Girard writes,

> not for rational reasons but because of a mimetic tidal wave against him/her, the populace feels better. [...] The hostilities that ferment inside the community are dissipated against an expendable victim, one whose violent elimination will not inflame the spirit of vengeance within the community.[22]

Girard's argument invites us to view conspiracism as a contemporary manifestation of mob violence akin to ancient public stonings, medieval witch hunts, and racist lynchings. In such cases, the principal aim of the crowd is to satisfy its collective outrage, not enforce justice dispassionately. A genuine exercise in truth-telling would require them to stop, bring their emotions under control, and carefully weigh the accusations heaped on the scapegoat against any proofs of its innocence. A genuine exercise in truth-seeking would also require them to coolly consider their own biases, unjustified fears, bloodthirst, greed, intellectual laziness, xenophobia, jealousies, self-righteousness, or exaggerated sense of victimhood. But lynch mobs don't function this way. Neither do conspiracist movements.

A genuine exercise in truth-seeking would also require that conspiracists recognize the influence of public opinion—to which they are an important contributor—in perpetuating confusion over the facts of JFK's assassination for well over half a century. This is where the scapegoating of "the military industrial complex," or simply "the government," as a distinct entity disconnected from the general populace has helped perpetuate the false and simplistic assumption that the world is divided into two warring camps: the establishment and its victims.

Intentionally or not, contemporary conspiracism borrows a page from the doctrines of Karl Marx, especially his theory of "dialectical materialism," which posits that all world history can be summed up as a war between the propertied classes (the financiers and factory owners, whom he called the "bourgeoisie") and the masses (the industrial working class or "proletariat") who, alienated from the product of their own labor, are compelled to serve the former.[23] In the eyes of modern conspiracists, the establishment is composed of elected and nonelected officials, their bureaucratic lackeys and agents, the heads of large corporations, and nongovernmental institutions like mainstream media, universities, professional associations, and leading religious organizations, all serve the will of a powerful secret cabal. Its victims usually includes anyone who remains free and untainted by the former—which implies, directly or indirectly, that ignorance, inexperience, and mistrust of institutions are badges of honor, of moral superiority, and of intellectual enlightenment.

Conspiracists rarely consider how deeply elected leaders and government agencies, as well as the "elites" who run and administer large corporations, are influenced by public opinion, particularly in a capitalistic democracy like the United States. Whether it be in their determination to fight communism, to make the world safe from terrorists, to export democracy to the Middle East, to create jobs, keep interest rates low, maintain a competitive consumer-price index, or simply "Make America Great Again," the agendas of those thousands of people we call "the establishment" hardly take shape in a vacuum. Indeed, when such people fail to take account of popular opinions and consumption habits, they soon find themselves out of a job or forced to adapt.

The main concern of "the establishment," then, is not to make sure that the slavish public remains under their yoke but to find ways to harness that multiheaded and unpredictable beast of public opinion—a creature driven by bias, self-interest, and emotional knee-jerks—into some sort of consensus, if only for a short while, to ensure that they get elected or sell enough widgets to fill their coffers. While the fickleness of politicians and wastefulness of corporations are worthy of blame, the public should not be absolved for its self-interested political behavior or consumption habits, which are often no less fickle or wasteful than those of the people in power. Critical thinkers should carefully consider whether the masses—and hence, themselves—bear some responsibility for undesirable social, economic, and political trends, and whether the engines of disinformation are solely controlled by the elites. Conspiracists, on the other hand, rarely concern themselves with the impact of the disinformation that they produce. They merely point the finger elsewhere.

Shining the searchlight of truth inwards might help the conspiracy-minded to discover that they are largely to blame for turning the facts of JFK's death into an Oak Island Money Pit. This was, in fact, one of the reasons for my "deconversion". They would also become more sensitized to the way public opinion shaped the tragic events for which they blame elites. Was it not, after all, to sway public opinion that Kennedy took part in open-top motorcades during the fall of 1963? Was it not also public opinion that pushed him to make an example of Castro by sponsoring covert attacks against Cuba and trying to have him murdered? Was it not in fear of public opinion that President Johnson limited the scope of the Warren Commission's investigation, convinced that nuclear war would ensue if the public was told the whole truth? Was it not with the backing of public opinion that Johnson escalated the war in Vietnam? And was it not in reaction to public opinion that Nixon felt compelled to put a swift and violent end to the conflict, even if it meant letting South Vietnam fall? And was it not to a certain extent in reaction to public opinion that an angry lone Marxist named Lee Harvey Oswald chose to take justice in his own hands—first by shooting at General Walker and then at President Kennedy—to protest America's generalized hatred of socialists? And was it not public opinion that got a paranoid bully like Jim Garrison elected numerous times and kept him in office long enough to make a spectacle of the Louisiana judicial system and a mess of the evidence of Kennedy's murder? And was it not also public opinion that gullibly took in and popularized conspiracy theories about JFK, MLK, Bobby Kennedy, John Lennon, 9/11, and Barack Obama's birth certificate? And was it not public opinion that put men and women who traffic in conspiracy theories in Congress and the White House during recent elections?

These are not the types of questions conspiracists are comfortable asking because they lead to the unsettling conclusion that what happened to Kennedy (and to America, Cuba, and Vietnam) was not a violation of the sacrosanct rules of democracy but rather a product of them. The halls of government and the board rooms of corporations are made up of human beings who wield more power than the average conspiracist, but they are usually no more and no less evil than the man on the street. In other words, the "government" is not a faceless consortium of amoral monsters and drones but a large collection of human beings with competing values, ideas, and prejudices, a community of citizens that may include our neighbor, our cousin, that guy we played ball with, that girl we once dated, some actor whose films we enjoyed, some local lawyers, and a few former college professors. The halls of political power and the general public are joined by a revolving door. Corporations have the power they hold because we purchase the products they make. Conspiracists ignore this to blame elusive boogeymen like the "military industrial complex" and a long list of scapegoats like Lyndon Baines Johnson, Allen Dulles, Edward Lansdale, J. Edgar Hoover, Clint Hill, James Humes, E. Howard Hunt, Carlos Marcello, David Ferrie, and Clay Shaw, a man who had nothing to do with JFK's death but paid for conspiracist bloodlust with his wealth, health, life, and legacy.[24]

If we delve into what made the Vietnam War a travesty, of which Oliver Stone said, "we must fix the blame for the only lost war in our history, for 56,000 American dead and for an as-yet unhealed split in our country and among our people,"[25] we would eventually have to ask whom we should blame for the My Lai massacre, one of the most reprehensible acts of cruelty perpetrated by American troops, causing the brutal and intentional deaths of over 500 Vietnamese peasants, over half of them women and children.[26] Was it President Johnson, the Pentagon, and the "military industrial complex," who financed and oversaw the buildup of US military forces in Southeast Asia? Was it the laboratories and corporations who developed weapons like Napalm and Agent Orange, which killed and terrorized thousands of unwitting peasants? All these groups were culpable of bloodshed, as were the communist revolutionaries whose methods were even more ruthless and ideologically driven than those of American and South Vietnam strategists. But none of these can bear the full guilt for what the villagers of My Lai endured on March 16, 1968, at the hands of Charlie Company,[27] a mob of working-class American G.I.'s who saw the "gooks" they were fighting as subhuman creatures, the peasant women they gang-raped as chattel, and the "Pinkville" hamlets they torched, along with the women and children inside them, as "collateral damage" and a sick source of entertainment. And although some of those servicemen went on to claim that they were compelled to participate, they did not risk their lives nor even their place in the pecking order to try to stop it, but rather just passed the buck to their superiors, claiming that they were just following orders. "What happened at My Lai 4 was not singular, not an aberration," writes journalist Seymour Hersh, who first broke the horrible truth in 1969, "My Lai was unique only in its size".[28]

The response of the mob to its own moral failures, Girard explains, is to pass blame onto some kind of scapegoat: they were victims themselves, they argue, someone else made them do it. Self-examination and the willingness to be wrong, two important precursors to critical thinking, are not conducive to scapegoating. Catharsis is possible only so long as the scapegoat's guilt remains assured, not because the facts say so, but because it has to be so. And so the blame game goes on. This helps explain why conspiracists draw a hard line between the so-called establishment and those who, like them, feel locked out of the system. While it may be true that power breeds smugness and dishonesty, it is false to assume that those who are locked out of power are somehow immune to these traits. As the influential Austrian psychiatrist and Holocaust survivor Viktor Frankl remarked, after witnessing the best and worst of humanity in Nazi death camps:

> There are two races of men in the world, but only these two—the 'race' of the decent man and the 'race' of the indecent man. Both are found everywhere; they penetrate into all groups of society. No group consists entirely of decent or indecent people.[29]

18.3 The orphans of Camelot

As Part I of this book explained, the life and sudden death of President Kennedy elicited several conflicting narratives. The Kennedy family and Johnson administration eulogized the fallen president as a champion of civil rights gunned down by the forces of hatred. This was done partly to counter the claims of many conservative pundits who painted JFK was part of a nepotistic Irish-Catholic "mafia," a corrupt liberal dynasty hostile to traditional American values. Many progressives and leftists countered these popular myths by claiming that he was a man of peace seeking to end the Cold War, and hence the victim of fascist warmongers inside the American political establishment.

Why did JFK's untimely death produce so many clashing interpretations of one of the most meticulously documented periods of history? Political scientist James Piereson offers this thought-provoking response:

> The assassination of a popular president by a communist should have generated a revulsion against everything associated with left-wing doctrines. Yet something very close to the opposite happened. [...] By 1968, student radicals were taking over campuses and joining protest demonstrations in support of a host of radical and revolutionary causes [...]. It is one of the ironies of recent history that many of those young people who filed in shocked grief past the president's coffin in 1963 would just a few years later embrace as

political activists the very doctrines that led Oswald to assassinate him. [...] The various conspiracy theories that arose in the wake of the assassination must be viewed [...] not so much as efforts to discover the truth but as aspects of the struggle to find meaning in a seemingly senseless event.[30]

In light of Piereson's assessment and of René Girard's scapegoating theory, let us consider the reasons for which Kennedy's murder gave rise to so many conspiracy myths.

18.3.1   Sin contexto, no comprendo

Few accounts of the JFK assassination present Kennedy's death from an emotionally neutral perspective. For almost everyone who has studied the crime, whether or not they are drawn to conspiracist explanations, there remains some sense that justice should have been served but was not. There was not only something flagrantly wrong about the manner Kennedy died; there was also little comfort to be found in the sudden murder of Oswald. These two killings robbed the public of a clear explanation for Kennedy's assassination. The fact that Oswald was neither a racist nor an organized criminal but an openly Marxist lone wolf living in a conservative state made the publicized facts even harder to process. For many, the climate of right-wing hatred that had been directed at the civil rights movement was, despite all evidence to the contrary, the likely cause of Kennedy's demise and many in the media, government, and academia wrote it that way. For acting President Johnson, the fear of reigniting the McCarthyist Red Scare or, worse, engaging Cuba and the Soviet Union in a nuclear showdown should it be learned that the assassin was under their orders, meant that Kennedy could not be described truthfully as a victim of the Cold War. The sort of right-wing radicalism that had produced the "Irish Mafia" mythology and sparked racist violence across the country was an appropriate scapegoat.

The Warren Commission's failure to ground Oswald's revolutionary Marxist worldview within the broader Cold War context led many to embrace the more comforting but no less inaccurate myth of Camelot popularized by Mrs. Kennedy in the days that followed the crime—a story in which JFK was recast as a peaceful idealist and champion of civil rights gunned down by the forces of bigotry, not a radical leftist striking a blow at the leading symbol of predatory Western capitalism.[31] As Piereson noted,

> our retrospective view of President Kennedy is now filtered through the legends and symbols [Jacqueline Kennedy] put forward at that time. The hardheaded politician devoted to step-by-step progress was transformed in death into the consummate liberal idealist. [...] Difficult as it may be to accept, the posthumous image of JFK reflected more the idealistic beliefs of Mrs. Kennedy than the practical political liberalism of the man himself.[32]

Henceforth, the distorted image of Oswald as a symbol of madness and bigotry and an enemy of civil rights (when there was no truth to this) laid itself wide open to criticism. Those who saw themselves as victims of capitalism—old socialists who suffered the witch hunts of the 1950s and the young adepts of the 1960s countercul-ture angered by the war in Vietnam—were the first to lash out at this nostalgic myth of American progress, leading them in the process to sympathize with Lee Oswald as a fellow victim of the establishment.

18.3.2 Alternative histories

Despite the widespread popularity of Kennedy-related conspiracy theories, the mainstream news media and academic publishers have largely stayed faithful to the Warren Commission's conclusion that the assassination was the work of one man. JFK buffs like Oliver Stone see this as an additional proof that the media are con-trolled by some powerful secret cabal. In a 1992 public debate over his film *JFK*, Stone offered the following remarks concerning the educational media's endorse-ment of the "official story":

> It makes me doubt all our history; all our history. I grew up [...] reading the Random House series of books on American history. I've come to have severe doubts about Columbus, Washington, the Civil War being fought for slavery, the Indian Wars, World War I, World War II, the supposed fight against Nazism and/or Japanese control of resources in Southeast Asia. I doubted everything; [...] I see the two paragraphs of American history on "Oswald did it alone," and that's all we get. These kids are not getting *an alternative version of American history.*[33]

What does he mean by "an alternative version" of history? A good example is presented in Stone's closing narration of an episode of his 2012 television series, *The Untold History of the United States*:

> In his inaugural address in the morning of that decade in January 1961, [Kennedy said] "let the word go forth from this time and place, to friend and foe alike, that the torch has been passed to a new generation of Americans." But with his murder, the torch was passed back to an old generation, the generation of Johnson, Nixon, Ford, and Reagan; leaders who would sys-tematically destroy the promise of Kennedy's last year as they returned the country to war and repression. Though the vision Khrushchev and Kennedy had expressed would fall with them, it would not die. The seeds they had planted would germinate and sprout again long after their deaths.
> For those of us who lived through the Nineteen Sixties, the Cuban Missile Crisis—coming on the heels of the war scare over Berlin—was a terrifying event. It was one of many nightmares, call it punches to the stomach of a new generation of American people who had never seen history unfold so quickly,

so dramatically and in such a violent fashion. It would soon be followed by the invasion of Vietnam, a blood bath, a nightmare of America's own making that would eat Vietnamese and Americans alive for almost a decade.

More horrifying things were to come by the end of that decade. But in hindsight, it was on that afternoon in Dallas when John Kennedy's head was blown off in broad daylight. It was as if a giant, horrific Greek medusa had unearthed its hideous face to the American people, freezing us with an oracle of things yet to come.[34]

In numerous other public outcries Stone has indicted the federal government, several law-enforcement agencies, and the loosely defined "military industrial complex" for planning and covering-up a right-wing coup d'état against Kennedy.[35] But to be consistent, his conspiracy theory must also involve numerous other suspects, including the world of educational publishing—which would, I presume, include this book's publisher. Indeed, Stone has inculpated thousands of privately funded journalists, academics, educators, editors, and publicists in this alleged affair, who have deliberately and collectively misled the public for decades by refusing to teach "alternative versions" of history. Stone's claims, sadly, are not exceptional.

No longer limited to the paranoid fringe, the concept of alternative history is a recurring theme in conspiracist media, especially online,[36] where JFK buffs display the same type of hostility toward historians as ufologists, young-earth creationists, and proponents of alternative medicines direct at accomplished scientists. Many conspiracists even promote a transcendental theory of knowledge similar to those of religious cults like Scientology, Falun Dafa, and Gnosticism, faith systems that hold that the visible world is a house of mirrors ruled by malevolent entities.[37] Better-grounded conspiracists might not go this far, but nonetheless speak as if most of what passes for history in textbooks is a subtle form of mind control orchestrated by rich Western powerbrokers. The Warren Report's lone gunman theory has thus become subsumed into a wider paranoid matrix, one that envisions an epic global deception that threatens to wipe out all freedoms lest it be exposed by a committed "resistance" of "open-minded" researchers. It is a story built on their fear of authority, held together by a single thread—global conspiracy—that connects all major historic events, from the rise and fall of ancient empires to the latest major catastrophe.

This is a central reason for which JFK assassination theories continue to spark widespread interest across each new generation. By promoting themselves as "alternative history," Kennedy assassination theories serve as a gateway drug into an anti-establishment culture. It invites its adepts to pursue their quest for a "higher truth" through self-guided research—a "truth" that can only be grasped through a radical personal awakening, or what philosophers call a paradigm shift. It becomes, simply put, something not unlike a cultish religion: a myopic community of enlightened initiates whose highest sacrament is to systematically doubt everything, and who commit themselves to liberating the minds of the ignorant from the controls of the reigning establishment and demonizing those who oppose them. What conspiracists ultimately seek, then, is not an *empirical* truth but an *existential* one: a story with the *appearance* of truth—what can rightly be called a doctrine or myth—that can help them claim the moral high-ground in their life story.

Myths usually contain some kernel of truth, but they do not chronicle past events dispassionately. What makes them myths and not histories or legends is the fact that, despite their lack of verifiable evidence, the believer assumes that the story is true because it has explanatory power. If the myth confirms the believer's impression that he is the victim of some powerful group (and conspiracy theories do this quite well), then the theory is simply assumed to be true because it offers the victim of alienation what the "official story" could not: simple answers, vindication of their frustrations, personal innocence, and a clearly identified—if poorly defined—source of evil to blame.

"Official" history—the sort that is subject to a peer-review process and rigid standards of evidence—does not typically offer its readers much comfort. It tells us that life is unpredictable, unfair, and complicated; that tragedy can strike anyone at any time; that cycles of violence may harm unwitting bystanders. It teaches us that no one is entirely good or evil; that yesterday's victims might be tomorrow's abusers; that a crowd can be as malicious as a tyrant. It tells us that, given a certain alignment of bad circumstances and unfortunate choices, no one is fully immune to becoming a Brutus, a John Wilkes Booth, or a Lee Harvey Oswald. "Alternative" history, on the other hand, can be simple to grasp and morally freeing, much like pagan mythology. It seemed obvious to ancient societies that unscrupulous gods were in charge of the world and that humans were either to serve them or suffer their whims. Likewise, if one presumes that all they've been taught is a lie and that hypercompetent secret cabals hold infinite power over their lives, there is no reason to look inside oneself for the causes of one's misfortune, and even less blame bad luck. When the entire record of history is suspect any new interpretation becomes merely an alternate viewpoint, a possible truth that holds as much weight as the reigning consensus or "official story". But when we carefully assess the truth-telling value of alternative histories in both their content and structure, they often turn out to be inconsistent, unduly alarmist, and self-serving.

Seen thus, conspiracy theorizing is the ultimate buck-passing device, serving a similar purpose as the fatalistic doctrines of ancient paganism. To the modern conspiracy mythmaker, the power brokers of our secular age may not look like Odin, Marduk, or Shiva the Destroyer, but their role in the story has not changed significantly. They are the bankers, weapons manufacturers, corporate lobbyists, amoral bureaucrats, shadow governments, and secret agents that lurk at the edge of perception, playing the same roles in modern folklore that anthropomorphous deities played in ancient times. Indeed, the modern power brokers imagined by conspiracy-mongers are often assumed to have superhuman abilities of mass persuasion and evidence-tampering. If, as I suggest, we see conspiracism as a modern and secular form of pagan religion—one that is deeply subjective but not self-reflecting, that thirsts for happiness now and not in some kind of afterlife—we can better comprehend why conspiracy theories have grown so popular in an age in which faith in a divine moral order and hope in its ultimate victory over evil have been largely abandoned in favor of a cold and impersonal scientism.

18.3.3   The substitute victim

In their attempts to make sense of their anger and grief, conspiracists often fall prey to emotional reasoning, especially self-pity. In many of the accounts discussed in this book, Kennedy's death is depicted as if the researcher's brother or father had been discovered one morning hanging from the rafters of the family barn. Police, government, news media, and academic investigations that peg the blame on an "angry lone nut" offer these authors little emotional closure because the angry lone nut explication cannot balance the ledger of their moral outrage.[38] The onus thus falls on the shoulders of the victim's "family" (i.e., the community of JFK buffs) to disregard expert opinion and reinvestigate the entire case on their own. After all, only they knew the "real" Jack. Only they "know" his death could not possibly be caused by an accident, incompetence, or the work of a lone sociopath. Only they know it *had* to have been the result of a finely coordinated attack against their "family"—that is, against whatever ideas, hopes, or concerns conspiracists might have projected onto their fallen hero, who serves as an idealization of their own sense of victimhood. In perceiving Kennedy's death as a *personal* tragedy, one whose "official" interpretation does not cohere with their own experience and expectations, conspiracists build their case up from the narcissistic conviction that somebody somewhere is lying *to them*. In this respect, JFK buffs can be seen as a generation of grieving Bobbys and Jackies charged with restoring the family's honor whatever the method or cost.

Of course, John Kennedy was no ordinary mortal. The handsome and charismatic statesman and his presidential court—later dubbed "Camelot"—were real-life theater to many. In a world not yet endowed with reality shows and 24-hour news cycles, the Kennedy family fulfilled a popular thirst for voyeurism, much as British royal scandals, The Osbournes and Kardashians, or Donald Trump's tweets did in later years. This is one reason why the mythic King Arthur could believably serve as an icon of the late President, one whose legacy was essentially still a blank page. Rightly or wrongly, the Kennedy White House came to symbolize that optimistic young generation who, on November 22, 1963, was left out in the cold. So it is to be expected that spending long hours reflecting on Kennedy's untimely death and unfulfilled promise of change would make any wide-eyed idealist feel like a collateral victim.

And so, the assassination of President Kennedy has become something like a religious event for many secular progressives, not unlike the crucifixion of Jesus for committed Christians: an event whose full significance can only be grasped through a leap of faith that calls the believer to fight in a war for the fate of humanity. The all-important difference, of course, is that Kennedy never rose from the dead. The conspiracists' hope for the future therefore resides solely in their own hands and not in a higher power, which may account for the despondent and desperate tone that permeates their literature.

But in another sense, conspiracism offers them an existential hope. Through the act of scapegoating, it gives its believers a simpler and more satisfying explanation for the problem of evil than the ones offered by philosophers, environmentalists, or mainstream theologians who argue that humans share a collective responsibility for the poor state of our world. Perhaps the fear of a bogeyman is more bearable than a guilty conscience. It is certainly more lucrative than books on critical thinking.

More evidence may come to light on Kennedy's assassination. It is quite possible that our knowledge of that event will change, as it did in 1975 when the CIA's secret program to assassinate Fidel Castro was first exposed and the failure of the Warren Commission to investigate Oswald's possible ties to Cuba grew clearer. But why should we assume that any new information would be accepted by the conspiracists? Would it count as a victory for them if it were revealed that Castro or Khrushchev made Oswald do it? Or that bureaucratic incompetence was largely to blame? Or that Kennedy carelessly put himself and his wife in danger, thinking he was invincible? I venture to say that none of these possible reasons for a cover-up would be acceptable simply because that isn't the story they want to hear—which is that some corporate "fascists" took over their government and are plotting to wreck their lives too. In other words, it would still prove that the principal motor of their suspicions—their irrational fear of a bogeyman—is feeding them a delusion.

Conspiracy theories are not attempts to elucidate the past so much as they are attempts to use historical claims to assert oneself in the present. The past—even a false one—can serve as a powerful vehicle to help us decide who we are and what sort of world we want to live in, and to inspire the powerless to "speak truth to power". Indeed, conspiracy myths offer believers something that most historians can't: a sense of serving a higher purpose. And that kind of "truth" can be hard to snuff out with cold logic and data.

According to Harold Weisberg, one of the earliest militant JFK buffs, millions of ordinary Americans have been the victims of an odious "whitewash" concerning the truth of Kennedy's death.[39] This is true. But the real deception lies not in the work of the Warren Commission. It lies in the misguided efforts of conspiracy theorists to wrongly and deceitfully acquit Kennedy's only known and demonstrably guilty assassin. It is those who believe in such myths who have become the orphans of history.

18.4 When Jack became Jesus

For those old enough to remember the troubling events of November 1963, JFK's murder was shocking enough to make them forever remember where they were and what they were doing when they heard the terrible news. Kennedy had many critics, but he was generally seen as a vibrant, young, and sophisticated individual dedicated to democracy, social justice and, to a certain extent, a more peaceful world. Those who perceived this as a façade nonetheless recognized him as a charismatic, capable, and shrewd tactician. But who exactly was JFK? As James Piereson remarked:

Kennedy, following his sudden death and solemn funeral, was turned into something different in public memory from how he was understood in life. Like Lincoln, Kennedy too was viewed as a martyr, albeit in devotion of a most uncertain cause. Here was a source of much bewilderment about the man and the event. What exactly did John F. Kennedy stand for? The great difference between Lincoln and Kennedy is that the former died at his moment of victory while the latter was killed before he was able to achieve any great success. [...] Lincoln was mourned but also celebrated for his magnificent achievement; Kennedy was mourned in a spirit of frustrated possibility and dashed hopes.[40]

The messianic aura that still surrounds Kennedy's memory has had a profound impact on the way his life story gets told, not just by conspiracy buffs but also by mainstream historians, journalists, and filmmakers. While many political leaders come to power as Kennedy did, wrapped in a cult of personality, their reputation is usually tarnished after the merciless game of partisan politics takes over and a series of unpopular decisions brings them back down to earth, not to speak of the ubiquitous scandals, muckraking media stories, and voyeuristic technologies that permeate contemporary news reporting, and which might have exposed Kennedy's private misdeeds had he been elected a few decades later. But none of that happened to John Kennedy, whose star power only waxed brighter after his death, as his wife and supporters turned him into a secular martyr. This made it all the more difficult for those who expected a post-Cold War, post-racial America to emerge at this time to separate the historical "John" from the mythical "Jack".

For those who, like me, were not even born when Kennedy died, their perspective is not much clearer. Every decade or so, a new series of books and films ensure that the conspiracy trail remains fresh with some claim of new evidence in the form of declassified documents, tell-all interviews with peripheral witnesses (many of whom turn out to be charlatans), photographic enhancements by self-appointed "experts," and disjointed "confessions" like those of Carlos Marcello or E. Howard Hunt.[41] Pop culture references are aplenty and usually take it as fact that JFK was killed by his own sycophants, some sinister criminal network, the "deep state," or some shadowy clique like the Freemasons. By the time I entered university in the early 1990s, the Kennedy assassination was front page news again thanks to Oliver Stone, the Vietnam vet with a grudge. Stone's *JFK* did not offer a novel explanation. In fact, it contained very little new content. What it did marvelously was to harmonize the disparate voices of umpteen JFK buffs and amplify them to an unprecedented level, capturing a whole new generation of gullible activists. The film touched a nerve because Stone's concerns about the evils of war, amoral investment banking, and political corruption were deeply familiar. Not only were these drummed into us through his previous films like *Salvador*, *Platoon*, and *Wall Street*, they were echoed in the films of other famous directors like Francis Ford Coppola, Stanley Kubrick, John Irvin, and Brian de Palma, who all helped turn Vietnam into a morbid obsession.

Stone's film was unusually powerful because it was timely. It reflected the spirit of 1991 better than the spirit of 1963. Discussions on *JFK* and the theories that inspired it appeared in the media alongside reports of the fall of the Soviet Union, the trial and conviction of Panamanian president Manuel Noriega, the liberation of Kuwait from the warmongering Saddam Hussein, the unstoppable spread of the AIDS virus, and the violent breakup of Yugoslavia—events that all triggered a stream of conspiracy stories. Stone's film was emotional flypaper for young paranoids of my generation, capturing our imaginations by tying every loose end the only way Hollywood films can, and by suggesting that Kennedy—much like Luke Skywalker, Frodo Baggins, Fox Mulder, and our other cultural icons—was an unflinching hero standing alone against an evil empire.

This was a very persuasive message during a period that saw the collapse of the Soviet Union and rapid expansion of American cultural, economic, and military influence overseas. In other words, *JFK* hit a nerve not because it offered us a correct historical picture of the 1960s (it didn't) but because it appropriated the historical theme of the assassination, rewrote the life of historical figures inside that story, threw in a spate of creepy (and irrelevant) suspects, and wrapped the whole thing in the anxieties of the early 1990s: a one-superpower world, growing government surveillance, out-of-control military spending, rampant deregulation of private industry, the militarization of outer space, the conglomeration of mass media, the destruction of the atmosphere, and the ulcer of cynicism that still lingered long after Vietnam, Watergate, and Iran-Contra were laid to rest. *JFK* was doubly convincing because the Russians were now to be pitied, not feared. The claim that an angry lone Marxist could manage to pull the trigger on Kennedy, a hero of peace, simply did not fit the zeitgeist of a capitalistic New World Order. And that is what made this film and its claims most compelling: it told me I was a victim of the "military industrial complex," that my enemy was an all-powerful (American) oligarchy, and that I had to resist it by demanding they "Release the files!"

This is my story. Not every JFK buff comes to "faith" in the conspiracist cause through the gospel of Oliver Stone, but they all come for similar reasons: mistrust of authority, feelings of helplessness, and the allure of a meaningful and empowering mission.

One could assume that the popularity of this conspiracy theory will wane as the short list of surviving suspects die off and the first generation of Kennedy buffs dies along with them (so far, all seem to have done so from natural causes), and as the trickle of new evidence dries up for good. But JFK conspiracism has not shown signs of disappearing any time soon. On the contrary, it receives new life every time a (mostly) left-wing reaction flares up against the ultrarich or a conservative wins the presidency.[42] But JFK conspiracism is no longer a necessarily left-wing phenomenon. It has now penetrated all political factions, including the Trump administration and the ultraconservative QAnon movement.[43] And yet we can cautiously hope that the tide has now turned. While popular beliefs JFK was killed by a conspiracy remains high, it has also begun to stall. The number of apostates—former conspiracists who repudiate all or much of their former beliefs—is also on the rise, not just on the subject of Kennedy's death, but as a general theme in media and publishing. The full or partial deconversion of recovering conspiracists like Dan Moldea, Gary Mack, David Reitzes, Edward Jay Epstein, Fred Kaplan, Fred Litwin, and Charlie Veitch (as well as my own) shows that conspiracism is not an inborn or lifelong condition but one we can grow out of.[44]

We are still far from seeing a massive movement of ex-conspiracists take shape. Although conspiracy theories frequently go out of style (consider how short-lived the *Da Vinci Code* hype lasted), they are often more quickly replaced by new theories than an increase in critical thinking. JFK conspiracism has enjoyed a long shelf life because of its universal appeal and because it (usually) steers clear of esoteric themes like time travel, mind control, and shape-shifting aliens. Nevertheless, a new form of counter-conspiracism is on the rise. More and more skeptical media, such as the podcasts of Joe Rogan, Michael Shermer, David McRaney, and Brian Dunning (as well as my own), are taking direct aim at conspiracist "logic". Academics like Joseph Uscinski and Kathryn Olmsted, journalists like Jonathan Kay and David Aaronovitch, and documentary filmmakers like James Lambert have also begun studying conspiracism, not as a mental illness but as a social phenomenon, and are trying to better assess its causes and effects.

This changing tide is also fueled by improvements in the tools of forensic science which, as we have seen, have recently allowed us to shed more light on the photographic, medical, and ballistic details of JFK's murder, proving even more strongly that the lone gunman theory proposed by the Warren Commission (with a few corrections) is still correct. When dealing with technical and scientific evidence, most conspiracists delve into waters that go deeper than their education, experience, or acumen can help them see through clearly. It then becomes easier for them to overgeneralize, misdiagnose, and fall prey to confirmation bias. This is why anyone who ventures into the "Oak Island Money Pit" of Kennedy assassination research, or any other form of conspiracism for that matter, should do so from their own expertise, should exercise excessive caution, and should always be willing to be wrong.

Of course, there may yet exist some shocking new revelation lying in wait, like a set of pictures stored in an attic, a misfiled document in the National Archives or dusty CIA vault, or some morbid heirloom in some long-forgotten safety deposit box. This is why many JFK buffs continue to wager that they will someday behold the elusive "smoking gun" that will vindicate all of their obsessive efforts. But the mountains of evidence now available, and the tools of logic discussed throughout this book, suggest that theirs is a losing bet, and I, for one, have stopped losing sleep over it.

WHAT IS FUTURE IS EPILOGUE

Notes

1 "Appendix G: Deposition of James J. Humes M.D., before the ARRB on 13 February 1996, Edited by David W. Mantik, M.D., Ph.D.," in Fetzer, ed.: *Murder in Dealey Plaza*, 451.

2 "Appendix G: Deposition of James J. Humes […] Edited by David W. Mantik," 452.

3 Appendices E, F, and G in Fetzer, 433–52.

4 Dr. D.L. Breo: "JFK's Death—The Plain Truth from the MDs Who Did the Autopsy," *JAMA (Journal of the American Medical Association)*, Vol.267, No.20, May 27, 1992, 2794–803.

5 Joe Nickell: "The Secrets of Oak Island," *Skeptical Inquirer*, Vol.24.2, March/April 2000, *CSICOP*.

6 At the time of writing this book, a History Channel reality show titled "The Curse of Oak Island," soon in its ninth season, continues to excavate vainly, financed by advertisements and cable TV subscriptions.

7 Richard E. Joltes: "History, Hoax, and Hype: The Oak Island Legend," *Critical Enquiry*, 2002. While the WHOI study acknowledged that the presence of decomposing coconut husks buried under the beach sand was unusual for this location, this does not imply that any underground engineering project took place on the island. While an intentional hoax was not discarded as a possible explanation for these, the WHOI's report suggested that early explorers or smugglers might have used the location as a stopover point or dumpsite for shipping materials, which would have likely included coconut fibers because these were formerly used in maritime freight the way polystyrene "packing peanuts" are used today.

8 Such deceptions include a stone carving found nearby that claimed Captain Kidd had left clues to the location of his hidden treasure (later revealed to be a hoax concocted by local youths), and a cipher stone that was allegedly found in the Money Pit (but disappeared in 1919) which read: "Forty Feet Below Two Million Pounds Are Buried". "Inscribed Stone Hoaxes," *Oak Island Treasure*; Nickell: "The Secrets of Oak Island".

9 The term is drawn from a Hebrew phrase that means "The goat that departs/is removed," or possibly "the demon Azazel's goat". It originates from Leviticus 16: 20–1, a passage of the Hebrew Torah that institutes rituals for the celebration of *Yom Kippur* (the Day of Atonement). Philologos (Hillel Halkin): "Why the Israelites Expelled a Scapegoat into the Wilderness on Yom Kippur," *Mosaic Magazine*, October 14, 2016.

10 Todd Merlin Compton: *Victim of The Muses: Poet as Scapegoat, Warrior and Hero in Greco-Roman and Indo-European Myth and History*, Hellenic Studies Series 11, 2006, *Center for Hellenic Studies*, Harvard University; René Girard: *I See Satan Fall Like Lightning* (2001).

11 For a discussion of scapegoating as a "mimetic psychosocial mechanism" in mythical, pagan, and Biblical contexts, see René Girard: "The First Stone," *Renascence*, Vol.52, No.1, Fall 1999. See also Christopher Hrynkow: "Girard, René, Theories of Mimetic Violence and Scapegoating," in Jeffrey Ian Ross, ed.: *Violence and Religion: An Encyclopedia of Faith and Conflict from Antiquity to the Present*, Vol. 2 (2011), and Gabriel Andrade: "René Girard," *The Internet Encyclopedia of Philosophy*.

12 David Cayley: "The Scapegoat: The Ideas of René Girard" (Parts 1–5), *CBC Radio 1: Ideas*, March 4–17, 2016.

13 Indeed, the poor reception given to *The Last Jedi* (2017) by Star Wars aficionados can be explained by director Rian Johnson's decision to stray from the traditional family storyline, which J.J. Abrams, the director of the subsequent sequel, *The Rise of Skywalker* (2019), was compelled to reclaim.

14 Cayley: "The Scapegoat…".

15 Uscinski and Parent, 6.

16 Cayley: "The Scapegoat…"; Cicero: *Selected Works*, Chapter 2: "Cicero's Life and Letters," 91, 97; John 11:50, *New International Version*.

17 Alison Flood: "'Post-Truth' Named Word of the Year by Oxford Dictionaries," *The Guardian*, November 15, 2016.

18 "Who Was Lee Harvey Oswald?" (1993) *PBS Frontline*, November 19, 2013; Olmsted: *Real Enemies*, 132; "Zach Sklar at Upstate Films in Woodstock, NY, after a Screening of Trumbo, November 28, 2015," *YouTube*; "George Sklar, 79, Dies; Playwright and Author," *New York Times*, May 18, 1988.

19 "We can only hope the free thinkers in the world," wrote Oliver Stone in the lead-up to his film *JFK*, "those with no agenda, will recognize our movie as an emotional experience that speaks a higher truth than the [*Washington Post*'s George] Lardners of the world will ever know". Oliver Stone: "Stone's 'JFK' A Higher Truth? The Post, George Lardner and My Version of the JFK Assassination," *The Washington Post*, June 2, 1991.

20 Richard S. Levy: *Introduction to Binjamin W. Segel: A Lie and a Libel: The History of the Protocols of the Elders of Zion* (1996).

21 "Catharsis," *Merriam-Webster Dictionary Online*.

22 Girard: "The First Stone," 11. Girard uses the term *mimesis* to describe the imitative (or bandwagon) effect of the mob that selects its scapegoat based on an emotional consensus instead of objective evidence.

23 Friedrich Engels, 1888 preface to "The Communist Manifesto," cited in W.T. Jones: *A History of Western Philosophy, Vol. IV: Kant and the Nineteenth Century*, 2nd Edition, 1976; G.A. Cohen: *Karl Marx's Theory of History: A Defence* (2000).

24 Patricia Lambert: *False Witness: The Real Story of Jim Garrison's Investigation and Oliver Stone's Film JFK* (1998).

25 Oliver Stone: "Making the Movie J.F.K.," Speech delivered to the National Press Club, January 15, 1992, *C-SPAN*.

26 According to Pham Thanh Cong, a child survivor of these events and current director of the My Lai Museum, the number of casualties included:

> five hundred and four victims, from two hundred and forty-seven families. Twenty-four families were obliterated—three generations murdered, with no survivors. Among the dead were a hundred and eighty-two women, seventeen of them pregnant. A hundred and seventy-three children were executed, including fifty-six infants. Sixty older men died.

These victims include those found at the nearby My Khe hamlet, who were killed by members of Bravo Company. Seymour Hersh: "The Scene of the Crime: A Reporter's Journey to My Lai and the Secrets of the Past," *The New Yorker*, March 30, 2015.

27 Charlie Company belonged to the 1st Battalion, 20th Infantry Regiment, 11th Brigade, of the 23rd Infantry Division.

28 Hersh, "The Scene of the Crime". A similar event occurred in the village of Truong Le on April 18, 1969, where American soldiers killed "forty-one children and twenty-two women, leaving only nine survivors".

29 Viktor E. Frankl: *Man's Search for Meaning* (2006), 86.

30 James Pie023on: *Camelot and the Cultural Revolution: How the Assassination of John F. Kennedy Shattered American Liberalism* (2007), x, xvi.

31 Olmsted, chap. 4; Theodore H. White: "For President Kennedy: An Epilogue"; Pie023on, chap. 7.

32 Pie023on: "How Jackie Kennedy Invented the Camelot Legend after JFK's Death," *The Daily Beast*, 11/12/2013.

33 "Hollywood & History: The Debate over 'JFK'" (Proceedings of a Panel Discussion on *JFK* at Town Hall, New York City, NY, March 3, 1992), *PBS Frontline*, November 19, 2013. Emphasis added.

34 Matt Graham, Peter Kuznick, and Oliver Stone: "JFK—To the Brink" (chap. 6), *The Untold History of the United States*, Showtime, 2012.

35 Oliver Stone interviews with Charles Kiselyak ("Oliver Stone's America," Warner Home Video, 2001, *YouTube*), Ken Paulson (*Speaking Freely* #312, March 1, 2002), Amy Goodman ("Oliver Stone on 50th Anniversary of JFK Assassination & the Untold History of the United States," *Democracy Now*, November 5, 2013), and Tyrel Ventura and Sean Stone ("JFK and the Untold History of Oliver Stone," *Buzzsaw* #75, November 6, 2013).

36 Some examples include Alex Jones' *Infowars*, Len Osanic's *Black Op Radio*, Joseph Farah's *World Net Daily*, Sean Stone's (Oliver Stone's son) *Buzzsaw*, and Cassim K. Igram's (aka: "Dr. K") *Nodisinfo*.

37 Joseph Heath: "What Makes Someone a Conspiracy Theorist?" *In Due Course: A Canadian Public Affairs Blog*, December 5, 2016.

38 William Manchester: "No Evidence for a Conspiracy to Kill Kennedy," *The New York Times*, February 5, 1992.

39 Harold Weisberg: *Whitewash: The Report on the Warren Report* (1965).

40 Piereson: *Camelot and the Cultural Revolution*, xiii–xiv.

41 See Chapter 6, and Erik Hedegaard: "The Last Confession of E. Howard Hunt," *Rolling Stone*, April 5, 2007.

42 Joseph P. Uscinski and Joseph M. Parent: *American Conspiracy Theories* (2014), 130–53.

43 Gabrielle Bruney: "Unpacking QAnon: A Batsh★t Conspiracy Theory Tailor-Made for the Trump Era," *Esquire*, August 5, 2018; Jeffrey Toobin: "Roger Stone's and Jerome Corsi's Time in the Barrel," *The New Yorker*, February 19, 2019.

44 Dan E. Moldea: *The Killing of Robert F. Kennedy* (1995); Michael E. Young: "Gary Mack and the Evolution of a JFK Conspiracy Theorist," *Dallas Morning News*, March 2, 2013; Will Storr: "The 9/11 Conspiracy Theorist Who Changed His Mind," *The Telegraph*, May 29, 2013; Fred Kaplan: "Killing Conspiracy: Why the Best Conspiracy Theories about JFK's Assassination Don't Stand Up to Scrutiny," *Slate*, November 14, 2013; Fred Litwin: *I Was a Teenage JFK Conspiracy Freak* (2018); Michel Jacques Gagné: "How Oliver Stone Turned Me into a Conspiracy Theorist," *The National Post*, November 22, 2013.

SELECT BIBLIOGRAPHY

1 Government documents

"1968 Panel Review of Photographs, X-Ray Films, Documents and Other Evidence Pertaining to the Fatal Wounding of President John F. Kennedy on November 22, 1963 In Dallas, Texas," (Clark Panel Report), February 26, 1968.

"ARRB Medical Testimony," 1996–1998, *Mary Ferrell Foundation* website.

Final Report of the Assassination Records Review Board (ARRB), September 1998, *National Archives: JFK Assassination Records.*

Final Report of the Select Committee to Study Governmental Operations with Respect to Intelligence Activities, United States Senate (Church Committee Report), Washington, DC: US Government Printing Office, 1976, *National Archives.*

JFK Assassination Reports and Records: Assassination Records Review Board (ARRB), Rex Bradford, ed.: *History Matters* website.

JFK Assassination Reports and Records: House Select Committee on Assassinations (HSCA), Rex Bradford, ed.: *History Matters* website.

JFK Assassination Reports and Records: Warren Commission Hearings and Exhibits, Rex Bradford, ed.: *History Matters* website.

Report to the President by the Commission on CIA Activities within the United States (Rockefeller Commission Report), Manor Books, 1975, *National Archives.*

Report of the President's Commission on the Assassination of President Kennedy (Warren Report), Washington, DC: United States Government Printing Office, 1964, *National Archives: JFK Assassination Records.*

Report of the Select Committee on Assassinations of the U.S. House of Representatives (HSCA Report), Washington, DC: United States Government Printing Office, 1979, *National Archives: JFK Assassination Records.*

Warren Commission Hearings and Exhibits, Volumes I to XXVI, 1964, Rex Bradford, ed.: *History Matters* website.

2 Articles and diaries

Attanasio, Paul: "The Long Inner War of Oliver Stone," *The Washington Post*, January 11, 1987.

Aynesworth, Hugh: "'One-Man Truth Squad' Still Debunking JFK Conspiracy Theories," *Dallas Morning News*, November 17, 2012.

Ayton, Mel: "The Truth about J. Edgar Hoover," *Crime Magazine*, July 19, 2005.

Bacher, Dannielle: "Oliver Stone Looks Back at 'JFK'," *Rolling Stone*, November 4, 2013.

Bethell, Thomas: "Inside the Garrison Investigation: The Thomas Bethell Diary," June 25, 1967 to April 1, 1968, John McAdams, ed.: *The Kennedy Assassination* website.

Billings, Richard: "Dick Billings's Personal Notes on Consultations and Interviews with Garrison: December 1966-January 25, 1967," David Reitzes, ed.: *JFK Online* website.

Dallek, Robert: "John F. Kennedy," Oxford University Press, ePub, 2011.

Ebert, Roger: "Oliver Stone Defends 'JFK' Against Conspiracy of Dunces," *Chicago Sun-Times*, December 22, 1991.

Epstein, Edward Jay: "The Second Coming of Jim Garrison," *The Atlantic Monthly*, March 1993.

Farid, Hany: "The Lee Harvey Oswald Backyard Photos: Real or Fake?" *Perception*, Vol.38, 2009.

Galbraith, James K.: "Exit Strategy," *Boston Review*, October/November 2003. See https://bostonreview.net/us/galbraith-exit-strategy-vietnam.

Girard, René: "The First Stone," *Renascence*, Vol.52, No.1, Fall 1999.

Gregory, Paul: "Lee Harvey Oswald Was My Friend," *The New York Times Magazine*, November 7, 2013.

Hersh, Seymour: "The Scene of the Crime: A Reporter's Journey to My Lai and the Secrets of the Past," *The New Yorker*, March 30, 2015.

Hofstadter, Richard: "The Paranoid Style in American Politics," *Harper's Magazine*, November 1964.

Holland, Max: "The Demon in Jim Garrison," *Wilson Quarterly*, Vol.25, No.2, Spring 2001.

Holland, Max: "The Power of Disinformation: The Lie that Linked CIA to the Kennedy Assassination," *2001, Center for the Study of Intelligence, Central Intelligence Agency*, April 14, 2007.

Holland, Max and Johann Rush: "J.F.K.'s Death, Re-Framed," *The New York Times*, November 22, 2007.

Hrynkow, Christopher: "Girard, René, Theories of Mimetic Violence and Scapegoating," in Jeffrey Ian Ross, ed.: *Violence and Religion: An Encyclopedia of Faith and Conflict from Antiquity to the Present*, Vol.2, M.E. Sharpe, 2011.

Janos, Leo: "The Last Days of the President: LBJ in Retirement," *The Atlantic Monthly*, July 1973.

Lane, Mark: "Oswald Innocent? A Lawyer's Brief: A Report to the Warren Commission by Mark Lane," *National Guardian*, Vol.16, No.11, December 19, 1963.

Lardner, George, Jr.: "On the Set: Dallas in Wonderland: How Oliver Stone's Version of the Kennedy Assassination Exploits the Edge of Paranoia," *The Washington Post*, May 19, 1991.

Lattimer, John K., et al.: "Could Oswald Have Shot President Kennedy? Further Ballistic Studies," *Bulletin of the New York Academy of Medicine*, Vol.48, No.3, April 1972.

Lattimer, John K., et al.: "Differences in the Wounding Behavior of the Two Bullets that Struck President Kennedy; an Experimental Study," *Wound Ballistics Review*, Vol.2, No.2, 1995.

Leman, Patrick: "The Born Conspiracy," *New Scientist*, Vol.195, No.2612, July 14, 2007.

Loebs, Bruce: "Kennedy, Vietnam, and Oliver Stone's Big Lie," *USA Today Magazine*, Vol.121, No.2576, May 1993.

McMillan, Priscilla: "A Word about Lee Harvey Oswald," June 11, 2007, *Washington Decoded* website.

Norden, Eric: "Playboy Interview: Jim Garrison—A Candid Conversation with the Embattled District Attorney of New Orleans," *Playboy*, October 1967.

Persico, Joseph E.: "Secrets from the Lubyanka," *New York Times*, October 31, 1999.

Phelan, James: "Rush to Judgment in New Orleans: District Attorney Jim Garrison Claims to Have Solved the President's Murder. What Evidence Does He Have? How Good Is It?" *Saturday Evening Post*, May 6, 1967.

Prouty, L. Fletcher, with Richard E. Sprague: "The Guns of August," *Gallery*, October 1975.

Russell, Bertrand: "16 Questions on the Assassination," *The Minority of One*, September 6, 1964.

Sabato, Larry J.: "The Kennedy Half Century: Acoustical Analysis of November 22, 1963 Dallas Police Recordings," *University of Virginia*, 2013.

Scott, Peter Dale: "From Dallas to Watergate: The Longest Cover-Up," *Ramparts Magazine*, November 1973.

Scott, Peter Dale: "The Doomsday Project and Deep Events: JFK, Watergate, Iran-Contra, and 9/11," *The Asia Pacific Journal*, Vol. 9, No. 47, Number 2, November 26, 2011.

Scott, Peter Dale: "The Fates of American Presidents Who Challenged the Deep State (1963–1980)," *The Asia Pacific Journal*, Vol. 12, No. 43, Number 4, October 20, 2014.

Selverstone, Marc J.: "It's a Date: Kennedy and the Timetable for a Vietnam Troop Withdrawal," *Diplomatic History*, Vol. 34, No. 3, June 2010.

Shermer, Michael: "Patternicity: Finding Meaningful Patterns in Meaningless Noise: Why the Brain Believes Something Is Real When It Is Not," *Scientific American*, December 1, 2008.

Swift, Art: "Majority in U.S. Still Believe JFK Killed in a Conspiracy: Mafia, Federal Government Top List of Potential Conspirators," *Gallup Politics*, November 15, 2013.

Tapley, Kristopher: "Oliver Stone and Kevin Costner Look Back at the Legacy of 'JFK,' 25 Years Later," *Variety*, December 20, 2016.

Zavada, Roland J.: "Analysis of Selected Motion Picture Evidence" *Zavada Report, Kodak Technical Report 31842OP*, September, 25, 1998.

3   Published interviews

Bugliosi, Vincent: "CBC Ideas: The Enright Files: John F. Kennedy," *CBC Radio 1*, November 4, 2013.

Dallek, Robert, "CBC Ideas: The Enright Files: John F. Kennedy," *CBC Radio 1*, November 4, 2013.

Hersh, Seymour: "Allan Gregg: Journalist Seymour Hersh on the Truth Behind JFK," *TVO*, December 8, 2010.

Lansdale, Edward Geary: "Interview with Stanley Karnow, 31 January 1979 (Raw Footage for the Program 'Vietnam: A Television History,'" *America's Mandarin (1954–1963)*, WGBH Educational Foundation. *WGBH: Open Vault*.

Moorman, Mary: "Transcript from Mary Moorman Interview by Gary Stover," *iAntique.com*, May 24, 2011.

Oswald Porter, Marina: "Marina Oswald," *Hard Copy*, November 19, 1990.

Prouty, L. Fletcher: "Gen. Ed Lansdale in Dealey Plaza," (n.d.), Len Osanic, ed.: *The Colonel L. Fletcher Prouty Reference Site*.

Prouty, L. Fletcher: "Interview with 'Mr. X' Col Prouty," *The Larouche Connection*, November 11, 1992.

Selverstone, Marc: "Kennedy Vietnam Tapes," *CSPAN*, October 16, 2013.

Shenon, Philip: "NPR Fresh Air: Botched Investigation Fuels Kennedy Conspiracy Theories," *National Public Radio*, Philadelphia, PA: WHYY, October 28, 2013.

Shenon, Philip: "NPR Fresh Air: The Still Unfolding Story of JFK's Assassination," *National Public Radio*, Philadelphia, PA: WHYY, August 10, 2017.

Sklar, Zachary: "Interview with Zachary Sklar, Co-Writer of the Movie 'JFK'," *Let'em Talk/ NWO Media*, January 14, 1992.

Sklar, Zachary: *Black Op Radio*, Show #38, May 17, 2001.

Stone, Oliver: "Oliver Stone's America," interview with Charles Kiselyak, *Warner Home Video*, 2001.

Stone, Oliver: "Interview with Ken Paulson at Comedy Arts Festival in Aspen, CO," *Speaking Freely*, #312, March 1, 2002.

Stone, Oliver: "Oliver Stone on 50th Anniversary of JFK Assassination & *the Untold History of the United States*," *Democracy Now*, November 5, 2013.

Tye, Larry: "NPR Fresh Air: From 'Runt of the Litter' to 'Liberal Icon,' the Story of Robert Kennedy," *National Public Radio*, Philadelphia, PA: WHYY, July 5, 2016.

4 Books

Allison, Graham T.: *Essence of Decision: Explaining the Cuban Missile Crisis* (1971), Harper Collins.

Barkun, Michael: *A Culture of Conspiracy: Apocalyptic Visions in Contemporary America*, 2nd Edition (2013), University of California Press.

Blaine, Gerald and Lisa McCubbin: *The Kennedy Detail: JFK's Secret Service Agents Break Their Silence* (2010), Gallery Press.

Blakey, G. Robert and Richard N. Billings: The Plot to Kill the President: Organized Crime Assassinated the President (1981), N.Y. Times Books.

Brotherton, Rob: *Suspicious Minds: Why We Believe Conspiracy Theories* (2015), Bloomsbury Sigma.

Bugliosi, Vincent: *Reclaiming History: The Assassination of President John F. Kennedy* (2007), W.W. Norton & Co.

Cassam, Quassim: *Conspiracy Theories* (2019), Polity Press.

Chomsky, Noam: *Rethinking Camelot: JFK, the Vietnam War, and U.S. Political Culture* (1993), South End Press.

Compton, Todd Merlin: *Victim of The Muses: Poet as Scapegoat, Warrior and Hero in Greco-Roman and Indo-European Myth and History*, Hellenic Studies Series 11 (2006), Harvard University Press.

de Haas, Frank and Wayne van Zwoll: *Bolt Action Rifles*, 4th Edition (2003), Krause Publications.

Douglass, James: *JFK and the Unspeakable: Why He Died and Why It Matters* (2008), Touchstone.

Fetzer, James, ed.: *Murder in Dealey Plaza: What We Know that We Didn't Know Then about the Death of JFK* (2000), Catfeet Press.

Garrison, Jim: *On the Trail of the Assassins: One Man's Quest to Solve the Murder of President Kennedy* (1991), Warner Books.

Girard, René: *I See Satan Fall like Lightning* (2001), Orbis Books.

Hellmann, John: *The Kennedy Obsession: The American Myth of JFK* (1997), Columbia University Press.

Hersh, Seymour: *The Dark Side of Camelot* (1997), Little, Brown, & Co.

Hill, Clint and Lisa McCubbin: *Mrs. Kennedy and Me* (2012), Gallery Books.

Hill, Jean and Bill Sloan: *JFK: The Last Dissenting Witness* (1992), Pelican.

Hurt, Henry: *Reasonable Doubt: An Investigation into the Assassination of John F. Kennedy* (1985), Holt, Rinehart & Winston.

Karnow, Stanley: *Vietnam: A History* (1983), Viking Press.

Kay, Jonathan: *Among the Truthers: A Journey Through America's Growing Conspiracist Underground* (2011), Harper Collins.

Kaye, Sharon M.: *Critical Thinking: A Beginner's Guide* (2009), Oneworld Publications.

Knight, Peter: *The Kennedy Assassination* (2007), University Press of Mississippi.

Lambert, Patricia: *False Witness: The Real Story of Jim Garrison's Investigation and Oliver Stone's Film JFK* (1998), M. Evans & Company.

Lane, Mark: *Rush to Judgment*, 2nd Edition (1992), Thunder's Mouth Press.

Leamer, Laurence: *The Kennedy Men, 1901–1963* (2001), William Morrow Publishing.

Lebow, Richard Ned: *The Politics and Ethics of Identity: In Search of Ourselves* (2012), Cambridge University Press.

Lewin, Leonard: *The Report from Iron Mountain on the Possibility and Desirability of Peace* (1967), Dial Press.

Lifton, David: *Best Evidence: Disguise and Deception in the Assassination of John F. Kennedy*, 2nd Edition (1984), Dell Publishing Company.

Litwin, Fred: *I Was a Teenage JFK Conspiracy Freak* (2018), NorthernBlues Books.

Litwin, Fred: *On the Trail of Delusion: Jim Garrison: The Great Accuser* (2020), NorthernBlues Books.

Mailer, Norman: *Oswald's Tale* (1995), Random House.

Manchester, William: *The Death of a President* (1967), Harper & Row.

Marrs, Jim: *Crossfire: The Plot that Killed Kennedy* (1989), Carroll & Graf.

McAdams, John: *JFK Assassination Logic: How to Think about Claims of Conspiracy* (2011), Potomac Books.

McWhorter, Diane: *Carry Me Home, Birmingham, Alabama: The Climactic Battle of the Civil Rights Revolution* (2001), Simon and Schuster.

Miller, Robert L. and Dennis Wainstock: *Indochina and Vietnam: The Thirty-Five-Year War— 1940–1975* (2014), Enigma Books.

Nashel, Jonathan: *Edward Lansdale's Cold War* (2005), University of Massachusetts Press.

Nevins, Allan and Henry Steele Commager (with Jeffrey Morris): *A Pocket History of the United States*, Ninth Revised Edition (1992), Simon & Schuster.

Novick, Peter: *That Noble Dream: The 'Objectivity Question' and the American Historical Profession* (1988), Cambridge University Press.

Olmsted, Kathryn S.: *Real Enemies: Conspiracy Theories and American Democracy, World War I to 9/11* (2009), Oxford University Press.

Oswald, Robert, with Myrick and Barbara Land: *Lee: A Portrait of Lee Harvey Oswald by His Brother* (1967), Coward-McCann.

Perlstein, Rick: *Before the Storm: Barry Goldwater and the Unmaking of the American Consensus* (2002), Hull and Wang.

Piereson, James: *Camelot and the Cultural Revolution: How the Assassination of John F. Kennedy Shattered American Liberalism* (2007), Encounter Books.

Pipes, Daniel: *Conspiracy: How the Paranoid Style Flourishes and Where It Comes From* (1997), The Free Press.

Posner, Gerald: *Case Closed: Lee Harvey Oswald and the Assassination of JFK* (2003), Anchor Books.

Prouty, L. Fletcher: *The Secret Team: The CIA and Its Allies in Control of the United States and the World* (1973), Prentice Hall.

Prouty, L. Fletcher: *JFK: Vietnam, The CIA, and the Plot to Assassinate John F. Kennedy* (1995), Random House.

Ramsay, Robin: *Who Shot JFK?* (2013), Pocket Essentials.

Ricklefs, M.C., et al.: *A New History of Southeast Asia* (2010), Palgrave Macmillan.

Robins, Robert S. and Jerrold M. Post: *Political Paranoia: The Psychopolitics of Hatred* (1997), Yale University Press.

Russo, Gus and Stephen Molton: *Brothers in Arms: The Kennedys, the Castros, and the Politics of Murder* (2008), Bloomsbury.

Scheim, David E.: *Contract on America: The Mafia Murder of President John F. Kennedy* (1988), Shapolsky Publishers.

Segel, Binjamin W.: *A Lie and a Libel: The History of the Protocols of the Elders of Zion* (edited and translated by Richard S. Levy) (1996), University of Nebraska Press.

Shaw, Gary, with Larry R. Harris: *Cover Up: The Governmental Conspiracy to Conceal the Facts about the Public Execution of John Kennedy* (1976), self-published.

Shenon, Philip: *A Cruel and Shocking Act: The Secret History of the Kennedy Assassination* (2015), Picador.

Swanson, James: *End of Days: The Assassination of John F. Kennedy* (2013), William Morrow.

Thompson, Josiah: *Six Seconds in Dallas: A Micro-Study of the Kennedy Assassination Proving that Three Gunmen Murdered the President* (1967), Bernard Geis Associates.

Toplin, Robert Brent: *History by Hollywood: The Use and Abuse of the American Past* (1996), University of Illinois Press.

Uscinski, Joseph P., ed.: *Conspiracy Theories and the People Who Believe Them* (2019), Oxford University Press.

Uscinski, Joseph P. and Joseph M. Parent: *American Conspiracy Theories* (2014), Oxford University Press.

Ventura, Jesse, with Dick Russell and David Wayne: *They Killed Our President: 63 Reasons to Believe There Was a Conspiracy to Assassinate JFK* (2014), Skyhorse Publishing.

Waldron, Lamar and Thom Hartmann: *Legacy of Secrets: The Long Shadow of the JFK Assassination* (2008), Counterpoint.

Wills, Chuck and Berman Museum of World History: *The Illustrated Encyclopedia of Weaponry: From Flint Axes to Automatic Weapons* (2012), Thunder Bay Press.

5   Films, documentaries, and public lectures

Cayley, David: "CBS Ideas: The Scapegoat: The Ideas of René Girard" (in five parts), *CBC Radio 1*, March 4–17, 2016.

"Cold Case JFK," dir. Rushmore DeNooyer and Scott Tiffany, *PBS: NOVA*, Lone Wolf Media, WGBH Educational Foundation, 2013.

Garrison, Jim: "NBC Presents: Jim Garrison's Response," *NBC*, July 15, 1967.

Giglio, James N.: "Hail to the Chiefs: John F. Kennedy," Kansas City Public Library, Truman Library Institute, and Missouri State University, March 20, 2012.

Graham, Matt, Peter Kuznick, and Oliver Stone: "JFK—To the Brink," (Chapter 6) *The Untold History of the United States*, Showtime, 2012.

"Hollywood & History: The Debate over 'JFK'," Panel Discussion between Norman Mailer, Edward J. Epstein, Nora Ephron, and Oliver Stone, Town Hall, New York City, March 3, 1992, *PBS Frontline*, November 19, 2013.

JFK, dir. Oliver Stone, Warner Brothers, 1991.

"JFK: The Lost Bullet," Prod. Robert Stone, written by David Konschnik, *National Geographic Channel*, 2011.

Lifton, David: "A Question of Authenticity," *The Zapruder Film: Is Seeing Believing in the Assassination of JFK?* University of Minnesota Duluth, May 2003.

McGee, Frank: "The JFK Conspiracy: The Case of Jim Garrison," *NBC*, June 1967.

On Trial: Lee Harvey Oswald, Dir. Ian Hamilton (Mock Trial of Lee Harvey Oswald, with Vincent Bugliosi, Prosecutor, and Garry Spense, Counsel for the Defense), London Weekend Television Productions, 1986.

"Peter Jennings Reporting: The Kennedy Assassination—Beyond Conspiracy," *ABC News*, 2003.

Sabato, Larry J.: *The Kennedy Half Century: The Presidency, Assassination, and Lasting Legacy of John F. Kennedy*, 2013, University of Virginia, Massive Open Online Course, *iTunes University*.

Stone, Oliver: "Making the Movie J.F.K.," Speech Delivered to the National Press Club, January 15, 1992, *C-SPAN*.

"The Men Who Killed Kennedy," Nigel Tuner Productions, *History Channel*, 1988 and 2003.

The Vietnam War, dir. Ken Burns and Lynn Novick, *PBS*, 2017.

Thompson, Josiah: "Why the Zapruder Film Is Authentic," November 20, 1998, Clint Bradford, ed.: *JFK Assassination Research Materials*.

"Two Men in Dallas," dir. Lincoln Carle, Alpa Productions, 1976. Written and narrated by Mark Lane.

"Unsolved History: JFK: Beyond the Magic Bullet," dir. Robert Erickson, *Discovery Channel*, 2004.

"Who Was Lee Harvey Oswald," dir. William Cran and Ben Loeterman, *PBS Frontline*, November 19, 2013.

6   Websites

Bojczuk, Jeremy: *22 November 1963: An Introduction to the JFK Assassination*, http://22november1963.org.uk/.

Bradford, Rex, ed.: *History Matters*, www.history-matters.com/.

Center for the Study of Intelligence: *Central Intelligence Agency*, www.cia.gov/library/center-for-the-study-of-intelligence/csi-publications/csi-studies.

Dunning, Brian: *Skeptoid: Critical Analysis of Pop Phenomena*, https://skeptoid.com.

Holland, Max: *Washington Decoded*, www.washingtondecoded.com.

John F. Kennedy Presidential Library and Museum, www.jfklibrary.org/.

Mary Ferrell Foundation, www.maryferrell.org/pages/Main_Page.html.

McAdams, John: *The Kennedy Assassination*, http://jfkassassination.net/home.htm.

Osanic, Len: *Black Op Radio*, http://blackopradio.com/.

Osanic, Len: *The Col. L. Fletcher Prouty Reference Site*, www.prouty.org/.

Reitzes, David: *JFK Online*, www.jfk-online.com/home.html.

Simkin, John: *Spartacus Educational*, www.spartacus-educational.com.

The Sixth Floor Museum at Dealey Plaza, www.jfk.org/.

Von Pein, David: *DVP's JFK Archive*, http://jfk-archives.blogspot.com.

GLOSSARY OF TERMS

See Appendices 1 and 2 for concepts relating to formal logic.

Anachronism: A chronological inconsistency, such as interpreting historical events, values, or culture through the distorted lens of the present.

Anecdotal evidence: An indirect or informal proof obtained through an intermediate source (e.g., a second- or third-hand eyewitness report), whose authenticity cannot be verified.

Artifact (in photography): The undesired or unintended corruption of an image caused by a foreign object or force (e.g., heat, water stains, scratches, and fingerprints).

Burden of proof: The responsibility to disprove the claims of others before declaring them false, especially when these represent the consensus of experts.

Centrality: An exaggerated sense of self-importance, such as believing that one is the target of a massive conspiracy.

Circumstantial evidence: Indirect evidence (like a bloodstain or physical wounds) that requires supplemental information, inference, or interpretation by experts to qualify as a proof.

Confirmation bias: To acknowledge only such evidence that confirms one's existing beliefs.

Cognitive dissonance: A state of tension that occurs when a person simultaneously holds inconsistent beliefs.

Corroborating evidence: Evidence that confirms (i.e., corroborates) the truth of a claim or the authenticity of another piece of evidence.

"Cui bono?": (From the Latin for "who benefits?") The fallacious assumption that those who benefit from an event or crime are guilty of causing it (see *post hoc* fallacy in Appendix 1).

Epistemic authority: A person who has expert knowledge, specialized training, or is endowed with a special investigative function.

Errant data: Information that is unaccounted for by, or stands in contradiction to, the widely accepted consensus (or "official story").

Flowchart conspiracism: The psychological tendency to ascribe all tragic events, nefarious organizations, or "evil" forces to the work of a single, omnipotent puppet master.

Forensic pathology: The medical study of the criminal circumstances and causes of unnatural deaths, and the cataloging of such evidence for use in legal proceedings.

Fortuitous data: Evidence that supports the reigning consensus (or "official" theory) but the existence or discovery of which seems "too good to be true".

Myth: A speculative story based on ostensibly historical events that offer a compelling explanation for how the world works, for the existence and nature of good and evil, and for determining one's purpose in life.

Ockham's Razor: "Entities must not be multiplied beyond necessity" (a saying ascribed to medieval philosopher William of Ockham). Also called the law of parsimony, it is the principle that the explanation with the fewest assumptions is more likely true.

Outlier: A piece of evidence that cannot be accounted for by any existing theory, often due to a statistical error, an incorrect memory, faulty analysis, or false expectations. It could also be proof that no existing theory is fully correct.

Paradigm shift: A radical transformation in the way one looks at the world, often as a result of cognitive dissonance and emotional stress caused by having incompatible values, beliefs, or theories for understanding reality.

Pareidolia: The tendency to perceive a meaningful image or pattern in a random or ambiguous set of visual stimuli (e.g., seeing a human face in a cloud or a sniper in some bushes).

Principle of charity (in debating):   The "gentlemanly" principle according to which one should consider an opponent's views in their strongest and most rational interpretation and so avoid resorting to straw man fallacies (see Appendix 1).

Projection (in psychology):   The tendency to attribute one's own (usually negative) feelings, impulses, or secret thoughts to someone else, or to perceive someone else as an extension of the self.

Pseudohistory: A form of historical research that mimics the methods and style of professional historians, but which relies on guesswork, circular reasoning, oversimplification, inappropriate authorities, or unsubstantiated rumors.

Scapegoating: To arbitrarily ascribe blame to an undesirable person or group without objective proof of their guilt.

Selection bias (in statistics):   Selecting a sample, purposefully or not, that reinforces the researcher's thesis, but which does not accurately represent the wider set of objects or people one is claiming to study. It is also called sampling bias.

Standard form (in logic): The "bare-bones" structure of an argument that is presented as a numbered list of premises (reasons) followed by a thesis (conclusion).

Syncretism: The combination of different beliefs or ideas (e.g., unrelated conspiracy theories) into a new hybrid idea.

Teleological reasoning (in philosophy): (From the Greek words for purpose (*telos*) and language or study (*logos*)). To explain a process or event in accordance with its purpose (or final end), not its causes (e.g., apples fall from a tree so that they might produce more apple trees).

Thought experiment (in philosophy): An imaginative scenario, the purpose of which is to "think through" the possible and impossible implications of a truth claim or unknown event.

Unfalsifiable: It is said of a claim for which no evidence can be found to prove or disprove its truth.

Weasel words: Vague or empty expressions that contain an implicit bias. It is also called glittering generalizations.

Whistleblower: An insider who takes the risk to speak out publicly against crimes or corruption in an institution.

APPENDIX 1

FALLACIOUS REASONING

With a list of frequently used fallacies

A fallacy is a statement, or set of statements, that contains misleading logic. While fallacies are sometimes used deliberately to deceive, for example, in advertising, they are usually committed unintentionally by careless communicators. Fallacies typically do one of three things: (a) they manipulate people's feelings, (b) they distract the audience from the issue being discussed, or (c) they draw a facile connection using vague or deceptive language between certain premises (alleged facts) and one's thesis (what one is trying to prove). In other words, a fallacy is a cheap shortcut used to win arguments under false pretexts. The deliberate and unscrupulous use of fallacies is called sophistry.

Conspiracy researchers often resort to fallacious logic because conspiracy theories are speculative by nature, requiring their authors to justify their beliefs with many unproven assumptions. The strong emotions that make such theories compelling can also skew one's ability to reason clearly. Since conspiracy claims habitually try to explain unresolved mysteries or expose secret plots conducted by powerful groups, conspiracists easily fall prey to paranoia and other types of emotional reasoning that prevent them from being objective. The most common conspiracist trap is to engage in circular reasoning, which is to begin an argument with the assumption that one's conclusion is true before sufficient evidence has been collected to support it. This leads researchers to cherry-pick only the evidence that favors their conclusion and to ignore any evidence that challenges it. Circular reasoning also leads conspiracists to "fill the gaps" in the evidence record with rhetorical questions that make their assumptions seem self-evident (e.g., "Why else would these files not be declassified?").

Reading only books or websites that suggest a theory is true, without being compelled to consider alternate viewpoints, will also prevent you, the reader, from learning about evidence that might change your mind. Circular reasoning may even make you believe in a hoax. Many examples exist of intentional forgeries that were accepted as true by thousands of willing believers: *The Protocols of the Elders of Zion*, the *Majestic-12* documents, Ray Santilli's alien autopsy film, Pierre Plantard's *Dossiers secrets*, etc. Kennedy assassination buffs are no less vulnerable. Consider the misleading "magic bullet theory," the many false witness testimonies (e.g., Perry Russo), and false assassin confessions (e.g., Loy Factor) reported as fact by conspiracist authors, many of whom readily claim they "smelled a rat" long before they came across any "proofs" of a cover-up. When the Warren Commission concluded, for instance, that Jack Ruby's shooting of Lee Oswald was the work of one man, many refused to accept it and went looking for any shred of circumstantial evidence—however lurid or unlikely—that might link Ruby to the mob or CIA. Others simply cannot accept that the most powerful man in the world, a president in whom they had vested their hopes as a symbol of change, could be gunned down at high noon by an insignificant loner. As William Manchester noted, the story lacked a certain moral and narrative proportionality—a scenario in which a great crime against a great man should have been committed by an equally great criminal, not a "wretched waif" like Oswald.[1] At least, that is what typically happens in novels and movies, and art greatly influences our perception of real-life events. It leads us to look for similar patterns in history, which is usually far more chaotic.

Fallacies come in two basic types. Formal fallacies are logical faults in the *structure* of the argument. Such an argument could contain only proven facts and still be wrong because these facts (premises) do not support the conclusion. Consider the following argument:

1. Oswald was either on the sixth floor of the Texas School Book Depository (TSBD) or he was not on the sixth floor of the TSBD.
2. No one saw Oswald on the sixth floor of the TSBD.

3. Therefore, Oswald did not shoot Kennedy.

The central problem with this argument is not that it makes factual mistakes. Although they are imprecise, the premises of this argument (statements 1 and 2) are arguably true. The main problem with this argument, rather, is that it is not logically consistent. Its premises, even if they were true, do not make the conclusion either necessary or probable (see Appendix 2 for a summary of inductive and deductive logic). One could equally conclude, for instance, that Oswald was on the sixth floor but hidden from view, or that he shot JFK from the rooftop, from another floor of the building, from the grassy knoll, or from some other location.

Informal fallacies are individual *statements* that are logically misleading or too vague to produce a specific conclusion. Most fallacies that appear in JFK conspiracy theories are of this type, and many examples are highlighted throughout this book. There are dozens of kinds of informal fallacies. Many are easy to spot with a little training and practice. Much the same way an experienced birdwatcher can identify a species by its song, color, or shape, you can teach yourself to sniff out misleading nonsense. All it takes is awareness and concentration. By teaching yourself to be on the lookout for fallacies, you can avoid being ensnared by these reasoning traps.

Students of conspiracy theories should study logic alongside their favorite conspiracy books. Below is a list of reasoning fallacies that frequently turn up in conspiracy literature. (For a longer discussion on fallacies, with links to critical thinking sources, see Bradley Dowden: "Fallacies," *Internet Encyclopedia of Philosophy*, https:// iep.utm.edu/fallacy/.)

List of common fallacies

1. *Ad hoc* rescue: An exceptional and untestable one-time explanation that defies trends, predictability, or the rules of logical consistency.
2. Appeal to emotions: Using language or symbols that manipulate the audience to accept a claim based on their feelings of pity, fear, anger, patriotism, etc.
3. Appeal to popularity: (aka: *Ad Populum* or "Bandwagon Effect") Claiming that X is true because a majority of people (or ancestors, or some well-known celebrities) believe it is true.
4. Appeal to an unqualified authority (aka: *Ad Verecundiam*): To claim that someone's viewpoint is true by virtue of their status or expertise in a different domain than the issue at hand.
5. Circular reasoning (aka: "Begging the Question"): Supporting a thesis with a premise that is only true if one first assumes that the conclusion is true.
6. Equivocation: Changing the meaning of a crucial term or concept in the middle of the argument.
7. Fallacy of composition: To make an inappropriate inference from the properties of the parts of a set to the set as a whole.
8. Fallacy of division: To make an inappropriate inference from the properties of a set to the properties of its constituent parts.
9. False dilemma: To offer a forced choice between two (or more) options when other possible alternatives exist.
10. Faulty analogy: To make an inappropriate inference between two things that are only superficially similar.
11. Furtive fallacy: The unjustified assumption that all events are guided by a hidden and malicious power.
12. Guilt by association: Ascribing blame on the basis that a person has some suspicious "connection" to other suspects.
13. Hasty generalization (aka: stereotyping): To make a broad generalization about a whole group, or about a person's possible actions, based on insufficient examples.
14. Moving the goalposts: To reject a piece of evidence by demanding it to meet an unnecessarily high criterion of legitimacy.

15. Personal attack (aka: *Ad Hominem* or "Poisoning the Well"): To criticize the person(s) presenting the argument instead of the argument itself.
16. Post Hoc Ergo Propter Hoc ("After this, therefore because of this"): To claim that the consequence of an event is a proof of its cause.
17. Red herring: An irrelevant fact or digression that draws the audience's attention away from the issue at hand.
18. Slippery slope: To assume that a possible action will inevitably lead to an unavoidable (and undesired) chain of events.
19. Straw man: Presenting an overly simplistic or distorted version of an opponent's argument to make them look silly.
20. Texas sharpshooter fallacy: Arbitrarily deriving a pattern from a cherry-picked set of random coincidences.

Note

1 William Manchester: "No Evidence for a Conspiracy to Kill Kennedy," *The New York Times*, Feb. 5, 1992.

APPENDIX 2

INDUCTIVE AND DEDUCTIVE LOGIC

With a flowchart to analyze each argument type

A2.1   Induction

Inductive logic is a form of reasoning that derives a *probable* conclusion from careful observations. Typically practiced in historical research, as well as scientific laboratories, forensic investigations, and criminal trials, induction cannot prove beyond all doubt that something is necessarily true (or false) because it relies on incomplete or contentious information. This is because historical and scientific data are subject to the limitations, miscalculations, and misinterpretations of the human agents who observe and record them. One must also consider the natural limits and possible malfunctions of the various technologies we use as imperfect extensions of our already imperfect senses, such as photographs, audio and video recordings, etc.

Inductive arguments must fulfill two obligations to be considered cogent (i.e., probably true):

1. Their premises (reasons), *assuming that they are true*, must support the conclusion to a high level of probability. In other words, no better conclusion can be inferred from these reasons. Premises may not contradict one another, nor may they have multiple interpretations. They must be clear and reinforce each other in supporting the stated conclusion. When this occurs, we say that the argument is inductively strong (or "forceful"). If the premises are contradictory, if they are not clearly related to the conclusion, or if they are too vague, the argument is said to be weak.
2. A strong argument whose premises are *also verifiably true* is said to be cogent. A cogent argument is an educated opinion founded on verified observations that best accounts for the known evidence.

In most historical and scientific research, new information may come to light to challenge our original conclusions. For this reason, a cogent inductive argument will never be indisputable but will remain a *compelling theory* (i.e., most likely true "beyond a reasonable doubt") until strong evidence can be found to disprove it. Compelling theories can rightly be called the "reigning consensus" or, if you prefer, the "official story".

Main types of inductive arguments

a Enumerative:	*P1: A is a P*
	P2: B is a P
	P3: C is a P
	_____
	C: Therefore, D is probably also a P
b Abductive:	*P1: P*
(aka: "Inference to the best hypothesis")	*P2: The best explanation for P is Q*
	_____
	C: Therefore, probably Q
c Argument by analogy:	*P1: P is like Q*
	P2: Q is an X
	_____
	C: Therefore, P is probably also an X

A2.2 Deduction

Inversely, deductive logic is a form of reasoning that derives *necessary* conclusions from universal generalizations. These include rules, definitions, and categorical claims, like "If A then B," "All As are Bs," "Either A or B," etc. Because of the nature of its premises, a properly structured deductive argument will lead to an *indisputable* conclusion.

Deduction is mostly used when rules of mathematics, language, science, or logic can help us establish, through a process of elimination, a single, logically necessary conclusion. For instance, a rule that is known to be true such as the logical principle of noncontradiction (i.e., that A and not-A cannot both be true) coupled with the verified laws of physics (e.g., that the same person cannot simultaneously be in two different places) would lead us to conclude that Jack could not have murdered Jill in Paris while he was simultaneously giving a speech in Chicago.

Deductive arguments must fulfill two obligations to be considered "sound" (or indisputable).

Main types of deductive arguments

a Categorical syllogism:
   P1: *All As are Bs*
   P2: *All Ds are Cs*

   _____

   C: *Therefore, all As are Cs*

b Disjunctive syllogism:
   P1: *Either P or Q*
   P2: *Not P*

   _____

   C: *Therefore, Q*

c Modus ponens:
   P1: *If P, then Q*
   P2: *P*

   _____

   C: *Therefore, Q*

d Modus tollens:
   P1: *If P, then Q*
   P2: *Not Q*

   _____

   C: *Therefore, not P*

e Hypothetical syllogism:
   P1: *If A then B*
   P2: *If B then C*

   _____

   C: *Therefore, if A then C*

f *Reductio ad absurdum:*
   P1: *A (according to theory X)*
   P2: *If A then B*
   P3: *But not B (i.e., B is not possible)*

   _____

   C: *Therefore, not A*

1. The structure of a deductive argument requires that its conclusion be logically necessary. It cannot leave room for doubt. Its premises, *assuming that they are true*, must support the conclusion to the level of logical certainty, to the exclusion of all others. An argument whose conclusion is logically certain is said to be valid. Anything else is invalid and must be rejected.

2. A valid deductive argument whose premises are *known to be true* is said to be sound. Soundness is the highest flattery an argument can receive. It is not merely an educated opinion, it is an established truth. However, sound arguments are rare and tend to be the product of mathematics, grammar, or pure logic, not of scientific or forensic observation. Nevertheless, soundness is the ultimate goal for anyone seeking to prove that what they believe is true.

FLOWCHART: ANALYZING DEDUCTIVE AND INDUCTIVE ARGUMENTS

1. Is it an argument?

> **NO.** It is only a set of facts, questions, a description, or an explanation.*

> **YES.** It is a series of reasons (premises) that support a truth-claim (conclusion).

2. Is the argument inductive or deductive?
   *a. Do the premises contain **a categorical statement** or only a set of **observations**?*
   *b. Is the conclusion presented as **indisputable** or only as **probable**?*

It contains one or more generalizations (laws, definitions...) **that lead to an <u>indisputable</u> conclusion.**	It contains a set of observations (measurements, frequency testimonies...) **that lead to a <u>probable</u> conclusion.**

DEDUCTIVE ARGUMENT

INDUCTIVE ARGUMENT

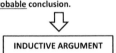

3. Is the argument **valid**?
   a. Do the premises (assuming they are true) make the conclusion <u>necessarily true</u>?
   b. Is this the <u>only</u> possible conclusion?

3. Is the argument inductively **strong**?
   a. Do the premises (assuming they are true) make the conclusion <u>highly probable</u>?
   b. Is this the <u>best</u> possible conclusion

YES   **NO**

YES   **NO**

> **INVALID ARGUMENT**

> **WEAK ARGUMENT**

VALID!

STRONG!

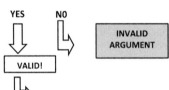

4. *Are all premises <u>known</u> to be true?*
   a. Clear and precise?
   b. No other meanings possible?
   c. a priori true (i.e., logically <u>necessary</u>)?
   d. a posteriori true (i.e., this <u>always</u> happens)?

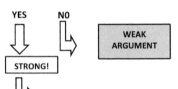

4. *Are all premises <u>acceptable</u>?*
   a. supported by a strong sub-argument?
   b. a priori or a posteriori true?
   c. common knowledge (<u>usually</u> happens this way)?
   d. supported by a <u>relevant</u> figure of authority?

YES   **NO**

YES   **NO**

> **VALID, BUT NOT SOUND**

> **STRONG, BUT NOT COGENT**

5. Does a strong counter-argument exist?
   a. Do any of the premises lack clarity or precision?
   b. Has some evidence been ignored?
   c. Are other explanations equally probable?

         YES   **NO!**

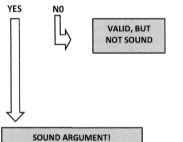

SOUND ARGUMENT!	**VARIOUS LEVELS OF INDUCTIVE STRENGTH:**	**COGENT ARGUMENT!**
Congratulations! You have achieved knowledge!	*e.g.,* *"Not very convincing because..."* *"Somewhat convincing..."* *"Thought provoking..."* *"Very convincing. However..."*	*Congratulations! You now have an authoritative and informed opinion!*

(*) A dark-shaded box indicates the end of the analysis.

(Explain clearly & debate)

INDEX

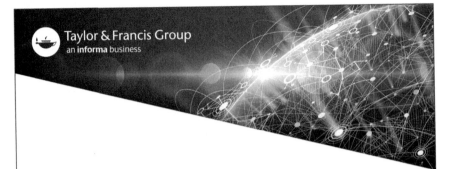